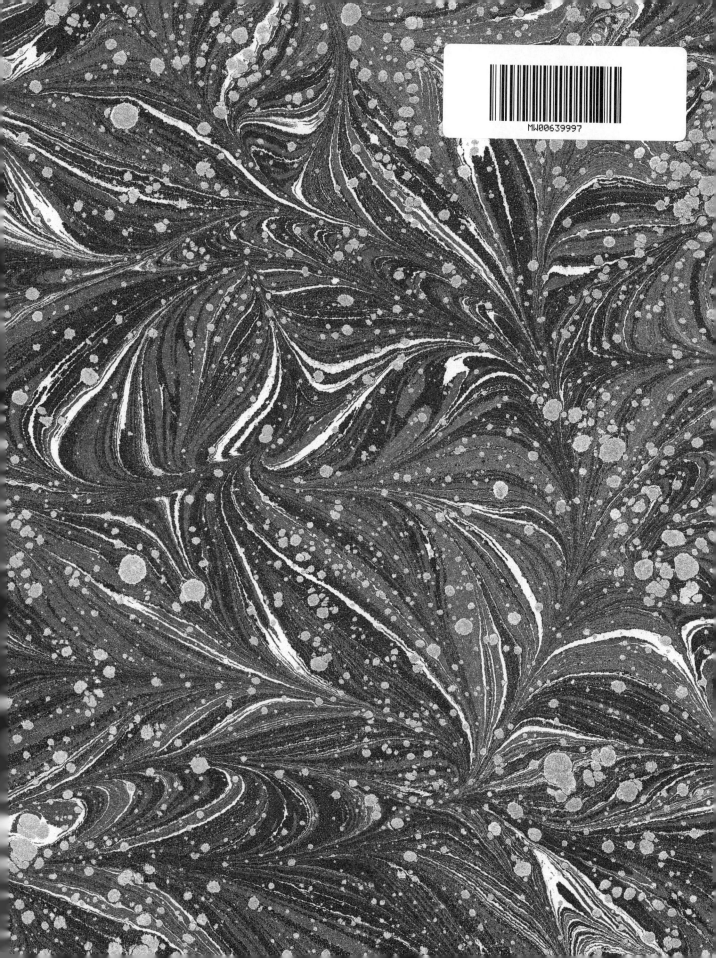

CULINARY BIOGRAPHIES

CULINARY BIOGRAPHIES

A DICTIONARY OF THE WORLD'S GREAT HISTORIC CHEFS, COOKBOOK AUTHORS AND COLLECTORS, FARMERS, GOURMETS, HOME ECONOMISTS, NUTRITIONISTS, RESTAURATEURS, PHILOSOPHERS, PHYSICIANS, SCIENTISTS, WRITERS, AND OTHERS WHO INFLUENCED THE WAY WE EAT TODAY

Edited by ALICE ARNDT

With Contributions by Numerous Experts

Title page illustration: Epicurus

Published by:

𝒴𝑒𝓈 Press, Inc.
P.O. Box 270744
Houston, Texas 77277-0744
U.S.A.
www.CulinaryBiographies.com

FIRST EDITION
Printed in the United States of America

Design and Production: Davis Design Partners
www.davisdp.com

Library of Congress Control Number: 2005936311
ISBN-10: 0-9718322-1-8
ISBN-13: 978-0-9718322-1-3

Jn dem namen der hailigen
trifaltigkaitt fach ich, sabina
welserin, das kochbúch an.
gott welle mir sein gottliche
gnad / vnnd weiß-
hait vnnd verstand vnnd ver-
núfft verleichen, das ich nach
seinem gottlichen willen leb
hie jn disser zeit vnnd beý
jm ewig amen. 1553 jar.

In the name of the Holy Trinity,
I, Sabina Welserin,
begin this cookbook.
God grant me His divine Grace
and Wisdom and Reason and Sense,
that I might live
according to His divine will
here in this time
and with Him for all time.
Amen. Year 1553

CONTENTS

INTRODUCTION

AT LAST—A BIOGRAPHICAL DICTIONARY OF CULINARIANS. IT'S ABOUT TIME! The success of books of biographies can be traced back at least as far as the first century, to Plutarch's classic *Parallel Lives*. Thereafter, various *Lives* of the Christian saints found enduring popularity. In the early nineteenth century, the number of books of biography began to increase, and has risen rapidly ever since. An early biographical dictionary of famous Swedish men, published in 23 volumes between 1835 and 1857, became a model for dictionaries of national biography in many other countries. The number of biographical dictionaries has become so large that many bibliographic volumes listing them have been published. Not only are biographical dictionaries numerous, but the groups they describe have become almost absurdly narrow. All sorts of groups have been "biographied," but for those who, throughout history, have influenced the way we eat and what eating means, there has been almost nothing. Until now.

In this volume, we have profiled a broad array of different types of historic culinarians. (For an elaboration of the latter term, see our protracted subtitle.) We selected from all time periods. By "historic" we mean to exclude living persons, whose careers are unfinished and still unassessed. We have stretched the definition of historic to include a few imaginary characters, such as **Aunt Sammy**, who played a role in the history of food. Our oldest subject is the philosopher **Pythagoras**, who was born in the sixth century BC, and the latest is **Julia Child**, whose passing on August 13, 2004, regrettably made her eligible for inclusion.

Some of our subjects, such as **Mike Butt** and **Minakshie DasGupta**, have never been profiled in print before. Others, such as **Alexander** the Great, are remembered more for their non-culinary accomplishments, but in this volume their food-related contributions are emphasized. Our diligent contributors have ferreted out a number of unknown or little-known facts about their subjects, for example, the identity of the mysterious **Ménagier of Paris**, and the place and date of **Elena Molokhovets**' death. Finally, this book corrects a few well-established errors, such as the purported collaboration of **Carême** and **Beauvilliers**.

In putting this book together, we were surprised to note how many of our biographees were renowned in their own time, yet had later been almost completely forgotten. The names of the most famous cooks of their day, the most influential writers and thinkers, the most fashionable restaurateurs, often bring blank looks when mentioned today. When the grave of **Mary Randolph**, one of America's most important nineteenth-century cookbook authors, was located during a 1929 renovation at Arlington National Cemetery, people were baffled as to who she had been. "Her intrinsic worth needs no eulogium," her tombstone declared, but a few words might in fact have been useful to introduce her to the twentieth century. Fortunately, a *Washington Star* article about this mysterious woman reached her descendents, who identified her for the public.

The fact is, it is not the significance of persons in their own period that causes them to be remembered, but the interests and activities of those who follow. Subsequent generations may be distracted by crises in their own time, or (inexplicably) lose interest in food and cooking, or decline to study history. It's really not the job of our historic subjects to make themselves remembered: We have that task! It is *our* responsibility to honor those whose contributions helped shape the world we live in. This book aims to restore these men and women to their rightful places in contemporary consciousness.

Our intention to make our roster of biographees as international as possible has run up against the fact that many cultures, less individualistic than those of the West, generally do not record the names of individuals involved with food. In those cultures, it is not the cook who is esteemed, it is the dish. Recipes and culinary techniques are handed down from master to apprentice, or from mother to daughter, and the great cook is not the innovator but the one who prepares the food in the way closest to the cultural ideal. This has left quite a few areas without a representative in the book. **Hildagonda Duckitt**, for example, represents just one of the many culinary cultures of South Africa.

There are, of course, many other culinarians who deserve to be in this work, and we'd like to hear about them, whether they've been omitted because of the nature of their culture, or our own ignorance, or the limitations of space and time. We look forward to receiving letters and emails that begin, "Why in the world [or words to that effect] didn't you include...." Please do send us your suggestions, and we'll try to add them to a future edition of *Culinary Biographies.*

While you're at it, we would also welcome your corrections and additions to the bibliographies at the ends of the biographies. Rather than citing secondary works about the subjects, we have endeavored to list their own culinary works, along with the date of first publication of each; but these titles and dates are notoriously difficult to sort out, and work remains to be done in this area.

We have gone to a great deal of trouble to find portraits to accompany the biographies whenever possible, in the belief that a face, and the way it is presented, assists a great deal in understanding the subject, especially in today's very visual culture. In the words of Thomas Carlyle, "Often I have found a Portrait superior in real instruction to half-a-dozen written Biographies.... [T]he Portrait was as a small lighted candle by which the Biographies could for the first time be read, and some human interpretation be made of them...." We think Carlyle underestimated the value of written biographies, especially given the gems that our contributors have provided here; we would prefer to value pictures and words at the usual one-to-1000 ratio. When we were not able to obtain a portrait, we often took the opportunity to show the title page of an important book, or some other relevant illustration.

Culinary Biographies is intended to be a contribution to food history, and we have tried to make clear the connections among these important historic individuals. Names written in bold type function as hyperlinks, to indicate that the person named has a biography of his or her own in this volume. We also have put together a chronological list of significant culinary texts, with their authors, to guide the reader from title to author to biography, where more information is waiting.

As with all dictionaries and encyclopedias, readers will get the most from this book by frequent use of the Index, which includes alternate names, variant spellings, and persons who are mentioned in someone else's biography.

Acknowledgements

I wish to thank, loudly and publicly, all the contributors to this volume. Without their expertise and knowledge, and their willingness to share it, there would simply be no book. Please turn to the list of contributors in the back of the book to see who they are and to read about their many accomplishments and activities.

In addition, I wish to acknowledge, with gratitude, those who supplied various other kinds of help: Ken Albala, Elizabeth Andoh; Nicole Arndt; Prudence Arndt; Joanne Badeaux, Esq.; Ethan and Susan Becker; Sharon Bemis; Inci Bowman; Terry Butt; Helen Chen; Sarah Coe; Renata Coetzee; Margaret Cousineau; Andrew Dalby; Manju Das; Jane Davidson; Matt and Karen Davis; Genevieve Dell; Elizabeth Driver; the East Asian Library, University of California, Berkeley; Beatrice Fink; Sophie Grigson; Barbara Haber; Emily Huffman and the James Beard Foundation; Sharon Hudgins; Vinod K. Huria; Priscilla Mary Işin; Tom Jaine; Patricia Kelly; Jamie Kennedy; Maria Baez Kijac; Robert Kline; Janice Bluestein Longone; Fiona Lucas; Anne Mendelson; May Mansoor Munn and the writers' group; Jill Norman; Sandra Oliver; Kyle Phillips; Jeffrey Pilcher; Jeri Quinzio; Elizabeth Ray; John and Joan Reardon; Alicia Rios; Arlene Shaner and the New York Academy of Medicine Library; the Schlesinger Library at the Radcliffe Institute, Harvard, and especially librarians Ellen Shea and Sarah Hutcheon; Özlem Sensoy; Laura Shapiro; Ann Sieber; Behnaz Smalley; Asele Surina; Martha Taylor; Betty Teel; Alice Thompson and the Institute of Culinary Education; Elizabeth Tosaris; Curtis Weeks; Debora Wells; Barbara Ketcham Wheaton; Ken and Amber Wickwire; Winnie Williams; Stephanie Wiltshire; and Paul Wolfson. A special word of thanks goes to Emilie Meislinger and the late Theresia Dengler, colleagues and heirs of **Erna Horn** and Julius Arndt, who were helpful in a number of ways. Finally, in the esteemed last-but-not-least position, I express my gratitude to Robert Arndt, *sous*-editor and *sine qua non* of this book.

— Alice Arndt

Friedrich Christian Accum ❧ 1769–1838 ❧

ALSO CALLED: Fredrick Accum

Friedrich Christian Accum was the first person to use chemical analysis to detect the presence of adulterants in foodstuffs. He was born in a small German town southwest of Hannover. His mother was Huguenot, his father a converted Jew who died a couple of years after his son's birth. The family soap-making business provided for Accum's education and his apprenticeship as an apothecary.

In 1793, at the age of 24, Accum moved to London to work with George Brande, a member of the London and Hannover firm who were apothecaries to George III. Fredrick (as he now called himself) married Mary Simpson and fathered eight children, only two of whom survived to maturity. He was fortunate enough to attract the attention of William Nicholson, publisher of the influential scientific and technological periodical *Journal of Natural Philosophy and the Arts*, who engaged him as a translator. In 1800, with Nicholson's patronage, he embarked on a successful career as a scientist-entrepreneur, something much commoner then than now. He gave classes and public lectures and wrote accompanying textbooks to sell to his students. He also sold chemical apparatus and supplies and offered his services as a chemical analyst. His book on gas lighting became the classic treatment of this new technology.

Engraving by J. Thomson after a portrait by S. Drummond, 1820

In 1820, Accum turned to food, producing within five years treatises on the scientific principles of cooking, brewing, bread baking, and wine making using native fruits. His *Treatise on Adulterations of Food* (1820) caused the greatest stir. The rapid growth of large cities provisioned by suppliers unknown to the inhabitants, and the increasing number of foods, beer prominent among them, being produced in factories, meant there were few checks on unscrupulous food producers and vendors, who added all kinds of adulterants to increase the weight or improve the appearance of their products. Although the government had made some efforts to control the problem by Parliamentary Acts that imposed fines on, for example, brewers who failed to maintain standards, it was only with the publication of Accum's exposé that the public began to wake up to the adulteration of their food and drink. The cover of his *Treatise* set the tone: Its design of snakes writhing around a fly trapped by a large spider was topped by a banner with a skull and crossbones and the words "There is death in the pot."

Not hesitating to name those involved, Accum devoted most of his attention to beer, still an important source of nutrition for much of the population. His tests showed that major London brewers added chemicals such as green vitriol (iron sulphate) and alum (aluminum potassium sulphate) to give beer a good head, and the poisonous extract of *Cocculus indicus* to give it a bitter taste. Furthermore, beer that left the brewery with an alcohol content of about 7.25 percent reached the public with only 4.5 percent alcohol. Other analyses showed that it was standard practice for bakeries to add alum to flour, that vintners passed off spoiled and colored cider as wine, that a small industry collected and dried blackthorn leaves to be sold as tea, that Gloucester cheese might well be colored with red lead, that cream was thick because of added flour or arrowroot, and that confectionary derived its brilliant colors from toxic salts of copper and lead.

The thousand copies of the first edition of the *Treatise on Adulterations of Food* sold out within a month. For Accum himself, though, the book heralded personal humiliation. Those he had accused were enraged by his outspoken attacks. Accum was arrested for having mutilated books in the library of the Royal Institution, London's leading center for education and research in chemistry. Although the case was eventually dismissed, it was widely believed that Accum's treatment would not have been so harsh had he not blown the whistle on the food adulterators. He fled London and spent the rest of his life in Berlin. Although he quickly acquired two technical professorships there, his entrepreneurial career was over.

With Accum's disgrace, the problem of adulterated food was dropped for many years. In 1860 Britain passed a largely unenforced Adulteration Act, but it was not until the passage of the Adulteration of Food Act (1872) and the Sale of Food and Drugs Act (1875) that analyses of the country's food were regularized.

— Rachel Laudan

Description of the process of manufacturing coal gas, for the lighting of streets, houses and public buildings, 1819

Treatise on adulterations of food, and culinary poisons, exhibiting the fraudulent sophistications of bread, beer, wine, spirituous liquors, tea, coffee, cream, confectionary, vinegar, mustard, pepper, cheese, olive oil, pickles and other articles employed in domestic economy. And ways of detecting them, 1820. 4th edition, 1822. American edition, 1820. German translation, 1822

A treatise on the art of brewing. Exhibiting the London practice of brewing, 1820. 2nd edition, 1821

A treatise on the art of making wine from native fruits, etc., 1820. French translation, 1825

A treatise on the art of making good and wholesome bread of wheat, oats, rye, barley and other farinaceous grain, 1821

Culinary chemistry: exhibiting the scientific principles of cookery, with concise instructions for preparing good and wholesome pickles, vinegar, conserves, fruit jellies, marmalades, and various other alimentary substances employed in domestic economy, 1821. French translation, 1825.

K. T. Achaya

ALSO CALLED: Dr. Konganda Thammu Achaya | Doc

K. T. ACHAYA, THE INDIAN CHEMIST AND FOOD HISTORIAN known as "Doc" to his many friends and colleagues, was a lifelong bachelor who half-jokingly referred to himself as a "cowboy" because he had worked so long in the chemistry of dairy products and milk production. His research later turned to oils and oil production, nutrition, and food technology. It was after his retirement that he ventured into the world of food history. "I had all these notes, and all this time," he explained, and he made excellent use of both. The book that made serious Western historians of food take note was *Indian Food: A Historical Companion* (1994). Here, at last, was a book on Indian food that went beyond curry, that didn't treat the cuisines of India as something beginning and ending with the British Raj. It had scope—the opening sentence begins, "Three hundred million years ago…"—and depth. There are footnoted references, glossaries, and several indices. A lifetime of research and intellectual curiosity led to that book, and it is a book that could well lead someone into a lifetime of research on the subject.

Born into a large family on October 6, 1923 at Kollegal (then in Madras Province, but now in Karnataka), Achaya graduated from Madras University with chemistry honors in 1943. He also received his MSc from that university while working at the Indian Institute of Science in Bangalore. He received a government scholarship for his doctoral studies, and sailed for England to work at the University of Liverpool, where he focused on the chemistry of cow and buffalo ghee. His research found a place in the *Proceedings of the Royal Society*. It was at that time that he published his first book, *Indian Dairy Products* (1948), co-authored with K. S. Rangappa. A revised edition was published in 1974, and it is still considered one of the most important books in the field.

In 1949, Achaya returned to India and was picked in 1950 to help establish what was later named the Regional Research Laboratory (RRL), an institute under the auspices of the Indian Council of Scientific and Industrial Research (CSIR). (RRL is now the Indian Institute of Chemical Technology.) During his 22-year tenure there, the institute garnered international recognition and was awarded several patents, and Achaya published another groundbreaking work, *Cottonseed Chemistry and Technology*, co-authored with K. S. Murti. During this period, Achaya went abroad twice, once to work on biological lipids at the University of Southern California, Los Angeles, and later to a laboratory of the National Research Council in Saskatoon, Canada, where he unraveled the glycerides of castor oil.

In 1971, Achaya became the executive director of the Protein Foods and Nutrition Development Association of India in Mumbai (Bombay), where one of his goals was to develop and distribute inexpensive, nutritious, ready-to-eat meals to the poor. Although a few products were test-marketed, the project never got off the ground. However, his book on nutrition, *Your Food and You,* became popular and was translated into several Indian languages.

Achaya next moved to Mysore to be closer to his home, Coorg, in Karnataka, where he became a consultant to the United Nations University Programme at the Central Food Technological Research Institute in 1977, a program designed to train people from developing countries in food science and technology. He retired in 1983 and published *Everyday Indian Processed Foods* the following year.

His retirement was productive. In addition to *Indian Food: A Historical Companion,* he published *Oilseeds and Oil Milling in India: A Cultural and Historical Survey* (1990), *Ghani: The Traditional Oil Mill of India* (1993), *The Food Industries of British India* (1994), *A Historical Dictionary of Indian Food* (1998), and *The Story of Our Food* (2000). When I visited him in Bangalore in March 2002, he had recently completed four articles on Indian food for an Italian encyclopedia, and claimed it was his last writing—though in conversation with my wife, he revealed a desire to write something about Indian classical music, a passion of his.

Achaya had many such extracurricular interests, among them photography, art, cinema, books, sports, and food, in addition to both Indian and Western classic music. Six months before his death, an article in *The Hindu* (February 25, 2001) had hailed him as "the Leonardo of Bangalore." I believe that the comparison with da Vinci embarrassed him, but however modest he was, there is no denying that when Achaya passed away on September 5, 2002 there was one fewer Renaissance man in the world. Every student of food and foodways in South Asia will be forever indebted to him.

— Bob Lucky *with* Vinod Huria

The Chemistry and Technology of Indian Dairy Products, with K.S. Rangappa, 1948. Revised edition, 1974
Science Perspectives, (Editor) with A. Rahman, 1969
Nutritious Foods for Everyone: PFNDAI, (Editor) with Rajat Mitra, 1972
Better Foods for Better Nutrition: PFNDAI, (Editor) with Rajat Mitra, 1973
Cottonseed Chemistry and Technology in its setting in India, with K.S. Murti, 1975
Your Food and You, 1975. Second edition, 1983. Translated into Bengali, Hindi, Tamil, Telugu, and Urdu.
Extruder-based Foods in India: PFNDAI, (Editor) with Rajat Mitra, 1976
Marketing of Foods for Children through the Public Distribution System: PFNDAI, Report of the New Delhi Workshop Held on July 9–10, 1977, (Editor) with Rajat Mitra,1977
First Indian Convention of Food Scientists and Technologists: AAFSTI, (Editor) 1978
Confectionary Industry in India: AFSTI, (Editor) 1979
Food Science and Technology: Proceedings of the UNU Workshop on the Management of R&D Institutions in Food Science and Technology Organized at CFTRI Mysore, (Editor) 1979
By-products from Food Industries; Utilization and Disposal: AFSTI, (Editor) 1980
Management of R&D Institutions in the Area of Food Science and Technology: Proceedings of the UNU Workshop Organized at CFTRI Mysore, (Editor), 1981
Food Challenges of the Eighties: Proceedings of the AFSTI International Conference AHARA, (Editor) 1982
Interfaces between Agriculture, Nutrition and Food Technology: Proceedings of the UNU Workshop Organized at CFTRI Mysore, (Editor), 1984
Everyday Indian Processed Foods, 1984

Interfaces between Agriculture, Nutrition and Food Science: Proceedings of the UNU Workshop organized at CFTRI Mysore, (Editor) 1984
Processed Foods for Special Dietary Requirements: AFSTI, (Editor) with M.R. Chandrasekhara, 1989
Oilseeds and Oil Milling in India: A Cultural and Historical Survey, 1990
Ghani: The Traditional Oil Mill of India, 1993
The Food Industries of British India, 1994
Indian Food: A Historical Companion, 1994
A Historical Dictionary of Indian Food, 1998
The Story of Our Food, 2000

Eliza Acton

❦ 1799–1859 ❦

ELIZA ACTON IS ONE OF THE GREAT ENGLISH COOKBOOK AUTHORS. HER writing is clear, her recipes are precise. She innovated the form of recipe we are all familiar with today, with an attached list of ingredients, with quantities, in the order in which they are called for. She estimates the time needed to prepare and cook a dish. She provides many useful hints, obviously derived from experience and attentive observation. Her books also contain interesting information and commentary. The first, *Modern Cookery* (1845), was immediately successful in England and was quickly adapted for readers in America. It continued to be revised and reprinted for half a century.

Acton was born in Sussex and grew up in Suffolk, the oldest daughter of a brewer of Ipswich. She lived for a while in France, where she was clearly influenced by the cuisine: Her books contain many recipes for French dishes. Rumors, to this day unsubstantiated, claim that she became engaged to a French officer but that, for some reason, the engagement was called off. What we know for sure is that Eliza Acton never married.

She returned to England and lived with her mother in Tunbridge and in Hampstead. Her skill with words first led her to write poetry, and she found subscribers and a publisher to bring out a volume of poems in 1826. (While poems like "Take Back Thy Ring" and "Go, Cold and Fickle Trifler!" lend some credence to the stories of a broken engagement, there are too many other poems of a different tone to allow for any certain conclusions.)

Acton must also have established a reputation as a good cook, because the publishers Longman and Company asked her to write a cookbook for them. This took her several years of careful work, during which she tested recipes and studied "a large number of works on cookery." Finally in 1845, *Modern Cookery in all its Branches* was offered to "private families"; it was not intended to be a work for professional chefs. Acton continued to tinker with this book for the rest of her life,

Frontispiece from the first edition of her Modern Cookery in All Its Branches, *published in 1845. The etching is by J. G. Spurgeon after a portrait by William Beechey.*

and numerous revised and enlarged editions appeared, with slight variations in title and subtitle. Indeed, the second edition of the work was published the same year the original edition appeared. At one point, Acton added a chapter on "Foreign and Jewish Cookery," and the 1854 edition acknowledged the new ideas of **Justus Liebig** and was retitled *Modern Cookery for Private Families: reduced to a system of easy practice, in a series of carefully tested receipts, in which the principles of Baron Liebig and other eminent writers have been as much as possible applied and explained.*

The publishers asked **Sarah Josepha Hale** to prepare an American edition of *Modern Cookery*, which she did in 1845, working from the second edition. Hale added a chapter on the "American Mode of Cooking Indian Corn, Pumpkins, etc." She added a recipe for cooking terrapins, remarking that "Many persons in Philadelphia have made themselves famous for cooking this article alone." The recipes Hale added stand out in the book because she failed to conform to Acton's practice of listing the ingredients. Hale also chose to omit several recipes which dealt with ingredients she apparently considered too exotic for America at that time, including chestnuts, olives, pheasant (for which she substituted chicken or pigeon), red herrings, Brussels sprouts, and salsify. The most significant difference between the Old World and New World editions is the subtle suggestion in Hale that the housewife is the cook, while Acton devoted more attention to the need to control the servants.

Acton's *English Bread-Book* (1857) is an impassioned plea for "*good, light* and *pure bread.*" She deplores the common practice of adulterating bread with alum and "other deleterious substances," and the false economy of laborers spending their wages on bread from the baker. Although she concedes that not all have access to an oven, she believes that many do not bake simply out of ignorance and fear. Acton mentions that she agrees in substance with the views of **William Cobbett** on bread for the poor, though not, perhaps, with the vehemence of his tone. The bread book offers an abundance of recipes for wheaten loaves, buns, rolls, and Sally Lunns, as well as breads made of rye, oats, potatoes, Indian corn, beans, parsnips, and other vegetables. She provides "very plain directions to a quite inexperienced learner for making bread." If the instructions in her book, Acton notes, "should prove sufficient to aid the reader effectually in becoming independent of the industry and skill of others, for the preparation of the most valuable portion of our daily food, the great aim of the author will be obtained."

After Acton's death in 1859, the publishers continued to bring out new editions of *Modern Cookery*, continuing nearly till the end of the nineteenth century. As recently as 1968, Acton's talents were again acknowledged with the publication of *The Best of Eliza Acton*, a selection of recipes with an introduction by **Elizabeth David**, who called *Modern Cookery* "the greatest cookery book in our language."

— ALICE ARNDT

Poems, 1826
Modern Cookery in all its Branches: reduced to a system of easy practice, for the use of private families: in a series of practical receipts, which have been strictly tested, and are given with the most minute exactness, 1845
The English Bread-Book: for domestic use, adapted to families of every grade: containing the

plainest and most minute instructions to the learner: practical receipts for many varieties of bread; with notices of the present system of adulteration, and its consequences; and of the improved baking processes and institutions established abroad, 1857

Modern Cookery in all its Branches:... "the whole carefully revised by Mrs. S. J. Hale," American edition, 1845

Aglaë Adanson

❦ 1775–1852 ❧

Frontispiece from the fifth edition of her Maison de Campagne, *published in 1845*

Aglaë Adanson, writer and gardener, was born in Paris on May 17, 1775. She was the daughter of Michel Adanson, a traveler, botanist, and member of the *Académie des sciences*, who had traveled to Senegal in the mid-eighteenth century, and Jeanne Bénard. Her parents separated when she was ten; she was educated in Paris at a convent school run by the Filles du Calvaire. In 1792, with the onset of the Terror, she and her mother fled to England, returning in 1794. She soon married one M. Lespinasse; the marriage ended in divorce. She subsequently married M. Doûmet, with whom she had two sons, Anarchises (named for the hero of a contemporary novel), and Emile-Auguste. Before the decade was over she was divorced for the second time, and did not remarry. She did, however, form an alliance with a third man, with whom she had a third son and, early in the nineteenth century, moved to the department of Allier in central France. This third partner disappeared along with their child, and Mme. Adanson, as she styled herself, settled down to live the rest of her long life on the estate of Baleine (or Balaine). Here, if her writings are to be believed, she led a life which exemplified both her joie de vivre and her love of gardening and domestic management.

It was at Baleine that she wrote, and in 1822 first published, her magnum opus, *La Maison de campagne* (*The Country House*). It was published in Paris by Louis Eustache Audot, himself a garden enthusiast and the author of France's leading nineteenth-century cookery book, *La Cuisiniere de la campagne et de la ville* (*The Town and Country Cook*). Adanson's *Maison de campagne* appeared in six editions at approximately five-year intervals, the last appearing in 1852, the year of her death.

Books on domestic management are usually dull at best. Aglaë Adanson's treatise is unique in its genre in reflecting an individual personality. She takes pride in her Enlightenment inheritance. The title page describes her as "the daughter of Michel Adanson." She recommends up-to-date domestic improvements, such as lightning rods, barometers, and window screens. She even dares to be original, telling her readers that they must conform to the practices of the locales in which they live, insofar as they take part in the local society, but that they should order their own domains as they please. She does, however, urge them to try her own way of doing things first. Half of each edition is devoted to gardening, which was plainly her passion. A solid section is devoted to a generalized essay on how one chooses one's country house, and organizes it. Another portion consists of a "little dictionary" of things one should know if one is to live in the country, and a quarter of her work is "a little book of home cookery."

Earlier writers, beginning with Nicolas de Bonnefons's *Jardinier François* (1653), had written books addressing the home cook, and subsequently François Menon's *Cuisinière bourgeoise* (1746) served as the basic cookbook for a century. **Mme. Mérigot**, a publisher's wife, may well have been the first Frenchwoman to publish a cookbook, a 34-recipe pamphlet on potato cookery; but Adanson was the first Frenchwoman to write her own substantial cookery book. It is a very pure expression of the nineteenth-century home kitchen. The recipes can be followed successfully today. They are simple, but clearly described, and require the excellent ingredients which would have been available to any reasonably prosperous countrywoman. Adanson draws heavily on the produce of her own estate. Based as she was in central France, she cooks with the carp that swam in her own canals and the migratory fish that came up the Loire watershed to spawn. She specialized in growing North American plants, from dogwood to tomatoes and sweet potatoes, and gives recipes for the latter two. The book evolves over its thirty-year life span: The recipes increase in number, and with each edition she revises the bibliography of books one needs to refer to for country life. Regularly she refers to her "dear readers" and the requests for information they send her. She disapproves of greenhouses, but her readers need advice, so she gives it. She urges compassion for the rural poor.

In the last year of her life she published a little pamphlet, *Le Livre des enfants de campagne* (*The Book for Country Children*) (1852), with the explanation that it was to be given to peasants in this backward region of France where poverty and superstition were widespread. In the introduction she tells landowners that there is nothing in the booklet that will harm piety or morals, and asks them to distribute it to their tenants. Teach your sons and daughters to read, to write, and to calculate, she urges them, so that they will not be taken advantage of. She accompanies this advice with a little rudimentary geography, and some brisk advice about the uselessness of superstition.

Adanson's life was richly lived, her opinions confidently stated. One must wonder why so few other women in her circumstances found their way into print.

— BARBARA KETCHAM WHEATON

La Maison de campagne (The Country House), 1822
Le Livre des enfants de campagne (The Book for Country Children), 1852

Kate Aitken

1891–1971

ALSO CALLED: Mrs. A

KATE AITKEN—FONDLY KNOWN AS "MRS. A"—WAS CANADA's first national culinary star. In the middle decades of the twentieth century, millions of Canadians listened to her dispense cooking advice—and much more—over CFRB radio in Toronto from 1934, later on CJAD in Montreal, and across the country on the Canadian Broadcasting Corporation (CBC) network from 1948 to 1957. Long after she died, families continued to consult her best-selling *Kate Aitken's Canadian Cook Book,* first published in 1945 by the *Montreal Standard* and reissued multiple times up to 1992.

1955

Aitken was born in the small town of Beeton, Ontario, northwest of Toronto, the first of seven children of Anne and Robert Scott, who ran the general store. She worked briefly as a school teacher before marrying Henry Aitken in 1914. The couple moved to Virginia, Minnesota, but soon returned to Beeton, where Henry managed a feed mill and Kate ran their farm. They had two children, Mary (Mrs. Robert Hortop) and Anne (Mrs. Clinton Thompson).

Kate had no professional training in agriculture or home economics. As a child in the 1890's, she learned about food and cooking from her mother and grandmother, including, for example, how to prepare favorite Ontario pickles and relishes, how to package farmer's butter for resale in the city (an activity that took place in the cool cellar), and how Ontario's nineteenth-century pioneers made brown-sugar pie for barn raisings: Five pounds brown sugar, 22 eggs, four quarts cream, and spices, baked in milk pans and served stone-cold from the milk house. Despite these humble beginnings, she was soon making a name for herself, breeding a world-record laying Wyandotte hen and starting up a canning business to process and sell her fruits, vegetables, and poultry.

At the request of the Ontario Department of Agriculture, she lectured to rural women throughout the province up to 1928. The "Country Kitchen" she set up at the Canadian National Exhibition in Toronto in 1923 to sell her goods led to a nearly 30-year connection with this annual fair: She organized its first cooking schools, ran the restaurants, did live radio shows on site, and in 1938 became the first director of women's activities. She wrote advertising booklets for Canada Starch Co., Ogilvie Flour Mills, and Tamblyn Drug Stores, often in conjunction with cooking schools for these companies. During World War II the federal government appointed her supervisor of conservation in the consumer branch of the Wartime Prices and Trade Board. From 1941 to 1951 she commuted weekly between Toronto (where she had moved from Beeton) and Montreal, where she was women's editor of the *Standard* newspaper. After retiring from broadcasting in 1957, she served on the Board of Governors of the CBC from 1959 to 1962 and also worked for UNESCO and UNICEF.

Prodigious energy and entrepreneurial drive, combined with the imagination and courage to set out on a different path from most of her contemporaries', fuelled Kate's self-made career, but a large part of her success lay in the close bond she established with home cooks through her demonstrations and radio shows. Audiences appreciated her repertoire of traditional Canadian fare, interspersed with new, but sensible, food fashions, and her practical advice for housewives. Kate's approach was the antithesis of the "scientific" method promulgated by the home-economics movement. Her warm, direct voice, preserved on recordings in the CBC archives, conveys the special rapport she had with her listeners. Her optimistic, "can-do" attitude positively beams from the pages of her two autobiographies, *Never a Day So Bright* (childhood) and *Making Your Living Is Fun* (adulthood). Other Canadian cooks rose to prominence in the 1920's and 1930's, among them Mary Moore, Nellie Pattinson, and Kay Caldwell Bayley, but the unique aspect of Kate's fame was that her broadcast journalism eventually reached beyond the culinary realm to political and cultural affairs. She traveled to every province and around the globe to report to her fellow citizens on international events seen through Canadian eyes, asking challenging questions in her interviews with such world leaders as Roosevelt, Hitler, and Mussolini. She was a giant in her time, and in *Kate Aitken's Canadian Cook Book* she captured the essence of the country's home cooking for a large part of the twentieth century. Kate died in Mississauga, Ontario, and is buried in Beeton United Church Cemetery.

— ELIZABETH DRIVER

Famous Royal Household Recipes, series for Ogilvie Flour Mills, 1934
52 Baking Secrets, 52 Cakes, 52 Desserts, 52 Pies, series for Canada Starch Co., 1940
Cooking Gossip, bulletins, Canada Starch Co.
Good News, monthly recipe bulletins, Tamblyn Drug Stores, 1940's–1950's
Feeding Your Family in Wartime, c. 1941–1945
How to Save Sugar in Cooking, 1942
Kate Aitken's Canadian Cook Book, 1945; new editions in 1950, 1953, and 1964; facsimile of 1945
    edition, with introduction by Elizabeth Driver and essays by the Aitken Family, 2004
Kate Aitken's Guernsey Gold Recipes for Christmas, Christie's Dairy Ltd, 1950's
Lovely You, 1951
Canadian Etiquette for Daily Living, 1953
It's Fun Raising a Family, 1955
Never a Day So Bright, 1956
Travel Alone and Love It, 1958
Making Your Living Is Fun, 1959

Akabori

Minekichi Akabori the First	✤ 1816–1904 ✤
Minekichi Akabori the Second	✤ 1853–1904 ✤
Minekichi Akabori the Third	✤ 1886–1956 ✤
Masako Akabori	✤ 1907–1988 ✤

ALSO CALLED: Akahori

MINEKICHI AKABORI IS THE INITIATOR OF COOKING EDUCATION FOR women in Japan and a founding father of modern Japanese home cookery. In fact, three personages are hidden behind this name. The "original" Minekichi (1816–1904) founded the first school of cookery for women and was the patriarch of a family of educators that has continued to influence Japanese culinary culture for the past century. His son Minekichi the Second (1853–1904), whose birth name was Kumauemon, assisted his father as a pioneer of cooking education and made sure that his own son, Minetarō (1886–1956), would be ready to take over as Minekichi the Third. Actually, it was during the activities of the third Minekichi that the scope of influence of the Akabori family expanded and began to shape Japanese cookery on a nationwide scale. Minetarō's daughter, Masako (1907–1988), topped off the family's mission during the 1960's, when her cooking shows were broadcast on radio and television, reaching practically every household in Japan. By that time, the cumulative number of graduates of the Akabori School of Cookery exceeded 800,000.

Minekichi the First was born in the provincial town of Kakegawa (now in Shizuoka prefecture) in 1816. The son of a family of tavern-keepers, Minekichi left for the capital at 18 and worked as a professional chef. He eventually opened a restaurant in the center of Tokyo in 1861 which he named after the hometown he had left 27 years earlier. However, it was his educational activities, which Minekichi undertook later, rather than his career as a chef, that earned him an honorable place in Japanese food history. In 1882, Minekichi established the Akabori Cooking Class (*Akabori Kappō Kyōjō*) in Tokyo. It was the first cooking school for women ever opened in Japan.

At first, the Akabori Cooking Class focused on Japanese cooking, but from 1887 onward classes in Western cookery—which fascinated Minekichi and was very much in vogue at the time—were also set up. Students were primarily wives and daughters of wealthy merchants, and they were not only taught how to cook, but also learned about the advantages of modern kitchen facilities, such as running water and gas. Minekichi the First and the Second also provided cooking classes at several prestigious women's schools in Tokyo. Aimed at upper-class women, the modern curricula of these schools included classes on nutrition and "scientific" cookery, principally under the influence of American home-economics education.

In 1892, Minekichi and Minekichi the Second, with three other reformers, founded the Kitchen Improvement Society (*Chihōkai*), with the aim of spreading the

Minekichi Akabori the Third

A

gospel of cooking education. Teachers from women's schools from all over the country attended lectures and presentations organized by the association, and in 1902 the Society published a cookbook. During this decade, Minekichi's recipes and advice also began to appear increasingly in the cooking columns of popular magazines.

The elder Minekichi's last book, *Home Recipes for Twelve Months*, appeared shortly after his death and was quite revolutionary, not least because it included a table of the nutritional value of various foods composed by the Tokyo Hygiene Laboratory. The book grouped recipes in twelve sections according to the time of the year, each focusing on ingredients in season and cooking techniques most appropriate in terms of weather and custom. This structure was very helpful for women running households and became the basis of dozens of Japanese cookbooks published during the following decades.

Although Minekichi the First and the Second were pioneers of the incorporation of Western dishes into Japanese home cookery, this aspect became particularly pronounced in the activities of Minekichi the Third. In 1909, he embarked on a three-year voyage to Europe and the United States, and the impact of the trip is evident in his publications. Along with introducing ingredients and dishes completely unknown in Japan and adapting them to local tastes, Minekichi the Third also brought fresh ideas and variety to Japanese home cooking by introducing new cooking techniques for well-known ingredients. His *New European and American Seafood Dishes*, for example, introduced several new ways of preparing lobster, oysters, crab, shrimps, snails, clams, anchovies, and many kinds of fish.

In 1904, Minekichi the Second died of stomach cancer, and two months later his father passed away. Now, the activities centered on Minekichi the Third, his wife, Michi, and his mother and aunt, both named Kiku. During Minekichi's travels, the three women took affairs entirely into their own hands. From the 1920's onwards, Minekichi and Michi's daughter, Masako, also joined the teaching staff. In fact, the entire family was involved in running the enterprise, in line with the *iemoto* tradition. *Iemoto*, or "house heads," were the hereditary masters of lineages or schools of tea, flower-arranging, poetry, kickball, archery, swordsmanship, calligraphy, and other arts who taught their skills to amateur disciples for fees. This system greatly enhanced the prestige and the influence of the Akabori family on Japanese home cookery.

— Katarzyna J. Cwiertka

Chihōkai ōnippon ryōrihō (Japanese Recipes of the Kitchen Improvement Society), 1902
Wayō katei ryōōrihō (Japanese and Western Recipes for the Home), 1904
Katei jûnikagetsu ryōrihō (Home Recipes for Twelve Months), 1904
Nippon ryōri kyōkasho, 1-3 kan (Textbook of Japanese Cooking, Vol. 1–3), 1905
Sokuseki sōzai ryōri (Quick Side Dishes), 1905
Wayō setchō katei ryōrihō (Japanese and Western Eclectic Recipes for the Home), 1905
Katei ōyō sōzai gohyakushu (Five Hundred Homemade Side Dishes), 1906
Nippon ryōrihō (Japanese Recipes), 1907
Katei ōyō yōshoku gohyakushu (Five Hundred Western Homemade Dishes), 1907
Sōzai ryōri (Side Dishes), 1908
Katei nichiyō ryōri, jōge (Everyday Dishes for the Home, Vol. 1 and 2), 1911
Eisei shokuhin chōrihō (Recipes for Hygienic Food), 1912

Katei nenjō ryōri no shikata (How to Cook at Home the Entire Year), 1912

Katei shin inryō (New Homemade Drinks), 1912

Nihon, seiyō, shina jitsuyō shin ryōri (New Practical Japanese, Western, and Chinese Cuisine), 1912

Ōbei gyokai shin ryōri (New European and American Seafood Dishes), 1912

Saishin yōgashi no chōsei (Latest Recipes for Western Sweets), 1912

Wayō kan'i ryōri (Easy Japanese and Western Home Cooking), 1913

Katei ōyō meshi hyakuchin ryōri (Hundred Unique Rice Recipes for the Home), 1913

Eisei shokumotsu wayō ryōrihō (Japanese and Western Recipes for Hygienic Food), 1913

Kasetsu gishiki ryōri (Official Cuisine for Auspicious Occasions), 1913

Katei shokumotsu ron (Homemade Food Theory), 1914

Shinshiki wayō katei ryōri (Japanese and Western Home Cooking New-Style), 1914

Nenjō ryōri no shikata (How to Cook the Entire Year), 1916

Katei nihon ryōrihō (Japanese Home Cooking), 1917

Shiki no ryōri (Seasonal Cuisine), 1917

Mainichi no sōzai (Side Dishes for Every Day), 1917

Ryōri no maki (The Recipe Book), 1917

Jitsuyō sōzai ryōri jōnikagetsu (Practical Side Dishes for Twelve Months), 1918

Katei jitsuyō seiyō ryōrihō (Western Practical Recipes for the Home), 1919

Saishin wayō ryōrihō (Up-to-Date Japanese and Western Recipes), 1922

Katei keiniku keiran ryōri (Homemade Chicken and Egg Dishes), 1924

Katei ōyō yōshoku gohyakushu (Five Hundred Western Dishes for the Home), 1926

Katei kaiseki jōnikagetsu ryōri (Homemade Kaiseki Banquets for Twelve Months), 1927

Akabori nihon ryōri hō (Akabori-Style Japanese Recipes), 1928

Akabori seiyō ryōrihō (Akabori-Style Western Recipes), 1929

Saishin shina ryōri (Up-to-Date Chinese Dishes), 1932

Akabori shiki sōza ryōri (Akabori-Style Side Dishes), 1936

Sokuseki ippin shina ryōri no tsukurikata (How to Cook Chinese Quick Dishes), 1936

Katei muki shina ryōri (Chinese Cuisine for the Home), 1941

Shina ryōri (Chinese Cuisine), 1941

Osōzai muki nihon ryōrihō (Japanese Recipes for Side Dishes), 1941

Nichijō jikken ryōri (Experimental Dishes for Every Day), 1942

Akabori seiyō ryōri zensho (A Full Collection of Akabori-style Western Dishes), 1948

Akabori nihon ryōri (Akabori-style Japanese Cuisine), 1949

Jisshō chōka ryōri zensho (A Full Collection of Practical Chinese Dishes), 1950

Sokuseki sake no sakana (Quick Sake Snacks), 1951

Seiyō ryōri no tsukurikata (How to Cook Western Food), 1956

Chōka ryōri no tsukurikata (How to Cook Chinese Food), 1956

Nihon ryōri no tsukurikata (How to Cook Japanese Food), 1956

A

Al-Baghdadi

ALSO CALLED: Muhammad ibn al-Hasan ibn Muhammad ibn al-Karim al-Katib al-Baghdadi

MUHAMMAD IBN AL-HASAN IBN AL-KARIM, KNOWN AS AL-BAGHDADI, MAY stand for all the compilers of the surviving medieval Arabic cookbooks in that practically nothing is known about him other than that he was a scribe living in Baghdad. As for the man who produced an expanded edition of al-Baghdadi's thirteenth-century book, *Kitâb al-Tabîkh* (*The Book of Dishes*), under the title *Kitâb Wasf al-At'ima al-Mu'tâda* (*The Description of Familiar Foods*), not even his name is recorded; internal evidence suggests that he might have lived in Cairo. The title under which a thirteenth-century Spanish Arabic cookbook is known, the *Manuscrito Anónimo*, speaks for itself.

We can deduce a certain amount about the compiler of another book entitled *Kitâb al-Tabîkh,* which dates from the tenth century. His name, Abu Muhammad al-Muzaffar ibn Nasr ibn Sayyar, indicates that he was descended from an eighth-century Muslim governor of eastern Iran, but the fact that he worked as a scribe shows that he had not inherited much. At any rate, he must have retained his family connections, because he was commissioned to write this book "assembling dishes of kings and caliphs and notables" at the behest of an unnamed patron, presumably Saif al-Daula, the culture-minded prince of Aleppo.

The caliphs of ninth-century Baghdad had adopted many practices from the pre-Islamic Persian court, one of which was a cult of gastronomy. They organized cooking contests among their boon companions, just as the Sassanid emperors had. It was fashionable for a nobleman to compile a book of his favorite recipes, even if he did not cook. These books have all disappeared, along with the cookbooks written by literary figures of the time. Fortunately for us, Ibn Sayyar had access to many of them, because he gives recipes from the collections of ten caliphs, from al-Mahdi (died 785) to al-Muktafi (died 908). Two dozen other notables (royals, viziers, poets, even a wife) are linked to recipes in the book, and four chefs are named. It is a remarkable legacy from the golden age of Baghdad.

One man we know a great deal about is Yahya ibn 'Isa ibn Jazla, but he was not, properly speaking, a cookbook writer. He was a physician of Nestorian Christian ancestry, like many of Baghdad's doctors since the eighth century. He studied medicine under Sa'id ibn Hibat Allah, the court physician of the caliph al-Muqtadi (died 1094). His enduring claim to fame was a monumental medical encyclopedia, *Minhaj al-Bayan fi ma Yasta' Miluhu al-Insan* (*The Pathway of Explanation as to That Which Man Uses*).

Among its thousands of prescriptions, however, are scores of recipes. It's not known how much involvement Ibn Jazla had in writing them: He might have altered a cook's recipe to suit his medical views. In any case, since they were written more precisely than usual in the Middle Ages and included discussions of the dishes' purported medical value, the recipes were immediately excerpted and circulated on their own as a cookbook and were freely plagiarized by later writers, including al-Baghdadi and the author of another thirteenth-century book, *Kitab al-*

Wusla ila al-Habib (*The Book of the Bond With the Friend*). Various manuscripts ascribe the latter cookbook to Yahya ibn 'Abd al-Azim al-Jazzar, to Ibn al-Adim al-'Uqaili, to an unnamed nephew of the sultan al-Malik al-Ashraf and to an unnamed head shaikh of Hama. In the thirteenth century, an obscure Spanish scholar living in Venice, Jamboninus of Cremona, translated 82 of Ibn Jazla's recipes into Latin.

The medieval cookbook author we know most about is the latest and the least of them, Jamal al-Din Yusuf ibn Hasan al-Salihi, known as Ibn al-Mibrad (died 1503), a Damascus legal scholar who wrote numerous short works on sundry topics, one of them being *Kitab al-Tibakha* (*The Book of Cookery*). Since the title of this collection of rather simple recipes could also be read *Kitab al-Tabbakha* (*The Book of the [Female] Cook*), we may suspect, even more than in the case of Ibn Jazla, that the author himself was not a cook.

— CHARLES PERRY

Kitâb al-Tabîkh (The Book of Dishes), thirteenth century

Alexander

※ 356–323 BC ※

ALSO CALLED: Alexander the Great

ALEXANDER THE GREAT WAS KING OF Macedonia from 336 to 323 BC and conqueror of the Persian empire. He was no cook, but there is good reason for his inclusion in a collection of culinary biographies. As a result of his Persian expedition some important foods from southern Asia first became available in the Mediterranean world. At the same time, foods familiar in earlier Greece were transplanted eastward. In each case this event marked a turning point in the development from local food to world commodity. In addition, Alexander's empire united Greek, Macedonian, and Persian traditions in a cultural melting-pot whose influence can be traced historically throughout Europe, North Africa, and the Middle East.

Born in 356 BC, Alexander was the son of Philip II, a warlord and statesman who ruled Macedonia from 359 to 336, and his first wife, Olympias. Philip dominated the squabbling Greek city-states to his south, as well as the Balkan kingdoms on his frontiers; meanwhile he encouraged the spread of Greek culture in Macedonia. He selected Aristotle, a Greek philosopher and scientist of astonishing achievements, as his son's tutor.

Alexander and his horse, Boucephalos, in a detail from a mosaic of the Battle of Issos, found in the House of the Faun in Pompeii. The mosaic dates from about 80 BC.

Philip married often. His latest marriage, in 337, produced a baby son; this fact threatened the previously secure position of Olympias and the young Alexander. Shortly afterward the king was murdered and Alexander succeeded him.

As king of Macedonia and leader of a Greek alliance, Alexander took up the project of eastern conquest that his father had planned. The vast Persian Empire extended from the shores of the Aegean Sea to the Indus Valley and the oases of Egypt. In ten years Alexander conquered the whole of that territory, replacing many Persian administrators with Macedonians and establishing new cities to be occupied by army veterans and Greek colonists. He planned further conquests, but died suddenly at Babylon in 323. His empire was eventually divided. The Seleucid dynasty, ruling Syria, and the Ptolemaic dynasty, ruling Egypt, were the most lasting and significant among the successors of Alexander, but both territories were eventually absorbed by the Roman Empire.

Under Aristotle's influence, scientists accompanied Alexander's expedition. Reports by botanists concerning important food plants of southwestern Asia, previously unknown in the West, are incorporated in the *History of Plants* (compiled 310 BC) by Aristotle's pupil Theophrastus. These include pistachio nuts, citrons (*Citrus medica*), and rice; peaches are mentioned in a later supplementary text. All these are now familiar foods in Mediterranean lands and in other parts of the world. Theophrastus also notes Indian fruits including jackfruit, banana, and mango, and describes edible Egyptian plants which few Europeans before Alexander would have seen: argun palm (*Medemia argun*), doum palm (*Hyphaene thebaica*), persea (*Mimusops schimperi*), sebesten (*Cordia myxa*), and sycamore fig (*Ficus sycomorus*).

Alexander's scientists tried planting European crops in the East. This had an important effect on the later agriculture of Egypt and Syria and of southern Iraq, where it was said that the Macedonians were the first to succeed with the grape vine. They contributed to the spread southeastward of several vegetables and fruits, including beet, turnip, asparagus, pear, walnut, and winter cherry (*Physalis alkekengi*); also, probably, to the eastward migration across Asia of the opium poppy, a minor food but an indispensable medicine in ancient times.

Although not mentioned by Theophrastus, asafoetida (*Ferula asafoetida*) was observed and used by Alexander's troops. They found that it closely resembled silphium, a now-extinct spice which was then produced in Libya and was of great importance in Greek food and medicine, and thus called it "Median silphium." (Media was a region of Iran.) As the supply of Libyan silphium dwindled, asafoetida took its place in Roman cuisine.

At Alexander's court Macedonian, Greek, and Persian customs (or vices, as some ancient writers thought) were intermixed. One member of his court was the official historian, Callisthenes, invited to join the expedition as Aristotle's nominee. "Lucky Callisthenes," someone said to the cynic Diogenes. "Not so very lucky," Diogenes replied. "He has to have his lunch and dinner when Alexander's hungry." Callisthenes had an unlucky end: He refused to kowtow to Alexander at dinner, in the new Persian fashion, and died in prison.

Alexander's steward or butler, Chares of Mitylene, wrote a memoir in which he included the information that at the monarch's court deep pits were used as a means of conserving ice through the summer. It seems likely, although Chares did not say so, that the method was learned from the Persians: Greeks and Macedonians, until that time, probably had no way of conserving ice. In times when refrigeration was otherwise impossible, ice was of great importance to wealthy gastronomes to chill wine, fruit, and other refreshing foods.

In the course of Alexander's expedition large-scale banquets, including a mass Macedonian–Persian wedding feast, were held in his famous hundred-couch tent. Greeks and Persians reclined on couches to dine, and they measured dining rooms by the number of couches they could accommodate, but there had never been any as large as this. Lavish display and costly luxury foods, far beyond the dreams of earlier Europeans, came into fashion for royal courts in Alexander's time. His *symposia* (drinking parties) formed the setting for several romantic and tragic incidents of his biography. There was competitive drinking of wine at these *symposia*, a custom which was all the more dangerous since Macedonians, unlike Greeks, drank wine unmixed with water, while Greeks, unlike Macedonians, drank all through the night. In unison, these customs certainly caused deaths at Alexander's court; some believed that they precipitated Alexander's own death.

— ANDREW DALBY

A

Ida Bailey Allen

1885–1973

ALSO CALLED: Mrs. Allen | Ida Cogswell Bailey Allen

WHEN SHE WAS EIGHT YEARS OLD, IDA COGSWELL BAILEY fell in love with cooking and the domestic life. She had dressed up in a "grown-up" dress from her grandmother's attic and gone to visit a neighbor. The neighbor received her graciously and, saying that "Grown-up ladies do useful things," she proceeded to give Ida her first cooking lesson. They made gingerbread. Her parents, Frank Garvin and Ida Louise Cogswell Bailey, encouraged her interest. They allowed her to bake her father's birthday cake, which he ate with gusto even though it had fallen.

Ida Cogswell Bailey was born in Danielson, Connecticut, in 1885. At age seventeen, she moved from her childhood home to Worcester, Massachusetts, to study domestic science at Oread Institute. She went on to study dietetics at Metropolitan Hospital in New York City, and served as dietitian in various hospitals. She was director of domestic science at the YMCA in Worcester and opened a small cooking school there. Later, in 1920, she founded Mrs. Allen's School of Good Cookery in New York City.

In 1912, she married Thomas Lewis Allen, an opera singer, and bore him a son and daughter. Widowed, she married William Brewster Chapman, an engineer, in 1921, but she kept the name Allen professionally.

Thus began the work of a long life-time, writing cookbooks and serving as contributor or editor at numerous magazines, beginning with *The Ladies' Home Journal*, and going on to *Good Housekeeping, Pictorial Review, Family Circle, Parade*, and many others. She wrote the syndicated column "Let's Eat" for 22 years. She also lectured at Chautauquas and, during World War II, to the Bakers' and Cooks' School of the Army's Quartermaster Corps. Seven times the National Newspaper Radio Editors' Poll named hers the most popular women's program on the air. Her book *Youth After 40* (1950), was translated into Japanese, French, Italian, and Spanish. She was awarded an honorary doctorate by Stanley College, Massachusetts, in 1956, and a Médallion de l'Arbalète by the Swiss in 1962.

Throughout her career, Allen worked to keep up with the times. She helped her "friend the Home-Maker" adjust to the First World War by publishing *Mrs. Allen's Book of Wheat Substitutes, Mrs. Allen's Book of Sugar Substitutes,* and *Mrs. Allen's Book of Meat Substitutes*. She immediately understood the importance of radio, and in 1928 launched "The National Radio Homemakers' Club." She took part in America's efficiency movement; an entire meal was cooked on a series of radio shows for CBS, with Mrs. Allen describing the procedures for the benefit of the listeners while an announcer used a stopwatch to time each step of the process. This all went into *Ida Bailey Allen's Time-Saving Cook Book*, published in 1940. (She wrote no books of temperance recipes. Rather, she wrote fondly of her sea-captain grandfather, John Bailey, who she said advocated adding rum to the pot of New England baked beans; and in 1934, just a year after the repeal of Prohibition, she published *Ida Bailey Allen's Wines and Spirits Cook Book*.) With the advent of television, she was seen in "Mrs. Allen and the Chef." Ever a close partner with industry, she served as spokeswoman for the Corn Products Refining Company, and her *Modern Method of Preparing Delightful Foods* (1926) featured Mazola oil. In the early 1930's, she wrote two cookbooks for the F. W. Woolworth Company, which sold them exclusively. After World War II, Mrs. Allen promoted pressure cookers, writing a cookbook about their use.

She continued to publish books and articles to the end of her life. Her publisher claimed in 1950 that "one of every three American homes owns at least one Ida Bailey Allen book." The last of her more than 50 cookbooks appeared a few months after her death in 1973. There is no doubt that from age eight on, she had devoted herself to doing "useful things."

Mrs. Allen was prolific and successful for more than half a century, but in the end her fans did not include the increasingly sophisticated among America's cooks and diners in the second half of the twentieth century. She did try to reach this group: Recognizing that "America has become food conscious," she published *Gastronomique: A Cookbook for Gourmets* in 1958. But this simply was not her strong point; she began the work by issuing a call "to purveyors of fine foods for samples of unusual products," thereby showing that she had missed the point. Her efforts were soon superseded by the likes of **James Beard**, with his emphasis on quality fresh ingredients, **Craig Claiborne,** who became food editor of *The New York Times* in 1957 and introduced America to many cuisines from around the globe, and **Julia Child**, who began in 1961, with *Mastering the Art of French Cooking*, to make French dishes accessible to all Americans.

— ALICE ARNDT

Mrs. Allen's Cook Book, 1916
Golden Rule Cook Book, 1916
Mrs. Allen's Book of Meat Substitutes, 1918
Mrs. Allen's Book of Wheat Substitutes, 1918
Mrs. Allen's Book of Sugar Substitutes, 1918
Temtor Tempting Recipes, 1920
Bride's Book, 1922
Home Partners, 1924
Mrs. Allen on Cooking, Menus, Service, 1924
One Hundred Four Prize Radio Recipes, 1926
Your Foods and You, 1926
The Modern Method of Preparing Delightful Foods, 1926
Vital Vegetables, 1927
Ida Bailey Allen's Modern Cook Book, 1932
When You Entertain, 1932
The Service Cook Book, 1933
The Round-the-World Cook Book, 1934
Ida Bailey Allen's Wines and Spirits Cook Book, 1934
The Service Cook Book No. 2, 1935
The Budget Cook Book, 1935
Satisfying Salads, [n.d.]
Cooking Within Your Income, 1936
Kitchenette Cooking for Two, 1938
Ida Bailey Allen's Kitchenette for Two Cookbook, 1938
The Everyday Cook Book, 1938, 1988
Ida Bailey Allen's New Modern Cook Book, 1939
Common Sense Cook Book, 1939
Ida Bailey Allen's Time-Saving Cook Book, 1940
Ida Bailey Allen's Money-Saving Cook Book, 1940
Successful Entertaining, 1942
Double Quick Cooking, 1943
Pressure Cooking, 1947
Picture Cook Book, 1947
Delicious Meals at Low Cost, 1948
Food for Two, 1948
Youth After 40, 1950
Solving the High Cost of Eating, 1952
Ida Bailey Allen's Step-by-Step Picture Cook Book, 1952
Ida Bailey Allen's Sandwich Book, 1955
Cook Book for Two, 1957
159 Exciting Easy-Do-Meals with Sausage, 1957
Gastronomique: A Cookbook for Gourmets, 1958
Best Loved Recipes of the American People, 1973

Juan Altamiras

ALSO CALLED: Raimundo Gómez

RAIMUNDO GÓMEZ WAS BORN IN THE TOWN OF ALMUNIA DE DOÑA GODINA IN the province of Zaragoza in northwestern Spain toward the end of the seventeenth century. He joined a Franciscan order and worked as a cook in several monasteries, spending his last years at the Colegio Mayor de San Diego de Zaragoza. The college, which had been established a century earlier on the grounds of the old Royal Monastery of San Francisco, was graced with a magnificent vegetable garden and was the residence of the Franciscan students attending the University of Zaragoza.

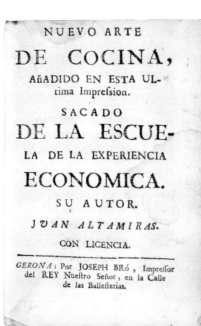

Title page of the enlarged 1770 edition of Nuevo Arte de Cocina

Raimundo Gómez was able to see the world through the eyes of these young monks and to understand the challenges they faced. He wrote his book for them, advocating a virtuous life that nonetheless excluded neither creativity nor enjoyment.

The title of his book is *Nuevo Arte de Cocina, sacado de la Escuela de la Experiencia Economica,* or *The New Art of Cooking, Derived from the School of Financial Experience.* The oldest known edition, printed in Madrid at the Imprenta Real, dates from 1745, but the work was republished on numerous occasions and in several formats. In 1770, 25 years after its first appearance, a new edition was published that included 125 new recipes and was dedicated to San Diego de Alcalá.

Published under the pseudonym Juan Altamiras, the *Nuevo Arte de Cocina* is a rich source of information on the culinary customs of the cooks of the Franciscan order, but Altamiras also incorporates comments on the foodways of other strata of society in Spain's golden age. His innovative spirit is evident in the way he emphasizes similarities and connections among different ways of life and the economic circumstances that underlie them.

The foundation of his cooking lies in Roman culture, but he acknowledges the influence of several centuries of Arab and Jewish presence in Spain, overlaid in turn by Christian culture. This millennial tradition, already complex, is renewed by the use of new products from the Americas, so different in aroma, taste, texture, and color.

Like all cooks in that era of transition, he had the honor and faced the challenge of overcoming the resistance to culinary innovation and the fear of new foods that doubtless manifested itself in his small society just as it did in the larger one outside the monastery. But he also gave literary form and structure to the practices that, in a spirit of joyful sobriety, regulated the kitchen of a Catholic monastery of the time—the spirit at the foundation of the everyday culinary traditions of his Aragonese countrymen.

Both introduction and text of *Nuevo Arte de Cocina* give us some insight into the personality of Raimundo Gómez. His candid and straightforward tone allows us to imagine a man of focused energy and intellectual curiosity. His comments, at times charming and funny, demonstrate a certain efficiency in financial matters. He was a modern man who valued simplicity and who believed that economizing on effort, time, and money was essential when working to turn a simple daily life into a paean to well-being and happiness.

He appears also to have had the gift of immense internal strength. He lived in harmony with the Franciscan spirit and sought perfection in the completion of his duties. He lived his religious calling and performed his work as a cook with complete integrity. His sole desire seems to have been to offer health and joy to his brothers and readers, with food and culinary wisdom as the utmost expression of his devotion to the Creator. The kitchen gave him the opportunity to fuse his creativity and his intellectual curiosity with the requirements of his religious service.

Brother Raimundo Gómez died about 1769.

— ALICIA RIOS

Nuevo Arte de Cocina, sacado de la Escuela de la Experiencia Economica (*The New Art of Cooking, Derived from the School of Financial Experience*), c. 1745. Enlarged edition, 1770. Modern edition with introduction by Jose M. Pisa Villarroya, 1994

Amphitryon

⁂ MYTHOLOGICAL CHARACTER ⁂

FOR THE PAST THREE AND A HALF CENTURIES, THE NAME OF AMPHITRYON HAS been used to designate a host at dinner, particularly one who is generous and lavish. This use of the word is especially common in France, where being labeled an "amphitryon" is a compliment to a gracious host.

Amphitryon is a character from Greek mythology. Homer and Hesiod, writing in the eighth century BC, placed him in the distant past, and his story was a favorite of many later Greek dramatists. The Roman playwright Plautus wrote a tragicomedy about him in the second century BC, which was followed by many other plays into the twentieth century. Elements of Shakespeare's *Comedy of Errors* also bear a marked similarity to the legend.

According to myth, Amphitryon was a Theban general married to the lovely Alcmene. The lustful god Zeus desired to spend a night with Alcmene while her husband was away at war. Knowing her fidelity, Zeus realized that the only way he could seduce her was to disguise himself as her husband. This he did, and the perfection of his disguise resulted in a great deal of confusion and consternation when the real Amphitryon returned home. Alcmene, entirely blameless since—to her knowledge—she had accepted only her husband, conceived a child by Zeus and bore the strong and courageous hero Hercules.

In Molière's comedy *Amphitryon* of 1668, much of the humor lies in the scenes of Amphitryon facing a copy of himself when he arrives home from battle. Amphitryon's servant Sosie, a comic character far more eager to have his dinner than to resolve the dilemma of who is really who, indicates his willingness to endorse whoever feeds him: *"Le vrai Amphitrion / Est l'Amphitrion ou l'on dine."* ("The true Amphitryon is the one who feeds you.") This popular line in a very successful play imparted an enduring new aspect to the character of Amphitryon.

In the early nineteenth century, **Grimod de la Reynière** entitled his guide for wealthy hosts *Manuel des Amphitryons*. A defining example of the amphitryon is Tallyrand who, employing the most illustrious chef of the age, **Carême**, used his magnificent dinners to advance his fame, power, and diplomacy.

— ALICE ARNDT

Anthimus

❧ LATE FIFTH/EARLY SIXTH CENTURY ❧

ANTHIMUS FIRST APPEARS ON THE HISTORICAL SCENE IN 478 IN CONSTANTInople, during the reign of the Emperor Zeno. He was caught in one of the political intrigues so common in the Byzantine Empire and was jailed, flogged, and sent into exile. The court of Theodoric, king of the Ostro-goths in Ravenna, took him in. Although he was already a trained physician, Anthimus must then have been a young man, because his famous treatise on dietetics wasn't written until at least a third of a century later.

After several years, Theodoric sent Anthimus to northwestern Europe as ambassador to Theudoric (also written Theodoric), a son of Clovis, the Merovingian king of the Franks. It is to Theudoric that Anthimus wrote his famous letter, *De Observatione Ciborum* (*Observations About Foods*), meant as a guide to a healthy diet for the king. Since Theudoric reigned from 511 to 534, we can date the letter to that period.

It is clear from his writing that Anthimus was not a native speaker of Latin. The language of Constantinople was Greek; perhaps he only learned his Latin in Ravenna. Philologists have used his work to study the transition of Latin to the romance languages of medieval Europe, but only recently have culinary historians looked at *De Observatione Ciborum* to study the foods and eating habits of the time.

As a physician, Anthimus is concerned with healthy foods and the best way to prepare them for good health. He says he is guided by the writings of various medical experts (which surely included **Galen**), but he has his own opinions on several matters and often takes the reader into new territory. He believes that the ancient principle "nothing to excess" should be applied to eating and drinking.

In Anthimus' discussions, we see evidence of the enduring culinary practices of the Roman Empire, but also of changes. There is still a long list of spices and herbs to be used in cooking, but a new Far Eastern spice is added to the repertory: Cloves, not available to **Apicius**, are now used in the kitchens of Europe. Anthimus bans the fish sauce (*garum*) so popular in earlier centuries, although he does allow a dilute version as a sauce for a sort of soufflé of egg whites and chicken.

In the Frankish kingdom Anthimus encountered the custom of eating raw bacon, which he extols as healthy. He views with more suspicion the fresh milk, butter, and aged cheeses eaten there. Fresh milk can be harmful, he suggests, unless it is so fresh that it is still warm from the animal. Baked or boiled cheese, along with smelly oysters or any stinking fish, he cites as tantamount to poison.

De Observatione Ciborum deals with many different meats and poultry, telling which should be boiled or steamed rather than roasted. Anthimus often recommends roasting meat far from the fire in order to ensure that it is not rare on the inside. He discusses numerous vegetables, fruits, grains, and pulses, some of which, such as rice and dates, would have been imported, like the cloves, from distant sources. Beer and mead are approved of; wine is not mentioned, although other evidence indicates that it was commonly drunk in Europe.

Since it was addressed to the king of the Franks and was probably written in his territory, Anthimus' letter has been called the first French cookery book. This is a beguiling idea, although it must be remembered that at that time there was no France.

— ALICE ARNDT

De Observatione Ciborum, between 511 and 534

Apicius

❧ FIRST CENTURIES BC AND AD ❧

ALSO CALLED: Marcus Gavius Apicius | *Earlier misidentified as:* Apitius Caelius

ONCE UPON A TIME IN ROME, IN THE FIRST CENTURIES BC AND AD, THERE LIVED a very rich gourmet who so loved dining, and went to such expensive extremes to indulge his ultra-refined tastes, that he became a legend in his own lifetime and in the brilliant, wealthy, hedonistic society of the early years of the Roman Empire. His name pops up in some of the best-known writers of the so-called Silver Age of Latin literature, and even in Greek, as Apicius, or Marcus Apicius, or even Marcus Gavius Apicius—but always as a gourmet, not as a man of affairs. The name is rare and otherwise undistinguished in Roman annals. Its first appearance is in the time of Julius Caesar, but the best authority for the gourmet has him flourishing under the first emperors, Augustus and Tiberius.

He is mentioned often in the literature of the first century of our era, including the *Natural History* of Pliny the Elder, where a particular method of killing mullets is attributed to "Marcus Apicius, who was born with a genius for every kind of extravagance...." He appears in Seneca, Juvenal, and especially in the epigrams of Martial, and it is Martial who ascribes his death to suicide by poison when he realized that he had spent 60 million sesterces on food, had only 10 million left, and could not face life at a reduced gastronomical level. A century later, toward the end of the second century, **Athenaeus**, born in Egypt, wrote in Greek a classic, only partly preserved, miscellany on dining, *The Learned at Din-*

Sketch of a wine pitcher by
Joseph Dommers Vehling,
from his translation of Apicius'
De Re Coquinaria

ner (Deipnosophistai), which told several stories of Apicius. One told of his sailing to Libya in bad weather because he had heard that he would find larger prawns there than those of Smyrna or his native place, Minturnae in Campania, but when he was not offered larger ones, he did not even land but sailed immediately back to Italy. And when the Emperor Trajan was in Parthia, far from the sea, Apicius had fresh oysters sent to him, preserved in a way of his own. As here, Athenaeus' chronology is often suspect, but there is no doubt that Apicius was a historic person whose name and fame lived after him.

Although we have no solid information on this Apicius the gourmet except the remarks of writers who knew or remembered him, we have long known the cookbook which bears the name of Apicius, entitled *De Re Coquinaria (On Cookery)*. It is a collection of about 470 Latin recipes in ten books, but classical scholars realized at least by the nineteenth century that they were quite unlikely to have come directly from any writer of the early years of the Roman Empire. The syntax and other stylistic characteristics are of the fourth century AD, but there is also a much smaller collection of 28 very similar recipes, titled *The Excerpts of Vinidarius*, which are considered to be from the fifth century. The ten books of Apicius survive in at least 18 manuscripts, the two oldest of which, from the ninth century, are in New York and the Vatican, while the *Excerpts* survive in only two, the older a beautiful eighth-century manuscript at Paris. The name Apicius in this collection has been explained as a generic term for a cookbook deriving from the name of the imperial gourmet, much as we use the words "frigidaire" and "kleenex" as generics.

This famous cookbook raises many questions, for it has not been considered a genuine work of the historic Apicius of Rome, since we have no evidence that he wrote such a book. But in his era the extravagant banquet was commonplace, well attested in both historians and satirists of the Silver Age of Latin literature in the first and second centuries. The best study of the sources of the "Apicius" collection is that of E. Brandt (Leipzig, 1927), from which he concluded that only about 60 percent of the recipes are drawn from gastronomy of Rome's apogee—which, like most of Roman culture of the time, had already been deeply influenced by Greek. He felt the rest were from a variety of agricultural, medical, and pharmaceutical writing, some of it in Greek. Some corroboration of this theory is obvious: The Greek titles for each of the ten books must be late, and much of the first book is advice on substitution of ingredients, preservation of foodstuffs, particularly in jars, and masking of inferior or spoiled items. Such useful hints may come from special manuals but would not seem to befit the kitchens of Apicius' own time.

Many of the main ingredients of the "Apicius" collection were fairly easily available, ordinary fare. In an era before refrigeration this was probably inevitable, but we are so dazzled by the kind of display made in such Roman classics as Trimalchio's banquet, in the *Satyricon* of Petronius, that we may miss the fact that most of its dishes also have quite ordinary ingredients, presented with most extraordinary inventiveness and flair. In the recipes of "Apicius," by far the most popular meat is pork, whether it is ham, suckling pig, large cuts, sterile sows' wombs, sausage meat, or bits or organ meat. Next in number are recipes using hare or rabbit, wild boar, kid and lamb, with beef, mutton, and goat far behind. Italy still lacks the broad grazing lands on which beef is usually produced. There are also many recipes for birds of all sizes and types, domestic, game and wild, from the ostrich and pheasant down to the song bird, with the chicken being most common, followed by duck and goose. The largest and most numerous class of main ingredients is that of the water-animals and amphibians—shellfish, sea food, fresh-water and Mediterranean fish of many sizes and varieties, eels, turtles, and frogs. No other type of ingredient was as accessible to many Mediterranean coastal dwellers as the products of the sea. There were, of course, sterile sows' wombs, which are not in our recipe books, and ostriches, flamingos, and moray eel, which cannot be purchased in every delicatessen, but these recipes were few.

Vegetables, legumes, and grains also appear in *De Re Coquinaria*, as do vegetarian dishes. Of course, the New World plants like corn, potatoes and tomatoes were not to appear for nearly a millennium, but there were many kinds of peas, beans, onions, carrots, turnips, leeks, garlic, broccoli, beets, cabbage, lettuce, celery, watercress, squash, and gourds, as well as nuts and the fruits and berries such as apples, peaches, pears, apricots, blackberries, and elderberries. These in themselves were not usually expensive fare, but the heart of the recipes of "Apicius" lies in their sauces and seasonings, the herbs and spices, leaves, berries or roots, whole or ground, which were imported into Rome from all over its known world. Pliny the Elder, in the time of the historic Apicius, tut-tutted about the imbalance of Roman trade (in which he included silk) by remarking that, at conservative estimate, Rome annually expended at least 100 million sesterces to China, India and Arabia for spices.

— MARY ELLA MILHAM

De Re Coquinaria, fourth century

Nicolas-François Appert   ❊ C. 1750–1841 ❊

BY FINDING A METHOD OF SAFELY PRESERVING FRUITS, MEATS, AND VEGETABLES in glass bottles, Nicolas Appert took an important first step toward the establishment of the modern canning industry. By his own account, Appert first learned about cooking and good food from his father, an innkeeper and brewer in the Champagne country. At the age of 31, after a decade working in various aristocratic kitchens, Appert opened a confectioner's shop in Paris. Among the products that confectioners commonly sold were gleaming jars of fruit preserved in sugar. Appert embarked on experiments to see if other foodstuffs could also be bottled in glass but without sugar. The potential rewards were great. Gourmets were prepared to pay handsomely to have a taste of summer in the depth of winter. Navies were desperate to find preserved foods that would not cause scurvy on long voyages. As a result, scientists and entrepreneurs had been experimenting with different ways of preserving for at least the previous century, although without success. By trial and error, Appert succeeded in preserving fruits, vegetables, and meats by bottling them in water or stock, sealing the bottles carefully, and submerging them in boiling water. This is still the basic method used in canning today.

With the outbreak of the French Revolution, Appert prudently moved to a small town a few miles outside Paris. There he employed 40 women to grow, prepare, and bottle his products in his four-room workshop. By 1804, he had a nice little business selling to gourmets under the patronage of **Grimod de la Reynière**, author of the famous *Almanach des Gourmands*.

Postage stamp issued in 1955

The French Navy, too, showed gratifying interest. In 1803, they carried out sea trials of Appert's bottled foods. In 1809, a committee issued a favorable report on his products. At war with Britain and deprived of sugar because of the British blockade and the loss of Haiti, the Navy was particularly interested in methods of preserving without sugar. Although they worried about ship's holds full of heavy, breakable bottles, Appert believed them to be considering giving him a contract. Influential French chemists including J. L. Gay-Lussac and C. L. Berthollet studied his process, and the French government awarded Appert a prize of 12,000 francs, a method of encouraging innovation as common as patents at the time. In return, he had to publish 200 copies of a book revealing the secrets of his method. In 1810, when Appert was 60, his *Art of Preserving Animal and Vegetable Substances for Several Years* appeared, running to four editions and being translated into both English and German.

Appert's fortunes, though, took a turn for the worse. He had explored other potential markets, employing an agent to sell his idea to France's enemy, Britain. In 1801, the probable buyer, Peter Durand, received a patent that he then sold to the engineer Bryan Donkin for 1000 pounds (about the equivalent of 40,000 pounds today). Donkin and his partners went into business preserving foods in tinned iron canisters, which had long been seen as an alternative to bottles even though they were more expensive. In 1814, as soon as the Napoleonic Wars had ended, Appert headed to London, apparently to try to get part of the profits. The trip was a failure. Meanwhile, back in France, his factory, which had been requisitioned as a field hospital during the war, had been left in ruins. His wife, about whom we know almost nothing, left him.

In 1831, when Appert was in his 80's, the government of the restored monarchy declared him a benefactor of humanity and helped him set up in business once more, this time producing tinned iron canisters of food with sales of over 100,000 francs a year. The lead in the canning industry, though, had passed first to the British and then to the Americans, who solved the difficult technical and marketing problems involved in transforming canned foods from expensive luxuries to pantry-shelf staples. After his death in 1841 Appert was forgotten until 1955, when the French government issued a postage stamp in his honor.

— RACHEL LAUDAN

L'art de conserver pendant plusieurs années toutes les substances animales et végétales (The Art of Preserving All Animal and Vegetable Substances for Several Years), 1810. German translation, 1811. English translation, 1812. Facsimile reprint as volume 1 in the Mallinckrodt Collection of Food Classics (St. Louis), 1965-1967(?)

John Arbuckle
❧ 1839—1912 ❧

JOHN ARBUCKLE, THE SON OF A WELL-TO-DO COTTON-MILL proprietor of Allegheny City, Pennsylvania, combined a penchant for invention with promotional genius to revolutionize the United States coffee industry in the late nineteenth century.

Arbuckle was born on July 11, 1839 in Allegheny City. He spent his boyhood there and in 1856 enrolled in Washington and Jefferson College at Washington, Pennsylvania. But business beckoned and he left college to join his brother and uncle in a wholesale grocery business in Pittsburgh. He received his first patent in 1868—the same year he married Mary Alice Kerr—for a process of coating green coffee beans with a gelatinous mixture of Irish moss, isinglass, gelatin, white sugar, and eggs to preserve their taste and aroma. According to Arbuckle, the gelatinous matter would also act as a "clarifying-agent when the ground coffee has been boiled in water." Subsequent improvements in designs of roasters allowed him to use only sugar and eggs.

The use of a machine which filled, weighed, sealed, and labeled coffee in paper packages similar to small bags of peanuts enabled Arbuckle to establish a market for convenient, reliable coffee. "Ariosa" coffee, a blend of hearty Rios and milder Santos beans, became the first successful national brand of packaged coffee in the United States. Other brands might be cheaper, but Arbuckle's was always considered superior, particularly among westerners.

The successful sales of pre-packaged coffee allowed Arbuckle to open a second office in Brooklyn, New York. It was the beginning of an entrepreneurial empire, Arbuckle Brothers, that eventually included branches in Kansas City, Chicago, Brazil, and Mexico as well as ownership of sugar plantations and a fleet of seagoing vessels to move the coffee beans from field to factory.

By 1891 Arbuckle was a multimillionaire; his company was the leader in the United States coffee market, and needed large quantities of sugar.

From John W. Jordan's Encyclopedia of Pennsylvania: Biography, Vol. VI, 1916

To acquire it at competitive prices, Arbuckle had to break up the sugar trust dominated by the Havermeyer families' American Sugar Refining Company, which was not hesitant about determining market prices and destroying those who did not adhere to their policies. During the trade war between the two industry giants, Arbuckle opened a sugar refinery in Brooklyn and Havermeyer acquired major interest in a rival coffee company. By the time Havermeyer admitted defeat, losses by the two firms were estimated at $25 million.

Arbuckle advertised with trading cards and folksy colored handbills. A coupon bearing Arbuckle Brothers' signature, redeemable for household goods, was placed on every package. A peppermint stick tucked inside the paper bag sweetened the deal. American homes, especially in the West, took on an Arbuckle's décor as consumers traded coupons for silverware, china, towels, and curtains.

Arbuckle Brothers introduced Yuban coffee in 1913, a year after John Arbuckle's death. The special blend had been his favorite, served only at his annual Christmas dinner or given to friends as gifts. Today, Arbuckle's "Ariosa" coffee, complete with the original Flying Angel trademark and a piece of peppermint candy in the bag, is again available on the Internet.

— JACQUELINE B. WILLIAMS

Archestratus

⚜ FOURTH CENTURY BC ⚜

ARCHESTRATUS HAS BEQUEATHED TO US A PRICELESS POEM ON FOOD THAT reveals much about Greek culture and a great deal about the style of Greek food in antiquity. Little is known of the author himself. **Athenaeus** of Naucratis in Egypt, who in his *Deipnosophistai* is our sole direct source for the poem, tells us that he came from Sicily, either from Gela or Syracuse. Of all the places named in the poem (and they are many), Syracuse and Gela remain the most important. It was in the Greek cities of Sicily and southern Italy that fine eating was first developed in the classical world, at the courts of tyrants such as Dionysius I and II in Syracuse, and earlier in the cities of Sybaris and Croton. The courts concentrated wealth derived from agriculture that was much richer than the equivalent in mainland Greece, and produced discerning diners who looked for new recipes and ingredients. Plato identifies a certain **Mithaecus** of Sicily as the author of the first Greek cookery book known to us; Archestratus follows soon after. Archestratus may have belonged to the elite and may have traveled extensively through the Mediterranean (with an emphasis on the Aegean and the seas around Sicily) but the biographer rests entirely on the internal contents of the poem for this information.

Athenaeus also tells us that different authorities reported different names for the poem, *Gastronomy, The Life of Luxury, The Science of Dining (Deipnologia)*, or *The Art*

A tuna-seller of the fourth century BC, from a krater in the Museo Mandralisca in Cefalú, Sicily

of Cooking. These many titles might suggest a wide distribution of the poem. (Note that the term 'gastronomy' is not known elsewhere, according to *Larousse Gastronomique* and the *Oxford English Dictionary*, until the nineteenth century.) The poem belongs to the fourth century BC, although there are arguments over the year.

The poem urges the reader to maintain an expensive life and to travel from city to city in order to find the best place for the best fish. The emphasis on place gives a strong impression of regional specialties. Archestratus plays on a double theme, of the best food cooked in the best way, often simply with oil and flavorings in order to bring out the essence of the fish or other food; and on the theme of luxury and the rejection of all things plebeian. Luxury often implied fish, in Greek thought, and a good three quarters of the surviving 62 fragments concern fish.

Archestratus plays on cultural concerns over excess, and playfully urges the reader to steal the most valuable fish if it can be acquired by no other means. This moral framework, and the concentration on fish, are a clever comment on two earlier epic poets, Homer and Hesiod. Homer famously excluded fish from his poems—so Archestratus puts them back into epic verse—and Hesiod gave advice on the best way to live—so Archestratus gives a satirical spin on the language of didactic poetry.

Archestratus is a clever poet; he also writes successful recipes. In Greek culture these two virtues were most frequently brought together in the literature of the "symposium," the drinking session that followed a meal. Much Greek poetry belongs to this cultural medium, and it is likely that *The Life of Luxury* was written for performance at such an occasion. People rarely read in private in the Greek world; rather, they heard literature recited to them at banquets and symposia. Archestratus even comments that a maximum of five men should be present at such occasions.

— JOHN WILKINS

Archestratus: The Life of Luxury. Translation of the poem, with gastronomic comments, by J. Wilkins and S. Hill, 1994

Giuseppe Arcimboldo   ❦ 1527–1593 ❧

A COURT PAINTER KNOWN LESS BY HIS NAME THAN BY HIS COLORFUL PAINTINGS of human heads cleverly composed of sumptuous fruits, vegetables, and flowers, Giuseppe Arcimboldo grew up in Milan, the son of a painter attached to the Milan Cathedral. He was highly educated, well read, and acquainted with the philosophical ideas of the ancient Greeks. A great-uncle who was archbishop of Milan introduced him as a young man to artists, scholars, writers, and important humanists, and this milieu formed his art, considered mannerist, and his character, considered eccentric by many of his contemporaries.

Arcimboldo made his debut as an artist at age 22, when he designed, with his father, several stained-glass windows for the Milan Cathedral. In 1551 he painted coats-of-arms for Ferdinand of Bohemia when the duke passed through Milan.

When Ferdinand became Holy Roman Emperor in 1558, he called Arcimboldo to his court in Prague; Arcimboldo accepted the position of court painter in 1562 and continued in that role under Ferdinand's successors, Maximilian II (1564–1576) and Rudolf II (1576–1612). Little is known of his personal life, his marital status, or his family.

Pen-and-wash self-portrait, made about 1575

Trade with the New World and with other non-European countries introduced a wealth of new plants to Europe in the sixteenth century. Collectors were eager to obtain exotic specimens; herbals, botanical encyclopedias, and other books were produced that attempted to organize scientists' rapidly expanding knowledge. At the same time there was a great increase in the European population that made the development of new agricultural methods a matter of high importance. Rudolph, like many other European princes, supported the advancement of scientific knowledge with great enthusiasm, assembling study collections and hiring artists of the first rank to illustrate them.

Arcimboldo's paintings "The Four Seasons," "Vertumnus," "The Vegetable Gardener," and "The Cook," often used today to illustrate cookbooks and food-history books, are part of a long history of food art that reaches back at least as far as Roman mosaics showing varieties of seafood and game and includes such Northern Italian painters contemporary with Arcimboldo as Annibale Carracci of Bologna ("The Butcher Shop") and Vicenzo Campi of Cremona ("The Fruit Seller"). Such works are rich sources of social, cultural, and food-historical information.

Arcimboldo painted the first series of "The Four Seasons" in 1563. The painter wrote that "man is a part of nature—a part of the elements and of time—and nature is a part of man." The painted seasons are thus personified, Spring as an adolescent, Summer as a young man, Autumn as a mature man with a beard, and Winter as an old man withered into the bark of a tree. The portraits are painted as two pairs of matching heads in profile, expressing a dialogue between summer and autumn and between winter and spring, and are entirely convincing as portraits from a little distance; it is only on closer examination that the full detail of the fruits and vegetables can be seen and Arcimboldo's remarkable skill in abstracting their shapes and colors can be appreciated.

In the first depiction of "Summer," fruits and vegetables of that season abound in glowing colors against a dark background, a garland of summer flowers framing the portrait. The personification boasts a small artichoke as a boutonniere. Into its broad collar of wheat are woven the words "Giuseppe Arcimboldo f[ecit, i.e. painted it]," and the date 1563 appears on its shoulder. The portrait of "Autumn" shows a profile head composed of sumptuous fall produce: a juicy pear for a nose, a ripe apple for a cheek, a chestnut protruding from its prickly burr for the lips, a chin of pomegranate, a gleaming blackberry for an eye, and a large red mushroom for an ear, with a bursting-ripe fig as a pendant earring. The head is crowned with red and white grapes and a large winter squash, and ears of different grains make up its sideburns, moustache, and goatee.

His next series, "The Four Elements," featuring animals, was painted in 1566. Humoral elements link the two series of paintings: Summer is hot and dry, like Fire. Winter is cold and wet, like Water. Spring and Air are both hot and wet, and Autumn and Earth are cold and dry.

As he approached age 60, Arcimboldo asked the emperor, who had heaped honors upon him, to allow him to return to his native Milan to enjoy his old age. Rudolf finally granted permission, and a pension, in 1587, but asked that Arcimboldo continue to paint for him in retirement.

Back in Milan, Arcimboldo painted two celebrated pictures for the emperor in 1591: "Flora" and "Vertumnus." The latter, perhaps the most famous of Arcimboldo's paintings today, is a majestic head-and-shoulders portrait of Emperor Rudolf II as Vertumnus, the god of horticulture and the seasons. The plants and produce of the entire year are gathered to express, with great imagination, Rudolf's majesty: a pear as nose, peaches as cheeks, cherries as lips, pomegranate seeds as teeth, peas as eyebrows, corn as ears, a pumpkin as chest, a cabbage leaf, artichoke and scallions as shoulder, and wheat as hair, with a flower garland over one shoulder.

The portrait is an allegory of the emperor as ruler of the seasons, and celebrates the harmony of the world under his rule. The detailed accuracy of the painted flowers, vegetables, and insects reflects the sixteenth century's interest in scientific illustration, and in symbolism: At Rudolf's court, natural science was thought to be the key to understanding the divine creative force working through man and nature, and the portrait celebrates the emperor as initiator of a golden age in which everything flourishes.

Rudolf was delighted with both paintings.

In his own time, Arcimboldo fitted naturally into the world of mannerist art, with its delight in style and paradox, in wit, fantasy, and illusion. He was famous especially for his festival designs and his most celebrated series of paintings. But he was soon forgotten after his death, and almost no mention of him is made during the seventeenth and eighteenth centuries. In the late nineteenth and early twentieth century, however, he was the object of renewed interest, and with the surrealist movement his "bizarre" paintings were rediscovered. In his 1987 book *The Archimboldo Effect,* Pontus Hulten salutes the director of the New York Museum of Modern Art, "Alfred H. Barr, Jr., who fifty years ago introduced Giuseppe Arcimboldo into the history of modern art."

— NANCY C. STUTZMAN

Pellegrino Artusi

PELLEGRINO ARTUSI WAS BORN IN FORLIMPOPOLI, A TOWN IN ROMAGNA, ITALY, on August 4, 1820, the only son in a family with six daughters. His father, Agostino, was the town pharmacist, and after a brief period in a seminary, Pellegrino began to work for him, traveling widely on family business.

He would likely have inherited the business and lived his life out in Forlimpopoli, had not Stefano Polloni, an infamous bandit, chosen to visit the town on the opening night of a play in January 1851. When the curtain went up, the audience was confronted by Polloni and his gang, pistols drawn. Before they were driven off, some of them broke into Artusi's home; his father fled, and though his mother gave them a sack full of silver, the brigands "despoiled and contaminated" Geltrude, the most beautiful of his sisters. She sank into a deep depression from which she never recovered, and shortly thereafter the family moved to Florence. Upon the death of his parents, he saw to marrying off his sisters ("I still had two sisters under my roof, who had begun to count their years and were frantic for husbands; anybody who's lived with spinsters will know what a trial tolerating them can be.") and set about earning his fortune. Though he was listed in the Encyclopedia of Italian Bankers, he was actually a silk merchant. He was also a shrewd and gifted investor, so much so that he was able to retire when he turned fifty. From then on he divided his time between Florence and Viareggio, a resort on the Tuscan coast.

He never married, though contemporary accounts describe him as engaging, pleasant, and witty. Rather, he lived the rest of his long life with his maid, Marietta Sabatini, his cook, Francesco Ruffilli, and, presumably, a long succession of cats, for he dedicated the first edition of *La Scienza in Cucina* to the two who were living with him at the time. In his will he ordered that part of his considerable fortune be used to establish a home for the elderly, and the rest be used to provide dowries for poor girls. His greatest gift, the royalties from *La Scienza in Cucina*, went to his servants, on the condition that they still be living under his roof at the time of his death. They were.

Though Artusi had published a book on Ugo Foscolo, an eighteenth-century intellectual, in 1876, he was unable to find a publisher interested in what amounted to his kitchen notes, with all sorts of tangents and asides thrown in. So in 1891 he paid a printer to produce a thousand copies of *La Scienza in Cucina e l'Arte di Mangiar Bene, The Science of Cookery and the Art of Eating Well.* Bookstores showed so little interest that he had to sell the book by subscription, and when he sent two copies to be raffled for charity in Forlimpopoli, his hometown, the winners sold them to the tobacconist, who used the pages to make snuff packets. Then a lecturer, Professor Paolo Mantegazza, mentioned it, and orders began to increase: Artusi prepared a second edition. It sold faster, so he brought out a third, expanding it and increasing the print run; by the time of his death in 1911, his book, which had grown to 790 recipes, was in its 35th printing and had sold 238,000 copies. Considering how few people read Italian at the time, this is impressive indeed.

Who purchased it? Middle class housewives: women who were wealthy enough to serve meat regularly, if not daily, but not so wealthy as to have many servants. They therefore had to cook, and greeted *La Scienza* with joy, because the recipes are tasty and thrifty, and because the book is written in clear, straightforward Italian without the French culinary terminology many professional chefs used in their books. As the economic conditions of the workers improved, especially after World War II, *La Scienza in Cucina* became popular with them too.

Because of its popularity, Artusi's book has had a profound influence on Italian cuisine. Though he concentrated on the dishes of his native Romagna and his adopted Tuscany, people throughout the Peninsula sent him recipes, and he added those he liked to the successive editions, thus providing cooks with a broad collection of recipes upon which to build, in addition to advice on serving combinations and menus. In this sense, as many food historians have pointed out, he laid the foundations for Italian cuisine as we know it.

In the years since the final edition of *La Scienza in Cucina*, many other cookbooks have come out, but Artusi continues to sell briskly, in part because many of his recipes are by now classics, but also because the book is simply interesting: Artusi read widely, corresponded with the intellectuals of his day, and had something to say about just about everything. Almost half his recipes contain anecdotes or snippets of advice on subjects as varied as regional dialects and public health, and while one may open his book to learn how to make minestrone or a German cake, one will probably read on to find out how he escaped cholera, or what the Austrian troops were like who occupied Northern Italy in the 1840's. In short, he produced a work of literature in an unlikely package, and since his book reached a much broader readership than did those that were primarily studied in school, he played an important role in helping to spread the use of modern Italian.

Despite his continued popularity with the general public, Artusi is controversial among food professionals. As a chef observed at the book's centennial celebration in Florence, he was an amateur, and many of his recipes are either approximate or incomplete. For example, he never goes beyond "put it in the oven" with baked goods, is hazy on cooking times in general, and frequently omits the amounts of ingredients, assuming the cook will know enough to get the proportions right.

The other reason some people object to Artusi is more profound: Though he took repeated digs at the French, they reigned supreme in the kitchen in his day and his book reflects their influence, especially in his use of butter as a shortening for dishes other than desserts, and in the inclusion of a number of obviously French dishes. At a deeper level, Italian cooking was and remains extremely regional. Because of his popularity, the dishes he proposed spread throughout the country and to a certain degree eclipsed the local specialties. During the 1960's and 1970's there was a backlash against his influence, with a flowering of regional cookbooks, one of which was entitled *L'Anti-Artusi*. So, in a roundabout way he contributed to the preservation of regional cultures and customs, because those unhappy with his influence sought out the members of older generations who still remembered the old dietary customs, talked to them, and took notes.

Finally, despite its age, *La Scienza in Cucina* remains surprisingly current. A nutritionist speaking at the centennial celebration pointed out that Artusi's cooking is remarkably healthy, provided one follows his advice as well as his recipes: Use rich ingredients sparingly, use a minimum of fat to make the food light and easy to digest, and remember that excess salt is the enemy of good cooking.

Artusi is in many ways a grandfather to Italian cuisine. Loved by some, condemned by others but acknowledged by all, his influence has been profound, and will continue for years to come. At the end of his recipe for *gnocchi alla romana* he says, "I hope you will like these as much as my guests have. If you do, toast me if I'm alive, or say a 'Rest in Peace' if I've gone to push up cabbages." He deserves many of both.

— KYLE M. PHILLIPS III

La Scienza in Cucina e l'Arte di Mangiar Bene, 1891

Athenaeus

ATHENAEUS IS THE AUTHOR OF *DEIPNOSOPHISTAI*, AN EXTENDED DIALOGUE IN ancient Greek on food and dining. Setting aside dietary texts, this work is the only significant source for classical Greek culinary recipes. The title means "Professors at Dinner"; the work is usually called *The Deipnosophists* in English.

An outline of Athenaeus' life can be gleaned from incidental remarks in the *Deipnosophists,* but there is no mention of him in any other contemporary source. He was born at Naucratis in Egypt, an ancient and historic Greek settlement in the Nile Delta. He lived in Egypt for some of his adult life: He writes familiarly of its capital city, Alexandria, and of the fine fish of the Nile. Later he moved to Rome, then capital of the Roman Empire. Athenaeus was a scholar, a habitué of libraries, and an amateur of rare old Greek manuscripts; how he made a living is unknown. He wrote two other books, one literary, one historical; neither survives. Having possibly lived in Rome from the AD 180's onward, Athenaeus wrote the *Deipnosophists* at some date between 200 and 230. His birth and death cannot be dated.

The *Deipnosophists*, divided into fifteen books, takes the form of a series of dinner discussions set in Rome. The discussions are reported, in a frame conversation, by "Athenaeus" to a friend, "Timocrates"; this unusual structure imitates the philosophical dialogues of Plato. The discussions are undoubtedly imaginary, because (a) they are much too long for any real dinner; (b) the speakers, though real and famous people, in some cases, were not really members of any such dining club, and did not spent their time searching out the obscure early sources that are woven together in these discussions. Therefore the book is a record of Athenaeus' own researches, not those of others.

The linking subjects are the food, drink, and entertainment of the Greeks and their neighbors in the first millennium BC. Over a thousand authors are quoted in the *Deipnosophists*—an astonishing number. The references to their works are usually careful and accurate when they can be checked; however, most of them cannot be checked, because, excepting Athenaeus' extracts themselves, the ancient texts are lost. That is the great value of the *Deipnosophists*: It is a collection of unique, otherwise unknown, original source texts on classical Greek food. The following are the earlier Greek culinary authors whose recipes are known via the *Deipnosophists*, with approximate dates:

Mithaecus, about 400 BC

Archestratus, about 350 BC

Glaucus of Locri, fourth century BC (one recipe, for a meat sauce)

Hegesippus of Tarentum, fourth century BC (one brief recipe, for a rich *kandaulos*)

Erasistratus, third century BC (one recipe, for a meat sauce)

Nicander of Colophon, second century BC (three verse recipes for lamb stew and vegetables)

Chrysippus of Tyana, second century BC (several recipes for bread and cakes)

Epaenetus, first century BC (one recipe, for a savory *myma*)

Artemidorus of Tarsus, first century BC (one recipe, for a dessert *mattye*)

Around the quotations Athenaeus weaves all kinds of explanations and arguments concerning social history, wining and dining practices, and the identification of foods. It is part of the enduring fascination of his work that many statements need to be questioned, and some arguments reach the wrong conclusion—but all of them are evidence of opinions held by at least one person in classical Greece or the Roman Empire. In spite of its complexities, the *Deipnosophists* is consulted by all those who work seriously on the food history and social history of the ancient world. Some of us who begin to read it never stop.

Athenaeus' preferred reading evidently consisted of comedy plays, memoirs, and popular history, full of scandal and gossip. There was plenty of food history in texts of that kind. However, he also quotes real food writers, including gastronomes like Archestratus (whose work would be totally unknown but for Athenaeus' quotations) and authors of recipe books like Mithaecus.

The text of the *Deipnosophists* survives in one beautifully written tenth-century manuscript now in the Biblioteca Marciana in Venice. This copy was damaged many centuries ago and now lacks all of books one and two and a few other pages, totaling a fifth of the whole. Earlier, however, an abridgement of the *Deipnosophists* was made by an unknown Byzantine scholar, and thanks to other manuscripts containing this abridgement, it is still possible to read an outline of the missing sections of Athenaeus' work. Gulick's edition incorporates extracts from the abridgement when necessary to fill the gaps in the full text.

— ANDREW DALBY

The Deipnosophists (*Professors at Dinner*, also translated as *Philosophers at Dinner* or *The Learned Banquet*), ed. and transl. by Charles B. Gulick, 1928. Reprinted 1957, 1967, 1987

Wilbur O. Atwater

ALSO CALLED: Wilbur Olin Atwater

IF TODAY WE THINK OF "FOOD" AND "CALORIES" TOGETHER, IT IS because of W. O. Atwater's early work in nutrition science. Wilbur Olin Atwater was born in Johnsburg, New York on May 3, 1844, but was raised largely in Vermont, where he attended the University of Vermont for two years before transferring to Wesleyan University in Middletown, Connecticut. He graduated from Wesleyan in 1865. Atwater taught school briefly, then entered Yale University as a chemistry student in the Sheffield Scientific School. His dissertation focused on feed corn and marked the first time in the United States that food had been chemically analyzed according to modern scientific methods. He received his PhD in 1869.

Since German scientists were, at the time, leaders in chemistry and physiology, Atwater spent the next two years studying abroad at the Universities of Leipzig and Berlin. From 1871 to 1873 the young professor held posts at the University of Tennessee, Maine State College and finally Wesleyan, where he would remain as a chemistry professor for the next 34 years. He always preferred research to teaching, and is best remembered today for research that began with further examination of fertilizers and feeds in farming and widened to include human metabolism and nutrition.

Within two years of settling in at Wesleyan, in 1875, Atwater became director of the first American agricultural experimental station, initially based in Middletown and later, from 1887 to 1902, at Storrs, Connecticut. His long-time connection to the stations—he served as the first chief of the U.S. Department of Agriculture's Office of Experiment Stations—and his growing interest in nutrition cemented the connections among the USDA, nutrition studies, and the emerging home-economics movement.

Between 1879 and 1882, Atwater analyzed various sorts of fish and animal matter to discover their chemical composition and determine their nutritional values. Returning to Germany in 1882 for about a year, Atwater studied mammal metabolism using German methods of measuring respiration. This work laid the basis for his own work, later in the U.S., on food digestibility and chemical composition; analysis of foods eaten by different groups of people; determination of how much of what sorts of food were needed to provide sufficient energy to work; and the effects of cooking on food's nutritional value.

During the last quarter of the nineteenth century, some basic information about food composition came to be understood. Generally, early nutritionists knew that animal food supplied muscle-building material, while grains provided carbon for energy. Atwater built on this knowledge to identify proteins, fats, and carbohydrates and their respective roles in diet. His development, with physics professor E. B. Rosa, a Wesleyan colleague, of a human-respiration calorimeter in 1892 gave him the tool with which to determine the energy values, or caloric content, of foodstuffs.

This information coincided with a rising awareness among the middle and professional classes in America that their diet did not match their nutritional needs. Dyspepsia, a term used for decades to describe the general digestive malaise of people eating too rich a diet for the energy they expended, was widespread. Many Americans were still eating as had their hard-working farmer forebears, despite living more sedentary lives. In 1894, Atwater became the first government official to advise Americans on their diet, cautioning them against consuming too much fatty or sugar-laden food. "It is a fair question," he wrote, "whether the results of [eating excess fats and sugars] have induced among us a large class of well-to-do people, with little muscular activity, [and] a habit of excessive eating and may be responsible for great damage to health, to say nothing of the purse."

Atwater would nonetheless recommend a diet for Americans which emphasized protein—meat, eggs, and milk—saying that Americans "live more immensely, work harder, need more food," than Europeans, and that Americans "have more money to buy it." To be accepted at all, clearly, nutrition science had to meet cultural standards.

In 1894 Atwater persuaded the USDA to fund nutrition research and recruited participation around the country from agricultural experiment stations, with $15,000 allotted annually to each. This enabled the Department of Agriculture, beginning in 1895, to publish tables of food composition values. Atwater's *Methods and Results of Investigations on the Chemistry and Economy of Food*, known as "Bulletin 21," is considered a landmark study, and "Bulletin 28," *The Chemical Composition of American Food Materials*, co-authored with A. P. Bryant and published in 1896, became the precursor of the USDA's *Agriculture Handbook 8*, nicknamed "the dietitian's bible." It reported the minimum, maximum, and average values of the nutrients in all American foods which Atwater and his colleagues had analyzed by July 1895.

Atwater's early emphasis on proteins, carbohydrates and fats skewed the nutrition-science picture at the turn of the nineteenth to twentieth century, and it would be another 20 years before nutritionists understood the role played by vitamins. His work was embraced nonetheless by diet reformers, scientific cooks, and home economists, and Atwater directly involved home economists in his nutrition research.

Atwater and his nutritionist colleagues took a very mechanistic view of food: food in, energy out. They hoped to establish a national standard for an economical and sufficient American diet, but their methodology, on which much modern nutritional work is still based, had many shortcomings. Their studies were rigorously rational, emphasizing careful weighing and record-keeping, but focused so closely on presupposed needs of designated ages, genders, and occupations that any variations in nutritional requirements within those groups were inadequately addressed.

Atwater died on September 22, 1907, in Middletown, Connecticut. In 1968 the Agricultural Research Service established the W. O. Atwater Memorial Lectureship, now considered one of the highest honors in the field of nutrition, to recognize scientists who make notable contributions to bettering world-wide nutrition.

— SANDRA L. OLIVER

Foods: Nutritive Value and Cost, 1894
Methods and Results of Investigations on the Chemistry and Economy of Food (Bulletin 21), 1895
Dietary Studies in Chicago in 1895 and 1896, 1898 (with A. P. Bryant)
The Chemical Composition of American Food Materials (Bulletin 28), 1896 (with A. P. Bryant)
Dietary Studies with Reference to the Food of the Negro in Alabama in 1895 and 1896, 1897
Dietary Studies in New York City in 1895 and 1896, 1898
Description of a New Respiration Calorimeter and Experiments on the Conservation of Energy in the Human Body, (Bulletin 63), 1899 (with E. B. Rosa)
A Respiration Calorimeter with Appliances for the Direct Determination of Oxygen, 1905 (with F. G. Benedict)

Aunt Sammy

❦ IMAGINARY CHARACTER ❦

Ruth Van Deman, an employee of the USDA, *wrote and read many of the recipes and scripts broadcast by "Aunt Sammy."*

IN THE EARLY 1920'S, RADIO IN AMERICA CEASED TO BE A CRYSTAL-set hobby of men and boys and became a wildly popular mass medium for everyone. "Wireless fever" swept the nation, with the establishment of broadcasting stations and the manufacture of receiver sets increasing faster and faster to keep up with each other. In 1920, there were only a handful of transmitting stations, with perhaps as many as 10,000 sets, mostly home-built, to receive their broadcasts; just two years later there were an estimated 60,000 radios in use. By 1923 the number of licensed stations had grown to 500, owned by entrepreneurs, newspapers, equipment manufacturers and dealers, universities, churches, municipalities, and others. Five years later, about seven and a half million homes in America had a radio.

People throughout the country were excited by this new phenomenon; magazine and newspaper articles speculated at length about the meaning and potential of radio. The programming required was envisioned as more than entertainment or information: It was seen as a means of uniting a vast country with diverse populations—and no one was to benefit more than the farm families, who were cut off from the nearest cities and even from their neighbors by great distances and poor roads. Relatively few farmers had automobiles or telephones; radio was an inexpensive way of ending their isolation.

Radio kept farmers up-to-date with weather reports, information on market prices, and lectures from agricultural colleges, and in 1926, the United States Department of Agriculture devised a new program for the benefit of farm women, based on the concept of a daily chat with Aunt Sammy, an imaginary character meant to be understood as the sister (or perhaps the wife) of Uncle Sam, the avuncular personification of the United States. Across the country, at 30 different stations, the identical script was read by 30 different women, each of them lending Aunt Sammy her own regional accent. (Ultimately, Aunt Sammy was broadcast from 194 stations.) For 15 minutes every day, Aunt Sammy was a warm, witty, and authoritative companion to the housekeeper as she discussed domestic problems and passed on household tips, jokes, recipes, and seasonal menus. The information she provided was "up-to-date and calculated to help the housewife in the intricate and vastly important task of managing a home," according to an article in *The New York Times*, October 3, 1926.

This type of programming was well received, and Aunt Sammy was not the only one offering a domestic chat on the air: In the same year that she went on the air, the equally fictitious **Betty Crocker** began broadcasting on NBC's Red Network and, just a couple of years later, the very real **Ida Bailey Allen** began her long career of bringing recipes and advice to housewives on radio, and later on television.

Because of the difficulties of interrupted or staticky reception, Aunt Sammy offered to send a free printed copy of her recipes to anyone who wrote in to request it. Within five months of the program's beginnings, the USDA had received nearly 41,000 requests. A 1927 printing of 100,000 copies of a collection of *Aunt Sammy's Radio Recipes* was exhausted within a year, and in 1931 a new, enlarged edition, *Aunt Sammy's Radio Recipes Revised,* was published. The following year it became the first cookbook to be published in Braille. With the help of members of Congress who gained favor by giving it away, the fifteen-cent *Revised* cookbook ultimately became a best-seller with two million copies distributed.

With a full decade of the Depression ahead, Aunt Sammy's cookbook guided housewives seeking to prepare economical, yet tasty and nutritious, dishes for their families. The from-scratch dishes she recommended still taste good, and even by today's standards the suggested menus are nutritious and varied. Menus were seasonal, and a typical February dinner of roast beef, Yorkshire pudding, scalloped parsnips, turnip greens, pickled cherries, and Washington pie (a basic white cake with jam or jelly between the layers and a dusting of powdered sugar on top) or a July supper of salmon cutlets, string beans, parsley potatoes, pepper relish (chopped green and red sweet peppers and onion in vinegar, sugar, and salt), and watermelon, would be as welcome this year as in 1931.

The USDA broadcasts continued until 1946, although in 1934 the fictitious Aunt Sammy was dropped and the discussion was led by an anonymous narrator. The name of the program was modernized from "Housekeeper's Chat" to "Homemaker Chats." Behind the scripts, as well as the menus and recipes, were Ruth van Deman and Fanny Walker Yeatman, employees of the USDA. Van Deman, the daughter of the Department of Agriculture's first pomologist, served as Chief of Information of the Bureau of Home Economics, later called the Bureau of Human Nutrition and Home Economics. During World War II, Van Deman managed the government's home food-preservation program, providing advice on home canning, freezing, and drying foods. As a prominent home economist, she contributed many articles to journals and popular magazines alike. She died in 1948 at the age of 59.

— ALICE ARNDT

Aunt Sammy's Radio Recipes, developed by the Bureau of Home Economics, U. S.
Department of Agriculture, 1927
Aunt Sammy's Radio Recipes Revised, Ruth Van Deman and Fanny Walker Yeatman, 1931

Avicenna

ALSO CALLED: Ibn Sina | Abu 'Ali al-Husain ibn 'Abd Allah ibn Sina

A MUSLIM PHILOSOPHER AND SCIENTIST WHOSE POLYMATH BRILLIANCE HAS been compared to that of Leonardo, Galileo, or Einstein, Avicenna (as he was known in Europe) made significant contributions to chemistry, botany, ethics, pharmacology, logic, physics, mathematics, and astronomy. His reputation is based largely on two of his more than 130 authenticated works, *Kitab al-Shifa'* (*Book of Healing [of the Soul]*) and *Al-Kanun fi al-Tibb* (*The Canon of Medicine*).

Avicenna was born in 980 in a small town in present-day Uzbekistan near Bukhara. His father was from Balkh, Afghanistan, the legendary birthplace of the prophet Zoroaster, and worked in government service for the Samanids. The Samanid dynasty controlled Transoxiania from about AD 900, with Bukhara as their capital. The splendid cities of Bukhara and Samarkand were the cultural centers of the empire, where arts and literature flourished.

Avicenna's native language was Persian, but he was educated primarily in Arabic. According to his autobiography, he had memorized the Qur'an and mastered the Arabic classics by the age of ten, and thereafter quickly outpaced his tutors. At thirteen he turned his attention to Greek medical texts, and he began to treat patients three years later. He then threw himself into mathematics, jurisprudence, natural science, and philosophy. By his own account, he perfected all the recognized sciences by the age of eighteen.

Avicenna's reputation came to the attention of Sultan Nuh ibn Mansur of Bukhara. As a reward for curing the sultan of an illness, Avicenna was given free rein in the royal library, where the Samanids had collected and translated much of the knowledge of classical antiquity—an experience that was crucial for Avicenna's intellectual development.

His father died when Avicenna was 22, obliging the young man to rely on his medical knowledge for a livelihood. But he soon became influential in government, for princes and others who found his medical judgment sound came to rely on him in political matters as well, and he acquired more than his share of enemies due to courtly intrigues and his own boorish personality, as well as his precarious ethnic and religious connections. His life was also greatly affected by the political instability that followed the Arab Islamic conquest of the area. For the remainder of his days, he moved from court to court as royal physician, or served variously as jurist and administrator, or was simply on the run or imprisoned.

While the quantity and range of Avicenna's writing was prodigious, perhaps the most remarkable aspect of his life was the quality of his production in the face of a furiously paced lifestyle. He is said to have written, without notes, even when traveling on horseback or while in prison.

Avicenna was an intellectual snob, a bachelor, and a sage for hire. Particularly telling is his fondness for poetry, song, wine, and women—a decadence some contend led to his demise. When chastised for his lack of sexual restraint, he replied that he wanted his years to be measured in breadth, not length. Avicenna wrote at night or in the early mornings, worked all day and, in the evenings, gathered with students for philosophical and scientific conversation. His pupil, secretary and subsequent biographer, al-Juzajani, recorded that, each night after working simultaneously on the *Book of Healing* and the *Canon of Medicine,* "…the various musicians would enter; vessels were brought out for a drinking party; and so we occupied ourselves." At the age of 57, Avicenna died of an overdose, intentional or otherwise, of celery seeds and opium taken in self-treatment for colic. He is buried in Hamadan, Iran.

Avicenna wrote *The Canon of Medicine* as a compilation of the medical knowledge of his era, supplemented by his own observations. Divided into five sections, the book summarizes and builds upon the Hippocratic and Galenic traditions and is loaded with food and dietary advice.

The ineluctable relationship of diet and health forms the basis of the humoral theories of medicine. There are several such theories worldwide, each with variations and modifications. Hippocrates, in the fifth century BC, is generally credited with setting down the Greek theory and **Galen** refined it in the second century of our era. Applying the Greek tradition to Indo-Iranian influences, Avicenna explains that the human body is made up of the four basic elements—earth, air, water, and fire—which are characterized by different elemental qualities: earth is cold and dry, air is hot and moist, water is cold and moist and fire is hot and dry. Four humors—essential fluids manufactured in the body—also exhibit these elemental qualities: Blood is hot and moist, phlegm is cold and moist, yellow bile is hot and dry, and black bile is cold and dry. The humors determine a person's physical constitution; their correct balance results in good health and their imbalance in disease. Because various foods can also be described by these qualities, eating the correct foods can help keep the humors in balance, or restore their balance and thus cure disease.

The humoral theory was such an accepted part of daily life that neither traditional medicine nor European medieval cooking—which relied heavily on Avicenna's principles—can be understood without it. Food and diet are central to the cause and treatment of disease, a viewpoint condensed simply to "most illnesses arise solely from long-continued errors of diet and regimen" and, as a consequence, "food is the best medicine." A healthy diet, Avicenna writes, requires varying the menu not only according to the season—for the seasons too are described as warm and moist (spring), cold and moist (winter), and so on—but also by the age, gender, physical constitution, and present condition of the diner as well. The ideal menu, as a rule, should consist of: (a) meat, especially of young sheep, ox, or goat; (b) unadulterated wheat, (c) a sweet dish which agrees with the individual temperament, and (d) a pure, fragrant drink.

Avicenna distinguishes between medicinal and nutritive foods—though honey, he believes, is "the food of foods, the drink of drinks, and the drug of drugs." He classifies alcohol, egg yolks, and meat juice as "highly nutritious." As he further delineates various foodstuffs, he places lamb on one end of the spectrum as "heavy, rich, and wholesome," whereas most vegetables are labeled "light, poor, and unwholesome." Though he opposes drinking water at meal times, Avicenna highly recommends mineral water throughout the day. To improve lactation in nursing women, he recommends white ants or dried earthworms given daily with barley water, or, equally effective, a cup of wine with an ounce of clarified cow butter. One of his sayings, particularly apt in a world of extreme wealth and poverty, concludes, "There is nothing so injurious as overeating during periods of prosperity and completely starving during spells of scarcity."

For more than a millennium, Avicenna's works on health have been a benchmark for herbal and dietetic medicine. His advice still has a tremendous influence: In Central Asia, laymen still classify most foodstuffs as humorally hot or cold, and Iranians, Turks, and Arabs alike claim him as a native son. Today, the *Canon of Medicine* remains the handbook for all practitioners of *unani* medicine in India and Pakistan. In Europe, that million-word opus was translated into Latin in its entirety in the twelfth century by several scholars, and from the twelfth to the sixteenth century the teaching and practice of medicine in Europe was firmly based on one of the 87 translations (some partial) that were produced. The *Canon* appears in the first known syllabus drawn up in 1309 for the School of Medicine in Montpellier, and Chaucer, in the Prologue of *The Canterbury Tales,* points out that no physician should be ignorant of Avicenna's work.

— GLENN R. MACK

Kitab al-Shifa' (Book of Healing [of the Soul])
Al-Kanun fi al-Tibb (The Canon of Medicine)
Al-Adwiyat al Qaliyya (Drugs for the Heart)
Arjozah (Poem on Medicine)
Kitab-ul-Tabir-e Roya (Book on Interpretation of Dreams)

B

Baldwin—*Cook*
Balzac—*Writer*
Barlow—*Diplomat, Poet*
Bavarchi—*Chef, Cookbook Author*
Beard—*Cookbook Author, Television Presenter, Teacher*
Beauvilliers —*Cookbook Author, Restaurateur*
Beck —*Cookbook Author, Teacher*
Beecher—*Cookbook Author, Teacher*
Beeton —*Cookbook Author*
Bekir—*Confectioner*
Benoît —*Cookbook Author, Radio/ Television Presenter, Teacher, Writer*

Betty Crocker—*Imaginary Character*
Bircher-Benner—*Physician, Reformer*
Bitting—*Cookbook Collector, Scientist*
Blot—*Cookbook Author, Teacher*
Bockenheim—*Chef, Cookbook Author*
Borden—*Entrepreneur*
Brady—*Gourmet*
Brillat-Savarin—*Gastronome, Jurist, Musician, Philosopher, Writer*
Brown—*Cookbook Author, Cookbook Collector, Writer*
Bushaq—*Poet*
Butt—*Entrepreneur, Restaurateur*

Bessie Baldwin

1818—AFTER 1849

BESSIE FLORENCE BALDWIN LEFT US A RECORD OF AUSTRALIA'S EARLIEST colonial cuisine. She got her culinary start in London, but practiced her art as a convict in Australia. Born on a farm in Kent, she came to town at age nineteen and studied baking and pastry-making with Thomas Edenwell near the House of Commons. Two years later, she demanded a raise of one penny per week to five pence. The ensuing uproar earned her a seven-year prison term for assaulting her employer "by striking him with a rabbit pie, and then beating him about the head with the pie dish."

With 182 other female prisoners and 24 children, Baldwin boarded the *Gilbert Henderson* on December 14, 1839, for transportation to the colony of Van Diemen's Land, today's Tasmania. En route, she earned a stay in the ship's brig for bashing Sir John Hamett, the ship's libidinous surgeon, with a candlestick for improprieties. He chose not to press charges and withdrew to his quarters for the remainder of the voyage.

At the Hobart penal colony in Tasmania, Baldwin passed directly to the "female factory," or workhouse, where convicts wore yellow garb during their incarceration. She was said to have been a ringleader of a scandalous escapade in which as many as 300 women convicts displayed their bare backsides to the lieutenant governor, Sir John Franklin, his wife and a clergyman, smacking their buttocks with their hands to make "a loud musical noise." Nonetheless, in 1842, Franklin assigned Baldwin to work as an assistant cook and pastry cook in the Government House kitchen, where she performed admirably. (The practice of "assigning" convicts as minimally paid servants to non-convict colonists was abolished during his tenure.) Before Franklin was removed from his post a year later, he determined that Baldwin had been rehabilitated, and pardoned her. Baldwin was then 31, and of her further personal history we know only that she did not marry in the colony, and that she left Tasmania for New South Wales in 1849.

Baldwin's legacy is a lengthy compendium of her recipes—recorded by a governess, perhaps the Franklins' Miss Williamson—that reflects the time when Tasmania was transforming itself from a penal to a constitutional colony. Baldwin's simple but nourishing food covers the spectrum of English cookery—mulligatawny, lemon sauce, savory tomatoes, fish hash, kidney on toast, date pudding, Cornish pasty, and ginger sponge. Added to the list were her own inventions, including an Australian salad dressing and steamed kangaroo. Like jugged hare, the preparation of the latter calls for tying layered kangaroo meat, bacon, and veal into a jar and steaming it for up to four hours.

Bessie Baldwin's recipe collection pre-dates the first Australian cookbook, *The English and Australian Cookery Book*, by Edward Abbott, but Abbott's book was printed in London in 1864, while Baldwin's recipes were finally published only in 1992, in the form of a 60-page booklet with the title *The Australian Convict Recipe Book: Featuring Ex-Convict Bessie Baldwin, Cook To Sir John and Lady Franklin at Government House 1842–1849.*

— MARY ELLEN SNODGRASS

The Australian Convict Recipe Book: Featuring Ex-Convict Bessie Baldwin, Cook To Sir John and Lady Franklin at Government House 1842–1849, 1992

Honoré de Balzac

❊ 1799–1850 ❊

PROLIFIC WRITER AND DEVOTED GASTRONOME, THE GREAT French novelist was born in Tours, in the heart of the Loire Valley, known for its medieval history, gastronomic tradition, and generous wines, from Chinon to Vouvray. Thanks to its mild harmonious climate, the area produces a variety of delicacies including pears, escargots, and the *asperges de Montlouis.*

During and after the French Revolution, his father, born Bernard François Balssa, held positions of some importance in the commissariat and hospital departments of the army; his mother, Anne Charlotte Laure Sallambier, was a beauty and an heiress. Balzac was educated in the *collèges* of Vendôme and Tours and later by private tutors in Paris, but left school at the age of 16. He trained in the law, obtained his *licence* and worked for three years in the office of a notary, but rebelled when his father wanted him to go into independent practice.

For two years, on a very small parental allowance, he starved in a Paris garret, attempting to write tragedies and novels; for another two years he did the same in his parents' home, and achieved publication in 1821 with the first of a spate of novels—thirteen of them, some pseudonymous, appeared by the end of 1825. His subsequent unsuccessful venture into business as a type-founder, printer, and publisher left him with debts that would oppress him the rest of his life, but this period probably also saw his first culinary publication: An 1827 *Code gourmand*, opening with a gastronomic calendar clearly inspired by **Grimod de la Reynière**, has been attributed to him.

In 1829, Balzac published his first major novel; 1830 saw the creation of a *Nouvelle théorie du déjeuner (New Theory of Lunch)* and *Physiologie gastronomique (Physiology of Gastronomy)*. The success of **Brillat-Savarin**'s text led Balzac to write a good number of *physiologies* on topics ranging from marriage to manners. He also wrote the article on Brillat-Savarin for the 1835 Michaud biography.

His prodigious productivity was achieved by a regimen of dining early, sleeping after dinner, then writing from midnight onward, often for sixteen hours at a stretch. During the days or weeks he was so occupied, Balzac would feed on fresh fruit and avoid overindulgence, except for his legendary consumption of coffee, which he regarded as an intellectual stimulant. He insisted on blending his own coffee from Martinique, Moka, and Bourbon beans. But once away from his writing regimen, Balzac relished good food and earned renown for his gargantuan appetite. At one dinner, a friend reports, Balzac feasted on "one hundred oysters, twelve lamb cutlets, a duckling with turnips, a brace of roast partridges, a Normandy sole, hors d'oeuvres, desserts, more than a dozen Doyenné pears, wines, coffee, liqueurs, and so on…"

Throughout his writings, Balzac theorized on the intellectual and physical consequences of excess, joining his fellow *Tourangeau* (citizen of Tours) **Rabelais** in advocating balance and sobriety so as not to hinder literary or other forms of production. Of particular interest is an afterword to an 1839 edition of Brillat-Savarin's *Physiologie du Goût (Physiology of Taste)* entitled "Traité des excitants modernes" ("Treatise on Modern Stimulants"). Coming after Brillat-Savarin's main course, the treatise serves more as a dessert or *digestif,* deliciously expounding the effects of alcohol, coffee, and tobacco on human reproductive abilities. Engrossed in questions of reproduction, and particularly the effects on sexuality of food and diet, Balzac follows one of the most modern aspects of Brillat-Savarin, who coined the term *génésique* to refer to a sixth sense which combines the other five and is responsible for the sexual attraction between individuals.

Balzac's greatest literary achievement remains *The Human Comedy,* a colossal project, conceived as a study of the customs of the nineteenth century, that regroups most of his social, scientific, and creative writings and comprises 90 novels and novellas. Among its many recurring themes and characters, we find innumerable tables, cafés, restaurants, and gastronomes from Paris of the 1830's.

Sylvain Pons (*Cousin Pons*, 1847), one of Balzac's most famous food lovers, has two obsessions: his antique collection and his never-ending quest for a good meal. Pons represents the archetypal bachelor gourmand for whom the source of all joy in life is the stomach, and food represents the only access to the world of sensation. Yearning for the smell of a good dinner as one might crave a lover's scent, Pons practically faints at the sight of a roasted quail, a glass of port, or a plum pudding with cream sauce. Seeking to please the bourgeois society on which he depends to accomplish his "gastronomic evolution," he is willing to compromise himself to the point of becoming not a man but only a stomach. The loss of his favorite table inducing a loss of appetite, he is left with a draconian diet and a sort of gastronomic nostalgia, painfully remembering dinners past.

With this gastronomically charged novel, Balzac reveals himself to be the rightful heir to Brillat-Savarin, adding to the latter's description of the gastronome's taste the real pleasure to be found at the table, and comparing the pleasures of digestion to the bliss of the act of love.

Balzac died at the age of 51, probably of overwork and excessive consumption of coffee. His chronicles of the gastronomic explosion of the early nineteenth century compel us to contemplate the importance of alimentary questions with regard to the acts of breeding and writing.

— PHILIPPE DUBOIS

Nouvelle théorie du déjeuner (New Theory of Lunch), 1830
Physiologie gastronomique (Physiology of Gastronomy), 1830
La Comédie humaine (The Human Comedy), 1842
Le Cousin Pons (Cousin Pons), 1847

Joel Barlow

1754–1812

Engraved by Asher B. Durand after a portrait of Barlow painted by Robert Fulton, developer of the steamboat

JOEL BARLOW, POET, DIPLOMAT, AND BUSINESSMAN, WON his fame in food history for the mock-epic poem "The Hasty Pudding," written in France during a 1793 stay in Savoy. A Connecticut Yankee, born in Redding on March 24, 1754, Barlow may have felt himself more a poet than anything else, but it was his diplomatic activity that assured his place in American history and, in December 1812, cost him his life, far from his native New England.

Barlow was the son of a prosperous Redding farming family, and was tutored by a local minister who prepared him for college. He first attended Dartmouth, known then as Moor's Indian School, in Hanover, New Hampshire, but when his father died, he was obliged to return to Connecticut, where he enrolled at Yale in 1778. He wrote poetry there and showed his interest in political philosophy and science. His first food-related poetry was from his Yale years, a broadside satire about the bad food served in the Yale common dining hall. While at Yale, he also met Ruth Baldwin, the sister of his friend and Yale tutor Abraham Baldwin, with whom he fell in love. Against Ruth's father's wishes, the young couple was secretly engaged in 1779, then married on January 26, 1781.

During this time Barlow served in the American Revolution as a chaplain to the Third Massachusetts Brigade, and at war's end began a printing business in Hartford, Connecticut, where he joined with other poets, all of a similar age and all from the western part of the state, in a group which became known as the Hartford Wits. Dr. Lemuel Hopkins, John Trumbull, David Humphreys, and Barlow published their poetry, often satires, in the newspapers of the day, but Barlow truly aspired to be America's epic poet. "The Vision of Columbus," which he published in 1787, best reflects this urge. The poem was read by George Washington, Ben Franklin, and Louis XIV of France, and was generally considered a success.

In 1788, Barlow was sent to France by Scioto Associates to sell Europeans land in what is now Ohio. The development scheme fell apart, but Barlow, ultimately accompanied by Ruth, spent seventeen years in Europe, coming to know literary and political people in France and England and even being awarded honorary French citizenship. His career in this era mixed literature, journalism, political commentary, business ventures, politics, and diplomacy—including service as United States consul in 1795 to negotiate the release of American prisoners captured by Algerian pirates. He observed the French Revolution at first hand, losing friends to prison and the guillotine.

Among his political activities was a run for office in the Savoy district of France. At an inn in Chambéry in 1793, Barlow was served a dish he remembered from his youth in New England, and the occasion prompted his mock-heroic and pastoral poem "The Hasty Pudding." According to an account of the meal (probably apocryphal in certain details and somewhat mock-heroic in its own right) recorded by Barlow biographer Charles Todd in *Life and Letters of Joel Barlow* (1886), "… on gathering with his grave compeers one day for the evening meal, he found smoking hot on the table the New Englander's national dish, Hasty Pudding. The bard could scarcely believe his eyes. He had sought it in vain in Paris, in London, at the hands of many a famous chef, and now beheld it under the smokey rafters of a Savoyard inn."

Whatever the impulse for writing "The Hasty Pudding," which was published in Europe in 1793 and in the United States in 1796, the poem stands as the one of all his works still popular today. It is a valuable reference to the use of cornmeal in Federal-era America, and it is clear that Barlow remembered how maize was used in various dishes, though his wife Ruth may have supplied some of the finer details that we so enjoy today. Over the course of the poem, he mentions descriptively, among others, succotash, hoe cake, cornmeal dumplings, and rich johnny cake—including the "dash of pumpkin in the paste" which New Englanders sometimes added, as we see in a recipe recorded later by **Lydia Maria Child** in *The American Frugal Housewife.* Barlow records directions for cultivating corn, and mentions husking parties at season's end. He even refers to regional nomenclature: "E'en in thy native regions, how I blush, to hear the Pennsylvanians call thee mush."

At the heart of the poem are detailed instructions for making and eating hasty pudding. Barlow captures its sound and appearance while cooking: It "puffs and wallops" and "rises to the brim" of its cooking pot. When it is ready to eat, he recommends putting milk and molasses on it and discusses what kind of spoon to eat it with. Further, he says, "Fear not to slaver; 'tis no deadly sin."

Joel and Ruth Barlow came back to America in 1805 and acquired a home outside Washington, D.C., which they named Kalorama, Greek for "a fine view," and where they entertained artistic and political figures. He promoted the idea of a national institution for science and the arts, a progressive notion which only caught on much later. In 1811, his friend President James Madison appointed Barlow U.S. Minister to France and sent him to negotiate a treaty with Napoleon. In December of 1812, Napoleon was retreating from Russia, where Barlow went to meet him. Then, back-tracking through Poland, Barlow caught pneumonia and died in Żarnowiec, Poland, on Christmas Eve. His grave is in the churchyard there, and a memorial stone was erected at the Great Pasture Road Cemetery in Redding.

— SANDRA L. OLIVER

The Hasty Pudding: A Poem in Three Cantos, Written at Chambery in Savoy, January 1793; U.S. edition, 1796

Bavarchi

ALSO CALLED: Hajji Muhammad Ali Bavarchi Baghdadi

BAVARCHI LIVED IN THE SIXTEENTH CENTURY DURING THE REIGN OF SHAH Isma'il Safavi (reigned 1501–1524). He is the author of the first manual of Persian cuisine in the Persian language (with the exception of the culinary poetry of **Bushaq**): *Karnameh dar bab-i tabbakhi va san'at ān (Manual on Cooking and Its Craft).*

Little is known about Bavarchi's life. He was chef to an unknown aristocrat in the court of Shah Isma'il, referred to as Mirza'i ("prince") in the introduction to the *Karnameh*. Bavarchi's father was also chef to a Safavid prince; he mentions this in one of the recipes in the *Karnama*, along with the fact that he had learned that recipe from his father. Being a chef may have been the hereditary family profession, as crafts did often run in families—cooking was considered a craft—and the name Bavarchi means "chef" in Persian. It is possible that **Nurallah**, the chef to Shah Abbas Safavi (reigned 1588–1629), was one of Bavarchi's descendants. Bavarchi writes that he learned the art of cooking as an apprentice to great chefs and by reading the books of learned men (the Persian word *hukama* covers all fields of learning, ranging from philosophy to mathematics), and he quotes some lines of poetry to this effect.

The term "Baghdadi" at the end of Bavarchi's name indicates that either he or his family were originally from Baghdad. The honorific "Hajji," taken by those who make the *hajj*, the Muslim pilgrimage to Mecca, implies that Bavarchi had attained a certain economic level, for the *hajj* only becomes incumbent upon someone who can afford to make the journey. The fact that Bavarchi was both literate and educated also places him in a higher social class—and indeed, chefs held a high position in Islamic societies even up to the twentieth century.

In 1520, Bavarchi went to Ardebil to visit the shrines of Shaykh Safi, the founder of the Safavid dynasty (1501–1722), and Sultan Haydar, the father of Shah Isma'il. In his introduction to the *Karnameh,* he says that he was so moved by the visit and his experience that he wished to make a unique offering to those holy men, but that he could not find anything worthy of them. A sudden revelation from beyond came to him, he continues, that he should write a cooking manual as an offering to the saints. This had never been done before and would benefit both the aristocracy and the general public, as well as bringing renown to the author.

The only extant copy of Bavarchi's manuscript is now in the central library of Tehran University. It was edited and published in 1981 in *Ashpazi-yi Dawra-yi Safaviya: Matn-i Dau Risala az an Dawra (The Cuisine of the Safavid Period: The Text of Two Treatises From That Time).* The editor, Iraj Afshar, explains in his introduction that the manuscript was originally in Turkey, but came into the hands of the bookseller Harrassowitz in Wiesbaden, Germany. Harrassowitz displayed the manuscript in 1976 as part of an exhibition at Tehran University, and Afshar obtained the manuscript for the University of Tehran the next year. According to the introduction, the manual originally contained 26 chapters. The Tehran manuscript, however, lacks chapters 23 to 26.

Regarding the recipes in the manual, Bavarchi states that they are based both on knowledge he acquired from master chefs and on his own experience and invention. The recipes are for large quantities, indicating that they are derived from the experience of cooking for a large, aristocratic household. However, they contain not only detailed measurements of the ingredients, but also the exact type of utensil to be used, the cooking heat required, and instructions for their preparation and presentation. Each of the chapters is assigned to a category or subcategory of food. Many of the ingredients and recipes (for example the different types of *ash*, *abgusht*, *pilaw*, *khurisht*, and *burani,* among others) are current in Iran and still exist in present day Persian cuisine.

In spite of the lack of biographical information on Bavarchi, some additional facts about his person and character can be gleaned from his introduction to the *Karnameh.* He was a religious man, he was an educated man, and, above all, he was a man with an original mind, for he conceived of writing a cooking manual, something not prevalent in his time. His wish of winning renown for himself by writing the manual has come true, as four hundred years later these lines are being written about him.

— SHIREEN MAHDAVI

Karnameh dar bab-i tabbakhi va san'at ān (Manual on Cooking and Its Craft), sixteenth century

James Beard

WHAT **Auguste Escoffier** WAS TO FRENCH CUISINE, JAMES Beard was to American cookery, and their differences are instructive. In contrast to Escoffier, who was diminutive, exacting, precise, and a skilled codifier of an ancient tradition, Beard was a giant of six feet four inches and 310 pounds (at his heaviest), a Paul Bunyan tramping out new territory from sea to shining sea, scattering larger-than-life legends in his wake. Beard was the first to give Americans a sense of the epic grandeur of our own culinary diversity and of our American do-it-yourself frontier style.

Born in Portland, Oregon, in 1903, Beard never lost a sense of the vast spaces and improvisatory nature of the West. He first learned about food from his English mother, who ruled a boarding house in the grand manner by subduing a series of maddened Chinese cooks. He also learned how to forage for food in the wild from his summers on the Oregon coast at Gearhardt. His childhood food memories, finely evoked in his memoir *Delights and Prejudices* (1964), gave continuity to a life spent largely in Europe and the American East.

A showman by instinct and training, he went abroad to study opera, hoping for a career as an Italianate tenor, or at least as an actor in theaters or movies. But by the time he was 35, he realized he needed to make money in order to eat, so he began to cook dinner for friends and in 1937 opened a catering shop on Park Avenue, New York, called Hors d'Oeuvre, Inc. The cookbook which followed in 1940, *Hors d'Oeuvre and Canapés,* proclaimed the open-handed Beard style, which turned French canapés into American "highball sandwiches." Soon after, in 1941, his *Cook it Outdoors* was the first serious book on outdoor cooking; it established his authority as a male home cook whose recipes were suitable for both sexes and for both indoors and outdoors.

After a brief stint in the army, he joined the United Seamen's Service and fulfilled his theatrical yearnings in USS clubs from Marseilles to Rio, picking up exotic food lore en route. At the war's end, he appeared in television's first cooking show, on NBC in 1946, advertising **Borden**'s Milk with Elsie the Cow: "Elsie Presents James Beard in 'I Love to Eat'." From then on, Beard's image was as important as his words, and his beaming bald-headed figure dominated the food world he was helping to create, first in New York and then across the nation, until his female counterpart, **Julia Child,** appeared on the screen in 1962.

In the 1940's, however, television was not yet ready for the full-scale cooking show Beard might have done, so he promoted his image largely through magazines, newspapers, books, and radio, and through his cooking classes. By 1955 he had published nine cookbooks, and in that same year established The James Beard Cooking School. For the next 30 years until his death, he held cooking classes not only in his own apartments in New York and at Seaside, Oregon, but also around the country in clubs, stores, auditoriums, restaurants, church basements, and professional cooking schools. He loved to teach as much as he loved to cook and eat, and he combined those pleasures with gusto.

Unlike **Craig Claiborne** or Child, Beard focused from the beginning on American rather than on French food, and he created new standards for home cooking. He was the first on our shores to emphasize good fresh ingredients, simply prepared, with flavor as the first priority. "Taste it," he would command his students. "Taste it until it tastes right to you." He was also our first celebrity chef with a branded name, and *The James Beard Cookbook* (1959) became an instant classic because the recipes were so simple and clear, the results so good, and the target so straightforwardly the solid middle ground between readers of *The Betty Crocker Cookbook* and **Earle MacAusland**'s *Gourmet* magazine. His gargantuan delight in a superabundance of butter, cream, garlic, bacon, and bourbon made **Fannie Farmer**'s texts sound like the mutterings of a pursed-lipped spinster. In *James Beard's American Cookery* (1972), he was the first to take a serious look at the rich literature of nineteenth-century American cookbooks other than Fannie, and to revel in their authors, especially the lady sensualist Miss **Eliza Leslie** of Philadelphia. *James Beard's Theory and Practice of Good Cooking* (1977) was a model of basic cooking principles that were American not just in ingredients, but in form and feeling.

American meant eclectic, for its people had come from everywhere, and Beard excluded nothing and nobody from his generous embrace. Many regretted his increasing plugs and endorsements for a host of manufactured products of diminishing quality and felt that he was eroding the authority of his name. But his ubiquitous image in promotions of all kinds did nothing to diminish Beard the myth. In the 1970's, with his Buddha smile and bow-tie, he'd become a logo of American prosperity and an icon of the good life. By 1983, however, when *Cuisine* magazine crowned him "King of Food," the age of excess had already given way to a new Puritanism called "health and diet." Beard himself was caught in the crossfire and tried to drop 50 pounds at his doctor's command, but it was far too late. Besides, it was not his style.

But if myths can't diet, neither can they die. When Beard died in 1985 at age 81, he had no thoughts of legacy. He'd requested that all his household effects be sold at auction as well as, upon the death of his longtime lover, his Greenwich Village townhouse. He'd never imagined that his house would be bought by friends like Julia Child, who wanted to ensure his legacy through the James Beard Foundation, which would provide a showcase for chefs known and unknown. Over twenty years, the Foundation's awards for excellence, in everything from cookbooks to chefs to restaurants to scholarship, has made the image of Beard as symbolic of American bounty as Bunyan, and as permanent.

— BETTY FUSSELL

Hors d'Oeuvre and Canapés, 1940

Cook It Outdoors, 1941

Fowl and Game Cookery, 1944

The Fireside Cookbook: A Complete Guide to Fine Cooking for Beginner and Expert, 1949

Paris Cuisine, 1952

The Complete Book of Barbeque and Rotisserie Cooking, 1954

Complete Cookbook for Entertaining, 1954

How to Eat Better for Less Money, 1954 (with Sam Aaron). Revised 1970

James Beard's Fish Cookery, 1954

The Casserole Cookbook, 1955

The Complete Book of Outdoor Cookery, 1955 (with Helen Evans Brown)

New Barbecue Cook Book, 1958 (re-publication of *The Complete Book of Barbeque and Rotisserie Cooking*)

The James Beard Cookbook, 1959. Revised 1961, 1970, 1987, 1996

Treasury of Outdoor Cooking, 1960

Delights and Prejudices: A Memoir with Recipes, 1964. Revised 1981, 1990

James Beard's Menus for Entertaining, 1965

James Beard's Party Cookbook, 1965

Jim Beard's Barbeque Cookbook, 1966 (re-publication of *The Complete Book of Barbeque and Rotisserie Cooking*)

James Beard's Barbeque Cookbook, 1966 (re-publication of *The Complete Book of Barbeque and Rotisserie Cooking*)

How to Eat (and Drink) Your Way Through a French (or Italian) Menu, 1971 (with Gino Cofacci)

Best of Beard, 1967, 1975

James Beard's American Cookery, 1972

Beard on Bread, 1973. Revised 1995

James Beard Cooks With Corning, 1973

Beard on Food, 1974 (with José Wilson)

Barbecue with Beard, 1975

James Beard's New Fish Cookery, 1976. Reprinted 1987

New Recipes for the Cuisinart Food Processor, 1976

James Beard's Theory and Practice of Good Cooking, 1977. Revised 1978, 1986, 1990

James Beard's Fowl and Game Bird Cookery, 1979 (re-publication of *Fowl and Game Cookery*)

The New James Beard, 1981. Revised 1989

The Fireside Cookbook, 1982 (re-publication of *The Fireside Cookbook: A Complete Guide to Fine Cooking for Beginner and Expert*)

Beard on Pasta, 1983

Best of James Beard, 1983

Beard on Birds, 1989 (re-publication of *Fowl and Game Cookery*)

James Beard's Simple Foods, 1993

Love and Kisses and a Halo of Truffles, 1994 (letters)

Beard on Pasta: A James Beard Cookbook, 1995 (re-publication of *Beard on Pasta*)

The James Beard Cookbooks, 1997 (series editor John Ferrone)

The Armchair James Beard, 1999 (editor John Ferrone)

The Grand Marnier Cookbook

Benson and Hedges 100's Presents: 100 of the World's Greatest Recipes by James Beard

Antoine Beauvilliers

✦ 1754–1817 ✦

IN 1814, TOWARD THE END OF HIS LIFE, ANTOINE BEAUVILLIERS IDENTIFIED himself as follows: *Ancien Officier de Monsieur, comte de Provence, attaché aux Extraordinaires des Maisons Royales, et actuellement Restaurateur, rue de Richelieu, No. 26, à la grande Taverne de Londres.* That is, he was a former steward to the Count of Provence (the future Louis XVIII), had been attached to royal households for special occasions, and was currently restaurateur at *La Grande Taverne de Londres*, with a prestigious location in the vicinity of the Palais Royal.

Beauvilliers' move from serving in royal households to opening a fine-dining establishment for the elite public was an unprecedented step in 1782. Beauvilliers called his establishment a *taverne* and named it for London in accord with a fashion for things English. The term "restaurant" was not yet in use, although M. Boulanger and others had already begun offering *restaurants*, or restorative bouillons, to those of delicate constitution.

Beauvilliers was the consummate restaurateur. As **Brillat-Savarin** wrote in his *Physiologie du Goût*, he was "the first to combine an elegant dining room, smart waiters, and a choice cellar with superior cooking." Beauvilliers dressed as a courtier, even wearing a sword. He "was the possessor of a prodigious memory: he could recognize and greet, after an interval of twenty years, persons who had only eaten once or twice in his establishment"; and "he knew all the heads of foreign contingents, and learned to speak all their languages as well as was necessary for his business."

"He also had a method of procedure peculiar to himself. When he was told that a party of wealthy people had sat down at one of his tables, he would approach them with an obliging air, kiss the ladies hands, and appear to honor his guests with special attention.

"He would point out here a dish to be avoided and there one to be ordered at once, before it was too late; a third which nobody dreamed of ordering, he would himself, at the same time sending for wine from a cellar to which he alone had the key; in a word, he assumed so gracious and engaging a tone, that all these additional items seemed so many favors on his part. But this **amphitryonic** role lasted only a moment; having played it, he withdrew from the scene; and before long the swollen bill, and the bitterness of **Rabelais**'s quarter of an hour [the period when the bill is paid], amply demonstrated the difference between a host and a restaurateur."

The *Taverne de Londres* remained pre-eminent for more than half a century, although Beauvilliers did take the precaution of closing it and moving to England for a few years after the Revolution. In 1814, he published his cookbook, *L'Art du Cuisinier*, which was esteemed in both France and England. He died in 1817.

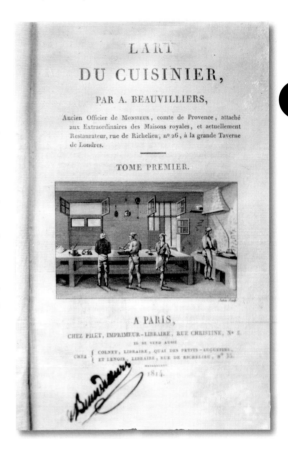

Title page of his L'Art du Cuisinier, *1814*

B

Beauvillier's cookbook, the summation of his long experience, appeared the year before the first of **Antonin Carême**'s books. Carême saw himself as a modernizer, and Beauvillier's classical art was precisely the sort of cuisine that Carême sought to modernize. For his part, Beauvilliers found Carême's famous *pièces montées* ridiculous. It is unlikely that either man would have been happy to know that in 1847 or 1848, years after their deaths, excerpts from their respective writings would be bound together (along with a small treatise on chocolate by Brillat-Savarin) in a two-volume work entitled *La Cuisine ordinaire*, and their two names shown as its authors. The statements found in the *Larousse Gastronomique* and other sources that Beauvillers and Carême *collaborated* on this book are entirely erroneous!

— ALICE ARNDT

L'Art du Cuisinier, 1814

Simone Beck

❧ 1904–1991 ❧

ALSO CALLED: Simca

Beck (standing) with Julia Child, 1970

SIMONE BECK WAS BORN ON JULY 7, 1904 INTO A PRIVILEGED Norman family passionate about food and wine. On her marriage in 1923, at the age of nineteen, she moved to Paris; she studied at Le Cordon Bleu with chef **Henri-Paul Pellaprat** in 1933. Her first marriage ended in divorce, and on April 30, 1937 she married Jean Fishbacher, a man as passionate about food and wine as she. It was he who gave her the nickname "Simca," after the Renault model she drove. Jean was a member of Le Club des Cent, a prestigious men's gastronomic society. He introduced Simca to the women's counterpart, Le Cercle des Gourmettes, open to women knowledgeable about food and of a certain class.

In early 1949 Simca met **Julia Child** in Paris and introduced her to Louisette Bertholle and to Le Cercle des Gourmettes, in which they became active. In 1952 Simca and Louisette were collaborating on a book on French food for an American audience. They had written a small cookbook, *What's Cooking in France,* and had plans to enlarge it. They sent it to Dorothy Canfield of the Book of the Month Club, who advised them to find an American to work with them. Julia was the obvious choice. In 1952 the three women opened L'École des Trois Gourmandes, teaching small groups of American women how to cook French food. The three taught and worked on Volume I of *Mastering the Art of French Cooking* for the next ten years.

In early 1958 they submitted the manuscript to Houghton Mifflin, which rejected it. They continued to work on it and in late 1959 submitted it to the publishing house of **Alfred A. Knopf** through Child's friend Avis DeVoto, who was a freelance editor. At Knopf, fortuitously, it came into the hands of Judith Jones, who loved French food. *Mastering the Art of French Cooking: Volume I* was published in 1961.

Simca and Julia began work on volume two while Louisette worked on a book of her own. Simca was the primary source of recipes for the second volume, which was published in 1970, while Julia did most of the testing. Though there were some books on French home cooking available for an American audience in the late 1940's and 1950's, such as the 1947 *Cordon Bleu Cook Book* of **Dione Lucas** and the various English translations, beginning in 1950, of Pellaprat's *L'Art culinaire moderne*, it was the two volumes of *Mastering the Art of French Cooking* that became essential for anyone wishing to cook authentic French food.

Following the publication of *Mastering*, Simca wrote several other books and gave cooking lessons in a number of places, including Bramafam, her home in the south of France. Her only book in French was about prunes, written for the prune industry. She explained being so much more widely known in the United States than in France with the statement that the French do not feel that they need to be taught to cook.

Simca died on December 20, 1991. Julia Child wrote that "hers was home cooking of the finest sort—*la bonne cuisine bourgeoise*." Beck's papers are in the Schlesinger Library, Radcliffe Institute, Harvard University.

— PATRICIA M. KELLY

Le Pruneau Devant le Fourneau: Recettes de Cuisine, c.1952
What's Cooking in France, with Louisette Bertholle and Helmut Ripperger, 1952
Mastering the Art of French Cooking: Volume I, with Julia Child and Louisette Bertholle, 1961
Mastering the Art of French Cooking: Volume II, with Julia Child, 1970
Simca's Cuisine, with Patricia Simon, 1972
New Menus from Simca's Cuisine, with Michael Jones, 1979
Food and Friends: Recipes and Memories from Simca's Cuisine, with Suzanne Patterson, 1991

Catharine Beecher

1800–1878

CATHARINE ESTHER BEECHER WAS BORN SEPTEMBER 6, 1800 IN EAST HAMPTON, New York. She was the oldest of thirteen children of Lyman Beecher and his wives, Roxana Foote Beecher and Harriet Porter Beecher. The Beechers were a family of activists. Lyman was an evangelical preacher; his male children also became ministers, and daughters Catharine, Harriet, and Isabella had public careers involving educational reform, abolition, and women's suffrage.

Catharine Beecher was educated at home and in a progressive private school for girls in Litchfield, Connecticut. Her formal education ended abruptly in 1816 when her mother died and Catharine assumed the role of mother and homemaker in the family, assisted by an aunt, until her father remarried. Catharine gave credit to her mother, her aunt, and her stepmother for her broad knowledge of housekeeping.

In 1821, Catharine became a schoolteacher, and the following year was engaged to a brilliant young professor at Yale. "Next came sorrow," she later wrote, "the heaviest and bitterest," when her fiancé was lost in a shipwreck.

In 1823, Catharine founded the Hartford Female Seminary with her sister Mary. The school was dedicated to the education of mothers and teachers, and was highly successful. In 1831, Catharine Beecher left Hartford to move to Cincinnati with her father. There she founded the Western Female Institute, which lasted only until the economic collapse of 1837. For the next 40 years, Catharine wrote and lectured extensively to promote women's education, the recruitment and education of teachers on the western frontier, and the founding of women's colleges in the Midwest. She died on May 12, 1878.

Early nineteenth-century American society was changing from a "home-centered" economic base as business and commerce became avenues by which men could support their families. Women became increasingly responsible for maintenance of the household and education of the children. The prevalence of servants was diminishing as a broad, literate middle class began to develop. Teaching was one of the very few socially acceptable occupations for women. Catharine Beecher believed that the most important role for women was to be the moral leader of the home and teacher of the children. It was her ambition to raise housewifery to a profession best performed by educated, knowledgeable women.

From Woman's Record *by*
Sarah Josepha Hale

In 1841, *A Treatise on Domestic Economy for the Use of Young Ladies At Home and At School* was published. In this book Catharine Beecher addressed myriad facets of domestic life, including healthful living and interior design. It was directed to the emerging literate female middle class, and was so popular that it was reprinted 15 times in as many years. A companion book, *Miss Beecher's Domestic Receipt-Book,* was first published in 1846. This important volume contains original recipes "tested by superior housekeepers and warranted to be *the best*." It was written in simple language with specific instructions to assist the American cook. Catharine Beecher introduced the custom of specifying quantities of ingredients in many of the recipes. She also advised on the best kind of cast-iron cooking-stoves. This book too was reprinted many times.

In 1869 Catharine Beecher and her sister, Harriet Beecher Stowe (the author of *Uncle Tom's Cabin*), published *The American Woman's Home, or Principles of Domestic Science. Being a Guide to Economical, Healthful, Beautiful and Christian Homes.* This book was reprinted in 1873 as *The New Housekeeper's Manual: Embracing a New Revised Edition of the American Woman's Home; or, Principles of Domestic Science. Being a Guide to Economical, Healthful, Beautiful and Christian Homes.* The recently published *From Catharine Beecher to Martha Stewart: A Cultural History of Domestic Advice* attests to the continuing relevance of this original "domestic diva."

— SUSAN MACDUFF WOOD

A Treatise on Domestic Economy for the Use of Young Ladies At Home and At School, 1841
Miss Beecher's Domestic Receipt-Book, 1846
Letters to the People on Heath and Happiness, 1855
The American Woman's Home, or Principles of Domestic Science. Being a Guide to Economical,

Healthful, Beautiful and Christian Homes, with Harriet Beecher Stowe, 1869
Principles of Domestic Science; as Applied to the Duties and Pleasures of Home. A Text-Book for the use of Young Ladies in Schools, Seminaries, and Colleges, with Harriet Beecher Stowe, 1870
The New Housekeeper's Manual: Embracing a New Revised Edition of the American Woman's Home; or, Principles of Domestic Science. Being a Guide to Economical, Healthful, Beautiful and Christian Homes, 1873

Isabella Beeton

❦ 1836–1865 ❦

ALSO CALLED: Mrs. Beeton

As EDITOR, COMPILER, AND JOURNALIST, ISABELLA BEETON managed to negotiate a powerful position for herself in the publishing world, and affected the domestic lives of myriad English women who turned to her for advice on cooking and running their households. She became a national figure who embodied matronly femininity, taking the role of mother to teach women how to manage themselves, their domestic environment, and even their husbands. Isabella was, and still is in many ways, a modern woman who has been held responsible for both the best and the worst of English cookery.

Portrait by Maull & Polyblank, ca. 1860–1865

Born Isabella Mary Mayson, she was the eldest daughter of Elizabeth (née Jerram) and Benjamin, who owned a small linen business at 24 Milk Street, off Cheapside, London, until his early death in 1841. Isabella was born at this address in March 1836 and was followed by two sisters, Bessie and Esther, and a brother, John. In 1843 Elizabeth married Henry Dorling, an old friend of her first husband, and moved to Epsom. They had thirteen children together, plus four from Henry's first marriage. When Henry became Clerk of the Grand Stand at Epsom, Elizabeth came up with the unusual idea of housing the children in this extensive building, with its many rooms. Along with Granny Jerram, Isabella and Bessie served as unpaid nursemaids to the younger children.

Isabella was first sent to school in Islington, but Henry soon sent her to a boarding school in Heidelberg, Germany, where she learned the conventional lady-like skills, including patisserie. In July 1856, she married Sam (Samuel Orchart) Beeton at Epsom Parish Church and enjoyed a reception at the Grand Stand before moving to their new house, No. 2 Chandos Villas, Pinner. By that time Sam had started his own publishing company under the sign of the Beehive and edited the enormously successful *Englishwoman's Domestic Magazine*. This was launched in 1852 and contained many novel features: essay-writing competitions, a problem page, and—something Isabella was to become intimately involved with—paper dress patterns of the latest fashions.

The Beetons had a loving and mutually beneficial relationship. Their working partnership began only a few months after their marriage when Isabella, somewhat reluctantly, agreed to write the cookery columns for the *Englishwoman's Domestic Magazine*. She was soon editing all the household aspects of the magazine. Mrs. Beeton's first biographer, her great-niece Nancy Spain, tells of a working holiday to Ireland during which the couple spent a rainy day in the hotel drawing room working on their respective columns, Sam on his *conversazione* and Isabella on the fashions. Isabella adopted for herself the aims of the magazine, which were the improvement of the intellect, the cultivation of morals, and the cherishing of domestic virtues, although it has been pointed out that, as a working journalist, she lived a very different life from most of her readers.

Since Isabella had only been running her own house for such a short time when she took over the cookery columns and was, her sisters insist, an "indifferent cook," she carefully studied many of the cookery books of the time, sought advice from her own cook, and experimented in her kitchen. She is said to have asked in frustration, "Why has no one written a book—a *good* book—for brides, to help them learn these things?" From her columns on household affairs grew a series of supplements which were published from 1859 to 1861. The recipes they included came from a variety of sources, not least because Sam had requested readers of *The Englishwoman's Domestic Magazine* to send in recipes in order that "the knowledge and skill of a few may be acquired by thousands." Isabella put her name to only three—Baroness Pudding, Pigeon Pie (Epsom Grand-Stand recipe), and Useful Soup for Benevolent Purposes—which suggests that she wanted to appear well-connected as well as charitable.

After four years' "incessant labour," these supplements were published in completed form in 1861 as *Book of Household Management comprising information for the Mistress, Housekeeper, Cook, Kitchen-Maid, Butler, Footman, Coachman, Valet, Upper and Under House-maids, Lady's-Maid, Maid-of-all-Work, Laundry-Maid, Nurse and Nurse-Maid, Monthly, Wet and Sick Nurses etc. Also, Sanitary, Medical & Legal Memoranda; with a history of the origin, properties, and uses of all things connected with home life and comfort, by Mrs. Isabella Beeton,* for sale at seven shillings sixpence—cheaper than rival publications. It was an attractive book, with wonderful color plates, and a layout that made it a pleasure to read and use.

Divided into four parts, the book opens with a preface in which Mrs. Beeton warns women that domestic mismanagement will send their husbands to seek comfort in clubs and taverns. She then empowers them by comparing the mistress of a household to the commander of an army, able to attain the highest feminine rank when she enters into the knowledge of household duties. The main text begins with a treatise on how to become an accomplished household manager. This is succeeded by nearly 1400 recipes, most of which are followed by useful information in the form of mini-essays on the scientific and botanical properties, processing, cost, and nutritional and culinary uses of a key ingredient, as well as more general and contingent information relating food to history, culture, art, politics, geography, anthropology, myth and legend, fable, folktales, and literature. At the back of the book are the duties of the lower and occasional servants; it ends with medical and legal information from male advisors.

Isabella was at heart an editor, as well as a compiler of recipes, who had to make numerous choices about what to include, where to include it, and how best to present her material. Her goal was not to present herself as a brilliant chef, nor to teach her readers to be first-class chefs, but to help them cook for their families in bourgeois domestic circumstances at a time when this type of knowledge was needed. She was not an adventurous cook, but concentrated on inventiveness of structure, on how a recipe was presented, explained, and organized. Isabella's success lay in her implicit and explicit methodology, which she applied equally to the layout of her recipes and to her own research, and which she tried to instill in her readers. "Method," she declared, "is most necessary, for when work is properly contrived, each part arranged in regular succession, it will be done more quickly and effectually."

The Beetons had four children, two of whom survived into adulthood: Orchart was born in 1863 and Mayson arrived two years later. The day after Mayson was born, Isabella developed a temperature and was diagnosed with puerperal fever, a common infection at the time, probably passed to her by a doctor or midwife during delivery or aftercare. Family rumors maintained that Sam had let her work too far into her pregnancy and had worried her with his business affairs. She died a week later, aged only 28, and was buried at Norwood cemetery. It was Sir Mayson Beeton who donated Isabella's portrait to the National Gallery in 1932 after a correspondence in the *Manchester Guardian* mistakenly identified Mrs. Beeton as **Eliza Acton**.

Isabella's only publications were *The Book of Household Management* in serialized (1859–1861) and full book form (1861); it was revised in 1863 and reformatted as *The Dictionary of Cookery* (1865) just before she died. The book, which in its various forms came to be known simply as "Mrs. Beeton," has, however, been constantly updated and re-branded to move with the times. Although most of the Mrs. Beeton titles which refer to household management have now disappeared, the cookery books, such as *Mrs. Beeton's Best of British Cooking* and the series Mrs. Beeton's Healthy Eating have continued to proliferate. The most popular titles today are those which refer to tradition or festivity, like *Mrs. Beeton's Christmas Book*, or to food as special gifts or as lifestyle.

"Mrs. Beeton" has become a highly successful culinary brand name that serves as an interface between women and the vast changes that consumer society has wrought on their lives. Perhaps more important, Mrs. Beeton—the book, the persona, and the person—has been a friend to countless women who have sought cultural approval over the years amid demands that they produce and present both simple and ceremonial home-cooked food as a measure of national and familial devotion.

— HELEN DAY

Book of Household Management comprising information for the Mistress, Housekeeper, Cook, Kitchen-Maid, Butler, Footman, Coachman, Valet, Upper and Under House-maids, Lady's-Maid, Maid-of-all-Work, Laundry-Maid, Nurse and Nurse-Maid, Monthly, Wet and Sick Nurses etc. Also, Sanitary, Medical & Legal Memoranda; with a history of the origin, properties, and uses of all things connected with home life and comfort, by Mrs. Isabella Beeton, 1861

Hajji Bekir

This representation of a benign and portly Hajji Bekir with customers may be imaginary, but it is universally familiar in Turkey as symbolizing the best in traditional sweets.

HAJJI BEKIR WAS BORN IN THE TURKISH BLACK Sea province of Kastamonu and was apprenticed as a young boy to a confectioner in Istanbul. He opened his own shop in the district of Bahçekapı in 1777. His *akide* (boiled sweets) and *lokum* (Turkish delight) were of such high quality that he was appointed chief confectioner to the Ottoman court, probably during the reign of Sultan Mahmut II (1808–1839). He is said to have made *akide* in many new flavors, such as cinnamon, rose, orange, lemon, and mastic. Lokum attracted the attention of foreign visitors to Istanbul early in the nineteenth century, and had acquired a considerable reputation outside Turkey by the 1830's. Although it was made by many confectioners, Hajji Bekir is said to have perfected the technique and formula of this sweetmeat, which became known in English at first as "lumps of delight" or "morsels of delight" and later as "Turkish delight." Hajji Bekir was exporting lokum to Europe in considerable quantities in the mid-nineteenth century.

Hajji Bekir's shop became one of the indispensable sights on tourist itineraries, recommended in nineteenth-century English guidebooks to Istanbul. Lady Dufferin, who lived in Istanbul between 1881 and 1883, visited the shop on her way back from the Hippodrome: "We called upon 'Hadji Baba,' the owner of a sweetshop, and tasted many things, and watched a yellow jelly converted, by pulling and beating, into a lovely shiny white bonbon." The misnomer "Hadji Baba" was common at this time, as was the assumption that the elderly shop owner was Hajji Bekir himself, who had in fact died in 1856. His son Mehmet Muhiddin was so generally identified with his celebrated father that a Turkish writer born in 1889 also claims in his memoirs to remember Hajji Bekir.

Dorina Lockhart Neave, who lived in Istanbul from 1881 to 1907, describes her visit to Hajji Bekir's shop. Although she confuses pulled sugar with Turkish delight, her account paints a lively picture of the establishment that would have been much the same in the time of Hajji Bekir himself:

"It was too late for any further sight-seeing, so we hurried back to the Bridge, paying on our return journey a visit, absolutely essential after seeing Stamboul, to Hadji Bekir's Turkish Delight factory. This is situated most conveniently near the Bridge head, and consists of one small room where, under the opening of a large chimney piece, huge copper pans were kept filled with sugar syrup. Young boys stirred these incessantly for two hours at a time, over a large wood fire, until the mixture thickened, when various flavours were added, such as mastic, rose or vanilla. I was much amused to note that Hadji Bekir, the owner, who welcomed us into his shop, never attempted to sell us his Turkish Delight. With great ceremony he offered us plaited straw-covered stools to sit on, and cups of coffee were supplied with generous helpings of *rahat loukoum* (Turkish Delight) and boiled sweets in many colours. We were then invited to watch the process of making Turkish Delight, which thrilled me, as we were just in time to see a man take out of the coppers a great coil of the thick syrup that had been cooking. With a dexterous twist of the wrist he threw the sticky substance, as thick as a coil of rope, into the air and caught it on a huge hook. With lightning speed it was spun through the cook's hands and thrown up again repeatedly onto the hook. Each time this process was resorted to the substance became thicker, and it shone with satin-like sheen. Finally, when the substance acquired the right consistency, the confectioner cut it up into squares, rolled these in the finest sugar procurable, and, when they were ready for consumption, handed them round to us to taste. From a shelf above his head he reached for a wooden drum-shaped box, and waited for orders for the quantity of Turkish Delight that was required. Until that moment we had in no way been given the slightest hint that we were expected to buy any of the goods for sale in the shop. We had been treated as honoured guests, with the usual beautiful manners of the courtly Turk, which always filled me with admiration; it was with the greatest diffidence that we asked what our account came to, and were surprised and relieved to find that we had been charged only for the boxes of Turkish Delight that we had been allowed to buy."

A portrait of the elderly Hajji Bekir (or possibly the son so often mistaken for him) was painted by the Maltese painter Amadeo Preziosi, who settled in Istanbul in 1851 and remained until 1882.

After Hajji Bekir's death in 1856, the shop was taken over by his son Mehmet Muhiddin, and then by his grandson Ali Muhiddin Hacıbekir, who was appointed chief confectioner to the court of Sultan Abdülhamit II in 1906 and to the khedive of Egypt in 1911. Confectionery produced by the firm won numerous medals at international expositions, including Vienna in 1873, Cologne in 1888 and Brussels in 1897. Hajji Bekir's original shop, run by his descendants, still exists in Bahçekapı, Istanbul.

—— PRISCILLA MARY IŞIN

Jehane Benoît

ALSO CALLED: Madame Benoît

1983

JEHANE BENOÎT, NÉE PATENAUDE—COOKBOOK AUTHOR, cooking teacher, food journalist, broadcaster, chemist, culinary historian, chef, and cooking consultant—was born at Montréal on March 21, 1904, and died at Sutton, Québec, November 24, 1987. During her long, eminent career, Madame Benoît tirelessly promoted the culinary arts and passionately advocated good Canadian food to Canadians of all ethnic backgrounds and walks of life.

"My [maternal] Grand'mère instilled in me a love of my culinary heritage by cooking in the old ways from an old handwritten manuscript receipt book inherited from her mother." Also, both her *grandpères*, one a professional bread baker, encouraged the young Jehane to appreciate fresh seasonal food. In 1925 she earned a degree in food chemistry from Université La Sorbonne under Dr. **Edouard de Pomiane**, whose influence continued through her life. She also attended Henri-Paul Pellaprat's Cordon Bleu Cooking School.

Returning to Montréal in the early 1930's, Benoît started a bilingual cooking school, Le Fumet de la Vieille France (The Flavor of Old France), and a landmark vegetarian restaurant called The Salad Bar. Both closed early in World War II. After a courtship begun in 1940, she married the much younger Lt. Bernard Benoît in war-stricken London, England, in August 1945. Together they later settled on a hilly sheep farm called Noirmouton (Black Sheep) near Sutton to raise Jehane's daughter, Monique, from an earlier marriage. Noirmouton became the geographic center of their life and work, and her husband her devoted companion.

Secrets et recettes du cahier de ma grand'mère, Benoît's first cookbook, was published in 1959, although it was preceded by several recipe pamphlets. Her last book, *Encyclopedia of Microwave Cooking*, appeared in 1985. Equally proficient in French and English, she made repeated appearances on radio and television, particularly the national CBC program *Take 30*, and she wrote countless articles for newspapers and magazines, as well as more than thirty cookbooks. Several of them became classic bestsellers in Canada. The best known was *L'encylopédie de la cuisine canadienne / The Encyclopedia of Canadian Cuisine*, first published in 1963 and reprinted many times. Readers valued her clear and friendly instructions, her folksy and lively manner, and her passion. Early in her career, media interviewers found "Jehane" difficult to pronounce correctly, so they took to calling her simply "Madame Benoît." The name became a national term of endearment.

Through the 1960's, 70's, and 80's, Madame Benoît traveled extensively across Canada, from Charlottetown on Prince Edward Island to Victoria, British Columbia, visiting urban housewives and countryside farms, old seamen in their shanties, and young agricultural exhibitors at fairs. Their many recipes told the story of what Canadians were eating. From a fisherman in Covey Cove, Nova Scotia, she learned how to cook lobster in icy-cold seawater. From a French epicure she heard of Potato Civette. An Irish nanny offered her An Honest Irish Stew and a Finnish friend a Jellied Tongue. Out of the seventeenth-century *Jesuit Relation* she reproduced Roast Wild Young Goose, adding the useful modern direction to roast "the equivalent of 20 minutes per pound in a 350°F oven."

"Antique recipe hunting can be a fascinating and rewarding pastime," she wrote. "There's always something new for us in what's old." For years she visited the Quebec City Archives and the National Archives in Ottawa, seeking material to understand Canada's culinary patterns, beginning with the First Nations, through her own Québecois background, then Upper Canada, Nova Scotia, and New Brunswick. She pioneered the recording of Canada's culinary history.

However, Madame embraced equally the old ways of nineteenth-century rural Québec and the new ways of the late twentieth. When metric measures and the microwave came along in the 1970's, she promoted them with great enthusiasm. The last years of her busy career were devoted to the microwave evolution under the auspices of the Matsushita Corporation of Japan, which produced Panasonic microwave ovens. She saw a continuum rather than a contradiction in cooking traditional recipes using modern technology.

In recognition of her lifelong commitment to celebrating Canada's native, francophone and anglophone heritages and to embracing Canada's other ethnic communities through their cuisines, Madame Benoît was named Officer of the Order of Canada in June 1974. In championing culinary regionalism and Canadianism with such great and intelligent verve, Jehane Benoît led the way toward today's culinary renaissance. For over thirty years Madame Benoît was a revered household name, the "cooking advisor to her nation" and the "first lady of Canadian cuisine."

— FIONA LUCAS

Secrets et recettes du cahier de ma grand'mère, 1959
Encyclopedia of Canadian Cuisine / L'encyclopédie de la cuisine canadienne, 1963
The Canadiana Cookbook: A Complete Heritage of Canadian Cooking, 1970
The Best of Mme Jehane Benoît: A collection of some of the most famous recipes and ideas from
    Canada's best known cook and most competent authority on Canadian foods, 1972
Madame Benoît's Library of Canadian Cooking, 12 vols, 1972
My Secrets for Better Cooking, 3 vols, 1973
Enjoying the Art of Canadian Cooking, 1974
Madame Benoît's Microwave Cook Book, 1975
Mme. Jehane Benoît's Complete Heritage of Canadian Cooking, 1976
Madame Benoît Cooks At Home, 1978
Madame Benoît's Lamb Cook Book, 1979
Madame Benoît's World of Food, 1980
Madame Benoît's Convection Oven Cook Book, 1981
My Grandmother's Kitchen, 1981 (translation of *Secrets et recettes du cahier de ma grand'mère*)
The Encyclopedia of Microwave Cooking, 1985
The New Revised Illustrated Encyclopedia of Microwave Cooking, 1986

Betty Crocker

Betty Crocker as she was portrayed in 1936...

THROUGHOUT MUCH OF THE TWENTIETH CENTURY, THE MOST famous and trusted authority in America on culinary matters was a woman who existed chiefly in the nation's collective imagination. Betty Crocker came to life in 1921 in the corporate headquarters of Washburn Crosby, the Minneapolis flour company that would become General Mills seven years later. Washburn Crosby had just run a highly successful promotion featuring magazine ads with jigsaw puzzles, which readers were invited to assemble and mail in for a prize. As tens of thousands of puzzles poured into company headquarters, the staff noticed that many women had included letters full of questions about home baking. ("Why won't my cakes rise?" "How long should I knead bread?") Washburn Crosby's home economists answered each letter personally, signing them with a name created for the purpose: "Betty" because it was homey, and "Crocker" in honor of a company executive.

At first she merely signed letters; but within a few years, ad hoc pictures of Betty Crocker started showing up in advertisements and recipe booklets. In 1924 she began the radio broadcasts that would usher in the most important and influential phase of her career, beginning with a local program in Minneapolis and moving to a national network two years later. The first of her many programs was *The Betty Crocker Cooking School of the Air*, in which home economists speaking as Betty Crocker offered recipes and instruction to homemakers across the country. The program lasted 24 years; more than a million of its listeners registered formally with the "school," prepared all the recipes in the curriculum, and received diplomas. Other Betty Crocker broadcasts had different formats, including dramas and celebrity interviews, but baking (and General Mills products) always figured prominently in the subject matter. The program that secured her identity as America's chief spokeswoman on right eating was *Our Nation's Rations*, which was commissioned by the War Food Administration and featured Betty Crocker dispensing advice and recipes to the home front. Her wartime booklet *Your Share* reached some seven million homes. In 1950, her first major publication—*The Betty Crocker Picture Cook Book*—was issued in a record-breaking first printing of 950,000 copies. By 1954, according to a company survey, 99 percent of American housewives were familiar with her name.

While various women played the part of Betty Crocker over the years, the one who did the most to establish her personality was Marjorie Child Husted (1892–1986), an ambitious businesswoman trained in home economics who directed the Home Service Department at General Mills for many years. Husted wrote ads, scripts, and speeches for Betty Crocker, played her in public, edited the recipe booklets and supervised the creation of the *Picture Cook Book*. Under Husted, absolute reliability became the fundamental ingredient in Betty Crocker's advice. Every scrap of information was the product of research, and every recipe was tested not only by professionals but by squadrons of home cooks. In addition, Husted's ongoing research persuaded her that homemakers felt ignored, and that they were hungry for praise and appreciation. She made sure that Betty Crocker's written and spoken texts took them seriously.

The persona that Husted developed so carefully was far more professional than motherly. Betty Crocker's radio voice was never cozy or intimate, and she never so much as hinted at a personal life. Instead, though she spoke warmly, she spoke as management. She made it clear that she loved and respected the kitchen; but it was just as clear that the only kitchen in her own life was the one at General Mills, where she supervised her staff as they developed and tested recipes. Her first official portrait, which General Mills commissioned in 1936 from the artist Neysa McMein, showed a woman of sober dignity, with only a tightly frilled collar to hint at femininity.

...and in 1996.

In 1950 General Mills hired a new Betty Crocker, looking outside the field of home economics for the first time. Adelaide Hawley (1905–1998) was a radio and television broadcaster specializing in fashion and women's news; she had no background in cooking and no interest in it, but she did have the height, the poise, and the calmly authoritative manner that Husted had built into the character of Betty Crocker. Hawley starred in two short-lived Betty Crocker television shows, conducted radio programs and appeared in numerous television ads for General Mills products during the 1950's. But by the early '60's, General Mills was advertising cake mixes and other short-cut products far more heavily than it was promoting flour, and with this shift in emphasis, Betty Crocker's personality changed. In her many cookbooks she remained a trustworthy source of wisdom on techniques, ingredients, and meal-planning; but in magazine and TV ads she became little more than a cheerleader for packaged foods.

Since then, while her cookbooks continue to thrive and General Mills updates her portrait constantly, Betty Crocker's vitality as a national domestic icon has faded. Her name is the only aspect of her that is still widely known, and she has outlived by decades the title she once held proudly: "America's First Lady of Food."

— LAURA SHAPIRO

The Betty Crocker Picture Cook Book, 1950
Over 200 Betty Crocker Cookbooks have followed the first book.

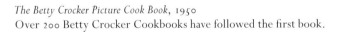

Maximilian Oskar Bircher-Benner ❧ 1867–1939 ❧

ALSO CALLED: Max Bircher

c. 1912

THE SWISS HOLISTIC PHYSICIAN MAXIMILIAN BIRCHER-BENNER was Europe's most important exponent of nutritional reform in the last decade of the nineteenth century and the first decades of the twentieth. His conception of medical treatment that included the patient's soul and spirit as well as his body, and his teachings about nutrition and dietetics, were ignored by his profession for decades, in spite of demonstrated successes, until in the 1930's—the last decade of his life—increasing numbers of clinics and teachers took them up and debated, tested, and confirmed them.

The second of five children of a notary, Max Bircher was born in Aarau, Switzerland, and graduated in 1885 from the cantonal high school, then considered the best classically-oriented high school in the country. Though economic adversity soon impoverished his family, benevolent friends financed his study of medicine at the universities of Zürich and Berlin. He opened his practice in 1891 in an industrial sector of Zürich, and it was there that he carried out his first experiments on the health benefits of raw food.

Bircher married Elisabeth Benner, the daughter of an old Alsatian family, in 1893 and thereafter used the double name Bircher-Benner. Their last of their seven children was born in 1904.

In 1897 he closed his practice and spent some months discussing his findings and his theories with one of his former teachers, Dr. Max Rubner, in Dresden. Late in that year he returned to Zürich and opened a small private clinic that provided him, from then on, with opportunities to further elaborate and test his ideas. At the same time he opened an institute for hydro- and other physical therapies, also in Zürich. He expanded his clinic in 1904, and by 1914 it had grown to include seven buildings and eighty beds, with five physicians. The writer Thomas Mann was a patient, and wrote to a friend about his stay at "Dr. Bircher's sanatorium, where one has to get up at six and turn out the light at nine. That is hard, and at first I kept struggling with rebellious impulses, suitcases at hand. But...I don't at all regret having stuck it out. My stubborn digestion improved to astonishing, to unprecedented levels."

Müsli, the much-imitated ancestor of present-day granola with which Bircher-Benner's name is still associated, was introduced at the clinic in 1900. At the time, a serving consisted of three tablespoons of rolled oats, soaked overnight; a tablespoon of condensed milk; the juice of one lemon; one grated apple; and a sprinkling of grated hazelnuts or almonds.

Economic circumstances at the end of World War I forced Bircher-Benner to scale back his clinic; personally, he also suffered from the disregard of the larger medical community for his ideas. In 1924, however, he began to publish a magazine called *The Turning Point in Life and Illness,* as well as a series of Turning Point books, largely drawn from the magazine, which instigated a broad discussion of nutritional therapy, and in his last years Bircher-Benner witnessed numerous scientific confirmations of his theories. Publication of *The Turning Point* continued through 1978.

During his lifetime, Bircher-Benner's three oldest sons, Max Edwin, Franklin, and Willy, all physicians, worked with their father in the clinic. His youngest son, Ralph, was editorial director of *Turning Point* for decades. His sister Alice was administrator of the clinic for ten years (then marrying a patient) and his sister Bertha held the same position from 1910 to 1945. Though its founder died in January, 1939, the clinic continued in operation until the early 1990's.

Bircher-Benner wrote and published prolifically. Besides the larger works listed below, he produced numerous articles, pamphlets, brochures and prospectuses, offprints of his journal articles and chapters, texts of his lectures and speeches and commemorative publications, as well as a translation into German of a work on uric acid by an English colleague, Dr. Alexander Haig.

— ECKEHARD METHLER & WALTER METHLER

Kurze Grundzüge der Ernährungs-Therapie auf Grund der Energie-Spannung der Nahrung (Essential Features of Nutritional Therapy on the Principles of the Energy Potential of Foods), 1903. Revised and quadrupled in length, 1906

Grundlagen unserer Ernährung (Foundations of Our Nutrition), 1921

Früchtespeisen und Rohgemüse (Fruit Dishes and Raw Vegetables), 1924. The first of the Turning Point series, co-authored with Dr. Max Edwin Bircher. Translated into 13 other languages. Revised 1926, 1939, 1944-1945, 1959

Eine neue Ernährungslehre auf Grund der Fortschritte der Naturwissenschaften u. der ärztlichen Erfahrung gemeinverständlich dargestellt in fünf Vorträgen für schweizerische Haushaltungslehrerinnen (A New Nutritional Doctrine on the Basis of Advances in Natural Science and Clinical Experience, Presented in Lay Terms in Five Lectures for Swiss Teachers of Home Economics), 1924

Der Menschenseele Not. Erkrankung und Gesundung (Affliction of the Human Soul: Sickness and Health), 1927. Expanded to two volumes which appeared in 1933 and 1940

Ernährungskrankheiten in gemeinverständlicher Darstellung: Erster Teil (Nutritional Diseases in Lay Terms: Part 1), 1927. Revised by Dr. Franklin E. Bircher, 1940

Ungeahnte Wirkungen falscher und richtiger Ernährung (Unsuspected Effects of Correct and Incorrect Nutrition), 1927

Die praktische Form der neuen vollwertigen Ernährung mit Einschluss der Rohkost (The Practical Form of the New Complete Nutrition With the Inclusion of Raw Fruits and Vegetables), 1930

Revolution der Ernährung, die neue vollwertige Ernärung des Menschen (Revolution in Nutrition: The New Complete Human Nutrition), 1931

Ernährungskrankheiten in gemeinverständlicher Darstellung: Zweiter Teil (Nutritional Diseases in Lay Terms: Part 2), 1932

Nährschäden in Wort und Bild (Nutritional Deficiencies in Words and Pictures), 1932

Frischgemüse im Haushalt (Fresh Vegetables in the Household), 1934

Die Verhütung des Unheilbaren (Preventing What Cannot be Cured), 1934

Diätetische Heilbehandlung: Erfahrungen und Perspektive (Dietetic Treatment: Experiences and Perspectives), 1935

Kinderernährung. Gemäß den Ergebnissen der neuen Ernährungsforschung (Pediatric Nutrition According to the Results of Current Nutritional Research), 1935

Vom Sinn einer therapeutischen Organisation (On the Purpose of a Therapeutic Organization), 1935

Vom Wesen und von der Organisation der Nahrungsenergie (On the Nature and Organization of Nutritional Energy), 1936

Kranke Menschen in diätetischer Heilbehandlung. I. Teil: Magen-, Darm- und Hautkrankheiten (Sick People In Dietetic Therapy. Part I: Stomach, Digestive and Skin Diseases), 1936

Kranke Menschen in diätetischer Heilbehandlung. II. Teil: Asthma, Bluthochdruck-, Herz- und Hautkrankheiten, Migräne, Kreislaufstörungen (Sick People In Dietetic Therapy. Part 2: Asthma, Heart and Skin Diseases, Migraine, Circulatory Diseases), 1936

Kranke Menschen in diätetischer Heilbehandlung. III. Teil: Vegetabile Heilkost, Fettsucht, Magerkeit, Verstopfung, Epilepsie, Melancholie, Schwangerschaftsleber, Schwindelanfälle, Hämorrhoidalblutungen (Sick People In Dietetic Therapy. Part 3: Vegetarian Curative Diet, Obesity, Emaciation, Constipation, Epilepsy, Depression, Fatty Liver of Pregnancy, Dizziness, Bleeding Hemorrhoids), 1937

Fragen des Lebens und der Gesundheit (Questions of Life and Health), 1937

Die Grippe (Influenza), 1937

Meine Stellungnahme in der Chiroprakfrage (My Position on the Question of Chiropractic), 1937

Vom Werden des neuen Artzes (The Development of the New Physician), 1938

Kranke Menschen in diätetischer Heilbehandlung. IV. Teil: Gelenk- und Nervenentzündungen, Gicht, Rheumatismus, Leber-, Gallen- und Nierenleiden, Grüner Star (Sick People In Dietetic Therapy. Part 4: Joint and Nerve Inflammations, Gout, Rheumatism, Liver, Gallbladder and Kidney Disease, Green Cataract), 1938

Kranke Menschen in diätetischer Heilbehandlung. V. Teil: Arterienverkalkung, Basedow, Heufieber, Kieferhöhlenvereiterung, Psychische Erschöpfung, Spinale Kinderlähmung, Tuberkulose, Zahnwurzelgranulome, Zuckerkrankheit (Sick People In Dietetic Therapy. Part 5: Arteriosclerosis, Goiter, Hay Fever, Sinus Infection, Psychic Exhaustion, Polio, Tuberculosis, Dental Abscesses, Diabetes), 1938

Ordungsgesetze des Lebens als Wegweiser zur Gesundheit (Rules for Life as Guides to Health), 1938

Die Rheumakrankheiten (The Rheumatic Diseases), 1939

Katherine Golden Bitting · 1869–1937 ·

THE KATHERINE GOLDEN BITTING MEMORIAL COLLECTION ON GASTRONOMY at the Library of Congress includes materials collected over 50 years by Katherine and Arvil Bitting. When the couple began collecting in the early twentieth century, they turned to Emile Nourry, a Parisian bookseller, for advice. According to Katherine, Nourry advised, "Make careful selection of books according to subject matter rather than by editions; purchase only what you can afford at a time; become familiar with them by use, thus learn to appreciate them, and maybe to love them."

The Bittings amassed a wide-ranging collection of approximately 4450 titles comprised of books on medicine, cookbooks, travel memoirs, agricultural manuals, dictionaries, almanacs, housekeeping books, regional cookbooks, herbals, confectioneries, and books on beverages. It included a number of manuscripts and rare items, such as one of the two known extant copies of Maestro Martino's *Libro de arte coquinaria*, printed between 1450 and 1460 and often regarded as the first modern cookbook because of its details about measurements and cooking times. (Martino is the chef who furnished the recipes for **Platina**'s *De Honesta Voluptate et Valetudine*.)

Katherine Bitting compiled a bibliography of their collection that was published in San Francisco in 1939. In the introduction to *Gastronomic Bibliography*, she states that the collection "represents a by-product on food research extending over a period of nearly fifty years. It covers the material which has been acquired or examined and is not compiled from outside sources. It is devoid of any element of inspiration or thought of reward other than the pleasure derived in doing it and making it easier for others who may be engaged in a similar or allied line of work." Her comments on each entry, and her research into other editions of individual works, however, demonstrate clearly that she had, as Nourry had suggested, come to love them.

Katherine Golden was born in 1869 in Canada. Her family came to the United States when she was young. She received a BS in 1890, and an MS in 1892, both from Purdue University. While obtaining her master's degree, she worked in the Purdue Agricultural Extension School and went on to be an assistant professor at Purdue from 1893 to 1901. This transition from research to a faculty position was highly unusual for a woman at the time. It was at Purdue that she met her husband, Arvil Bitting, a chemist. They married on December 26, 1904 and went on to work together in various laboratories for most of their careers.

From 1907 until 1913 Katherine Bitting worked as a microbotanist in the United States Department of Agriculture's Bureau of Chemistry, then under the direction of **Harvey Wiley**. Wiley, believing that the use of preservatives in food was harmful, gave her the task of finding a way to make commercial ketchup without the use of preservatives. Among other accomplishments, she devised a process by which spoiled tomatoes could be detected using microscopic analysis.

Her subsequent career included working as a microanalyst for the National Canners' Association (1913–1918) and as a biologist for the Glass Container Association (1913–1923). She died in 1937.

Most of her publications appeared in technical food-chemistry journals, but she also produced two important gastronomic works: her *Gastronomic Bibliography: Compiled by Katherine Bitting*, and her translation of **Nicolas Appert**'s *The Art of Preserving*. Her introductory material in that work discusses Appert's importance to the food-preserving industry.

— PATRICIA M. KELLY

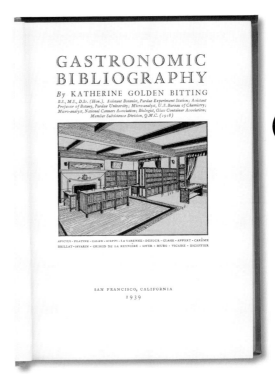

Title page of Bitting's Gastronomic Bibliography, *1939*

Microscopic Examination, 1915
Canning and How to Use Canned Foods, with A.W. Bitting, 1916
The Effect of Certain Agents on the Development of Some Moulds, 1920
The Book for All Households or The Art of Preserving Animal and Vegetable Substances for Many Years, translated from Appert, 1920
Gastronomic Bibliography: Compiled by Katherine Bitting, 1939. Facsimile reprint, 1981

Pierre Blot

ALSO CALLED: Professor Blot

THE JURY IS STILL OUT ON THE ROLE OF FRENCH CUISINE IN THE DEVELOPMENT of American cookery. And indeed, not all the evidence has been gathered, nor all the leads investigated. One piece of evidence involves Pierre Blot and the first French cooking school in New York City. Given Blot's importance and the almost unbelievable publicity he enjoyed during his lifetime, it is strange to find so little known about him today. Few records can be found of his early life and work in France, including his purported editorship of the *Almanack Gastronomique* of Paris and numerous other gastronomical works. Those credentials are listed on the title page of his first documented cookbook, but research has so far failed to turn up copies of any such publications. Blot appears to have been a political refugee, arriving in the United States in the mid-1850's.

In 1863 Blot published his first cookbook in America, *What to Eat and How to Cook It*. It is a large and systematic cookbook which must have thoroughly captured the imagination of New Yorkers, as numerous publications began to trumpet him and his activities. On February 5, 1865, *The New York Times* began a series of lengthy and idolatrous articles on the man they most often referred to as "Professor Blot." His reforms, they said, "will be more acceptable to the people of New York than any which have heretofore been derived from pleasure-loving and extravagant France."

In 1865 Blot opened his New York Cooking Academy, the first cooking school in New York. Full details of the school and its classes were enthusiastically reported in *The New York Times*. At Blot's Cooking Academy, the professor explained the processes to the ladies in his audience, while a female assistant demonstrated by preparing the dishes. Then the foods were sampled, and questions asked. "All of the pupils," the *Times* reported, "were the heads of the families of our most distinguished and wealthy citizens, with the exception, perhaps, of five or six, who, we should suppose, were the daughters of parents whose good sense and love of humanity had induced them to send them to Prof. Blot, that they might be instructed in the art which has so much to do with the temper of the sterner sex." There was also a class scheduled for servants.

Blot's successes in New York induced him to establish a branch of his Academy in Brooklyn, and in 1866, the Professor took his show on the road, giving a series of fourteen lectures in Mercantile Hall in Boston. Each was fully reported in the *Boston Daily Evening Transcript*. The lectures, later published, were "sketched by a Lady" whose identity I have been unable to uncover. Blot traveled throughout the Northeast, teaching and lecturing, always receiving glowing reviews in the local papers.

Over the years, Blot contributed several articles to *The Galaxy*, a very popular and influential literary magazine of its day. In his 1867 article "American Cookery," he opines that "America is not behind other countries in ability to appreciate a good dinner," but that "American cookery is, generally speaking, worse than the cookery of any other civilized nation." Blot continues, "It may be pronounced a custom peculiar to this country to pay little attention to the quality and preparation of food, and great attention to quantity...."

In 1867, Blot authored a new work, the *Hand-Book of Practical Cookery, for Ladies and Professional Cooks*, innovatively marrying sophisticated French methods and recipes to the startling—to him—bounty of America. Dishes inspired by **Carême** were included, but also corn cakes and the preparation of possum, coon, skunk, fox, and woodchuck from American forests. Delicious fish preparations were given with comments on how the American Indian prepared his fish. *The New York Times* reviewed it positively: "The book will supply a great want that has long been felt by many housekeepers—namely, of preparing food in an economical way."

The *Times* adds, "Many of the cook books are written or compiled by those who have no practical knowledge of cookery, and of the physiology of man, and who care nothing about the mass of people who have to live on moderate incomes. Prof. Blot's maxims are 'Make use of everything good,' 'Waste nothing, however small.'"

It is almost unimaginable that the *Times* reviewer could have made those statements about existing cookbooks. Books such as **Lydia Maria Child**'s *The American Frugal Housewife*, **Catharine Beecher**'s *Domestic Receipt-Book*, **Eliza Leslie**'s *Directions for Cookery*, **Mrs. E. A. Howland**'s *The New England Economical Housekeeper* and numerous other female-authored books addressing just these questions had been published in multiple editions prior to this time. The *Times* reviewer simply ignored a complete body of cookbook literature, yet this uninformed writing simply enhanced Blot's reputation.

Blot's fame was such that in 1870 he was asked if the recipes using potatoes in his recent book might be included in a new work about to be published. He graciously agreed, and so a fourth title by him can be found in the National Union Catalogue. In addition to his two major works, mentioned above, and the *Lectures on Cookery Delivered at Mercantile Hall*, we have *The $100 Prize Essay on the Cultivation of the Potato. Prize offered by W. T. Wylie and awarded to D. H. Compton. How to Cook the Potato. Furnished by Prof. Blot*.

Yet as early as 1868, *The New York Times* published a series of articles about Prof. Blot regarding his prospective opening of a group of eating clubs. Nothing appears to have come of this plan, and I have been unable to unearth specific details, but some mysterious aftertaste of controversy and disillusionment with Blot was apparent in the articles. In a letter to the *Times*, Blot claimed that although there was wide public support for such clubs, the city's "leading citizens" failed to support him with the necessary capital and leadership.

And even while Blot's most successful articles were being published in *The Galaxy*, some people were beginning to question his work. Late in 1871, a column in *The Galaxy* made specific complaints: "Whatever has become of 'Professor' Blot? Have his instructions borne much fruit? We fear not a great deal; and we also suspect this result to be not altogether chargeable to the blindness of the natives; though to be sure some of their objections to him certainly were ridiculous enough, such as that his cooking was too "Frenchy," which is like finding fault with a trotting horse for being too American, or with music for being too Italian.

But however learned M. Blot may be in the principles of his art, or however good a practical cook, his book, as a receipt book, is very open to criticism. Some of his directions are positively erroneous and others unintelligible and useless...."

Prof. Blot had clearly fallen out of favor with the public and the press by this time. *The New York Times* did not even bother to print his obituary in 1874.

I could not better summarize Blot's contributions to, and place in, American culinary history than to excerpt some paragraphs from an 1876 *Galaxy* article entitled "What Shall We Eat?" The author, Albert Rhodes, laments the state of cooking and eating in America, and then goes on to talk about attempts at kitchen reform:

"Pierre Blot in our country worked hard to bring about a change in the way of preparing food, a few years ago, but there is no trace of his passage left. He probably made the same mistake which **Soyer** made in London, in trying to teach cookery to those who from their station in life could not become practical cooks—who were beyond the necessity of doing so. He however followed up his work with sufficient energy to produce a stir, which he kept up for several years, in the well-to-do class of women. They followed his lectures, accompanied with practical illustration, in sufficient numbers to lead many people, especially husbands and fathers, to believe that a radical reform was about to be inaugurated. The enthusiasm of M. Blot, too, was contagious, according to those who listened to him, and as long as the learners were in sound of his voice and under his eye, they really believed they were going to become disciples worthy of their master. They returned to their homes and essayed to put the lesson thus learned into practice, and succeeded perhaps twice or thrice in doing so, in the spirit of amateurs; but to cook is to work, as they were not long in discovering, and then they turned the responsibility of the charge to the Irish servant, appeasing their conscience with a theoretical exposition of the method of operating, which fell on the ear of Bridget like an unknown language. M. Blot later, recognizing the mistake he had made in working among the upper instead of the lower stratum of society, made an effort to teach the people who were already in the kitchen the mysteries of his art; but as no marked results followed this effort, the presumption is that the teacher's energy was spent, or that the masters and mistresses had lost interest and ceased to require true qualifications in those whom they employed."

Blot's name does appear in some books on American culinary history, though simply as the founder of the first French cooking school in New York City. Blot's *Hand-Book of Practical Cookery* was included in a series of reprints of American culinary classics edited by Louis Szathmary in 1973, and was published yet again in facsimile in 2001; he is also listed briefly in two classic biographical reference works of the nineteenth century: *Appleton's Cyclopedia of American Biography* and *Allibone's Critical Dictionary of English & British & American Authors*. No other records of Blot and his contributions to American culinary history exist. All of the details of his life beg further study: his background in Europe; his early years in the United States; the question of a possible scandal relating to the dining clubs in New York City; his business enterprises in New York, Brooklyn, and New Jersey; and his final years in sad obscurity until his death in Jersey City, New Jersey.

— Janice Bluestein Longone

What to Eat and How to Cook It, 1863

Lectures on Cookery, Delivered at Mercantile Hall [Salem?], 1866

Professor Blot's Lectures on Cookery: The Substance of His "Immensely popular" Course of Lectures Delivered in Mercantile Hall, and Reported With Great Care [Boston], 1866

Hand-Book of Practical Cookery, for Ladies and Professional Cooks, 1867. Reprinted 1973, 2001

The $100 Prize Essay on the Cultivation of the Potato. Prize offered by W. T. Wylie and awarded to D. H. Compton. How to Cook the Potato. Furnished by Prof. Blot, 1870

Johann von Bockenheim

✤ FIFTEENTH CENTURY ✤

B

JOHANN VON BOCKENHEIM WAS COOK TO POPE MARTIN V, WHO DIED IN 1431. He was the author of a fascinating and unusual cookery book. Very little is known of his life outside his religious career. He is assumed to originate from Bockenheim, near Worms, in Germany: Certainly he held titular benefices (priesthoods) in the Frankfurt region. In the best manuscript of his book his name appears as Jo. Bockenheym and he describes himself as "former cook to the Lord Pope Martin the Fifth." Other documents give his full name in Latin as Johannes Herbordi de Bockenheim.

Already a member of the priesthood, he was appointed cook on December 4, 1417, only a few days after the pope himself was elected. The papal household, initially established at Konstanz, in southern Germany, where the election took place, moved to Rome in 1420. Bockenheim probably retained his post until the death of Martin V, afterward returning to a more normal career in the church. He must have compiled his book very soon after 1431, however, because the two surviving manuscripts, neither of which is his original, were both written before about 1450. He refers to the book as his *Registrum Coquinae* or *Cookery Record*. It is a short compilation of 74 recipes, most of which are relatively brief.

One of the manuscripts of Bockenheim's cookery book is in the Bibliothèque Nationale in Paris; the other (which seems closer to the original) is in a private collection in London. His work was practically unknown until the Latin text was published by Bruno Laurioux in 1988. Laurioux's edition includes full discussion, information on variations between the manuscripts, and an important index-glossary. There is now a translation into Italian based on Laurioux's text.

In two features Bockenheim's *Registrum Coquinae* differs from most other early modern cookery books. The first is that it has no direct ancestors and no descendants. Many compilers worked on the basis of an existing collection, adding revisions and new ideas, eliminating unfashionable recipes, rearranging the sections. No one, however, drew on Bockenheim's cookery book: It was not printed until modern times, and the manuscripts found few if any readers. Nor did Bockenheim himself rely on earlier manuscripts by others, and it is interesting to consider why. If he did not learn his skills from books, did he pick them up in Germany, before joining the papal household, or from the kitchen staff over which he then presided?

The second remarkable feature of this cookery book is the care taken by the author to indicate for which sorts of guests each recipe is best suited. This feature is noted in Bockenheim's preface and a specific recommendation appears at the end of most of the recipes, though no reasons are ever given.

The reader finds that over half the recipes are said to be suited to people from a specific region of Europe. For example, No. 5, boiled beef, concludes, "It will be good for Germans." No. 20, small birds parboiled and roasted with a juniper sauce, "will be good for Frisians and Slavs." No. 26 is pepper sauce to serve with peacock, a classic combination which is mentioned in passing in many medieval texts; this recipe, according to Bockenheim, "is good for Romans." No. 37 is headed "Another pie for Hungarians and Bohemians." Laurioux has shown that a few of these recipes really are linked with the typical cuisine of the places named by Bockenheim. For example, No. 22, *vigitelli de porco*, recommended "for Romans," is a version of a typically Roman dish now called *fegatelli di maiale*.

An additional large group of recipes is said to be suitable for specific social groups. No. 14, for a spit-roasted hog with an elaborately spiced stuffing, "will be for the rich." No. 19, for *piperatum nigrum* (stewed kid in a black pepper sauce), is "for men of power." No. 38, for hard-boiled eggs in a sauce, "will be good for clerics and monks." No. 45, for farm goose, "will be good for citizens." Some of Bockenheim's recommendations deal with people whom a papal cook might not have been expected to encounter professionally. No. 47, for roast fowl, is recommended for "freebooters on campaign." No. 49, an egg dish flavored with orange, "will be for pimps and lecherous women," while No. 50, a sweet made with almond milk, "will be good for prostitutes." This unexpected and challenging feature of Bockenheim's cookery book was recently the focus of a study by Luigi Ballerini in *Gastronomica*. In the last section of his paper Ballerini raised the special problems of recipe No. 50: What are the "sponges" used during the cooking process? Why is the finished dish recommended for prostitutes? These issues have attracted the attention of a dozen authors from different disciplines, whose various proposals have now been gathered in a symposium moderated by Ballerini.

In spite of this scholarly attention, no one has yet given a fully satisfactory answer to the question of how Bockenheim arrived at his recommendations, either for this dish or for many of the others. Some answers might well be found in the details of his biography, if it were better known. Bockenheim's own earlier life in Germany, along with the German origin of the new papal entourage, may suggest why numerous recipes are listed as suitable for Germans, for inhabitants of individual regions of Germany, and for other northern Europeans. A study of the succession of visitors to the papal court between 1417 and 1431—many of whom must have been honored by an invitation to a banquet—could probably help to explain many of the other recommendations.

— ANDREW DALBY

Registrum Coquinae (Cookery Record)

Gail Borden, Jr.

≉ 1801–1874 ≉

WITH LESS THAN TWO YEARS OF FORMAL SCHOOLING, THIS SURVEYOR, PUBLISHER, Texas patriot, tax collector, land agent, and devout Christian completely changed the world's dairy industry. Dairymen dependent on local customers, armies, travelers without access to fresh milk, and children sick or dying from contaminated milk—all were helped by this tinkerer who believed wholeheartedly in his inventions. Gail Borden's greatest accomplishments came after he was 50, quite old for a nineteenth-century entrepreneur.

He was born in Norwich, New York on November 9, 1801, the son of Gail and Philadelphia Wheeler Borden. The family moved several times, eventually settling in New London, Indiana. In his early twenties, he and a brother headed south in search of a milder climate. Gail Borden settled in Mississippi, thinking that would alleviate his persistent cough, while his brother, Thomas Henry Borden, moved on to the Mexican territory that would become Texas. While in Mississippi, Gail taught school, held several surveying positions, and in 1828 married Penelope Mercer.

In 1829, he moved to Fort Bend County, Texas, where he raised cattle, farmed and surveyed land for Stephen F. Austin's colony of Anglo-Americans. He quickly became involved in the region's politics. He established *The Telegraph and Texas Register,* a small eight-page newspaper that recorded the war with Mexico and the new government's activities. In 1837, Borden sold his share of the newspaper and became the first collector of fees for the Port of Galveston. Borden held a number of jobs while in Galveston, but being settled in one place for fourteen years gave him time to pursue many new interests. His long-standing friend, Dr. Ashbel Smith, encouraged him to experiment with growing Rohan potatoes. He established orchards of fig and citrus trees and raised cattle on the island's grasslands.

Borden was enchanted with new ideas, constantly experimenting and building new machines. He was famous for saying, "I never drop an idea except for a better one." He moved quickly, always running between his offices and home, seeming to need little sleep. By 1845 he had experimented with mass production and canning of preserves made from the figs and other fruit on his property. He was convinced that condensing was the wave of the future—exhorting one local minister to condense his sermons while he himself condensed the time spent eating a meal to a mere fifteen minutes. After the death of his first wife, Borden married Mrs. A. F. Stearns (her first name is thought to have been Augusta), who cared for his five children while he devoted his time to experimentation.

He was familiar with the Texas Indian trail-food mixture of dried buffalo meat, hominy, and mesquite beans, and also with pemmican, a similar mixture of dried meat and berries preserved with bone-marrow grease or tallow. He felt that his own invention, the meat biscuit, was a far superior food for travelers and armies. Eleven pounds of meat were boiled until one pound of syrupy extract remained; this was then kneaded with flour and baked. Exactly when Borden developed his meat biscuit is uncertain, but in 1850, when he was granted the American patent, he dropped all other employment to market his life-sustaining product. Despite favorable notices in *Scientific American*, testimonials from military officers, and a gold medal at London's Great Council Exhibition in 1851, the meat biscuit was never widely accepted. Borden moved to New York in an effort to establish an international center for marketing his invention. Meanwhile his various Texas properties were sold or mortgaged while his two youngest children and his wife were sent to live in various places. Finally, faced with debts amounting to perhaps $60,000, Borden set his meat-biscuit venture aside. He had found a better idea—condensed milk.

In 1853, while living in a cellar in Brooklyn, Borden became convinced that his new ideas—condensed milk, condensed coffee, and other foods—were the wave of the future. A Texas visitor reported that a mere teaspoonful of Borden's condensed milk and coffee made a very good cup of *café au lait* and that Borden was waiting for a patent for his new low-temperature condensing process for milk. Borden had purchased a vacuum machine, similar to the one used by the Shaker colony in New Lebanon, New York for condensing fruit juices, for his experiments. After many trials, modifications of the equipment, and failures, he found a way to condense whole milk. In 1856, he finally persuaded the British and U.S. patent offices that his was a new invention. Borden seldom disputed the claims that others had earlier discovered a vacuum process; his major claim to novelty was in the fact that, from the beginning of the heating and vacuum process until the milk was hermetically sealed in cans, all air was excluded.

Borden's exclusion of air, his strict codes of cleanliness in the dairies supplying milk to his factory, and his temperature control of the milk all preceded **Louis Pasteur**'s discovery of and work with bacteria. Borden produced milk that could be shipped long distances and stored for long periods because he had unwittingly eliminated the bacteria that caused spoilage and disease. With the backing of Jeremiah Milbank, a wholesale grocer who paid Borden's many debts, he founded the New York Milk Company in 1857. This became the Borden Company, which propelled the dairy industry into a profitable nation-wide business.

Orders for canned milk came slowly in the first few years, but when the Civil War began and the Union Army placed orders for more condensed milk than Borden's factory could produce, the financial success he had long sought was assured. In 1860, Borden married his third wife, Emeline Eunice Church. At her suggestion, Borden looked westward for new markets and established the Elgin Milk Condensing Company outside Chicago in 1865. Here, he experimented with all his pet projects— cheese, condensed coffee, extract of beef, jelly, and—once again—meat biscuits.

Separated from his friends, children, and grandchildren during the Civil War, Borden could hardly wait to visit Texas again. He also had business there, having transferred most of his beef-extract business to Borden, Texas, a small community named for his family. At his advanced age, he found northern winters too harsh and chose to pass the cold months in Texas. Here he could spend time with family and on philanthropic endeavors for new churches and schools. He died in Borden on January 11, 1874. His body was taken by rail to White Plains, New York for interment at Woodlawn Cemetery.

— ELIZABETH BORST WHITE

Letter of Gail Borden, Jr., to Dr. Ashbel Smith, setting forth an important invention in the preparation of a new article of food, termed Meat Biscuit; and the reply of Dr. Smith thereto; being a letter addressed to the American Association for the Promotion of Science, at their semi-annual meeting, to be held at Charleston in March next, 1850

The meat biscuit, invented, patented and manufactured by Gail Borden..., 1851

Directions for cooking Borden's meat biscuits or the extract of beef dried in flour, invented and manufactured in Galveston, Texas, 1855

James Buchanan Brady

❧ 1856–1917 ❧

ALSO CALLED: "Diamond Jim" Brady

ONE COULD ARGUE THAT, BECAUSE ALL RESTAURANTS need customers and all chefs need appreciative audiences, the diner may be an equal partner in the public dining phenomenon. If that is so, then James Buchanan Brady was a significant figure in late nineteenth-century American food, since he was surely the greatest diner in American history. Both gourmand and gourmet, "Diamond Jim" Brady is the very symbol of the Gilded Age, an era of gross materialism, political and corporate greed, and saturnalian dining by the beneficiaries of the period's unbridled corruption.

The son of an immigrant Irish saloon keeper, James Brady was born on Manhattan's Lower East Side in 1856. Lacking formal education but not pluck, the slum-raised boy left home at eleven to become a bellhop at the toney St. James Hotel. Jovial, smart, and hungry, the already plump lad learned how to ingratiate himself with wealthy patrons and how to behave among them. By the age of fifteen he had been hired as an office boy by the New York Central Railroad. Brady quickly rose to become a salesman for a railroad-equipment company, thus beginning his career as America's first "supersalesman." By garnering financial tips from his many wealthy friends, and thanks to his sharp wits, Brady made millions and entered the ranks of America's newly rich. He adorned himself with diamond rings and stickpins, declaring, "Them as has 'em, wears 'em." Newspapers dubbed the more than 300-pound bon vivant "Diamond Jim."

Diamond Jim at the race track in 1915

Brady's dining exploits are legendary. His breakfasts routinely consisted of a few dozen oysters, pork chops, beefsteaks, eggs, and pancakes, all gulped down with pitchers of orange juice with milk chasers. Lunches and snacks throughout the day were of the same scope. Dinners were rarely fewer than twelve courses composed of balanced food groups: canapés and turtle soup, followed by fish, poultry and meat, shellfish, lobster *à l'Américaine* in a chafing dish, and roasted meats. After a break for sherbet came canvasback duck, terrapin, and—when in season—fresh asparagus, followed by mousses, pastries, and fruit. Two to five pounds of his favorite chocolates finished the meal. (He bought a Boston chocolate factory to supply himself and his friends.)

Like that of a renaissance prince, Brady's eating was a spectator sport. Rector's, Delmonico's, and the other great New York restaurants were his arenas. Surrounded by his many friends, he shared gigantic meals, especially with his great "pal" Lillian Russell, the original American Beauty. No slim reed herself, Russell could and sometimes did match Brady dish for dish, on occasion having to shed her corset. Brady would sit four inches from the table and when his stomach reached the edge, the meal was done.

No mere glutton, Diamond Jim demanded to try every new dish that he heard about. When a friend told him about a Sole Meunière he had eaten in France. Brady sent restaurateur Charles Rector's son, then in law school, to France to spy on the restaurant kitchen. Upon hearing that the recipe had been obtained, Brady rushed to the dock, grabbed the purloined recipe and had Rector's make it at once. The dish became a standard and young Rector became a restaurateur.

Generous to one and all, Brady's large donations helped found the nation's first urological institute at Johns Hopkins University, where he had been treated for kidney stones. His death in 1917, brought on by years of massive food intake, marked the symbolic end of a golden age of groaning tables and coffers swollen with ill-gotten wealth.

— BRUCE KRAIG

Jean-Anthelme Brillat-Savarin   ❦ 1755–1826 ❦

HAD SOMEONE TOLD BRILLAT-SAVARIN THAT THE BOOK HE HAD WORKED ON as an afterthought, in tongue-in-cheek mode, and published shortly before he died, would ensure his celebrity for all eternity, he would surely have invented an appropriate aphorism and feasted the occasion with truffled turkey along with a *grand cru*, while philosophizing on the merits of readership taste.

That book, of course, is his *Physiologie du goût, ou méditations de gastronomie transcendante; ouvrage théorique, historique et à l'ordre du jour, dédié aux gastronomes parisiens, par un professeur, membre de plusieurs Sociétés littéraires et savantes (Physiology of Taste: or, Meditations on Transcendental Gastronomy: A Theoretical, Historical and Up-to-Date Work Dedicated to the Gastronomes of Paris, by a Professor and Member of Several Literary and Learned Societies).* The book's subtitle tells us as much about the author's mind-frame as it does about the work he wrote. The same may be said of its contents, for it abounds with colorful personal anecdotes depicting an adventuresome existence. In the "Brillat-Savarin" entry in the *Dictionnaire Napoléon*, our eclectic author is labeled "gastrologue, gastronome, musician, jurist, philosopher." One might have added "professor," since this is how he refers to himself in his book.

Jean-Anthelme Brillat-Savarin was born to a family of the lower nobility, many of whose members were jurists and magistrates—a path that he himself was later to follow. The Brillat family became Brillat-Savarin in order to inherit the wealth bequeathed by a maiden aunt in 1733, whose will specified that her family name be attached to theirs. Another fortunate family tie—having the famed beauty Juliette Récamier as a cousin by way of his mother's relatives—opened many a prestigious *salon* door for Brillat-Savarin in the post-Revolutionary period. It also accounts for the delightful tuna omelet episode in *Physiologie*.

Until the French Revolution, Brillat-Savarin led a life of privilege and learning, surrounded by a doting family that included eleven siblings and an enlightened father grounded in the teachings of the *philosophes*. Always the brilliant scholar, the son received his law degree in Dijon, pursuant to which he practiced law in his native and beloved Bugey, the province in which Belley was located. Among the earliest signs of the *savant* gastronome and author he was to become were his interest in chemistry and medicine, two disciplines he also pursued in his studies. Thierry Boissel's recent biography mentions the boy Jean-Anthelme's thrill whenever he entered the family kitchen and experienced its many wonders. A love of music was instilled by his father, who played the violin and saw to it that his son did likewise, little realizing that this particular skill would provide a means of livelihood for Brillat-Savarin in the future.

In 1789, the complacency of this existence, as that of countless others, was abruptly shattered by the French Revolution. Like many another liberal member of the privileged class, Brillat-Savarin was reform-minded and, upon being elected in March 1789 to represent Bugey at the Estates General, he chose to be grouped with the Third Estate rather than the nobility, and was one of the signatories of the famed *Serment du Jeu de Paume* (the Tennis Court Oath) the following June, whose adherents vowed to establish a national constitution. Soon thereafter he became a highly vocal reformist member of the Constituent Assembly's Third Estate section, aiming for a system of government that would provide for a constitutional monarchy.

Not being eligible to serve in France's follow-up Legislative Assembly in 1791, Brillat-Savarin returned to Belley, was elected its mayor in 1793, served in the National Guard with the rank of commander, and held a judgeship in the freshly minted administrative *département* of Ain. In the meantime, France had become a republic, and extremist factions were in control. Brillat-Savarin was denounced as a moderate and forced to flee for his life across the border to Switzerland. *Physiologie* commemorates the denunciation with a spicy recipe for "Sauce de la trahison" dedicated to his betrayers.

Brillat-Savarin then led a precarious, if rather picturesque, existence as an émigré for almost three years, after which he returned to post-Robespierre France. Nearly all of these years of exile were spent in the United States, in and around New York, where he was obliged to eke out a somewhat bohemian existence by playing first violin in a major theatre and giving French lessons to young ladies. (He spoke quite acceptable English.) During this time he made a number of helpful social contacts. More of this below.

When Brillat-Savarin returned to France in 1796 he resumed his legal activities, briefly served on the staff of General Augerau in Germany, and held a number of judgeships in appellate courts until his death. During these years of rapidly shifting regimes (Directorate, Consulate, Empire, Restoration, Hundred Days, Second Restoration) he managed not only to stay afloat, but also to gain recognition through his legal activities and writings, in the process being honored with the *Légion d'honneur* and named a Knight of the Empire. His best-known publications prior to *Physiologie*—they differ significantly from this masterpiece—are *Vues et projets d'économie politique (Views and Plans of Political Economy)* (1800), a manuscript fragment titled *Théorie judiciaire (Judicial Theory)* (1808), *De la Cour suprême (On the Supreme Court)* (1814), *Essai historique sur le duel (A Historical Essay on Dueling)* (1819), and *Notes sur l'archéologie de la partie orientale du départment de l'Ain (Notes on the Archeology of the Eastern Part of the Départment of Ain)* (1819).

I now turn to Brillat-Savarin the gastronome, but the other, far less known Brillat-Savarin—the politically and ideologically committed persona described above—cannot be brushed aside. In fact, parts of *Physiologie* bear the hallmarks of a legalistic style, and more than one critic—among them Jean-François Revel and the historian Louis Trénard—has been struck by the fact that this work is basically a satire or parody of the thought and writing of the Ideologues. Members of this philosophical leaning, with whom Brillat-Savarin was well acquainted, included the physician and physiologist Pierre Jean Georges Cabanis. Trénard claims that Brillat-Savarin's main target was Cabanis.

Brillat-Savarin's biographers point out that their subject not only appreciated a fine repast to the point of dissecting its every part, but also enjoyed nothing more than hosting a gourmet meal in grand style, frequently entertaining his guests by playing the violin. *Physiologie* reflects this penchant in nearly every page, albeit in differing ways. This unique work, drafted during the more relaxed final years of his life, is in fact first and foremost a reflection of its many-faceted author's personality: his gregariousness, witty humor, and fancifulness, his embrace of both cosmopolitanism and nationalism, and his world view. It is likewise a repertoire of autobiographical vignettes, among the most interesting and amusing of which are those concerning his years of exile in America, a land his imagination tinted in rosy utopian hues. A forerunner of Alexis de Tocqueville in more ways than one, Brillat-Savarin envisioned the young democracy's institutions as models for France.

Anecdotes in *Physiologie* variously recount drinking bouts, gastronomic dishes prepared by the author, odd prandial company, and a string of food-related events. The most involved, and in many ways most prototypical, is the tale of the "professor's" exploit in Meditation vi, Section iv. While visiting the farm of a family named Bulow during a stay in Hartford, Connecticut in October 1794, Brillat-Savarin recounts with no little pride how he shot a wild turkey during a hunting expedition and prepared it for his dinner guests the next day. The eaters labeled it "a glorious bit." The delight the dinner host takes in his double achievement is contagious, and turns into a metaphor of his relationship to fine cuisine and convivial meals. Nor should his depiction of the idyllic family as represented by Mr. Bulow and his entourage of four daughters, all "buxom lasses," be forgotten, especially since papa Bulow was wearing socks hand-knit by daughter Mariah! This home-sweet-home projection is most likely a metaphoric depiction of America as a whole, seasoned with no little amount of spicy good-will and humor.

Physiologie has gone through innumerable complete editions in the original French since 1825, some fancy and illustrated, some with substantive introductions by well-known authors (that of Roland Barthes is a case in point), some as facsimile reprints, some in paperback, and some in electronic form—the most recent, to my knowledge, appearing in 1997. It has been translated into many languages, most frequently into English: The Library of Congress catalog alone accounts for seventeen English-language editions, the best known by far being that of **M. F. K. Fisher**, first published in 1949.

— BEATRICE FINK

Vues et projets d'économie politique, 1800

Fragment d'un ouvrage manuscrit, intitulé Théorie judiciaire, 1808

De la Cour suprême, 1814

Essai historique sur le duel, 1819

Notes sur l'archéologie de la partie orientale du départment de l'Ain, 1819

La Physiologie du Gout, ou méditations de gastronomie transcendante; ouvrage théorique, historique et à l'ordre du jour, dédié aux gastronomes parisiens, par un professeur, membre de plusieurs Sociétés littéraires et savantes, late 1825, 2 vol.

Bob Brown

❦ 1886–1959 ❧

ALSO CALLED: Robert Carlton Brown II | The Browns, Cora, Rose, and Bob

BOB BROWN WAS BORN AND RAISED IN AND AROUND CHICAGO, ILLINOIS. He entered the University of Wisconsin at Madison but flunked out in 1906 after one year. He began writing short stories, which he sold to New York magazines. In 1909, he married Lillian Fox; they moved to New York, where Brown opened a literary agency. He continued writing fiction and in 1913 published his first two novels, *What Happened to Mary* and *The Remarkable Adventures of Christopher Poe*.

Bob Brown and his wife commenced a vagabond life, living, traveling, and writing in many different countries around the world. In 1913 they moved to Seville, and the following year his first book of poems, *My Marjonary*, was published. In 1916, Bob and Lillian were divorced. He returned to New York, where he opened a restaurant on 57th Street. Two years later, he married Rose Watson, and the couple moved to South America, settling in Buenos Aires, where Brown founded *The Brazilian American Weekly*. During the following decade, Bob and Rose Brown traveled extensively in Turkey, Spain, Austria, France, Mexico, and the United Kingdom, and he continued to publish articles and books.

With Prohibition about to end, Brown wrote *Let There Be Beer!* (1932), a humorous, light history of beer brewing and drinking. It was also his first book concerned with culinary matters, which most likely encouraged him to write his next book collaboratively with his mother and wife. In 1933, the Browns moved to Atlantic Highlands, New Jersey, where Bob, his wife Rose and his mother, Cora, completed *The Wine Cook Book* (1934). During the next seven years, "The Browns, Cora, Rose, and Bob" as the author credit read, turned out nine more cookbooks: *The European Cook Book* (1936), *The Country Cookbook* (1937), *10,000 Snacks: A Cookbook* (1937), *Salads and Herbs* (1938), *Most for Your Money Cookbook* (1938), *The Wining and Dining Quiz: A Banquet of Questions and Answers from Soup to Nuts* (1939), *The Vegetable Cook Book from Trowel to Table* (1939), *America Cooks: Practical Recipes from 48 States* (1940), and *The Fish and Sea Food Cook Book* (1940). Cora Brown was likely the driving force behind these: Her name appears first in the author sequence and, after her death in 1939, Bob and Rose completed only one additional cookbook, *Look Before You Cook: A Consumer's Kitchen Guide* (1941).

From 1940 to 1945, Bob and Rose lived in South America, where Bob continued to write fiction and nonfiction and worked on film scripts. Rose Brown died in 1952, and Bob married his third wife, Eleanor Parker.

The Browns had collected cookbooks for years, and Bob planned to compile a bibliography of American cookbooks—mainly "the regionals," as Eleanor Brown called them in her introduction—intended to supplement and complement Eleanor Lowenstein's *American Cookery Books, 1742–1860*. When Bob Brown died in 1959, Eleanor saw the project through to its completion. *Culinary Americana: Cookbooks Published in the Cities and Towns of the United States of America During the Years from 1860 Through 1960* was published in 1961. It remains the best bibliography of American cookbooks for that period.

— ANDREW F. SMITH

Let There Be Beer!, 1932 (Bob Brown)
The Wine Cook Book, Being a Selection of Incomparable Recipes from France, from the Far East, from the South and Elsewhere, All of Which Owe Their Final Excellence to the Skillful Use of Wine in Their Preparation, 1934 (The Browns)
The European Cook Book for American Homes (from Italy, Spain, Portugal, and France), 1936. Also published as *The Four-in-One Book of Continental Cookery.* (The Browns)
The Country Cookbook: Cooking, Canning, and Preserving Victuals for Country Home, Farm, Camp & Trailer, with Notes on Rustic Hospitality, 1937 (The Browns)
10,000 Snacks: A Cookbook, 1937. (The Browns)
Homemade Hilarity: Country Drinks Both Hard & Soft, 1938 (Bob Brown)
Salads and Herbs, 1938 (The Browns)
Most for Your Money Cookbook, 1938 (The Browns)
The Wining and Dining Quiz: A Banquet of Questions and Answers from Soup to Nuts, 1939 (The Browns)
The Vegetable Cook Book from Trowel to Table, 1939 (The Browns)
The South American Cook Book, 1939 (The Browns)
Soups, Sauces and Gravies, 1939 (The Browns)
America Cooks: Practical Recipes from 48 States, 1940 (The Browns)
Outdoor Cooking, 1940 (The Browns)
The Fish and Sea Food Cook Book, 1940 (The Browns)

Look Before You Cook: A Consumer's Kitchen Guide, 1941 (Rose and Bob Brown)
*Culinary Americana: Cookbooks Published in the Cities and Towns of the United States of America
During the Years from 1860 Through 1960,* 1961 (Eleanor and Bob Brown)

Bushaq

DIED C.1427

ALSO CALLED: Bushaq At'ameh | Abu Is'hāq

VERY LITTLE IS KNOWN ABOUT THE LIFE OF FAKHR AL-DIN IBN HALLAJ ABU Is'hāq, otherwise known as Bushaq or Bushaq At'ameh (Bushaq of Food). He was born in Shiraz, Iran toward the end of the fourteenth century and is thought to have died in about 1427. Shiraz at that time was the center of Persian politics, poetry, and culture. Despite the fact that he was born into the trade of wool-carder, his wit and poetic talent soon brought him to the notice of the Persian court in Shiraz. He was a favorite of Iskandar Omar Shaykh Mirza, Timurid governor of Fars from 1409 to 1415.

It is said that his taste for superior food was developed at court, and his poetic reflections soon turned to the glories of Iranian cuisine. He felt that all the finest poetry had already been written, so he took to parodying the great poets of the time, turning their deeply spiritual philosophy into amusing culinary parodies.

One of his first works, "A Treasury of Appetite," is said to have been inspired by the fact that his lover had lost her desire for food. He promised to compose a poem that would stimulate her appetite. To this end "he girded his loins and cooked a meal garnished with verbal artifices and rhetorical devices, baking it in the oven of reflection with the dough of deliberation." A lengthy poem consisting of 105 rhyming couplets, it was a parody of a work by an earlier poet written to reawaken the sexual appetite of his patron.

A further long poem concerns "The Battle of Saffron Rice and *Bughra*" (*bughra* is a sort of dumpling) in which he describes the careful and exhausting work required in the cultivation of both rice and saffron.

It is difficult to appreciate the humor and flair of his poetry in English translation, but a few examples are given below, brief couplets parodying the works of Hafez, the most popular mystic poet in Iran since the fourteenth century.

Hafez:
I aspired towards seclusion and abstention
But my alluring lover is too tempting.
Bushaq:
I aspired towards fasting and abstention
But that alluring roast lamb is too tempting.
Hafez:
My Turkish beloved went out drunk today.

I wonder whose eyes will shed tears for her now.

Bushaq:

My finest cook went out to buy onions today.

I wonder whose eyes will shed tears for him now.

Hafez:

I am a stranger in your land, Oh friend of the exile;

Attend for an instant to the needs of this exile.

Bushaq:

I am a stranger thanks to my love of onions and bread;

O cheese, attend for an instant to the needs of my table.

Such was Bushaq's fame in his lifetime that gourmands and epicures came from as far away as India to consult him. He occasionally left Shiraz to research famed foods in the Isfahan and Khorasan regions of Iran. In Iran he remains famous, and is frequently quoted. Indeed, local people still visit his tomb in a suburb of Shiraz, quoting verses from his poetry and from the Qur'an in the hope of receiving some rich food for their tables.

Today his works are hard to find. Only one complete edition of his *Divan,* or collected works, was printed sometime in the 1880's by Mirza Habib Isfahani, an Iranian expatriate in Istanbul, and this was reprinted in Iran in the 1950's by Ali Ashgar Hekmat. An anthology of extracts was also published in 1971 in Dushanbe, capital of Tajikistan.

Bushaq remains a valuable resource for food historians. His comments on the food of Iran precede the two earliest Persian-language cookery books, written by the chefs **Bavarchi** and **Nurallah** in the sixteenth and seventeenth centuries, respectively, and follow one written in Arabic by **Al-Baghdadi** in the thirteenth century. Bushaq's works are thus the only serious and knowledgeable primary material on Iranian food during a gap of three centuries, a period that included the Mongol conquest.

— MARGARET SHAIDA

"A Treasury of Appetite," early 15th century
"The Battle of Saffron Rice and *Bughra,*" early 15th century
Divan [collected works], c. 1880

Mike Butt

ALSO CALLED: Mahmood Butt

MAHMOOD (MIKE) BUTT WAS BORN IN NAIROBI, KENYA ON MAY 7, 1926. His parents were Indians from Lahore and Amritsar. He moved to London, then in the late 1940's came to Ireland with a civil-service cricket team for what was intended to be a six-week stay. He never left.

He met and, in 1955, married Terry Foy of Dublin, a graduate of the College of Catering, who was manager of the Green Rooster Restaurant in O' Connell Street. Mike's first business, called "Fruity Frost," involved the production of fruit ices on a stick. He had a factory near Mespil Road but was refused funding when he tried to expand. An Irish company took the concept, received the funding, and prospered.

At this point, Mike had two options: to return to Kenya or to set up a new business. Terry did not want to leave Ireland, so they decided to use her catering experience and his Indian cooking knowledge to open one of Ireland's first Indian restaurants. They searched for premises and took a long lease on 27 Lower Leeson Street, which was in a residential area, and opened the Golden Orient Restaurant in February, 1956. The restaurant had six tables; a curtain separated the kitchen from the dining room. Fortunately, Terry O' Sullivan of the *Irish Press* came in on the opening night and wrote a great review of the restaurant that helped secure it a loyal following from early on. The restaurant became like a club, staying open until three a.m.; students from University College Dublin, in nearby Earlsfort Terrace, would often work waiting tables just to get their dinner for free.

As pioneering restaurateurs, Mike and Terry had to import all the spices, rice poppadoms and even tomato purée from London and store them in their garage at home. The English firm Evans, Gray and Hood blended the restaurant's curry powder specially. It was not until the early 1980's that these ingredients became more widely available in Ireland. In the April, 1956 issue of *Good Cooking*, Ireland's first food and wine publication, Mahmood Butt was featured in the "Chef's Choice" section, giving recipes and advice on producing a good curry and accompaniments.

Mike noticed that his winter-time business was not as healthy as in the summer, when tourists were more plentiful. To keep busy and also to educate the Irish public on Indian food, hence increasing future custom, he traveled around the provinces in the winters, running Indian food festivals in hotel restaurants from Donegal to Clare. In the 1960's he set up Golden Orient Foods, producing frozen Indian TV dinners—but he was ahead of his time, as very few people then had freezers. He worked with Irish meat packers to produce a range of canned Golden Orient curry products that held pride of place in many gourmet shops' window displays.

In the early 1970's he noticed the appearance in England of gourmet or "fine-dining" Indian restaurants, evolving from the simpler curry houses. He decided to move first to preempt the competition, and opened the Tandoori Rooms in the basement of his Leeson Street premises. He drew up plans for a tandoor oven and had it made by a friend who worked in a foundry. His style of food was eclectic:

He would often take crayfish and monkfish from Hanlons fishmongers that might have been in their window display but would never have been sold and create Indian dishes with them. Recipes from the Tandoori Rooms appeared in many publications, including *Gourmet*, and the restaurant was listed in the Gault Millau guide and in every Egon Ronay guidebook from the first edition.

Mike Butt was the founding president, in 1970, of the Irish Restaurant-Owners Association (IRA), which soon changed its name to the Restaurant Association of Ireland (RAI), for obvious reasons. John D. Carroll, Mark Kavanagh, Peter Robinson, Maurice Cohen, Heather Gay and Rachael Bewley were the other founding members. The main purpose of this organization was to lobby for reduced taxation and a special licence that would permit restaurants to serve spirits and beer as well as wine. Mike was also director of Dublin Tourism for a period, as well as being honorary cousul of Pakistan in Ireland.

In 1975, Golden Orient, Ltd. started a service called "Dine Around" which allowed visitors to Ireland to book meals in top Irish restaurants before leaving home and pay for them with special vouchers purchased from their local tour operators.

The 1980 *Good Food Guide* found the tastes and the bonhomie of the Tandoori Rooms unchanged as the restaurant completed a quarter-century of business. At this stage Mike was sharing the cooking tasks with Mohamad Yusuf and Kevin Pigot. In 1986, however, because of Mike's ill health and a severe downturn in the economy, the restaurant closed.

Mike Butt enjoyed shooting pheasant and was an avid fly fisherman, favoring particularly the Connemara lakes. He loved to drive fast cars and was the proud owner of a Bristol 404, Austin Martin DB4 and the first MGB GT in Ireland. In his latter years he took up painting and became an Irish citizen. He died on January 15, 1988.

— MÁIRTÍN MAC CON IOMAIRE

Poppy Cannon

❦ 1905–1975 ❦

ALSO CALLED: Lillian Gruskin

REMEMBERED CHIEFLY AS THE BEST-SELLING AUTHOR OF *The Can-Opener Cookbook* (1952), Poppy Cannon had a far livelier and more provocative career than such a book title suggests. She was one of the most popular culinary authorities of the mid-twentieth century; and though few of her recipes deserve immortality, in the course of an immensely productive working life she developed a perspective on food, cooking, and the woman in the kitchen that was considerably ahead of her time.

Cannon was born Lillian Gruskin in Capetown, South Africa in 1905 and grew up in Pennsylvania. She graduated from Vassar in 1927; hoping to become a writer, she moved to New York with her first husband, a librarian named Carl Cannon. ("Poppy" was a longtime nickname). After they divorced she married Alf Askland, an engineer, who died in 1938; later she married Charles Claudius Philippe, known as "Philippe of the Waldorf," the culinary mastermind at the Waldorf-Astoria Hotel. She divorced him in 1949 to marry Walter White, executive secretary of the National Association for the Advancement of Colored People, with whom she had been secretly in love for many years.

Straight through this busy and tempestuous romantic life, which brought her three children, Cannon worked prodigiously. Married or single she was determined to support herself, and her writings are notable for the lack of any apologizing or temporizing when she mentioned working women. She simply took it for granted that modern women worked for pay just as men did, and that there was no need to debate the issue—a frame of mind that set her well beyond most of her peers.

Her career began in 1935 at Maxon, Inc., an advertising firm where she specialized in food accounts. The food industry was already deeply invested in promoting packaged products—an effort that would balloon to vast proportions after the war—and Cannon developed an abiding faith in convenience foods. She genuinely loved good food, but she wasn't a natural or instinctive cook, and the idea that wonderful dishes might appear in minutes with the help of boxes and jars was irresistible to her. Women as well as men deserved to come home to a delicious, relaxing dinner at the end of the day, she believed; hence she would teach home cooks how to "doctor up" and "glamorize" packaged foods. From her travels, her visits to restaurants, and her own huge culinary library, she gathered a wide array of recipes and set about creating short-cut versions of them. Bouillabaisse, chicken curry, minestrone, nesselrode pie—"In this miraculous age it is quite possible... to be a 'chef' even before you can really cook," she proclaimed in *The Can-Opener Cookbook*; and it was her creed for many years. The difference in quality between the originals and the imitations was a subject she largely ignored.

Cannon's first journalism job was a branch of her advertising job: From 1940 to 1951 she produced a food column laced with brand names for *Mademoiselle*. In 1953 she became food editor of *House Beautiful*; later she contributed regularly to *Town & Country* and *Ladies' Home Journal* as well as writing a syndicated column, hosting a radio program and making television appearances.

Over the years, as her social and professional circles widened and she came into contact with the most sophisticated cooks of her time—**James Beard, Alice B. Toklas, M. F. K. Fisher**—her approach to food became more discerning. She began writing less doggedly about saving time, and more about the importance of understanding ingredients and honoring flavor. A prime influence was Walter White, who introduced her to his huge, diverse circle of famous friends in politics and the arts and was himself a well-known gourmand. When they were finally wed—prompting such headlines as "Negro and Vassar Graduate Married"—Cannon settled into the happiest years of her life. She was working as hard as ever, but the food itself relaxed. She never lost her affection for short-cut cookery, but by the 50's convenience foods no longer dominated her thinking. In the book she was proudest of, *Poppy Cannon's Eating European Abroad & At Home* (1961), she openly reveled in the pleasures of authentic local food, and the recipes called for traditional, hands-on cooking.

White died in 1955, and Cannon dealt with her grief the way she dealt with her happiness: by writing. She eulogized their years together in a memoir, *A Gentle Knight* (1956), and then produced eight more cookbooks. By the 70's, however, she was struggling with mental illness. Numerous efforts at treatment failed, and in 1975 she jumped to her death from the balcony of her New York apartment.

Along with the works already mentioned, Cannon's cookbooks include *The Bride's Cookbook* (1954), *Aromas and Flavors of Past and Present* (with Alice B. Toklas) (1958), *Unforbidden Sweets* (1958), *The Electric Epicure's Cookbook* (1961), *The Frozen Foods Cookbook* (1964), *The Fast Gourmet* (1964), *The Presidents' Cookbook* (with Patricia Brooks) (1968), *Poppy Cannon's All-Time, No-Time, Any-Time Cookbook* (1974), and *Italian Cooking* (1975). Most of these have been forgotten. What makes her a figure worthy of memory is that passionate hunger with which she searched for the ultimate recipe—the recipe that would unite women, work, and great food in a single, manageable dinner.

— LAURA SHAPIRO

Antonin Carême

※ 1783–1833 ※

ALSO CALLED: Marie-Antoine Carême

MARIE-ANTOINE CARÊME WAS A CHILD OF THE FRENCH REVOLUTION who became a culinary revolutionary. He died, not yet fifty, as a proudly self-made man who had not only survived but thrived in the multiple changes of regime in France between 1789 and 1830. As he himself told his story, he was one of fifteen children, and was abandoned by his impecunious and improvident father in the streets of Paris with the injunction to make his own way. As fortune (and legend-in-the-making) would have it, the eleven-year old followed a providential light to an inn, where he began working in the kitchen.

Carême moved on to work for a fashionable pastry-maker, where his *pièces montées*, the spectacular architectural pastry creations with which he would first make his career, caught the eye of the influential Duc de Talleyrand, soon to become Napoleon's most trusted counselor. More important for the future of French cuisine, this consummate gastronome also served as the official host for the definitely ungastronomic emperor. Carême ever after cited Talleyrand as the ideal patron, a full collaborator in the realization of culinary greatness—though his greatest virtue seems to have been his willingness to open his pocketbook. Such generosity was essential, for Carême's vision of French cuisine depended upon prodigality—of funds, provisions, and invention. This culinary extravagance ill suited commercial enterprises, which explains why Carême soon divested himself of the pastry shop that he had opened early in the century and never had anything to do with restaurants, which were fast becoming Parisian landmarks and a characteristic urban institution.

In these years, as he takes care to inform his readers, Carême assiduously frequented the royal library to prep himself in the history of cuisine, and he included a brief "Parallel of Ancient and Modern Cuisine" in his *Le Maître d'hôtel français*

From Favre's Dictionnaire universel de cuisine, *1903*

(*The French Steward*) (1822). Greatly appreciated by his wealthy and titled patrons from the Prince Regent of England and the Tsar of Russia to Baron Rothschild in France, Carême made his first mark on French cuisine with two treatises on the art of pastry making (which at the time included savory as well as sweet dishes). *Le Pâtissier pittoresque* (*The Picturesque Pastry-Maker*) and *Le pâtissier royal parisien* (*The Royal Parisian Pastry-Maker*), which both appeared in 1815, boasted detailed engravings, drawn after Carême's own designs, to accompany the recipes. He famously proclaimed cuisine as the fifth branch of architecture and was proud to be known as the Palladio of French cuisine.

Yet, however exquisite the meals that he served his grateful employers and their fortunate guests, however spectacular his pastry edifices, it was not cooking that made Carême's lasting contribution to French cuisine. This "chef of kings" was even more significantly the "king of chefs," authorized by King Louis XVIII to sign himself simply "Carême de Paris" (Carême preferred the classically inflected "Antonin" to the more plebeian "Marie-Antoine"). To see why, we must look to his great works, *Le Maître d'hôtel français*, *Le Cuisinier parisien* (*The Parisian Chef*) (1828), and, finally, the work to which he devoted his last years and which had to be completed by others, *L'art de la cuisine française au dix-neuvième siècle* (*The Art of French Cuisine in the Nineteenth Century*) (1833). Where previous chefs had offered collections of recipes, Carême proposed a total culinary system. He detailed not one sauce but a comprehensive system of sauces—and of soups, of pastry, of meats, and of vegetables.

Ever the professional, Carême aimed to instruct practitioners and consumers alike and also, more generally, to convince both groups that his was the path, the only path, to culinary excellence. He insisted that his works were treatises that were both elementary and practical, that is, fundamental and doable. In contrast to regional cuisines defined by given products, Carême conceived French cuisine as a body of knowledge and a repertory of techniques that could be put into practice anywhere by anyone who had mastered the principles. This culinary code constructed a whole that no other French cookbook had attempted, much less achieved. In rationalizing culinary practice, in reducing it to principles, Carême created the vehicle that took French cuisine around the world. Almost a century later, the great chef **Auguste Escoffier** acknowledged how much he and everyone else were in Carême's debt: "The fundamental principles of the science [of cooking], which we owe to Carême,...will last as long as cooking itself."

That Carême was able to impose himself virtually unchallenged has much to do with his tireless promotion of himself, his profession, and the practice that he claimed as both a science and an art. He was, in a word, an extraordinary cultural entrepreneur, who considered his writing even more important than his actual cooking. If cooking made his career, writing made his reputation, in the eyes of his contemporaries and his successors alike. Although we now look on Carême's creations as overblown and overcomplicated, his culinary system was decidedly modern. He eagerly took up innovations (the pastry tube receives special mention) and proposed a number of his own, including a reduction of stock to an essence that is surely the ancestor of our bouillon cubes. He explicitly aimed to translate his practices for lesser kitchens, even those without a proper staff.

That his model ruled French cuisine for at least a century, and made its influence felt well beyond, would have been taken by Carême as a foregone conclusion. Yet, however confident he was of his culinary contribution, Carême would not have been surprised to see French cuisine moving in directions that he had never dreamed of, for, better than most, he knew that every *nouvelle cuisine* worked off the old. Those to come would work off his cuisine as he had worked with (and against) the culinary practices of his illustrious predecessors.

In the intensely competitive culinary market of early nineteenth-century Paris, Carême stood, if not alone, then assuredly head and shoulders above his contemporaries; he was characterized by Alexandre Dumas (no mean gastronome himself) as the "apostle of gastronomes," and was the only chef honored with a full entry in Dumas' encyclopedic *Grand Dictionnaire de Cuisine* (1873). As with other Romantic heroes who turn out to be very much a part of their times, Carême's genius lay in the ways he capitalized on and magnified trends well in evidence. For this we admit him as a modern. His all too familiar hype, bordering on vanity, should not blind us to his absolute dedication to the culinary enterprise. For better and for worse, French cuisine even today harks back to Carême.

— Priscilla Parkhurst Ferguson

Le Pâtissier pittoresque. ou Traité élémentaire et pratique de la pâtisserie ancienne et moderne, de l'entremets de sucre, des entrées froides et des socles suivi d'observations utiles aux progrès de cet art, d'une série de plus de soixante menus, et d'une revue critique des grands bals de 1810 et 1811, 1815
Le pâtissier royal parisien ou traité élémentaire et pratique de la pâtisserie ancienne et moderne, 1815
Projets d'architecture dédiés à Alexandre Ier, 1821–1826
Le Maître d'hôtel français ou Parallèle de la Cuisine ancienne et moderne selon les quatre saisons, 1822. 2 vols.
Le Cuisinier parisien, ou L'Art de la cuisine française au dix-neuvième siècle. Traité élémentaire et pratique des entrées froides, des socles et de l'entremets de sucre suivi d'observations utiles aux progrès de ces deux parties, 1828
L'art de la cuisine française au dix-neuvième siècle. Traité Élémentaire et Pratique suivi de dissertations culinaires et gastronomiques utiles aux progrès de cet art, 1833. 2 vols.

Cato

234–149 BC

ALSO CALLED: Cato the Censor | Cato the Elder | Marcus Porcius Cato

MARCUS PORCIUS CATO, ROMAN POLITICIAN, WAS THE AUTHOR OF A FARMING handbook and collection of recipes that is the earliest surviving work of Latin prose.

Cato was born in 234 BC in Tusculum (near modern Frascati), a self-governing city fifteen miles south of Rome. His father had a town house there but worked a farm at Venafrum in the mountainous Sabine country to the southeast. "I spent my boyhood in frugality, privation, and hard work," said Cato later, "reclaiming the Sabine rocks, digging and planting those flinty fields."

He joined the Roman army at seventeen, reached the rank of military tribune, and began a political career which culminated in 195 in his election to the consulship. Successive military and political postings took him to Sicily, North Africa, Sardinia, Spain, and Greece, in all of which he served with success and extended Roman rule. He was an inflexible disciplinarian and a difficult subordinate. Already from Sicily he had launched a political attack on his superior, Scipio Africanus; this and other such disputes ran on, occupying much of his political life. In 184 Cato was elected censor, an occasional and prestigious office whose duties were to review the lists of the Senate, the Knights, and the Citizens, expelling the unworthy. In later life Cato continued—as senator, advocate, and prosecutor—to target corruption and misbehavior by Romans serving overseas. His rhetorical skills were used in political quarrels, in policy debates, and in defending his own past acts. He died in 149 BC, aged 85. His last major contribution to public affairs had been to urge war against Carthage, Rome's long-standing rival. In every speech in the Senate, whatever the subject, he repeated his watchword, *Carthago delenda est*, "Carthage must be razed." The war was fought after Cato's death and did indeed end with the destruction of Carthage.

Cato had married Licinia, a member of an aristocratic family, about 195. He was said to have joked that his wife never put her arms around him except when there was a thunderstorm: "I am a happy man when Jupiter thunders." Their son, Marcus Cato Licinianus, was born c. 192, but died relatively young, as did his mother. At the age of 80 Cato married a much younger woman, Salonia, the daughter of one of his secretaries, and had a second son, Marcus Cato Salonianus.

Cato is famous for strongly stated moral and traditional opinions. He publicly criticized luxury expenditure and unwaveringly opposed the spread of Greek fashions. Yet he wrote a handbook, *De Agri Cultura, On Farming,* which draws on Greek experience and includes recipes for flavored wines and cakes in the Greek style.

Evidently composed to assist a farm owner and a *vilicus* (farm manager, usually a slave) and drawing on Cato's own experience, this fascinating but uneven work gives instruction on the making of olive oil and wine and the growing of cereals, fruit, and other crops. Cato sometimes focuses on a property near Rome (like his own at Tusculum) which would sell produce at city markets, sometimes on a larger slave-run farm in the Sabine hills (like his own at Venafrum), where the aim would be to make a profit from olive oil. He writes what comes to his

Joyce Chen

JOYCE LIAO WAS BORN IN BEIJING, CHINA ON SEPTEMBER 14, 1917. She began her culinary endeavors at a young age, making miniature pastries while the family chef made some for the adults. Her father, Liao Xin Shi, a railroad administrator and city executive, and her mother both encouraged her to do things for herself and to learn to cook. That was unusual in a family with staff and one whose grandfather had been a governor of China. At the age of eighteen, Joyce cooked a banquet, using household help to wash and cut all ingredients while she gave orders. She was pleased with the success of the meal; it inspired her future endeavors and a career in things culinary.

Joyce married Thomas Chen in Shanghai. Her daughter Helen and son Henry were born there. In 1949, the family left China for Cambridge, Massachusetts to start a new life. A third child, Stephen, was born in the United States. In Cambridge, without help, Joyce began entertaining Chinese students at Harvard and other local universities inviting them home to dinner. She also made egg rolls for her children's school bazaar that were so successful that she was asked to make more of them. These led recipients and friends to ask her to give them cooking lessons. They also helped her to understand that many Americans wanted to taste and learn more about the authentic foods of her homeland.

Thus encouraged, she opened the Joyce Chen Restaurant in Cambridge, near Harvard University, in 1958. It became a popular Chinese eatery that set the tone for Americans to expect and get authentic Chinese cuisine. Two years later, Mrs. Chen began to teach Chinese cooking in Cambridge and Boston at adult-education centers. There were waiting lists for her classes, and their popularity encouraged her to think about writing a cookbook for those not able to take the classes or see her popular demonstrations in department stores and other venues in the region.

She wrote the *Joyce Chen Cook Book,* which included recipes from northern, southern, eastern, and western Chinese cuisines; it was self-published in 1962. The book provided colorful historical background for the recipes and thorough information about ingredients, and it had a tear-out Chinese and English shopping list with descriptions of the more than forty items on it.

The success of the book led to a weekly public television program called *Joyce Chen Cooks* in 1966. The program made Chinese food popular all over the country, and helped many people understand and begin to cook Chinese food in their own homes. Thanks to these programs also, many viewers could purchase cookware and specialty items from the Joyce Chen Products company, founded in the 1960's.

Joyce Chen returned to China in 1972, soon after President Nixon's visit, and with her two children, Helen and Stephen, made "Joyce Chen's China," a PBS special about her homeland.

In 1973, Mrs. Chen opened a larger restaurant, also in Cambridge; like its predecessor, it was highly regarded and very popular. It closed when, due to illness, Joyce Chen was not able to continue teaching and feeding people the foods that she loved and made so well.

After she died in 1994, her children maintained and expanded the Joyce Chen business until it was sold to a large Chicago-based corporation. Joyce Chen's superb teaching was passed on, as Helen followed in her mother's footsteps, writing a cookbook of her own.

— JACQUELINE M. NEWMAN

The Joyce Chen Cook Book, 1962

Julia Child

❀ 1912—2004 ❀

SINCE JULIA CHILD'S TELEVISION DEBUT ON BOSTON'S WGBH ON February 11, 1963, few practitioners in the culinary field have enjoyed such instant name recognition. Few hostesses have wined and dined so many vicarious guests on the small screen. Few authors have remained in continuous print and sold over two million copies of their first book. And even fewer food personalities have been honored with one-man shows, cartoon caricatures, or have teamed up with symphony orchestras and White House chefs, celebrated birthday parties from coast to coast, or have been the recipients of honors, medals, degrees, and citations as diverse as France's Legion d'Honneur, the Emmy Award, and the Presidential Medal of Freedom. Julia Child achieved all this and more.

"I think people were just interested in cooking, and I happened to be the right woman at the right time," Julia responded when an interviewer asked about her coast to coast success in nine TV series from *The French Chef* in 1962 to *Julia Child and Jacques Pepin: Cooking in Concert* in the 90's. Although **Dione Lucas**, **James Beard**, and, to some degree, **Poppy Cannon** had experimented with TV as a culinary vehicle in the late 40's and 50's, Julia Child established the basic television format for food appreciation and cooking instruction for scores of imitators who specialized in everything from ethnic cuisines, frugal meals and thirty-minute dinners to celebrity menus cooked by celebrity chefs. In the vanguard it was Julia initiating viewers into the art of French cooking, following the example of her hero **Auguste Escoffier** to "faites simple."

Commenting on her background, Julia liked to say; "I was a real hayseed, having never been outside the USA, except to Tijuana." But her disclaimer belied her impressive lineage. Julia's maternal grandmother was a descendant of Governor William Bradford of the Plymouth Colony, and her paternal grandfather followed the Gold Rush to California where he made substantial investments in land. When his son John McWilliams, Jr. married Carolyn Weston in 1911, the union of the second-generation pioneer and Princeton graduate and the red-haired, free-spirited Smith College graduate decided the social as well as genetic DNA of their three children. Julia was born in Pasadena, California, on August 15, 1912, followed by John McWilliams III two years later, and Dorothy Dean McWilliams in 1917.

From her mother, Julia inherited her Weston *joie de vivre,* independent spirit, and uncritical acceptance of other people. From her father, she fell heir to the intelligence, organization, stubbornness, and longevity that characterized the McWilliams clan. Growing up in Pasadena where her father worked with her grandfather managing the family's business interests, Julia was accustomed to associating with children of other well-to-do families in the thriving community that boasted country clubs and rose parades. Her mother introduced her to tennis, swimming, horseback riding, and other sports as well as to books, music, and the theater. A housekeeper kept the house running smoothly, a gardener tended the spacious grounds, a nurse took care of the children, and a cook prepared the meals except on her night off, when Carolyn made buttermilk baking-powder biscuits, codfish balls, and Welsh rarebit. During the summer the family retreated to a beach house in Santa Barbara.

Julia went to Pasadena's Montessori School, and to Polytechnic School until tenth grade. She then traveled to the Bay area to attend the Katherine Branson boarding school for girls. Enrolled in Smith College by her mother the day she was born, Julia earned a reputation at college for being a madcap, the tallest member of her class, and a history major. After graduation in 1934, Julia returned to Pasadena for a year before taking a job writing advertising copy at New York's toney home furnishings store W. & J. Sloane. Two years later she returned to Pasadena shortly before her mother died on July 21, 1937. After a year as an active Junior Leaguer, she took a job as advertising manager of the Beverly Hills branch of W. & J. Sloane, but her duties far exceeded her expertise, and she was asked to leave after four months. In 1942 she went to Washington as a typist for the Office of War Information. She was soon promoted to administrative assistant in the Registry of the OSS. Transferring to Kandy in Ceylon, she met Paul Child, a cartographer in the War Room of the OSS China Command. He was urbane, a linguist, and an aspiring artist who had lived in Paris in the 20's. He was also ten years her senior. But his knowledge of ethnic cuisine and their frequent dinners in Chinese restaurants gradually led to a more serious relationship when they worked together in the cities of Kumming and Chungking. After the war ended on August 15, 1945, Julia returned to Pasadena, where she corresponded with Paul and took some basic cooking classes because she was feeling "nesty." A year later Paul came to California to meet his future father-in-law and persuade Julia to travel east with him.

After Julia and Paul's wedding on September 1, 1946, they settled into a small house on Wisconsin Avenue in Washington and eventually purchased a house in Georgetown when Paul rejoined the State Department. Julia depended on *The Joy of Cooking, Gourmet* magazine, and cooking in tandem with her sister-in-law and other friends to prepare meals for the dinner parties she hosted, while Paul selected appropriate wines. They complemented each other, and Julia became a magic catalyst to an ever-growing circle of friends.

On October 27, 1948, Julia accompanied her husband to Paris, where he served as exhibits officer for the U.S. Information Service. Renting an apartment on the rue de l'Universite only fifteen minutes from the American Embassy, they sought out small restaurants to dine in, and Paul introduced Julia to Paris. While he worked, Julia explored the city, took French lessons at Berlitz, and in the fall of 1949 she enrolled in the professional chef's ten-month course offered at the Cordon Bleu cooking school. In the company of eleven U.S. veterans on the G. I. Bill, Julia spend twenty-five hours a week doing hands-on cooking and attending classes in the demonstration kitchen. Her favorite instructor was Chef Max Bugnard, who had trained with Escoffier in London and specialized in sauces and meat and fish cookery. She also learned pastry from Claude Thillmont, and *garde manger* from Pierre Mangelotte, chef of the Restaurant des Artistes. After six months of learning the basics of French cooking, Julia left Cordon Bleu, preferring to study independently with Chef Bugnard.

"Until I got into cooking," Julia said, "I was never really interested in anything." And, although she eagerly developed a pattern of entertaining embassy staff members as well as visitors from the States, she longed to belong to a group of women involved in French cooking. Fortuitously, at a party in the home of the first president of Sears International, Julia met **Simone Beck**, who, along with Louisette Bertholle, had self-published a forty-eight page spiral-bound cookbook called *What's Cooking in France*. The synergy between the two women was instant and soon they also invited Louisette Bertholle to join them in giving cooking lessons to embassy wives and visitors in the kitchen of Julia's fourth-floor apartment. Their school, which they called L'Ecole des Gourmandes, led directly to collaboration on a cookbook to teach the basics of French cooking to an American audience. By the time that Paul was transferred to Marseille in 1953, Julia was testing recipes and was an active participant in writing "the great big book" that would eventually become *Mastering the Art of French Cooking*.

Six years in France had changed Julia. Not only had living in Paris and Marseille broadened her horizons, but the experience had also propelled her into a purposeful career. When Paul was transferred to Bonn in 1954 and then to Oslo in 1959, Julia had opportunities to shop in American supermarkets while vacationing in the States and to use frozen ingredients purchased in the American commissaries in Germany. In her frequent letters to Simone Beck, she was continually adjusting U.S. ingredients to French recipes, and writing about her discoveries. She was also pursuing the publication of the book with friends in the States.

Shortening the scope of what the three women planned as a sequence of books on Sauces, Soups, Meats, Fish, and so on into a single volume for Houghton Mifflin, the authors were devastated when the Boston publisher eventually turned the book down. Largely through the efforts of William Koshland and Judith Jones, however, **Alfred Knopf** recognized that the book was a *working* French cookbook incorporating "the tradition of *cuisine bourgeoise* with touches of *haute cuisine*," and the prestigious house accepted the manuscript. Published in September 1961, *Mastering the Art of French Cooking* demystified dishes that Americans had only dreamed about savoring in French restaurants and provided the means to prepare those dishes with detailed instructions and the use of blenders and timesaving procedures.

When Paul retired from government service in 1961, the Childs sold their Washington home and moved into a large rambling house on Irving Street in Cambridge, Massachusetts. Because of the rush of journalists and food critics who wanted to interview Julia, they immediately began to remodel the kitchen. And Paul joined the coast-to-coast publicity tours that Julia and Simone Beck undertook to promote *Mastering the Art of French Cooking*. After Julia demonstrated the making of an omelet during a television book review show on WGBH, the station received so many fan letters that the producer Russell Morash and his assistant Ruth Lockwood asked Julia if she were interested in making three pilot programs. She was, and Paul, by now her willing assistant, transported the necessary cooking equipment and ingredients to a makeshift set. *The French Chef* successfully premiered on February 11, 1963. From the early black and white films to color films in 1970, from studio sets to outtakes of French cheese makers and Provencal markets, and from dinner party formats to cooking with up-and-coming chefs, Julia's TV series broke new ground and introduced ever-growing audiences to the pleasures of the table.

From 1963 until her death on August 13, 2004, Julia Child starred in nine TV series, along with regular appearances on ABC-TV and The Food Channel. She also made a sequence of educational videotapes and filmed single shows for special events. At various times during her long career, she wrote articles for *The Boston Globe, Food & Wine, McCall's,* and *Parade.* A tireless advocate for advanced degrees in gastronomy, she also lent her prestigious support to various culinary organizations and was always willing to demonstrate the making of a mousse or a pâté to raise money for worthy causes. And of enduring value, in addition to the collaborative *Mastering the Art of French Cooking, Vols. 1 & 2,* Julia published many other best-selling cookbooks, including her magnum opus, *The Way to Cook.*

Her signature sign-off, "*Bon Appétit!*" became synonymous with the best in television cooking programs, and Julia Child will always be remembered as the teacher *extraordinaire* who invited American audiences into the kitchen and taught them the way to cook with a French accent.

— JOAN REARDON

Mastering the Art of French Cooking, Vol. 1 (with Simone Beck and Louisette Bertholle), 1961
The French Chef Cookbook (drawings and photos by Paul Child), 1968
Mastering the Art of French Cooking, Vol. 2 (with Simone Beck), 1970
The French Chef With Julia Child, 1970
From Julia Child's Kitchen, 1975
Julia Child & Company (with E.S.Yntema), 1978

Julia Child & More Company (with E.S.Yntema), 1979
The Way to Cook, 1989
Julia Child's Menu Cookbook, 1991
Cooking With Master Chefs, 1993
In Julia's Kitchen With Master Chefs (with Nancy Verde Barr), 1995
Julia's Delicious Little Dinners (with E.S.Yntema), 1998
Julia's Menus for Special Occasions, 1998
Julia's Kitchen Wisdom (with David Nussbaum), 1998
Julia's Casual Dinners, 1999
Julia's Breakfasts, Lunches, and Suppers (with E.S.Yntema), 1999
Julia & Jacques Cooking at Home, 1999

Lydia Maria Child

1802–1880

From Harper's Monthly, *January, 1880*

LYDIA MARIA CHILD, AUTHOR OF *THE FRUGAL HOUSEWIFE, DEDICATED to Those Who are Not Ashamed of Economy*, was one of nineteenth-century America's most influential women. This book of cookery and household management was first published in Boston in 1829. By the eighth edition of 1832, its title was changed to *The American Frugal Housewife* so as not to confuse it with an earlier English work, *The Frugal Housewife*, by Susannah Carter, first published in London in 1765 and in Boston in 1772. Mrs. Child's eighth edition most pointedly informs the reader that the title was changed to differentiate her book from that English work which was "not adapted to the wants of this country."

The American Frugal Housewife quickly became the standard American cookbook of its time, following in the footsteps of **Amelia Simmons**' *American Cookery* (1796) and **Mary Randolph**'s *The Virginia Housewife* (1824). It was reprinted at least 35 times between 1829 and 1850, when it was allowed to go out of print because of Mrs. Child's increasing public work, unpopular in some quarters, in the cause of anti-slavery, and because of the publication of newer, more modern books. It is sobering to note, however, that her work was reprinted in England as late as 1860.

Lydia Maria Francis Child was born in 1802 in Medford, Massachusetts, the youngest of six children of Susannah Rand and Convers Francis, a baker and businessman. From her parents she learned to live simply and to be generous to others. The dominant influence of her early years was her brother Convers who, being male, was given the Harvard education Lydia Maria always wished she had had. By 15 years of age she was reading *Paradise Lost* and writing to her brother of Milton's misogyny and male chauvinism. Women's rights and the rights of the poor, especially of black and native Americans, were to be the dominant themes of her long and productive life.

In 1824 she published her first novel, *Hobomok*, which catapulted her to instant fame. The novel was daring in a number of ways: It was one of the earliest books to help define a distinctive American literature and it dealt with the unmentionable subject of a white woman's marriage to an American Indian. Two years later came *The Rebel*, a tale of the American Revolution. In 1826, she founded *Juvenile Miscellany*, the first American monthly periodical for children, and for the next several years she wrote short stories and articles for a variety of newspapers and magazines.

She married the improvident David Lee Child, a Boston lawyer, in 1829. From then on, due to the legal and social problems arising from their work in the abolitionist movement (including David's imprisonment and large debts), Lydia Maria became the family breadwinner.

Thus, a work for "those not ashamed of economy" seemed a natural next book to the author, both to help the American housewife during the hard times following the recession of the 1820's and to help the Childs pay their bills.

Mrs. Child could indeed be frugal—and a bit severe. Assuredly, this was the result of the Puritan ethic in which she was raised as well as her own personal experiences. In her introduction, she sets the tone of the book:

"The true economy of housekeeping is simply the art of gathering up all fragments, so that nothing be lost. I mean fragments of *time,* as well as *materials*.

"Whatever the size of a family, every member should be employed, either in earning or saving money.

"I have attempted to teach how money can be *saved*, not how it can be *enjoyed*.

"Look frequently to the pails, to see that nothing is thrown to the pigs which should have been in the grease-pot. Look to the grease-pot, and see that nothing is there which might have served to nourish your own family, or a poorer one."

That last line, about helping others poorer than yourself, is perhaps the key to Lydia Maria Child. This woman cared about that "poorer" family. She did, in fact, devote most of her life to those less able to help themselves or to raise themselves out of poverty and humiliation, whether these were due to slavery or to prejudicial laws and education policies.

In addition to hundreds of recipes from Apple Pie to Whortleberry Pudding, *The American Frugal Housewife* contains household hints, medical remedies, practical information on buying, cooking and storing food, and moral and social observations on the role and education of women. This latter section included the opinion that marriage was not the end-all and be-all for females.

Although many of the recipes are for economical cooking, the touch of a knowledgeable cook is often obvious. Clearly, all households were expected to have a variety of alcoholic beverages readily available, and Lydia Maria expected even a poor household to have and be able to use a surprising variety of herbs, spices, and seasonings. In addition to the use of herbs in cooking and preserving,

Mrs. Child offers herbal remedies, many with a rather modern touch.

Following the success of *The American Frugal Housewife,* Lydia Maria published anti-slavery tracts, biographies of famous women, and three companion works to *The Frugal Housewife*: *The Little Girl's Own Book* (1831), *The Mother's Book* (1831), and *The Family Nurse* (1837). In 1833 her life, and the life of the nation, changed when she published *An Appeal in Favor of That Class of Americans Called Africans.* Child found herself socially ostracized, and the sales of her works dwindled. The mass cancellation of subscriptions to the *Juvenile Miscellany* forced her to give up its editorship in 1834.

In 1841, Mrs. Child moved to New York to edit the *National Anti-Slavery Standard*, the foremost such journal in the country. She also began publishing a series of "letters from New York," which dealt with a wide range of social and political issues. The remainder of her life was devoted to writing, proselytizing, and working for abolition, and, after the Civil War, for the education and advancement of the freed slaves, for universal suffrage of black men and all women, and a number of other social causes.

For half a century, Lydia Maria Child was a household name in America. There was much calumny and much praise. William Lloyd Garrison, famed anti-slavery agitator, hailed her as "the first woman in the republic." Senator Charles Sumner, suffragist leader Elizabeth Cady Stanton, the transcendental theologian Theodore Parker, and author Edgar Allen Poe all praised her work. Child continued her writing and crusading until the end of her life, in Wayland, Massachusetts, in 1880.

I have the feeling that Lydia Maria Child would consider her one and only cookery book to be a lesser contribution among her life's works, yet it painted so vivid a picture of domestic life in the first quarter of the nineteenth century in America that it has become an invaluable tool for social historians and all those interested in America's past.

— JANICE BLUESTEIN LONGONE

Hobomok (novel), 1824
The Rebel (novel), 1826
The Frugal Housewife, Dedicated to Those Who are Not Ashamed of Economy, 1829; name changed to *The American Frugal Housewife*, 1832
The Little Girl's Own Book, 1831
The Mother's Book, 1831
An Appeal in Favor of That Class of Americans Called Africans, 1833
History of the Condition of Women, 1835
Philothea (novel), 1836
The Family Nurse, 1837
Progress of Religious Ideas, 1855

Chiquart

ALSO CALLED: Master Chiquart

THE NAME OF MASTER CHIQUART APPEARS IN ONLY A COUPLE OF CONTEMPORARY documents. The first of these is a household account for the court of Duke Amédée I of Savoy, dated 1416; it enumerates the spices that *magister Chiquardus* requisitioned and received from the household apothecary for saucing a roast lamprey. In another household account for 1428 *Meistre Chicart Amiczo* is designated "cook," the senior of two, and entitled to receive a new issue of the Savoyard livery. At the head of the table of contents of his book we read, "...*On the Matter of Cookery* [*Du fait de cuisine*], compiled by Master Chiquart, cook of our most respected Lord, the Duke of Savoy, in the course of the year of the nativity of Our Savior Jesus Christ one thousand four hundred and twenty, and written down by me, John of Dudens, clerk burgess of the town of Annecy." Finally, Master Chiquart names himself four or five times in his book *On Cookery*.

In the prefatory dedication address to his master the duke, which brims with formal deferential language, Chiquart states that the duke had persistently urged him to leave some abiding legacy that testified to his contribution to the glory of the court of Savoy. Thoroughly flattered, but claiming he has no model, has never seen a cookbook, he accedes to the duke's wishes.

Throughout *On Cookery* we hear a real person speaking, advising a neophyte, patiently explaining, passing on helpful practical hints, proud of his abilities, accomplishments, and experience. He is a literate man, quoting Latin authors and contemporary medical treatises, finally composing a 48-line poem to express his gratitude to the Trinity and to his master's family, the duke, the duchess, and their children, for all the support they have consistently given him. With pride he records what he prepared for a two-day banquet in a minor Savoyard castle to mark the moment his master, at that time the eighth count of Savoy, aged twenty, received his eighteen-year-old betrothed Marie from the hand of her father, Duke Phillip the Bold of Burgundy. The banquet, in October of 1403, called for an exceptional tour de force consisting of some 40 "lean" prepared dishes—that is, suitable for a fast-day. *On Cookery* takes that event, obviously capital in its author's young professional life, as its framework.

Chiquart's book is as remarkable as its author. It is unique: The manuscript was never copied; no other version of it exists, before or after. Rather than by a traditional generic arrangement Chiquart organizes his 78 recipes according to their possible use in a two-day banquet: dinner (two servings) and supper (a single serving), 41 preparations, for 21 of which he provides recipes. Then he repeats himself, supposing that the cook must prepare the same two-day banquet for lean days of the week or year: another twenty complex recipes among the 36 lean dishes that a competent cook should know how to prepare. Always aware that a

The second page of Chiquart's manuscript begins with a preamble in Latin: "Man's unretentive memory often reduces clear things to doubt; as a consequence, the noble foresight of the ancients decreed that ephemeral things should be rendered immortal by being written down...."

whim may decide his master to prolong a banquet, a cook should be ready to keep even more dishes coming, so Chiquart supplies recipes for 24 additional preparations. A final selection of sixteen dishes is intended for convalescents because, Chiquart writes, in any group of your master's guests there are apt to be a number of sick or sickly individuals.

Chiquart is far more detailed in his instructions and more generous in his practical suggestions—some of his recipes taking up two or three manuscript pages—than any previous recipe writer. An interesting, again unique, section catalogs precisely the kitchen furnishings, utensils, and provisions needed for a large two-day banquet. He advises on the necessary quantities of foodstuffs (including 25 pounds of saffron, twelve baskets of candied figs and, for *each* day, 6000 eggs), the textiles, the amounts of firewood and coal, and the lead time necessary to gather in game meats and fowl.

Chiquart's cookery is still medieval in its ingredients. It does not know turkey, potatoes, or eggplant but still uses spices judiciously and sugar generously. His menus give some space to the roasts, sauces, and broths of the previous century, but add in a wide variety of sops (a sauced foodstuff on bread or toast), *tortes* (standing pies with a compound filling), and delicately stuffed birds, mutton shoulders and crayfish. His dishes, always tasty and often complex, depend more on the fine judgment and professional competence of the cook than in previous generations. The constructed centerpieces for his banquet hall are remarkable with their meat-paste Castles of Love, peacocks fully feathered but roasted, and fire-breathing piglets—the impressive spectacle concealing an ensemble of live minstrels.

The watchwords of Chiquart's work, words that recur continually in *On Cookery*, are care and cleanliness; the cook's reward is honor, the honor that derives from doing thoroughly good and worthy work.

— TERENCE SCULLY

On Cookery, 1420

Grace Zia Chu

1899–1999

ALSO CALLED: Madame Chu

THE WOMAN WHO INTRODUCED CHINESE COOKING TO THOUSANDS OF AMERICAN home kitchens was born in Shanghai in 1899, the "bossy big sister" of the nine children of Zia Hong-lai, a teacher, and Sochen Sze. In 1918 she graduated from the McTyeire School for Girls, whose students were mostly from Chinese Protestant families or families connected with foreign firms in China, and she won a scholarship to Wellesley College.

At college, as she told the *Wellesley* magazine in 1982, she found herself "far from home, in a world full of tall strangers and inedible food." When possible, she shopped in Boston's Chinatown, tiny at the time, for familiar foods that she brought back to the dormitory and cooked on a hotplate.

After graduating in 1924 with a certificate in hygiene and physical education, she returned to her birthplace to teach physical education at a girl's high school. She was also a coach to the 1936 Chinese Olympic team, and served as international vice-president of the YMCA.

In 1928, she married Chu Shih-ming, an arch-supporter of Chiang Kai-shek, and soon became a diplomat's wife, planning, but not cooking, Chinese meals in the embassies he was posted to, including Paris, Moscow, back in China, and then in Washington, D.C. At this last posting, she decided to help raise funds for China Relief by giving Chinese cooking lessons for American military wives. This was one of her first forays into cooking Chinese food for others.

1961

Grace Chu moved to the United States and became a citizen in 1955. Her Chinese cooking classes at her upper west side Manhattan home were extremely popular. "Madame Chu," as her students called her, regaled her students with stories of China and its foods. She taught them four regional ways to prepare Chinese Roast Duck and how to grow bean sprouts; her lessons included dishes for a Chinese banquet at a time when few Americans had heard of or ever attended one. She developed their Chinese taste buds, and sent them home with copies of the recipes made in her classes. These handouts and the urging of her students were the foundation of her first Chinese cookbook, *The Pleasure of Chinese Cooking*, published in 1962 by Simon and Schuster. About that time, she founded New York's China Institute Cooking School, and taught there for many years. She also taught at the Modern House Cooking School. Many of the dishes taught after the first book became sources for the 1975 one titled *Madame Chu's Cooking School*, also published by Simon and Schuster.

Committed and concerned, she leapfrogged the United States to teach in many cities and states. Her goal was to expand the cookery of her homeland in as many places as she could in her adopted country. She did this humbly, always thanking her students for their interest, inspiration, and suggestions. **Craig Claiborne**, food editor of the *New York Times*, called her the doyenne of Chinese cooking teachers as she opened eyes and stomachs to the wonders of Chinese cuisine.

Grace Chu also taught Chinese cooking in cities of other countries including Rome and Venice, and she taught it on the *Queen Elizabeth 2* on its way to, from, and in Bermuda. In her later years, she proudly spoke about having lived on three continents and dining with four national leaders, namely Chiang Kai-shek, Stalin, Hitler, and Franklin Delano Roosevelt. She died in 1999, having influenced tens of thousands to eat, enjoy, and make good Chinese food.

— JACQUELINE M. NEWMAN

The Pleasure of Chinese Cooking, 1962
Madame Chu's Cooking School, 1975

Craig Claiborne

1980

AMERICA'S FOOD REVOLUTION BEGAN AFTER WORLD War II ended, and it was Claiborne who named the day: June 17, 1947. This was the day Pan American Airlines sold its first round-the-world ticket for $1700 a person. For the first time ever, ordinary middle-class Americans, released from wartime restrictions, jumped at the chance to circle the globe and gobble up the world's foods. Claiborne, during his thirty years as food critic and food editor at *The New York Times*, became America's guide and translator on a journey of culinary discovery that coincided with the nation's coming of age as a superpower.

Born in Sunflower, Mississippi, on September 4, 1920, Claiborne was as Southern and as genteelly poor as his birthplace. His mother ran boarding houses as they moved their wagonload of furniture from town to town. Thus began "a lifelong series of humiliations," he wrote in his memoir, *A Feast Made for Laughter* (1982). Graduated from the school of journalism at the University of Missouri, he joined the U.S. Navy in 1942 and saw the world as secretary to Admiral John Leslie Hall. Later, the G.I. Bill took him to the Ecole Hotelière in Lausanne, Switzerland, for a year and a half, and from then on, he recalled, his sole ambition was "to be food editor of *The New York Times*."

It was a singular ambition for a man at a time when food was thought to be a subject fit only for women. When Claiborne replaced Jane Nickerson at the *Times* in 1957, he instigated a national revolution in restaurant reviewing and in food talk, eventually transforming the Women's Page into the Living Section. His authority as a serious critic stemmed in part from the fact that he was a small quiet man with a shy smile who seemed to fade into the background. Looking anonymous was useful for a critic who set unheard-of standards of objectivity in reviews that were strictly segregated from the advertising department. He gained further credibility by inaugurating a rating system that was based on the quality of the food rather than on the social cachet of the site or its ambience.

He became our stand-in when he entered culinary temples like New York's Pavillon and both demystified and extolled its pomp. He admired elegance in table settings, with champagne in crystal glasses, but he was equally enthusiastic for grits or chili con carne, properly made, in their own down-home settings. He lured us into savoring foods of all kinds, high and low, familiar and strange, and taught us to scorn what was insipid, mediocre, or fake. He believed that both cooking and eating were arts that anyone could learn to enjoy, so he set about to instruct us with humor and clarity. In 1961, he spread the word through *The New*

York Times Cookbook, which was a comprehensive and sophisticated compilation of 1500 recipes, ranging from scrambled eggs to truffled pâtés. While **Julia Child**'s first book, *Mastering the Art of French Cooking*, appeared the same year, Claiborne's book was far more accessible to a far greater number of people.

Because he thought of himself as a translator of expertise rather than a chef, collaboration was natural to him. His most important team effort was with another country boy, Pierre Franey, who had left his native village of Tonnère ("Thunder") in France to become eventually head chef at Le Pavillon in New York City. In 1964 Claiborne began the long collaboration with Franey that translated for American stoves and palates the home cooking of France. In the process they became close friends and neighbors at Gardiners Bay in Long Island and collaborated on seven books before they left the *Times* to start *The Craig Claiborne Journal* in 1970, a food newsletter that was ahead of its time. When the journal went bankrupt four years later, they returned to the *Times,* as a team, and became notorious in 1975 for eating a dinner, won at a charity auction, at a restaurant of their choice, no matter where, with food and wines of their choice, no matter how costly. The fact that their 31-course meal at Chez Denis in Paris cost $4000 put the boys from Sunflower and Thunder on the front page of the *Times,* with much disapproval and controversy resulting.

While introducing his readers to the standards of French high, middle, and low cuisine and to a galaxy of male chefs, Claiborne became at the same time an enthusiastic expositor of cuisines from every corner of the globe, from Ethiopia to Szechuan, usually transmitted by women cooks. Through Claiborne, we learned Chinese cooking from Virginia Lee, Italian from Marcella Hazan, Indian from Madhur Jaffrey, Mexican from Diana Kennedy, and British from **Jane Grigson**. Again, he collaborated as a writer with profiled cooks to fashion recipes from their own native cultures that Americans could actually cook in their own kitchens, adapting equipment and ingredients as necessary. Because Claiborne was genuinely curious about people and their foodways, he was able to seduce the most traditional meat-and-potato-minded Americans to experiment with Chinese wontons and Mexican tamales. He loosened us up to new pleasures. As Americans traveled the world, we were more and more eager to recreate at home the exotic flavors we'd sampled abroad. Claiborne's *New York Times International Cookbook* of 1971, which arranged recipes by countries, helped us in our quest to experience a broader culinary geography.

Despite his public successes, his private life was shadowed by alcoholism, his struggle with homosexuality, and loneliness. Ever courteous in the Southern way, he also compulsively quarreled with his best friends, including Franey, and the break was irrevocable. Claiborne liked to say, "I love music and sex and food, and outside of that, forget it." His transformation from a humiliated boy in a puritan Southern town to a globe-trotting connoisseur was never quite complete, but he found lots of good company along the way by means of the written word. He was 79 when he died, alone, in his apartment in New York City.

— BETTY FUSSELL

The New York Times Cookbook, 1961
An Herb and Spice Cookbook, 1963
New York Times Guide to Dining Out in New York, 1964
Cookbook for Booksellers, 1965
The New York Times Menu Cookbook, 1966
A Kitchen Primer, 1969
Cooking With Herbs and Spices, 1970
Classic French Cooking (with Pierre Franey), 1970
The New York Times International Cookbook, 1971
The Chinese Cookbook (with Virginia Lee), 1972
Craig Claiborne's Favorites From the New York Times, *Volume One*, 1975; *Volume Two*, 1976; *Volume Three*, 1979; *Volume Four*, 1984
Veal Cookery (with Pierre Franey), 1978
Craig Claiborne's New York Times Cookbook (with Pierre Franey), 1979
Craig Claiborne's Gourmet Diet (with Pierre Franey), 1980
A Feast Made for Laughter, 1982
Master Cooking Course (with Pierre Franey), 1982
Cooking with Craig Claiborne and Pierre Franey (with Pierre Franey), 1983
Craig Claiborne's The New York Times Food Encyclopedia (compiled by Joan Whitman), 1985
Memorable Meals, 1985
Craig Claiborne's Southern Cooking, 1987
Elements of Etiquette: A Guide to Table Manners in an Imperfect World, 1992
Best of Craig Claiborne (with Pierre Franey), 1999

William Cobbett

❧ 1763–1835 ❧

FARMER, JOURNALIST, POLEMICIST, AND SELF-MADE MAN, WILLIAM COBBETT was born in Farnham, Surrey, England on March 9, 1763 to a farming family. Living a roller-coaster life between peaks of prosperity and political influence and valleys of exile from England and imprisonment for his radical views, Cobbett once wrote, "The reasonings of the belly are more powerful than those of the brain." He never lost sight of the correlation between a peaceful and just society and a sufficiently fed population.

Cobbett left home at age twenty and worked a while as a London law clerk, an unsuitable occupation for such an active person. Cobbett rose early every day, read, and taught himself grammar. He later joined the army and was assigned record-keeping work. He noticed much graft, and when Cobbett finished his army service, the first of many tangles with reform revolved around reporting on abuses by army officers. Unsuccessful in his attempt to sue them, Cobbett was forced into the first of two political exiles to the U.S., taking himself and his new wife to France, thence to the States, where he lived nearly eight years before returning to England. Wherever Cobbett settled he would observe some injustice or become indignant about some political activity, write about it, and irritate his opponents so much that he would be either sued for great sums of money, forced into exile, or at least obliged to retire to his country home for a while. At least once, he was sent to prison. At least once, he was also sent to Parliament. During none of these episodes, however, did he cease observing and writing. He deplored the enclosures in Great Britain, the loss of agricultural land for common laborers, and the wage slavery of England's increasingly industrial economy. In the spirit of reform that Charles Dickens would later promote in his writing, Cobbett vigorously criticized industrialization and fought for agrarian and political reforms.

For nearly all his adult life, he wrote and sold weekly broadsheets full of political commentary, and a whole raft of history and advice books including two of particular relevance to food history, both published in 1821. Cobbett spoke and wrote often about food. His personal love of farming and gardening led always to his establishing gardens, orchards, and fields. His farm life observations in his book *A Year's Residence in America* are valuable to American agricultural history, and his frequent references to the food supply interest American food historians.

Another smaller piece of work of interest to food historians is the *Instructions for Using the Meal and Flour of Indian Corn*, published by Mrs. Cobbett in 1846. This booklet provided instruction for making all forms of corn-meal breads; mush and porridge forms including polenta, hominy, suppawn, and samp; puddings, dumplings, and hot cakes. (Years later, the Cobbetts' daughter Anne continued the family tradition, writing a household manual, *The English Housekeeper,* 1835.)

While he lived in the United States Cobbett observed that Americans were less likely than the British to have household gardens, in his opinion a great omission. *The American Gardener* resulted. In it he promotes vegetable and small fruit growing, describing each sort, recommending varieties, and giving information about growing habits, care and culture, and, not infrequently, preparation. By reading between the lines, we can see which plants were, in his opinion, underutilized, such as, for example, rhubarb, and a Cobbett favorite, the rutabaga or Swedish turnip. We can also see by his suggestions on improving them what was the true state of early nineteenth-century American vegetable gardens.

Cobbett's *Cottage Economy*, addressed to Britons, describing English practice, reflects his great hope of reconnecting laborers to the land and habits of self-sufficiency in the face of so many having been evicted from farms and expected to provide for themselves on slender wages. *Cottage Economy* richly describes making bread, brewing beer, keeping cows, pigs, bees, ewes, goats, poultry, and rabbits; preserving meat; making cheese—in short living well and independently on a small plot of ground.

With *Cottage Economy*, Cobbett clearly hoped to point impoverished workers away from desperate measures; and at the same time he took a swipe at smug politicians and clergy, saying, "A couple of flitches of bacon are worth fifty thousand Methodist sermons and religious tracts. The sight of them upon the rack tends more to keep a man from poaching and stealing than whole volumes of penal statues, though assisted by the terrors of the hulks and gibbet."

He faulted strenuously a government which turned a deaf ear to hungry people, and viewed as insurrection any food riot. In his July 4, 1812, *Political Register* he wrote about a woman hanged for stealing potatoes, "Far be it from me, to attempt to justify people in the commission of unlawful acts.... But there is, I hope, no harm expressing my compassion for her; ... I cannot and I will not allow, that her forcibly taking some potatoes out of a cart at Manchester, was any proof of a treasonable design and of hatred against the whole form of our Government."

Cobbett sought economic reform, setting his own example by advertising for unemployed men to dig over a piece of his land. He reasoned that since labor-saving devices had done such an effective job of putting laborers out of work, he would hire work in exchange for payment not in money, but in food—bread, meat and cheese—which would have cost more for the men to buy but which Cobbett himself produced. This example was embraced by later reformers, but the trend toward mechanization and commodification of most domestic and trade processes was well on its way.

In tones that could sound familiar today, Cobbett commented in *Cottage Economy* about bread-making that many English women, servants and housewives alike, "appear to think that loaves are made by the baker, as knights are made by the king; things of their pure creation, a creation in which no one else can participate. ... they would all know how to make it ... if they had been fed on bread of their mothers' and their own making."

In fact, in 1857, cookbook author **Eliza Acton** commented in her *English Bread-Book*, "Mr. Cobbett, in his wish to impress forcibly on the minds of his readers the facts he set forth, is sometimes rather more vehement in his expressions than the occasion seems altogether to demand. It is improvident and imprudent of the labourer to send to the bread-shop; but he has not always a free choice in the matter.... The ignorance of which Mr. Cobbett speaks as prevailing so generally in his time is, strangely enough, when our vaunted 'progress' is considered, more than ever perceptible at the present day, —when a better state of things might naturally be expected from us; and it is often less easy to obtain, at any price, a loaf of really good homemade bread in an English household, than the rarest foreign dainty ...."

Cobbett is famous for, and often quoted on, his disdain for tea. ("I view the tea drinking as a destroyer of health, an enfeebler of the frame, an engenderer of effeminacy and laziness, a debaucher of youth and a maker of misery for old age.") He also had little use for potatoes, and had he lived but another decade he could have seen the devastating effects of over-reliance on them which he predicted. He was a great believer in traditional English bread, meat, and beer and promoted the growing of maize and the drinking of milk.

During one visit to America, Cobbett noted a conversation he had with a tavern-keeper, related in G. D. H. Cole's biography of his life. The tavern-keeper observed that Cobbett appeared "fresh and young" and Cobbett told him that "I rise early, go to bed early, eat sparingly, never drink anything stronger than small beer, shave once a day, and wash my hands and face clean three times a day, at the very least." William Cobbett lived a long, apparently vigorous if turbulent life, dying peacefully in 1835 at 72 years of age.

— SANDRA L. OLIVER

The American Gardener, 1821
Cottage Economy, 1821

A Year's Residence in America, Part I, 1818, Parts II and III, 1819
In addition, William Cobbett produced a constant stream of political or historical
   books, articles, pamphlets and broadsides.

Josephine Cochrane

JOSEPHINE GARIS COCHRANE WAS AN UNLIKELY INVENTOR. BORN IN
Shelbyville, Illinois, in 1838, she was the great-granddaughter of inventor John
Fitch, who had engineered hydraulic pumps and built steamboats. She married
William Cochrane, a wealthy Illinois merchant and politician, and lived in a large
home well-staffed with servants. Widowed in her early forties, she remained active among her circle of friends. In 1882, after a dinner party, she contemplated
delicate glassware and china waiting to be washed and worried that her kitchen
staff would break, crack, or chip her fine dishes.

Tired of washing dishes herself and ruining her hands with hot soapy water, in
1886 Cochrane measured her dishes and mapped out a schematic drawing of jets
of water striking dish surfaces from several angles. The concept surpassed that of
inventor L. A. Alexander, who, in 1865, had patented a hand-cranked geared device that spun a rack of dishes through water. Cochrane hired an engineer to build
a mechanical dishwasher comprising dish compartments atop a wheel and a brass
boiler. In a woodshed, he assembled wire brackets and pulleys to be levered into
the washtub. With a soap and water assembly at the base, the user hand-pumped
a continuous spray for the wash cycle. The washing procedure ended with boiling
rinse water poured on by hand. Dishes then air-dried in the rack.

After patenting the idea, Cochrane hired an Illinois firm to build her iron
dishwasher, which she sold to female friends. For her company, the Garis-Cochrane Dish-Washing Machine Company, she wrote ad copy for periodicals aimed
at hoteliers, stewards, restaurateurs, innkeepers, and managers of hospitals. Chicago's two largest hotels installed her washers at a cost of $150 each. At the 1893
World's Columbian Exposition in Chicago, she promoted the apparatus, winning
first prize in international competition for a durable, adaptable mechanical construction. Her booth drew nine buyers from concessions needing a dishwasher.

Cochrane's appliance incurred some difficulties. Some interested parties did
not have enough hot water available to operate the whirling jets. The idea of saving
women labor earned the scorn of male clergy, who believed kitchen work the God-
assigned task of females, as specified in the book of Genesis. Considering the fate
of seamstresses after the invention of the sewing machine, professional kitchen
staff also objected to any device that would replace them or deny them work. The
most irate in Chicago and New York attempted to unionize to fight mechanization. Nonetheless, Cochrane's corporation produced numerous upgrades, including the Garis-Cochrane Dishwashing Machine, patented in 1900, which featured

an oscillating dish rack that could wash and dry 120 dishes in one minute. Her other innovations added a revolving washer, centrifugal pump, and draining hose to the initial machinery.

At her death from exhaustion and stroke in 1913, Cochrane left a healthy business that her heirs sold a decade later to the Hobart Corporation, founders of the KitchenAid brand, which they introduced in 1949.

— MARY ELLEN SNODGRASS

Sophie Coe

1933–1994

Coe in about 1968, with some of her brood

SOPHIE COE, AUTHOR OF IMPORTANT STUDIES OF THE PRE-Columbian cuisines of the Americas, was raised in a scholarly environment. She was born in Pasadena, California where her father, the famous geneticist Theodosius Dobzhansky, was teaching at the California Institute of Technology; she grew up largely in New York, where he taught at Columbia University and Rockefeller University.

While attending Radcliffe College, she met her husband-to-be, Michael D. Coe, in a joint Radcliffe–Harvard physical anthropology laboratory. As they worked side by side measuring the cranial capacity of skulls by filling them with mustard seeds and then counting the seeds, he realized that this was the girl his roommate had told him about, the one who kept a tarantula in her dormitory room. (It was a pet collected on one of her father's expeditions to South America). They married in 1955, the year of her graduation. The marriage produced five children.

Sophie Coe obtained a doctorate in anthropology from Harvard University nine years after her bachelor's degree, writing a thesis on a subject (saints of the northwestern Mediterranean) which gave no hint of her later specialty, and joined her husband, by then a professor at Yale University, on many anthropological expeditions to Central America, where he was to become an important scholar of the ancient Mayas.

She once wrote that most anthropologists spend a lot of time studying pots but don't know anything about cooking. That was certainly not true of her; she was an adventurous cook and a lifelong collector of cookbooks. Still, first ventures into food writing did not come until 1983, when she published two articles in the whimsically scholarly English magazine *Petits Propos Culinaires:* one on the Russian festival bread *kulich* (she always baked hers in an ancient coffee can so thoroughly broken in by use that whenever the family moved the movers had to be carefully instructed not to throw it out as trash) and the second on Russian-language cook-books of the Soviet nationalities.

Those brief notes scarcely prepared the magazine's readers for her next six articles, "Aztec Cuisine" (three articles, 1985), "Inca Food: Animal and Mineral" (1988), "Inca Food: Vegetable" (1989), and "Inca Food: The Inca and the Span-ish." Drawing on sixteenth- and seventeenth-century Spanish documents and the latest research in Latin American anthropology, she presented a rich and often surprising portrait of pre-Columbian food and foodways, from the systematic farming of protein-rich *Spirulina* pond scum in Mexico and of guinea pigs in the Andes, to the Inca taste for certain kinds of clay and the Aztec ritual in which din-ner party guests would cross-examine their host about the wholesomeness of his ingredients and his intentions in giving the dinner. A series of papers presented at the Oxford Symposium from 1988 to 1993 explored particular topics, such as what flavorings the Aztecs used in chocolate (red pepper, among others, which was quite good, she added, characteristically having tried it); the 13-layered Maya tamale that represents the levels of the cosmos (a question that bedeviled Catholic authorities at one time); and whether the iguana should be considered licit food during Lent (or perhaps just its tail).

All these researches fed into her magisterial study *America's First Cuisines* (Uni-versity of Texas Press, 1994). Unfortunately, she died quite unexpectedly of can-cer just weeks after its publication. Michael Coe finished the second book she had been working on, *The True History of Chocolate,* which would be published by Thames & Hudson in 1996.

An annual Sophie Coe Memorial Prize has been established. This is awarded at the Oxford Symposia on Food and Cookery for an essay in food history. Any aspect of food history is considered, and the prize is open to all.

— CHARLES PERRY

America's First Cuisines, 1994
The True History of Chocolate, 1996

Christopher Columbus   ❧ 1451–1506 ❧

LIKE **Alexander** THE GREAT NEARLY TWO MILLENNIA BEFORE HIM, CHRISTO-pher Columbus effected an enormous cultural and geographic exchange of goods, plants, animals, peoples, diseases, and foodstuffs. Unlike Alexander's, the "Co-lumbian exchange" was between the Old World and the New.

Until Columbus, the peoples of Europe and Asia had never seen nor heard of tur-keys, maize, tomatoes, papayas, guavas, avocados, pineapples, pumpkins, most kinds of beans, potatoes, sweet potatoes, cassava, chocolate, vanilla, allspice, or chiles, to name only a few edibles—although that last hot little item spread around the world so rapidly that some historians have wondered if in fact it had a head start on Columbus.

Columbus and his successors also brought Old World foods to the New, planting wheat and grapes, which were so important to the Church. Ginger and sugar cane were early imports, followed by bananas, cabbages, cauliflowers, chickpeas, figs, melons, onions, oranges and other citrus, pomegranates, and radishes. The Spaniards' horses changed the lives of the native populations thousands of miles distant from the Spanish possessions, affecting how they hunted for their food. Cattle and swine too became feral and spread rapidly on their own. Chickens, cinnamon, pepper, cloves, coriander, and cumin became embedded in the cuisines of the Americas. Many other foodstuffs traveled the Atlantic in one direction or the other.

There are many stories concerning Columbus' origins, and not a few mysteries. He was born, probably in 1451, in Genoa, to a family of weavers. He received little education, but being from Genoa naturally absorbed a great deal of knowledge of sailing, navigation, and colonization. His voyages to the Genoese colony of Chios in the Aegean Sea acquainted him with the valuable commodity mastic, and after his discovery of America he kept wishfully thinking that he had spotted mastic trees on the islands.

In the late fifteenth century, the Portuguese had taken the lead in navigation and exploration. Christopher and his brother Bartholomew made their living in Lisbon as cartographers, while Christopher tried to persuade the Portuguese crown to support his plan to reach the fabled East, the land of gold and spices, by sailing west. In Portugal, Columbus learned to read and write in Catalan and Latin, and he married into one of Portugal's prominent families. His bride, Doña Felipa Perestrello e Moniz, gave him a son, Diego, in about 1480, but died within a few years of the birth.

Columbus and his young son left Portugal in haste in 1485, probably to elude his creditors, and settled in Spain. There he tried to present his plan—his obsession—to King Ferdinand and Queen Isabella. In 1488, while he was still waiting to see the sovereigns, his mistress, Beatriz Enríque de Harana, gave birth to Columbus' second son, Ferdinand; this son ultimately became his father's biographer. Finally, in 1492, the same year that the royal couple reconquered the last fragment of the Iberian peninsula from the Arabs and expelled the Jews, Columbus was given permission and resources to proceed on his fateful journey.

Columbus made four voyages to the New World, bringing settlers, seed, and animals and returning with ships laden with valuable and exotic products. Like Alexander, Columbus was primed to exploit the wealth of the lands he laid claim to. He thought he spotted nutmegs and other spices; he had his men load the ships with American agave, thinking it was aloe; and when he observed the natives eating *aji* (chiles), "which is their pepper," he said, he planned to bring quantities of it back to Spain.

Ultimately, the effects of his discovery altered the entire Earth. European diseases were carried across the Atlantic, and it is possible, though not yet definitively determined, that Columbus' crews brought a strain of venereal syphilis from America to Europe. The influx of American precious metals contributed to the intense monetary inflation that Europe experienced in the sixteenth century. A budding increase in human population was exacerbated by the availability of additional foods from America. This increase has continued as American foods spread around the world: Since the middle of the seventeenth century the number of people on earth has quadrupled; today, though the rate of growth has slowed, the total population is still increasing. Ironically, population pressures in the Old World prompted an enormous migration to the Americas, especially during the nineteenth century.

The exchange initiated by Columbus differs from that of Alexander to such a huge degree that it differs in kind. Columbus not only discovered a New World, he made the whole world new. To find something comparable to this event, we have to look not to the past but to the future, to something that has not happened yet: the invasion of our planet by aliens from another part of the universe.

— ALICE ARNDT

Columella

FIRST CENTURY

LUCIUS JUNIUS MODERATUS COLUMELLA, A WRITER ON AGRICULTURE AND household work, lived in Spain and Italy in the early years of the Roman Empire. Columella wrote, in Latin, *Res Rustica (Country Work)*, the best and fullest textbook of farming that survives from the ancient Mediterranean world. The last section of this work, Book XII, is a collection of recipes for household conserves. It is much fuller and clearer than any similar text in Greek or Latin; Columella is therefore a major early culinary author and an important source of information on the foods and flavors of ancient Rome.

Most of what is known about Columella comes from references, in his book, to his own life and experience. His dates of birth and death are unknown, but (a) he quotes **Varro** as an author from "our grandparents' time"; (b) Pliny the Elder, who wrote in the 60's and 70's of our era, quotes Columella. This, with other evidence, leads to a dating for Columella's work in the 40's or 50's. He does not mention his parents, but often writes of his uncle, Marcus Columella, an innovative stock-breeder who farmed in the Roman province of Baetica (southwestern Spain). The oldest city of this region was Gades (modern Cadiz): It is interesting that Plutarch, a Greek author of the second century, mentions a philosopher, Moderatus of Gades, who could have been a relative of Columella.

It seems that Columella as a young man worked on his uncle's farm, and at some later time moved to Italy, where his property included a farm at Caere (modern Cerveteri) on the Tuscan coast not far from Rome. He also had a military career. An undated inscription found at Taranto names him as a tribune serving with Legio VI Ferrata. It is known that this legion recruited in Spain and served in Syria, and Columella himself happens to mention, while discussing crop planting, that he had seen sesame planted in June in Syria.

Columella's *Res Rustica* is the most systematic of all the Roman farming manuals. It draws on his own and his uncle's experience and on numerous earlier writers, Greek, Carthaginian, and Roman. It is written in stylish, clear Latin prose, except that Book X, on gardening, is in verse: This book is intended as a tribute and supplement to Vergil's famous poem on farming, the *Georgics*. These are the sections of Books I to XI that are most relevant to food studies: cereal crops (Book II sections 6–10); vines, olives, and other fruit trees (Books III to V); domestic animals (Book VII); beekeeping and honey (Book IX sections 2–16); and the kitchen garden (Book X, supplemented by Book XI section 3). Of special interest are some extended discussions of food production practices that were typically Roman. Columella deals with a wide range of domesticated and semi-domesticated birds: barnyard fowl, guinea-fowl, woodcock, pigeons, turtle-doves, thrushes, peafowl, geese, and ducks (Book VIII sections 2 to 15). He discusses fish ponds and gives a useful list of fish that could be bred for the market (Book VIII sections 16–17). He discusses the keeping of game animals, including deer and wild boar (Book IX section 1).

Book XI, a calendar of farm work, is set out as a manual for the *vilicus,* or farm manager, who was usually a slave, and ran the farm when the owner was absent.

Book XII, its sequel, is a guide to household tasks for the *vilica* or manageress (also a slave, the unofficial wife of the *vilicus*). Her work consisted largely of storing and conserving farm produce. This was essential because a typical large Roman farm was expected not only to produce a profit in cash crops such as olive oil and wine, but also to keep the farm's labor force and the owner's city household supplied with food. Columella includes, early in this section, instructions for making vinegar, brine, honey water, and grape syrup for pickling and conserving. Recipes for all kinds of pickles and conserves follow, arranged by the seasons of the farming year. There are long lists of vegetables that can be pickled, with careful instructions. Fruits to be conserved and dried include several varieties of pears, apples, figs, grapes, quinces, pomegranates, and sorbs (*Sorbus domestica*); there are also detailed instructions for several kinds of medicinal herb-flavored wines. For salted wines, which were popular in the ancient world, we are told the methods followed by Columella's uncle in his Spanish vineyards; for raisin wine we are given a recipe, translated from Phoenician, from the Carthaginian farming manual by Mago. There are many interesting recipes for table olives, using several different conserving methods and including various herbs and spices.

— ANDREW DALBY

Res Rustica (Country Work), first century. Translation *(On Agriculture)* by Harrison Boyd Ash, E. S. Forster, and Edward H. Heffner, 1941–1955 (3 vols)

Laurie Colwin

❀ 1944–1992 ❀

IN HER INTRODUCTION TO *HOME COOKING*, A COLLECTION OF FOOD essays, Laurie Colwin summed up her philosophy of food and eating: "One of the delights of life is eating with friends; second to that is *talking* about eating. And, for an unsurpassed double whammy, there is talking about eating *while* you are eating with friends." This philosophy permeates her essays on food, drawing the reader into her kitchen as a participant and a friend. Though a minor part of her writings, Colwin's food essays are among her best loved and best selling. Ruth Reichl has noted that Colwin was one of the "best-loved contributors" to *Gourmet* during the 1980's and early 1990's.

She was born in Manhattan in 1944 and died there of a heart attack at the age of 48. She attended Cheltenham High School in suburban Philadelphia, where she edited the *Cheltonian*. After high school she studied at a number of colleges including Bard College, Columbia University, the Sorbonne, and the New School for Social Research. In 1965 she began working for a series of publishers such as Viking, Putnam, E. P. Dutton and Pantheon. She continued in publishing until 1977, when she began to write full-time.

Colwin sold her first story in 1969 to the *New Yorker*. This was followed by stories in a variety of publications including *Harper's, Mademoiselle*, and *Playboy*. She was a prolific and popular writer, publishing numerous articles and books between 1974 and 1993. Her books were about middle-class family, love, and life. In addition, she translated some of the works of Isaac Bashevis Singer.

She took food seriously. During the student protests at Columbia University in 1968 she cooked for the protestors. She also donated time cooking for homeless shelters, edited a newsletter for the Coalition for the Homeless, and in 1991 participated in an evening to benefit the homeless with Garrison Keillor and Maya Angelou, among others.

Colwin's food essays in *Gourmet* ran from 1984 through 1993. When she died, she had written enough pieces for *Gourmet* that the magazine was able to publish them through a full year after her death. Her essays in *Gourmet* and other publications were collected and published in two volumes, *Home Cooking* and *More Home Cooking*, which remain in print; they bring us into her world and invite us to share her experiences in the kitchen and around the table. Her optimism and humor come through in each piece. John Thorne, editor of the newsletter *Simple Cooking*, has said of her: "She was a paragon of what food writing ought to be and so rarely is: honest, smart, open, brave."

During her career, Colwin received a number of awards, including a Guggenheim fellowship in 1987 and the O. Henry Award for short fiction.

— PATRICIA M. KELLY

Home Cooking: A Writer in the Kitchen, 1988
More Home Cooking: A Writer Returns to the Kitchen, 1993

Juliet Corson

JULIET CORSON WAS ONE OF THE NINETEENTH-CENTURY CULINARY AUTHORITIES who made a difference in the life of all Americans. Her short life was dedicated to teaching others, of all classes, how to cook and feed their families both nutritiously and economically. She was especially noted for her work with the poor and with the early dietetics and home-economics movements.

Corson was born to Mary Ann Henderson and Peter Ross Corson in the Roxbury section of Boston on January 14, 1841. The family moved to New York City when she was six years old. Too frail to attend school, she was educated by her maternal uncle, Dr. Alfred Upham, who encouraged her to make use of his large library. Corson was sixteen when her mother died. Two years later, when her father remarried, according to one biographer, "the animus of a step-dame barred her father's door to her and she began the battle of life."

One of her earliest jobs was as a librarian at the Working Women's Library, where her salary of four dollars a week was later augmented by the privilege of sleeping in the room. This initiation into the problems of the poor set her upon her life's course. From 1863 to 1870 she supplemented her meager income by writing articles of interest to women in various newspapers and journals, including the New York *Leader* and the *Courier.* Offered the job of indexing the *National Quarterly Review,* she was soon writing articles for it. There she made many friendships among newspaper personnel who were to help her in her subsequent career. This may explain why Corson's life and work were so regularly chronicled by *The New York Times.*

In 1873 Corson became involved with the Women's Educational and Industrial Society of New York, which had recently been organized to offer aid to poor women forced by the financial panic of that time to seek employment. Since many of the women had no training for any kind of work, the society set up a free training school for women where subjects such as bookkeeping, shorthand, sewing, and proofreading were taught. A year later, a cooking class was added to the curriculum. Corson taught the cooking classes, educating herself in the culinary literature of France and Germany. The *Times* reported regularly on the progress of the cooking classes and their graduates.

By 1876 Corson started her own New York Cooking School, accessible to all and charging tuition on a sliding scale. Her school and her increasing reputation led to invitations to lecture throughout the United States and Canada, and her appearances often resulted in domestic economy being introduced into the local public-school curriculum. She was a frequent guest instructor at missions, orphanages, and industrial training schools, including those for nurses in hospitals in New York and elsewhere.

For the next twenty years, Corson followed a very busy and productive schedule of teaching, lecturing, and writing. Her major works include several which derived from her teaching of cooking, including *The Cooking Manual* and the *Cooking School Text Book.* From her work with hospitals and nurses, she compiled her

Manual of Cookery for the Sick. For the poor, she wrote *Fifteen-Cent Dinners for Families of Six.* She had hoped to have this pamphlet underwritten for free distribution "among the families of workingmen earning One Dollar and Fifty Cents, or less, per day." When the country faced hard times following the railroad strike of 1877 and she could not find an underwriter, she published it at her own expense. This warning was prominently printed on the title page: "All persons are cautioned not to pay for this book. This edition of 50,000 copies is published for free circulation only." For those of moderate means she wrote *Meals for the Million* and *Twenty-Five Cent Dinners for Families of Six.* And for everyone, she wrote *Family Living on $500 Dollars a Year, Juliet Corson's New Family Cook Book,* and her magnum opus, *Miss Corson's Practical American Cookery.*

The genesis of this last book is unique. In a conversation with her friend John Eaton, U.S. Commissioner of Education, concerning the state of American cookery, he commented that her own works showed much European—especially French—influence. She countered that that was because the public demanded it, though she herself felt that "genuine American cookery is both wholesome and palatable, and has lost none of the traditional excellence which characterized it in our grandmothers' days." They then arranged for her to write a letter to Commissioner Eaton which he would circulate throughout the country under the auspices of the Bureau of Education. In her letter, Corson explained that her work thus far had been mainly in the northeast and that she now wanted to write a national cookbook, including the western and southern states, especially considering the "marked social changes attendant on the Civil War" in the latter. She asked respondents to send her information on the principal foods in local use and their average price in the market, and accurate recipes for preparing such materials in popular dishes. The response was "abundant" and she augmented it by material she had gathered during recent lectures and tours throughout the country.

The book that resulted, *Miss Corson's Practical American Cookery,* is an American classic. It includes chapters on "The Kitchen, Pantry and Cellar," "Marketing," "Methods of Cooking," "Carving," "The Dining-Room and its Fittings," "The Dinner Table and its Appointments," "Flowers, Bills of Fare, and Wines," "The Etiquette of Dinners and of Various Entertainments," "Beverages" and "Suggestions for the Diet of Invalids and Children"—and 400 pages of recipes. These include such traditional American dishes as Stewed Hominy, Succotash from Dried Samp and Beans, Dried Apple Pan Dowdy, Beaten Biscuits, Okra Soup with Crabs, Knickerbocker Dried Beef, Squirrel-Pie, Philadelphia Canvas-Back Duck, Maple-Sugar Sauce and Graham Gems. It also contains many useful black-and-white illustrations.

Corson remained fully active in her final years even as her health failed. In 1893 she conducted a cooking school at the World's Columbian Exposition in Chicago under the auspices of the New York Board of Lady Managers. Before her final illness, she wrote a series of well-received columns for *Harper's Bazaar* and for *The New York Times.*

Corson found herself close to destitution toward the end of her life and an appeal was made to her many supporters for financial assistance. About ten months before her death, a *New York Times* article ("Aid for Miss Corson: The Appeal in Her Behalf Brought Generous Responses") presented a list of those who had sent money to help pay for her medical care. She died at home on June 18, 1897 at age 56 and is buried in Greenwood Cemetery, Brooklyn. On June 20, *The New York Times* published a lengthy and laudatory obituary entitled "Death of Juliet Corson. The Well-Known Writer and Teacher of Cookery and Dietetics Expires Almost Alone." According to the obituary, the French consul-general in New York had applied to Corson in the name of his government for her plan of work and for the list of her books with the intention of introducing her system into the public schools of France.

— JANICE BLUESTEIN LONGONE

The Cooking Manual of Practical Directions for Economical Everyday Cooker, 1877
Fifteen-Cent Dinners for Families of Six. New York: Juliet Corson, 1877
Twenty-Five Cent Dinners for Families of Six. New York: By the author, at the Office of the N.Y. Cooking School, 1878
Cooking School Text Book; and Housekeepers' Guide, 1879
Meals for the Million: The People's Cook-Book, Juliet Corson, 1879
Juliet Corson's New Family Cook Book, 1885
Miss Corson's Practical American Cookery and Household Management, 1885
Family Living on $500 Dollars a Year. New York: Harper & Brothers, 1888
Manual of Cookery for the Sick. Adapted for Hospitals and Private Families, 1892 [Published anonymously but firmly identified as by Juliet Corson.]

Almost all of Corson's books appeared in numerous editions and printings, often in enlarged or revised formats and/or with different publishers. She also wrote many newspaper and magazine articles and a Bureau of Education circular on training-schools of cookery (1879). Along with many of the leading nineteenth-century culinary authorities, she also authored or contributed to promotional publications (advertising ephemera). Among them are:

Every-Day Cookery, Table Talk and Hints for the Laundry. Chicago: Adams & Westlake Manufacturing Co., 1884 [Promotion for stoves and other products]
600 Selected Recipes. **N. K. Fairbank** *& Co., Chicago*, 1892 [Promotion for Cottolene shortening]

D

Nils Gustaf Dalén

1869–1937

AN ENGINEER AND INVENTOR, DALÉN INVENTED SELF-LIGHTING AND self-regulating lights for marine buoys and lighthouses and developed the fuel-conserving AGA stove, the most important appliance in many country households in Scandinavia, England and northern Europe to the present day.

Dalén was born to a dairy-farming family in Stenstorp, Sweden. As a boy, he invented a morning alarm system to turn on a coffee maker, and a threshing machine powered by a spinning-wheel. He was sent to an agricultural school after his primary education, and took over operation of the family farm, but in 1892 he invented a device to measure the butterfat content of milk that brought him to the attention of Gustaf de Laval, an engineer active in the dairy field. Laval encouraged him to get a technical education instead.

In 1896, Dalén received a degree in mechanical engineering from Chalmers Institute of Technology in Göteborg; after a further year of study at the Swiss Federal Technical Institute in Zurich, he returned to Sweden to work as a designer at de Laval Ångturbinen. He formed the firm Dalén & Celsing with a fellow student; the partners devised a new way of producing and using acetylene gas, mainly for municipal lighting. In 1901, Dalén joined Svenska Karbid- och Acetylen, a company that was developing acetylene technology, and introduced welding and metal-cutting using acetylene gas in 1902.

After joining the Gas-Accumulator company, Dalén turned to ways to automate the collection, safe release and ignition of this high-energy hydrocarbon gas that fueled lighthouses, marine beacons, and harbor buoys. He perfected a compound of asbestos and diatomaceous earth that permitted the storage of acetylene in capillaries too fine to permit explosion, and invented a "sun valve" that allowed acetylene-fueled lights to turn themselves off at dawn and on at dusk, as well as a device to permit such lights to flash in desired patterns and a mixing valve to keep the fuel-air balance correct. His refinements made possible cheaper and more reliable marine buoys, low-energy lighthouses that could run unattended for as long as a year, and improved headlights on trains and other vehicles. When his firm was reorganized as Svenska Aktiebolaget Gasaccumulator, or AGA, in 1909, Dalén became its managing director. AGA won an enormous $150,000 order in 1911 to provide an entire lighthouse system for the Panama Canal.

In September 1912, during a test of safety devices on cylinders of acetylene, a valve failed and Dalén was blinded. His brother, Dr. Albin Dalén, a famous ophthalmologist, could not restore his sight. Weeks later, while still bedridden, Gustaf Dalén was awarded the Nobel Prize in Physics; because of his severe impairment, he sent his brother as proxy to receive the award.

In permanent darkness, but with strong support from his wife and four children and his company, Dalén returned to work in 1913 as researcher, inventor and executive, relying on telephone, radio, readers and a phenomenal memory. During his recuperation at home, he had noticed his wife's difficulties in keeping a wood-burning kitchen stove lit and in stoking the firebox to the right temperature for cooking; in 1929, he completed his design of a better stove. The cast-iron AGA stove, originally coke-fueled, produced precisely controlled radiant heat in a firebox insulated with diatomaceous earth. It used minimal fuel and could burn smokelessly and unattended for 24 hours; there were no knobs or dials, the various ovens and hot surfaces maintaining different temperatures by their varying distances from the single heat source. His design resulted in another patent— one of almost 100 granted Dalén over his lifetime—and a new, rather divergent, product for AGA that sold extremely well. Throughout Europe, the AGA stove became the most popular kitchen appliance of the era, particularly in regions not served by gas companies.

The massive AGA stove typically came with two ovens and an internal hot-water boiler, a boon to the cook who constantly boiled water for laundry, cleaning, and cooking. Additional features included a boiling plate, simmering plate, warming oven, and roasting oven with door thermometer that regulated an air damper. Unlike the grim black iron stove of the past, the AGA's creamy enamel surfaces wiped clean. Manufactured for both private homes and restaurants, and eventually adapted to burn wood, coal, peat, oil and natural gas, the AGA cooker had sold more than 100,000 units internationally by 1948. Today, though the Swedish company no longer manufactures them, AGA stoves are still produced under license in Britain, hand-built and installed by technicians for each customer, and are a standard throughout the world for serious food preparation in private homes, guest houses, bed-and-breakfasts, hotels, restaurants, and institutional kitchens.

Dalén married Elma Persson in 1901. Of their four children, one son, Gunnar, also became an engineer and a director of AGA; the younger son, Anders, became a physician in his uncle's footsteps. Dalén died, laden with many honors, in Lidingö, Sweden.

— MARY ELLEN SNODGRASS

Nobin Chandra Das

1846 ?

As befits the legendary reputation of Bengali sweets throughout the Indian subcontinent, their origins are shrouded in myth and mystery. The primary ingredient, *chhana* or acid-curd cheese, is not to be found in the sweets of other regions of India. Many believed that deliberately spoiling milk with acid was a sin. Nor is chhana mentioned as an ingredient for sweets in medieval Bengali writings about food. Historians speculate that the Bengalis might have learned about this kind of cheese-making from the Portuguese settlers in seventeenth- and eighteenth-century Bengal. Others believe that it might have been a happy instance of necessity being the mother of invention: Confronted with large quantities of spoiled (separated) milk, some enterprising Bengali started mixing it with sugar to make it palatable. However, it was not till the nineteenth century that the Bengali culinary imagination transformed chhana into the building block of a whole new order of confectionery.

Perhaps the most famous Bengali sweet—one that is almost synonymous with the plump, gastronomically obsessed Bengali himself—is the *rosogolla*. Literally, the term means "balls in sweet syrup." Although the confectioner Nobin Chandra Das is credited with its creation, the brand name now associated with it is that of his son, K. (Krishna) C. (Chandra) Das. The family-owned sweet shops in Calcutta are called "K. C. Das" and the company's rosogollas are canned for export under the same logo.

If family historiography is to be believed, the creation of the rosogolla is intimately linked to the history of British colonialism in Bengal. Nobin Chandra Das was the son of a wealthy merchant family based in the village of Sutanuti on the bank of the Ganges—one of the three villages that the British East India Company had acquired in 1698 to create the port of Calcutta. The Das family made their money by exporting cane sugar crystals. By the 1860's, however, the British had expropriated this business. In 1864, Nobin Chandra Das decided to set up shop as a confectioner. His marriage to the granddaughter of Bhola Moira, a famous sweet-maker, may have provided inspiration. As he prospered, he also gave rein to his imagination. In 1868, he created the rosogolla, and its overnight popularity changed the landscape of sweet making in Bengal. Soon, he moved to the Baghbazar area of British Calcutta and opened a bigger shop. His customers were so in love with the rosogolla that they even made up a couplet in his honor:

Baghbazarer Nobin Das / Rosogollar Columbus.

A translation would read: "Nobin Das of Baghbazar, the Columbus of rosogolla." Americans can surely identify with the sense of discovery that Das provided his fellow Bengalis.

Nobin Das' only son, K. C. Das, modernized the family business and streamlined the production of sweets in a more scientific way. He opened the first of several shops bearing his name in 1930. But K. C. Das was not merely a talented businessman. Like his father, he too had a creative imagination and came up with another legendary product, in which the rosogollas float in a rich sauce of evaporated milk perfumed with cardamom and saffron and sometimes garnished with pistachio chips. K. C. Das called it *rosomalai* and, over time, it has acquired a status as legendary as that of the rosogolla.

Through the years, hundreds of confectioners have replicated these sweets, but the K. C. Das brand name survives as a mark of excellence even today. The company, still family owned, is even considering setting up operations in Australia, where milk is cheap, plentiful, and of high quality. But perhaps what would please Nobin Chandra Das most, were he alive today, is the fact that the rosogolla has been declared the National Sweet of India.

The creation of the other famous Bengali sweet, *sandesh*, is attributed to Paran Chandra Nag, a confectioner from Janai, a village near Calcutta. In 1826, he opened a shop in the Bowbazar area of Calcutta and started selling sandesh—a dry sweet made by mixing chhana with different grades of sugar and cooking it to different consistencies. His son, Bhim Chandra Nag, had an even greater flair, as evidenced by the thirty to fifty varieties of sandesh he made in a wide range of flavors and textures. Like rosogolla, sandesh too was immensely popular among the rich and famous of Calcutta. Bhim Nag was also esteemed for his *pantuas*—a deep-fried sweet made with a combination of chhana and *kheer* (evaporated milk that has been boiled down to a solid, fudge-like consistency). The generic *gulabjamun* available in Indian restaurants in the West is an inferior descendant.

Bhim Chandra Nag's fame as a confectioner attracted clients from the top layers of society. The poet Rabindranath Tagore, the first Indian to win a Nobel Prize, was particularly fond of sandesh from Bhim Nag's store. But possibly Nag's most memorable contribution is associated with the colonial British rulers. Once when the viceroy, Lord Canning, and his wife were visiting Calcutta from Delhi, Bhim Nag created a sweet—a variant on the pantua—to please the vicereine. The new product, spherical, succulent, and fragrant, was named "Lady Canning." Over the years, the Bengalis have adapted the English name and it is now popularly known as "ledikeni."

— CHITRITA BANERJI

Minakshie DasGupta   ⚜ 1931–1994 ⚜

ALSO CALLED: Kewpie

IT IS A PARTICULARLY HAPPY COINCIDENCE THAT THE FIRST WOMAN TO WRITE a modern Bengali cookbook in English, with precise measurements, clear directions adapted for the modern kitchen, and including a wide range of dishes, should be named Minakshie. The term, meaning "she whose eyes are shaped like fish," derives from Sanskrit, the mother language of Bengali. According to the esthetics of ancient India, fish was the ideal shape for a woman's eyes. In South Asia's eastern region of Bengal, the concept resonates with potency, since fish, along with rice, is the staple of the Bengali diet.

Minakshie did not choose her name, of course: Her parents did. But in keeping with Bengali tradition, they also gave her a nickname. (Most Bengalis have two names, one for the home and one for the world.) The nickname, Kewpie (the brand name for a fat-cheeked British doll), was as untraditional as it could get. But this bipolarity is happily reflected in Minakshie's culinary interests and achievements, which encompassed both Bengali traditional cookery and the fusion cuisine of Eurasians in India.

Growing up in a family of food enthusiasts in Calcutta, Minakshie began to frequent her mother's kitchen from the age of three. As family lore has it, by the time she was seven, she insisted on accompanying her nanny on trips to the local market to select ingredients for items she would make for the family's Sunday lunch. From these simple beginnings grew a lifelong curiosity about the cuisines of the world. After completing her school and college education in Calcutta, Minakshie married Mitu DasGupta, whose enthusiasm for food not only complemented hers, but also bore unexpected fruit in the late 1990s.

With her husband, she traveled extensively in India and around the world and missed no opportunity to explore the cuisines of each place, whether it was a provincial bistro in France or a roadside sushi joint in Japan. Her personal library grew with the collection of recipes and stories from each of her stops. Through all this, she also raised three children, a son and two daughters, who learned to share her enthusiasm for food from an early age.

Minakshie published her classic *Bangla Ranna* (*Bengali Cooking*) in 1982. For the first time, there was a cookbook in English that demystified the complexity of Bengal's elaborate cuisine and brought its delicacy and variety within the reach of any interested reader and cook. The book became a best seller and is currently in its tenth edition. The cookbook's debut was notable as well, for Minakshie launched it at the 1982 Festival of India in London. A discriminating art lover, Minakshie had become a champion of the art and culture of India's many overlooked tribal communities. As vice-president of the Calcutta Crafts Council, she represented the organization during the Festival in both London and New York.

The success of the book prompted her to work on another project. *The Calcutta Cookbook*, co-authored with two food historians, Jaya Chaliha and Bunny Gupta, deals with the contribution of various non-Bengali communities to the city's unique cuisine. Sadly, however, Minakshie DasGupta did not live to see the publication of this book, having succumbed to a kidney ailment that had been taking its toll for several years. The last three years of her life were also darkened by the untimely death of her only son in 1991.

Minakshie DasGupta will certainly be remembered as a gifted cook and the author of a classic cookbook. But her legacy reaches far beyond these personal accomplishments. The reason for that lies in the nature of Bengali cuisine and the way it has been affected by a rapidly globalizing urban culture. As in many traditional societies, cooking and food preparation in Bengal was mostly the domain of women. In this lush, tropical region where the economy was primarily agricultural for many centuries, large extended families were the norm. Every household had many women who collaborated in the kitchen, each bringing her special talents to create the varied dishes that Bengalis love to eat with rice. The presence of several generations under one roof, as well as the infusion of new ideas and techniques brought by brides from their own families, enriched and reinforced this tradition of cooking. Among Hindus, widows had a special role. Their lot was a sad one—they were not permitted to remarry, nor were they allowed to eat any animal foods like fish, meat, or eggs and even certain vegetables, including lentils, onions, and garlic. But many of them overcame these limitations by creating innovative vegetarian delicacies that are justly famous. They also used their free time to make a wealth of pickles and chutneys that added zest to their vegetarian meals.

With time and industrialization, however, came the growth of big cities and urban life. In the more than sixty years since India's independence, family structure and eating habits have significantly changed. Small or nuclear families are increasingly replacing the multi-generational extended families of the past. Few homes now have a host of elderly women busying themselves in the kitchen with the production of delectable tidbits or elaborate specialties. As a result, there are fewer and fewer people to transmit the art of cooking and serving food by example and instruction. Modernity has undone the continuity of tradition, without replacing it with other accessible methods of learning about cuisine.

Even the positive aspects of modern life, which include advances in women's education and the opportunity to pursue careers outside the home, have contributed to the loss of valuable culinary lore. For many younger working women, cooking seemed more an activity that had chained their forebears to long hours in the kitchen than an art they could acquire and take pride in. When one also considers the effect of mobility (in search of economic opportunities) in a once-stable society, it is easy to see why diet and eating preferences in urban Bengali society now reflect trends similar to those in the West. Eating out has become more and more common. But the absence of a restaurant culture in Bengal has meant the proliferation of restaurants serving the food of other regions of India—primarily the meat-based cooking of Punjab in the north, such as that of **Kundan Lal Gujral**, and the vegetarian food of Tamil Nadu in the south—as well as establishments serving Chinese and some kinds of European food. More recently, the incursion of Western fast food chains like McDonald's, Dominos, or Pizza Hut have dealt a further blow to the perpetuation of traditional foods. While reports of the demise of Bengali cuisine, like that of Mark Twain, may be exaggerated or premature, it is definitely becoming an endangered species.

In this context, the impact of Minakshie DasGupta's book is nothing short of inspiring. Like so many American women who were once intimidated by the mere idea of French cooking but lost their fears after reading and watching **Julia Child**, many Bengali women were emboldened to try their hand at traditional recipes because of the accessibility of Minakshie's book.

But the story does not end there. Four years after her death, in May 1998, her husband Mitu and her two daughters, Pia Promina and Rakhi Purnima, decided to open a restaurant named Kewpie's that would celebrate her memory by serving authentic Bengali cuisine. Eating out in Calcutta would never be the same again. Bengali food is notoriously hard to produce on a mass scale, as one realizes when tasting one of Kewpie's signature dishes—tiny shrimp tossed with finely sliced onions, ground mustard paste, turmeric, salt and fiery mustard oil, and slowly baked inside a green coconut. That may be why fine dining was always at home rather than in a restaurant. This fact makes Kewpie's even more remarkable. Despite doing brisk business, the restaurant has sacrificed neither authenticity nor sophistication. The family is determined to keep it as a family-owned business, follow Minakshie DasGupta's legendary recipes, and plan the menu according to seasonal offerings. This means that both discerning Bengali food lovers as well as outsiders will continue to have the opportunity to taste a cuisine whose delicacy, elegance, and richness reflect the natural bounty of its native region. Many may be motivated to go home and try their hand at some of Minakshie DasGupta's recipes. Over time, the domino effect of these eating and cooking experiences can only help to ensure the survival of Bengal's ancient culinary heritage.

— CHITRITA BANERJI

Bangla Ranna (Bengali Cooking), 1982
The Calcutta Cookbook: A Treasury of Recipes from Pavement to Palace (with Jaya Chaliha and Bunny Gupta)

Elizabeth David

❦ 1913–1992 ❦

ELIZABETH DAVID WAS THE SECOND OF FOUR DAUGHTERS OF RUPERT Gwynne, member of parliament for Eastbourne, and his wife Stella, née Ridley. She grew up in a manor house in Sussex, with nanny and governess, as was the norm for children of her class. Her earliest pleasure in food came from mushrooms gathered in the fields and cooked illicitly over the nursery fire by Nanny, and not from the meals sent up from the kitchen: "Junket was slippery and slimy, jam roly-poly greasy...." At sixteen she was sent to Paris to study art history and French literature. She lodged with the family whom she called the Robertots in *French Provincial Cooking,* and here she had her first taste of excellent French cooking.

Her father had died when Elizabeth was ten years old, and when she returned to Britain she knew she would have to earn her own living. Beautiful and self-possessed, she joined the Oxford Repertory Company against her mother's wishes, and later the Regent's Park open-air theater. Here she fell in love with the actor Charles Gibson Cowan, a married

man, and sailed off with him to France just before the outbreak of World War II. She was away from England for seven years.

In Antibes she met the writer Norman Douglas; in Messina she and Cowan were interned and their boat impounded when Italy entered the war. They went on to the Greek island of Syros, where, "in a bare white cube of a house," Elizabeth learned to rely on the basic foods of the Mediterranean, and to make English pickles and Christmas pudding on charcoal fires for the "friendly tyrants" of the village. When the Germans entered Athens she and Cowan were evacuated via Crete to Egypt, where Elizabeth worked for the Admiralty and the Ministry of Information until the end of the war. There she met and married Tony David, an Indian Army officer. Elizabeth and Tony lived together briefly in New Delhi, but the marriage was not a success and the climate did not suit Elizabeth. In 1946 she returned to Britain.

In an England still stricken by post-war deprivations, she scribbled down her recollections of the food of the Mediterranean. These aromatic memories and recipes were published as *A Book of Mediterranean Food* in 1950. In the next decade there followed four more books, regular columns for *Vogue, The Sunday Times*, and *The Spectator,* and many other publications.

Elizabeth read widely all her life in the literature of food, travel, and history; in her writing she always put food in context, using literary material to illustrate the recipes she chose. Her articles for *Vogue* on the markets of Europe were the first examples of food-travel journalism. "Why does a barrow-boy selling bunched radishes and salad greens in the market at Chinon know by instinct so to arrange his produce that he has created a little spectacle as fresh and gay as a Dufy painting, and you are at once convinced that unless you taste some of his radishes you will be missing an experience which seems of more urgency than a visit to the Chateau of Chinon?"

Her elegant, lucid prose and her quiet authority ensured a substantial readership for her work that still persists today. Her respect for tradition, her passion for accuracy, and her insistence on first-class ingredients made millions of people want to cook. Her artist's eye brought alive the fish market in Venice, the vegetable stalls in Carpentras, and the village girl cooking in southern Spain. Her observations were no less keen when being critical; Elizabeth had a deadly sense of ridicule when dealing with the absurd, the pretentious, or the downright bad. She spoke out against the drab and the disgusting and took on food manufacturers, poor chefs, greedy restaurateurs, and food writers who peddled ersatz dishes.

In the 1960's she opened one of the first kitchen shops, selling equipment and tableware she imported from France. It led the way for Robert Carrier, Terence Conran, and others to follow, but Elizabeth was not good at being a shopkeeper, and she went back to writing, turning her attention to English cooking. *English Bread and Yeast Cookery* kick-started the British bread revival; after attacking the millers and bakers with scorn and fury, she told readers how to make their own. People scoured London for live yeast and unbleached flour; the book sold and sold. Elizabeth continued researching and writing until her death; her last work, *Harvest of the Cold Months*, a scholarly account of the history of ice and ices, was published posthumously.

Elizabeth David had a stubborn integrity. She detested fuss, and was wary of grand restaurants and of journalists seeking interviews. She was a private person who said that everything she thought worth knowing about her was contained in her books. She never ran a restaurant or a cookery school, she never taught on television, yet her writing made it possible for today's celebrity chefs and television supercooks to find a receptive audience. She was awarded the OBE in 1976 and made a Chevalier de l'Ordre du Mérite Agricole in 1977; the universities of Essex and Bristol conferred honorary doctorates on her in 1979 and 1988 respectively. In 1982 she was elected Fellow of the Royal Society of Literature, and in 1986 was awarded the CBE. In spite of receiving so many honors, she refused to be a public figure.

Elizabeth treated her readers as equals; her comments on the writing of **Edouard de Pomiane** could have been applied just as well to her own work: "It is creative because it invites the reader to use his own critical and inventive faculties, sends him out to make discoveries, form his own opinions, observe things for himself, instead of slavishly accepting what the books tell him." In *French Country Cooking* she wrote, "Good cooking is honest, sincere and simple, and by this I do not mean to imply that you will find in this or any other book, the secret of turning out first-class food in a few minutes with no trouble. Good food is always a trouble and its preparation should be regarded as a labour of love...." These two statements are her epitaph and offer guidance to anyone wishing to write or to cook well.

— JILL NORMAN

A Book of Mediterranean Food, 1950. Revised 1955, 1958, 1965, 1988. New introduction 1991
French Country Cooking, 1951. Revised 1958, 1966
Italian Food, 1954. Revised 1963, 1969, 1977, 1987
Summer Cooking, 1955. Revised 1965
French Provincial Cooking, 1960. Revised 1965, 1967, 1970
Spices, Salt and Aromatics in the English Kitchen, 1970. Revised 1973, 1975
English Bread and Yeast Cookery, 1977
An Omelette and a Glass of Wine, 1984
Harvest of the Cold Months, 1994
South Wind through the Kitchen: The Best of Elizabeth David, 1977 (compiled by Jill Norman)
Is There a Nutmeg in the House?, 2000 (compiled by Jill Norman)

Henriette Davidis

1801–1876

HENRIETTE DAVIDIS, GERMANY'S MOST FAMOUS AUTHOR OF COOKBOOKS, household manuals, and behavior guides, decisively shaped German culinary culture. Born in the village of Wengern an der Ruhr (today called Wetter) as the tenth of thirteen children of pastor Ernst Davidis and his Dutch-born wife Katharina Litthauer, Davidis' life followed an unusual course for a nineteenth-century woman. We cannot trace all its stages, however, because her autobiography, *Erin-*

nerungen aus meinem Leben und Wirken (Memories From My Life and Work), which she wrote in 1874, was never published, and the manuscript has been lost.

In her childhood and youth, Davidis was taught all aspects of middle-class homemaking and propriety by her mother, a skilled housekeeper and excellent cook. This course of instruction was to determine her direction at a number of important junctures in her life. She left her parents' house soon after her confirmation in the Wengern village church in May 1816 and went to live in Schwelm with one of her sisters, who was married to a local landowner. Martfeld Castle, with its extensive estate, was to be her home for about two years.

This 1994 portrait by E. Hegemann is in the Henriette-Davidis-Museum in Wetter, Germany.

Life at Martfeld during Davidis' time there was strongly influenced by the squire's grandmother, Wilhelmine Wichelhausen, an open-minded, tolerant and cultured lady who had opened her home to clergy, writers, physicians, and other intellectuals, whether local people or visitors to Martfeld's healing springs, which attracted gentry and "beautiful people" from a wide radius. There was a playhouse there where Schiller, Shakespeare, and Kotzebue were performed, and we may assume that Davidis followed the advice she herself was later to give her readers: "Sharpen...eyes and ears for learning; focus on putting your time to good use in gathering in stores for your heart and spirit, so that later you do not lack the fruits you desire."

Davidis was one of 28 pupils enrolled in a girls' school in Schwelm in 1817 and 1818. It was advanced for its time; the school's co-rector, Peter Heinrich Holthaus, believed that "the written expression of thought is more important than many another subject in the curriculum." He valued Davidis' ability to write clear and elegant prose, and she was fortunate to benefit from his teaching for two years. She then moved on to Elberfeld in the Rhineland and was trained as a teacher at a well-regarded school established by Karl Ludwig Theodor Lieth.

Her first position was as tutor to the four children of another of her sisters, her beloved Albertine, a farmer's wife in Bommern bei Witten, but she left that post after her father's death in 1828 to return to Wengern to live with her mother. During her ten years in Wengern, she often vacationed in Stemwede-Levern. She enjoyed cooking in the local post hotel, where travelers passing through often had higher standards and more sophisticated tastes than the local people there or in Wengern; she earned a considerable reputation for her culinary skills. On other occasions, she visited her friend Katharina Ewers in Medebach-Küstelberg, whose abilities as a cook had been recognized even by the Prussian royal household and some of whose recipes were later to find their way into Davidis' own cookbook, which she began to work on in 1836.

Following the death of her mother in 1838, Davidis traveled to Switzerland as a lady's companion. Her observations of Swiss agricultural practices were later to appear in her *Praktisches Gartenbuch (Practical Garden Book).* In 1839 or 1840 she moved to Windheim, in Lower Saxony, and in the spring of 1841 to Sprockhövel, where she took over direction of the local *Mädchenarbeitsschule*—a school where girls were taught the middle-class domestic skills that they would need to run their own households in the future—and seemed to settle for a time, filling her home with memorabilia, furniture from the manse in Wengern, and potted plants on pedestals.

This was a period of growing economic and social change, when "Germany" was still a geographical, not a political, concept that referred to more than a score of separate entities (like "Europe" at the end of the twentieth century). The industrial revolution was rapidly gathering steam; factories and railroads were being built at breathtaking rates, workers were being drawn off the farms into manufacturing, and the explicit and quasi-professional teaching of cherished cultural norms—as exemplified by the *Mädchenarbeitsschulen*—was a defensive response to the expectation of greater and more sweeping changes to come.

In Sprockhövel, Davidis remained active as a cook and collector of recipes from all over Germany. There were more than 400 German-language regional cookbooks in print, and Davidis collected, tasted, and tested all across the culinary landscape, selecting and often changing and improving, until she had created not only the first pan-German cookbook but in fact a multifaceted German cuisine—the primary achievement of her career. Hardly less important, however, is the picture that Davidis' cookbook provides of its particular moment in German social history, when the comfortable middle class demanded books that would teach its daughters how to achieve the housewifely virtues that it valued so highly. It was a demand that Davidis felt called to meet.

Her book, completed in 1844, was rejected by three publishers before finding its home with Velhagen & Klasing in Bielefeld, who brought it out in 1845 under the title *Zuverlässige und selbstgeprüfte Recepte der gewöhnlichen und feineren Küche (Reliable and Personally Tested Recipes for Ordinary and Finer Cuisine)*. It was not until the third edition that the title became *Praktisches Kochbuch für die gewöhnliche und feinere Küche (Practical Cookbook for Ordinary and Finer Cuisine)*, the name under which it sold 264,000 copies in the author's lifetime. In her inexperience, Davidis sold all rights to the book, receiving 450 thaler; she later realized that the publisher had taken advantage of her, and in her future relationships with Velhagen & Klasing and other publishers she stoutly insisted on better treatment: additional fees for revised editions; separate publication of her new works; attention to her opinions on advertising, printing paper, format, and other matters; and larger fees. She was not always successful: The firm refused her request for a 200-thaler fee for revision of the eighth edition, in which all quantities had to be converted to a new system of standard measurements, and had that work done by an employee.

The appearance of the fifteenth edition of *Praktisches Kochbuch* in 1870 marked the book's 25th anniversary; by that time Davidis was generally recognized as Germany's greatest authority in the combined fields of cooking and household management. She spent her afternoons replying to letters from her readers, with whom she felt a close bond. The sixteenth edition, in 1871, was particularly thoroughly revised, with each recipe re-edited for economy, the favorite virtue of the time, and with all quantities revised to metric units, now legally required in Germany. **Justus von Liebig**'s meat extract first appeared in that edition; Davidis had written an advertising pamphlet for the product in 1870. The 20th edition appeared in 1874, Davidis' last and most productive working year; its new material included gourmet recipes from the Rhineland, rabbit recipes from Hannover, and preserving recipes provided by the steward of a ducal family. By then a very experienced and self-confident author, Davidis coolly rejected recipes proposed by the publisher for inclusion, and received an honorarium of a thousand thaler for her work.

Praktisches Kochbuch was by no means Davidis' only publication. In 1847, the year before she left the school at Sprockhövel, she produced *Arrangements zu kleinen und größeren Gesellschaften,* a 51-page guide for hostesses of "higher station" who were preparing "breakfasts, luncheons, suppers, coffees, and teas." The next year, for those of lower station, she published *Praktische Anweisung zur Bereitung des Roßfleisches (Practical Instructions for the Preparation of Horse Meat)* and in 1950 the first edition appeared of *Der Gemüse-Garten oder Praktische Anweisung, einen Gemüse-Garten mit Berücksichtigung der Schönheit und des reichlichsten Ertrages zu besorgen (The Vegetable Garden or Practical Instructions for Care of a Vegetable Garden with a View to Beauty and Maximum Productivity).*

Davidis had apparently proposed a children's cookbook to Velhagen & Klasing some time before the very successful publication of just such a book in 1854 by the unknown Julie Bimbach. Davidis communicated advocacy and complaint to her publisher in equal measure: "Would you now, perhaps, be kindly inclined to publish [my] dolls' cookbook? As you are no doubt aware, a dolls' cookbook was published last year before Christmas and found so many purchasers that stocks were entirely exhausted. That little work, which contains few ordinary recipes and those not at all suitable for children's cooking, will be no impediment to us, though it is a pity that my idea was not carried out immediately at the time [I suggested it]." Velhagen & Klasing hesitated, then offered too little money, and Davidis' *Puppenköchin Anna (Anna, the Dolls' Cook)* was published by Grote in 1856. "I sincerely regret that I could not see the little book brought out by you," Davidis wrote to Velhagen & Klasing. "The honorarium was far too small, and I did not want to see still more dolls' cookbooks appear before mine."

With *Puppenköchin Anna,* Davidis was able to integrate her pedagogical purpose into imaginative play without adhering too closely to the model of an adult cookbook, as Bimbach had done. Her "flower kitchen" gave her readers—girls of eight to fourteen years—opportunities for imaginative and playful creativity in the kitchen that encouraged them to grow gradually into their future roles as housewives and mothers. Her next book, *Puppenmutter Anna (Anna, the Dolls' Mother)* continued this task. A book that seemed to answer exhaustively every possible housekeeping question, it was intended to "awaken impulses of domesticity and economy" in its young readers, Davidis wrote. Nonetheless, Anna's mother was depicted in it as a very well-educated woman, and Anna herself as receiving a good education: Davidis believed that training for a profession should be a normal part of a girl's growing up, because it would permit her to be independent as an unmarried woman. Yet though Davidis herself made her way independently all her life—she was engaged twice but both her fiancés died—she too found it difficult to resolve the conflict of work and family obligations. In 1855 she left the manuscript of *Puppenköchin Anna* unfinished to take over operation of her relatives' farm at harvest time. Life in the familiar, loving family circle offered great conveniences, she wrote later, but it was a hindrance to a writer, "because everything that happens there, joy and sorrow alike, makes demands on one's emotions."

In 1857 Davidis published *Die Jungfrau (The Young Woman),* a guide to self-understanding and life preparation for young women. (The book was retitled *Der Beruf der*

Jungfrau [The Young Woman's Vocation] in its second edition.) Her foreword, written during a visit to Wengern in 1856, reveals Davidis' view of the social position of women, and shows the degree to which she was both a product of her own time and a visionary. She lent the marginalized middle-class unmarried women of the nineteenth century—more than half the female population of Germany at the time!—a new dignity with her advocacy of professional training for women, which would make independent living possible for them and would open to them lifestyles, other than those centered on marriage and family, that were nonetheless socially recognized. She laid out a wide range of possible professions: nursing, teaching and training, household work, art, secretarial and bookkeeping work, or independent commerce in passementerie, millinery, or white goods. "In recent times," she added, "a number of other occupations have been suggested as suitable for women and some of them have already been successfully entered into." Davidis' conception and advocacy of the role of the independent woman, conscious of her own worth, intellectually and economically self-sufficient, coincided with the ideas of the early women's movement—yet she never freed herself of conventional notions of the social supremacy of men.

In 1857 she moved to Dortmund, "quite close to my sisters," where she was to spend the rest of her life. Her most important new production in those years was *Die Hausfrau (The Housewife),* a comprehensive guide on housekeeping matters that appeared in 1861. She was otherwise fully occupied with new editions of her other books, which more and more were becoming standard works for German women, revising them collectively into a sweeping educational and cultural program whose unprecedented influence has shaped women's lives and German society even into the present day. She also found time to write for magazines and to produce, in 1860, a belletristic collection of "contributions to women's emotional education."

In 1875 Davidis' health deteriorated considerably, but her desire to keep working on the latest—the 21st—edition of her *Praktisches Kochbuch* was undiminished. She wrote to Velhagen & Klasing that she would "do whatever is possible to maintain the quality of this work, which has won such universal recognition." In fact, she did not live to see the 21st edition published, but her desire to maintain the quality of her cookbook was well served by her publisher's selection of outstanding editors to produce posthumous revisions of the work: Luise Rosendorf, Luise Holle, Ida Schultze, and **Erna Horn**.

The copyright on *Praktisches Kochbuch* expired in 1906, and a number of other publishers promptly brought out their own versions of Davidis' book or mined it to produce derivative works, activities that continue to the present day. German- and English-language adaptations were also published in the United States and translations in Holland.

Henriette Davidis died of a stroke on April 3, 1876 and is buried in Dortmund's East Cemetery, where her headstone bears the incorrect birthdate 1800. In her birthplace, Wetter, the stones of the hearth at which she tested many of her recipes have been used to build a memorial to her, and a street and a square in the town have been named after Wetter's most famous citizen and one of the great women of nineteenth-century Germany.

— ECKEHARD METHLER & WALTHER METHLER

*Zuverlässige und selbstgeprüfte Recepte der gewöhnlichen und feineren Küche. Praktische
Anweisung zur Bereitung von verschiedenartigen Speisen, kalten und warmen Getränken, Gelees,
Gefrornem, Backwerken, sowie zum Einmachen und Trocknen von Früchten, mit besonderer
Berücksichtigung der Anfängerinnen und angehenden Hausfrauen* (Reliable and Personally
Tested Recipes for Ordinary and Finer Cuisine. Practical Instructions for the Preparation of
Different Sorts of Foods, Cold and Hot Drinks, Jellies, Frozen Dishes, and Baked Goods, as
well as for Preserving and Drying Fruits, With Particular Attention to the Needs of Beginners
and Prospective Housewives), 1845. Revised 1846. Revised as *Praktisches Kochbuch für
die gewöhnliche und feinere Küche. Zuverlässige und selbstgeprüfte Recepte zur Bereitung der
verschiedenartigsten Speisen, kalter und warmer Getränke, Gelees, von Gefrornem, Backwerken,
so wie zum Einmachen und Trocknen von Früchten. Mit einem Anhange, enthaltend
Arrangements zu kleinen und größeren Gesellschaften, zu Frühstücks, Mittags- und Abendessen,
Kaffee's und Thee's, und einem Küchenzettel nach den Jahreszeiten geordnet. Mit besonderer
Berücksichtigung der Anfängerinnen und angehenden Hausfrauen* (Practical Cookbook for
Ordinary and Finer Cuisine. Reliable and Personally Tested Recipes for the Preparation of the
Most Various Sorts of Foods, Cold and Hot Drinks, Jellies, Frozen Dishes, and Baked Goods,
as well as for Preserving and Drying Fruits. With an Addendum Containing Arrangements
for Small and Larger Functions, for Breakfasts, Luncheons, and Suppers, Coffees and Teas,
with a Menu Arranged According to the Seasons. With Particular Attention to the Needs of
Beginners and Prospective Housewives), 1847. Revised 1849, 1851, 1854. Pocket edition,
1854. Revised, fourteen words removed from title, 1858. Revised, 1861. Revised as
*Praktisches Kochbuch für die gewöhnliche und feinere Küche. Zuverlässige und selbstgeprüfte
Recepte zur Bereitung der verschiedenartigsten Speisen, kalter und warmer Getränke, zum
Einmachen und Trocknen von Früchten, etc., und einer Hinweisung auf schnell zu machende
Speisen. Mit einem Anhange, enthaltend Arrangements zu kleinen und größeren Gesellschaften
und einem Küchenzettel nach den Jahreszeiten geordnet. Mit besonderer Berücksichtigung
der Anfängerinnen und angehenden Hausfrauen* (Practical Cookbook for Ordinary and Finer
Cuisine. Reliable and Personally Tested Recipes for the Preparation of the Most Various Sorts
of Foods, Cold and Hot Drinks, for Preserving and Drying Fruits, etc., and a Note on Quickly
Prepared Foods. With an Addendum Containing Arrangements for Small and Larger Functions,
and a Menu Arranged According to the Seasons. With Particular Attention to the Needs of
Beginners and Prospective Housewives), 1862. Revised 1865, 1867, 1869, 1871, 1873,
1875, 1876. Posthumous revision by Borchling and Otterbruch (anonymously), 1877.
Posthumous revision by Luise Rosendorf as *Praktisches Kochbuch für die gewöhnliche
und feinere Küche. Unter besonderer Berücksichtigung der Anfängerinnen und angehenden
Hausfrauen von Henriette Davidis. Nach dem Tode der Verfasserin fortgeführt von Luise
Rosendorf* (Practical Cookbook for Ordinary and Finer Cuisine. Revised and Edited With
Particular Attention to the Needs of Beginners and Prospective Housewives by Henriette
Davidis. Continued by Luise Rosendorf After the Death of the Author), 1882. Revised 1884,
1888, 1890, 1891. Posthumous revision by Luise Holle as *Praktisches Kochbuch für die
gewöhnliche und feinere Küche. Unter besonderer Berücksichtigung der Anfängerinnen und
angehenden Hausfrauen neu bearbeitet und herausgegeben von Luise Holle* (Practical Cookbook
for Ordinary and Finer Cuisine. Revised and Edited With Particular Attention to the Needs
of Beginners and Prospective Housewives by Luise Holle), 1892. Revised 1893, 1894, 1900,
1901, 1903, 1904, 1906, 1907, 1909, 1910, 1912, 1929, 1935. Posthumous revision by
Erna Horn as *Praktisches Kochbuch für die einfache und feinere Küche* (Practical Cookbook for
Simple and Finer Cuisine), 1960. Revised, 1963

Many other republications, revisions, and derivative works exist by (among others) Elsa
Bier, Nanette Burg, Helene Faber, Roland Glööck, Kurt Hensch, Burgi Kühnemann,
Ilse von Lagerström-Zerbe, Maria Lehnert, Laura Leopold, Eva May, Annie Juliane
Reichert, Helene Reinhold, Helene Richter, Elisabeth Schmitz, Karl Schneider,
Fritzi Schreiber, Ida Schulze, Charlotte Täuber, Theodore Trainer, Marie Walter,
Marie Wesenberg, Gertrude Wiemann, and Rudolf Zäch.

First U.S. edition, *Praktisches Kochbuch für die Deutschen in Amerika. Zuverlässige und selbstgeprüfte Anweisungen zur Bereitung der verschiedenartigsten Speisen und Getränke, zum Backen, Einmachen u.s.w. Eine Bearbeitung des anerkannten besten deutschen Kochbuches der Frau Henriette Davidis. Vermehrt und verbessert durch Aufnahme von Recepten zu den in Amerika landesüblichen Speisen, Backwerken etc., und durch Übertragung des deutschen in Amerikanisches Maß und Gewicht, sowie durch Hinzufügung eines Speisezettels für Kranke aller Art (Practical Cookbook for the Germans in America. Reliable and Personally Tested Instructions for the Preparation of the Most Various Sorts of Foods, for Baking, Preserving and so on. A Revision of Henriette Davidis' Cookbook, Recognized as the Best German Cookbook. Expanded and Improved by the Inclusion of Recipes for Dishes and Baked Goods Common in America and by the Conversion of German Weights and Measures to American Units, as Well as by the Addition of a Menu for Those Suffering From Every Sort of Illness)*, 1879. Revised 1889. Revised and expanded by Hedwig Voß, 1897, reprinted 1899. Other U.S. titles in German: *Praktisches Kochbuch für die gewöhnliche und feinere Küche*, 1897; *Praktisches Kochbuch für die Deutsch–Amerikanische Hausfrau*, 1904; *Praktisches Kochbuch für die Bürgerliche und feinere Küche*, c. 1915. First U.S. edition in English, *Practical Cookbook. Compiled for the United States from the 35th edition. Containing an Appendix of Receipts for Dishes prepared in Styles peculiar to Cooking as done in this Country. With the German Weights and Measures according to the American System. Supplemented by an English–German and German–English Vocabulary of Culinary Terms*, 1897. Revised as *German National Cookery for American Kitchens…*, 1904, reprinted c. 1910

Arrangements zu kleinen und größeren Gesellschaften, zu Frühstücks, Mittags- und Abendessen, Kaffee's und Thee's und einem Küchenzettel nach den Jahreszeiten geordnet (Arrangements for Small and Larger , for Breakfasts, Luncheons, and Suppers, Coffees and Teas, with a Menu Arranged According to the Seasons), 1847. Thereafter absorbed into *Praktisches Kochbuch*, above.

Praktische Anweisung zur Bereitung des Roßfleisches (Practical Instructions for the Preparation of Horse Meat), 1848

Der Gemüse-Garten oder Praktische Anweisung, einen Gemüse-Garten mit Berücksichtigung der Schönheit und des reichlichsten Ertrages zu besorgen;... (The Vegetable Garden or Practical Instructions for Care of a Vegetable Garden with a View to Beauty and the Greatest Productivity;...), 1850. Reprinted 1850, 1857. Revised 1859. Revised as *Der Küchengarten für Hausfrauen (The Kitchen Garden for Housewives)*, 1863. Revised as *Der Küchen- und Blumengarten für Hausfrauen (The Kitchen and Flower Garden for Housewives)*, 1866. Revised 1869, 1872, 1874. Reprinted 1876, 1877, 1879, 1880, 1882. Posthumous revisions by J. Hartwig, Otto Mohrmann, Paul Schmielke, and Heinrich Schaefer were published until 1913.

Puppenköchin Anna. Ein praktisches Kochbuch für kleine, liebe Mädchen (Anna, the Dolls' Cook. A Cookbook for Dear Little Girls), 1856. Revised 1858, 1864, 1869. Revised by 1874. Posthumous revisions by Theodore Trainer, Emma Heine and Emma Merkel were published until c. 1930.

Die Jungfrau. Worte des Raths zur Vorbereitung für ihren Beruf (The Young Woman. Words of Counsel in Preparation for Her Vocation), 1857. Revised as *Der Beruf der Jungfrau. Eine Mitgabe für Töchter gebildeter Stände (The Young Woman's Vocation. A Parting Gift for Daughters of the Educated Classes)*, 1864. Revised as *Der Beruf der Jungfrau. Mit einem Anhange: Albumblätter für Stille Stunden. Eine Mitgabe für Töchter bei ihrem Eintritt in's Leben (The Young Woman's Vocation. With an Addendum: Poems for Quiet Hours. A Parting Gift for Daughters as They Begin Their Lives)*, 1867. Revised 1871. Reprinted 1874, 1876. Posthumous revisions by Albertine Frielinghaus and others were published until 1925.

Puppenmutter Anna oder wie Anna sich beschäftigt und ihren Puppenhaushalt führt. Nebst Geschichten und Gedichten (Anna, the Dolls' Mother, or How Anna Amuses Herself Running her Doll-Household. With Stories and Poems), 1858. Revised as *Puppenmutter Anna oder wie Anna sich beschäftigt und ihren Puppenhaushalt führt. Nebst Geschichten für kleinen Knaben und Mädchen (Anna, the Dolls' Mother, or How Anna Amuses Herself Running her Doll-*

Household. With Stories for Little Boys and Girls), 1868. Posthumous revisions by Emma Heine were published until 1890.

Natur- und Lebensbilder. Kleine Beiträge zur weiblichen Gemütsbildung (Sketches From Nature and From Life. Little Contributions to Women's Emotional Education), 1860

Die Hausfrau. Prakische Anleitung zur selbständigen und sparsamen Führung des Haushalts, eine Mitgabe für junge Frauen zur Förderung des häuslichen Wohlstandes und Familienglücks (The Housewife. Practical Instructions for Independent and Economical Housekeeping, a Parting Gift for Young Women to Promote Domestic Comfort and Familial Happiness), 1861. Revised 1863, 1865, 1869. Revised as Die Hausfrau. Prakische Anleitung zur selbständigen und sparsamen Führung von Stadt- und Landhaushalten. Eine Mitgabe für angehende Hausfrauen (The Housewife. Practical Instructions for Independent and Economical Housekeeping in Town and Country. A Parting Gift for Prospective Housewives), 1870. Revised 1872, 1874, 1876. Reprinted 1877. Revised 1879. Posthumous revisions by Theodore Trainer, Emma Heine, and Elisabeth Schmitz were published until 1920. First U.S. edition, Die Deutsch–Amerikanische Hausfrau, 1895

Kraftküche von Liebig's Fleischextract für höhere und unbemittelte Verhältnisse erprobt und verfaßt von Henriette Davidis (Strengthening Cuisine With Liebig's Meat Extract, Tested and Recorded by Henriette Davidis for Those in Better-Off and Impecunious Circumstances), published in English as Improved and Economic Cookery, 1870. Reprinted c. 1875, 1878, 1878 or 1879, 1879 or 1880, 1880. English edition (Modern Cookery. Liebig Company's Extract of Meat. A Collection of Recipes for Rich and Poor. Composed and Carefully Tried by Henriette Davidis), 1885

Alan Davidson

❧ 1924–2003 ❧

ALSO CALLED: Alan Eaton Davidson

Davidson received the 2003 Erasmus Prize for contributions to social sciences. "By your personal approach to the study of food...," his encomium read, "you have been a source of inspiration for all those who regard food as their chosen perspective to the study of culture."

ALAN DAVIDSON WAS BORN IN LONDONDERRY, NORTHERN Ireland in 1924, the son of an inspector of taxes—a peripatetic calling at the beginning of the last century. He was educated at Leeds Grammar School and Queen's College, Oxford, where he took a double first in classical greats, interrupted by military service in the Royal Naval Volunteer Reserve in 1943, first as an ordinary seaman, later as a lieutenant. He served in the Mediterranean, North Atlantic, and Pacific until 1946.

After coming down from Oxford in 1948, he joined the British foreign service. His diplomatic career commenced in Washington in 1950, then took him to The Hague, Cairo, Tunis, Brussels, and finally Laos, where he was ambassador from 1973 to 1975. In 1951 he met and married Jane Macatee, the daughter of an American consular official. They had three daughters.

Although his diplomatic career was long and distinguished, he decided to retire long before his time was up. He put that down to strong pressure from his wife and daughters—who feared, he said, that "he would become insufferably pompous if he had another ambassadorial post"—to irritation with life behind a desk when confined to Whitehall, and to the siren call of a new avocation as a writer with a particular interest in food.

His first glimpse of new horizons did not arise until he was head of chancery at the British Embassy in Tunis in 1961. His wife was understandably muddled by the various names proffered for one sort of fish or another in the local markets, and he promised to compile a list. At this juncture he was fortunate in the arrival of the Italian professor Giorgio Bini, the world's greatest living authority on seafish in the Mediterranean, as part of an official delegation to discuss the irrepressible dynamiting of their catch by Sicilian fishermen in the Gulf of Tunis, a method more rapid than discerning. As the negotiations were long and largely political, Bini, no politician, was able to instruct the Briton in elementary ichthyology. Out of these lessons, *Seafish of Tunisia and the Central Mediterranean* was born. Published by Davidson himself in 1963, it was shortly followed by *Snakes and Scorpions Found in the Land of Tunisia*. At that stage, his passion seemed to be for taxonomy rather than fish dinners.

A colleague who had known the food writer **Elizabeth David** when she was working in wartime Cairo sent her a copy of the fish book; she reviewed it in her column for *The Spectator*. From this first contact flowed the process of its conversion from pamphlet to the full-blown work *Mediterranean Seafood*, published by Penguin in 1972.

Once he was embarked as a writer, diplomacy did not lose him but books kept appearing. While part of the British delegation to NATO in Brussels from 1968 to 1971—a posting mired in international protocol—he buoyed the spirits by composing a diplomatic thriller of quixotic inventiveness called *Something Quite Big*.

He was posted to Laos in 1973. As he navigated the streets of the elegant capital, Vientiane, in his stately Bentley motor-car, the new ambassador was witness to the final days of the uneasy coalition between the royal dynasty and the Pathet Lao communist insurgents. When Vietnam and Cambodia fell to the communists, they assumed control of Laos. Davidson's curiosity about that country and its culture resulted in his unearthing a cookery text used in royal circles. This was to become *Traditional Recipes of Laos*, published in 1981. His investigations into fish in the Mekong and other inland waters were published as *Fish and Fish Dishes of Laos* in 1975.

The first years of his retirement saw a flurry of work, from a translation and abridgement (in partnership with his wife) of Alexandre Dumas *père*'s *Le Grand Dictionnaire de Cuisine* to the private publication of *Seafood of South-East Asia* in 1976 (later commercially published in Singapore in 1977 and London in 1978). His trio of seafood catalogues was completed by *North Atlantic Seafood* in 1979. In 1976, he put in place a deal with Oxford University Press to commence his magnum opus, *The Oxford Companion to Food*, which was not to see the light for 22 years. His literary output was by no means cut off by work on the *Companion*, however: Other titles include *Seafood* (1989) and *Fruit* (1991), both with Charlotte Knox as illustrator; an anthology of writings on food, *On Fasting and Feasting* (1988); and a collection of his food essays and journalism, *A Kipper with My Tea* (1990).

He also found a nascent community of interest in food and cookery that pushed the subject further than mere composition of recipes for weekend maga-

D

zines; that enjoyed fine writing and additions to knowledge, but did not indulge the bibulous fatuities of gourmets and gastronomers. His mindset was questing pragmatism, leavened by surreal, puckish humor. People of a like mind purchased the reprinted classics of the kitchen shelf that he began to issue under the imprint of Prospect Books in the 1980's, and a wider public still was to applaud his handsome edition of Patience Gray's timeless *Honey from a Weed*. Prospect Books and its associated journal, *Petits Propos Culinaires*, were to swallow much time—too much, indeed, for speedy completion of the *Companion*. So, too, did the annual gatherings of food enthusiasts at St Antony's College, Oxford, that he organized with the historian Theodore Zeldin. (He was careful always to call them "semi-academic": He disliked arid scholarship almost as much as gastronomy.)

These activities on behalf of others made Alan and Jane's house in Chelsea an international caravanserai of scholar-cooks, many contributing his or her tithe of knowledge to the slowly accumulating *Companion*. Progress on that work never had a disciplined air until his indefatigable assistant, Helen Saberi, imposed calm order. It was also held up by a serious heart attack in the early 1990's, which contributed to his selling Prospect Books in 1993 and transferring *Petits Propos Culinaires* in 2000.

The Oxford Companion to Food appeared at the end of the millennium to just acclaim. Its more than a million words, mostly his own, displayed wit, humanity, curiosity, and knowledge in equal measure. He eschewed the anthropology or sociology of cookery, and indeed the Byzantine ramifications of *haute cuisine*, for a delight in describing the most arcane ingredients or the complex lineage of food customs, recipes, and techniques.

Alan will be remembered for his charm, which was rarely used knowingly; his innocence, which engendered a constant public optimism; his stubborn itch for accuracy, perhaps encouraged by diplomatic training; and his handsome daily turnout in gay but never garish clothing (with an affection for silks and American checks), complete with impressive shopping bag, or even three.

In November 2003, just a month before his death, Alan Davidson was awarded the Erasmus Prize by the Dutch government at the Royal Palace in Amsterdam. This prize, founded in 1958 by Prince Bernhard, is awarded annually to individuals who have made an important contribution to European culture.

— TOM JAINE

Seafish of Tunisia and the Central Mediterranean, 1963
Mediterranean Seafood, 1972
Fish and Fish Dishes of Laos, 1975
Seafood of South-East Asia, 1976
Dumas on Food (translation and abridgement, with Jane Davidson, of *Le Grand Dictionnaire de Cuisine*), 1978
North Atlantic Seafood, 1979
Traditional Recipes of Laos, 1981
On Fasting and Feasting, 1988
Seafood, 1989
A Kipper with my Tea, 1990
Fruit, 1991
The Cook's Room, (Editor), 1991
The Oxford Companion to Food, 1999

Adelle Davis

ADELLE DAVIS WAS POSSIBLY THE FIRST SUPERSTAR NUTRITIONIST IN the United States. Deemed "the high priestess of popular nutrition" by *Look* magazine in 1970, her books sold millions of copies, and she appeared regularly in national news magazines and on television talk shows. She raised awareness of the importance of nutrition for health and fostered concern with where our food originates.

Davis' core philosophy—that virtually any disease or health problem could be prevented or cured by proper diet—introduced many twentieth-century Americans to the benefits of fresh foods, whole grains, milk, and vitamins, as well as to the dangers of pesticide residues and over-processed food products. "We are indeed much more than what we eat, but what we eat can nevertheless help us to be much more than what we are."

Although she was a trained nutritionist with a degree in biochemistry, Davis was viewed with suspicion and scorn by much of the medical establishment, which regarded her research as unsound and her recommendations as fallacious and possibly dangerous. While many of her dictums have since been validated, her ideas are still debated by nutritionists and doctors.

c. 1971

Daisie Adelle Davis was born on a farm in Union Township near Lizton, Indiana, the youngest of five girls. Ten days after her birth, her mother suffered a paralytic stroke; she died seventeen months later. Bottle-feeding was uncommon, and Davis' early sustenance was delivered by eyedropper; she attributed her lifelong interest in nutrition to her infant deprivation of suckling and mother-love.

Raised by her strict father and an elderly aunt, Davis worked hard on the farm, pitching hay, plowing cornfields, and sacking wheat. She learned to cook before she learned to read and, as an avid 4-H Club member, she regularly won competitions for canned produce and homemade bread.

After graduating from Lizton High School in 1923, Davis studied dietetics at Purdue University, where fellow students dubbed her "Vitamin Davis." Her enthusiasm was quite advanced: This was only about a dozen years after vitamins had been generally recognized by the scientific community, and a great many vitamins still remained to be discovered in the late 1920's and 1930's. After two years at Purdue, Davis transferred to the University of California at Berkeley, where she received a BA in dietetics in 1927. She continued her studies at Bellevue and Fordham hospitals in New York City and worked as a nutritionist for the Yonkers public school system and at the Judson Health Center in Manhattan.

By 1931, Davis was a consulting nutritionist at the Alameda County Health Clinic in Oakland, California. She moved to Los Angeles two years later as consultant at the William E. Branch Clinic in Hollywood and in 1938 earned an MS in biochemistry from the University of Southern California School of Medicine. From 1931 through 1958, Davis built a thriving private practice with patients referred by physicians. She estimated that she advised 14,000 clients, often developing individualized diets to address specific health problems.

Davis' first publication was a promotional pamphlet for a milk company in 1932. Two privately printed tracts followed, *Optimum Health* (1935) and *You Can Stay Well* (1939), as did a nutrition handbook, *Vitality Through Planned Nutrition* (1942).

In 1947, Davis published *Let's Cook It Right*, in which she presented straightforward recipes and basic information about preparing nutritious food. She was critical of most cookbooks, including *The Joy of Cooking* by **Irma Rombauer**, about which she wrote, "That is the worst. Food should taste good but also build health. That book doesn't do either."

Let's Have Healthy Children (1951) contained nutritional advice for infants, children, and pregnant and lactating women. A breastfeeding proponent, Davis denounced prepared baby foods because of additives and pesticide residues.

Let's Eat Right to Keep Fit (1954) was a primer on nutrition for laypeople. It explained the functions and sources of more than 40 nutrients—vitamins, minerals, proteins, and essential fatty acids. She eschewed high sodium, refined sugar, growth hormones, and preservatives. "Thousands upon thousands of persons have studied disease," she wrote. "Almost no one has studied health."

Let's Get Well (1965) presented nutritional therapy for a panoply of ailments, including heart disease, high cholesterol, ulcers, diabetes, and arthritis. It contained over 2000 references to medical journal studies, many of which were later shown to be erroneous.

Also, during psychotherapy that began in 1953, Davis participated in early LSD experiments before the drug became illegal. She documented her experiences in *Exploring Inner Space* (1961) under the pseudonym Jane Dunlap.

With each book, Davis became more popular and more controversial. She stressed protein and natural foods in cooking, and had no use for vegetarian and macrobiotic diets, such as that advocated by Michio and **Aveline Kushi**. She disapproved of vitamin pills, but considered them necessary to compensate for inferior food. "Ideally, everything should come from wholesome food, the kind our grandparents ate at every meal."

As her books' popularity skyrocketed in the 1970's, selling 10 million copies, criticism from the medical and scientific communities mounted. Drawing on her own regimen and patient studies for examples, she preferred testimonials and anecdotes to scientific analyses. She described herself as a mediator between the medical profession and the lay consumer. "I think of myself as a newspaper reporter, who…gathers information from hundreds of journals, which most people can't understand, and I write it so that people can understand."

On the lecture circuit and in her numerous print and television interviews, Davis was an imposing figure, expounding her theories with supreme assurance. In *Cosmopolitan*, C. Robert Jennings described her "deep-throated, hell-for-leather voice that seemed better fitted to handing down Mosaic law."

From 1943 through 1953, Davis was married to George Edward Leisey and adopted two children, George Davis Leisey and Barbara Adelle Leisey (later Frodahl). In 1960, she married Frank Vernon Sieglinger, who had been her patient.

From 1948 until her death, she lived in Palos Verdes Estates near Los Angeles, where she raised organic fruits and vegetables in her yard, wrote, consulted, and played tennis and swam every day.

In 1973, at the pinnacle of her popularity, Davis was devastated to learn that she had bone-marrow cancer. She attributed it to "too many X-rays," and said, "I thought this was for people who drink soft drinks, who eat white bread, who eat refined sugar.…" Davis died in 1974.

— MM Pack

Vitamilk, 1931
Optimum Health, 1935
You Can Stay Well, 1939
Vitality Through Planned Nutrition, 1942
Let's Cook it Right, 1947, 1962
Let's Have Healthy Children, 1951, 1972
Let's Eat Right to Keep Fit, 1954, 1970
Let's Get Well, 1965

Lorenzo Delmonico

❧ 1812–1881 ❧

BORN INTO A FRENCH-SPEAKING SWISS FAMILY, LORENZO DELMONICO WAS preceded in America by his uncle John (originally and on all legal documents, Jean) and Peter (Pierre). John had been a sea captain, but in 1825 he settled in New York City, setting up a shop importing and dispensing French and Spanish wines. After a couple of years, he was joined by his older brother Peter, a confectioner. The two men established a café and pastry shop on William Street near the business district. Their high-quality food was such a success that they opened a French restaurant next door, hiring a French cook. Soon they called for other family members, including their nineteen-year-old nephew Lorenzo, to come from Switzerland to help them.

Very much a family business, Delmonico's employed many family members, and profits from the business were used to educate the younger ones. The family built a succession of new restaurants, each grander than the preceding one, moving steadily uptown to keep pace with the fashionable, wealthy set that provided their best customers. In all, the Delmonicos established about a dozen eating places, sometimes operating two or three at once; they also ran a hotel for a while. Altogether, the business lasted just short of a century, from 1825 to 1923, being sold outside the family only in 1919, the year that Prohibition was voted in.

In 1842, John Delmonico died and six years later Peter retired to his large property on Long Island, leaving the family business in the hands of Lorenzo, who

1881

remained in control of the entire operation until his death in 1881. He rose early each morning to do the marketing himself, rested at midday, and was ever-present in the restaurant in the evening, ensuring that his high standards of good food, good service, and proper decorum were strictly maintained.

Delmonico's became the place for everybody who was anybody, or wished to be somebody, to be seen. Every U.S. president who came to New York ate there, from James Monroe to William McKinley; the president after McKinley, Theodore Roosevelt, was a native New Yorker and well-acquainted with Delmonico's throughout his life. The Delmonico restaurants also hosted the soprano Jenny Lind, the war hero and gourmet Winifred Scott, and in 1860 the Prince of Wales ([much] later Edward VII). New York society's "Four Hundred" chose Delmonico's for countless balls and banquets. Mark Twain celebrated his seventieth birthday there. In 1868, Charles Dickens spoke at a dinner at Delmonico's; the quality of food, setting, and service prompted him formally to retract his earlier critical remarks about American dining, which he had published in *Martin Chuzzlewit* and *American Notes*, and he promised to add a correction to future editions of these books. **Diamond Jim Brady** was a regular, often accompanied by his good friend Lillian Russell. There were of course other exquisite restaurants in New York—the Maison Dorée, the Waldorf-Astoria, or Sherry's—but Delmonico's was always in the top tier.

The food at all the Delmonico restaurants was always good. Among the outstanding chefs who worked there over the years were John Lux; Felix Delice; Charles Lallouette; Eugene Laperruque; M. Grevillet; Jules Harder (who moved to San Francisco's lavish new Palace Hotel in the early 1870's); Alessandro Filippini, who also managed one of the Delmonico restaurants and wrote *The Table* (1889), a household book for housewives, as well as cookbooks for railroads; and the incomparable Charles Ranhofer, who oversaw every detail of the kitchen, personally tasting each dish, and who wrote the 1183-page *The Epicurean* (1894) for professional chefs. Numerous chefs all over New York got their start in the kitchens of a Delmonico's restaurant. Not only the chefs, but many of the waiters also achieved prominence: The names of the untiring Louis, of Oscar Tschirky (later known as "Oscar of the Waldorf"), of the loyal headwaiter Philippe, and of old John Klages at the bar are still recognized today.

The Delmonico family was active in the French community of New York City; they supported the construction of the first French church there, St. Vincent de Paul, and of Our Lady of Grace in Hoboken. At the mature age of 41, Lorenzo chose a bride from this community. Clemence Charon Miège had been born and raised in Sèvres, France, where her father was director of the famous porcelain factory. She was a widow, and Lorenzo treated her children and grandchildren as his own.

At Lorenzo's death, control of the Delmonico empire passed to his nephew, Charles Delmonico, who apparently suffered a nervous breakdown: In 1884 he wandered off in a blizzard and perished in the snow. Control of the business— but not ownership—then passed to Charles' nephew, Charles Delmonico Crist, who obtained permission from the state legislature to call himself Charles Crist Delmonico. In 1897, he opened the final Delmonico's restaurant, even further uptown at Fifth Avenue and Forty-fourth Street, and even more luxurious than any of the earlier ones. At Charles Crist's sudden death in 1901, his aunt Rosa Delmonico, who had inherited half-ownership of the business from the first Charles Delmonico, took over nominal control but in fact left management to the staff. This method was adopted in turn by her niece and successor, Josephine Crist, who also added Delmonico to her name. The restaurants continued to uphold their fine reputation, but the company's debts began to mount, due mostly to unwise loans, family squabbles, heavy spending by Josephine, and perhaps increased competition. The private family firm became a stock company in 1908, giving it a fresh infusion of capital; nonetheless, by 1919 the company had sold off all its properties.

World War I changed the nature of society, and Prohibition changed fine dining in America. In 1923, the new owner closed the restaurant. But the cachet of the name Delmonico's remains so potent that to this day many other establishments make good use of it.

— ALICE ARNDT

Jack Cecil Drummond

1891–1952

DRUMMOND, AN ENGLISH BIOCHEMIST, FOOD HISTORIAN, AND nutritional-policy advisor, was born in Leicester on January 12, 1891. He studied chemistry at East London College, where he met Mabel Helen Straw; they were married in 1915. His first position was as research assistant in physiology at King's College, London. In 1914 he moved to a similar post at the Cancer Hospital Research Institute, where the biochemist Casimir Funk had already begun a series of pioneering "vitamine" studies. As Funk's colleague and successor at the institute and, after 1919, as research assistant at University College, London, Drummond participated in much early vitamin research and was responsible for amending Funk's term *vitamine* (based on an erroneous chemical assumption) to *vitamin*. Named professor of biochemistry at UCL in 1922, he was instrumental in the rapid growth of biochemistry as a research field in the 1920's and 1930's.

Drummond also took a lively interest in food from other standpoints. He was an early member of **André L. Simon**'s Wine and Food Society. In the late 1930's he began working on a history of English food in collaboration with his former student and secretary, Anne Wilbraham, whom he married in 1940 after divorcing his first wife. *The Englishman's Food: A History of Five Centuries of English Diet* was published in 1939. (The revised version that Drummond was planning at the start of the 1950's would be posthumously realized by his colleague Dorothy Hollingsworth and published in 1957.) The work surveyed the changing makeup of the English food supply for people of varied circumstances—rich and poor, young and old, city-dwellers and country folk—from roughly the fifteenth to the twentieth century. The focus, as the subtitle suggests, is on nutrition rather than cookery, but as a history of a nation's food, combining scholarship and popular appeal, the work remains unsurpassed.

After the outbreak of World War II, Drummond at once began working with the newly instituted Ministry of Food. On February 1, 1940 he was named scientific advisor to the ministry. He was thenceforth the person principally responsible for devising national nutrition initiatives to be publicized and popularized by the Minister of Food, Lord Woolton. Among these measures were encouraging commercial vegetable production and private "Dig for Victory" gardens, along with increased consumption of raw salads and vegetables prepared so as to conserve vitamins; increasing domestic milk production and imports of milk-based products; introducing dehydrated foods like powdered egg; and mandating the use of "National Flour"—calcium-fortified flour that contained at least 85 percent of the wheat endosperm—in bread.

Drummond and a team of experts also drew up a rationing and distribution system for fair allotment of scarce commodities, including meat, fats, sugar, and tea, with extra allowances of items like milk and orange juice and such supplements as cod-liver oil for pregnant women, nursing mothers, and small children. Though the food program was widely disliked and such patriotic dishes as "Woolton pie" (a baked farrago of potatoes and any available vegetables) were endured rather than enjoyed, the incidence of deficiency diseases in England fell to historic lows during the war, while infant and child mortality declined sharply. Counter to all previous experience, the nutritional status of the British population *improved* during more than five years of wartime privations. The Ministry of Food's wartime work, as largely planned by Drummond, is widely regarded as one of the most successful governmental applications of nutritional knowledge to public-health purposes.

In 1944 Drummond was knighted for his services to the nation. He was active in devising food-relief measures for both general civilian populations and concentration-camp victims in liberated Europe. In 1945 he left the university to accept a position as director of research at Boots Pure Drug Company Ltd., a pharmaceutical firm that also owned a chain of drugstores, and in 1946 he retired from the ministry. In 1952 Sir Jack, Lady Drummond, and their only child, the ten-year-old Elizabeth, were motoring in the foothills of the French Alps when all three were found (August 5) brutally murdered in a field near Lurs, where they had apparently been camping overnight. The crime, of which an elderly local resident was eventually convicted, has been the subject of various Cold War conspiracy theories, none ever corroborated by definite evidence.

— ANNE MENDELSON

The Englishman's Food: A History of Five Centuries of English Diet (with Anne Wilbraham), 1939
The Englishman's Food: A History of Five Centuries of English Diet, Revised and with a new chapter by D. F. Hollingsworth (with Anne Wilbraham), 1957

Hildagonda J. Duckitt

1840–1905

HILDAGONDA JOHANNA DUCKITT, WHO HAS BEEN CALLED "SOUTH AFRICA'S **Mrs. Beeton**," wrote one of the earliest, and one of the most popular, South African cookbooks, which was reprinted for more than two and a half decades. Her cooking combines the favorites of her English paternal ancestors with the dishes of her Dutch mother. In addition, she gathered recipes from various South African families living on or near the Cape Peninsula, and from travelers, so that East Indian, Malay, German and Huguenot influences were represented in her repertory as well.

Hilda was born and grew up at "Groote Poste," a large farm occupying land that had once belonged to the East India Company. With her parents and nine siblings, and numerous servants and workers of all kinds on the farm, it was necessary to kill a sheep every morning, and sometimes a stall-fed ox as well, to feed them all. Since the farm was so far from any town, everything possible was made at home. Candles and soap were made from the fat of sheep and goats. Grapes were converted into wine, jam, and raisins. The oven was heated twice a week for baking bread, cakes, and other dainties. Fruits and some vegetables were preserved as a matter of course. The cook might also wrestle with the hind leg of an ox, from which she would "cut out in a long tongue-shape" about six or eight pounds of beef "from the thigh-bone down to the knee-joint. There are two such pieces in each leg, being quite encased in a fleecy skin." In addition, the daughters of the family supervised the dairy, gardened, and sewed their own dresses. "I often wonder," Hilda mused late in her life, "whether people had more energy or strength in those days, for certainly nothing seemed to be a trouble or worry then, though we did so much of planning, arranging, and carrying things out ourselves ....and with all these home supplies it never seemed a difficulty to have friends staying in the house."

The family played as hard as it worked. Day-long drives in horse-drawn carts over what Hilda called "heavy roads" brought them, with baskets full of provisions, to visits on other farms in the area. Officers and distinguished guests were included in the picnics, dinners, and balls whenever their ships stopped at the Cape. Hilda met such people as the distinguished botanical artist Marianne North, the future King George V, and Queen Mary, and of course the naval lieutenant William Brown, to whom she became engaged in about 1860.

Hilda waited for seven years while Lt. Brown pursued his career in the Navy. At last she set out from home for the ship that would take her to their wedding in England, but on the way received a letter from her fiancé that ended the engagement.

After her parents' deaths, her older brother Jacob inherited the farm; Hilda and her sisters ran the household for him for several years until he married. Hilda continued to perfect her culinary skills. Her baked goods and preserves were in great demand at church bazaars. She also gave cooking demonstrations to young housewives.

In 1891, the London publishers Chapman and Hall brought out *Hilda's "Where Is It?" of Recipes* both in England and South Africa. The book was an enormous success. In it, Hilda lists her recipes alphabetically, and for many of them she credits her source: "Bobotie: A Delicate Indian Minced Curry. Malay or Indian. My Mother's," "Ginger Beer: Mrs. J. Cloete's" (her eldest sister married into the Cloete family), "Punch–Milk: Admiral Etheridge's, Madras," "Pudding–Bread and Butter: From a Dutch Family Cookery Book, Over One Hundred Years Old," and so on. A few dishes are marked as being particularly delicious. Hilda's recipes are clearly and succinctly written, and there are many hints for making the recipes turn out well, or for attractive presentations.

Although perhaps the most popular of her time, Hilda's was not the first South African cookbook. Four others preceded hers. The earliest was *Mondprovisie Boekje* (1710) written in South Africa by Johanna van Riebeck, who offered dishes suitable for long sea voyages. In 1889, Mrs. A. B. Barnes published *The Colonial Household Guide by a Housewife of the Colony* for newly arrived British women; Hilda noted that "all Colonists should get it." The following year saw both *De Suid Afrikaanse Kook-, Koek- en Resepte Boek*, the first cookbook in Afrikaans, by E. J. Dijkman, the English bride of an up-country missionary, and *Cape Cookery: Simple yet Distinctive* by Allie G. Hewitt.

At the end of her life, Hilda and her sister Bessie kept house, with one servant, in a small house with a garden and a poultry run in a suburb of Cape Town. There she wrote down her happy memories, along with more recipes and housekeeping advice, in her *Diary of a Cape Housekeeper*. She died in 1905. Since her death, several collections of recipes taken from her two books have been published with titles such as *Hildagonda Duckitt's Book of Recipes* and *Traditional South African Cookery*.

Hildagonda Duckitt's cookbooks, representing the tastes of well-to-do white burghers at the end of the nineteenth century, remain of great historical as well as practical interest. However, it would be a mistake to regard her recipes as representative of all of South African cooking. South African culinary historian Renata Coetzee points out that there are several other culinary cultures prominent in South Africa: the foods of the veld from the Khoi-Khoi and San people of the Cape; the cuisines based on grains, such as sorghum, from the tribes further north; Malay foods with their fine spices and *halal* principles; Jewish dishes from both Ashkenazi and Sephardi traditions; and Indian cookery, beginning with that of the sugar workers who came to Durban from Calcutta in 1860.

— ALICE ARNDT

Hilda's "Where Is It?" of Recipes: Containing, amongst other practical and tried recipes, many old Cape, Indian, and Malay Dishes and Preserves; also directions for polishing furniture, cleaning silk etc. and a collection of home remedies in case of sickness, 1891
Hilda's Diary of a Cape Housekeeper: Being a chronicle of daily events and monthly work in a Cape household, with numerous cooking recipes, and notes on gardening, poultry keeping, etc, 1902

E

Eisai

✲ 1141–1215 ✲

ALSO CALLED: Myōan Yōsai

MYŌAN EISAI (ALSO KNOWN AS YŌSAI) BROUGHT TEA SEEDS FROM CHINA to Japan and spread the practice of drinking *matcha*, or whipped pow-dered green tea. He was a Japanese monk, the founder of the Rinzai sect of Zen Buddhism in Japan.

Eisai was born in 1141 in Bitchū province, which is now part of Okaya-ma Prefecture. His father reportedly served as the chief priest of the Kib-itsu Shrine and at one time studied Tendai Buddhism. Through his father's various connections, Eisai entered Annoyji temple and began studying Buddhism in the Shingon tradition. At age thirteen, he went to Enryakuji, the famous Tendai temple on Mount Hiei, just outside Kyoto. There he became a monk and, for the next fourteen years, studied the Lotus Sutra, along with the writings of Saichō, founder of the Tendai sect of Buddhism.

In those times, little distinction existed between religious and secular life—the Buddhist clergy participated in the concerns of the state and the ruler of the state oversaw the affairs of the Buddhist clergy. Convinced the Buddhist schools needed moral and social reform, Eisai made a five-month-long pilgrimage to Song (Sung) China in 1168. For the next five months he visited Tendai (Chinese: T'ien-t'ai) monasteries and gathered numerous Tendai texts. When he returned home, he immersed himself in the Tendai teachings, hoping to help rekindle the true nature of the faith among the Buddhist community.

In 1187 Eisai sailed, once again, to China. From there, he hoped to journey to India to see where Buddha had lived and taught. When the Chinese government refused to grant him permission to travel beyond its borders, Eisai made a life-changing decision: he would travel to Mount T'ien-t'ai near Hangzhou and begin studying Zen (Chinese: Ch'an) Buddhism under the Rinzai (Chinese: Lin-Ch'i) master Xu'an Huai-chang, who eventually would certify Eisai's enlightenment.

For the next four years Eisai's spiritual practice consisted of meditation, koan study, and various monastic rituals. He also closely followed the drinking customs

Portrait of Eisai on a silk hanging scroll from the 14th or 15th century. The scroll belongs to the Ryōsoku-in Temple in Kyoto.

and medicinal uses of tea, sharing with fellow monks the benefits of drinking whipped green tea as a stimulant during their meditations. When he returned to Japan in 1191 at the age of 50, he brought back his newfound Rinzai Zen teachings, along with high-quality tea seeds and supplies of powdered green tea. The seeds were cultivated near Kyoto and produced what tea connoisseurs would consider Japan's "true tea," later used in the tea ceremony.

Eisai's passion for tea sprang from his conviction that it could cure numerous ills. He promoted its health benefits in a written work, *Kissa Yōjōki (On Drinking Tea and Nourishing Life)*, of which two slightly different versions exist, one dated 1211 and the other 1214. Based on predominantly Chinese sources, the first half of the treatise focuses on the health properties of tea and continually states, "Tea is an elixir for the maintenance of life." The text's second half discusses various natural remedies for preventing and curing disease. In 1214 Eisai gave a copy of the *Kissa Yōjōki* to the shogun Minamoto Sanetomo, along with some powdered green tea, in part to cure the leader's hangover after a night of heavy drinking, but also to help promote the use of tea for its curative properties.

Following the traditional Chinese method, Japanese Zen monks would steam, dry, and then grind the tiny green tea leaves into a fine powder and whip it with a bamboo whisk in boiling water to create a thick medicinal drink. Over time, many of the monks became tea masters and started whipping green tea for the imperial court, and by the early fourteenth century tea-drinking had become a social event, and powdered green tea became a standard item on the imperial court's list of imported luxuries.

The communal drinking of tea began to take on a spiritual dimension under several tea masters including, in the sixteenth century, **Sen no Rikyū,** a Zen practitioner universally heralded as the most important tea master who ever lived.

While Eisai's proposals for tea-drinking garnered much support from the monks at Enryakuji, they rejected his Chinese Zen teachings. In 1199 he moved to Kamukura to seek the patronage of the Minamoto clan in the newly established Kamakura shogunate. The Minamotos received him warmly and gave him funds to establish two Zen temples: Shofukuji in Kyushu and then Kenninji in Kyoto. Eisai moved to Kenninji in 1202, where he served as its founder-abbot and practiced Zen meditation, along with Tendai textual study, Shingon trantric practices, and preceptual discipline.

Eisai died in 1215 at the age of 75. Upon his death he was given the title "Master of a Thousand Lights," in part because his body was said to have become radiant upon performing a rain dance in China, but also because he brought the light of Zen to Japan.

— VICTORIA ABBOTT RICCARDI

Shukke taikō (Essentials of Monastic Life), 1192
Kōzen gokoku ron (Promulgation of Zen as a Defense of the Nation), 1198
Nihon buppō chūkō gammon (A Plea for the Revival of Japanese Buddhism), 1204
Kissa Yōjōki (On Drinking Tea and Nourishing Life), 1211 and 1214

Emy

⁂ FL. 1768 ⁂

IN 1768, MONSIEUR EMY WROTE THE FIRST BOOK EXCLUSIVELY DEVOTED TO ICES and ice creams. That much we know. We do not know his first name, the dates of his birth or death, the names of his employers, or how he came to be a wonderfully talented confectioner.

Emy's book was called *L'Art de Bien Faire les Glaces d'Office; ou Les Vrais Principes Pour congeler tous les Rafraichissemens. La manière de préparer toutes sortes de Compositions, la façon de les faire prendre, d'en former des Fruits, Cannelons, & toutes sortes de Fromages. Le tout expliqué avec précision selon l'usage actuel. Avec un traité sur les mousses. Ouvrage très-utile à ceux qui font des Glaces ou Fromages glacés. Par M. Émy, Officier.* It was published in Paris by Le Clerc.

The title *officier* meant Emy was in charge of the *office* or cool kitchen, now called the *garde manger*, where pastries, ices, distilled liqueurs, marzipans, jellies, and other confections were prepared. It was a responsible position and, in a large household, the *officier* would supervise one or more assistants.

L'Art de Bien Faire les Glaces d'Office was a manual that explained everything one needed to know about creating ices and ice creams. Written for other *officiers*, it covered the science and techniques of freezing, the necessary utensils, and even health issues. Emy thought eating too much ice cream caused colic, but also believed that people got sick when they didn't have enough ice cream.

Emy wrote about the quality and characteristics of cream, fruits, and other ingredients, told his readers what to do if ices didn't freeze properly and, most important, gave them lots of recipes. His ice creams included anise, chestnut, chocolate, clove, coffee, crème brulée, orange-flower, pistachio, rye bread, saffron, strawberry, truffle (the fungus, not the chocolate), vanilla, and an ice cream made with Parmesan and Gruyère cheeses. Among his ices were apricot, cherry, peach, pear, pineapple, pomegranate, quince, rose, strawberry, and violet. He also provided recipes for uncooked frozen creams and mousses.

Frontispiece from L'Art de Bien Faire les Glaces d'Office

A man of strong opinions, Emy wrote that earlier ices had not been well made despite their popularity and despite the fact that they were served at the most sumptuous tables. Now, he claimed, they were "*parfaites.*" He crowned the pineapple king of fruits and the strawberry queen. He preferred the oranges of Malta to those of Provence.

Emy knew that professional cooks were often called upon to create dishes they might not like or even approve of, so he gave instructions for them even as he expressed his disapproval. For example, he didn't think it was a good idea to use wines or spirits in ices because they didn't freeze properly—but he offered recipes for them anyway. He couldn't resist adding that he did not regard the mixtures as excellent.

Emy prized the beauty of ices and ice creams that were molded and tinted to resemble peaches or lemons or even a bunch of asparagus. But, he wrote, some people were afraid colored ices contained poison, and since food should inspire desire rather than fear, it was better not to tint them. Then he gave instructions for coloring them anyway in case one were asked to do so.

A believer in the seasonal approach to ice cream, Emy preferred cinnamon or chocolate ice creams in winter, strawberry in summer when the berries were bursting with flavor. Many of his recipes start with a phrase such as, "Pick the most fragrant…" or "Choose the ripest…." But he included recipes that substituted marmalade for fresh fruit in winter, since a professional would need to know how.

Emy urged his readers to taste, taste, taste, and even suggested they wash their mouths out between tastings so one flavor wouldn't affect the next. He pointed out that freezing diminished flavor, so ices had to taste almost too strong when warm to be just right when icy cold. He warned that the bitter white pith under lemon and orange peel shouldn't be used. It's all sound advice today. Clearly Emy was a consummate professional who knew what he was writing about. If only we knew more about him.

L'Art de Bien Faire les Glaces d'Office closes with two pages of very small type wherein Louis, by the grace of God, King of France and Navarre, gave Emy permission to publish it. We are grateful.

— JERI QUINZIO

L'Art de Bien Faire les Glaces d'Office; ou Les Vrais Principes pour congeler tous les Rafraichissemens. La manière de préparer toutes sortes de Compositions, la façon de les faire prendre, d'en former des Fruits, Cannelons, & toutes sortes de Fromages. Le tout expliqué avec précision selon l'usage actuel. Avec un traité sur les mousses. Ouvrage très-utile à ceux qui font des Glaces ou Fromages glacés (The Art of Making Ices for the Garde Manger; or The True Principles Behind Freezing All Kinds of Refreshments. The Way to Prepare All Sorts of Mixtures, How to Make Them Set, How to Shape Them Into Fruits, Cannelons & All Sorts of Cheeses. All Explained Precisely and According to Current Practice. Along With a Treatise on Mousses. A Very Useful Work for All Those Who Make Ices and Ice Creams), 1768

Epicurus

※ 341–270 BC ※

Bust of Epicurus in the National Archaeological Museum in Naples

TODAY, AN EPICURE, OR EPICUREAN, IS AN INDIVIDUAL WHO ENJOYS, AND IS knowledgeable about and desirous of fine foods and wines. He is seen as tasteful, refined, and elegant; and many food companies proudly label themselves "epicurean." At various times in the past, however—as in some circles today—the hedonistic epicure was regarded as reprehensible for his self-indulgence and love of luxurious living.

Epicurus, the eponymous Greek philosopher of Epicureanism, was born in 341 BC of Athenian parents on the island of Samos. His father, Neocles, a school teacher, was probably his first instructor; later he traveled to various Greek cities in Asia Minor to continue his studies.

Epicurus' philosophy was atomistic: Everything, including the human body and soul, is composed of atoms. At the death of an individual, the atoms of the soul are simply disbanded; therefore, since there is no afterlife, there is no need to fear death. The gods, Epicurus taught, are uninterested in the affairs of mortals, so there is no need to fear them either. Thus the mind is relieved of two common sources of distress. Knowledge is obtained through the senses, and pleasure is the good sought by each person. However, the pleasures of the original Epicureans were quite restrained; rational thought, they believed, would reject the type of sensual pleasure that costs too much in distressful consequences. Happiness is based on tranquility and peace of mind.

In 306 BC Epicurus bought a house and a garden in Athens; he lived there the rest of his life, teaching and writing. The fact that women were accepted into the Epicurean school led to the slander that sexual orgies took place there, and the joyful meals of the community were sometimes labeled excessive, when in fact meals often consisted of water, barley bread, and the vegetables they grew themselves in the garden.

Epicurus inspired great love in his followers, and he was generous and affectionate toward them. Friendship was highly valued by both teacher and students. Epicurus bore admirably the painful disease—possibly prostatitis—of which he died in 270. There is some speculation that he used a prototype of the wheelchair to get around Athens at the end of his life.

Epicureanism continued to be popular in the Greek world, and later in the Roman world, for eight centuries. Excavations at Herculaneum, a town buried by the eruption of Mt. Vesuvius in AD 79, have unearthed papyrus scrolls of Epicurean works, and many Roman writers, including Cicero, Lucretius, and Seneca, commented on or adopted parts of Epicurean thought. This school of philosophy, along with Stoicism and other pagan beliefs, was eclipsed by Christianity around the fourth century, although it has been revived occasionally, most notably in the Renaissance and in modern times.

— ALICE ARNDT

Henriette Schønberg Erken ❦ 1866–1953 ❦

The cover of the 23rd edition of Erken's cookbook boasts of 240,000 copies in print.

NORWAY'S FIRST FOOD GURU, HENRIETTE SCHØNBERG Erken, was a prolific cookbook author. Through teaching and demonstrations in addition to writing, she influenced nearly two generations of the Norwegian people, shaping their habits with regard to both daily food and food for special occasions.

Such a career was not what her parents had in mind when Henriette was born in Oslo in 1866. Her father, a professor at Oslo (then Kristiania) University, tried to dissuade her from writing a cookbook: His opinion was that a lady of her good background should not deal with public cooking!

But Henriette's interest in cooking could not be curbed and she developed her culinary abilities at home, supervised by her mother, who was an excellent cook. She completed a six-week course for teachers of what would later be called "domestic science" and, in 1893, at the age of 27, was given an appointment as a teacher at Miss Bonnevies' School in Oslo. After a few years she felt she wanted to increase her competence, and she joined the newly started State (that is, National) School for Domestic Science. She also took courses in cookery in Berlin and later passed the diploma examination at the Edinburgh School of Cookery, one of Europe's pioneer institutions in this field. (It is now the Edinburgh College of Domestic Science.) Desiring to publicize her own ideas, she began in 1897 to write a regular column for the women's magazine *Urd*. At the same time she was the head of Norwegian Women's Association, which taught home economics to young mothers and housemaids.

In 1902 Henriette married Colonel Albert Erken and moved with him to Levanger (northeast of Trondheim) when he was stationed there. Henriette taught cooking courses there as well. Then in 1908 they bought a big farm, Dystingbo, in southeastern Norway, where she lived for the rest of her life. She died in 1953.

It was at Dystingbo that Henriette wrote her most important cookbooks. A hard worker, she would get up at four o clock in the morning to have two hours' peace for writing before the rest of the house started to stir. They had 40 people—not counting her students—at table every day.

Dystingbo became the center for her teaching. She started ten-month courses and later on two-year courses for teachers. She continued this activity until 1927, even after being widowed in 1916. She also traveled around the country to give demonstrations and lectures. Her lectures could be quite dramatic: Often she would not appear on stage as she was being introduced; then suddenly a stage curtain would open, revealing Henriette in front of a table filled with tantalizing dishes.

But even if Henriette Schønberg Erken was a power in herself, it is as an author of cookbooks that she is most famous. She was very productive, and her books disseminated useful information about healthy ways of eating and rational housekeeping. A practical person, she emphasized the importance of keeping food costs low while nonetheless including the right nourishment. Her standard Norwegian work is *Stor Kokebok (The Big Cook Book),* first published in 1912, which covers cooking, baking, preserving, winemaking, slaughtering, canning, menus, and menus for sick people.

In her introduction to *Stor Kokebok,* she writes, "My primary aim with this book has been, after twenty years of teaching, to collect my recipes, the simpler as well as the fancy ones, into one big volume. Housewives will see that monotony does not have to occur in their households, and that they themselves will be able to create their own menus according to their budgets, for both everyday and festive occasions."

— Kari W. Çağatay

Cook Book for School and Home, 1895 (Originally co-authored with physiologist Caroline Sten). Ninth edition, 1914
Cook Book 1, 1903
Cook Book 2, 1904
Cook Book for Frugal Housewives, 1905
Home Baking and Practical Hints, 1908
Stor Kokebok (The Big Cook Book), 1912. Revised 1916
Reasonable Food, 1914

Auguste Escoffier

⚜ 1846–1935 ⚜

ALSO CALLED: Georges Auguste Escoffier

OF ALL THE FAMOUS CHEFS IN MODERN WESTERN HISTORY, NONE HAS HAD greater impact or been more emulated than Auguste Escoffier. Resounding down the years, his name has come to represent *haute cuisine,* specifically a now classic French style. He was an innovator in public dining, a revolutionary in the kitchen, and the creator of the popular image of the star chef. In a larger cultural sense, Escoffier's name implies a cultural style: a good and rich life through appreciation of the subtle arts of cookery.

Escoffier was born into family of modest but comfortable circumstances in Villeneuve-Loubet, near Nice. He was named Georges Auguste Escoffier, but the great chef always signed his books simply "Auguste Escoffier," or even just "A. Escoffier." His father was a blacksmith, school teacher, and village mayor who gave his son a formal education to the age of thirteen and then apprenticed him to his brother, François, who owned a popular restaurant in Nice. It was just as well that Auguste had learned much about country cooking from his grandmother, whose Provençal recipes he used through the rest of his life.

Like all culinary apprenticeships of the era, Escoffier's was hard. The kitchen was from hell: hot, badly organized, and under the absolute control of a demanding chef who enforced his will with foul language, blows, and kicks. From this experience arose Escoffier's resolve to reform the organization and culture of professional cooking. *Chefs de cuisine* should no longer be mere tradesmen but honored for practicing what was, after all, a science and art. These principles informed all of Escoffier's career.

Endowed with impeccable gustatory ability—he claimed to be able to tell the ingredients in a dish by smell alone—and a capacity for hard work, Escoffier climbed up the restaurant hierarchy. In 1865 he was called to the celebrated Parisian restaurant, Le Petit Moulin Rouge. There he filled every position, finally becoming head chef in 1873, after his service in the army during the Franco-Prussian War. Fame for his brilliant cooking brought celebrities, theater performers, and nobility alike, all of whom the rising culinary star cultivated. He began the practice of naming newly created dishes for them; *pêche Melba*, named in 1893 in honor of the opera diva Nellie Melba, is among the most famous.

In 1884 Escoffier accepted manager **César Ritz**'s invitation to run the kitchens of Monte Carlo's popular Grand Hotel. Ritz and his chef formed a team that would create the modern hotel, with splendid cuisine as one of its important features. Escoffier immediately began in Monte Carlo the kitchen and menu reforms already begun in Paris. Among them were changes in the canons of French cuisine set out by **Antonin Carême** early in the century, although Escoffier paid sincere tribute to his predecessor. Recipes were simplified, in accordance with the watchword *faites simple*, by which was meant a refinement of taste and balance of flavors. Presentations changed dramatically. Instead of

Frontispiece from his
Les fleurs en cire

the grand sculptures in which Carême gloried, table decor referred to the dishes served, like a good sauce enhancing a central ingredient. (A fine artist, the chef was not averse to ice sculptures.) Finally, Escoffier embraced and popularized a new trend in service: Instead of large numbers of varied dishes served all at once, the Grand Hotel did it *à la Russe*, one dish per course, presented in sequence. Though his menus called for appetizers, Escoffier thought that a good soup was the best beginning for a meal, and not some sharply flavored starter that would spoil the diner's taste for what was to follow. He also hated smoking in restaurants for the same reason.

Ritz had developed new standards of hospitality emphasizing luxury, convenience, and comfort for guests. Like the industries of the day, hotels were to be run with new standards of efficiency that meant division of labor according to specific task. Escoffier shared this view and when both men were brought to the new Savoy Hotel in London in 1890, they instituted the new methods. First, new standards of cleanliness were effected—kitchens were scrupulously cleaned each day and kept spotless. With a view towards speedy service at correct temperatures, Escoffier divided his staff into teams headed by chefs. Each *brigade de cuisine* was specialized, from fish, meat, and vegetable preparations, to *saucier* and *garde-manger*. To compose a single dish each team prepared one element at roughly the same time, adding each as the dish was passed to it. After inspection by the head chef, the dish was sent to the table. These methods remain the standards for restaurants and hotel dining rooms.

Escoffier was a snob about food and wine, never learning English during his twenty years in that country for fear that it would coarsen his French cookery (he thought even less of German). Though he actively courted celebrities—the playboy Prince of Wales, later King Edward VII, was one of his admirers—Escoffier was also interested in educating a broad public about good cooking. *Le Guide Culinaire* first published in 1903 is the virtual bible of classic French cookery, as is *Ma Cuisine* (1934). Many Escoffier recipes remain in the modern repertoire, from *Tournedos Rossini* to Peach Melba, but others seem antiquated: *Sole Normande* calls for poached oysters, shrimp tails, mushrooms, meat glaze, truffles, smelts, and crayfish.

Escoffier was a prolific writer; his many articles in culinary journals often delved into aspects of food, and he was keenly interested in food history, particularly if it were French. His interest in regional cuisines and wines set a standard for culinary studies the world over. One might see his insistence on the centrality of French cuisine as an act of patriotism or chauvinism. The great chef was certainly a French patriot, a war veteran, but also an advocate for peace. Engaged to cater meals on the German cruise ship, *Amerika* in 1906, Escoffier met Kaiser Willhelm II and pleaded for peace. The Kaiser is reported to have told him, "I am the Emperor of Germany, but you are the emperor of chefs."

Though a member of world's social elite by reason of celebrity and personality (a small dapper man, fastidious in grooming and attire) he had a social conscience. In 1910 he published a tract calling for national social programs in Britain to aid the poor, principally by cutting arms expenditures. Seeing education as a way out of poverty, he helped found England's first culinary school in 1910, at the Westminster Technical Institute. Among other charitable organizations he helped was the Little Sisters of the Poor to whom he donated kitchen leftovers for impoverished Londoners. Thus Escoffier anticipated modern chefs' interest in modern social programs and culinary education.

By his 50's Escoffier was a world-wide celebrity, honored and cheered wherever he went. His publications, food products made by his own company under the Escoffier label, the many brilliant chefs he trained, and his rubbing elbows with the great and famous made Auguste Escoffier the very model of the modern celebrity chef. Only he was the original.

— BRUCE KRAIG

L'Aide Mémoire culinaire: suivi d'une étude sur les vins français et étrangers à l'usage des cuisiniers, mâtres-hôtel et garçons de restaurant, 1900

Le Guide Culinaire: Aide-Mémoire de cuisine pratique, 1903. Revised 1907, 1912, 1921

A Guide to Modern Cookery, 1907

Les Fleurs en Cire, 1910

Le Carnet d'Epicure, 1911

Le Livre des Menus: complément indispensable du Guide culinaire (with Philéas Gilbert et Emile Fetu), 1912

Le Riz: l'aliment, lemeilleur, le plus nutrite, 1927

La Morue, 1929

Ma Cuisine: 2500 recettes, 1934

Le Guide Culinaire: The Complete Guide to the Art of Modern Cookery, 1979. (Complete translation) Reprinted 1983

The Escoffier Cookbook and Guide to the Fine Art of Cookery for Connoisseurs, Chefs, Epicures, 1941. (U.S. edition, partial translation with fewer than 3000 recipes) Reprinted 1969, 1989

Souvenirs inédits: 75 ans au service de l'art culinaire (Writings by Auguste Escoffier, compiled by his grandson Pierre Escoffier and his great-grandson Marcel Escoffier), 1985

Auguste Escoffier: Memories of my Life (translation of Souvenirs inédits, by Auguste Escoffier's great-granddaughter-in-law Laurence Escoffier), 1997

F

N. K. Fairbank

❧ 1829–1903 ❧

ALSO CALLED: Nathaniel Kellogg Fairbank

The American industrial revolution gave rise to a great many highly successful manufactured food products, among them N. K. Fairbank's Cottolene, a factory-made shortening sold as a replacement for lard. It was the first such product on the market; later competitors were Swift's Cotosuet (1893) and Proctor and Gamble's Crisco (1911).

Born in Sodus, New York, Fairbank found his calling in the growing Midwest, a region of considerable opportunity. In 1855 he moved to Chicago, then a city of 80,000 people, to work for David Dow in grain merchandizing, and a decade later launched his own career by developing stockyards and processing canned meats and lard. His success may be judged by the fact that, immediately after the great fire of 1871, he was named head of the Employment Committee of the Chicago Relief and Aid Society; by 1879 he was president of the trustees of the University of Chicago. By the 1880's, he not only owned the Standard Cattle Company, an important meat packer, but had also invested heavily in new railroad lines connecting Chicago to its southern and midwestern resources and customers.

Fairbank recognized the possibilities in the food industry's waste products; he was no doubt aware that one such product, cottonseed oil, was exported to Europe and used as an olive-oil adulterant and, in the 1870's, was being successfully substituted for animal fat in the manufacture of oleomargarine, first produced in France and, in 1873, in the United States. He concocted Cottolene from beef tallow (ten percent) and cottonseed oil (ninety percent); production began in the early 1880's.

The great success of Cottolene was due to Fairbank's ability to produce an inexpensive and durable product that presumably raised the nutritional standards of its day, and then to market it with great energy, flair, and imagination. This involved the kind of vertical integration that journalistic muckrakers and anti-trust laws would later attack: In Fairbank's case, ownership of cattle, stockyards, food-processing factories, and distribution channels. N. K. Fairbank and Co. measured its success internationally, with offices in Canada, the United

Kingdom, and Germany as well as Chicago, St. Louis, New York, Boston, Philadelphia, and Pittsburgh.

Fairbank was doubtless ahead of his time in offering two competing products, lard and Cottolene, and advertising them both. On behalf of Cottolene, his company contributed to giving lard a bad name, calling it a product of "filthy swine," and describing it as impure and indigestible. Fairbank broadsides carried such headlines as "The Passing of Lard" and "Are You a Lard Eater?" One wonders whether he foresaw the demise of pork fat and produced Cottolene simply to keep up with the market. And one wonders how it was that housewives did not see for themselves the superiority of lard.

Fairbank made the case for Cottolene by hiring physicians, nutritionists, and noted cookbook authors—such as **Juliet Corson**— to write testimonials, which he included in Cottolene pamphlets and cookbooks. Perhaps the most famous of these was *Home Helps* (1900) by Mrs. **Sarah Tyson Rorer**, principal of the Philadelphia Cooking School. Some of his pamphlets, such as *What Hetty Learned at School* and *Poems for Pinafore People*, were aimed at children, on the assumption that their mothers would read aloud the entertaining and somewhat educational stories and verses and be influenced by the advertising content. ("Molly's in the kitchen / Baking pumpkin pies, / With COTTOLENE to help her; / which shows that Molly's wise.") Others, like *Cooks of All Nations,* aimed at the mother's edification. Fairbank also promoted baking contests and gave away trade cards, calendars and such items as tip trays, doughnut cutters, pie tins, and measuring cups in apparently inexhaustible quantities. His advertising was nothing if not entertaining: Early lard trade cards illustrated handsome pigs in human roles; one series satirized Aesop's fables.

Some credit must be given to Fairbank's sensitivity to the changing culinary concerns of American housewives. He was aware that a semi-scientific approach would make Cottolene appear to be an intelligent choice nutritionally and economically. His clever advertising slogans reflected changing nutritional priorities: "Cheaper than butter, better than lard" and "Shortens your food, lengthens your life." He was aware of slaughterhouse conditions, and of the attractions of cleanliness and purity. And he understood the value of certain types of cooking in developing women's social reputations, and positioned Cottolene as a superior medium for newly fashionable foods. Women of the period were enlarging their cooking repertoires to include more deep-frying—particularly of doughnuts, cookies, timbales, and meats—and broadening their traditional pie-making skills. Icons of the new popular cookery of the 1880's and 90's, these favorites were fostered by the developed cook stove, inexpensive ingredients, and an expanded social life that required a regular exchange of hospitality, desserts, and snacks.

The Cottolene trademark—a cow's head wreathed in cotton plants—was known everywhere, and the product became a staple nationwide. It appeared in agricultural exhibits at the World's Columbian Exposition in Chicago (1893), Buffalo's Pan-American Exposition, and the St. Louis World's Fair (1904). It featured not only in store inventories but also in expedition provisioning lists, and was studied for scientific reports. With the success of Cottolene, Fairbank turned his hand to a line of soaps, another use for waste fats. His "Gold Dust Twins," a pair of African-American children depicted in cleanliness-related scenes, were possibly America's first long-lasting product trademark. The use of African-Americans as targets of humor, very common at the time, was an intrinsic theme in Fairbank's advertising for the products, as it was throughout popular white American culture.

As these enterprises grew, Fairbank continued to expand his holdings. He bought a mining claim in Tombstone, Arizona and organized the Grand Central Mining Company—both a mining town and a mineral were named for him—and he was involved in the Elk Rapids Iron Company of Michigan and in Louisiana pine forests. His leadership in business and social affairs was well recognized, and he took on the role of philanthropist, supporting Chicago's St. Luke's Hospital and becoming a founding trustee of the Chicago Symphony Orchestra. He operated a private fish hatchery and maintained wildlife at Lake Geneva, Wisconsin, where he summered with his wife, Helen Livingston Graham, and their eight children. Fairbank died in Chicago at the age of 74.

— ALICE ROSS

Fannie Merritt Farmer

❧ 1857–1915 ❧

FANNIE FARMER IS CHIEFLY REMEMBERED FOR HER COMPENDIOUS AND LASTING work, *The Boston Cooking-School Cookbook,* published in 1896. She was one of a group of late–nineteenth-century women who achieved celebrity as cookbook authors, cooking-school directors, teachers, and lecturers. These women worked at careers in a time when the middle-class urban social ideal required women to marry, to eschew personal ambitions in the market place—overwhelmingly a male preserve—and to contribute their efforts instead to home, church, and community. Women who remained single and were compelled to support themselves often found work that was congruent with the period's ideal of "separate spheres" of activity for the genders. Farmer was one of these, and made major contributions to her time through cookery.

She was born to a middle-class Boston family on March 23, 1857. She suffered extended ill health during her adolescence, was left with a limp, and could not complete high school. Her first efforts at self-sufficiency were domestic, initially in her parents' home and then in a job as a mother's helper. There her clear talents and enthusiasm for cooking and eating led her to enroll in the Boston Cooking School in 1888, an institution dedicated to training teachers, cooks, and other food professionals. She joined the school's staff after graduation as assistant director and ultimately served as principal from 1893 to 1902. She then opened her own Miss Farmer's School of Cookery to offer instruction to nurses and non-professional homemakers. At her death in 1915, her school was still in operation and, in fact, continued to function until 1944. An inveterate teacher, Farmer also taught a course at Harvard in cooking for invalids, and lectured widely across the nation.

Farmer's primary contributions were through teaching and writing. Her published works enriched her classrooms as well as the housewives who lived too far away to attend Boston classes. Her books had a considerable influence in the new directions of American cooking at the beginning of the twentieth century.

Before her time, most women had learned to cook by watching their mothers, using printed recipes only for variations of processes and dishes with which they were already familiar. They depended on the age-old sensory approach to cooking—that is, the use of smell, touch, taste, sight, and hearing to gauge amounts, temperatures, and mixing and cooking times. This approach worked well with a fairly stable and somewhat limited culinary repertoire.

However, by the end of the nineteenth century, American cuisine was expanding. Changing costs and kinds of ingredients, such as spices, sugar, and packaged products, enlarged the possibilities of home cooking. Increased urban leisure, new technologies, a new taste for travel, and the desire to entertain fashionably brought previously unfamiliar regional and international dishes (or their simulacra) to the American kitchen. For their tea tables, ladies' luncheons, and important family functions, women aspired to learn the new processes—such as home preserving and candying—and high-status foods: iced and filled layer cakes, salad and sandwich lunches, soft drinks, and frozen desserts. To do this, they often equipped themselves with the instructive works of Fannie Farmer and the standardized measuring equipment and techniques that she espoused.

Farmer's *Boston Cooking-School Cookbook,* an updated and expanded version of the text written by her predecessor as principal, **Mary J. Lincoln**, was highly influenced by reshaped culinary patterns, new concepts of nutrition and biochemistry, and the growing influence of science on daily life. Her book was one of the true parents of modern cookbooks in that it was used by people who had neither tasted nor prepared many of the dishes before and who could expand their repertoires by relying on the printed word for direction.

To this end Farmer's carefully scientific notation was of great importance. She was dedicated to precise, level measurement with the new standardized equipment—calibrated cups and spoons—as well as systematic and complete directions. In contrast to the somewhat anecdotal form and the vague quantities that were typical of earlier recipes, her format became the model in current use: a listing of ingredients followed by step-by-step directions. Despite the rigor of her notation, however, she did not omit the cook's personal involvement in the food itself, guiding with careful descriptions of the stages each dish passed through and including cautions and suggestions for trouble-shooting common problems. Her clear and voluminous instruction was rich and easily visualized, and encouraged women at home to undertake the new cooking techniques of baking, candying, saucing, and preserving that had become fashionable by the end of the century.

— ALICE ROSS

The Boston Cooking-School Cookbook, 1896
Chafing Dish Possibilities, 1898
Food and Cookery for the Sick and Convalescent, 1904
What to Have for Dinner, 1905
Cresca Dainties: A Collection of Practical Recipes, 1908
Catering for Special Occasions, With Menus and Recipes, 1911
A New Book of Cookery, 1912
A Book of Good Dinners for My Friend or "What to Have for Dinner", 1914
Fannie Farmer also wrote a regular column for the *Women's Home Companion* from 1905
   to 1915.

F

Joseph Favre
1849–1903

IN HIS SHORT LIFE OF ONLY 54 YEARS, JOSEPH FAVRE MANAGED TWO SUCCESSFUL
careers: first, as a highly regarded chef, and second, as a promoter of the culinary
profession.

He began at a disadvantage, being orphaned at a young age. He was interested in science and thought he would like to become a physician, but his circumstances limited his choice to the priesthood or a manual craft, which included
cooking. Favre chose the kitchen, and left his hometown of Vex in the Swiss
canton of Valais and apprenticed himself in the city of Sion, capital of Valais.
After the requisite three years of apprenticeship, he moved to the Hotel
Métropole in Geneva. Next, Favre found work in Paris, and was soon
hired at the prestigious La Maison Chevet, in the Palais Royal. He was
eighteen years old.

M. Chevet sent the young man to work in his restaurant in Wiesbaden,
and Favre embarked on the peripatetic life of a successful chef, working for
the nobility and in hotels and restaurants all over Europe. During the Franco-
Prussian War of 1870-1871, Favre, a Swiss citizen, joined a group of French and
Italian volunteers led by Garibaldi to fight against the Prussians. After the war,
Favre continued to travel, working in London, Berlin, Lausanne, Freiberg, Luga-
no, and many other cities. This lifestyle brought him fame, wealth, and—what's
more—the opportunity to fulfill his earlier dream of serious academic study, as
he arranged to spend his winters taking courses at the University of Geneva.

In 1877, he began to publish *La Science culinaire*, the first trade journal for professional chefs, and two years later he founded *l'Union universelle pour le progrès de
l'Art culinaire*, the first society for the protection and promotion of the profession.
His socialist leanings inspired him to set up a program of courses teaching cuisine
to the masses. In 1882, Favre moved from Geneva to Paris to organize a culinary
exhibition, and he remained in Paris for the rest of his life. Following a dispute
with some fellow chefs in *l'Union,* he founded a rival *Académie de Cuisine,* and served
for a time as secretary general of this organization.

From the Dictionnaire
universel de cuisine, 1903

Expanding greatly on the many culinary articles he had written for his journal over the years, Favre published his four-volume encyclopedia of cuisine in 1894. The work remains valuable to this day, giving menus, recipes, biographies of prominent chefs and restaurateurs, descriptions of traditional foods, and a history of cooking. Favre died in 1903, just before publication of the second edition. He left a wife and young son; in fact, this edition was completed by his wife. A biography of Joseph Favre, written by his colleague E. Darenne, was added to the work.

— ALICE ARNDT

Dictionnaire universel de cuisine: Encyclopédie illustrée d'hygiène alimentaire (Universal Dictionary of Cuisine: Illustrated Encyclopedia of Food Hygiene), 1894; second edition, 1903

Abby Fisher

❧ C.1832—BETWEEN 1910 AND 1920 ❧

ALSO CALLED: Mrs. Fisher

FROM THE RECORDS OF THE 1870 US CENSUS, THE FIRST CENSUS TO INCLUDE African-Americans, we learn that Abby Fisher was born in South Carolina in about 1832. Her father was born in France and her mother in South Carolina, and since Abby herself is classified as mulatto, it is almost certain, given the time and place, that her mother was a slave and her father one of the many Huguenot landowners of that state. She probably grew up and learned to cook on a plantation, judging by her later references to plantation life. We do not know when or why she moved to Alabama, nor how she met Alexander Fisher, who became her husband, but we find them in 1870 living in Mobile, Alabama, with four young children, the eldest of whom was five. Sometime after this, the family made the long trek to San Francisco; their last child was born along the way in Missouri in 1877.

Soon after their arrival in San Francisco, Abby Fisher won a diploma at the 1879 Sacramento State Fair, and the following year she received two medals at the San Francisco Mechanics' Institute Fair for her pickles, sauces, jellies, and preserves. Alexander and Abby Fisher established a successful pickle manufacturing business, and she developed a following among the prominent citizens of the area, who urged her to publish a book on her "knowledge and experience of Southern Cooking, Pickle and Jelly Making." Since she was illiterate, this work was presumably dictated to those patrons whose names are listed, "by permission," in the book.

What Mrs. Fisher Knows About Old Southern Cooking appeared in 1881, and was intended to be "a complete instructor, so that a child can understand it and learn the art of cooking." There are 160 recipes for delicious Southern dishes, such as "Maryland Beat Biscuits," "Plantation Corn Bread," "Fried Chicken," "Sweet Potato Pie," "Ice Cream," "Peach Cobbler," and those prize-winning pickles and preserves.

The book includes a recipe for a blackberry syrup used to check dysentery in children, which Mrs. Fisher notes is "an old Southern plantation remedy among colored people," and also instructions for making a pap of boiled flour and milk for infants. In a note accompanying the pap recipe, she tells us, "I have given birth to eleven children and raised them all, and nursed them with this diet." We have seen her and Alexander Fisher with five children born in Alabama or Missouri, but where and when her six older children were born is impossible to say, except that it was before the end of the Civil War and quite likely while she was still enslaved. How long would she have been allowed to keep those children with her? When she speaks of "raising" her children, it seems she is speaking—with justifiable pride at a time of horrendous infant mortality—of getting them past infancy. Certainly, little Alexander, Jr., who was three years old in 1870, did not make it from Alabama to California with the family in 1880; he does not appear in the census records for that year. The 1900 census form indicates that Abby was the mother of eight children and that three were living. If we interpret that cursory notation to mean that eight were deceased (or lost to her because of slavery) and three were alive, then that would account for the eleven children she referred to. Only three of the Fisher children can be located in the census records from 1900 on.

Abby Fisher's rare cookbook was reprinted in 1995 with historical notes by Karen Hess, who began uncovering the story of Mrs. Fisher's life and brought to the subject her own extensive knowledge of the culinary history of South Carolina. At the time, Hess and others believed that *What Mrs. Fisher Knows* was the first cookbook written by an African-American. (She excluded two earlier works which, although they contain some culinary recipes, are not primarily cookbooks: *The House Servant's Directory* by **Robert Roberts**, published in 1827, which may well be the first book of any kind written by an African-American; and *Hotel Keepers, Head Waiters and Housekeepers' Guide*, 1848, by the politically active Tunis Campbell.)

Since then, Janice Bluestein Longone, curator of the new Longone Center for American Culinary Research at the University of Michigan, has identified an earlier candidate for the role of first African-American cookbook: *A Domestic Cookbook: Containing a Careful Selection of Useful Receipts for the Kitchen* by Malinda Russell, published in 1866. Russell was born free in Tennessee, almost emigrated to Liberia as a teenager, and worked as a cook in the South before being obliged to leave during the Civil War. She moved to Michigan and published her book in the town of Paw Paw. Longone believes there are other early African-American cookbooks waiting to be discovered.

— ALICE ARNDT

What Mrs. Fisher Knows About Old Southern Cooking, Soups, Pickles, Preserves, Etc., 1881

M. F. K. Fisher

1942

IN 1954, CLIFTON FADIMAN REVIEWED *THE ART OF EATING: The Collected Gastronomical Works of M. F. K. Fisher* and said, "Of all the writers on food now using our English tongue M. F. K. Fisher seems to me to approach most nearly in range, depth, and perception, the altitude of **Brillat-Savarin** himself." Half a century later, time has only enhanced her reputation, broadened interest in her work, and crowned her achievement. Born on July 3, 1908, in Albion, Michigan, Mary Frances Kennedy was the oldest child of newspaperman Rex Brenton Kennedy, and banker's daughter Edith Oliver Holbrook. As native Iowans, both of her parents were comfortably middle-class, educated, and somewhat emancipated from their parents' religious practices. They were also peripatetic, moving from Iowa to Michigan and then on to Washington State and California, where they settled in Whittier when Rex Kennedy became part owner and editor of *The Whittier News* in 1912.

Mary Frances, along with two younger sisters and a brother, lived in a household, where the presence of Grandmother Holbrook and her special dietary needs dominated the family meals, and the occupation of her father dictated a large library and collection of magazines and newspapers. Add to that, her mother's fondness for novels and Anglo-authors, and the result was a climate where children learned to read before they went to grammar school and wrote poems and even "novels" before attending high school.

Although she attended private boarding schools, Illinois College, Whittier College, and Occidental before continuing her education at the University of Dijon in 1929 as the newly married Mrs. Alfred Fisher, she did not distinguish herself academically or obtain a college degree. In 1931 after her husband completed his doctoral dissertation, the Fishers resided in Strasburg and Cagnes-sur-Mer before returning to California the next year. Unable to find employment, the Fishers lived in the Kennedy beach house in Laguna Beach, doing odd jobs and writing. Fisher published her first article, "Pacific Village" in *Westways* in 1934. The same year her husband obtained a position in the English department at Occidental College.

Spending her mornings in the Los Angeles Public Library before going to a clerking job in the afternoon, Fisher became fascinated with the library's collection of old cookery books and contemporary translations of classics like ***Apicius***: *Cooking and Dining in Imperial Rome,* Petronius' *Trimaldino's Dinner Party,* and **Grimod de la Reynière**'s *L'Almanach des Gourmands.* She began writing witty essays about the sauce *garum*, Roman dining habits, Florentine cooks introducing sherbet to the French court, and **Vatel**'s precipitous suicide. She showed these pieces to her friend and soon-to-be lover Dillwyn Parrish, who gave them to his sister, a

Harper & Brothers author, who, in turn sent them to Gene Saxton, her editor. He offered Fisher a contract if she would substantially expand the manuscript. *Serve It Forth* was published in June 1937, and it launched Fisher's publishing career. She divorced Al Fisher the same year, and resided with Dillwyn Parrish in Vevey, Switzerland, at an idyllic restored *vigneron's* cottage named Le Paquis.

Fisher's personal life drove her professional career. When her second husband suffered an embolism in his leg in 1938 and Europe erupted into World War II, they both returned to the States and purchased a hilly, rocky, deserted piece of property beyond the city limits of Hemet, California, in 1940. Diagnosed with fatal Beurger's disease, her husband was in constant agony, and Fisher compensated by writing a jovial book of legend and lore as well as well-known recipes for oysters in a book called *Consider the Oyster*. It was published shortly after Parrish committed suicide on August 6, 1941.

Drawing on her pre-war experiences in Switzerland and the imminence of war in the States, Fisher then wrote a book on survival during a time of stress and rationing. *How to Cook a Wolf* (1942) with its glamorous photo by George Hurrell attracted the attention of Paramount Studio, and Fisher was soon employed as a junior screenwriter. In 1943, she wrote the story of her gastronomical coming of age, which she titled *The Gastronomical Me,* gave birth to her first daughter Anne, and left Hollywood. She wrote monthly columns for *House Beautiful,* contributed to *Coronet,* and supported herself as a single mother.

In 1945, while spending the summer in New York City, she met Donald Friede, of the former Covici-Friede publishing house, and precipitously married him. That fall she was pregnant with her second daughter Kennedy, and she and Friede returned to Hemet to write their respective books. Working with editor Patrick Covici who had moved to Viking, Fisher published a book of banquet literature, *Here Let Us Feast* (1946), a novel *Not Now, But Now* (1947), and a revision of articles formerly published in *Gourmet* called *An Alphabet For Gourmets* (1949), the same year her translation of Brillat-Savarin's *The Physiology of Taste* appeared in a slip-case edition for the Limited Editions Club.

The death of Fisher's mother in 1949, ill health, and estrangement from Friede led to a permanent separation. Fisher and her two daughters moved to the family Ranch in Whittier where she resided with her aged father until his death in 1953. Fisher then moved to the Napa Valley and took her daughters to Aix the following year. A collection of her first five gastronomical books, *The Art of Eating* appeared while she was in France. Dedicating most of her time to the education of her daughters, Fisher did not publish another book until *A Cordiall Water* appeared in 1961.

Trying to escape the hot stove of culinary writing, Fisher wrote about "places"—Aix-en-Provence, Marseilles, Dijon, and the people she met and befriended in those places, but the lure of the Faire Gastronomique, Marseilles' Old Port seafood restaurants, and Left Bank cafes interjected the memories of food, the pleasures of wine, and the experience of eating into her every essay and story.

In 1966, when Time-Life hired her as writer for the first volume in the *Foods of the World* series, she spent time in Paris, Provence, and Placassier, working on *The Cooking of Provincial France* (1968) with Michael Field. She met **Julia Child**, another consultant on the book, when she returned to Boston. They became friends, and Fisher joined the ranks of **James Beard**, **Craig Claiborne**, and Julia Child as important figures in the culinary revolution sweeping the country. Fisher's most significant magazine articles appeared in *The New Yorker* from the mid-60's until the 80's. Under the title "Gastronomy Recalled," she published a sequence of articles that were republished as *With Bold Knife and Fork* in 1969. The following year, she published another sequence, "The Enclave," that **Alfred Knopf** republished as *Among Friends* in 1970. She also wrote articles for *Holiday, Esquire, Ladies Home Journal, Architectural Digest, Vogue,* and *Atlantic Monthly.*

Fisher moved from Napa to the Sonoma Valley in 1971 when David Pleyell-Bouverie built a two-room home for her on his ranch, and during the 70's Fisher visited and spent time in Provence on four different occasions, completing *Sister Age,* and *A Considerable Town.* North Point Press republished Fisher's major works in handsome paperback editions in the 80's, and a continuing number of aspiring culinary writers, film-makers, and journalists made their way to Fisher's Last House when she was unable to travel. During her lifetime she received many awards for her contribution to America's culinary landscape. In 1991, however, her work received the ultimate recognition when she was elected to the American Academy and National Institute of Arts and Letters.

Afflicted with Parkinson's disease and bed-ridden, Fisher died on June 22, 1992. Three posthumous volumes: *To Begin Again; Stay Me, Oh Comfort Me;* and *Last House* collected fragments of her journals, essays, and memories. A scrapbook of photographs, *A Welcoming Life,* annotated and edited by Dominique Gioia appeared in 1997. *M. F. K. Fisher: A Life in Letters,* selected and compiled by Norah Barr and Marsha and Patrick Moran, collected many of her letters to family, friends, and fans.

— JOAN REARDON

Serve It Forth, 1937
Consider the Oyster, 1941
How to Cook a Wolf, 1942
The Gastronomical Me, 1943
Here Let Us Feast, 1946
Not Now, But Now, 1947
An Alphabet For Gourmets, 1949
The Physiology of Taste; or, Meditations of Transcental Gastronomy. A New Translation by M. F. K. Fisher, with Profuse Annotations by the Translator and Illustrations by Sylvain Sauvage, by Brillat-Savarin, 1949
The Art of Eating: The Collected Gastronomical Works of M.F.K. Fisher, 1954
A Cordiall Water, 1961
The Cooking of Provincial France (with Michael Field), 1968
With Bold Knife and Fork, 1969
Among Friends, 1970
A Considerable Town, 1978
Sister Age, 1983
To Begin Again, 1992
Stay Me, Oh Comfort Me, 1993
Last House: Reflections, Dreams, and Observations, 1943-1991, 1995
A Welcoming Life, annotated and edited by Dominique Gioia, 1997
M. F. K. Fisher: A Life in Letters, correspondence 1929-1991, selected and compiled by Norah Barr and Marsha and Patrick Moran, 1997

Theodora FitzGibbon

THEODORA ROSLING WAS BORN OCTOBER 21, 1916, in London. Her Irish parents lived apart for most of their marriage, and she was brought up by her maternal grandmother. She attended convent schools but was, as she wrote later, "always a recalcitrant child at school." At age sixteen, she refused to go on with her formal education and instead traveled, alone, to Calcutta to join her father, Adam Rosling, a veterinary surgeon. After a time in India, he brought her to France where she spent a term in finishing school. Theodora aspired to be an actress, and appeared in a few plays and films. Being quite beautiful, she supported herself between acting jobs by modeling. (She was perhaps never entirely secure in her view of herself since she had grown up in the shadow of a great beauty, often overhearing "She'll never have half the looks of the mother.")

From 1938 to 1943, she lived with the photographer and painter Peter Rose Pulham, first in Paris, from which she escaped by bicycle, pedaling just ahead of the invading Germans, then in London during the Blitz. Theodora and Peter lived a very social, Bohemian life, making friends with the many artists and writers she found so stimulating—including Norman Douglas, Augustus John, Donald Maclean, and Caitlin and Dylan Thomas—most of them as penniless as they were creative. They scrabbled daily to find enough to eat. She made pâté from horse liver and often served rook and other lesser-used wild birds at her soirées.

Although Theodora and Peter maintained an affectionate relationship, she fell in love with Constantine FitzGibbon and married him in March 1944. After the war, Constantine began his writing career. It took some time to complete his first novel and find a publisher and, although Constantine taught at a local school for a while, the couple was quite impoverished, a condition that remained constant for much of their marriage.

During all this time, Theodora served as a muse for others, but made no attempt to do any writing herself. One day while she and Constantine were entertaining Derek Verschoyle, he commented that she always prepared wonderful meals and suggested that she write a cookbook, which he himself would publish. The result was *Cosmopolitan Cookery in an English Kitchen* [1952], with recipes from the countries she had lived in, adapted to the rationing in England. This was a huge success, and was followed by other cookbooks, magazine articles, short stories, a novel, and broadcasts on the BBC. Ultimately, she published more than 30 books.

Constantine's jealousy over his wife's success helped bring to an end their already deteriorating marriage, and the couple divorced in 1960. At that time Theodora began work on her encyclopedia, *The Food of the Western World* [1976], which includes roughly six thousand entries from 34 countries. From the late sixties she lived in Dublin and produced a steady stream of books and articles, writing a cookery column for the *Irish Times* for over twenty years. She was cookery editor for *Image* magazine and the *Irish Times,* and she lectured widely.

Theodora also wrote two autobiographical volumes, *With Love* [1982] and *Love Lies a Loss* [1985]. The later volume concludes with a reference to her years of happiness during the last period of her life in Dublin, working on her "life-giving career of writing." She married George Morrison, the film-maker and photographic archivist; with whom she collaborated on the "*A Taste of…*" series; Morrison compiled and prepared the period photographs that accompanied these volumes. Theodora FitzGibbon died in Dublin on March 25, 1991, at the age of 74.

— MÁIRTÍN MAC CON IOMAIRE

Cosmopolitan Cookery in an English Kitchen, 1952
Weekend Cookery, 1956
Country House Cooking, 1958
The Young Cook's Book: For All Ages From 6 to 15, 1958
Game Cooking, 1963
The Art of British Cooking, 1965
Flight of the Kingfisher (novel), 1967
A Taste of Ireland, 1968
Eat Well and Live Longer: Cookery Without Animal Fat, 1969
A Taste of Wales, 1971
Theodora FitzGibbon's Cookery Book, 1972
A Taste of England—The West Country, 1972
A Taste of London, 1973
A Taste of Paris, 1974
A Taste of Rome, 1975
The Food of the Western World, 1976
A Taste of the Sea, 1977
Making the Most of it: A Cookery Book Which Examines the Past as a Guide to Good Food on a Budget, 1978
Crockery Pot Cooking, 1978
Theodora FitzGibbon's Irish Kitchen Map, 1978
A Taste of Scotland, 1979
A Taste of Yorkshire, 1979
A Taste of the Lake District, 1980
Pleasures of the Table, compiled by Theodora FitzGibbon, 1981
Traditional West Country Cookery, 1982
With Love, 1982
Irish Traditional Food, 1983
Your Favourite Recipes from Theodora FitzGibbon, 1985
Love Lies a Loss, 1985
A Taste of England, 1986
Good Housekeeping Good Food for Diabetics, 1988

Charles Elmé Francatelli

❧ 1805–1876 ❧

CHARLES ELMÉ FRANCATELLI, VICTORIAN ENGLAND'S MOST FAMOUS CHEF, WAS able to commiserate with the struggles of the poor to feed their families.

He was born in London of Italian ancestry. Trained in France by the esteemed chef **Antonin Carême**, Francatelli worked his way up to *chef de cuisine* and returned to England at a time when it was fashionable among the wealthy to employ French cooks. His years of serving the best of dishes and the most expensive wines to the earl of Chesterfield were followed by employment by other members of England's aristocracy and then by some of London's most exclusive clubs, including the Melton Club and Crockford's. In 1841 and 1842, he was Queen Victoria's chief cook and *maître d'hôtel;* the brevity of his service there was probably due to the royal family's preference for "plain food," as distinct from the elaborate multi-course dinners he prepared—one of them including 70 dishes.

Francatelli returned to club cooking, working first at the Coventry Club, then for seven years as *chef de cuisine* at the Reform Club, and then serving as executive chef at St. James's Hotel (1863–1870) and the Freemason's Tavern (1870–1876). He published his first cookbook, *The Modern Cook: A Practical Guide to the Culinary Art in All Its Branches*, in 1845; it contained 1462 recipes, among them French, German, and Italian dishes as well as Indian curry. In its preface, he wrote of the excellence of English ingredients and the poverty of English cooking. *The Modern Cook* went to 29 editions.

For the poor, Francatelli published *A Plain Cookery Book for the Working Classes* (1852). To critics mocking his production of a laboring-class cookbook, he retorted that he could nourish a thousand families entirely on the food London wasted daily. In the book's introduction, he established, with exact prices, the necessary equipment for a kitchen, beginning with a stove with workable draft and a boiler for heating water. He specified one oval boiling pot, two lidded saucepans, a potato steamer, a frying pan, a gridiron, a copper for washing or brewing, a mash tub, and two cooling tubs, which the thrifty household could make from a recycled wine or beer cask. The total cost was six pounds, twelve shillings and fourpence, and he exhorted "those of my readers who, from sickness or other hindrance, have not money in store," to "strive to lay by a little of your weekly wages to purchase these things, that your families be well fed, and your homes made comfortable." Although his tone was condescending, his intentions were good and his recipes practical.

In the 240 recipes in Francatelli's *Plain Cookery Book*, he explained in a conversational style how to melt jelly into sauce, boil beef, and stuff and roast a goose. His compendium incorporated such English national dishes as Christmas plum pudding, toad in the hole, and bubble and squeak. He gave instructions for home-brewed beer and elderberry wine, baked stuffed bullock heart, sheep's pluck, cow-heel broth, and rice gruel. For a freshly slaughtered pig, he spoke with authority to cottagers on debristling the carcass with burning straw, scraping the surface dry with a knife, and cleansing the gut before removing pluck, fat, and chitterlings. For curing, he gave precise measures of salt, molasses, saltpeter, herbs, and spices. He suggested pressing hams between boards weighted with stones before smoking them in a shed or chimney.

Francatelli maintained his focus on economy in recommending Patna rice as the cheapest and easiest to boil and suggesting how to make salt herring palatable and savory. He introduced the English reader to the French haricot bean, "a principal part in the staple articles of food for the working-classes, and indeed for the entire population." The ovenless cook he consoled, "You can easily roast your potatoes by placing them on the hobs, bars, and under the fire-grate; and if you are attentive to their being well roasted, by turning them about now and then, so that they may be done all over alike, you need not be deprived of a baked potato for the want of an oven." He outlined how to cook a veal knuckle or neck end and make a hot cottage supper from common root vegetables by rubbing them through a colander for a vegetable porridge.

A separate section on sickroom cookery suggested beef tea and chicken or mutton broth strained through a clean cloth as a suitable diet for invalids. Francatelli's list of ingredients offered variety for the recovering patient, whom the cook might tempt with oatmeal, groats, blancmange, and isinglass or Iceland moss jelly. Advice on a single-serving bread pudding concluded reassuringly that any pudding constituted safe food for the most delicate patient. He was conversant with making tea for coughs and gout, balm for fever, red cabbage for scurvy and skin ailments, rice water for diarrhea, wine whey and cordials for colds, and peppermint sugar for flatulence.

In 1870, Francatelli married Elizabeth Cooke, the daughter of a hotel keeper. Six years later, after a half-century of cooking and food writing, he died on August 10, 1876, at Eastbourne in Sussex.

— MARY ELLEN SNODGRASS

The Modern Cook: A Practical Guide to the Culinary Art in All Its Branches, 1845
French Cookery: The Modern Cook: A Practical Guide to the Culinary Art in All its Branches, 1846
A Plain Cookery Book for the Working Classes, 1852
The Royal Confectioner: English & Foreign. A Practical Treatise on the Art of Confectionary in All Its Branches, 1862
Cook's Guide and Housekeeper's & Butler's Assistant: A Practical Treatise on English and Foreign Cookery in All Its Branches, 1864

G

Galen

❧ AD 129—AFTER 210 ❧

GALEN WAS BORN IN PERGAMUM IN ASIA MINOR (MODERN BERGAMA, TURKEY) under the Roman Empire. His father, Nicias, was a member of the Greek-speaking elite, an architect, who put his son through a wide-ranging education before directing him to philosophy and then to medicine.

Galen's contribution to philosophy is still highly regarded, but is outweighed by the vast number of his medical works, which came to dominate Western and Arab medicine until the seventeenth century. He studied at the medical schools of Smyrna, Alexandria, and Corinth before becoming a doctor attached to the school of gladiators in Pergamum. In 162 he moved to the imperial capital, Rome, and began to establish himself as the most formidable physician in the city. After alarming encounters with armies and plague, and a return home to Pergamum, he became physician to the emperor Marcus Aurelius. We know a great deal about his life from personal anecdotes in his treatises and from important short works that review his vast output, *On My Own Books* and *On the Order of My Own Books*.

Galen was at the heart of contemporary medical polemic, and gives the best, if not an unbiased, account of rival medical thought. His tradition is broadly Hippocratic, with adaptation of the Hippocratic authors, who wrote in the period 430—300 BC. Nutrition and dietetics lay at the heart of Hippocratic medicine; Galen calls that the most useful of the three branches of medicine, and links it to the second branch, pharmacology, through close cross-referencing between his main food treatise, *On the Properties of Foods*, and an important work on drugs, *On the Properties and Mixtures of Simple Medicines*. These treatises are of the greatest importance for the history of food.

Galen is the master of the anecdote: He recounts his triumphs over lesser rivals in Rome; that peasants boil wheat flour and get indigestion; that wet-nurses give babies skin diseases because they eat wild plants in the spring; and that a young man lived healthily for four years on a vegetarian diet. This imperial physician witnessed the diet of the poor: He notes that peasants send their best grain to the city; that they are forced to adapt their diet to cattle food such as vetches in the Mediterranean spring; that ditch-diggers are strong and can eat bad food, but die young.

Galen is also the master of research; he comments valuably on problems of identification, nomenclature, and the taxonomy of species. He also has a wide geographical scope, noting rabbits from Spain and rye from the Black Sea, and he helps to build a picture of regional foods and styles of eating, based on observations during his extensive travels, especially in Asia Minor. As a Hippocratic, he has environmental concerns, since the human animal is as much subject to climatic variation as any other. Urban pollution in the Tiber and other rivers near towns is a major hazard, he notes. As a technical writer, he is less prone to complain about the excesses of the Roman elite than satirical writers such as Juvenal: He simply says he cannot understand why people would go out of their way to eat the livers of red mullet and other such delicacies.

— JOHN WILKINS

On Cooking
On Prognosis
On My Own Books
On the Order of My Own Books
On the Properties of Foods
On the Properties and Mixtures of Simple Medicines

Petrona Carrizo de Gandulfo ❦ 1898–1992 ❦

ALSO CALLED: Petrona C. de Gandulfo

IRONICALLY, ARGENTINA'S MOST FAMOUS COOK SPENT HER CHILDHOOD avoiding the kitchen. Born in the northwestern province of Santiago del Estero on June 29, 1898, to parents of Italian, Basque, and indigenous descent, Petrona Carrizo spent most of her time reading rather than helping her mother prepare food for their boarding house. However, as Petrona herself remarked, "The one who never wanted to cook ended up cooking for everybody." Indeed, over the course of her career, Petrona became the most influential food expert in Argentine history, thanks to her landmark cookbook, *El libro de Doña Petrona*, along with her frequent talks, magazine contributions, and radio and television programs.

Her career began in the late 1920's, when she enrolled in classes at the Cordon Bleu after moving to Buenos Aires with her future husband, Oscar Gandulfo. In 1928, she landed a job with the British gas company Primativa, where she worked as a home economist, teaching women how to use the new gas stoves. In this capacity, Petrona began giving cooking lessons to small neighborhood crowds across Buenos Aires. By the 1930's, she was hosting a national radio program, and she published the first editions of her cookbook. In the 1960's she became the lead cook for a tremendously successful televised variety program, *Buenas Tardes, Mucho Gusto*, which was broadcast until the early 1980's.

Petrona's ubiquitous presence as the predominant cooking expert in Argentina fueled an enormous demand for her cookbook. First published in 1934, *El libro de Doña Petrona* has been reprinted more than 100 times, establishing itself as one of the three best-selling books in Argentine history, after the Bible and the national novel, *Martin Fierro*. Petrona published and energetically promoted her cookbook and was joined in this effort by her second husband, Atilio Massut, whom she married in 1946 after being widowed. Their only son, Marcelo Massut, had two children, Alejandro and Marcela; Marcela collaborated with her grandmother to "modernize" her cuisine in the 1980's, and continued to publish new editions of the cookbook after Petrona's death in Buenos Aires on February 6, 1992.

El libro de Doña Petrona represented the first major attempt to synthesize Argentine cuisine on a national scale. Thanks to the large influx of European immigrants during the late nineteenth and early twentieth centuries, people across Argentina enjoyed a wide variety of meals influenced by Spanish, Italian, Eastern European, and indigenous culinary traditions. Inspired by her French culinary training at the Cordon Bleu, Petrona included some high-end French recipes in the first edition of her cookbook, such as oyster *vol-au-vents* and caviar canapés—dishes that had previously been served only in elite homes and expensive restaurants. At the same time, her book also reflected her more modest provincial upbringing and her desire to reach a mass audience, and she included numerous recipes for stews, steaks, empanadas, and preserves. The influence of large-scale Spanish and Italian immigration on Argentine cuisine is apparent throughout, in such recipes as Spanish tortilla and Spanish-style cod together with Italian pastas and Neapolitan-style pizza.

Petrona did not simply assemble French, Spanish, and Italian recipes; she creolized and augmented them with recipes inspired by Argentine home cooking. For example, she incorporated several recipes for flan, a Spanish egg-yolk custard, and made one version with *dulce de leche*, an Argentine milk caramel. She also included several recipes for beef, which served as the foundation of many Argentines' diets, including *asado al horno*, oven-roasted beef ribs traditionally cooked out-of-doors by men. Petrona devoted significant energy to the presentation of all of these dishes, emphasizing the importance of stylized, decorative flourishes. Hand-drawn color illustrations and, later, photographs in her cookbook and her frequent magazine contributions depict piped potato roses, hard-boiled eggs fashioned into bunnies, fruit pyramids, and cakes built to resemble houses, soccer fields, or churches.

Petrona faithfully updated *El libro de Doña Petrona* and published new editions throughout her life. She also published other specialized collections that included new recipes and advice responding to the current interests and preoccupations of Argentines. Capitalizing on her reputation as a dessert maker and decorator extraordinaire, she published the first edition of *Para aprender a decorar (Learning to Decorate)* in 1941. In 1953, she published another collection that sought to demystify the pressure cooker titled *Cómo cocina Doña Petrona con ollas a presión (How Doña Petrona Cooks With a Pressure Cooker)*. In the midst of the deteriorating Argentine economy in the early 1960's, she published a cookbook that aimed to provide less expensive and less time-consuming recipes, aptly titled, *Recetas económicas (Economical Recipes)*. Tapping into concerns about diet and weight in the 1970's, she also published two low-calorie collections, *Coma bien y adelgace (Eat Well and Lose Weight)* and *Bajas calorías (Low Calories)*. However, while all of these books sold well, *El libro de Doña Petrona* outsold and outlasted them all.

Even today, Doña Petrona remains famous in Argentina not only for her groundbreaking cookbook, but also for the extravagance of her recipes (despite her attempts at economizing) and her harsh relationship with her on-air assistant, Juana "Juanita" Bordoy. In Argentina's current economic downturn, some Argentines remark that this is "no longer the day of Doña Petrona," referring to her extravagant ingredients and portion sizes and mentioning recipes such as the flan made with a dozen eggs. Even so, Petrona's cookbook retains a privileged place in kitchen cupboards and bookstores across Argentina, and her cooking program continues to be replayed on the television channel Volver. Both older and younger generations of Argentines are thus intimately acquainted with Petrona's frequent, brusque commands to Juanita on television, as a result of which Petrona developed a reputation as a harsh taskmaster. Even today, Argentines utilize the name "Juanita" to refer to a helper; they might say, "You be my Juanita" if they want someone to help them prepare a dish, or ask "What do you think I am, your Juanita?" if they want to make fun of someone ordering them around in the kitchen.

Despite these criticisms, Doña Petrona remains a beloved figure in Argentina. Many credit her with their ability to cook and suggest that her cookbook is present "in every Argentine home." While this overstates the access that Argentines (especially in the poorer and more rural sectors of society) have had to Petrona and her relatively expensive cookbook, there is no doubt that she was an influential national icon for over fifty years. This achievement is due not only to her business acumen and food savvy, but also to the emergence of new forms of domestic and media-related technology such as the gas stove, radio, and television; the expansion of the consumer market; and the increasing focus on female consumers during this period.

Doña Petrona's success reveals increasing efforts on the part of both private and public interests to encourage Argentine housewives in the expanding middle-income sections of the population to consume new technologies, products, and foods in order to maintain the perfect home and thereby fulfill ideals of Argentine domestic modernity. It also demonstrates the deep and enduring commitment of a great many Argentines to food, family, and friendship—all of which were championed by Petrona throughout her long career.

— REBEKAH E. PITE

El libro de Doña Petrona, 1934
Para aprender a decorar (Learning to Decorate), 1941
Cómo cocina Doña Petrona con ollas a presión (How Doña Petrona Cooks With a Pressure Cooker), 1953
Recetas económicas de Doña Petrona (Economical Recipes of Doña Petrona), 1962; reprinted 2002
Coma bien y adelgace (Eat Well and Lose Weight), 5th ed., 1977
Bajas calorías (Low Calories), 1970's

Fabiola Cabeza de Baca Gilbert ❧ 1894–1991 ❧

FABIOLA CABEZA DE BACA GILBERT PRESERVED NEW MEXICAN food folklore and pioneered in popularizing New Mexican cookery as a distinctive regional cuisine. Her *Historic Cookery* and *The Good Life: New Mexican Food* have been the inspiration for many subsequent Southwestern cookbooks.

She was born on May 16, 1894 at La Liendre, New Mexico Territory, into a large, politically active clan. Like other elite Hispano families, the Cabeza de Bacas owned vast lands and raised cattle. Growing up on the family ranch, Fabiola learned food preservation and cooking from her grandmother and other Hispanic women, as well as from Anglo-American homesteaders in the area. At a time when few Hispanics had an opportunity for higher education, Fabiola received a degree in education from New Mexico Highlands University in 1921 and taught in public schools before earning a BS in home economics from New Mexico State University in 1929. Hired that same year by New Mexico's Agricultural Extension Service, Fabiola spent the next 30 years in extension work and published cookbooks, articles, and a novella about Mexican cookery. By the time she retired in 1959, UNESCO and the federal Department of Agriculture had recognized her as an authority on regional foods. In later years she served as a trainer and consultant for the Peace Corps and wrote articles for Santa Fe newspapers and magazines. Fabiola was married to Carlos Gilbert, but the marriage ended in divorce, and they had no children. She died in Albuquerque, New Mexico, on October 14, 1991.

Soon after Fabiola joined the Extension Service, its work concentrated on the goals of progressive reformers (and later New Dealers) who wanted to keep farm families on the land, increase their production for home use, and improve the nutritional content of their meals. As a home economist, Fabiola firmly believed in the new scientific guidelines that emphasized vitamins and minerals. As a Hispana, she was well aware that many Hispanos lived in poverty despite owning small plots of land, and as a member of the Hispano elite, she believed it her responsibility to improve their condition and educate them in more modern ways. Yet she also wished to preserve the cultural legacy of her people, including their food traditions.

Fabiola's first efforts were directed toward teaching New Mexican women to can. Hispanics and Pueblo Indians had dried foodstuffs for centuries, but Fabiola encouraged them to save time and provide better nutrition for their families through home canning. To further the process, she wrote a canning manual in Spanish in 1931, and within a decade most Hispanic families in northern New Mexico had learned to can. The larger amounts of food they were able to preserve allowed them to survive on their land rather than seek wage work elsewhere, even during the drought and the great depression of the 1930's.

Even as she worked to modernize Hispano food practices, Fabiola maintained a strong sense of ethnic pride. By the 1930's, Anglo-Americans who had discovered the Southwest were eagerly consuming New Mexican dishes, and Anglo-American authors had published two cookbooks about New Mexican cookery. In response, Fabiola and other Hispanas wrote their own cookbooks, asserting their authority as true inheritors of Hispanic culture and cuisine. (One of those authors was Fabiola's cousin, from whose work Fabiola borrowed liberally and without attribution.) Fabiola's *Historic Cookery* (1939) was the most influential of these volumes because it provided exact measurements and detailed instructions and, as an Extension Service circular, enjoyed wide distribution. The collection emphasized dishes made with chiles, corn or meat, many of which represent New Mexican cookery of the mid-nineteenth century. But more modern influences were also reflected in the references to canned food and pressure cookers.

Historic Cookery also made New Mexican enchiladas and tacos accessible to the Anglo-Americans who poured into New Mexico during and after World War II. By 1954, the cookbook was so popular that it was reissued in an expanded version that has been in print ever since. The new edition eliminated some recipes while adding others, particularly in the meat and dessert categories. Some of the added recipes came from Fabiola's nostalgic novella *The Good Life, New Mexican Food* (1949), the story of a year in the life of a fictional New Mexican family. Food traditions illustrate the changing of the seasons, tie members of the community together in bonds of reciprocity, and mark religious observances. The last half of *The Good Life* is a cookbook that evokes an agricultural past in which families butchered their own livestock and wasted nothing. Recipes include *espinacito,* a chile dish made with kid's spine, and *morcilla,* blood pudding, which later appeared in *Historic Cookery* accompanied by Fabiola's plea to give them a try.

Fabiola's recollections also led to her memoir *We Fed Them Cactus* (1954), which related her experiences in a cattle-ranching family. One of the few Hispana autobiographies, *We Fed Them Cactus* is her best-known work and has been widely studied since the 1980's by scholars of the Hispana experience. It contains few references to food, however.

Fabiola Cabeza de Baca Gilbert not only recorded recipes and food traditions that were disappearing, but also provided instructions that allowed others to survive and thrive. In part because of her work, New Mexico chiles are renowned throughout the United States and are New Mexico's most important crop.

— CHERYL J. FOOTE

"Boletin de Conservar" (New Mexico Agricultural Extension Service Circular #106), 1931
"Los Alimentos y Su Preparacion" (New Mexico Agricultural Extension Circular #129), 1934; reprint 1942
Historic Cookery, 1939. Reprint, 1942. Revised and expanded edition, 1954. Reprints, 1958, 1970, 1996
The Good Life, New Mexican Food, 1949. Second edition, *The Good Life, New Mexico Traditions and Food*, 1982
We Fed Them Cactus, 1954. Reprint 1994

Lillian Moller Gilbreth

In the offices of the President's Unemployment Commission, 1930

LILLIAN EVELYN MOLLER GILBRETH, ENGINEER, MANAGEMENT consultant, industrial psychologist and professor, has been called "the mother of modern management" and "the first lady of motion study." She was certainly the best known female engineer of twentieth-century America.

Born into a well-to-do family in Oakland, California, the eldest of nine children of a store-owner and a homemaker, Lillian Moller was shy and timid. She was initially educated by her parents and by tutors, entering public school only at age nine. Her mother's poor health often left her the responsibility of taking care of her younger siblings, and despite her excellent grades in high school her family's expectations for her did not include college. Rather, she was expected to marry well and run a comfortable household for her husband. Lillian herself thought she was too plain to be likely to marry and planned to become a teacher instead, and she succeeded in persuading her parents to let her attend the University of California at Berkeley—on condition that she live at home and continue to take care of her siblings.

At Berkeley, she studied English literature, foreign languages, philosophy and psychology, all with a view to her teaching career. She graduated with honors in 1900, and was the first woman student to give a commencement speech at Berkeley. Lillian began her graduate studies at Columbia, where at least one professor refused to admit her, a female, to his classroom. She contracted pleurisy and returned to Oakland to recuperate, thereafter enrolling at Berkeley again and earning a master's degree in literature in 1902. She promptly entered a Ph.D. program in English and psychology.

To celebrate her master's degree, Lillian planned to travel to Europe the following summer with a group of other young women, chaperoned by a high-school teacher named Minnie Bunker. In Boston, Bunker introduced the group to her cousin, Frank Bunker Gilbreth, the handsome, high-school educated, 35-year-old bachelor owner of a construction company. Moller and Gilbreth immediately fell in love, and when the group returned from Europe three weeks later Gilbreth was waiting for Moller with flowers. The two were married that October.

Frank Gilbreth had been interested in efficiency in the workplace since the age of seventeen, when as an inexperienced bricklayer he studied the different work styles and movements of the old hands around him. He had come to believe that, with study and analysis, the "one best way" to do any job, or any component of any job, could be determined, and that doing the job that way would bring substantial increases in productivity and decreases in effort and fatigue. For his own workers, he devised divisions of labor and invented devices that simplified construction tasks, and by analysis taught his masons to lay a brick with four and a half discrete motions instead of 18, with increases in productivity approaching 200 percent.

Lillian Gilbreth continued her studies in Boston, changing her concentration from literature to psychology to be able to help Frank run his company, and joined him in his passion for efficiency and productivity through analysis. She encouraged him to start a consulting business to disseminate his ideas. Their joint advances streamlined production processes, improved factory layout and materials, and increased the functionality of product design. They tapped into research conducted by Christine McGaffey Frederick, author of *Household Engineering: Scientific Management in the Home* (1915), a work that applied time-and-motion analysis to efficient kitchen design.

The Gilbreths began their family—it eventually came to six girls and six boys, exactly as they had planned—and moved to Rhode Island in 1910. Lillian earned her doctorate from Brown University in psychology in 1915, with her four children at the ceremony. Working with her husband, who focused more on the mechanical aspects of worker efficiency, Lillian Gilbreth paid greater attention to its human aspects, noting that workers were motivated both by such direct incentives as job satisfaction and such indirect ones as money. She was one of the first in her field to recognize that stress and fatigue affected workers' time-management ability.

An innovator in ergonomics and career assessment, Lillian Gilbreth stressed the physical and psychological isolation that impaired workers. With her husband, she published two monographs, *A Primer of Scientific Management* (1912) and *Applied Motion Study* (1917); on her own, she published *The Psychology of Management* (1914), the touchstone of a new field of study. She patented an electric mixer, home lighting fixtures, and a domestic trash can equipped with a foot-pedal that lifted the lid, thus saving the housekeeper repeated hand-washing. Her labor-saving kitchens, designed for the Brooklyn Gas Company and featured at an international training center at New York University, aided homemakers, particularly the disabled, whom she studied at the Institute of Rehabilitation Medicine.

After Frank Gilbreth's sudden fatal heart attack in 1924, Lillian Gilbreth took over Gilbreth, Inc. while also managing a household of twelve children. (Two of her children, Frank Junior and Ernestine, later commemorated their unusual family in two humorous memoirs, *Cheaper by the Dozen* [1949] and *Belles on Their Toes* [1950]). She sent the children to college on her earnings as a consultant to such firms as Johnson & Johnson, Arma, and Macy's and as a world-renowned expert on workplace enhancement. She wrote *The Home-Maker and Her Job* in 1927 and *Living With Our Children* in 1928, in which she acknowledged that individual needs, fulfillment and happiness—including those of wives and mothers—must be integrated with home-management principles.

From her studies of domestic work came articles for women's magazines and two books, *Normal Lives for the Disabled* (1945) and *Management in the Home* (1954). In the former, which she wrote in collaboration with engineer and mathematician Edna Yost, she encouraged the handicapped to seek jobs in 24 categories, including operating a meat market and managing a restaurant. In the latter text, co-authored with writers Orpha Mae Thomas and Eleanor Clymer, she named specific ways of expediting culinary work, such as baking, vegetable preparation, and roasting, by applying the industrial concept of organizing work centers.

Gilbreth applied other principles of efficiency, such as work simplification, to her designs for homes, which included intensely detailed specifications on such matters as placement of appliances, doors and windows; multiple use of spaces and facilities; and traffic patterns. She proposed such time-savers as storing food in the quantities used and assembling complete meals in a single freezer container. One of her home plans suited a housewife with a heart condition; others were designed for farm families. Writing for housewives with outside jobs, Gilbreth urged thinking beyond restrictive names like "dining room" and "attic," and suggested making a chart that divided uses of home space into four categories: quiet activities, living, feeding, and working. After pairing these with a parallel list of available rooms, the housewife could draw lines from activities to rooms and label each line with the names of the family members who participated in the activity. To complete these shifts in purpose and use, she instructed the reader to "draw a floor plan to scale...[with] two-dimensional scale models of your furniture out of cardboard so you can move them about.".

Gilbreth put her principles of efficient work to good use. As a spokesperson for women, she served on the President's Emergency Committee for Unemployment Relief in 1930, creating a successful national program called Share the Work. During World War II, she advised the government on the conversion of factories to war production. She also lectured at the Dartmouth College Conference on Scientific Management and the First World Power Congress and taught industrial engineering at Bryn Mawr, Rutgers, Newark College of Engineering and, from 1935 to 1948, at Purdue, where she was the first woman professor of engineering.

Lillian Gilbreth retired from Purdue at age 70 but continued to write and consult until late in her eighties. She died in Phoenix at 93.

— MARY ELLEN SNODGRASS

A Primer of Scientific Management (with Frank Gilbreth), 1912

The Psychology of Management: The Function of the Mind in Determining, Teaching and Installing Methods of Least Waste, 1914

Applied Motion Study (with Frank Gilbreth), 1917

The Home-Maker and Her Job, 1927

Living With Our Children, 1928

Normal Lives for the Disabled (with Edna Yost), 1945

Management in the Home: Happier Living Through Saving Time and Energy (with Orpha Mae Thomas and Eleanor Clymer), 1954

The Quest of the One Best Way: A Sketch of the Life of Frank Bunker Gilbreth, 1990

As I Remember: An Autobiography, 1998.

Hannah Glasse

HANNAH GLASSE MAY BE THE ONLY COOKBOOK AUTHOR—CERTAINLY OF HER day—celebrated in epic poetry. *The Mince Pie: An Heroic Epistle* (1800) compares Glasse's mighty treatise, *The Art of Cookery, Made Plain and Easy*, to novelistic effusions that excited the senses of her contemporaries:

What lips unmoisten'd speak that glorious name?
What bosom burns not with charcoal flame?
Yet when reflection views her ardent mind
Kindling the kitchen range of human kind;
When all the culinary art is found
In one octavo volume neatly bound;
From rapt amaze to liq'rish fancies tost,
We scarcely credit what delights us most:
Till, led by appetite, our thoughts advance,
And grave receipt books look like gay romance.

Glasse was no ordinary cookbook author, and with **Elizabeth Raffald** was one of only two female culinary writers of the eighteenth century noticed by the *Dictionary of National Biography*. Indeed, *The Art of Cookery* went through no fewer than seventeen editions between 1747 and 1803, adding recipes and graphics even after Glasse's death. The text became synonymous with the type of encyclopedic culinary tome popular well into the nineteenth century. Moreover, it had personality. Glasse frequently appended "Notes" to her recipes offering variations, procedural advice, or outspoken opinions on some aspect of the dish, intimating that she was right in the kitchen cooking along with the reader. The text inspired confidence.

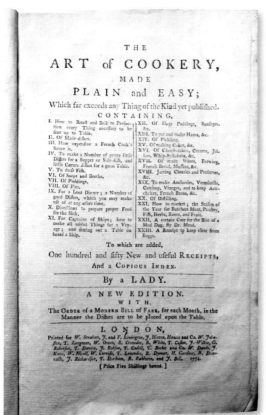

The title page of the first edition of *The Art of Cookery Made Plain and Easy,* 1747

Like most early cookbooks, *The Art of Cookery* borrowed liberally from its predecessors. What distinguished it, was Glasse's simplifications and clarifications, which made the recipes suitable for inexperienced cooks. This was a concern of female cookbook authors, who unlike their male counterparts were not writing for chefs in great houses, but for servants and middle-class mistresses, who often had no one at home to demonstrate culinary technique. Glasse claimed that her text would relieve mistresses of the need to supervise, that is, it would "improve the Servants, and save the Ladies a great deal of Trouble." The frontispiece to later editions shows a lady copying a recipe from the text and handing to a servant, who takes it off to the kitchen by herself.

Naturally, Glasse was caught up in the love/hate relationship that British cookbooks carried on with France. She repeatedly denounced French cooking as extravagant, but smuggled in French-inspired recipes anyway. While she claimed that some such dishes only had French "names," she was obviously fascinated by high Gallic cuisine, and printed several expensive recipes probably because she knew that her readers wanted them. Indeed, by the mid-eighteenth century, British food was becoming cosmopolitan, and *The Art of Cookery* also included recipes from the rest of the Continent and even the first recipes from the colonies—for example, Indian curry and pilau. Clearly, Glasse had long sea voyages in mind when she produced a chapter "For Captains of Ships," which included a recipe for "Ketchup to keep twenty Years."

Like many cookbook authors of her day, Glasse was not a professional cook. She wrote because she needed money. She was the illegitimate daughter of the educated, but unemployed Isaac Allgood of Hexham, and an Irish widow named Hannah Reynolds. Glasse's husband—John Glasse—was also markedly unsuccessful. He was said to be feckless, an adventurer, and 50 years old rather than 30, as he claimed to be. To raise money for her large number of children, Glasse tried selling a patent medicine for a while, until she finally wrote her magnum opus. As the book was launched, she also became a fashionable habit-maker, advertising "Riding Habits, Josephs, Great Coats, Horsemens Coats, Russia Coats, Hussar Coats, Bed-Gowns, Night-Coats, and Robes de shambres, Widows Weeds, Sultains, and Cantouches." If nothing else, Glasse was entrepreneurial. Yet by 1754 she was bankrupt, owing the astronomical sum of 10,000 Pounds. How she arrived at this condition is unclear, though it may have stemmed from her involvement with the set surrounding the Prince of Wales. As part of the resolution of her debt, Glasse sold the copyright to *The Art of Cookery*, as well as the printed sheets of the fifth edition, the last to have been edited by Glasse herself (and the first to feature a recipe for ice cream). After that, the book lived on its reputation, but was constantly changed. Glasse produced two other books, *The Compleat Confectioner* (1760/61) and *The Servant's Directory* (also 1760), neither of which were as successful as her first. Like her first book, the *Confectioner* was to a considerable degree a confection of others' recipes, notably from Edward Lambert's *The Art of Confectionary* (1744). *The Servant's Directory* was more like a conduct book, and is of interest today because, in addition to the usual officious admonitions, it gives detailed descriptions of each servant's obligations in maintaining a household. It went through at least four editions.

There are few records pertaining to Glasse's life after the bankruptcy. Not too ironically, however, many later cookbooks stole recipes from hers. Perhaps their authors recognized staying power. *The Art of Cookery* might be remembered as the first cookbook to become an institution, to take on a life of its own independent of that of its author. In this sense, it is a precursor to perennials such as **Irma Rombauer**'s *The Joy of Cooking*, whose longevity still does not come close. In the world of cookbook classics, *The Art of Cookery* takes first place, establishing the whole idea of cookbook classics.

— SANDRA SHERMAN

The Art of Cookery, Made Plain and Easy, 1747
The Compleat Confectioner, 1760/61
The Servant's Directory, 1760

Gogol

ALSO CALLED: Nikolai Gogol

NIKOLAI GOGOL, ONE OF NINETEENTH-CENTURY RUSSIA's greatest writers, was born on March 19, 1809, in Sorochintsy, near the Ukrainian city of Poltava. Although his family claimed noble Cossack ancestry, that was a fabrication on his grandfather's part, and Gogol suffered from an awareness of his modest background. He attended boarding school in Poltava and high school in Nezhin, another provincial Ukrainian town. In 1829 he settled in St. Petersburg, where for some years he served in the civil service, taught history at the Patriotic Institute, and worked as a private tutor.

In 1831, when Gogol published his first stories, Russian literature was still dominated by poetry, but Gogol's linguistic genius and original vision ushered in the golden age of Russian prose. His fantastic transformations of nature and reality have been compared to those of Edgar Allen Poe, and his writing affected all who followed. (Fyodor Dostoevsky is reputed to have said that "we have all come out from under Gogol's 'Overcoat,'" in reference to Gogol's famous story of that name.) Gogol was, however, anxious about the public reception of his work, and he chose to live abroad for twelve years, from 1836-1848, making only brief visits to Russia. He died in Moscow on February 21, 1852.

Gogol's work frequently depicts eating as both an art and an obsession. Well over one hundred different foods are mentioned in his oeuvre, and not just in passing or as backdrop. Characters are often defined by the foods they like or by the amount they consume, and Gogol details methods of preparation and presentation. In "Old World Landowners," a remote country estate with its never-ending bounty represents a kind of land of Cockaigne, as well as a lost way of life. A typical day of eating includes an early breakfast with coffee; a mid-morning snack of lard biscuits, poppy-seed pies, and salted mushrooms; a late-morning snack of vodka, more mushrooms, and dried fish; a dinner at noon of various porridges and stews, their juices tightly sealed in earthenware pots; an early afternoon snack of watermelon and pears; a mid-afternoon snack of fruit dumplings with berries; a late-afternoon snack of yet other delicacies from the larder; and supper at half past nine. The woman of the house, Pulkheria Ivanovna, typifies a great hostess—she "always liked to prepare more than was needed, to have some on hand"—and the rhythm of her life is determined by the meals she serves. Her husband, Afanasy Ivanovich, spends much of his time watching the servant girls run in and out of the larder, and he is aroused by the secret aspect of the place with its promise of sensual pleasures. In another of Gogol's works, the novel *Dead Souls*, the hero, Pavel Chichikov, travels from estate to estate in his quest for deeds to serfs ("souls") who have died, in the process moving from dinner table to dinner table. Gogol characterizes each household by the fare it provides.

Contemporary critics objected to so much food and drink in Gogol's work; so did his friends, who complained that they were "living in Gogol's stomach." By all accounts Gogol's appetite was prodigious, even unhealthily so. He had a particular fondness for macaroni, which he had learned to make in Italy, and he often prepared it for his friends. Gogol proclaimed the stomach the human body's "most noble" organ. He was obsessed with what he ate, partly because he suffered from severe digestive problems. Gogol was convinced that his stomach was malformed—upside down, in fact, a position he claims the "renowned doctors" in Paris had discovered. His letters to friends are filled with descriptions of his gastric distress, which was brought on by both nerves and overeating.

Gogol's source of torment—his appetite—ultimately became his inspiration, his muse, transforming into entertainment the hunger that affected his whole being. Yet his gourmandizing bespoke something beyond a mere physical urge; his hunger was existential, and not easily satisfied. If hunger is life, then for Gogol, it was also art. Plagued with self-doubt about his writing, Gogol could no longer eat. Instead, after years of gastric and psychic distress, he crafted for himself a state of spiritual grace, which he could attain only through starvation. Under the influence of Father Matvei Konstantinovsky, Gogol began to fast, and in the end starved himself to death.

Vladimir Nabokov has noted "the curiously physical side of Gogol's genius. The belly is the belle of his stories, the nose is their beau." At the end of Gogol's life, his stomach was nearly gone—in Nabokov's words, it "had become so soft that [the doctors] could feel his backbone." From his mouth and nose leeches dangled. Gogol refused all food and medication and refused to speak, apart from begging that the leeches be removed. In a gesture full of irony, loaves of hot bread were placed all around his chilled body to warm it. After Gogol died, following Russian custom his corpse was laid out on the dining table, a symbolic end to a life that had been so viscerally lived.

— DARRA GOLDSTEIN

Evenings on a Farm Near Dikanka, 2 vols, 1831-32
"Old World Landowners," 1835
"The Inspector General," 1836
"The Nose," 1836
"The Overcoat," 1842
Dead Souls, 1841-46

Charles Goodnight

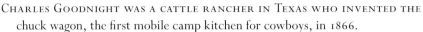
1836–1929

CHARLES GOODNIGHT WAS A CATTLE RANCHER IN TEXAS WHO INVENTED THE chuck wagon, the first mobile camp kitchen for cowboys, in 1866.

Born on March 5, 1836, on a farm in Macoupin County, Illinois, Goodnight moved to Texas as a young boy with his family in 1845 and started his own cattle business there in 1856. During the American Civil War (1861–1865), Goodnight fought with a unit of Texas rangers defending the western frontier of the state, primarily against Indian raids. When his military service ended in 1864, he returned to the cattle business and joined other cattlemen in rounding up thousands of cattle that had roamed free in Texas during the disruptions of the Civil War.

In 1866, in partnership with another rancher, Oliver Loving (1812–1867), Goodnight organized a cattle drive of two thousand animals overland from Fort Belknap, Texas, westward to Fort Sumner, New Mexico, where the cattle could be sold for a higher price than in Texas. The trail they blazed became known as the Goodnight-Loving trail, with subsequent branches of their later-legendary cattle trail extending northward into Colorado and Wyoming.

Prior to 1866, cowboys riding on the open range had carried their own food in saddlebags on their horses, cooking it themselves over an open fire wherever they camped for the night. On longer journeys additional food supplies were sometimes carried in "chuck boxes" strapped onto pack mules. ("Chuck" is cowboy slang for "food.") But for his first long trail drive, Goodnight arranged to supply the food, a cook, and a mobile kitchen for his crew of eighteen cowhands who would be camping out for a month as they moved the cattle over 700 miles of rough, dry terrain.

Goodnight purchased an Army-surplus four-wheeled wooden wagon, which he then had rebuilt to his own specifications. At the back of the wagon he fitted a "chuck box," a large wooden cabinet with shelves and drawers that held cooking ingredients and small utensils. A horizontally hinged door covering the chuck box folded down to form a work table for the cook. Another storage space known as the "boot" carried heavier equipment such as Dutch ovens, iron skillets, grill racks, pothooks, and a large enamelware coffee pot. A length of cowhide or canvas was secured under the wagon as a sling to hold wood and dried cow dung to fuel the cooking fire. The front of the wagon held additional food supplies (flour, dried beans, coffee, salt pork, lard, molasses, sourdough starter), a water barrel, kerosene lanterns, a toolbox, and the cowboys' bedrolls, personal gear, and ropes. The top of the wagon could be covered with waterproof canvas, stretched over arched wooden bows, to protect against the weather. Goodnight's first chuck wagon was pulled by a large team of oxen, but later wagons were pulled by smaller teams of horses or mules.

Goodnight never patented his original design for the chuck wagon. Copies of it (with a few modifications) were made by wood-workers and wagon-build-

A photograph taken c. 1888 and in the possession of the Bugbee family of Clarendon, Texas.

ers throughout the American West. From the late 1860's through the mid-1880's, chuck wagons accompanied the great cattle drives from Texas to markets in the American West and to railheads in Kansas and Missouri where the cattle were shipped by train to markets in the Midwest and East. Many of these migrations of cattle and cowboys took three months or longer, during which time the crew had to be fed every day—breakfast and supper at the chuck wagon, with lunch (usually breakfast leftovers) often eaten on horseback as the cowboys drove the cattle along the trail.

As the railroads extended farther into the American West and Southwest, and as refrigeration became more widespread, long cattle drives overland to railheads and distant markets became unnecessary. But ranchers soon realized the value of chuck wagons as portable kitchens for use during cattle roundups and branding seasons. Thus Goodnight's original concept of the chuck wagon as a mobile kitchen that moved every day in advance of the cattle on the trail evolved into the "ranch wagon" that was set up in outlying areas of the cattle-owner's land, staying in one place for two or three weeks to feed the cowhands working on that part of the ranch.

During the late nineteenth century, despite fluctuations in his personal finances, Goodnight continued in the cattle business, establishing ranches in both Texas and Colorado. He was recognized for his innovations in agriculture, land irrigation, stock breeding, and marketing, including crossing domesticated buffalo with Angus cattle to produce the first "cattalo."

In 1870 Charles Goodnight married Mary Ann (Molly) Dyer (1839–1926), with whom he lived for fifty-six years but had no children. Although Goodnight had very little formal schooling, he and his wife, a former teacher, took a great interest in education and founded Goodnight College, a co-educational academy that operated from 1898 to 1917 in the small Texas Panhandle town of Goodnight. In 1927, on his ninety-first birthday, he married twenty-six-year-old Corrine Goodnight (not a blood relative). He died on December 12, 1929, at his winter home in Phoenix, Arizona, and was buried next to his first wife in the community cemetery in Goodnight, Texas. In 1958 Charles Goodnight was one of the first five people inducted into the National Cowboy Hall of Fame in Oklahoma City, Oklahoma, and later he became the model for the character Woodrow Call in the novel *Lonesome Dove* (1988), written by Larry McMurtry.

— SHARON HUDGINS

Sylvester Graham

SYLVESTER GRAHAM, A NEW ENGLAND CLERGYMAN NOW known only for the brown crackers and whole wheat flour that bear his name, is commonly regarded as the father of American food reformers. His advocacy of puritanical vegetarianism made early "Grahamites" of such influential figures as newspaper editor Horace Greeley, Seventh Day Adventist Church co-founder, Ellen White, and the director of the Church's legendary dietary sanitarium, John Henry Kellogg and his wife **Ella Eaton Kellogg**, whose innovations in grain-and-nut-based foods would become the basis of America's breakfast-food industry.

Graham was born in West Suffield, Connecticut, the last of seventeen children of the 72-year old Reverend John Graham, Jr. Following his father's death, his mother became mentally deranged, leaving the child to be raised by various relatives. He later studied languages briefly at Amherst College in 1823, was ordained as a Presbyterian minister in 1826, began preaching in New Jersey after a long illness, and became general agent for the Pennsylvania Temperance Society in 1830. His shaky health inspired a passionate interest in nutrition and human physiology that formed the basis of popular lectures he gave throughout the East on what came to be known as the Graham System. Later published in several collections that included the widely read *Lectures on the Science of Human Life* (1839), his talks encouraged abstinence from meat, alcohol, and tobacco as well as all hot and spicy foods, too much food, and excessive sexuality. In their place, he advocated a Spartan grain-based diet with fresh fruit and vegetables, clean water, hard mattresses, fresh air and exercise, sexual restraint, and cheerfulness at meals.

Graham's recommendations came at a time when America's diet consisted largely of corn, pork, molasses, puddings, and pies, with potatoes cooked in lard and plenty of whisky to wash it all down. Early in his speaking career Graham seized upon the sorry state of commercial bread that had begun to enter the New England marketplace after the 1830's. In his *Treatise on Bread and Bread-Making* (1837), Graham advocated homemade brown bread made of unbolted flour and bran instead of the light, thin-crusted loaves then being sold which he condemned for being adulterated with unwholesome fillers and additives. (For such criticism, the lecturer once had to be rescued from a mob of angry Boston bakers.) Farinaceous foods were also promoted as a way of dealing with masturbation and other forms of unrestrained sexuality, which seemed to Graham the cause of innumerable mental and physical illnesses that he detailed at length. (His public accounts of sexually related ailments had to be curtailed when he found women fainting during his lectures.) In his view, the best way to curb sexual appetite and enjoy a long healthy life was to live "entirely on the products of the vegetable kingdom and pure water." To be avoided were all condiments and spices such as pepper, ginger, cinnamon, and horseradish, which he considered "all highly exciting and exhausting." Dairy products—including milk, eggs, and butter—were not altogether forbidden but should be used only sparingly and carefully. Cheese was permitted if it was mild and not aged. Besides alcohol and tobacco, coffee and tea were also considered poisons, as were any drugs offered by physicians and other medical practitioners of the day. "All medicine, as such, is itself an evil," Graham insisted, at a time when all medical licensing laws were rescinded or unenforced and any quack could call himself a doctor.

Graham's personal popularity was greatest in the 1830's when Grahamite boarding houses were established in Massachusetts and New York and the American Physiological Society published a weekly in Boston in 1937 and 1938 called the *Graham Journal of Health and Longevity* which illustrated and supported his principles. Disciples of Graham also figured prominently in the Brook Farm utopian community and other American reformist circles. With fame also came derision from contemporaries like Ralph Waldo Emerson who called Graham "the poet of bran and pumpkins." His nutritional philosophy did little to help his own health which was never robust and began progressively to falter after 1840 along with his career as a speaker and author. Graham died at the age of 57 in Northampton, Massachusetts, before completing a last collection of lectures, *The Philosophy of Sacred History*, which related his teachings to scripture. Yet the influence of Sylvester Graham is still felt after more than a century and a half and can be seen in the lifestyle choices promoted by many of today's nutritionists and diet experts who continue to favor largely vegetarian regimens and healthy physical activity.

— BARBARA HABER

A Treatise on Bread and Bread-Making, 1837
Lectures on the Science of Human Life, 1839
Letter to the Hon. Daniel Webster, on Compromises of the Constitution, 1850
The Philosophy of Sacred History, 1855

Jane Grigson

1928–1990

JANE GRIGSON WAS A NATURAL-BORN RESEARCHER WHO TURNED TO FOOD writing in the mid-1960's. Born to a middle-class family and raised in Gloucester and Sunderland, in northeast England, she earned a degree in English from Cambridge in 1949, then worked in art galleries and publishers' offices, and became a translator of Italian. In 1966 she shared the John Florio prize for her translation of Beccaria's "Of Crime and Punishment."

In the early 1960's, Jane and her husband, the poet Geoffrey Grigson, bought a tumble-down house in Trôo, in the Loire Valley of France. They divided their time between there and Strand Hill, Wiltshire. In Trôo, cooking for Geoffrey and their daughter, Sophie, she became fascinated with the range of ingredients and artisanal products available in her small village, as well as the serious French approach to food.

By happy accident, a friend of hers from the village, Adey Horton, had been commissioned by a publisher to write a book about charcuterie. Jane was to be the researcher, but in the end Horton was unable to write the book, and Jane completed it alone.

The book, *Charcuterie and French Pork Cookery* (1967), was "a real novelty and a wonderfully welcome one," wrote **Elizabeth David** in an introduction to a posthumous anthology of Jane Grigson's writing. "Now that the book has long since passed into the realm of kitchen classics we take it for granted, but for British readers and cooks in the late 1960's its contents, the clarity of the writing, and the confident knowledge of its subject and its history displayed by this young author were new treats for all of us."

The book has been translated into French, a singular honor for an English food writer.

In 1968 Elizabeth David recommended Jane for a job as weekly food columnist at *The Observer*, a position she herself had declined. Jane's association with *The Observer* continued until her death.

Jane approached her newspaper articles as she had done her book: by putting food in a wider cultural context, using diligent but not pedantic scholarship. She would combine humorous quotes from Chaucer on the subject of pike galantine, for example, with a careful recipe for a modern chicken-and-pork version of the same ancient dish. On watermelon, she would evoke the hot summers of Florence and the icy fruit salads displayed in café windows, and then go on to quote the tenth-century Japanese author Sei Shonagon on fruit sherbets. And she would end her piece with practical advice on storing and freezing a hollowed-out watermelon-half fruit "container" for re-use another time!

Her prose style was inimitable. *Charcuterie and French Pork Cookery* begins, "It could be said that European civilization—and Chinese civilization too—has been founded on the pig. Easily domesticated, omnivorous household and village scavenger, clearer of scrub and undergrowth, devourer of forest acorns, yet content with a sty—and delightful when cooked or cured, from his snout to his tail."

Jane's next books were *Good Things* (1971), a collection of essays from *The Observer*; and *The International Wine and Food Society's Guide to Fish Cookery* (1973). In 1974 came *English Food,* in which she denounced the poor quality of food and cooking in England, and showed how it might be put right.

She next wrote *The Mushroom Feast* (1975) and the prize-winning duo *Jane Grigson's Vegetable Book* (1978) and *Jane Grigson's Fruit Book* (1982). Between them came *Food with the Famous* (1979), in which she indulged her fascination with historical figures by trying to better understand some of the great authors—Jane Austen, **Thomas Jefferson**, Marcel Proust, Emile Zola, and others—through their writings about food.

The Observer Guide to European Cookery (1983) and *The Observer Guide to English Cookery* (1984) reflected further work for the newspaper. *Exotic Fruits and Vegetables* (with paintings by Charlotte Knox) expanded her range, while *The Cooking of Normandy* (1987) brought her back to the food of her beloved France.

Jane's attitude on learning is worth noting. When the English food writer Geraldene Holt professed a lack of confidence in choosing a subject for her second cookbook, Jane told her firmly, "That's how you learn. Find something that you are interested in, write it well, and go out and teach it to others." It is this straightforwardness and lack of pretension that spurred **M. F. K. Fisher** to liken Jane to "a freshly baked loaf."

She is also recognized for her warmth and sense of humor. **Alan Davidson** wrote in an obituary for *The Independent* that "she was above all a friendly writer, … the most companionable presence in the kitchen…."

Jane was always a crusader. For years a champion of top-quality ingredients, she began to see her efforts to promote small producers take hold in the late 1980's. However, successive health scares about chickens, milk, and eggs made her very angry. "I advise action, not just another research committee," she said in a speech to the Guild of Food Writers in London in 1988, denouncing the government policy of allowing salmonella in eggs. "You may get away with allowing agribusiness to poison our drinking water; it cannot get away with eggs."

Jane died of cancer at age 62. After her death, her daughter Sophie and a group of colleagues and friends set up the Jane Grigson Trust, which awards scholarships and encompasses a growing cookery library where Jane's own cookbooks form the core of the collection.

— Elizabeth Field

Charcuterie and French Pork Cookery, 1967
Good Things, 1971
The International Wine and Food Society's Guide to Fish Cookery, 1973
English Food: An Anthology, chosen by Jane Grigson, 1974
The Mushroom Feast, 1975
Jane Grigson's Vegetable Book, 1978
Food with the Famous, 1979
Jane Grigson's Fruit Book, 1982
The Observer Guide to European Cookery, 1983
The Observer Guide to English Cookery, 1984
Exotic Fruits and Vegetables, 1986
The Cooking of Normandy, 1987

Alexandre Balthazar Laurent Grimod de la Reynière

❧ 1758–1837 ❧

AN ORIGINAL, ECCENTRIC HERO IN THE GASTRONOMIC PANTHEON, GRIMOD de la Reynière is widely considered the first modern Western food critic. His finest work is the eight-volume *Almanach des Gourmands* (1803-12). The *Almanach* contained the earliest narrative restaurant guide to Paris, and it was the first European food guide to become wildly popular among readers.

It is not for the timid to imagine a day in the life of the La Reynière family, with its clashing personalities and class conflicts. Grimod's bourgeois father Laurent amassed immense wealth working as a tax farmer. His aristocratic mother Suzanne de Jarente, daughter of a marquis, forever resented having married down. When Grimod was born with malformed hands, Madame de la Reynière blamed her husband, while he neglected to have his son's birth certificate properly drawn up, and so Grimod remained a bastard in the eyes of the law. He later blamed both parents for his "monstrous" heritage, although the metal prostheses he wore under white gloves were not a social impediment, and he was able to write and draw comfortably. His paternal grandfather Gaspard, a renowned gourmand, knew Voltaire. The liberal censor Malesherbes, minister to Louis XVI, was Grimod's uncle by marriage.

From Favre's Dictionnaire universel de cuisine, *1903*

After training as a lawyer, Grimod reviewed plays for Republican journals during the last decades of the *ancien régime*, a practice which gave him entree into the theatrical demi-monde and guaranteed him regular contact with Parisian actresses. Beginning in the 1770's he hosted *philosophical dinners* and *mystifiers dinners*, most infamously staging sustenance as spectacle on February 1, 1783. This dinner became the talk of Paris even before it happened. The twenty-two people who had received invitations to a "burial and supper" at the La Reynière family *hôtel* at 1, Champs Elysées made their way through a maze of grotesquely decorated rooms, finally to be seated at a table disguised as a catafalque. During dinner Grimod loudly announced the provenance of each item brought in for consumption. The many grocers and butchers, bread-makers and pâtissiers whose wares composed the meal were all humble relatives of Grimod's distinguished parents. Later in the evening an additional 300 people filed into an upper gallery to watch as dessert was eaten below. The coffin reminded all present that progress toward death, like digestion, is democratic. Grimod's carefully choreographed ceremony mocked not only court spectacle and aristocratic pretension, but also the rituals beloved of exclusive societies such as the Freemasons, paradoxically associated with Enlightenment despite its universalist aims.

Expectedly, the funeral supper scandalized Grimod's parents, who had their son banished from Paris by means of a *lettre de cachet* or sealed letter, used by *ancien régime* kings to discipline troublesome subjects without the bother of a hearing. Grimod married the actress Adélaïde Feuchère while exiled in Lyon, where he briefly worked as a traveling salesman hawking spices, pharmaceuticals, and perfumes. Following the Revolution, and learning of his father's death in 1793, Grimod returned to the house on the Champs-Elysées to live with Adélaïde and his mother. The family fortune was all but gone. During these thin years Grimod reputedly made his own bread to save money and guarantee a loaf of decent quality. He again turned to writing, this time to support himself.

A general climate of indulgence followed the rigors of the Revolution and the Terror, and the number of boutiques and caterers in Paris increased rapidly. Publishing the *Almanach des gourmands* (beginning in 1803) was an opportunistic coup—a savvy response to changing times that also put food on the author's table. In the *Almanach* Grimod proposed to educate his readers, exchanging his knowledge of Paris and of gastronomic culture for his readers' buying power. Combining practical advice with hyperbolic fantasy, Grimod describes each month and season in terms of available foodstuffs, and he walks his readers through Paris, neighborhood by neighborhood, evaluating shops and restaurants for quality. The style is urbane and idiosyncratic. The *Almanach* provides a lovingly detailed catalogue of the edible pleasures of Paris, while digressions show an outrageous sense of humor and an ironic view of recent history. The first *Almanach* volume established the formal paradigm for the restaurant guidebook that has been followed for the last two centuries.

In a further burst of inspiration described in the second volume (1804), Grimod created a tasting jury as well as a *légitimation* or food-judging process by which caterers and restaurateurs were persuaded to trade food items for a write-up in the *Almanach*. Merchants benefited from having their names publicized, and Grimod came away well fed. The *légitimation* professionalized informed eating and fostered commercial success for caterers and food-writers alike. It further bound together cook (producer) and eater-reviewer (consumer), implicating the medium of print in influencing culinary cultural production. It is a suggestive coincidence that in the same year Napoleon forcibly invited Pope Pius VII to France to have himself crowned Emperor of the French, Grimod, too, created for himself a position of authority, as gastronomic law-giver for the "Gourmand Empire."

Having cooked up a successful commercial enterprise, it is curious that in later *Almanach* volumes, Grimod proceeded to critique his own literary invention as well as his own self-created position of gustatory authority. He shortened the guide-book section of the *Almanach* and relegated it to the back of the later volumes, complaining that for a "real" writer the task of keeping a guide current was boring and repetitive. He focused instead on broad-ranging essays or short articles, sometimes expanding upon or correcting statements from earlier volumes. These articles cover a variety of topics: the history of tablecloths, the advantages of **Nicolas Appert**'s new preserving process, the utility of placing pewter balls under the dining room floorboards to retain heat in winter, the cannibalistic symbolism of Louis XVI's decapitation a decade earlier. His writing became increasingly multi-layered. Through the lens of food, Grimod scrutinized literature, history, and the contemporary world. Through the metaphor of gastronomy, he critiqued commercialism at home in France as well as Napoleon's policy of military expansionism across Europe. He even promoted gastronomic writing as the new common tongue for a transnational, peace-loving Republic of Letters for the nineteenth century. As it emerges in the later *Almanach* volumes, Grimod's food-writing tends to blur the borders delineating national culinary customs. He favors enriching the cook's practice and the eater's diet with cosmopolitan diversity. Grimod championed comfort and convenience as well as quality, variety, and knowledge. He was little concerned with tradition for its own sake, nor did he care about elegance or ostentation.

While the business of writing almanacs flourished, Grimod paid high overhead in fatigue and hours worked. In a damning comparison in a late *Almanach* volume, he likened the professional gastronome's body to a machine. To be a food writer, he concluded, required becoming a food processor that must run constantly to keep pace with food samples and publication deadlines. Grimod's table talk prefigures and mirrors our own food culture and industry. His gastronomic writing is remarkable for promoting knowledgeable enjoyment without shying from aesthetic self-critique and exploration of the ethical implications of commercialization.

Although the *Almanach* remains Grimod's most important contribution to gastronomic and culinary history, two other publications deserve mention. As a complement to the yearly *Almanach*, Grimod established the monthly *Journal des Gourmands et des belles* in January 1806. He imagined the magazine would function as an organ of communication for enlightened, educated eaters everywhere on the continent. But idealism soon ceded to disillusionment, and following the November 1807 issue, Grimod abandoned the periodical, which was taken over by others. He then published the *Manuel des* **Amphitryons** (1808), a one-volume, semi-serious reference work for wealthy hosts. The section on "Elements of Gourmand Etiquette" is largely culled from earlier *Almanach* volumes, while the menus are cobbled together from Grimod's extensive cookbook library, and the "Treatise on the Dissection of Meat" draws on a tradition of illustrated carving guides published in the Italian and German states, the Netherlands, and France over the preceding two centuries and more. The *Manuel* encrypts *ancien régime* mores in words and pictures, but it also modifies older customs for contemporary times. In the *Manuel*, Grimod reforms the grand traditions of hosting evoked in the work's title, to make them both more democratic and more humanistic.

Following the appearance of the last *Almanach* volume, Grimod retired from Paris to Villiers-sur-Orge and ceased to publish, although he lived another quarter-century. It is not clear what motivated Grimod's untimely abdication of the gourmand imperial throne. Pressure from Napoleon's censors as well as criminal and civil lawsuits waged against him for corrupt practices surely contributed. Competition from the now-flourishing gastronomic publishing industry may have been another factor. Finally, it is possible that Grimod became disillusioned with the publishing and tasting enterprise he had invented and in which he participated, and whose practices were quickly co-opted to promote commercial interests and nationalistic sentiment.

— JULIA LUISA ABRAMSON

Almanach des Gourmands, 8 vols., 1803-12
Manuel des Amphitryons, 1808

Kundan Lal Gujral

❧ 1910—1987 ❧

ALSO CALLED: Kundan Lal

TODAY TANDOORI CHICKEN, BUTTER CHICKEN, TANDOORI ROTI, AND DAL makhani are staples of Indian restaurants around the world, but sixty years ago they were virtually unknown, even on the Indian subcontinent. They were the creation of one of India's most dynamic and innovative restaurateurs, Kundan Lal Gujral, founder of India's most influential restaurant, Moti Mahal in Delhi.

Kundan Lal, as he was called, was born in 1910 near Peshawar, which is now in Pakistan but was then part of the North West Frontier province of British India. He was a Hindu of Punjabi and Pathan origin. As a child he worked in a small catering shop in Peshawar, which eventually expanded into a restaurant called Moti Mahal ("Pearl Palace" in Hindustani). It served such local specialties as kabobs—pieces of chicken or goat with very little spicing roasted on skewers over hot coals in a *tandoor,* a large clay oven buried in the ground that originated in Iran or Central Asia. The kabobs were accompanied by rotis, round unleavened wheat bread baked in the tandoor. Kundan Lal's tremendous energy and ebullient personality helped to make the restaurant a local success.

In 1947, British India was partitioned into Pakistan, a Muslim state, and India, a secular state with a Hindu majority. Millions of people left their homes and crossed the new borders to settle in the other country. Often they had few resources other than their energy and determination to succeed. Kundan Lal and his family ended up in the Indian capital Delhi, where he set up a little roadside café on Daryaganj, a street in Old Delhi, the ancient capital of the Moghul dynasty. He called the restaurant Moti Mahal. Kundan Lal found a tandoor maker, a fellow refugee, who experimented with different designs until he came up with an aboveground version that would work in a restaurant kitchen.

To make the bland food of his region more palatable to Indian tastes, Kundan Lal tried different spice mixtures until he settled on the blend used in the restaurant today. Its recipe is a secret but it includes ground coriander seeds, black pepper, and a mild red pepper that gives tandoori chicken its characteristic red color. Pieces of chicken and whole chickens were marinated in this mixture and yogurt and roasted in the tandoor. To please richer palates (and, it is sometimes claimed, to use left-over tandoori chicken), he created butter chicken: pieces of roasted chicken cooked in a tomato, cream, and butter sauce. Another Moti Mahal specialty was dal makhani, black lentils cooked slowly overnight and mixed with tomatoes, butter, and fresh cream.

In the tradition of many great restaurateurs, Kundan was a consummate showman, easily identified by his lambswool fez, curled moustache, and courtly manners. The restaurant became a favorite of Indian political leaders, including India's first Prime Minister Jawaharlal Nehru and his daughter Indira Gandhi, who later became Prime Minister, who brought many visiting VIPs there. An Indian official once told the Shah of Iran that coming to Delhi without eating at Moti Mahal would be like visiting Agra without seeing the Taj Mahal or New York without seeing the Statue of Liberty. The restaurant also catered many important events, including a state dinner for visiting First Lady Jacqueline Kennedy and the wedding reception of Nehru's grandson Sanjay Gandhi.

Kundan Lal opened branches in Delhi and Moosoorie but remained a fixture at his original restaurant until the end of his days. His grandson Monish, who studied restaurant management, recently launched a more upmarket version of the restaurant called Moti Mahal Deluxe Tandoor Trail restaurants. Today Moti Mahal has countless imitators in India and throughout the world. And, in one of the ironies of culinary history, tandoori chicken is regarded as the quintessential Indian dish!

— Colleen Taylor Sen

H

Fritz Haber

❦ 1868–1934 ❦

CHEMIST FRITZ HABER, A DEVOTED SCIENTIST, A PATRIOTIC GERMAN, and a Jew, made possible both the lives and the deaths of millions. He was the first to efficiently synthesize ammonia, the raw material for making nitrogen fertilizer, without which about a third of the world's present population of six billion people would starve. He was also an active proponent of using poison gas as a weapon of war, played the leading role in its development, and was personally present at the front lines in 1915 when the first extensive poison-gas attack was carried out. And, after his death, the Nazis used a pesticide he had developed, Zyklon-B, to murder large numbers of Jews in concentration camps.

Haber was born in Breslau, Silesia, Prussia (now Wrocław, Poland) as the son of a prosperous chemicals merchant. His mother died in childbirth, and his father remarried when Fritz was nine. The boy remained very close to his stepmother all his life. He attended a *humanistisches Gymnasium,* that is, a high school focused on Latin, Greek, philosophy and literature, which contributed to his lifelong affection for literature and his striking conversational brilliance. He studied at the universities of Berlin and Heidelberg and at the Imperial Physico-Technical Institution in Charlottenburg (Berlin), earning his Ph.D. at age 23. The following year he converted from Judaism, a step that may have had more to do with his German nationalism than any strong religious conviction.

1917

He accepted an assistantship at the Technical Institute in Karlsruhe in 1894, where he taught himself physical chemistry and carried out research in electrochemistry and thermodynamics, becoming a full-fledged professor in 1906. The introduction of his 1898 textbook, *Grundriss der technischen Elektrochemie auf theoretischer Grundlage (Basics of Technical Electrochemistry on a Theoretical Foundation),* made explicit his goal of deriving industrial processes from theoretical chemical research, and his work over the next decade was focused on industrial and physiological measurement techniques, energy loss in steam engines and motors, determination of flame temperatures, and other topics at the boundary of theory and application.

In this same time period, Sir William Crookes, president of the British Association for the Advancement of Science, expressed a widespread concern. In his 1898 presidential address, he warned of a crisis in world food supplies that would arrive, he estimated, by 1931: "England and all civilized nations stand in deadly peril of not having enough to eat," he said, because farmers would be unable to meet the increasing demand for food with available supplies of nitrogen, the main nutrient plants need to grow. At the time, nitrogen fertilizers were made from sodium nitrate—obtained from deposits of nitrate-bearing caliche rock discovered in Chile early in the century—and ammonium sulphate, obtained from coal gas. (Manure from humans, animals, and birds also provided nitrogen, but not in significant long-term quantities.) Crookes reminded his audience that nitrogen gas makes up 79 percent of the earth's atmosphere, though not in a form plants can take up, and he suggested that, to meet the world's increasing nitrogen needs, "it is the chemist who must come to the rescue": Chemists must develop artificial methods for "fixing" atmospheric nitrogen.

The nitrogen molecule (N_2) is inert. To tear it apart so its atoms are free to combine with others requires considerable energy. Lightning bolts do this naturally, allowing the nitrogen atoms to combine with oxygen; the resulting nitrogen oxides dissolve in rain and fall to earth as plant-accessible nitrates. Certain microbes, often in symbiosis with plants—mostly legumes such as peas, clover, soybeans or alfalfa—provide the only other non-artificial pathway for nitrogen fixation, using energy from plant nutrients to turn N_2 into ammonia (NH_3) that is used in turn to make proteins and other nitrogen compounds. Legumes are thus often alternated with other crops because they increase the available nitrogen in the soil.

In the laboratory, imitating lightning by discharging electrical sparks through the air did indeed produce oxidized, or fixed, nitrogen, and the method was also used industrially in the few places where cheap hydroelectric power made it cost-effective. Haber began to study the thermodynamics, or energy relationships, of gas reactions in about 1904, and soon succeeded in synthesizing ammonia—itself a useful fertilizer and the raw material for other fertilizers—from nitrogen and hydrogen. He used an iron catalyst and carried out the reaction at a temperature of 1000°C. But the yield he achieved was low, and the conditions required for the reaction were too demanding for production on an industrial scale. Three years later, with more data from other researchers who had used his theoretical work in thermodynamics, he concluded that, with an osmium or uranium catalyst, it should be possible to reduce the reaction temperature to a more practical 500°C, thus showing the "impressive progress [that] was necessary to awaken technical [that is, industrial] interest in the subject" of synthesizing ammonia.

In June, 1908 he and his English collaborator, Robert Le Rossignol, produced the first 100 grams of ammonia in a demonstration attended by Carl Bosch, a chemist and engineer, and Alwin Mittasch, an expert on catalysis, both employees of the chemical firm Badische Anilin- und Soda Fabrik (BASF). In 1912, after more than 20,000 experiments, Bosch and Mittasch succeeded in industrializing the process (it is today called the Haber-Bosch process) and the first commercial synthetic-ammonia plant went into operation in Oppau, Germany in 1913, with a production capacity of 8700 tons a year.

In 1911, Haber was appointed head of the Kaiser Wilhelm Institute for Physical Chemistry in Berlin-Dahlem. With the outbreak of World War I, the Institute was placed under military control and its work focused on the war effort. Haber's biographer, Margit Szeolleosi-Janze, says that he "considered it his duty, and that was the Prussian in him. It was his duty as a scientist to work with all his might for the goals of the state to win the war." Haber took on research on the supply of war-critical raw materials, of which nitric acid, necessary for the manufacture of high explosives, was the most important. Ammonia is essential in the production of nitric acid, and the Oppau ammonia plant, along with a much larger one subsequently built at Leuna, supplied about half of Germany's needs, contributing greatly to her ability to continue to fight.

Haber also persuaded the initially uninterested German military to support research into chemical weapons and protective devices against them, and urged their use, provided the war could be ended within a year of their first deployment—the time he estimated it would take the Allies to develop their own chemical weapons. Ultimately more than 150 Institute personnel and a staff of 2000 worked on these weapons, developing chlorine and mustard gas and a primitive delivery system. At sunrise on April 22, 1915, near Ypres, France, Haber directed the first large-scale use of poison gas in warfare. Between 5000 and 15,000 Allied troops were affected, of whom half died within ten minutes; 2000 were taken prisoner. German casualties numbered in the hundreds. The German high command, delighted at the new weapon's effectiveness, immediately ordered Haber to the eastern front to set up gas-warfare capabilities there. Haber's wife, chemist Clara Immerwahr, who had objected to his work on gas warfare with increasing vehemence and revulsion, committed suicide.

Many scientists shared Immerwahr's view that Haber's work on poison gas was a perversion of the values of science, and many outside Germany regarded Haber as a war criminal responsible for 1.3 million gas casualties. There was considerable protest when he received the 1918 Nobel Prize in Chemistry for the synthesis of ammonia. However, he continued as head of the Institute in Dahlem, winning admiration for his mentoring of younger scientists, his organization of research, the freedom he gave his department heads, and the "Haber colloquia" at which he brought together people from different disciplines to speak about their work and often himself pointed out convergences or synergies across disciplinary lines. He also continued secretly to assist the German military, in violation of the Versailles Treaty, and, in the hope of helping Germany pay the reparations that the treaty imposed, Haber exhausted himself in a six-year attempt to devise a process for extracting gold from seawater. (It turned out that previous analyses had overestimated the gold content of seawater by a factor of 100 or more.) He carried out further fruitful research in the 1920's, contributed to the establishment of scientific links between Germany and Japan and, in 1930, the establishment of the Japan Institute, and was deeply respected both as a scientist and a citizen.

In 1933, however, the Nazi government purged German universities of Jews; Haber was ordered to dismiss the Jewish scientists working at the Institute. His own position was not then threatened, thanks to his service in World War I, but he responded to the order by stating that he had always chosen his fellow workers on the basis of their professional qualifications and their character, and not their ethnicity. "You will hardly expect a man of 65 to alter the mode of thought that has guided him in the 39 years of his academic career," he added, "and you will appreciate that it is the pride with which he has served his German homeland throughout his life that now dictates his request for retirement."

The same year, Haber left Germany and accepted an invitation to Cambridge University, where he opened a small laboratory. But he was neither happy nor healthy there, and hoped to find an academic home in Switzerland. Traveling through Basel on his way to Palestine to investigate a possible position at what is now the Weizmann Institute of Science in Israel, he suffered a heart attack and died in a hotel room on January 29, 1934.

Today, worldwide ammonia production, mostly in plants using improved versions of the Haber-Bosch process, is 159,100,000 tons.

— MARIO ANDERS

Grundriss der technischen Elektrochemie auf theoretischer Grundlage (Basics of Technical Electrochemistry on a Theoretical Foundation), 1898
Thermodynamik technischer Gasreaktionen (The Thermodynamics of Technical Gas Reactions), 1905

Sarah Josepha Hale

❧ 1788–1879 ❧

SARAH JOSEPHA HALE WAS AMONG THE MOST INFLUENTIAL WOMEN IN nineteenth-century America and the arbiter of the nation's taste for a good portion of that century. She achieved this position mainly through her longtime editorships of the *Ladies' Magazine* and *Godey's Lady's Book*. *Godey's* is considered the forerunner of modern women's magazines. It is difficult for us in the fast-paced, news-overloaded early 21st century to comprehend the influence of these early magazines. Eagerly sought and read, they shaped the lives of nineteenth-century Americans, both in the cities and on the farms.

Sarah Josepha Buell was born to Martha Whittlesey and Gordon Buell in Newport, New Hampshire, in 1788. Her father had been an officer serving under General Horatio Gates during the American Revolution. Returning home wounded and in ill health, he was always extremely proud of his role in American independence. His patriotism was clearly a major influence in Sarah's life, but her mother, with her unusual love of books and learning, had perhaps a greater influence. This combination of pride in America and belief in the importance of learning and education was the guiding principle of Sarah's long and productive life. Her brother Horatio was her closest friend and companion, especially in

Frontispiece of her
Woman's Record

matters of learning. Formal education for women was not an option in those days. Thus, when Horatio went off to Dartmouth, he literally shared his studies with Sarah, providing her with the same textbooks and supervising her progress, so that upon his graduation, she had received the equivalent of a college degree.

Sarah taught in a private school and then, upon her mother's early death in 1811, helped her father run a small inn in Newport. It was there that she met, and in 1813 married, David Hale, a lawyer. Their marriage appears to have been a most congenial one, with David encouraging Sarah in her love of books and in her own writing. Sarah wrote, "We commenced, soon after our marriage, a system of study and reading, which we pursued while he lived. The hours allowed were from eight o'clock in the evening till ten; two hours in the twenty-four; how I enjoyed those hours!"

Then, suddenly, in 1822, shortly before the birth of their fifth child, David Hale died, leaving Sarah a widow with the necessity of raising and educating her five children, the eldest only seven years old. After several attempts at a new career, first as a milliner and then a poet (both professions partially subsidized by David's fellow Freemasons), Sarah decided that her future lay in full-time authorship. In 1827, her first novel, *Northwood*, was published to much acclaim. Its success brought her an offer to edit the *Ladies' Magazine*, which she developed into one of the first successful women's periodicals in America. Sarah edited the *Ladies' Magazine* until 1837, when it was acquired by the publisher Louis A. Godey of Philadelphia. She then became the editor of *Godey's Lady's Book*, serving with distinction for forty years.

Many people today remember *Godey's* simply for its collectible color fashion plates, but in its own day it was an influential arbiter of social and civic values, women's rights and responsibilities, literature, language, intellectual life, music, home design and furnishing, fashion and home-making, and cooking. On the eve of the Civil War, *Godey's* was the most widely read periodical in the United States, boasting 150,000 subscribers. Sarah and Godey literally invented the American magazine, with an American outlook and using American authors (and paying them well). In the magazines she edited, Sarah rejected the then current practice of "clipping," that is, reprinting, without permission or acknowledgement, pieces from other journals, especially British publications. This was possible as there were then no international copyright laws. Sarah championed and promoted, tirelessly, American authors—especially women writers. She not only published their works but promoted them in her editorials and book reviews. Sarah published, among many others, works of Hawthorne, Irving, Longfellow, Holmes, Emerson, Bryant, Whittier, Poe, **Lydia Maria Child**, **Eliza Leslie**, Lydia Sigourney and Harriet Beecher Stowe.

In addition to stories, serials, essays and poems, *Godey's* contained architectural patterns and plans; hand-colored fashion plates; music and dance compositions and instruction; sewing patterns; a "Ladies' Work Department" with detailed instructions for crocheting and other handiwork; advice on home furnishings, health, etiquette, home nursing, family medicine, and consumer goods; science;

cooking recipes; book reviews and an editorial section. Inclusion of the architectural patterns began in 1846 when *Godey's* encouraged private home ownership by establishing the first "own-your-own-home" department, Godey's Model Cottages. As for the fashion plates, *Godey's* published them against Sarah's own wishes, as she felt the clothing depicted was often either unhealthy or inconvenient for the modern American woman.

Above all, it was the book reviews and the editorials that Sarah used to endorse her position on many issues: the importance of women's education; property rights for women after marriage; daycare for children whose mothers had to work; greater job opportunities for women; fresh air, physical exercise, healthy clothing, and good food to cure ills; encouragement of the training of women doctors, nurses, and medical missionaries; playgrounds and open spaces for those in the cities; and a thousand other causes. We should mention, though, that Sarah always clothed her preaching in "ladylike" garments and was in favor neither of women's suffrage nor of women competing with men in their own spheres.

Using her editorial position, and through her private efforts, Sarah accomplished many other good deeds: She founded the Seaman's Aid Society and Homes for Sailors; she was instrumental in having President Lincoln mandate Thanksgiving as a national holiday; she raised funds for the completion of the Bunker Hill Monument to soldiers of the American Revolution, and helped preserve George Washington's Mount Vernon for posterity. She was influential in the founding of Vassar College, the first major school of higher education for women in America; she worked with Mary Lyon of Mt. Holyoke and Emma Willard, the pioneer educator of young women. She encouraged and publicized **Catharine Beecher**'s American Women's Educational Association, which trained women as teachers for Western settlements.

Busy as she was, Sarah still found time to write prolifically. She authored novels, poems—her most famous poem is "Mary Had a Little Lamb"—short stories, essays, plays, children's books, etiquette manuals, and cookbooks, and edited anthologies and the collected letters of famous literary figures. Her most lasting contribution, perhaps, was her *Woman's Record; A Biographical Dictionary of all Distinguished Women from the Creation to A.D. 1850 ... With Selections from Feminine Writers from Every Age*. This massive compilation, first published in 1853, had more than a thousand pages and was illustrated with hundreds of portraits. It was revised and enlarged in subsequent editions until 1870 and is still used as a reference book.

When Sarah wrote *The Good Housekeeper* in 1839, the number of original American cookbooks published was quite small, fewer than thirty. Thus, Sarah felt that there was a need for a new *American* cookbook. She explains that those who wanted to learn the art of "good living" could turn to *The Cook's Oracle* (by Dr. William Kitchiner**)** while those who wanted to learn about "cheap living" could consult the *American Frugal Housewife* (by Lydia Maria Child). Sarah's aim was "to select and combine the excellences of these two systems, at the same time keeping in view the important object of preserving health, and thus teach *how to live well, and to be well while we live*." Sarah does this quite nicely. This book is full of information about cooking and health and economy, yet it always takes pains to be concerned with taste and comfort. Many of the recipes offer personal, savory touches that result in delicious dishes. Sarah's discussion of the role of bread in family life and her vindication of meat-eating make intriguing reading today.

Sarah's cookbooks all went through many printings, often with variant titles. In addition, she revised and prepared for the American market one of the most important contemporary English cookbooks, **Eliza Acton**'s *Modern Cookery in All Its Branches*.

Sarah once wrote that she had entered into her literary life not for fame and fortune, but because she needed to support and educate her children. How proud she must have been of them. Both her daughters studied to be teachers and graduated from Emma Willard's School in Troy, New York. Sarah Josepha taught in a private school in Georgia for a number of years before opening her own successful and fashionable Boarding and Day School for Young Ladies on Rittenhouse Square in Philadelphia. Frances Ann married Dr. Lewis Boudinet Hunter, a naval surgeon; Sarah spent the last years of her life in their home, surrounded by adoring grandchildren. Her oldest son, David Emerson, graduated from West Point and died young in the service of his country. Her youngest son, William George, graduated from Harvard and practiced law in Virginia before moving to Texas, where he played an invaluable role handling the old Spanish claims that immediately flooded the courts of Texas upon its separation from Mexico. Sarah's middle son, Horatio, a renowned ethnologist and linguist, conducted the pioneer investigation into the customs, languages, and dialects of North American Indians, both in the United States and in Canada.

Sarah Josepha Hale retired from *Godey's* in 1877 and continued writing until her death at ninety-one in 1879.

— Janice Bluestein Longone

Cookery books of Sarah Josepha Hale (Most of her books went through many editions and printings, sometimes with variant titles, sometimes spine titles differ from title-page titles.):

The Good Housekeeper: The Way to Live Well, and to be Well While we Live, 1839

Keeping House and House Keeping, 1845

Modern Cookery in All Its Branches, by Eliza Acton. Revised and prepared for American housekeepers, by Mrs. Sarah J. Hale, 1845

The Ladies' New Book of Cookery, 1852

The New Household Receipt Book, 1853

Mrs. Hale's Receipts for the Millions, 1857

Mrs. Hale's New Cookbook, 1857

Woman's Record; A Biographical Dictionary of all Distinguished Women from the Creation to A.D. 1850 … With Selections from Feminine Writers from Every Age, 1853

Marion Harland

ALSO CALLED: Mary Virginia Hawes Terhune

Marion Harland was about 30 and the author of three novels when this photograph was made in 1860.

IN 1894, THE LEAD PARAGRAPH OF AN ARTICLE PUBLISHED in *The Richmond Dispatch* stated: "Every one has heard of Marion Harland. Grandmothers tell of the sensation produced by her first book 'Alone'.... Mothers chime in with praises of her 'Common Sense in the Household,' the kitchen classic that has reached its majority. ...Girls who read her stories and helpful articles yield her humble and hearty allegiance...." More than a hundred years later, however, the mention of Marion Harland's name, world-famous during her lifetime, is usually met with a blank stare. This despite the fact that she produced a extraordinary number of works that included fiction and short stories, books on travel, biography, and colonial history, as well as articles and some twenty-five books on domestic affairs, homemaking, and women's issues.

Mary Virginia Hawes Terhune spent her formative years in rural Virginia counties, where her father ran a successful mercantile business. Born in December 1830, Virginia was the second daughter of Samuel Hawes, a Massachusetts native, and his wife, Judith Anna, a Virginian with ties to the planter elite.

From her early childhood, Virginia's exceptional intelligence was recognized by her parents, who provided ample educational opportunities for their children. In an age during which most southern girls were provided with little more than rudimentary book-learning, Virginia was encouraged to excel. Her father wanted his daughters educated "as if they were boys and preparing for college," and tutors were engaged to instruct the children in music, French, Latin, history, literature, and geometry. They were encouraged to read the classics and enjoyed lively conversations with their parents on topics that ranged from politics to literature. When Virginia was thirteen, she and her older sister spent a year away from home to further the education their father felt was so important, and when the family moved to Richmond, their education continued at an exclusive Presbyterian school where the girls completed their studies.

Marion Harland's life as a writer began years before her first book was published. A precocious child, she had begun writing essays and stories before she reached her teens. By the time she was fourteen, she was contributing anonymously to two religious newspapers distributed throughout the upper South. Two years later, she began to write the book that was to become her first novel.

In 1853, the Sons of Temperance sponsored a literary contest with a prize of $50. Virginia entered the contest, using for the first time the pen-name, "Marion Harland," by which she became best known. To her great delight, Virginia won the prize. Success inspired her to rework the novel she had started several years earlier. When it was turned down by a Richmond publisher, her father, always convinced of Virginia's abilities, had the book privately printed. Titled *Alone,* the novel was published in 1854. It was enthusiastically received, going into seven printings in Richmond before being acquired by a New York publishing house in 1856. *Alone* became a national best seller, with more than 100,000 copies bought by readers all across America. Her second novel, *The Hidden Path,* was published in 1855, and Marion Harland's career was launched.

In the late summer of 1854, Virginia was introduced to Edward Payson Terhune, a young Presbyterian minister from New Jersey. They were attracted to each another immediately and became engaged about a year later. They were married in Richmond in September, 1856, after which they settled in Charlotte Courthouse, Virginia, described by the new Mrs. Terhune as "a rambling hamlet." Throughout her long life, Virginia Terhune looked back nostalgically upon their three years in the rural community. She credited that time as pivotal, for not only did it intensify her interest in Colonial history, it directly affected her later domestic writings.

When Edward accepted a pastorate at the First Reformed Church of Newark, New Jersey, in 1859, the Terhune family relocated to that city where they remained for the next 18 years. There, Mary Virginia continued writing while carrying on a range of domestic and parish work. She considered herself fortunate that the Newark parishioners tolerated her writing career, although some of them did have problems with the fact that Virginia made more money than her husband. There were others who disapproved of the Terhunes' elegant lifestyle, for the couple enjoyed living well. They entertained often in their elegant Newark mansion and built a summer home which they named Sunnybank, located on twenty-four lakeside acres in Pompton, New Jersey.

By 1870, Virginia Terhune had published a dozen novels, as well as numerous stories and articles for a variety of magazines. The following year, she published her first cookbook, *Common Sense in the Household.* It was an immediate best seller. In it, she wrote that she longed to spare other women the "mortifications and bewilderment" of her first year of marriage when she had had to learn housewifery basically on her own. Despite the domestic training received from her mother, Virginia saw herself as poorly equipped to run a household and manage servants. She realized that "there was no printed manual that would take the tyro by the hand and show her a plain path between pitfalls and morasses." Over time, Mrs. Terhune wrote, she "learned by degrees to regard housewifery as a profession that dignifies her who follows it, and contributes, more than any other calling, to the mental, moral, and spiritual sanity of the human race." She was convinced that she was fit to supply through her "own shortcomings and battles" what American women lacked. "A rule without exception," she emphasized, is that "no American woman, however exalted ...her social rank... can afford to remain ignorant of practical housewifery." *Common Sense* remained in print for fifty years; was translated into French, German, and Arabic; and ultimately sold over a million copies. The book contained household advice as well as recipes, and had "familiar talks" that sympathized with the problems of housekeeping. It was filled with sensible advice on ways for women to avoid the pitfalls of their household duties. *Common Sense,* as well as other domestic works that followed, influenced millions of women in this country and abroad.

By the mid-1870's, Mrs. Terhune was in failing health and in 1876, she was diagnosed with tuberculosis. Soon after, the Reverend Terhune resigned his Newark pastorate and took the family to Europe where they spent the next two years, giving Virginia the opportunity she needed to recover her health.

After their return, Mr. Terhune accepted a series of pastorates, the last in Brooklyn, New York, where the Terhunes remained until 1895, when Edward's own ill health forced his retirement. He died in 1907 and was buried at a church near Sunnybank, their Pompton, New Jersey home. Virginia Terhune had been fortunate in having in Edward Terhune a husband who supported her writing career throughout their fifty-one years of life together. By all accounts, their marriage was one of mutual support and devotion.

Virginia Terhune continued to write on a variety of topics. *The Story of Mary Washington*, for instance, published in 1892, helped arouse interest in erecting a monument over the grave of the first president's mother. Her book, *Eve's Daughters* (1875), provided women of her generation with advice that ranged from coping with pregnancy, marital infidelity and beyond. She played a dominant role in the lives of her three surviving children, all of whom became authors. Her daughters, Christine Terhune Herrick and Virginia Van de Water wrote on household topics; her son, Albert Payson Terhune, was especially successful, a noted writer of books and articles that focused on dogs, collies in particular.

What was she really like, this multi-faceted woman? The author, Kate Sanborn, wrote a chapter on Marion Harland for a book, *Our Famous Women*, published in 1884. Sanborn described the 50-ish Virginia Terhune as a woman "with a great deal of individuality and energy. Perfectly natural, a fine talker, full of anecdote, repartee, and humor..." Witty was a word often used to describe Virginia, and in most of her writing, that wit came across, as illustrated in the mince pie directions she gave in *Common Sense in the Household*:

> I take this opportunity of warning the innocent reader against placing any confidence whatever in dried currants. I years ago gave over trying to guess who put the dirt in them. It is always there! Gravel-stones lurking under a specious coating of currant-looking paste, to crucify grown people's nerves and children's teeth; mould that changes to mud in the mouth; twigs that prick the throat, not to mention the legs, wings, and bodies of tropical insects .. It is all dirt! although sold to use at currant prices.

After emphasizing that the offending fruit must be thoroughly washed and drained, Mrs. Terhune instructed her readers to "spread the currants upon a large dish, and enter seriously upon ... geological and entomological researches."

Terhune was a paradox, a woman who had an active, lucrative career during an era when women stayed home, but saw no contradiction in glorifying a purely domestic role for women. Firmly convinced that females should be well educated, prepared to support themselves if the need arose, she nevertheless espoused the role of "wife, housekeeper, and mother" as a "high and holy sphere." Terhune attacked the feminist movement in her writings, stating that women didn't need the vote but needed to make voters. "If the American nation ... is to maintain a continued and vigorous existence," she wrote in *Eve's Daughters*, "it is by and through the birth of American infants. These must be borne by American women."

Virginia Terhune's remarkable energy was boundless and remained so up until the last months of her life. Early on, she had organized her days for maximum efficiency, determined that every minute would be occupied. According to Kate Sanborn, this self-discipline was the secret of Terhune's ability to do so much more than the rest [of her contemporaries]. To Sanborn, Mrs. Terhune was a "versatile and successful author... a *perfect* housekeeper, a model minister's wife..., a devoted mother, a queen of society, and a sympathetic, satisfying friend."

Virginia Terhune can be viewed as a "bridge-figure," a witness to life that reached back to the antebellum south, and forward into the twentieth century. In the introduction to her autobiography, she acknowledged that fact herself. "... of all the authors still on active professional duty in our country," she wrote, "I am the only one whose memory runs back to the stage of national history that preceded the Civil War by a quarter-century. I, alone, am left to tell, of my own knowledge and experience, what the Old South was... [Others] have portrayed scenes of those days ... but theirs is hearsay evidence—second-hand testimony... What *I* [emphasis mine] have to say ... is of what I saw and heard and did—and <u>was</u> in that hoary Long Ago."

In one of her last interviews, Terhune was asked how she had been able to maintain the working pace that after so many years was finally slowing down. She replied that the secret of her youthful attitude lay in a happy blend of religion and humor. "If you want to stay young, have some work you like, something to get you up in the morning. I don't mind growing old," she said, "Up on the tableland of age, the air is invigorating." In August 1919, her final novel, *The Carringtons of High Hill*, was published. On June 3, 1922, after a brief illness, Virginia Terhune, better known to the world as Marion Harland, died at her home in New York City. She was in her ninety-second year.

— NANCY CARTER CRUMP

A selection of non-fiction books related to cookery:

Common Sense in the Household , 1871
Breakfast, Luncheon & Tea , 1875
The Dinner Yearbook, 1878
The Cottage Kitchen , 1883
Housekeeping & Homemaking, 1883
Cookery For Beginners, 1884
House & Home, 1889
The Premium Cook Book, 1894
The Art Of Cooking By Gas, 1896
The Ladies' Home Cook Book, 1896
The National Cook Book, 1896
The Comfort Of Cooking And Heating By Gas, 1898
Cooking Hints, 1899
Household Management, 1899
Marion Harland's Cook Book Of Tried And Tested Recipes, 190?

365 Desserts, 1900
Marion Harland's Complete Cook Book, 1906
Everyday Etiquette: A Practical Manual of Social Usages, 1905
The New England Cook Book, 1905
Marion Harland's Complete Etiquette, with Virginia Terhune Van de Water, 1907
The Story Of Canning And Recipes, 1910
House Making, 1911
The Helping Hand Cook Book, 1912
The New Common Sense in the Household, 1926 (posthumous)

Dorothy Hartley

1892–1985

ONE OF THE MOST RESPECTED RESEARCHERS INTO BRITISH FOLKWAYS, DOROTHY Rosaman Hartley was born in Skipton, Yorkshire. Her father was headmaster of the local school and a science enthusiast, and from him she no doubt inherited her wide-ranging interests and passion for accuracy.

Dorothy Hartley took an interest in British folklore from an early age, and it informed her projects throughout her life. In the 1930's, she traveled around Great Britain on a bicycle, taking photographs and making sketches of rural life. When recounting her adventures, she would explain that in those days there were no bed and breakfast places to stay overnight and, "There weren't youth hostels then, you know." She enjoyed living in the open air. "When I say in the book [*Food in England*] that I cooked on an open fire, it's true, I did…. One can make a fire and boil a billy of water within 20 minutes. I could do it on a wet Irish bog if I had to." She often slept in the open air. Her pragmatism even led her to test out Jack London's theory that one can sleep quite safely in the snow! The result of her wanderings was a series of self-illustrated articles for the *Daily Sketch*, a national newspaper. She also wrote for several popular magazines of the time.

Hartley's research into traditional British folkways, customs and, above all, crafts of all kinds was meticulous and unique, since at the time academics considered this kind of subject beneath them. But Great Britain was on the verge of the sea change caused by World War II. Had she not written in such detail about ways of life that were fast disappearing—the lives of the poorer sections of the rural population, the craftspeople and farm workers—the knowledge would certainly have been lost forever.

Another of Hartley's interests was medieval life, and she moved to London for a while to study the subject. In 1931, she produced a handsome, lavishly illustrated volume entitled *Mediaeval Costume and Life* (recently republished as *Mediaeval Costume and How to Recreate it*, Dover, 2003). Her interest in medieval customs also extended to food, and she once cooked a medieval meal for a dining club in Hampstead, London.

Hartley was not only a researcher and writer but also a talented artist, graduating from art school in 1919. She illustrated her own books, and is credited with producing several oil paintings, all now in private collections, including one of a monk drinking from a forest pool. The monk is reputed to be Geraldus Cambrensis, one of the medieval characters about whom she wrote at length.

Hartley had spent World War I working in a munitions factory and during World War II she served in the Women's Royal Air Corps as a Leading Aircraftswoman I. After the war, she spent much of her time lecturing and teaching at various colleges and societies, especially on the subject of food. She continued to live with her mother in a cottage in Froncysyllte, near Llangollen, Wales. She later inherited Fron House from her grandfather, and moved there in the 1960's.

It is for her work on food that Hartley is best known. She claimed to have cooked for the household since the age of 12 and the practicality of her recipes comes through clearly in all her writings. Her 1954 *Food in England* is one of the great classics of English cookery, and is still in print. The book deals with local and regional dishes from all over the British Isles, comparing techniques and usages rather than dividing Britain up along geographical lines. As she states in the introduction, *Food in England* was written for cooks, and the recipes and eclectic array of information are all useful and workable. The *British Weekly* reviewer went so far as to say: "The woman who owns this book can throw away all the others." It is the elegant and poetic style—concise, yet full of evocative imagery—that makes it such a timeless book. Line drawings supplement descriptions of cooks' tools and cooking pots, methods of folding, etc. Many cookery and food history writers have said that it is among their favorite works of all time.

Hartley claimed to have invented the term "tracklements" as a collective word to mean condiments of various types (mustards, jellies, bottled sauces), which she first used in this book. She wrote that it is borrowed from an English dialect word meaning "appurtenances" or "impedimenta" but did not give the original dialect word or the part of England from which it originates. In fact, there are several similar dialect words with this meaning in different parts of the country.

Hartley died at the age of 93 and is buried in the churchyard of St. David's Church, Froncysyllte.

— JOSEPHINE BACON

Thomas Tusser ... his Good Points of Husbandry, Life and Work of the People of England, 1931
Mediaeval Costume and Life, 1931 (republished as Mediaeval Costume and How to
    Recreate it, 2003)
Here's England, 1934
Irish Holiday, 1938
Made in England, 1939
The Countryman's England, 1943
Food in England, 1954
Water in England, 1964
The Land of England: English Country Customs Through the Ages, 1979
Lost Country Life, 1979

Fred Harvey

FRED HARVEY HELPED CIVILIZE THE AMERICAN WEST BY INTRODUCING it to fresh, well-prepared food at his impeccable railroad hotel and depot restaurants where travelers were served by well-groomed respectable young waitresses that Harvey recruited from the East. These were the Harvey Girls who were later featured in a popular 1946 movie musical of that name with Judy Garland.

Harvey's career in food service began humbly enough when he migrated from London to New York at the age of fifteen and took a job as a busboy at two dollars a week. Hoping to open his own restaurant, he traveled first to New Orleans in 1856 and the following year to St. Louis where he married and started a thriving café venture that soon succumbed to the privations of the Civil War and an absconding business partner. After the war, Harvey took a series of clerical and freight-agent jobs with railroads that were rapidly expanding into the West and witnessed first-hand the wretched food and unsanitary dining conditions at train stops throughout that part of the country. He opened successful restaurant cafés in Kansas and Colorado but could not persuade his new partner to maintain the high standards he demanded for food and service. He had better luck with the fledgling Atchison, Topeka and Santa Fe Railway which became a dominant train route to the American Southwest and California in the last two decades of the century. Harvey Houses were eventually established every hundred miles along the line from Chicago to San Francisco. By 1901 when he died of intestinal cancer and left the business to his sons, Harvey's chain included fifteen hotels, forty-seven restaurants, thirty dining cars, and food services on the ferries across San Francisco Bay.

A Harvey House dinner menu of 1888 featured a choice of bluepoint oysters, fillets of whitefish with Madeira sauce, or lobster salad, and entrees such as capon with Hollandaise, roast sirloin of beef au jus, sugar-cured ham, duck, or stuffed turkey with cranberry sauce. Desserts included apple or mince pie, assorted cakes, New York ice cream, oranges and grapes, all followed by Edam or Roquefort cheese and coffee. The price for such a quintessentially American meal was seventy-five cents, cheap even then, considering that ingredients were brought by rail from all over the country. Meat came from Texas by way of slaughterhouses in Kansas City or Chicago, fresh vegetables from the Midwest when not locally grown, refrigerated fresh fruit from California or as far away as Mexico, and fish and seafood in railway ice cars from the east or the Gulf. Also shipped by rail were coal, ice and water, the latter for cooking, coffee and tea in place of water from alkaline-laden streams in the West.

According to Lesley Poling-Kempes, author of *The Harvey Girls*, the Harvey Houses maintained a full, well-paid staff that typically included "a manager, a chef, a head waitress, between fifteen to thirty Harvey Girls, a baker, a butcher, several assistant cooks and pantry girls, a housemaid and busboys." Harvey insisted on fastidious cleanliness and impressive food presentation, with polished English sliver and freshly-laundered Irish linen, and on the speed and efficiency of table service. Orders would be telegraphed ahead and the gracious waitresses used ingenious methods for serving food quickly and correctly so that sixty to a hundred travelers could be fed in the twenty to thirty minutes allowed at train stations. Menus were also rotated along rail lines so that passengers could eat at different Harvey restaurants for four days without repeating meals.

Harvey's dining service was an effective loss leader that cost the Santa Fe thousands every year but attracted passengers and kept them loyal in the face of competition from other rail lines. For over half a century, the statement "Meals by Fred Harvey" on a menu or railroad advertisement was a guarantee of high quality at low cost to hungry travelers and Westerners fortunate enough to live close to one of Harvey's restaurants. It took competition from air and automobile travel, especially after World War II, to force the eventual closure or sale of the Harvey Houses and associated food services. To their lasting credit, Fred Harvey and his eating places helped prove that the West was not just a primitive place of violence and vulgarity. In this regard, perhaps his greatest legacy was not the standards he set for regional dining but his adventurous, hard-working Harvey Girls who helped settle that part of the country by marrying and raising families.

— BARBARA HABER

Nika Hazelton

♦ 1908–1992 ♦

NIKA HAZELTON WAS BORN MARGUERITE DITTMAN IN 1908 IN THE PALAZZO Colonna, in the historic center of Rome. Her mother, Maria Leoni, was Roman, her father, Otto Dittman, a German diplomat. At the end of her life, Nika liked to think of herself as Italian, but she always presented herself in a stereotypically Germanic style. Her first cookbook, *Reminiscence and Ravioli,* was published in 1946, and if the caricature in it is a fair reflection of her looks at the time, Hazelton was a veritable Brunhilde: large and imposing, with her very long hair woven into a braid that crowned her head from ear to ear. When she got older and even larger and used two canes to get about, she was even more intimidating. Her bearing was regal. Her wit was very quick and cutting.

Hazelton liked to say that her parents' characters were the opposite of what you'd expect. Her German father was the soft one, a cultured and socially liberal man; her Italian mother was the stern keeper of the hearth, instilling in her daughter the necessity of a well-organized home, a well-set table, and a well-cooked meal. Her father was not indifferent to food and the pleasures of the table, but her mother was the one who taught her the pleasure she might receive by knowing how to prepare a good meal and serve it well. To the very end, as stern and difficult, sophisticated and blasé as she could be, Nika Hazelton loved nothing more than to sit at the table at the end of a meal and peel fruit for the men sitting

Eating in Germany, 1967

around her. She was a bright, provocative and humorous conversationalist who often resorted to silliness because, she said, it was so opposed to the carefully cultivated severity of her appearance. One of her favorite cocktail party ice-breakers, for instance, was, "What do you think of string?" She surrounded herself with lively, intelligent people who didn't have to be celebrated or rich, but often were one or the other or both. Her most famous friend—aside from her brother-sister relationship with the poet James Agee in her twenties and thirties—and her biggest benefactor was William F. Buckley, Jr., for whose *National Review* she wrote an eating and drinking column for more than twenty years. Buckley paid for her stay at the Margaret Manning Walsh Nursing Home and for her funeral in April, 1992 at the famous St. Agnes church, where Bishop Fulton Sheen used to preside. Priscilla Buckley, William's sister and the editor of the *National Review*, was among her closest female friends.

Hazelton always said that she wrote the first cookbook out of necessity after her ugly divorce from Anthony Standen. She needed work that she could do without leaving home and her two children. She'd received a liberal education in London and had trained as a journalist; she cooked and she had opinions about cooking, food and entertaining: The choice seemed obvious. On the cover of the book, she billed herself as "the literate housewife." But by the 1950's she was more than that: She was entrenched in New York City's professional food world, which centered around **James Beard**. Helen McCully, the influential food editor of *McCall's*; Cecily Brownstone, the long-time food editor of the Associated Press, and Ann Seranne, an editor at *Gourmet*, were in this crowd and among her good friends. They met regularly at Beard's Greenwich Village apartment on West Twelfth Street.

Hazelton is best known by the surname of her second husband, Harold, an accomplished amateur pianist and professional genealogist. She was still Nika Standen, however, for the first cookbook. Her first husband, Anthony (Tony) Standen, came in and out of her life twice, the second time fathering her two sons, Tony, Jr. and Julian. But their relationship ended so badly that she always referred to him as "The Unlamented." She had an uneasy relationship with her sons, too, and they with each other, which is why, she always said, Tony lived in London and Julian lived in Los Angeles, while she settled in New York, on Riverside Drive and 102nd Street, where she and Harold and a couple of cats had a large, book lined apartment facing the Hudson River.

Nika and Harold Hazelton loved to travel—first class if possible—which explains the subjects of several of her cookbooks. Harold Hazelton made very little money, but the books were a way to finance trips, especially to her favorite places—the Scandinavian countries, Switzerland, Belgium, Germany, and her beloved Italy. Her everyday home cooking was mostly Italian, but at her dinner parties she would branch out, often composing shocking menus for the amusement and delectation of her guests.

Her two most outrageous and famous dinners were in honor of Bill Buckley. He loved asparagus, so Hazelton prepared an all-asparagus dinner, ending the meal with some fantastic desserts. Buckley commented at the end of the meal that he could easily eat only dessert for dinner, so at the next party she gave in his honor, she served only a big dessert buffet, ending the meal with mugs of hot beef consommé.

Besides the 26 cookbooks she wrote, and her columns for the *National Review,*

Hazelton was also, from the early 1970's and until just a few years before her death, the cookbook reviewer for the *New York Times Book Review*.

— ARTHUR SCHWARTZ

Reminiscence and Ravioli, 1946
The Art of Cheese Cookery, 1949
The Continental Flavor, 1961
The Art of Danish Cooking, 1964
Classic Scandinavian Cooking, 1965
Family Circle Encyclopedia, 1966 (special project editor)
The Best of Italian Cooking, 1967
The Swiss Cookbook, 1967
Chocolate!, 1967
Stew!, 1968
The Picnic Book, 1969
The Cooking of Germany (Time-Life Food of the World series), 1969
Eggs!, 1969
I Cook as I Please, 1974
Hamburger!, 1975
The Raggedy Ann and Andy Cookbook, 1975
What Shall We Cook Today?, 1975
American Wines, 1976
The Unabridged Vegetable Cookbook, 1976
The Belgian Cookbook, 1977
The Regional Italian Kitchen, 1978
American Home Cooking, 1980
The Russian Tea Room Cookbook, 1981 (with Faith Stewart-Gordon)
Nika Hazelton's Pasta Cookbook, 1984
From Nika Hazelton's Kitchen, 1985
Ups and Downs, 1989

Annabella Powell Hill   ❧ 1810—1878 ❧

ALSO CALLED: Mrs. A. P. Hill

BORN IN MADISON COUNTY, GEORGIA IN AUTUMN OF 1810 TO VIRGINIA NATIVES Major John Edmonds and Annabella Burwell Dawson, Annabella was the youngest of five children. She married The Honorable Edward Young Hill in December of 1827. The couple lived first in Monticello, Georgia, where Judge Hill was on the circuit court. In 1845 the judge was elected to the superior court and the family moved to LaGrange, Georgia. There they enjoyed a large home on Newnan Street (later renamed in Judge Hill's honor), a home that Troup County historians believe the Hill's may have built. They had eleven children, six of whom survived infancy, but only two of them were to survive Mrs. Hill when she died in 1878.

Well-to-do and socially prominent, the Hills were widely known in both religious and educational circles. They were especially active in the politics of the Baptist church in Georgia, and helped found at least one girls' academy. Mrs. Hill's elder brother, The Rev. John Edmonds Dawson, Jr., was a Baptist minister and educator, and the couple was involved in several of his endeavors. Their commitment extended into home life: for a time they even opened their home to board students from a local female academy.

Judge Hill died in early December of 1860, on the eve of the War Between the States. Though the Hills had opposed secession, they remained loyal to Georgia. Their two eldest sons enlisted in the Confederate Army and died in combat in 1862. Judge and Mrs. Hill had sold their large home on Hill Street and moved to a more modest house on Greenville Road in 1853. Nonetheless, in the lean years of reconstruction that followed, economic hardship forced Mrs. Hill to sell all her property in LaGrange and move to Atlanta, where she became principal of the lottery-funded orphans' school from around 1868 until shortly before her death a decade later.

Mrs. Hill is not, however, remembered for her work in education, or for the short biography that she wrote of her brother the cleric, but for her single writing on cookery, *Mrs. Hill's New Cook Book*, a work probably composed in the late 1850's. It was not published until after the War, in 1867, but proved to be a seminal work, enjoying numerous editions through the remainder of the nineteenth century and was frequently referenced in later cookbooks. (Since 1995, the second [1872] edition, has been reprinted in facsimile by University of South Carolina Press under her originally intended title *The Southern Practical Cookery and Receipt Book*.)

According to contemporary accounts, unlike so many upper-class matrons who only baked (if indeed they cooked at all) and had at best a detached general knowledge of cooking, Mrs. Hill was an accomplished cook and was widely known for her table. Contemporary accounts describe a handsome, patrician, and accomplished matron and hostess. The recipes, rich with humor and illuminating detail, confirm that she was indeed accomplished in the kitchen.

This remarkable woman was a natural food writer—funny, insightful, and wise. She also stood on the cusp of a technological and social revolution. As war altered forever the old socio-economic system of the South, wood-fired ranges were revolutionizing the kitchen, bringing the biggest changes to cooking technology in more than a thousand years. Her book, with its almost exclusive use of the open-hearth, was a bit old fashioned when it was published, yet she lists a range as essential to a well-equipped kitchen.

It is this old-fashioned quality and yet forward looking sensibility that makes Mrs. Hill's work so important as a critical link back to the old foodways of the early nineteenth century. It also provides one of the only printed records of antebellum cookery in Georgia and a clear illustration of the complicated blending of cultures and cuisines that shaped Southern cooking. Including more than eleven hundred culinary and medicinal recipes, it was comprehensive and encyclopedic in its scope and unparalleled in its carefully detailed instructions. This detail, combined with the fact that Mrs. Hill carefully credited other cookbook authors by name, if not always by work, makes the book an invaluable reference for historians. The breath of her education and reading is seen in the long list of authors cited, including: Dr. William Kitchiner (her favorite), **Alexis Soyer**, Izzak Walton, Mrs. Hannah Moore, **Count Rumford**, **Baron Justus von**

Liebig, Mary Randolph, **Sarah Josepha Hale**, and **Eliza Leslie**, among others.

Mrs. Hill is frequently misplaced as a Reconstruction era author, in part because of the publication date of her book, in part because of the foreword by the Rev. E. W. Warren, written at the time of publication, and in part because she occasionally renames old recipes with contemporary names like "Jeff Davis Pudding" and "Confederate Fruit Cake"; but the old-fashioned method of her recipes and the sensibility of her text clearly date the work as antebellum.

— DAMON LEE FOWLER

Mrs. Hill's New Cook Book, 1867; the second [1872] edition, has been reprinted in facsimile by University of South Carolina Press under her originally intended title *The Southern Practical Cookery and Receipt Book* (1995).

H

Erna Horn

❦ 1904–1981 ❦

TALL, BEAUTIFUL, ENERGETIC, AND CONFIDENT, THE GERMAN cookbook author Erna Horn began her career early, publishing her first book when she was 24 years old. She continued to work and write steadily until her death more than 50 years later. Her output was enormous, and her books were important. After World War II she addressed the needs of a changed society and a nation in distress and turmoil. As Germany struggled to find its feet politically and economically, her publications on cooking, etiquette, and household matters of all kinds helped to bring domestic stability to the country. Later in the century she kept home cooks current in the new kitchen technology and in culinary fashions. Her constant work with the food industry and with manufacturers of kitchen appliances extended her influence throughout the country.

Erna Horn was born in Munich in 1904, the daughter of a physician, Dr. Franz Horn. She was educated at Munich's Höhere Töchterschule, a prestigious old institution for girls that provided a serious academic grounding while acknowledging that many of its graduates would seek employment and support themselves. Her mother, and especially her grandmother Francisca Hoberkeisen, taught her cooking and all the skills of household management: gardening, preserving, baking, caring for the sick, washing, sewing, decorating, grooming, and so on.

This portrait of Erna Horn still hangs in Schloss Buchenau, the stately home in Bavaria where she lived, wrote, and ran her test kitchen and photo studio.

As a young woman, Horn combined her home training with her schooling and wrote newspaper articles on food and household matters for the *Hanoverischer Anzeiger*. In 1928 she self-published a book of chocolate recipes with the up-beat subtitle *How the Housewife can Create Chocolates, Pralines, Candied Fruits and Other Sweets Cheaply, Easily and Well*. This was the first German cookbook on chocolate geared to the home cook; it was re-issued, in eight editions, until 1952.

In 1929, she complained to the state radio network, Bayrischer Rundfunk, that they provided no programming for women. Their response was to ask her to do a program for them, and she began to broadcast "The Women's Hour," which dealt primarily with cooking and housekeeping.

The following year, Erna Horn published the first edition of her comprehensive, illustrated handbook, *Der neuzeitliche Haushalt (The Modern Household)*. This book became a standard gift to German brides, or a helpful present from mother to daughter, and it was enlarged and updated regularly for the next half-century, with over a quarter million copies printed.

A dispute with a newspaper editor over her fees prompted her to go directly to the publisher of the newspaper chain to state her case. The publisher, Dr. Julius Arndt, felt that the economy of the time required that he keep her fees low, but he later admitted that this had not been a wise decision because, just one year later in 1932, he and Erna Horn were married.

With Hitler's rise to power, Arndt resigned from his position as newspaper publisher and the couple moved to the Bavarian countryside. They established a test kitchen, hired a staff of cooks, photographers, and secretaries. With the help of her husband, Erna Horn continued to research, write, and publish her cookbooks.

At the end of the war, Germany's economy, agriculture, and society were in great disarray. In a time-period labeled "the hunger years," housewives struggled to feed their families. Addressing the situation, Horn published a series of pamphlets, each containing a few of the most basic recipes for ordinary dishes, using available ingredients such as potatoes, sugar beets, and baking powder. The publishing house Winkler approached her to write a cookbook along these lines, and in 1948 Winkler brought out *Das Kochbuch für Heute (The Cookbook for Today)*. A similar impulse to help German society steady itself led her to write a compendious book on all aspects of etiquette and deportment. *Die Hohe Schule der Lebensart (An Advanced Course in the Art of Living)*, published 1953, clearly filled a need, as more than forty thousand copies were sold within a year.

Horn worked closely with the food industry, initially helping firms adapt their bulk recipes to a scale that could be utilized by the housewife in her home kitchen. Food products and kitchen appliances, as well as recipes, passed through Erna Horn's test kitchen. She traveled to food-industry fairs all over Germany to keep in close contact with manufacturers, for whom she also wrote advertising brochures and recipe pamphlets. The firm Maggi broke with its hundred-year tradition of publishing its advertising literature anonymously and put Erna Horn's name on a pamphlet of recipes entitled *Aus der Küche geplaudert: Ein Gang mit Erna Horn durch die Küche der Monate (Chat from the Kitchen: A Stroll with Erna Horn through the Culinary Calendar)*. Horn appears on the cover in a white lab coat, along with a notebook, a scientific scale, a dish of prepared foods—and, of course, a bottle of Maggi Würze sauce.

While working with industry, Horn continued to produce her own books at a lively pace, garnering medals along the way from the Gastronomic Academy of Germany and the International Culinary Art Exhibition in Frankfurt. She was astonishingly prolific, and indeed it is impossible to track precisely all of her publications through the maze of updates and revisions, altered titles, and undated editions. She also wrote under a pseudonym ("Maria Anders"), and produced several works with co-authors. Some of her books were translated into other European languages, including Dutch, Polish, Italian, and English. A few cookbooks continued in print twenty years after her death.

Julius Arndt and Erna Horn assembled a collection of bibliophile cookbooks and other food-related books in German; at one time, theirs was the largest culinary book collection in Germany. Arndt hired a bibliographer, Marie Sachs, to produce a catalogue which, however, due to ill health, was finished and published only after the deaths of both collectors. It appeared in 1982 as *Schöne alte Kochbücher: Katalog der Kochbuchsammlung Erna Horn und Dr. Julius Arndt (Beautiful Old Cookbooks: Catalogue of the Cookbook Collection of Erna Horn and Dr. Julius Arndt).* The collection can now be found in Passau, on the Danube River, in the museum residing in the group of fourteenth-century buildings that make up the inn "Der Wilder Mann."

A chronological look at Erna Horn's publications reveals a developing interest in culinary history. She made good use of the antique books in their possession to write several culinary and cultural histories of Bavaria and surrounding states. Erna Horn was a devoted Bavarian. Several typical dialect words were allowed into her books, as in her 1977 *Bayrische Kuchl (Bavarian Kitchen)*, in which she proudly presents herself as a native of that region. She had high regard for local foods, and claimed that the breads of Bavaria were superior to those of the rest of Germany because of the fine soft wheat that grows in its comparatively sunny climate.

Erna Horn always addressed her readers affectionately in her brief remarks in introductions and asides—even in her etiquette books when she was telling them how to behave. She characterized all her work when she reported in *Kalt, Bunt, Lecker (Cold, Colorful, Delicious)* that she had gathered her material and tested, cooked, arranged, photographed, and written it all "with much love."

— ALICE ARNDT

Das Schokaladebuch (The Chocolate Book), 1928
Der neuzeitliche Haushalt (The Modern Household), 1930
Das Kochbuch für Heute (The Cookbook for Today), 1948
*Koche mit mir: praktisches Kochbuch der Gegenwart (Cook With Me: Practical Present-Day Cookbook),*1950
Für liebe Gäste und häusliche Feste: gesellschaftlicher Ratgeber mit Koch-Rezepten für festliche Gelegenheiten
    (For Welcome Guests and Homey Holidays: Party Tips and Recipes for Holiday Occasions), 1951
Backe backe Kuchen (Pattycake, Pattycake), 1952
Die Hohe Schule der Lebensart (An Advanced Course in the Art of Living), 1953
Lux Koch Lexikon von A–Z (The Lux Kitchen Dictionary From A–Z), 1954
Der Arzt spricht und Mutter kocht: ärztlich betreutes Reform- und Diätkochbuch (The Doctor Speaks and
    Mother Cooks: Medically Approved Health and Diet Cookbook), 1955 (with Hans Wiegmann, MD)
Kochen mit Wein und Weinbrand (Cooking With Wine and Brandy), 1957
Kalt, Bunt, Lecker; Neubearbeitung Henriette Davidis (Cold, Colorful, Delicious: A Revision of
    Henriette Davidis), 1960
Salate für jede Jahreszeit (Salads for Every Season), 1963
Kalte Platten für jede Jahreszeit (Cold Dishes for Every Season), 1963
Die Welt der Küche (The World of the Kitchen), 1964 (with Richard Schielicke and others)
Vom himmlischen Theriak (Of Heavenly Theriak), 1965 (with Julius Arndt)
Erna Horn's Buntes Sandwichbuch: Leckere Brötchen in Rezept und Farbbild (Erna Horn's Colorful
    Sandwich Book: Delicious Sandwiches With Recipes and Color Photos), 1966
Gaumenfrohe Küchenweisheit (Tongue-Tickling Kitchen Tricks), 1968

Fisch in der Küche (Fish in the Kitchen), 1968
Wild in der Küche (Game in the Kitchen), 1968
Bunte Beeren (Bright Berries), 1968
Der Apfel (The Apple), 1968
Leuchtend Rote Kirschen (Radiant Red Cherries), 1969
Citrusfrüchte (Citrus Fruits), 1969
Nüsse Datteln und Rosinen (Nuts, Dates, and Raisins), 1969
Erna Horn's köstliche Salate (Erna Horn's Scrumptious Salads), 1972
Internationale Cocktails (International Cocktails), 1974 (with Julius Arndt)
Endlich einmal preiswerte Fleischgerichte (Economical Meat Dishes At Last), 1974
Das Altbayrische Küchenjahr: Ein kulinerischer Kalender (A Year in an Old-Fashioned Bavarian Kitchen: A Culinary Calendar), 1974
Bavaria Antiqua: Drei altbairische Koch- und Kultur Dokumente (Bavaria Antiqua: Three Old Bavarian Cook- and Culture-Documents), 1974
Schmankerl aus Bayern (Delicacies From Bavaria), 1975
Weissblaue Gaumenletzen: culinarisch-historische Betrachtungen aus Bayern im Schatten seiner Dome, Klöster und Burgen (Delights for the Tastebuds, in Blue and White: Culinary-Historical Reflections from Bavaria, in the Shadows of its Cathedrals, Monasteries, and Castles), 1976
Das grosse Kochbuch: über 1550 Rezepte (The Big Cookbook: More Than 1550 recipes), 1976
Von Knötelein, Knödchen und Knödeln: kulturhistorische Betrachtungen rund um Knödel und Klösse (Reflections on Cultural History Relating to Dumplings), 1976
Die Königlich-bayerische Küche (The Royal Bavarian Kitchen), 1976
Oberpfälzer Kost aus Bauern-, Bürger- und Pfarrhäusern (Cuisine From the Farmhouses, Middle-Class Homes and Rectories of the Upper Palatinate), 1977 (with Adolf J. Eichenseer)
Bayrische Kuchl: alte bayrische Originalrezepte (Bavarian Kitchen: Original Recipes of Old Bavaria), 1977
Köstliches und Curieuses aus alten Kloster- und Pfarrküchen (Delicious and Unusual Dishes From Old Monastery and Rectory Kitchens), 1979
Bayern tafelt: vom Essen und Trinken in Altbayern. Franken und Schwaben: Ein kulinarische Kulturgeschichte (Bavaria at Table: Of Eating and Drinking in Old Bavaria, Franconia and Swabia: A Culinary Cultural History), 1980

Esther Allen Howland ❧ 1801–1860 ❧

Esther Allen Howland was born in 1801, married Southworth A. Howland, gave birth to five children, four sons and one daughter, and died in 1860. Along the way she lent her name to a small, inexpensive, and very popular volume of recipes entitled *New England Economical Housekeeper*, first published in 1844 and frequently thereafter by her husband, a printer and bookseller in Worcester, Massachusetts. The little *Economical Housekeeper* is as much a monument to Yankee enterprise as Esther herself is a mystery.

Unlike some of her contemporaries, like **Lydia Maria Child** or the **Beecher** sisters for whom a book of recipes and household advice was part and parcel of other literary activities, or **Eliza Leslie** or **Mary Randolph** who were famous for their cooking, Mrs. Howland apparently just gave her husband a helping hand with his need for a cookbook in his product line, which included a lurid little volume of disaster stories. There are other recipe books of this sort issued by various publishers, often lacking author's identity, with contents that very often resemble one another.

Mr. Howland apparently felt that a female name affixed to the title page would lend credibility. The Preface to the 1845 stereotype edition was very frank about the origins of many recipes: "Many of the receipts are new, having been prepared, or furnished, expressly for this work. Selections have also been made from various works on this subject, such as have been proved to be good by use." It is very hard to tell for what portion of the writing Mrs. Howland herself may have been directly responsible. Some recipes seem lightly rewritten from others in print at the time, or merely copied as, for example, in the 1845 edition, "34. Election Cake" and "35. Sponge Cake, No. 1" which are verbatim from Mrs. Child's *American Frugal Housewife*. Others are conversational, but hardly original, giving advice for just about every operation of plain food preparation in common use. At the end of the book is a standard Medicinal Department. Among the most charming aspects of the book are two items: one, numbered 274, a Course of Dinner for a Week, with daily menus which ring practical and true; and the other, item 275 which lays out all that is required for a replete Thanksgiving meal.

The little work sold very well, and was reprinted annually for at least a decade, and a version of it titled *Practical Cookbook and Economical Housekeepers Guide* was in print in 1868. Besides the Worcester one, editions of *New England Economical Housekeeper* were printed in Montpelier, Vermont; New London, Connecticut; and Rochester, New York. Within a year of its appearance in 1844, a version entitled *American Economical Housekeeper* was printed in Cincinnati, Ohio. While the title *American* appeared on the cover, the inside title page still bore the words, *New England*, and it varied not the least from the original. Apparently the Ohio publishers felt a name change would suit the market better, and, since much of Ohio was settled by transplanted New Englanders, the recipes within would appeal.

The content of the book, however, probably mattered less than its commercial appeal, than its place in a line of booksellers' products. Southworth Howland was a sharp enough businessman to cover all the publishing bases. He was prosperous enough to send his children to college. The Howland's only daughter, also named Esther Allen Howland, was enough her father's daughter to found a thriving greeting card industry. Known as the Mother of American Valentines, Miss Howland graduated from Mount Holyoke in 1847 and began making Valentines by hand, but when orders exceeded her capacity she expanded to an assembly line operation which she ran until 1881 when she retired.

Mrs. Howland was no reformer with an agenda of diet improvements to pursue—she included some **Graham** flour recipes but only conventional, mainstream ones. She was not a temperance follower—there are beer recipes. Speed, simplicity, and economy are the book's hallmarks, with plentiful use of chemical leavenings, plain daily recipes, and commonly available ingredients. Her unremarkable cookbook with its every appearance of being largely a commercial enterprise, has given Esther herself an accidental immortality.

— SANDRA L. OLIVER

New England Economical Housekeeper, 1844; aka *American Economical Housekeeper, 1845*

J

Louis Jammet ❖ 1894–1964 ❖

LOUIS JAMMET CREATED A LAVISH FRENCH RESTAURANT THAT SERVED AS A gathering place for the well-heeled and artistic of Dublin for over half a century.

The legacy began with Louis' father, the well-known French chef Michel Jammet, a native of Quillan in the French Pyrenees. The elder Jammet had first moved to Dublin as chef to Henry Roe, the wealthy whiskey distiller known for restoring St. Patrick's Cathedral. Michel Jammet returned to Dublin in 1895 as chef to the Lord Lieutenant, the Earl of Cadogan at the Vice Regal Lodge. Louis had been born in London in July the previous year.

In 1900 Michel and his brother François bought the Burlington Restaurant at 27 St. Andrew Street, known for its oysters from the red bank oyster beds of the Burren in County Clare. The restaurant was renamed Jammet's two years later, and became one of the few restaurants accommodating prosperous Dubliners. Irish historian Peter Somerville-Large describes the Dublin social scene of the day: "Bowler-hatted citizens could attend a few good restaurants like the Bailey or the one opened by the Lord Lieutenant's chef, Monsieur Jammet, in Andrew Street which moved to Nassau Street in 1926."

Michel's brother François returned to Paris in 1908 but the restaurant traded at 26-27 Andrew Street and 6 Church Lane until the lease reverted back to the Hibernian Bank in 1926, at which point Michel acquired Kidd's Restaurant at 45-46 Nassau Street. However, Michel died just a year following the move.

Meanwhile, Louis Jammet had pursued his education at Belvedere College, Dublin, and joined the French army as a soldier during World War I. He was wounded in his right arm and came close to losing it. After the war he studied engineering in l'École Centrale in Paris where he met his wife, Yvonne, a second cousin from a strong restaurant family. One side of the family owned the Hotel Bristol and on the other the Le Boeuf à la Mode, both in Paris. Louis worked as an engineer in France until his father's death. Following the bereavement, Louis and Yvonne decided to move to Dublin and run the business. He bought out his sister's share of the business, and expanded on his father's reputation as proprietor of Ireland's best restaurant.

The new premises on Nassau Street were sumptuous. A regular customer, John Ryan, described them: "the main dining room was pure French Second Empire, with a lovely faded patina to the furniture, snow-white linen, well-cut crystal, monogrammed porcelain, gourmet-sized silver-plated cutlery and gleaming decanters." The centerpiece was a set of four murals depicting the Four Seasons painted by the artist Bossini—given to the old Burlington Restaurant in order to discharge his bill.

Jammet's became the hub for the artist and the literary set. The posh crowd came in through the Nassau Street entrance, while plainer folks entered through an alley into the smoking room and oyster bar, where one could perch on a high stool and eat lunch at a wide marble counter. The literati drank here, figures like Liam O' Flaherty, Seán O' Sullivan and the artist Harry Kernoff. (You can see Kernoff's painting of Jammet's at Patrick Guilbaud's Restaurant in Dublin's Merrion Hotel.) Yvonne, Louis' wife, had a reputation of her own as an excellent painter and sculptor and as a member of the avant-garde collection of painters known as the White Stag Group.

As Dublin's only French restaurant, Jammet's became a sought-after respite from war-time food shortages and rationing in Britain. Customer John Ryan described how American GI's, "cigar-chomping and in full uniform, were streaming across our neutral border to sample the fabulous food in the prodigious quantities available here. Jammet's could not and did not fail." One satisfied customer described the fare during the World War II years as "the finest French cooking between the fall of France and the Liberation of Paris."

After the war, when films began to be made in Ardmore Studios, the stars would converge on Jammet's. It continued as the place to be seen during the 1950's and early 1960's.

Louis died quite suddenly in October 1964 and the running of the restaurant fell to his son Patrick, the only member of the family who had worked in the business. But Patrick's health had been poor most of his life and when his mother died in 1967 he decided to close the restaurant for good.

Louis Jammet contributed to the formation of some of the leading figures in the Irish restaurant industry over the years. These included Willie O' Regan, Jimmy Beggan, Christy Sands, Charles Opperman, Mark Fore, Vincent Dowling, Frank Farren, Liam Kavanagh, and P.J. Dunne. Many of these chefs and waiters went on to become the future teachers, mentors, and standard bearers of the culinary world both in Ireland and abroad.

— MÁIRTÍN MAC CON IOMAIRE

Thomas Jefferson ❦ 1743–1826 ❦

OUR MOST ILLUSTRIOUS EPICURE WAS BORN TO PETER JEFFERSON and Jane Randolph Jefferson on April 13, 1743, in what is now Albemarle Country, Virginia. He died July 4, 1826, at Monticello, the baronial home he built near Charlottesville, Virginia. Much of his boyhood was spent at Tuckahoe, and he entered the College of William and Mary in 1760, graduating two years later. Along the way he learned classical Greek and Latin, as well as some French. His social position was assured by being a Randolph. Among his many accomplishments, he penned the Declaration of Independence, served as American ambassador to France (1784-1789) and as our third president (1801-1809).

Jefferson was to fall madly in love with the cuisine and wines of the royalist France, but his first love was gardening, and here the record dates to 1766 with the first entries in his Garden Book. This passion stayed with him to the end of his life.

Jefferson played a most important role in the introduction of French influences to Virginia cookery, this was by two paths; during his sojourn in France he had the enslaved James Hemings trained in some of the best kitchens in France. Hemings was later to train his brother Peter in the kitchen at Monticello, this in return for his manumission. Further, Jefferson's *maître d'hôtel* at the President's House was Étienne LeMaire and from him he cadged innumerable descriptions of the great dishes of the courtly cuisine of France, some of which have survived. His *chef de cuisine* was Honoré Julien, and the enslaved Edy, described as Mr. Jefferson's "favorite cook," learned her craft in his kitchen at the President's House. Many recipes in the hands of his granddaughters, Virginia Jefferson Randolph Trist and Septimia Anne Randolph Meikleham attributed to LeMaire and Julien survive in manuscripts penned in mid-nineteenth century. Many of those recipes had earlier found their way to **Mary Randolph**, a cousin of Jefferson and a sister-in-law of Jefferson's daughter, Martha Jefferson Randolph, who was also Virginia Trist's mother. It was Mary Randolph who incorporated the recipes into her cookbook, *The Virginia House-wife*, published in 1824. Those recipes were not attributed, to be sure, but there are innumerable identical tell-tale phrases which bespeak their origin.

Jefferson, however, did not forsake his "native vittles." What may be described as the English warp of Virginia cookery remained in evidence. Perhaps even more important, it must be remembered that no white hand ever stirred the pots at Monticello, so that the presence of African ways and products—most notably okra—permeates all.

— KAREN HESS

Thomas Jefferson's Garden Book, 1766-1824, with relevant extracts from his other writings, annotated by Edwin Morris Betts, 1999

Thomas Jefferson's Farm Book, with commentary and relevant extracts from other writings, edited by Edwin Morris Betts, 1999

Ella Eaton Kellogg

1853–1920

ELLA ERVILLA EATON WAS BORN IN 1853, IN ALFRED CENTER, NEW York, and graduated from college in 1872 at the tender age of 19, the youngest graduate of Alfred College. Four years later, she and her sister were vacationing in Battle Creek, Michigan, when her sister was stricken with typhoid fever. Ella brought her to the Battle Creek Sanitarium, a Seventh Day Adventist institution headed by Dr. John Harvey Kellogg (1852–1943).

Dr. Kellogg was so impressed with the skills Ella displayed nursing her sister that he invited her to join his staff as a charter member of his new School of Hygiene. She soon became a dietician, writer, advocate for children, and social reformer. Ella and John were married in 1879. Devoted working partners, they never consummated their marriage and lived in separate quarters. However, they did raise 40 foster children, and founded the Haskell Home for Orphans in Battle Creek. The couple ran kindergartens, supervised children's play and development, and conducted classes for area mothers and foster mothers.

The Battle Creek Sanitarium subscribed to the credo that the secret to health was good nutrition combined with pure living. The Adventists avoid coffee, tea, tobacco, and meat, replacing them with fruit, vegetables, bread, and vigorous exercise. Feeding patients at the Sanitarium led to the development of several new foods .The doctor constantly experimented with whole-grain foods, whose healthfulness had been proclaimed earlier in the century by reformers such as **Sylvester Graham**; in 1890 Dr. Kellogg was credited with perfecting peanut butter, useful protein for people who had problems with their teeth. Ella's brother-in-law, Will Keith Kellogg (1860–1951), also experimented with grains and, almost by accident, stumbled upon a flaked mixture, which—once processed, dried, and served with milk—was an instant hit with the patients.

Many other entrepreneurs in the Battle Creek area manufactured cereal products, among them a former Sanitarium patient, C. W. Post (1854–1914), who produced a cereal-based coffee substitute called "Postum." Post's "Grape Nuts," along with W. K. Kellogg's "Corn Flakes," and other cold cereal dishes, were not just

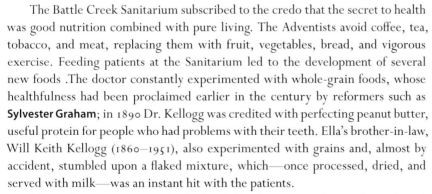

intended for patients but were aggressively advertised around the country. They revolutionized the composition of breakfast in America and much of the world.

Ella Kellogg founded and was dietitian at the Sanitarium's School of Home Economics and the School of Cooking. She created a new field, which came to be known as dietetics, or what she termed, "the hygiene of cooking." Much later, in 1917, she and Sanitarium colleague Lenna Cooper were involved in the formation of the American Dietetic Association. Dr. John Kellogg readily acknowledged, "Without the help derived by this fertile incubator of ideas, the great food industry of Battle Creek would never have existed. They are all a direct or indirect outgrowth of Mrs. Kellogg's experimental kitchen, established in the fall of 1883."

Ella Kellogg's major work, published in 1892, was *Science in the Kitchen: A Scientific Treatise on Food Substances and Their Dietetic Properties Together with a Practical Explanation of the Principles of Healthful Cookery and a Large Number of Original, Palatable and Wholesome Recipes*. In the book, she states, "There is no department of human activity where applied science offers greater advantages than in that of cookery." She analyzed the "food elements"—starch, sugar, fats, albumen, mineral substances, indigestible substances—as they were understood at the time, and emphasized her belief, "The brain and other organs of the body are affected by the quality of the blood which nourishes them, and since the blood is made of the food eaten, it follows that the use of poor food will result in poor blood, poor muscles, poor brains, and poor bodies, incapable of first-class work in any capacity." She declared that a taste for spices and condiments to season food is "a degradation of the sense of taste," which "was given to us to distinguish between wholesome and unwholesome foods, and cannot be used for merely sensuous gratification." She also presented an argument about the unsafe methods of meat packing in a time before federal meat standards were legislated.

All her life, Ella Kellogg was extremely energetic. In addition to her day-to-day work, she formulated dietetic courses for nurses, founded the School of Domestic Economy, and was assistant editor of Adventist *Good Health* magazine from 1877 to 1920, which she published with her husband. Her column *Science in the Household* ran for many years. She also wrote other domestic books, including *Everyday Dishes and Everyday Work* (1900), *Studies in Character Building* (1905), and *The Good Health Birthday Book: A Health Thought for Each Day* (1907).

Her activities extended outside of the Battle Creek area as evidenced by her activity at the national level in the Women's Christian Temperance Union; at the National Department of Mothers' Meetings and Child Care Circles; and as Superintendent of Hygiene at the National Department of Social Purity. Locally, she was a charter member and honorary president of the Michigan Women's Press Association; chairman of the World's Fair Committee on Food Supplies for Michigan; and a member of the National Congress for Mothers, the American Home Economics Association, the Women's League, and the YWCA.

Toward the end of Ella's life, she lost her hearing. To her remarkable credit, she learned lip-reading and moderation of her own speech so successfully that few realized she had this handicap. She was inducted into the Michigan Women's Hall of Fame in 1999.

— MARTY MARTINDALE

*Science in the Kitchen: A Scientific Treatise on Food Substances and Their Dietetic Properties
Together with a Practical Explanation of the Principles of Healthful Cookery and a Large
Number of Original, Palatable and Wholesome Recipes,* 1892
Everyday Dishes and Everyday Work, 1900
Healthful Cookery: A Collection of Choice Recipes for Preparing Foods, 1904
Studies in Character Building: A Book for Parents, 1905
The Good Health Birthday Book: A Health Thought for Each Day, 1907

Alfred A. Knopf

⁂ 1892–1984 ⁂

K

ALFRED A. KNOPF WAS BORN IN NEW YORK CITY, SEPTEMBER 12, 1892.
He was the most successful member of a new generation of twentieth-
century American publishers who cultivated the discovery of new authors and interesting literary endeavors. With close attention paid to
book design, typeface, and paper quality, Knopf publications from the
beginning held a particular cachet that showcased their subject matter.
His first publications, Russian literature in translation, were announced
under the Borzoi Books imprint in 1915. The subject was chosen deliberately to distinguish his list from those of other small publishers.

Knopf married Blanche Wolf in 1916, and she, almost unique among
women in the publishing industry, worked as an equal business partner
in the firm throughout her life. She became Director and Vice President
in 1921, and President in 1957. Borzoi Books incorporated as Alfred A.
Knopf Inc. in 1928, and merged with Random House in 1960.

During Prohibition, Knopf issued several wine books from its London office, but directly after repeal of Prohibition in 1933 brought out
Julian Street's *Wines* as a reintroduction to wine for an American readership. The book remained in print for almost 30 years. Knopf continued
the lifelong pursuit of his wine interests through publications. A week
after reading Alexis Lichine's book manuscript in 1950, Knopf's enthusiasm led him to France to meet the author—the first American owner of
a French vineyard—and tour the wine country with him. Lichine's *Wines of France*
was published upon Knopf's return.

In large part, the gastronomic aspect of Knopf publications reflected Alfred
A. Knopf's own tastes. As a gourmand and wine aficionado, Knopf structured
much of his business and personal life around the art of eating. "Alfred likes quality, and this is as true for printing as it is for music, food, and wine," wrote Knopf
illustrator Warren Chappell. "He has chosen to share his enthusiasm, in the form
of better-looking trade books, just as he shares his extraordinary cuisine and cellar with his friends ...."

Although the firm went on to publish the gastronomic writing of **Elizabeth David**
and several other books on wine, cookbooks were not big business in the U. S. before

the early 1960's. With its publication of *Mastering the Art of French Cooking*, Knopf not only set the standard for American cookbooks but established its culinary authors as catalysts in what would become a renaissance of cooking in the United States.

After Houghton Mifflin rejected **Julia Child** and **Simone Beck**'s manuscript for *Mastering the Art of French Cooking* as being "too formidable to the American housewife" (the original ran almost to a thousand pages), it was brought to Knopf's attention. The cookbook was accepted largely due to the efforts of its ultimate editor, Judith Jones. "The enthusiasts around here are absolutely convinced that this book is revolutionary," she wrote, "and we intend to prove it and make it a classic."

Mastering the Art of French Cooking was published in 1961 after much debate over the title, which Knopf thoroughly disliked but Child declared, "Saved by a participle!" The book was an immediate success, hailed repeatedly as "authoritative" and "a fundamental work" which demystified French cuisine for the American cook. "The recipes are glorious," wrote **Craig Claiborne** in the *New York Times*. "All are painstakingly edited and written as if each were a masterpiece, and most of them are."

The second volume, published in 1970, was dedicated to Alfred Knopf as "the ideal publisher for this kind of book, just as he is the ideal dinner guest...." The two-volume set has gone through 34 printings, sold over two million copies and was reissued in a 40th anniversary edition in 2001.

Judith Jones went on to cultivate a Knopf stable of culinary writers, which includes Lidia Bastianich, **James Beard**, Penelope Casas, **M. F. K. Fisher**, Pierre Franey, **Jane Grigson**, Maida Heatter, Ken Hom, Madhur Jaffrey, Irene Kuo, Edna Lewis, Joan Nathan, Elisabeth Lambert Ortiz, Jacques Pepin, Waverley Root, Nina Simonds, Raymond Sokolov, and Jeffrey Steingarten. Many of its titles, such as Marcella Hazan's *Classic Italian Cookbook*, Claudia Roden's *A Book of Middle Eastern Food* and Anna Thomas's *Vegetarian Epicure* volumes became standards on their subjects. Jones looked to transform the genre from household reference works and entertainment guides to serious examinations of techniques and ingredients. "I've always thought that the best cookbooks are teaching books, that they introduce you to a different culture," she said.

Knopf's successful reissue of the 1896 **Fanny Farmer** *Cookbook*, revamped for a new generation of cooks by Marion Cunningham, underscored the explosion of interest in American cooking in the 1970's. Jones was convinced American food merited further exploration best told "in parts, exploring a region or a typically American theme." From this came the celebrated eighteen-book series "Knopf Cooks American," which investigated American foodways through recipes, reminiscences, and histories.

After Blanche's death in 1966, Knopf married former Knopf author Helen Hedrick in 1967. He officially retired from the firm in 1972, actively serving as chairman emeritus until his death on August 11, 1984.

The Alfred A. Knopf, Inc. Records archive is held by the Harry Ransom Humanities Research Center, University of Texas at Austin. "The Company They Kept: Alfred A. and Blanche W. Knopf, Publishers" celebrated the couple and the company in a major exhibit at the University of Texas in 1995. A complete archival inventory is available online at http://www.hrc.utexas.edu/research/fa/knopf.html.

— LISA JONES

Ray Kroc

RAYMOND ALBERT KROC WAS BORN IN OAK PARK, ILLINOIS, ON OCTOBER 5, 1902. His father worked for Western Union and his mother was a piano teacher. He quit high school in the tenth grade and, lying about his age, attempted to become an ambulance driver in World War i, but the war ended too soon for him to be shipped out. Thereafter, he made a living as a piano player and a salesman in a variety of jobs. At age 52 Kroc was a salesman of multimixers—a machine that made large volume milk shake production possible as it had five spindles arranged around a pedestal for making up to five shakes simultaneously.

Kroc at age 69

Kroc paid a call on his best customers—the McDonald brothers in San Bernardino, California to see what made their operation so successful. What he discovered was a hamburger restaurant where the production process was precise and efficient, the menu limited, and the prices low. He was so impressed with the operation that he bought the right to franchise the operation from Richard and Maurice McDonald on the spot in April 1954.

His mission was to replicate the restaurant <u>exactly</u> and to provide customers with a casual, identifiable restaurant with cheap food and no waiting. Kroc also insisted on high standards of cleanliness and service. The franchise was the operating system that was so specific that food would taste identical in Maine and Mississippi. Later, Kroc established "Hamburger University" to teach his methods to franchisees.

Kroc built the first demonstration restaurant in Des Plaines, Illinois. With the process well defined, franchises were sold. In 1961, he bought out the McDonald brothers. The key to the growth of the corporation was a real estate strategy whereby the corporation identified and purchased property that was then leased to the franchisee. In the first ten years of operation the company spread to forty-four states and made an initial public offering. Eventually, the McDonald's Corporation became the largest restaurant company in the world. Ronald McDonald, one of the most identifiable clowns in history, developed as an image that helped bolster McDonald's sales by appealing to children. Further, expansion first to Canada and Puerto Rico (in 1967) then to Europe, Asia, and South America followed.

In 1977, Kroc resigned from the day-to-day operations of the McDonald Corporation and became Senior Chairman of the company. He purchased the San Diego Padres baseball team in 1974, and for a time was flamboyantly involved in its operation. In addition he supported numerous philanthropies including the Kroc Foundation which supported research into diabetes, arthritis, and multiple sclerosis.

Ray Kroc died of heart failure in San Diego on January 14, 1984. He had been married three times. His surviving widow, Joan Kroc, was also a philanthropist and donated a large portion of the family fortune to unusual charitable causes, including the establishment of centers for world peace at Notre Dame University and the University of San Diego.

— SUSAN MACDUFF WOOD

Grinding It Out: The Making of McDonalds, 1977

Peter Kump

Kump in about 1981

VISIONARY. INDEFATIGABLE. CHARISMATIC. THESE ARE SOME OF THE WAYS THAT friends and colleagues have described Peter Clark Kump, who is best known for his instrumental role in creating the James Beard Foundation and for teaching legions of professional and amateur cooks at the eponymous Peter Kump's New York Cooking School and School of Culinary Arts.

Born in Los Angeles on October 22, 1937 to Ernest and Josephine (née Miller) Kump, Peter (few refer to him by his surname, even 10 years after his death) spent his childhood in Los Altos, California. Family mythology credits the young Peter with dual affinities for teaching and cooking: he is rumored to have taught his younger sister Ramonda and other neighborhood children to read. His mother also claimed that she heard strange noises one night in the kitchen, only to discover the two-year-old Peter busily stirring an unorthodox concoction of milk, pudding mix, and ant poison. The family moved to Switzerland when Peter was 15, where he attended the elite Le Rosey boarding school.

Peter returned to the United States to study Speech and Drama at Stanford University. He founded the Comedia Repertory Company, which he ran for a murkily defined period from the late 1950's to the early-mid 1960's. Peter married Carolyn Davis in 1960; they had one son, Christopher, but the marriage soon ended in divorce. Peter earned an m.f.a. degree from Carnegie-Mellon University in the mid 1960's, supporting himself by teaching speed reading as part of the Evelyn Wood Reading Dynamics empire. His interpersonal skills vaulted him to the position of national director, where Peter received the plum assignment of teaching the Nixon White House staff speed reading. He wrote *Breakthrough Rapid Reading*, with editions published from the 1970's through the 1990's.

But speed reading was meager fare for Peter's insatiable curiosity. He studied cooking in the early 1970's with **Simone Beck**, Diana Kennedy, Marcella Hazan, and **James Beard**, and sojourned in Europe on a gourmand's tour of Michelin-starred restaurants for both lunch and dinner. In 1974, Peter taught his first cooking class to a group of five friends from his small apartment kitchen in New York City. Focusing on what he considered the basics, Peter's vision of creating "recipeless cooks" materialized in his French techniques approach to curriculum: the first class taught sautéing, and every dish repeated that cooking technique, with students feasting on sautéed lamb chops, sautéed potatoes with garlic and parsley, and sautéed broccoli, all finished with a generous knob of butter. Classes were pedagogical devices, not exercises in menu planning.

An article by *New York Times* restaurant critic Mimi Sheraton, plus Peter's business savvy to advertise in such venues as *Gourmet* magazine, an unprecedented step for cooking teachers in the 1970's, boosted the school's profile. The physical reality, however, did not yet match Peter's ambitions. For those seeking professional training, "Peter Kump's New York Cooking School" led a peripatetic existence, with instructors and assistants transporting equipment and ingredients by taxi to different rented kitchens around New York City. Peter continued to teach amateurs at home under the name "Peter Kump's School of Culinary Arts."

In 1979, Peter found a permanent home for his cooking schools in a funky former carriage factory with notoriously rickety stairs on East 92nd Street. Again Peter's aspirations temporarily outpaced reality: difficulties with Con Edison meant no gas service for the first six months of the schools' operation, with students cooking on camp stoves. Nonetheless, Peter emphasized the art and profession of fine cooking for small numbers, rather than the banquet training prevalent in other vocational schools. Typical of Peter's holistic approach to the culinary universe was the list given to entering professional students: two pages naming exotic ingredients, figures in culinary history, cooking terminology, and contemporary chefs, with a round-table discussion personally conducted by Peter. No student left without at least hearing the names **Apicius** and **Carême** and Peter's breathless joy of why these figures mattered. The 92nd Street location became a self-sustaining culinary enclave, with professional students baking most of the bread served in the school and avocational students enjoying a broad range of classes, from basic techniques classes that tracked the professional curriculum, pastry and baking lessons (borrowed from the professional pastry and baking program developed in the 1980's), and ethnic classes. Many of the most renowned cooking teachers taught specialty classes, among them Madeleine Kamman and **Julia Child**.

When James Beard died in 1985, Peter was instrumental with Child in forming the James Beard Foundation to honor his mentor. They raised money to purchase and renovate Beard's Greenwich Village townhouse, convincing prominent chefs to donate their time and energy for the Foundation's benefit. The first dinner at the Beard House was cooked in 1987 by Wolfgang Puck, and since that time, the house has been a high-profile stage for chefs to exhibit their talents. In 1991, through the Foundation, Peter established the James Beard Awards to celebrate excellence in the culinary field, now with more than 70 awards for chefs, restaurants, cookbook authors, and food journalists. Seen as the Oscars of the food world, with this single idea, Peter did more to elevate chefs to celebrity status than any other food event in the twentieth century, with the exception of television's Food Network. Peter remained as president of the Foundation until his death.

Peter also found time to write, with a weekly column in *The Chicago Tribune*, and occasional pieces in *The New York Times, Bon Appétit, Food & Wine*, and other publications. His one cookbook, *Quiche and Pâté*, part of the "Great American Cooking Schools" series, received a Tastemaker Award in 1983. Peter was president of the International Association of Culinary Professionals and the New York Association of Cooking Teachers, where he also was honored in 1994 for his contributions to culinary education. By this time, Peter was planning a major expansion of the school to modern space on Manhattan's West 23rd Street (several impermanent branches had met varying success outside New York City). Construction was nearing completion when Peter succumbed to liver cancer on June 7, 1995 at his weekend home in East Hampton, New York. He negotiated a deathbed sale of the school to entrepreneur Rick Smilow; the school has continued to grow, but was renamed The Institute of Culinary Education in 2001. Peter was survived by his father, son, sister, and companion, Andrew Semons.

— CATHY K. KAUFMAN

Breakthrough Rapid Reading, 1979
Quiche and Pâté, 1982

Aveline Kushi

ALSO CALLED: Tomoko Yokoyama

No matter what culture she was in, this was an extraordinary woman, full of energy, drive, and discipline. She was born Tomoko Yokoyama in a small mountain village in Japan's agricultural region of Izumo. Her family was Christian; her father having joined the Salvation Army as a teenager. She learned cooking and sewing from her mother, and silk-screen painting from her father.

Born in the Year of the Boar, she was typically active and headstrong, and was an outstanding athlete and scholar. When she finished high school, Tomoko, who wanted to be a teacher, scored highest among 70 girls on the college exams. It was unusual for girls in that area to go to college, and her mother was opposed, but her father supported her wishes and she enrolled in the Women's Teachers' College, five hours from home on the Sea of Japan.

Her college curriculum was very broad, including both Eastern and Western history and literature. Toward the end of her studies came the news of Pearl Harbor, as great a shock to the Japanese people as it was to the American people. Rationing of rice, soy sauce, and other essentials began. The school's tennis courts were dug up, and gardens were planted to grow food.

After graduation, Tomoko began teaching girls in an elementary school near her home village. She encouraged them to write poetry, a practice she followed all her life. Rural Izumo was spared the air-raids so familiar in other parts of Japan, but everyone had a family member in the war, and anxiety was high. The Japanese government's control of the news kept the people from knowing that the country was losing the war. The major newspapers even minimized the atomic destruction of Hiroshima and Nagasaki for a few days until August 15, 1945, when the emperor went on the radio and announced that the country would surrender.

Tomoko tried to carry on with her teaching in the aftermath of the war, but she became seriously ill and depressed, and returned to her family home where she lay weakly on her futon for several months. With the gradual return of her strength she heard talk of world peace that inspired her. Early in 1950, she traveled to Tokyo to meet George Ohsawa, one of the leading proponents of world government, peace, and healthy eating.

As a teenager, Ohsawa had cured himself of tuberculosis by turning to the traditional Japanese diet of brown rice and vegetables, with miso soup and seaweed. He began to travel widely in the 1920's and 1930's, and wrote prolifically about diet and society. If humanity regained its health through proper balance of yin and yang, the world would become more peaceful, he believed. In his lifetime, he wrote more than a hundred books, in several different languages. Perhaps the most influential in America was *Zen Macrobiotics* (a term he coined), written in English and first published in 1960.

George Ohsawa had renamed himself, changing his name from Yukikazu Sakurazawa after his cure. He renamed many of his followers as well, and called Tomoko "Aveline," a made-up name he felt was suitable for a Christian girl. Aveline studied with Ohsawa for more than a year, supporting herself by selling his

World Government newspapers illegally at Tokyo's train stations. She was the top salesman in the group. Then in 1951, she completed the difficult task of gathering funds and visas, and traveled, alone, to the United States.

Michio Kushi, a graduate student at Columbia and a friend of George Ohsawa's, met her at the station when her bus came in to New York. She was already half in love with him on the basis of his letters to Ohsawa's group and his beautiful handwriting. Their early years in New York were occupied with learning English, taking odd jobs, or launching small businesses, and avoiding deportation by the U.S. immigration service. Michio gave lectures and Aveline taught cooking classes at special macrobiotic summer camps, which emphasized peace and harmony through diet. A daughter Lilly was born to them, and when Aveline became pregnant again, the couple decided to legally marry. Ultimately their family grew to include four sons and one daughter.

In the early 1960's, the family moved to Boston. They expected to find intellectuals in the Boston area flocking to their cause; instead they got hippies from the West Coast. But they welcomed any and all. Natural, whole foods of the type the Kushis were using were difficult to find in America at that time, and Aveline established one of the first natural food stores, Erewhon. The name came from Samuel Butler's utopian novel and is said to mean "nowhere," with the word spelled backwards and adjusted to make it pronounceable. There were already some health stores in America, but their emphasis was on vitamins and mineral supplements, such as those recommended by the popular **Adelle Davis**, rather than on the foodstuffs advocated by the Kushis for a macrobiotic lifestyle. Erewhon offered organic brown rice and other whole grains, soybeans, azuki beans, lentils and other legumes, as well as seeds and nuts. They encouraged farmers to grow organically for the store, sometimes guaranteeing their first crops. Erewhon also innovated a natural peanut butter without sugar or artificial ingredients, and packaged a variety of healthful granolas.

Without consulting her accountants or anyone else, Aveline opened a second Erewhon in Los Angeles. This store, too, was very successful. In her enthusiasm, Aveline grew the organization too fast, taking on too much debt. The Kushis were also distracted by their many other activities. Erewhon employees were now drawn less from those devoted to macrobiotics and more from those who wanted a well-paying job. The workers unionized and joined the Teamsters. Ultimately, Erewhon was forced to file for bankruptcy. Never ashamed to cry, Aveline wept bitterly and profusely at the signing of these papers. Soon, with many apologies to those who had been hurt, she sold the company. Over the years, many of the Kushis' students went on to found natural food stores of their own, or futon companies, or other related businesses.

The Kushis also established several macrobiotic restaurants, and set up macrobiotic centers around the country. They continued to lecture and to teach cooking; Aveline's classes were described as "delicious and fun." The couple traveled extensively, visiting Europe, Central America, Africa, and ultimately Japan. Aveline wrote that the Japanese were embracing all things Western and found macrobiotics "too Japanese."

With her world travels, Aveline began to understand that dietary needs varied with climate and with the individual. She added more vegetables, and used less salt and oil; she experimented with traditional dishes from many other countries. A good diet, she said, should be assessed by its effects on health and peace of mind.

The Kushis continued to work hard spreading the word about health and harmony. Several celebrities, such as Gloria Swanson and John Denver, endorsed macrobiotics. The Kushi Institute was established in Brookline, Massachusetts, adding a large retreat center in the Berkshires.

In 1983, *The Cancer Prevention Diet: Michio Kushi's Nutritional Blueprint for the Relief and Prevention of Disease* was published. Its theories were supported by the experience of Anthony Sattilaro, an MD who cured himself of advanced cancer with a macrobiotic diet. Nevertheless, while the low-fat, high-fiber macrobiotic diet is widely accepted as ideal in preventing heart disease, its effectiveness with cancer has not yet been established.

In 1993, both Aveline and her daughter Lilly were diagnosed with cancer of the cervix. This was a great shock to both the family and to the macrobiotics movement; they struggled to explain it in some way that would not invalidate the macrobiotic diet: Did she follow the diet properly? Was she too busy with her work schedule? Was she affected early in her life by her father's paints? Did the diet in fact allow her to survive this long, when otherwise she would have been stricken much earlier? Aveline consented to take conventional medical treatment, receiving radiation that put the cancer into remission, but later it entered her bones. Lilly died in 1995 and Aveline died in 2001 at the age of 78. In 2004, Michio Kushi had a malignant tumor surgically removed from his colon. After this crisis in his health, he chose to rest and to follow a stricter macrobiotic diet.

Macrobiotics has been an important movement in the United States and other parts of the world since the 1960's and 1970's. The Smithsonian Institution in Washington, DC has in its collection a bag of brown rice, donated by Michio and Aveline Kushi, to commemorate this phenomenon of American History. For half a century, Aveline Kushi worked tirelessly, educating and inspiring thousands of students. Today, natural foods are widely accepted, and organic crops represent a rapidly-growing segment of agriculture. In addition, her efforts to promote world peace are felt in the hearts of many individuals around the world.

— ALICE ARNDT

Aveline Kushi's Complete Guide to Macrobiotic Cooking for Health, Harmony, and Peace (with Alex Jack), 1985
Changing Seasons Macrobiotic Cookbook (with Wendy Esko), 1985
Cooking for Health: Allergies, 1985
Cooking for Health: Diabetes and Hypoglycemia, 1985
Aveline: The Life and Dream, of the Woman Behind Macrobiotics Today (with Alex Jack), 1988
Macrobiotic Cancer Prevention Cookbook, 1988
The Quick and Natural Macrobiotic Cookbook, 1989
Food Governs Your Destiny, by Namboku Mizuno, translated by Michio and Aveline Kushi (with Alex Jack), 1991
Good Morning Macrobiotic Breakfast Book, 1991
Diet for Natural Beauty: A Natural Anti-aging Formula for Skin and Hair Care, 1991
Thirty Days: A Program to Lower Cholesterol, Achieve Optimal Weight, and Prevent Serious Disease (with Tom Monte), 1991
Macrobiotic Diet/Michio and Aveline Kushi, edited by Alex Jack, 1993
Raising Healthy Kids, by Michio and Aveline Kushi (with Edward and Wendy Esko), 1994
The Complete Whole Grain Cookbook (with Wendy Esko), 1996

L

Vincent La Chapelle ❧ FIRST HALF OF THE 18TH CENTURY ❧

CHEF TO THE FAMOUS, AND AUTHOR OF WHAT IS ARGUABLY THE most intriguing, if not best-selling, cookbook of his time, this versatile master chef's life is as intriguing as his sole contribution to culinary literature. The known facts of La Chapelle's biography are few and far between, and filling the gaps requires some detective work. There are seemingly no available vital statistics for this French émigré, or son thereof, who was in all likelihood a Huguenot seeking refuge in England in order to escape from Louis XIV's persecution of Protestants in France. The title pages of the English and French editions of his cookbook indicate he served in the households of the Earl of Chesterfield in London and thereafter in that of William, Prince of Nassau and Orange, at the Hague, as head chef. Holland, of course, was another well-known refuge for fleeing French Protestants. Alec Mellor's *Lord Chesterfield et son temps* [Tours: Mame, 1970] describes Chesterfield's "master chef, a certain Vincent de la Chapelle [sic] whom William of Orange had recommended," as being "the venerable of a Masonic lodge as well as the author of a gastronomic treatise dedicated to his master," and indicates that he was "of an inventive mind, and one is entitled to think that most of his outlandish creations remained theoretical." [Pp. 168-69. My translation. I shall discuss the "outlandish" parameter further on.]

From Le Cuisinier Moderne, *1742*

The Masonic connection helps unravel some of this author-chef's mystery. An article by Bro. W. McLeod titled "John Coustos: His Lodges and his Book" in the official and reliable Masonic periodical *Ars Quatuor Coronatorum* reveals the following regarding Vincent La Chapelle (variously spelled as De la Cappell, De la Chappelle, and La Chappell): that as early as 1730 he was listed as being a member of the Grand Lodge of England no. 75 and subsequently no. 9; that the former lodge had as many as 15 members with French names, and that the latter was known as the "Union French Lodge".[*Ars Quatuor Coronatorum. Transactions of Quatuor Coronati Lodge No. 2076.* Vol. 92, 1979. Pp. 113-15] These facts are corroborated on file cards in the Bibliothèque Nationale's Masonic collection, under the de la Chapelle, Vincent [sic] entry, with the following additional information: "considered to be the founder of FM [Freemasonry] in Holland"; "founder of the 1st lodge in the Hague 11-8-1734....founder, Lodge of the Grand Master of the United Provinces [Holland] and of the Generality of The Hague, 1734." [FM Impr. #3357. My translation.] His several functions purportedly included that of choirmaster.

All three editions of his cookbook were published at author's cost and were very luxurious—the finest paper, generous amounts of intricate engravings as illustrations and fold-outs—which points to his having been paid generously for his services. (Aside from George Vicaire's mention in his *Bibliographie gastronomique* of another English edition in 1744—of which no apparent trace exists—there have been no further editions of *The Modern Cook,* except for Morcrette's 1984 facsimile reprint.) He was also jealous of his rival **Massialot**, whose *Cuisinier royal et bourgeois* became a best-seller in its English translation, outshining La Chapelle's book on the latter's English territory, which led to a bout of plagiarisms, insults, and counter-insults involving these author-chefs in the thirties.

The cookbook's content is as diversified as the spellings of La Chapelle's name, domicile, and commitments. True, some of its overly-long recipes are indeed outrageous and would require a regimental size kitchen staff and days of preparation. The same may be said of several outlined banquet layouts in the form of centerfolds. La Chapelle's was a visionary artist's view of culinary creations. However, sections on how to feed the sick and poor, food supplies and recipes for lengthy maritime journeys, and other down-to-earth considerations such as an avant-garde version of today's bouillon cube, belie the one-sidedness of ostentatious courtly cooking. Flavors of the exotic also run through his pages, doubtless attributable to surroundings in which the Dutch East Indies Company and its fleet were major players of the day. Did La Chapelle ever travel on a Dutch tall ship to far-away places? Most likely in his imagination, but otherwise most probably not. We shall never know, for as of now nothing more is known of this disciple of modernity with a distinctly personal slant.

— BEATRICE FINK

The Modern Cook, London, Printed for the Author, 3 vol., 1733
Le Cuisinier Moderne, La Haye: de Groot, 4 vol., 1735
Le Cuisinier Moderne, La Haye, aux dépens de l'Auteur, 5 vol., 1742
Facsimile reprint of 1742 ed., Luzarches: D. Morcrette, 1984

Antonio Latini

DURING THE LATTER HALF OF THE SEVENTEENTH CENTURY, fresh breezes were blowing through European kitchens and dining rooms. New World foods, new philosophies of health, and scientific discoveries all combined to transform the way wealthy Europeans, then nearly everyone else, ate. Antonio Latini not only participated in this transformation, he recorded it for posterity.

Portrait from Lo scalco alla moderna, *1692*

Latini was a *scalco*. The Italian equivalent of *maître d'hôtel*, a *scalco* oversaw the food, wine, and entertaining for a noble household. He planned the meals and merriment, kept the books, and supervised the cooks, carvers, and helpers. He made sure everything from the food to the service, from the linens to the entertainment was carried out perfectly and with great panache. The nobility relished spectacle and style, and status often depended on how well one entertained. Latini's patrons entertained lavishly and stayed *au courant.*

When he was 50, Latini published a two-volume treatise on the foods of his time, *Lo scalco alla moderno.* He also wrote an autobiography, which was only recently discovered. According to the authors of *Italian Cuisine,* Alberto Capatti and Massimo Montanari, the manuscript was found in the public library of Fabriano, Italy. It had been copied by Fra Francesco Maria Nicolini in 1690. A book based on the manuscript has been published by Furio Liccichenti; it is titled: *Autobiografia (1642–1696): La vita di uno scalco.*

Latini's humble origins would not have predicted a future as either a *scalco* or an author. Born in the town of Coll'Amato in the Marche province of Italy in 1642, Latini was orphaned at the age of five and had to beg for food and shelter. When he was still very young, he went to work as a servant and learned the rudiments of reading and writing from a priest-cook in the household where he worked. At sixteen, he traveled to Rome to apprentice in the service of Cardinal Antonio Barberini, nephew of Pope Urban VIII. There he was trained in the skills of *cuoco* (cook), *trinciante* (carver), and *scalco.*

Continuing to learn and improve his skills, he worked for important officials in Macerata, Mirandola, and Faenza. In 1682, he became master of the household of don Stefano Carrillo Salcedo, first minister of the Spanish viceroy in Naples. It was an important position since Spain ruled much of Italy and all of Sicily, and Spanish nobles entertained lavishly and were famed for their confections. In 1693, Latini was honored with the title of *Cavaliere Aureato e Conte Palatino.* He died in 1696.

The first volume of *Lo scalco alla moderno* was published in 1692, the second in 1694. The book begins with sonnets to Latini by anonymous friends, anagrams of his name,and other laudatory notes. Then Latini describes the qualities and responsibilities of the *cuoco, trinciante,* and *scalco* in detail. He writes that a cook should be good and faithful, should know how to do his job very well, and shouldn't be overly fond of wine. In detailing the duties of a *trinciante,* Latini explains how to carve turkey, veal, every sort of fish, and *frutti di mare* as well as the fruits of the earth. One of the book's illustrations of the carver's art shows razor-thin ribbons of peel spiraling gracefully around a pear. Another shows a crown carved atop an apple. According to Latini, the *scalco* had one of the major posts in court, and a good *scalco* owed complete fidelity to his master. He devotes several pages to his description of a *scalco*'s duties.

The two volumes include everything from how to select fish to how to drink wine and avoid drunkenness. There are recipes for soups, pasta dishes, sauces, meat, and fish. Latini cites specialties of various regions of Italy, such as the saffron for which Aquilla, capital of the Abbruzzo province, is famous.

He describes the ornate centerpieces called "*trionfi,*" literally triumphs, that adorned tables at banquets. Marzipan figures molded into representations of Justice and Prudence, a bull in combat with a lion sculpted from butter, and a ham carved from ice and served in a basket made of sugar paste are just a few. He lists menus for lavish wedding banquets, dinners for nobles, and a regal trip out to view the eruption of Vesuvius. The menu for one wedding celebration numbered 15 courses plus a *credenza*, or cold buffet, at the beginning of the banquet and another as its finale.

In addition to recipes, the book contains many serving suggestions. For example, Latini writes that he serves Parmesan cheese with sage under it and laurel leaves painted silver and gold over it. He suggests stuffing spit-roasted pork with diverse ingredients, without specifying what those ingredients might be, and recommends decorating it with a crown of lemon. He serves fresh strawberries generously bathed in wine with sugar over them and snow under them. Snow was an important ingredient, served under or over fruits, vegetables, and candies. The penultimate course of many of the banquets described in the book consists of fresh fennel, pears, fresh almonds, black and white grapes, and tender artichokes, served with snow and bunches of carnations and other flowers. The last course is often an abundance of cookies, pastries, and *sorbetti*. At the conclusion of festivities, according to Latini, there was excellent music by the finest voices and most famous instrumentalists of Naples and much rejoicing.

Latini's foods include many we recognize as Italian, such as lasagna, fettucine, prosciutto, and pizza, along with wines such as Orvieto, Montepulciano, and Chianti. Although there are such medieval leftovers as heavily sugared pasta, *Lo scalco alla moderna* makes it clear that times were starting to change.

Latini was one of the first to describe using New World foods. His recipe for tomato sauce is the first one recorded in Italian. He calls it sauce in the Spanish style, and makes it with two "*Poma d'oro,*" as well as onions, peppers, mint, salt, and oil. He serves chocolate as a drink and also makes chocolate ices. Although his recipes for ices are the first published in Italian, Latini writes that everyone in Naples was born knowing how to make ices. Latini's recipes include a lemon ice, two chocolate ices, and a "*sorbetta di latte*" made with milk and candied citron or pumpkin. None call for cream or eggs, and all were made with so much sugar that they would have been unlikely to freeze very solidly.

In one brief chapter, Latini introduces the idea of using fresh herbs such as parsley, thyme, and mint in cooking rather than sweet spices like cinnamon and clove. He claims health benefits for the new style and cites its use among Capuchin monks to recommend it. This was the beginning of the end of the elaborately sugared and spiced style of dining in Europe, and Latini was leading the way.

He was a modern *scalco* indeed.

— JERI QUINZIO

Lo scalco alla moderno, vol.1, 1692; vol.2, 1694; republished Milan, with introduction by Claudio Benporat, 1993
Autobiografia (1642–1696): La vita di uno scalco, (based on Latini's autobiography)

La Varenne

C. 1618–1678

ALSO CALLED: François Pierre

MOST HISTORIANS ACCEPT 1500 AS THE END OF THE MIDDLE Ages, but cuisine, ever conservative, lagged behind the other arts and sciences. Changes in cooking from the medieval style become evident in Europe toward the end of the sixteenth century, with the publication of the *Opera* (1570) by **Bartolomeo Scappi** in Italy, *Ein New Kochbuch* (1581) by **Marx Rumpolt** in Germany, and Hugh Platt's *Delights for Ladies* (c. 1600) in England. In France, however, the entire century from the mid-1500's to the mid-1600's saw no new cookbook, and, as Barbara Wheaton reasons in her *Savoring the Past,* (page 114) it is probable that none of the earlier cookbooks were still in use either.

Then, in 1651, *Le Cuisinier françois* burst upon the scene, showing that a new cuisine had indeed been developing in the kitchens of France. The book brings organization and method to the preparation of a growing culinary repertory, and introduces many new dishes, including omelets and potages. Fewer spices are used than in the medieval period; the author calls for a *bouquet garni* and mushrooms as seasonings. Several New World foodstuffs are mentioned in the cookbook, as well. *Le Cuisinier* was a tremendous success; it was reprinted for a century, translated into English, and widely plagiarized.

Le Pastissier françois, another important cookbook, which appeared only two years later, has also been attributed to La Varenne. However, the styles of the two books are very different and, since pastry-making and cooking were two separate professions at that time, it seems likely that at best La Varenne worked with another author on this book. La Varenne is also sometimes given credit for *Le Confiturier françois* and *L'Ecole des ragoûts*.

The author of *Le Cuisinier françois* and perhaps the other works, François Pierre, called La Varenne, was chef to Louis Chaalon du Bled, the Marquis d'Uxelles. In

CUISINIER FRANCOIS

From the third edition of Le Cuisinier françois, *1658*

his dedication to the Marquis, La Varenne asserts that "During a whole ten years employment in your house, I have found the secret how to make meats ready neatly and daintily. I dare say that I have exercised the profession with a great approbation of the princes, of the Marshals of France, and of an infinite number of persons of quality, who did cherish your Table...." [Translation by "I.D.G." in the first English version of the book, published in 1653]. It is thought that La Varenne created the mushroom condiment *duxelles* in honor of the Marquis, but there is no recipe for it in the *Cuisinier,* although several other mushroom recipes are given. (Among the variations, many recipes for duxelles call for finely chopped mushrooms, shallots, and herbs; the sautéed mixture is used as an ingredient in sauces and stuffings.)

Little is known about François Pierre. A chronicler, writing in the eighteenth century, reported that he was born in Burgundy and died there, in Dijon, in 1678, aged over 60. He himself alludes to his humble background in the dedication of his book, stating, "my condition doth not afford me a Heroick heart." The significance of the nickname "La Varenne" is a mystery; there was a chef of that name in the employ of Henri IV a few decades earlier, but he was better known for assisting the king with his love affairs than for cooking. (The contemporary joke was that this La Varenne had done better by carrying *poulets* ("love letters") than by larding them.)

— ALICE ARNDT

Le Cuisinier françois, 1651
Le Pastissier françois, 1653

Pierre Jean-Baptiste Legrand d'Aussy

❦ 1737–1800 ❦

PIERRE JEAN-BAPTISTE LEGRAND, WHO LATER ADDED D'AUSSY TO HIS NAME, was born in Amiens on July 3, 1737. He came from a bourgeois background, and was educated by the Jesuits prior to joining their order himself. Following the Jesuits' 1764 dissolution in France and subsequent suppression by the Pope, he moved to Paris, mingled in learned circles, and put his talents to work in the area which fascinated him most, namely a conflation of cultural and material history.

He assisted the noted medievalist Lacurne de Sainte-Palaye in the painstaking research required for the latter's projected glossary of old French, in the process whetting his appetite for digging into the roots of French customs and life-styles. Legrand d'Aussy spent most of the 1770's researching France's bygone traditions, whether transmitted orally or in writing, which in turn led to his translation into modern French of medieval texts in prose and verse titled *Fabliaux ou Contes du XIIe et du XIIIe siècle(Fables and Tales from the Twelfth and Thirteenth Centuries),* 1779–1781.

This ambitious five-volume edition's annotations and "observations" are in and of themselves the first manifestations of a projected four-part *opus* covering the private sphere of Frenchmen's lives throughout the ages, to have been divided as follows: living accommodations, food and meal customs, clothing, and entertainment.

In fact, only the second of these categories, the one dealing with food, ever saw the light of day. This material from the notes to *Fabliaux*, which also includes aspects of cookery, meals, and table conduct, was published in three volumes, with the title *Histoire de la vie privée des Français, depuis l'origine de la nation jusqu'à nos jours*, (*History of French Private Life from the Beginnings of the Nation to the Present*) in 1782. This was the first *bona fide* food history in French context.

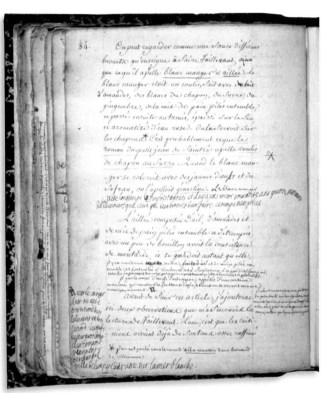

And now, the intriguing genesis and no less intriguing epilogue of this publication: The work owes its existence to the opportune encounter of an erudite author in search of desirable research conditions and a well-heeled bibliophile marquis in search of a learned researcher. Enter Antoine-René de Voyer d'Argenson, marquis de Paulmy (1722–1787), whose family ranked among the upper crust of France's aristocracy. Lodged in the vast quarters of the royal arsenal which he administered, yet more interested in books than weapons, the enlightened marquis put together a library (the future Bibliothèque de l'Arsenal). His impressive collection soon attracted high-level scholars who were then put to work drafting savant reports whose authorship was subsequently claimed by the marquis.

From the manuscript of Histoire de la vie privée des Français, depuis l'origine de la nation jusqu'à nos jours

In 1776, one of these scholars, Contant d'Orville, was tasked with researching and documenting what was meant to become a general history of Frenchmen's private lives, beginning with the section on food. The demanding marquis, soon dissatisfied with the level of Contant d'Orville's scholarship, began looking for a replacement, thereby summoning Legrand d'Aussy to his side in 1778. The latter took on where the former left off, sharply criticizing the manuscript left by his predecessor, titled "De la nourriture des français," which was later deposited in the French National Library. He then spent twelve months at the Arsenal, researching and filing notes non-stop while exchanging comments with the marquis, frequently during a meal. Neither actually had a reputation for being a connoisseur of fine food or even a gourmet, their interests being primarily scholarly.

This collaboration verging on camaraderie was soon to end, however. The former Jesuit, feeling increasingly that he was working for, rather than at the side of his aristocratic benefactor, began to fear for his autonomy and the freedom to sign the work he had researched and drafted. At first, he published a prospectus of the ongoing *Histoire* at the end of his *Fabliaux ou contes,* whereupon the marquis parried by using a selection of the former Jesuit's manuscript fragments and notes to publish a *Précis d'une histoire générale de la vie privée des Français…*under his own name in 1779. In response, Legrand d'Aussy proceeded to fine-tune and publish, in 1782, what he had written thus far, namely the three volumes of *Histoire de la vie privée des Français,* which had become "Part One" of his never-to-be-completed four-part *magnum opus.* The marquis, noting that he had initiated the project himself with Contant d'Orville, was swift to react. He published an open letter to Legrand d'Aussy , and, while not accusing him outright of plagiarism, gave indications that this was in fact the case. That ended the polemic, but the suspicion of plagiarism remained, with the result that the erudite scholar abandoned the rest of the project and turned his efforts elsewhere, namely the Auvergne region, and published a *Voyage d'Auvergne (An Avergne Journey)* seen in naturalist perspective in 1788.

In 1795, after the French National Library was transferred from the royal to the public domain, Legrand d'Aussy was named its curator of manuscripts. He died in Paris, December 5, 1800.

Paradoxically, a learned man with no particular previous or subsequent ties with the world of food, one who was not even an *aficionado,* authored the first French historical treatise on food. True, this was favored by chance, to which one can add the overall codification tendencies of Enlightenment thought and a nascent interest in the rituals of the table. Legrand d'Aussy's three volumes thus fit into context. Its seven parts cover the gamut: vegetarian foods; animal-derived foods; prepared foods; dining utensils and furniture; decorative table arts; feasts and banquets; prandial civility. An interesting sideline is a history of civilization seen in culinary perspective: Refinement in the culinary arts is viewed as marching alongside that of civilization in general. Part carefully researched reference tool, part reflection of an era when food, cookery, and meals became a valid subject of inquiry, Legrand d'Aussy's heads a series of *Histoires de la vie privée…* to follow, such as that of Alfred Franklin and more recently that of Georges Duby. A second (posthumous) edition of Legrand d'Aussy's work appeared in 1815 followed by a recent one dated 1999–2000. A manuscript version, titled "Recherches sur la nourriture des Français," exists at the Arsenal Library in Paris (see illustration).

— BEATRICE FINK

Fabliaux ou Contes du XIIe et du XIIIe siècle, 5 vols., 1779–1781
Histoire de la vie privée des Français, depuis l'origine de la nation jusqu'à nos jours, 1782; second
    edition, 1815; republished 1999-2000
Voyage d'Auvergne, 1788

Eliza Leslie

~ 1787–1858 ~

ALSO CALLED: Miss Leslie

ELIZA LESLIE WAS THE AUTHOR OF *DIRECTIONS FOR COOKERY*, THE MOST POPULAR American cookbook of the nineteenth century, to judge by the number of editions and printings, topping such successful works as the *Virginia House-wife* (1824) by **Mary Randolph**; the *American Frugal Housewife* (first published as *The Frugal Housewife* in 1829) by **Lydia Maria Child**; **Eliza Acton**'s *Modern Cookery in all its Branches*, as revised for America by **Sarah Josepha Hale** (1845), or any of Mrs. Hale's own cookbooks; *Miss Beecher*'s *Domestic Receipt-Book,* (1846); and even the influential *Mrs. Lincoln*'s *Boston Cook Book*, (1884).

Eliza Leslie was born November 18, 1787 in Philadelphia, the eldest of five children. Her father was a watchmaker with a strong interest in mathematics and science, through which he became acquainted with Benjamin Franklin and **Thomas Jefferson**. Eliza received her early literary education in London as her father moved the family there when she was five. They returned to Philadelphia in 1800 and Eliza remained there for the rest of her life. When her father died in 1803, she and her mother ran a boardinghouse to provide for the family. Eliza was perhaps improving herself for this task when she enrolled in Mrs. Goodfellow's cooking school for young ladies, where she ranked among the best students. The Leslie family managed to prosper. Eliza's younger brother, Charles Robert Leslie, was successful as an artist in England, and Eliza matched that success in America with her writing.

Eliza Leslie's first publication was *Seventy-five Receipts for Pastry, Cakes and Sweetmeats* (1828), probably derived from her study at Mrs. Goodfellow's school. Repeat editions of this publication occurred 20 times in the following 20 years. Miss Leslie wrote for the American homemaker, using ingredients and cooking implements available in American markets. She expected her readers to cook on an open fireplace.

In 1831 she published *The American Girl's Book* (a volume which emphasizes the importance of play in the lives of children) and in 1837, the very popular *Directions for Cookery* was published. In it, her directions are always clear, dry ingredients are measured by weight and the book incorporates nuances regarding the importance of freshness and quality ingredients. For example, the receipt for cat-fish soup begins "Cat-fish that have been caught near the middle of the river are much nicer than those that are taken near the shore where they have access to impure food. The small ones are the best. . . ." Sixty editions of this cookbook were published between 1837 and 1870.

Miss Leslie published several additional cookbooks and companion books intended to educate American women in household management. A lesser-known of her books entitled *The Indian Meal Book* was first published in London during the potato famine to teach the Irish how to use corn meal as a staple.

Miss Leslie also wrote novels, literature for children, and stories for several prominent magazines of the day, including the *Saturday Evening Post* and *Godey's Ladies Book*, edited by Sarah Josepha Hale. Hale also included Eliza Leslie in her tribute to distinguished women, *Women's Record*.

Engraved after a portrait by Thomas Sully, from Woman's Record *by Sarah Josepha Hale*

To Miss Leslie's mind, her fiction represented her best and most important work—she saw recipe books as "unparnassean"—but her popularity was due primarily to her cookery books and domestic manuals, and she is remembered today as a cookbook author.

Eliza Leslie died on January 1, 1858.

— SUSAN MACDUFF WOOD

Miss Leslie's culinary and household books:
Seventy-five Receipts for Pastry, Cakes and Sweetmeats, 1828
The American Girl's Book, 1831
Domestic French Cookery, 1832
Domestic Cookery Book, 1837
Directions for Cookery 1837
The House Book, 1840
The Ladies' Receipt Book, 1846
The Indian Meal Book, 1847
Miss Leslie's Lady's New Receipt-Book, 1850
More Receipts, 7th edition, 1852
The Behavior Book, 1853
New Receipts for Cooking, 1854
Miss Leslie's New Cookery Book, 1857

Justus Liebig

1803–1873

ALSO CALLED: Baron Justus von Liebig

1860

JUSTUS LIEBIG WAS BORN IN DARMSTADT, GERMANY. AT THE AGE OF TWENTY he moved to Paris, where he studied under Joseph Gay-Lussac, a prominent scientist. The following year, 1824, when he was 21 years old, Liebig became professor of chemistry at the University of Giessen, where he established a large chemistry laboratory. He developed unique equipment for analyzing inorganic and organic substances. By 1827, he had a major research laboratory there with a staff of twenty researchers. As a result of experiments conducted in the lab, Liebig concluded that living tissue consisted of carbohydrates (sugars), fats (fatty acids), and proteins (amino acids). He then focused his studies on protein compounds and concluded that muscular exertion required mainly protein, not carbohydrate or fat. He summarized his conclusions in his *Animal Chemistry* (1842). He also worked extensively in agricultural chemistry and the production of fertilizers. Although many of his views were later proved erroneous, Liebig's methods sparked extensive research into organic chemistry, and for this he is frequently identified as "the father of organic chemistry."

In 1845, Liebig was made a *Freiherr* (baron) by the Duke of Hesse-Darmstadt. Later he moved to the University of Munich, where he was freed of teaching obligations. He remained in Munich for the rest of his life, and died there April 10, 1873.

Liebig was interested in cookery since childhood, when he had watched the family cook prepare meals. As an adult, he occasionally threatened to write a cookbook, but this was a task he never completed. However, he had a great influence on cookbooks and an even greater influence on food processing. Beginning in 1844, he published several food-related articles and books, the most important of which was translated into English as *Researches on the Chemistry of Food,* and published in England in 1847. In this work, Liebig reported that the most important nutrients were contained in meat's fluids, and that these nutrients were lost during boiling or roasting. He recommended searing meat by boiling at a high temperature to form an outer crust to retain juices, then lowering the temperature of the water. He also recommended "beef tea," a broth composed of beef juices and water. If this tea were boiled down, it formed a concentrated extract which, when wanted, could be reconstituted to make soup by simply adding boiling water. These were both touted as particularly helpful for workers and for those with illness.

Liebig was incorrect in his belief that the most important nutrients were contained in the muscle fluid and that they were lost in cooking, but his procedures for boiling meat had two major effects. The first was in cookbooks: The 1854 revised edition of **Eliza Acton**'s *Modern Cookery* was newly subtitled, *Reduced to a system of easy practice, in a series of carefully tested receipts, in which the principles of Baron Liebig and other eminent writers have been as much as possible applied and explained;* in the United States, **Sarah Josepha Hale**'s *New Cook Book* (1857), published Liebig's procedures for making his tea and extract; and in Germany, the sixteenth edition of **Henriette Davidis**' influential *Praktisches Kochbuch* (1871), introduced Justus von Liebig's meat extract. Subsequent writers began to include other "scientific" matter in their cookbooks, and the tradition of cooking as an art began to swing toward cookery as a science.

The second effect of Liebig's work was on the application of his ideas to commercial ventures. Several food companies tried to manufacture the extract that Liebig had proposed, but it was an expensive process since it required beef. The cost problem was solved by Georg Christian Giebert, a German engineer, who built railroads in South America. Cattle in South America were killed mainly for their hides, and very little of the meat was used. With Liebig's agreement, Giebert and others set up a small plant to manufacture beef extract. This small-scale experiment was successful, and in 1865 Giebert established the Liebig Extract of Meat Company in London. In return for allowing the company to use his name, Liebig received a directorship and a large cash payment, as well as a salary. The company quickly set up subsidiaries in most European countries as well as the United States, Australia, and Latin America.

Liebig was by no means a silent partner. He used all his contacts to promote his Extract of Meat, which was meant to be used to make broths, sauces, and many other dishes. The company was one of the first in Europe to issue cookery booklets as a promotional device. In 1870 it published *Improved and Economic Cookery,* written by Henriette Davidis**,** in both Germany and England. A second

English-language cookbook by Davidis, *Modern Cookery: Liebig Company's Extract of Meat: A Collection of Recipes for Rich and Poor,* was published about 1876. Based on this experience, the company concluded that it needed to publish different editions compiled by nationally-known cookery experts from each country, with the help of nationally-known cookery experts. Thus the U.S. edition was compiled by **Maria Parloa** and published under the title *Liebig Company's Cookbook: One Hundred Ways to Use Liebig Company's Extract of Beef. A Guide for American Housewives* (1893). Parloa's recipes included American ones, such as Creole Soup and Oysters à la Baltimore, and—unlike the British edition—incorporated canned foods. Yet another English text, *Liebig Company's Practical Cookery Book* (1893), was compiled by Hannah Young. The Liebig Extract of Meat Company changed its name to its initials, Lemco, and the cookbook was revised and reissued by Young under the title *The Lemco Cookery Book* (1897). Most recipes in these books used Liebig's Beef Extract as an ingredient.

Liebig made other contributions to the culinary arts. One of his most famous students during the early 1840's was the American chemist Eben N. Horsford. Liebig encouraged him to investigate the nitrogen content of vegetable foods. After his return to the United States, Horsford was appointed **Rumford** Professor of Science at Harvard, where he built a laboratory modeled on Liebig's at Giessen. He patented a new baking powder in 1856 and, to produce it, became a partner in the Rumford Chemical Works in Providence, Rhode Island. Liebig, noting Horsford's success with baking powder, became interested in bread-making. He concluded that white bread contained few, if any, nutritious elements and he attempted, unsuccessfully, to devise a way to put the bran back into bread. His next venture—an attempt to make powdered coffee—was similarly unsuccessful, although it presaged a popular twentieth-century product.

One of Liebig's ideas that did come to fruition was "humanized milk," a liquid made from wheat and other products, which he developed in response to Europe's high infant mortality rates. His product was intended for mothers who could not nurse their babies and for infants who were allergic to cow's milk. To promote it, he set up several corporations, such as Liebig's Registered Concentrated Milk, Ltd., in England. While sales never amounted to much, others manufactured similar products in the United States and England. Inspired by Liebig's interest in infant mortality, Henri Nestlé succeeded in developing powdered milk in Switzerland. Due to his pioneering work, Liebig is frequently considered to be the inventor of infant formula and one of the first to develop baby food.

— ANDREW F. SMITH

Liebig's food-related books include:
Agricultur Chemie, 1840
Tier Chemie (Animal Chemistry), 1842
Researches on the Chemistry of Food, 1847

Mary J. Lincoln

❀ 1844–1921 ❀

ALSO CALLED: Mrs. D. A. Lincoln

From The Congress of Women…, *1894*

IN 1946, THE GROLIER CLUB, ONE OF THE MOST PRESTIGIOUS BIBLIOPHILE societies, opened its exhibition "One Hundred American Books Printed Before 1900," books chosen on the basis of their influence on the life and culture of the people. The purpose of the exhibition was to display books that "would arouse in all who saw it a feeling of pride in the accomplishments of our country."

Only one cookbook was selected for this exhibition: *Mrs. Lincoln's Boston Cook Book*, first printed in 1884. It was included among such noble and important documents as Stowe's *Uncle Tom's Cabin*, Audubon's *Birds of America*, Paine's *Common Sense,* Holmes's *Common Law*, the Constitution, the Declaration of Independence, the Emancipation Proclamation, and Webster's *Dictionary*. In describing the *Boston Cook Book*, the selection committee declared that this book

> …marked a change in culinary literature. Having directed the Boston Cooking School (est. 1879), she was able to arrange her material in an orderly plan, and to set it forth in plain, sensible language that housewives could understand. While it instantly became the standard kitchen companion, it had still greater effect in shaping the course of early work in domestic science in grade and normal schools. **Fanny** [sic] **Farmer**'s Cook Book is a direct outgrowth from this.

Mary Johnson Bailey Lincoln was born in South Attleboro, Massachusetts, to the Rev. John Burnham and Sarah Morgan (Johnson) Bailey in 1844. She lost her father when she was seven years old and was reared by her mother, who taught her three children good character and usefulness in their formative years. These traits seem to have shaped Mary Lincoln and her works for the remainder of her life.

Lincoln's mother moved her family to Norton, Massachusetts, so that her daughters could attend Wheaton Female Seminary, from which Mary graduated in 1864. She married David A. Lincoln in 1865 and happily settled down to life as a housewife. But her husband's reduced circumstances and ill health soon forced Mrs. Lincoln to earn her own living. She faced the future courageously and spent the rest of her life becoming one of America's most respected and influential cooking authorities.

She became the first principal of the Boston Cooking School at its incorporation in 1879, and served until 1885.

In 1884 she wrote the *Boston Cook Book*, which immediately became the standard by which other books of the era were judged. It was in print, in original and revised editions, for forty years, a 23rd printing being recorded in 1923. The praise for the books in newspapers and journals of the day was simply superlative, if not hyperbolic. A quote from the *Christian Intelligencer* illustrates this:

> Mrs. Lincoln's "Boston Cook-Book" is no mere amateur compilation, much less an *omnium gatherum* of receipts. Its title does scant justice to it,

for it is not so much a cook-book as a dietetic and culinary cyclopaedia. Mrs. Lincoln is a lady of culture and practical tastes who has made the fine art of *cuisine* the subject of professional study and teaching.

In addition to the *Boston Cook Book*, Mrs. Lincoln wrote numerous other books and pamphlets, all of which received much praise in the press. Among her other major works, some of which were in print for nearly thirty years, are: *Peerless Cook Book* (1886), *Carving and Serving* (1886), *Boston School Kitchen Text-Book* (1887), *What to Have for Luncheon* (1904) and *The Home Science Cook Book* (co-authored with Anna Barrows, 1902). In addition, she wrote many commercial pamphlets for food and cooking-equipment companies. She allowed her name to be used as an endorsement for a wide variety of products, and she was a principal in Mrs. Lincoln's Baking Powder Company, which flourished in Boston at the turn of the century.

Among Mary Lincoln's most influential contributions was her ten-year stint as culinary editor of the *American Kitchen Magazine* (also variously titled the *New England Kitchen* and *Home Science Magazine*). In her monthly column, "From Day to Day," she answered thousands of letters from readers in all parts of the United States. It is in reading this column that one learns to appreciate the practical turn of mind and attention to detail for which Mrs. Lincoln was famous, as well as her poise and literacy. She undertook to educate her questioner: No question was too simple, nor too complicated, to answer; the reader must understand the reason behind the answer. Mrs. Lincoln seems to have been a born teacher.

One can picture this dedicated woman consulting her large personal library of clippings, magazines, and books in order to answer each question. In one column Mrs. Lincoln described her research methods, indicating voluminous reading and clipping of articles (duplicating information by longhand in those days before easy copying) and reliance on a detailed filing system.

In addition to her regular monthly column in the *American Kitchen Magazine*, she also wrote other columns, often with a very modern concern for historical and sociological perspectives on gastronomy—and always making use of her massive personal archive.

Mrs. Lincoln spoke at expositions, Chatauquas, colleges, conferences, department stores, cooking schools—any place she was invited. One lecture series at a Long Island Chatauqua led to a long editorial in the *New York Sun* on the pros and cons of teaching domestic science in the public-school system. Another lecture series in Boston led to a column on outfitting a modern (1894) kitchen. This column created much discussion on the introduction and use of modern kitchen utensils.

Mrs. Lincoln was active in the Cooking Teacher's Club of Boston, the Cooking School Teachers' League, various domestic-science and home-economics organizations and the New England Women's Press Association. She was asked to contribute an article to the new *Encyclopedia Americana*. She gave a major address at the Congress of Women at the 1893 World's Columbian Exposition in Chicago. She prepared the *Boston School Kitchen Text-Book* for use in the Boston Public Schools. (This was the forerunner of the book I used during my own childhood in Boston fifty years ago.) The *Text-Book* and her *Boston Cook Book* were used in public and private schools throughout England, Scotland, Scandinavia, Canada, and the United States. The *Boston Cook Book* was the text used at the Biltmore School of Domestic Science (Asheville, North Carolina) "to train colored girls between the ages of sixteen and twenty-five to fill creditably any position in the home." Mary Lincoln's students taught in schools and colleges throughout the United States and helped to shape the home-economics movement.

Mary Lincoln died in Boston in 1921.

— JANICE BLUESTEIN LONGONE

Mrs. Lincoln's Boston Cook Book, 1884
Peerless Cook Book, 1886
Carving and Serving, 1886
Boston School Kitchen Text-Book, 1887
Frozen Dainties: Fifty Choice Recipes for Ice Creams, Frozen Puddings, Frozen Fruits, Frozen Beverages, Sherbets, and Water Ices, 1898
The Home Science Cook Book, with Anna Barrows, 1902
What to Have for Luncheon, 1904

Kenneth Lo

❦ 1913–1995 ❦

KENNETH H.C. LO WAS BORN IN 1913 IN FUZHOU, CHINA. HE WENT to London at the age of six with his father, who was appointed consul to the Chinese Embassy there. He returned to China and lived in the south and other regions until he went to study physics at Yenjing University in Beijing, then called Peking. In China, Mr. Lo was a professional tennis player who became the champion of North China, and he played for the Chinese in the Davis Cup. Later, in 1946, he also played at Wimbledon.

Mr. Lo returned to London in 1936 to study English literature and art at Cambridge University. Later, he became an industrial relations officer dealing with labor and welfare issues for Chinese seamen in Liverpool. Later still, he was a vice-consul in Manchester. Also before his culinary career, Kenneth Lo was a publisher of Chinese prints, a frequent speaker on a myriad of topics, a journalist, broadcaster, etc.

Kenneth Lo popularized Chinese cooking in England and later abroad. He founded the Chinese Gourmet Club of London, and became a legendary figure as a prolific author who penned dozens of Chinese cookbooks and touted Chinese cooking in a myriad of other ways. One of these was opening a Chinese restaurant with his wife Anne Brown, called Memories of China. It became exceptionally popular. Before that he had opened others, some with other partners, one of which sprouted satellite branches. In addition to these efforts, he and his wife founded the Kenneth Lo Cooking School in London which was run by his daughter Jenny; and he popularized the cuisine with a line of Chinese packaged and frozen foods called Memories of China. These were produced and marketed by the Heinz company of the United Kingdom, for whom he was a consultant. And, in 1982–1983 two television films were made of his myriad of activities in a series about Chinese food done by Thames TV; they aired several times in Great Britain.

Kenneth Lo wrote more Chinese cookbooks than did anyone else in the western world. The very first was *Cooking the Chinese Way*, published in London in 1955 by Arco. The last one located in English, republished by Crescent Books in New York in 1995, the year he died, was a reprint of the *New Chinese Cooking School* originally published by HP Books in Tucson, Arizona ten years earlier. Also in the year he died, Faber and Faber republished *Chinese Vegetable and Vegetarian Cooking*, a book originally published in New York as *Chinese Vegetarian Cooking* by Pantheon Books. A year after his death, Penguin Books of London released a revised and expanded edition of *Chinese Food*, first published in 1974 by Faber and Faber. Clearly his large number of volumes published on both sides of the Atlantic had major influences that expanded knowledge about Chinese food, as did those books translated and published abroad in other languages. The exact number of books is difficult to assess as some were republished with different titles. Stony Brook University in New York, which holds the largest collection of English-language Chinese cookbooks, has many more than thirty where Lo is the sole author, a couple where he is the editor, and several he co-authored.

In addition to writing books, Mr. Lo authored quite a few articles in magazines and newspapers, and did a lot of restaurant consulting in his adopted country and for the government of his birthplace. His two daughters are following in his footsteps, Vivienne the writer and Jenny the chef have published, in 2000, a Pavilion of London cookbook titled *Secrets from a Chinese Kitchen*. They also opened and run a café restaurant called The Teahouse on Eccleston Street in London.

— JACQUELINE M. NEWMAN

Cooking the Chinese Way, 1955
Quick and Easy Chinese Cooking, 1970
Peking Cooking, 1971
The World of Food: China, 1973
Chinese Food, 1974; revised and expanded edition, 1996
The Chinese Cooking Encyclopedia, 1974; published in the US as *The Encyclopedia of Chinese Cooking*, 1979
Chinese Vegetable and Vegetarian Cooking, 1974
The Encyclopedia of Chinese Cooking, 1974
Cheap Chow, 1976
Chinese Cooking on Next to Nothing, 1976
A Guide to Chinese Eating, 1976
Food the Chinese Way, 1976
The Love of Chinese Cooking, 1977
Chinese Provincial Cooking, 1979
Chinese Regional Cooking, 1979
New Chinese Cooking School, 1985; republished 1995
New Chinese Vegetarian Cooking, 1986
The Feast of My Life, 1993

Dione Lucas

⁂ 1909—1971 ⁂

Dione Lucas was one of the most influential food professionals in America from the mid-1940's until her death in 1971. She had one of the first cooking programs on television, and through these programs, her many restaurants, cooking schools, and books, she reached a wide audience, introducing French home cooking to Americans.

Lucas prepares an omelet in her cooking school.

Dione Narona Margaris Wilson was born on October 10, 1909 in Italy, daughter of British artist Henry Wilson. She studied cello at the Conservatoire in Paris but found her life's work after taking courses at L'École du Cordon Bleu under the tutelage of Henri-Paul Pellaprat. She received a diploma and was the first woman to complete a formal chef's apprenticeship at the restaurant Drouant. In 1933, she worked with Rosemary Hume to open the cooking school Le Petit Cordon Bleu in London.

Later in the 1930's, she worked as a chef at one of the grand hotels in Hamburg. Adolph Hitler used to dine there, and Lucas records that stuffed squab was a favorite dish of his. "Let us not hold that against a fine recipe, though," she wrote in her *Gourmet Cooking School Cookbook*, (page 89).

Her marriage to architect Colin Lucas ended in divorce and she and her two young sons, Mark and Peter, came to New York in the early 1940's. She opened her first Cordon Bleu Restaurant and School in New York in October, 1942. Her small, hands-on classes of five or six students teaching the techniques of French classical cooking were comprehensive and structured. Among the students who studied with her and went on to careers in food are Julie Dannenbaum, Paula Wolfert, and Bert Greene.

From the mid-1940's through 1953 she had two television cooking programs: "To a Queen's Taste," was broadcast from her restaurant, and later "The Dione Lucas Cooking Show" aired on local and major networks. Her shows were the first to focus on French cooking for the American home.

In the 1950's Dione Lucas opened the Gourmet Cooking School in New York, and in 1956, The Egg Basket Restaurant, where she prepared omelets in view of her customers. When these closed she continued to open a variety of restaurants and schools.

She was considered eccentric and described by those who worked with her as neurotic, bossy, a hypochondriac, severe, and dry, given to dramatic fainting spells. She was also described as charming, a great showman, an excellent teacher. **Julia Child** has called her the "Mother of French Cooking in America" and "a wonderful technician." Though considered dry, giving the impression that French food was difficult to master, in her books she advises her readers to "have fun."

Her books and articles were not just compilations of recipes but were well structured and provided a wealth of information including material on cooking techniques, shopping, freezing food, menu planning, equipment, the time needed to prepare a recipe, plate presentation, and they often contain a glossary of cooking terms. Her 1947 *Cordon Bleu Cook Book* was, until the publication of Julia

Child's *Mastering the Art of French Cooking* in 1961, the major source of information and recipes on French cooking for Americans.

In 1980 her *Cordon Bleu Cook Book* was installed in the **James Beard** Cookbook Hall of Fame and there is a Hall of Fame Scholarship in her name. She was honored by Les Dames d'Escoffier in 1994 at a Women in Gastronomy Event.

Dione died in December, 1971. Her papers are in the Schlesinger Library, Radcliffe Institute, Harvard University. The library's edition of *The Dione Lucas Book of French Cooking* was donated to the library by Julia Child, whose comments are found throughout.

— Patricia M. Kelly

Au Petit Cordon Bleu: Recipes by Dione Lucas and Rosemary Hume, 1936; revised edition, 1953 and reissued in 1956
Cordon Bleu Cook Book, 1947
French Cookery, Smith College Club Scholarship Benefit, 1953
The Dione Lucas Meat and Poultry Cook Book, with Ann Roe Robbins, 1955
The Gourmet Cooking School Cook Book, with Darlene Geis, 1964; reissued as *The Dione Lucas Gourmet Cooking School Cookbook*, 1982
The Cordon Bleu Cook Compendium, with Marion Gorman, 1972
The Dione Lucas Book of French Cooking, with Marion Gorman, 1973

Lucullus

117—56 BC

ALSO CALLED: Lucius Licinius Lucullus

Lucullus, from a prominent family in ancient Rome, had a long and successful career as a general and a provincial administrator. He spent many years fighting against King Mithridates of Pontus on the Black Sea, but in 66 bc he was abruptly recalled to Rome. His financial reforms in the provinces had created enemies among some influential Romans.

Lucullus retired to his studies and to active enjoyment of his many villas and parks, his fish ponds and aviaries near Naples, and the splendid Gardens of Lucullus on the edge of Rome. He is credited with introducing sweet cherries to Rome from the eastern regions where he had been campaigning.

Lucullus entertained lavishly, with the degree of sumptuousness of the meal depending on the importance of the guests. The story goes that one evening Lucullus dined alone, and his staff brought him a dinner of the moderately expensive sort. When he objected, they defended themselves on the grounds that there were no guests, but Lucullus insisted that the meal should be especially grand because "tonight, Lucullus is host to Lucullus."

Today, a Lucullan feast is one which is rich in both senses of the word, and many restaurants and food businesses have appropriated those connotations by taking "Lucullus" as their name. Numerous elaborate dishes have been tagged Lucullus, and a favored variety of Swiss chard has been given that name as well.

— Alice Arndt

MacAusland—*Entrepreneur*
Makhmudov—*Cookbook Author,*
    Food Historian, Philosopher
Markham—*Cookbook Author,*
    Farmer, Writer
Marshall—*Cook, Cookbook Author,*
    Entrepreneur, Inventor, Teacher
Massialot—*Chef, Cookbook Author*
Maurizio—*Food Historian,*
    Reformer, Scientist
Ménagier de Paris—*Cookbook Author,*
    Householder, Knight

Mérigot—*Cookbook Author*
Messisbugo—*Cookbook Author, Scalco*
Mikoyan—*Communist Party Leader,*
    Food Industrialist
Mithaecus—*Cook, Cookbook Author*
Molokhovets—*Cookbook Author*
Montiño—*Chef, Cookbook Author*
Mukhopadhyay—*Cookbook Author,*
    Food Historian, Writer
Muro—*Cookbook Author, Writer*

Earle R. MacAusland

❧ 1892—1980 ❧

M

IN JANUARY OF 1941, EARLE R. MACAUSLAND LAUNCHED *Gourmet: The Magazine of Good Living.* World War II raged in Europe, Africa, and Asia. America was just turning the corner on twelve years of the Great Depression. Some would have thought this a less than auspicious time for such a venture, but not Earle MacAusland.

Earle MacAusland was born in Taunton, Massachusetts in 1892, one of three sons and a daughter born to Scottish immigrant parents. His father was an accomplished silversmith who worked for the venerable firm of Reed and Barton Silversmiths. When the elder MacAusland was promoted to general manager, he moved the family to Beacon Hill in Boston. Although the MacAuslands were not wealthy, there was always sterling silver on the table, and Earle grew up believing that one needn't be rich to appreciate the finer things in life.

Earle was expected to become an orthopedic surgeon like his older brothers. But, as he later explained, he couldn't bear the sight of blood and, having flunked Latin, he could not get into Harvard. After one not very successful year as an engineering student at the Massachusetts Institute of Technology, his father suggested he move to New York and seek employment more to his liking.

He was hired to sell advertising space for the publisher of a national ladies magazine. Later he was made vice president and advertising manager of *Parent Magazine*, whose financial success he characteristically attributed to his own efforts. It prompted him to start his own magazine—which proved a disastrous decision.

The venture left him bankrupt at age 40. The Great Depression was in full swing and he was penniless. He was primed for any idea that might bring him success. It came in the form of a catalogue from S. S. Pierce, a purveyor of very high-quality canned and prepared foods who supplied the well-off with imported products from various parts of the world and quality foods from elite suppliers in the United States.

As MacAusland explained, "I was sitting in my Packard convertible with my poodle by my side, driving out to the suburbs to see a lady friend and I was thinking about the S. S. Pierce catalogue." Why not a *magazine* devoted to good food, he thought.

Despite his past failures, he persuaded his brothers and father to lend him the money to put out the first issue of *Gourmet*. By the time the second issue was ready, he had acquired two wealthy backers: Gladys Guggenheim Straus, of the publishing house Farrar, Straus and Giroux, and Ralph Reinhold. The first year he had to sell advertisements during the day and edit copy at night; yet also within the first year he had moved from the old art-deco building at 330 West 42nd Street in Manhattan to a penthouse duplex in the Plaza Hotel. The headquarters were elegant, as befitted a magazine devoted to fine living, and reflected MacAusland's belief that "if you can't go first class, better not go at all."

Earle MacAusland was the epitome of the elegant gentleman. When he appeared in the lobby of the Plaza wearing an English handmade suit and homburg hat, with his poodle on a leash, no one could deny that he looked every inch the publisher of *Gourmet*. Nevertheless, his employees knew that he might fly into a rage at the slightest provocation. One day some visiting subscribers witnessed a screaming, very angry MacAusland dragging some hapless employee through the rotunda where the receptionist sat. When they were out of sight, the quick-witted receptionist smiled at the visitors and explained, "It's a rehearsal for our Christmas play."

MacAusland's was a noisy, quick-to-ignite anger, but it also dissipated rapidly, and since he forgot quickly he was surprised that others did not. Opposition often triggered his tirades, and perhaps it was his angry displays that prompted Samuel Chamberlain and James Beard to leave the magazine after many years.

A reading of the magazine from its inception to just after the war in 1945 shows clearly that MacAusland intended *Gourmet* to appeal as much to men as to women. Articles written by Chamberlain, M. F. K. Fisher, Stephen Longstreet, and others were meant to entertain the reader and instruct in the preparation of fine food (primarily French) and fine wine (Californian, because French wines were inaccessible) and in the enjoyment of elegant living. Since the publisher was intimately engaged in its production, the magazine generally reflected his personal preference for France and its cooking, with occasional excursions to Nantucket for chowders. (He was said to "make a mean clam chowder.")

Through the pages of *Gourmet*, readers were painlessly educated in the art and language of French cuisine. *Sauce béchamel* substituted for the ubiquitous white sauce of their childhood, and *bavaroise au fraises* elbowed strawberry jelly molds off dessert tables. From an amusing tale told by Stephen Longstreet, readers learned that their knives and kitchen tools were, in fact, *poignées,* their wire whisks were *fouets,* and that, years before Julia Child's wonderful television series, one could pick dropped food off the floor and with a smile and great élan call it *coup de ballet Parisien.*

Travel articles by writers like Samuel Chamberlain, who had contributed since the first issue, and Naomi Barry were so precise and enticing that readers used them as travel, hotel, and restaurant guides. Recipes from these restaurants and hotels made it possible for readers to duplicate what they had enjoyed in their travels. Given its international flavor, it wasn't surprising that *Gourmet* became a favorite source of recipes for entertaining, nor that for many years the largest number of subscribers lived in the Washington, D. C. area, where elegant entertaining was, and still is, a professional imperative.

For many years, Earle MacAusland and his wife Jean lived on Nantucket. He commuted to New York every week by private plane. Jean MacAusland was said to be responsible for covering the island with daffodils, a particular passion of hers.

Earle R. MacAusland died in 1980, and was buried on Nantucket. For 39 years, he had exerted his influence on the magazine that chronicled good taste and fine living. He always resisted change, except for the better. Food fads ran counter to his philosophy and he protected his readers from them. Those who grew up reading *Gourmet* owe MacAusland a real debt of gratitude, for he produced a magazine that read like amusing and enlightened dinner conversation, never just an instructional manual, never crass or common. For many, *Gourmet* was a window on a world of gustatory pleasures that revealed views of better and better cooking and eating.

Gourmet and MacAusland were sometimes accused of being elitist, and perhaps they were. However, both the magazine and its originator aimed at reflecting an ever higher quality of life, and offered all their followers a gastronomic style to match their rising expectations—a style to which <u>anyone</u> could aspire.

The Gourmet Cookbook, edited by MacAusland, was published by Rand-McNally in 1950. Numerous revisions and supplements followed. In 2004, another cookbook of the same name (subtitled *More than 1000 Recipes*) was produced by Ruth Reichl, the current editor of *Gourmet* magazine.

— Margaret Leibenstein

The Gourmet Cookbook, 1950

Karim Makhmudov

1926–1993

As author of the first book on Uzbek cuisine, Karim Makhmudov significantly shaped the culinary culture and national identity of Uzbekistan. He was born in 1926 at the western edge of the lush Ferghana Valley, in a small village near the city of Andijan. A philosophy professor and cultural nationalist, he is both praised and criticized for his representation of Uzbek dishes and his zealous historical approach to regional food, customs, and traditions. Makhmudov's life coincided almost exactly with the period of Soviet power in Uzbekistan, yet his research illuminated Uzbek culture before Russian dominance and his books continue to influence the national character of the new republic.

In his career Makhmudov wrote twenty-eight books and over seventy-five articles on Uzbek food and hospitality. He was the most prolific culinary author in Central Asia and by far the best known and best selling. His milieu no doubt greatly influenced his thinking. The Ferghana Valley comprises less than 5% of the territory of Uzbekistan, but contains a third of the country's population. The region is considered the political and religious heartland of the nation. Uzbeks hold up the language and traditions of the valley as a national cultural standard. Home to a branch of the Silk Road, Ferghana was also one of the earliest cultivated areas in the world, with fruit and vegetables in abundance. Makhmudov naturally chose culture and food as key elements in his ethnographic approach to nationalism.

Makhmudov received a PhD in Philosophy from Tashkent State University. In 1952 he began to lecture at his alma mater, the country's premiere university. For the next 38 years he taught philosophy there. He also organized extracurricular sessions on Uzbek traditions for college students. His academic research covered two main areas—labor (fitting for a Soviet scholar) and Uzbek customs (arcane, but not anti-establishment). The latter subject became his sole focus with the death of Stalin and a corresponding popular interest in the cultural heritage of Central Asia. In 1956 the Congress of Intelligentsia of Uzbekistan affirmed that Central Asia was an ancient center of human cultural development. The Uzbek Communist Party boldly urged the Congress delegates to take the lead in developing the nation's culture, essentially ignoring Moscow's nationalities policy—nationalist in form, socialist in content.

The Russians, after all, generated ethnic profiles, languages, histories, and territories for Central Asia. Uzbekistan was a full Soviet Socialist republic with a parliament, prime minister, and local governments—all the trappings of political nationality. After Khrushchev denounced Stalinism in 1956, Uzbek cultural nationalists brought language issues to the fore and advocated the use of Uzbek language. Furthermore, history books were rewritten and literature flourished. Not surprisingly, Makhmudov's first cookbook, *Uzbek Dishes*, appeared in 1958.

The stated goal of Makhmudov's cookbooks was to help housewives prepare authentic Uzbek dishes. With Uzbekistan essentially enduring a colonial existence, the tone of his writings reflects nostalgia for a disappearing Uzbek way of life in the face of escalating Russification. To place the recipes in a cultural and historical context, Makhmudov studied written sources, observed food customs, and consulted with tribal elders and local chefs. Though he is often criticized for not being a chef, he made special efforts to work closely with chefs and credited them profusely in his texts. He also modified recipes and created new ones, retaining the essence, in his view, of Uzbek cuisine.

As a member of the Communist party, Makhmudov had to reconcile Soviet ideology and Uzbek tradition. Cookbooks in the USSR had become a non-threatening vehicle for boasting the diversity of culture within the Soviet brotherhood of nations, while appeasing nascent nationalist sentiments. His writings are sprinkled with quotes from Marx, Engels, Lenin, and even Brezhnev, juxtaposed with the advice and science of Avicenna, the eleventh-century Central Asian philosopher and physician. He awkwardly credits Russian soldiers and restaurants for introducing new foods to the region and refers to the feudal conditions and the impoverishment of local diet before the socialist revolution. At the same time he speaks of the uniqueness and greatness of Uzbek culture, cuisine, and history.

Uzbek Dishes, published in multiple Uzbek and Russian language editions from 1958–1982, is clearly Makhmudov's most influential work. It includes descriptions and illustrations on nutrition, cooking methods, equipment, table settings, serving, and the culinary arts. It also includes sections on regional herbs and spices, products, preserves, and menu suggestions. In an exercise of good-spirited ethnic rivalry or cultural superiority, Makhmudov attempts to prove that Uzbek cuisine has more than only a couple dozen dishes, as claimed by unnamed experts. He presents over 500 recipes—including classical, well-known, original, and many old or forgotten recipes. Makhmudov reclaims or revives traditional dishes and methods of cooking lost via industrialization, urbanization, and Sovietization. In the style of the pioneering Russian cookbooks *Book on Tasty and Healthy Food* (1939) and the Stalin era *Kulinaria*, the book is organized around the structure of a menu, with non-Asian sections such as salads, soups, main courses, and desserts. Further evidence of Russian European influence is an illustration of classical French cuts.

M

Unlike the majority of Soviet cookbooks, Makhmudov's works are not simply a listing of ingredients illustrated with poor-quality or retouched photographs. He provides commentary, anthropological observations, and history, though at times spurious. In his role as cultural nationalist, Makhmudov searches for the essences and origins of identity, culture, and nationality to piece together a long and continuous history of the Uzbek people and nation. For example, he concludes that the culinary arts in Uzbekistan are ancient, based on the remains of ancient cooking and charred animal bones, intimating that the Uzbek themselves reach into antiquity. It is generally agreed that the Uzbeks settled in the area not earlier than the fifteenth century. His critics also charge that he is too Uzbek-centric, a sensitive accusation given the complicated demographics of the region. While comprising 70% of their country, Uzbeks still make up 30% of the entire population of Central Asia.

Makhmudov maintains that hospitality and tradition, more than the dishes themselves, define Uzbek culinary culture. Following eastern and Islamic traditions, a meal emphasizes the ritual of receiving guests and paying respect to elders. Makhmudov identifies the core Uzbek dishes as *plov* (mutton and rice pilaf), *hasip* (mutton and rice sausage), *manti* (steamed mutton dumplings), and *mastava* (mutton and rice soup). He wrote two books solely dedicated to the flagship of Uzbek cuisine, plov, recording sixty regional and classical variations. Beyond recipes and methods, Makhmudov extols its curative and dietary properties. He describes making plov as a rite of passage for young Uzbek men. His books on tea and bread follow the same pattern—covering history, nutrition, service, ceremony, and accompaniments, in addition to the recipes.

Given chronic food shortages and few restaurants in the Soviet era, Makhmudov focused on domestic cookery and his books have offered guidance to generations of Uzbeks. In Uzbekistan, Makhmudov is considered the father of modern national cuisine. His works on tea, noodles, flatbread, hospitality, and food traditions are a continuing staple for housewives, young chefs, and anthropologists. One and a half centuries of Russian influence in Central Asia have not diminished the social role of cuisine. Makhmudov, in no small part, helped revive and form the modern culinary cultural heritage of Uzbekistan.

— Glenn R. Mack

Uzbekskie bliuda (Uzbek Dishes), 1958, 1962, 1974, 1976, 1982
Muchniye bliuda Uzbekskoi domashnei kukhni (Farinaceous dishes of Uzbek Domestic Cookery),
*   1963, 1986*
Uzbek taomlari (Uzbek cuisine), 1963, 1970, 1977, 1986
Uzbekskii Plov (Uzbek pilaf), 1979
Uzbekskaya domashnaya kukhnya (Uzbek Domestic Cookery), 1984
Qiziqarli pazandalik (Interesting Art of Preparing Fine Cuisine), 1987
Ochil dasturhon (Spread out the tablecloth), 1988
Plov na liuboi vkus (Pilaf for any Taste), 1988
Mehmonnoma (All About Hospitality), 1989
Delikatesy Uzbekistana Uzbek Tansiq Taomlari (Delicacies of Uzbekistan), 1989
Khleb nash nasushnym Non-aziz rizq ruzimiz (Our Daily Bread), 1991
Choinoma (All About Tea), 1993

Gervase Markham ❦ 1568–1637 ❦

Frontispiece of The Perfect
Horseman or the Experienc'd
Secrets of Mr Markham's
50 Years Practice

OUR HOUSEWIFE…MUST NOT BE BUTTER-FINGERED, SWEET-TOOTHED, NOR FAINT-HEARTED;
for the first will let everything fall, the second will consume what it should increase,
and the last will lose time with too much niceness.

Markham, Gervase. *The EnglishHousewife*, 1615
[Edited by Michael Best. Kingston: McGill-Queen's University Press, 1986. p.64]

It is virtually impossible to study the daily life of seventeenth-century Englishmen and women without bumping up against the voluminous work of Gervase Markham. A minor poet and playwright, Markham's most important contributions are undoubtedly his comprehensive, practical, and authoritative works on a range of topics from veterinary medicine to country pastimes to the many and varied "arts of housewifery" described in his notable domestic work *The English Housewife.*

Gervase Markham was probably born in the year 1568, ten years into the reign of Queen Elizabeth I. He was the third son of a noble Nottinghamshire family in serious financial (and therefore social) decline. In 1601, Markham married Mary Gellsthorpe and in 1627 claimed to have "many children and great charge of household." In addition to writing, Markham was a soldier in the Netherlands and Ireland, a noted horse breeder (he is credited with bringing the first Arabian horses into England) and a husbandman—a small landowner/farmer. All of the experiences and observations gained through his varied career became ready fodder for Markham's writings.

Markham produced only a single work on housewifery—but what a work! *The English Housewife* was first published in 1615 as the second book of *Countrey Contentments.* (The first book, *The Husbandman's Recreations,* described the rural pastimes of a landowner including riding, hunting, and hawking.) The frontispiece of *The English Housewife* describes its comprehensive nature: "The English Hus—wife, containing the inward and outward virtues which ought to be in a compleat woman. As, her skill in Physicke [medicine], Cookery, Banqueting Stuffe, Distillation, Perfumes, Wool, Hemp, Flax, Dayries, Brewing, Baking, and all other things belonging to an Household."

This popular book was reissued, repackaged, and revised both during and after Markham's lifetime. A surviving bill of lading for a ship bound to Virginia in 1620 included "Markhams worke of husbandry & huswifry," which makes *The English Housewife* the first cookbook known to be imported to the English colonies.

To historians, *The English Housewife* is remarkable and valuable on many counts. It clearly illuminates the breadth and scope of a housewife's duties and responsibilities in the first half of the seventeenth century, presenting her for the first time as a vital and active partner in the household economy and domestic order. *The English Housewife* is one of the earliest English cookbooks written for rural housewives and gentlewomen—earlier cookbooks were clearly intended for courtly nobility. Markham's intended audience was the wealthy, landed, and literate housewife, though, not the common laborer's spouse. Topics including dairying, baking, and brewing, received their first thorough treatment in print in this work. The presentation of information in *The English Housewife* follows a logically organized path, whereas the organization of earlier domestic works was haphazard, with recipes, remedies, and household advice all mingled together. For example, Markham's section on cookery is arranged according to the order of service to the table, with recipes for sallets (salads) first, and fried dishes, boiled meats, roasted items, and baked goods following. The recipes in the cookery section include everything from fancy and costly "made dishes" to the ordinary daily fare of rural households, providing us with the best glimpse we will ever have into the kitchens (and stomachs) of England at that time. Markham's clarity of organization, his practical and detailed eye regarding his subject matter, and the very readable nature of his writing make *The English Housewife* one of the most important works on English cookery and the domestic realm.

Like many writers of practical guides in his time, Markham did not claim to be the sole author of any of his works. Part of his contribution was in compiling, editing, organizing, polishing, and augmenting (with his practical observations) the books and manuscripts of others. Michael Best, who edited the definitive version of *The English Housewife*, wrote that "Markham was no slavish copier of received opinion; both as a writer and an editor he approached his subjects with a balanced skepticism, transmitting the opinions of those 'esteemed famous'... but always prepared to test them by experience, and to approve or criticize them accordingly."

Despite a truly impressive body of published works, Markham found some fame but little fortune in his lifetime. In his day authors were paid for their manuscript by the publisher but received no additional payments even if the book was republished over and over again. Markham, however, got a bit of his own back by re-selling some of the same books under new titles—until 1617 when a bookseller put a halt to that practice.

Gervase Markham died in 1637 with little apparent wealth and was buried at St Giles's, Cripplegate, London.

— KATHLEEN CURTIN

Cavelarice, or The English Horseman, 1607
Markham's Maister-peece, 1610
The English Husbandman, 1613-1615
Cheape and Good Husbandry, or the Well-Ordering of All Beastes and Fowles, 1614
The Husbandman's Recreations, published as Book i of Countrey Contentments, 1615
The English Hus-wife, first published as Book ii of Countrey Contentments, 1615
Markham's Farewell to Husbandry, 1620
A Way to Get Wealth, 1631

Agnes Bertha Marshall

1855—1905

ALSO CALLED: Mrs. A. B. Marshall

AN ENTREPRENEUR, INNOVATOR, AND INVENTOR, AGNES Marshall was probably the foremost Victorian cookbook writer, and made unique contributions to the development of ices and ice cream. She apparently originated the edible ice-cream cone.

Unlike **Mrs. Beeton**, who edited a part-work that contained readers' recipes, Mrs. Marshall was a cook. The introduction to her first book assures the reader that "every recipe in it has been tried out by myself, and that I have written each accordingly, and have not copied any from other authors." Yet she is no longer famous, as she was in Victorian times and as Mrs. Beeton still is, for the rights to her books were purchased after her death by Ward Lock, Mrs. Beeton's publishers, and suppressed. Her most notable contributions were her two classic books on ice cream and her unique design of a fast-freezing ice-cream machine, patented in her husband's name.

She was born at Walthamstow, in Essex, England, the daughter of one John Smith, a clerk. She had at least one brother; her father died young, and her mother, Susan, married Charles Wells. Of the four children of that marriage, John later became the manager of Marshall's School of Cookery and Ada became Agnes' housekeeper.

In August, 1878, Agnes married Alfred William Marshall. They had four children: Ethel (1878), Agnes (1879), Alfred (1880), and William (1882). No details are known about her early education or where she learned to cook, but her husband was quoted in the *Pall Mall Gazette* in 1886 as saying, "Mrs. Marshall has made a thorough study of cookery since she was a child, and has practised at Paris and with Vienna's celebrated chefs." Agnes herself, in the preface of her first cookbook, refers to her "practical training and lessons, through several years, from leading English and Continental authorities, as well as a home experience earlier than I can well recall...."

In January, 1883, Agnes opened Marshall's School of Cookery in London. The school's records have been destroyed, but from other evidence it appears that she bought it as a going concern, using her own money. The Married Women's Property Act had just come into force, so she would have been able to own the school in her own right, and certainly it was made clear from the outset that Mrs. Marshall was the owner and driving force of the establishment. It included a cook's registry, warehouses, and a shop selling kitchen equipment; Agnes pioneered the sale of "house brand" food and equipment, especially Marshall's Patent Freezers, which she claimed to have invented.

England's burgeoning middle class, familiar with fine food from hotel restaurants or large-scale banquets prepared by professional caterers, was eager to achieve this level of cuisine in its own households. As one of the most perceptive of Victorian culinary entrepreneurs, Marshall recognized the scope this unfilled demand offered her remarkable personal skills. Her cooking school, cookbooks, weekly paper, and branded equipment and supplies were all targeted to the numerous nouveau-riche middle-class ladies who wanted their cooks or housekeepers to produce top-quality dishes for their dinner parties and similar entertainments. Those setting up or modernizing their kitchens had only to get in touch with Mrs. Marshall, who advertised that she would provide free estimates "for the entire furnishings of kitchens, in accordance with the requirements of Modern Cookery, thus avoiding the numerous superfluous articles often supplied by those who have had no practical knowledge of the use of the goods they sell."

Marshall published her first book, *The Book of Ices,* in 1885. It remains a model of its kind: Well and clearly written, the recipes are easy to follow, and it includes line drawings and four superb chromolithographs of some of her ices in many marvelous shapes, including swans and baskets of fruit. The next year, Marshall started *The Table,* "a weekly paper of Cookery, Gastronomy, Food amusements etc." whose publication continued into 1939. For the rest of her life, she contributed a weekly recipe page; for the paper's first six months, and again from 1889 onward, she also contributed a weekly article, chatty, witty and ironic, on the widest range of topics.

In 1887, Marshall decided to publish her second book, but—in light of the favorable but mostly provincial notice *The Book of Ices* had received—decided first to undertake a nationwide lecture-demonstration tour of "high-class cookery." Besides some 16 other cities, it included two very successful and widely reported appearances in London, at which she lectured before 600 people for more than two hours while preparing a complete eight-course meal. The tour made her the most talked-about cook in England, and when *Mrs. A. B. Marshall's Book of Cookery* appeared in 1888, sales were brisk.

The *Book of Cookery* was practical, well planned and arranged, lucid, accurate, and comprehensive, with a good and extensive index. In it, foreshadowing her contemporary, **Auguste Escoffier**, Marshall codified all the main processes of cooking. She included a chapter on "The Art of Dinner Giving." And in a recipe for Cornets with Cream, she wrote, "These cornets can also be filled with any cream or water ice, or set custard or fruits...." This is the earliest presently known mention of the edible ice-cream cone, sixteen years before the St. Louis world's fair of 1904, at which ice-cream cones are sometimes said to have been invented.

In 1891, Marshall published *Mrs. A. B. Marshall's Larger Cookery Book of Extra Recipes,* as much a prestige publication as a practical cookbook, and aimed at the *haute cuisine* end of the market. The following year, she again embarked on an author's tour of the country, lecturing and demonstrating and selling not only her book but also her branded equipment, supplies, and food articles. In 1894 she published *Fancy Ices,* which included a recipe for Margaret Cornets—made with ground almonds, sugar, flour, eggs, vanilla, and orange-flower water and filled with ginger water ice and apple ice cream—and Christina Cornets, to be filled with a frozen mixture of vanilla custard, whipped cream, dried fruit, and spices.

In her lectures, Marshall insisted on the need for absolute cleanliness in the kitchen, and she was an outspoken and ceaseless campaigner for improvements in food hygiene. She was forward-looking and progressive in her thinking, supporting the rights of women, foreseeing the use of refrigerated trucks to transport produce, and predicting both that pure drinking water would be supplied "to all dwelling places as a matter of course" and that "small provision shops will be entirely swallowed up" by larger stores. *The Table* was advertising dishwashing machines in 1902, and the front door of the paper's office was a "Sesame Door" that opened automatically as people approached it.

By the early 1900's, Marshall was frequently in ill health, probably suffering the first manifestations of the cancer that was to kill her. She died at Pinner, the estate she had bought in 1890, on July 29, 1905. Marshall's School of Cookery continued to operate until the outbreak of World War II and Marshall's Ltd. was finally wound up in 1954.

— ROBIN WEIR

The Book of Ices, 1885
Mrs. A. B. Marshall's Book of Cookery, 1888
Mrs. A. B. Marshall's Larger Cookery Book of Extra Recipes, 1891
Fancy Ices, 1894

François Massialot

1660(?)–1733

AS IS OFTEN THE CASE FOR PRE-1700 COOKBOOK AUTHORS, LITTLE IS KNOWN about Massialot the man, notwithstanding the fact that his *Cuisinier Roial et Bourgeois* (1691) was a watershed book in more ways than one. In fact, his name does not even appear in any of this work's editions. However, since his later book, *Le Nouveau Cuisinier* (1712), in which Massialot's name does appear, is basically a reworking of the former, incorporating some elements of his *Nouvelle instruction...*(1692), it has been safely assumed by all scholars in the field that the attribution is water-tight.

Massialot was born in Limoges, probably in 1660, and died in Paris in 1733. He is reputed to have been chef in the households of the highest French nobility, including those of the dukes of Chartres and Orléans (who became regent after the death of Louis XIV). This throws light on the first part of *Cuisinier*'s title and justifies the preface's insistence on the author's familiarity with meals served "recently at the Court or by Princes and persons of the highest standing" (translation mine).

Thanks to *Cuisinier*'s multiple editions and its rapid translation into English, Massialot's renown spread accordingly on both sides of the Channel. Voltaire refers to him on several occasions, most pointedly in his famed poem *Le Mondain* (1736) and heralds him as an icon of enlightenment in matters culinary. While the innovative character of Massialot's recipes and their related meal-sequence "instructions" is debatable (in fact, his very title suggests fence-straddling) the inclusion of "bourgeois" surely pleased Voltaire and was in fact a significant first in French cookbook titles. The departure—at least in name—from strict courtly cuisine and its implicit recognition of an evolving social structure is paired with another sign of changing times, one auguring the era of the dictionary and encyclopedia. *Cuisinier* is the first cookery book, at least in France, to order recipes alphabetically.

The book's English translation, along with its appealing double-pronged title, circulated at a time of flux when liberal, cosmopolitan Whigs wished to emancipate themselves from the chauvinistic grip of culinary Englishness, thus facilitating the inroads of French cookery. Massialot's recipes were, on the whole, easier to handle than those of **La Chapelle**, which doubtless accounts for the fact that the former, who in all probability had never set foot on English soil, was more appreciated as an author than his émigré compatriot and chef to Lord Chesterfield. A battle of the cooks ensued in which both authors engaged in various forms of plagiarism and derision of the other, curiously enough for the most part after Massialot's death in 1733!

— BEATRICE FINK

Le Cuisinier Roial et Bourgeois: qui apprend à ordonner toute sorte de Repas, & la meilleure manière des Ragoûts les plus à la mode et les plus exquis. Ouvrage très-utile dans les Familles et singulièrement nécessaire à tous les Maîtres d'Hôtel, & Ecuiers de Cuisine, 1691

Nouvelle Instruction Pour les Confitures, les Liqueurs, et les Fruits: Avec la manière de bien ordonner un Dessert, & tout le reste qui est du devoir des Maîtres d'Hôtel, Sommeliers, Confiseurs, & autres Officiers de bouche. Suite du Cuisinier Roial & Bourgeois, 1692

Court and Country Cook: giving new and plain directions how to order all manner of entertainments, and the best sort of the most exquisite a-la-mode ragoo's. Together with New instructions for confectioners...Faithfully translated out of French into English by J.K., 1702

Le Nouveau Cuisinier Royal et Bourgeois: Qui apprend à ordonner toute sorte de Repas en gras & en maigre, & la meilleure manière des Ragoûts les plus délicats & les plus à la mode; & toutes sortes de Pâtisserie: avec des nouveaux desseins de Tables, 1712

Adam Maurizio

※ 1862–1941 ※

ADAM MAURIZIO WAS BORN ON SEPTEMBER 26, 1862, IN KRAKOW (currently Poland, at the time under the reign of the Habsburg Empire) as a Swiss citizen. His parents, Paris and Maria, were both economic migrants from the Bergell Valley near St. Moritz. In the nineteenth century, Swiss-Italian sugar-bakers successfully ran bakeries and cafés all over Central and Eastern Europe. Café Maurizio, which was managed by Adam's father and later by his brothers, was famous for its confectionary and its flavored vodkas, and was considered the best establishment in Krakow.

While growing up surrounded by delicacies, Adam was from his teens sensitive to social injustice. He became involved in a socialist movement that at the time began to take root among young Krakow intellectuals. The family business and the early encounter with socialism were largely responsible for his later interest in the history of bread and other plebeian foods.

In 1884, Maurizio was arrested for his socialist activities, imprisoned for several months, and finally expelled from the state's borders. Taken care of by the family in Switzerland, he graduated from the gymnasium in Chur and studied chemistry and botany at the University of Zurich (1888–1889), as well as universities in Geneva (1889–1890) and Bern (1890–1894). The entire time, Maurizio remained in close contact with the European socialist movement and published widely on the topic in newspapers and journals. In the mid-1890's, however, he left political activism behind and devoted himself entirely to scientific work. Possibly, his marriage in 1892 with the Polish Helena Landau was a factor in this decision.

After acquiring his PhD in 1894, Maurizio worked first at the Wädenswil Research Institute near Zurich and subsequently at the Grain Processing Research Institute in Berlin, where he developed a botanical interest in grains. Also, his concern with social issues found a new articulation—he became increasingly involved in fighting against adulteration of flour, animal fodder, and fertilizers.

In 1900, Adam Maurizio became employed as assistant botanist at the Agricultural Department of the Zurich Technical Institute, and seven years later was appointed Professor of Botany and Commodity Studies at the Chemical Department of the Lwow Technical Institute. (The city of Lwow, also known as Lemberg, is currently in the Ukraine, but at the time was a Polish territory under the Habsburg Empire.) Fate had brought Maurizio back to the land of his birth, and he remained in Poland for almost 30 years.

Maurizio became a botanist of international standing, and his pioneering work on the history of staple foods—porridge, ashcakes, and bread—was highly esteemed. Today, his *Histoire de l'alimentation vegetale* remains a *vade mecum* for French food historians. The rest of the world, however, has only recently began to rediscover the wealth of Maurizio's legacy; the fact that his publications have never been translated into English greatly restricted their readership.

Maurizio was enormously productive. Most of his writing appeared in German, but he also published widely in Polish and Italian. Between his first paper in 1894 and his last in 1940, Maurizio covered a vast range of subjects, from the pathology of fish to the analysis of food habits during periods of food shortage. Over time, the technical side of his research became less dominant, giving way to a more socio-cultural approach. Next to thorough library research, he paid much attention to fieldwork and relied on local informants. Adam Maurizio brought a materialist and historical outlook to the study of food, addressing issues that remain highly relevant today.

He retired from his position in 1926 due to eye illness, but prior to his departure for Switzerland in 1935, he was appointed honorary professor at Warsaw University, where he lectured on food commodities. He died in Bern on March 4, 1941, at the age of 79, leaving his wife Helena and two children, Julius and Anna.

— KATARZYNA J. CWIERTKA

ACKNOWLEDGMENT: My study on Adam Maurizio has been supported by the European Institute of Food History (IEHA).

Getreide, Mehl und Brot (Grain, Flour and Bread), 1903
Die Getreide-Nahrung im Wandel der Zeiten (Staple Foods through the Ages), 1916
Die Nahrungsmittel aus Getreide, Bd. I. (Food from Grain), vol. 1, 1917
Die Nahrungsmittel aus Getreide, Bd. II. (Food from Grain), vol. 2, 1919
Pożywienie roślinne i rolnictwo w rozwoju dziejowym (Vegetable Food and Agriculture in Historical Development), 1926; German edition published as *Die Geschichte unserer Pflanzenernahrung von den Urzeiten bis zur Gegenwart (The History of Our Vegetable Food from Earliest Times to the Present)*, 1927; French translation of the German edition published as *Histoire de l'alimentation végétale depuis la préhistoire jusqu'à nos jours (The History of Vegetable Food from Prehistory to Our Times)*, 1932
Geschichte der gegorenen Getränke (The History of Fermented Beverages), 1933

Ménagier de Paris ❧ FOURTEENTH CENTURY ❧

ALSO CALLED: Guy de Montigny | Goodman of Paris

MEDIAEVALISTS INTERESTED IN CULINARY HISTORY HAVE LONG BEEN fascinated by the *Ménagier de Paris,* a fourteenth-century treatise preserved in three manuscripts under the deadening label of *anon*. It was my good fortune, recently, to be able to identify this Parisian householder (*ménagier*) and thus to throw new light on this important work.

Nowhere in his book does the author identify himself through names, dates, places, or connections. Yes, hints abound, but they are made in passing and are scattered among a variety of topics. When collating these hints (which may be classified into several categories: thumb-nail sketches of people and places he knew or mentions; casual remarks about his and his wife's life; general or more specific events, one is already faced with a tenuous yet cogent framework all the more tantalizing for being evanescent.

In its variety of approaches—all tending to a common aim—the ménagier gives a compendium of his experiences as a householder both in Paris and in the provinces for the benefit of his young wife. His deep Christian commitment colors his advice on religious, moral, and practical subjects and reveals a strong sense of social awareness and responsibility. The alimentary typology is backed by detailed instructions on gardening, agriculture, and animal husbandry, and the running of a country-estate and a Parisian establishment.

The ménagier *and his wife in a medieval miniature from the Bibliothèque Nationale*

Probably born in the 1330's, he married his fifteen-year old wife around 1386–1387 to save her from an uncertain future following the Flemish conflicts of 1385. By the time he was writing his treatise he already had children by her, and the work was designed to help her after his death when she would remarry and have to organize her household and hold her rank socially.

The author's clear connection with the Duke of Berry, together with his obvious knowledge of the Bassigny region of Eastern Champagne and especially of the *Bailliage* of Chaumont led me, through the perusal of documents in the *Archives de France* and *Archives départmentales* to identify a "simple chevalier" (as he calls himself) among the Officers listed as such in the muster-rolls of the Duke of Berry. After various eliminations, one name only remained: Guy de Montigny, *chevalier* and *chambellan* in the ducal household, envoy on numerous missions in the service of the Duke of Berry. Nothing, so far, is known of Guy de Montigny's time or place of death.

The Montignys' Parisian residence, in the elegant Saint-Antoine district, had all the best appointments available at the time: a kitchen-block with bread-oven, separate from the body of the house, a kitchen-garden and orchard as well as a pleasure garden and a well. There were cellars for storage of wine and food, for charcoal and lumber; a stable for, at least, two horses. The house is still extant today in Paris, and inhabited! The servants included a majordomo, a housekeeper, kitchen-staff and house-maids. The district was well-provided with markets and shops and street-hawkers.

Just outside Paris, Guy de Montigny had a farm which provided him with dairy produce, meat and fowl as well as fruit and grain; whereas his Paris garden had a dual function, producing the more unusual vegetables and herbs and some fruit for the table as well as flowers and fronds for house-decoration. It also provided the Montignys with a haven of rest and fresh air.

To add to his stock of consumables, Guy de Montigny could also avail himself of the bounty from his country estate in the Vosges region, especially for furred and feathered game, including venison and boar and bear.

From local sources he would get milk and cheese, eggs, vegetables, herbs, and fruit to supplement his own garden resources and, of course, wines of various kinds, including the luscious *Grenache*, still highly-valued today but rarely found in its original single-estate condition. Various kinds of meat were available from several butchers near their residence.

In those days, the river Seine was unpolluted in its upstream Parisian reaches and a large variety of fish abounded in specialized markets—for those who could afford it. Salt-fish and shellfish could be bought in the central market (*Les Halles*) within 12 hours of catching on the Normandy coast.

Most important for households of comfortable means was the possibility to buy a variety of spices and, above all, salt, so essential in food preservation. And mostly honey and sugar, the latter still an expensive rarity.

So, here is our ménagier having at his disposal this great variety of foodstuffs. What does he do with it all?

His motto could have been "Comfort with economy," and we must always keep in mind that his mode of life was primarily governed by his strong Christian principles. Thus he had to reconcile these principles with his social obligations. If we keep in mind that there were between 182 and 227 meatless days in the year and that, on some occasions, milk, eggs, and cheese were also forbidden, one can easily understand that the housewife and the cook had to be resourceful in order to serve substantial, appetizing, and often ceremonial meals year in and year out. The second part of the work (articles 4–10) deals with food preservation and presentation.

In a time when there was no possibility of obtaining certain foods out of season, it was essential to observe a sensible policy of preservation thus, mindful of economy, ensuring a continuous enjoyment of foodstuffs. Grains had to be kept aired (all breads and pastries were baked at home); wine had to be checked for acidity; vegetable matter was air- and oven-dried or buried in sand or peat, away from the light. Honey and vinegar were used in the preservation of fruit and the author gives us a number of succulent recipes for fruit preserves, especially walnuts. Animal matter could be salted, dried, smoked, or treated in various combinations of these. Fish could be kept alive in fish ponds and birds in cages. The variations were countless. Milk could, of course, be kept as butter or cheese.

With such an array of food at his disposal (which can sometimes put our generation to shame!) the ménagier could instruct his cook as to his duties. The kitchen was well-equipped and menus, from the simplest to the most elaborate, could be produced as the need arose. The author gives us 24 menus.

All through that long section on cookery, the author, who had had the opportunity to observe how things were done in the Duke of Berry's household, gives us a great number of cooking tips and techniques which can successfully be applied nowadays (and are, often, by me!). The great strength and interest in this section is that, whereas the author assumes that the cook has an essential basic knowledge of culinary techniques, he can give precise and elaborate details when a certain dish, especially a regional one, needs special attention.

It is certain that the ménagier used various sources to write this section, and especially **Taillevent**'s *Viandier,* but his keen observation of methods noted in the course of his travels enabled him to offer novel recipes as well as improvements on well-known ones. Potages and roasts; pies and egg preparations; fish and sauces; entremets and glazed dishes offer an exciting and tempting array of several hundred recipes which must have delighted Guy de Montigny's young wife and can successfully be prepared to-day.

As one reads the *Ménagier,* one gets a deep sense of a well-organized, comfortable and prosperous household whose Christian and civic virtues predominate; where kindness to others overrides personal needs and where awareness of social status excludes wasteful ostentation. These various traits find their best expression in the culinary section of the book. During his service with the Duke of Berry, Montigny had had ample opportunity to witness both gracious living and wastefulness. In the ménagier's household, harmony governed dining and entertainment, and this arose from his keen desire to give pleasure to his guests. The ménagier's entertaining offered joy to the five senses: the sight of a well-appointed dining-hall, soberly decorated; the feel of crisp linen and polished silver; the perfume of flowers and candles, and the fragrance of dishes whose well-balanced taste progressed to a lovely apotheosis of entertainment, pleasing to the ear and to the eye. All this ensured success achieved, not through insolent opulence, but gentle concern. We are fortunate to be able to enjoy, six hundred years later, the wisdom of the ménagier.

— NICOLE CROSSLEY-HOLLAND

Ménagier de Paris, early 1390's

Madame Mérigot

C. 1795

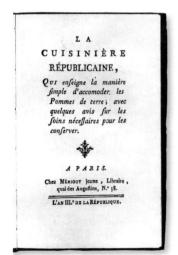

The title page of Mme. Mérigot's revolutionary potato cookbook

WHO WAS MME MÉRIGOT? THE AUTHOR OF *LA CUISINIÈRE RÉPUBLICAINE,* THAT TINY 42-page cookbook published during the third year of the young French Republic? Although her name appears nowhere in the book, its authorship is attributed to her by the top authority, Antoine Alexandre Barbier, in his bibliography of anonymous and pseudonymous works (1806–1808). The attribution remains uncontested to this day. A glance at the name of the book's publisher underscores the attribution. Whereas professional women and women authors remained a rare species in *ancien régime* France and quite some time thereafter, bookseller/publisher's wives or widows were a notable exception. We can thus claim to know two facts about Mme Mérigot: She is the author of *Cuisinière,* and the wife (or, more likely, the widow) of its bookseller/publisher.

The cookbook's culinary content is hardly worth a second glance and its author was most likely inspired by recipes contained in Antoine Parmentier's *Examen chymique des pommes de terre* (1773, subsequent editions). It is, however, most interesting from a social and historical viewpoint, and first of its kind in France several times over. It is the first cookbook ever authored by a woman in France. Contrary to England, where cookbooks written by women during the eighteenth century were the rule, in France such books had remained an all-male fiefdom. *Cuisinière* was also the first cookbook to be published under the Republic that was proclaimed in September 1792 (An I). In addition, and more pointedly, it was the first cookbook to contain exclusively potato recipes. Potatoes were a revolutionary rallying cry in times of severe wheat shortages and overall food scarcity. Mme Mérigot's book is thus a revolutionary act in and of itself at a time when, official proclamations urging people to cultivate and eat potatoes notwithstanding, the vast majority of the French population still regarded *Solanum tuberosum esculentum* with a great deal of suspicion.

In addition to its 34 rather undistinguished recipes, *Cuisinière* contains a foreword stating the author's hope that her recipes would make potato dishes more appealing and thus increase the tuber's popularity, while stressing the virtues of simplicity and economy. No sign of gastronomy here to be sure, but much patriotism, buttressed by practical advice as to how best select, store, and prepare potatoes. Small wonder that this unique—and today exceedingly rare—aptly-titled book was reprinted in facsimile by Daniel Morcrette (well-known for his culinary reprints) with the symbolic Phrygian cap impressed on its leather-bound cover.

— BEATRICE FINK

La cuisinière républicaine, qui enseigne la manière simple d'accommoder les Pommes de terre; avec quelques avis sur les soins nécessaires pour les conserver. Paris : Mérigot jeune, an III (1795)

Cristoforo di Messisbugo ❦ FIRST HALF, 16TH CENTURY BC ❦

MESSISBUGO WAS ONE OF THE FIRST GREAT COOKBOOK authors of the modern era. His *Banchetti, Compositioni di vivande, et apparecchio generale*, published posthumously in 1549, not only offers 323 recipes organized by subject but also detailed descriptions of spectacular meals served at the ducal court of the Este family in Ferrara between 1529 and 1548. It is intended as a practical guide for rulers who hope to imitate such banquets, and even details the equipment required down to every last plate and the entire kitchen and wait staff, a veritable army of servants. It thus offers the first fairly complete picture of what was involved in banquet organization in the early sixteenth century.

There exist scant details of Messisbugo's origins. Some accounts contend that his family was an ancient one of Ferrara, others that he arrived from Flanders. His name is certainly unusual. In any case, he was definitely living in Ferrara around 1524, given that he worked there for 25 years and married a noblewoman of that city, one Agnese di Giovanni Gioccoli. He was also at some point given the title Count Palatine by the Emperor Charles V. That is, his position at court was a fairly exalted one. As *scalco* or banquet manager for one of the most opulent of Renaissance courts, he should not be thought of as a mere cook, but account manager, organizer, and general impressario of ducal festivities. Although the banquet would typically center around food, served in up to a dozen courses and lasting many hours from 11 or 12 late into the night, it was punctuated by musical interludes, dancing, plays by renowned authors such as Ludovico Ariosto, and even side shows with animals. These were no mere state functions but multimedia spectacles meant to astound and overwhelm the guests' five senses.

The recipes included in his cookbook are typical of the era; there is a heavy use of cinnamon and sugar in places we might find incongruous today, as well as acidic sauces, almonds and raisins and other flavor preferences inherited from the Middle Ages. But there are also modern touches, such as an increased use of dairy products and vegetables. What makes his recipes distinct, however, is the large number of international dishes of German, French, Spanish, Turkish, and even Hebraic origin. There are also striking similarities among the recipes he labels as French and those found in contemporary French cookbooks, which suggests that these cuisines exerted a mutual influence upon each other. Clearly his audience was cosmopolitan and appreciated anything exotic and new—including coral and pearls ground into the food. The great majority of recipes are thoroughly Italian, though, with a good contingent of pastas, soups, and sausage recipes among them. There are also many pies with edible butter-laden crusts and delicate pastries and fritters far beyond the standard medieval repertoire. In the well stocked larder Messisbugo suggests a good store of biscotti and breads, sausages, prosciutto, cheeses, olives, fruits, and truffles. He explains how to make pickles, conserves, and *mostarda*. There is also a staggering variety of fresh fish and meats, including every organ and body part imaginable. It is clear from these details alone that Italian ingredients that still form the backbone of the cuisine were already in place, especially considering the wide variety of vegetables used both cooked and in salads. The book even carefully specifies dishes appropriate for Lent.

What immediately strikes the modern reader, however, is the apparent lack of order in each course served. Apart from salads to begin and fruits to end, every single course contains sweet and savory dishes, soups, pastries, meats, and fish. Diners were apparently expected to choose whatever they liked from the melée, but in many cases individual dishes were presented or larger platters, meant to be divided on each table or for several people. It seems as though the aesthetic sensibilities governing these banquets was precisely that of the art of the period, known as Mannerism. The profusion of details, willful lack of focus, and preoccupation with ingenious inventions and marvels—in this case basic ingredients presented in as many guises as possible in order to display the skill and ingenuity of the chef—are characteristic of all the arts at this time.

Messisbugo's legacy is that this style of dining was indeed imitated by other European courts, just as they imitated other late Renaissance arts. This type of grand banquet, combined with other forms of pomp and entertainment, provided not only a delightful escape from the rigors of daily life, but served as a visible and edible expression of the power of the state—in other words, as superb propaganda.

— KEN ALBALA

Banchetti, Compositioni di vivande, et apparecchio generale, 1549

Anastas Ivanovich Mikoyan ❦ 1895–1978 ❦

ALSO CALLED: Artashes Mikoyants

AN IMPORTANT FIGURE IN THE HISTORY—AND ESPECIALLY the food history—of the Soviet Union was born the son of an illiterate carpenter in the Armenian village of Sanain (Sanahin). A visiting bishop arranged for his education in the Nestorian seminary in Tiflis (today's Tblisi, Georgia), which was, like many seminaries in the Russian Empire at that time, a breeding ground of atheists and revolutionaries. Mikoyan was further politicized by the poverty he experienced after leaving school. He joined the Bolshevik wing of the Communist Party in 1915, was active as an organizer and revolutionary journalist in the Baku region, took part in the communist insurrection in Baku in 1917, and—apparently by an oversight—was the only one of the 26 Baku Commissars not executed when Soviet power was overthrown in Baku in 1918.

During a visit to the United States in 1959, Mikoyan (holding a steak) toured a Giant supermarket in Washington, paying particular attention to the meat department.

The following year, in the midst of the Civil War, he was elected to the Central Executive Committee of the Russian Federation. He remained a member of the highest governmental bodies of the USSR—the Central Executive Committee and the Supreme Soviet—for the next 55 years, surviving successive regime changes and purges to which many of his colleagues succumbed, thanks equally to agility and ability. Mikoyan was married and had five children. One of his sons, a pilot, was killed during World War II in the battle of Stalingrad. He died in Moscow just a month short of his 83rd birthday.

It was under Stalin's rule that Mikoyan marked the most significant part of his career. A member of Stalin's Politburo along with such personalities as Beria, Molotov, and Kaganovich, he was *ipso facto* an ominous figure, and though he certainly shared responsibility for the terror and brutality of the time, he is generally more associated with positive developments than with repression and state criminality. Mikoyan was in charge of the food industry, and that niche served him as refuge; his name is mainly linked with the culinary achievements of the Soviet Union.

Stalin appointed Mikoyan People's Commissar [minister] of Trade in 1926, and in 1934 he became head of the newly established Ministry of Food Industry. For the overwhelming majority of citizens of the USSR, food supplies were very meager in the 1930's; there was no shortage of basic foods in years of good harvest, but the food industry was underdeveloped, and a system of food service was almost non-existent. The comparatively rapid development, in that decade, of many branches of the food industry—canned goods, sugar, candy, chocolate, cookies, sausage, fats, baked goods, and tobacco—was thanks largely to Mikoyan's initiative and leadership.

Mikoyan's 1936 trip to the United States, with other Soviet leaders, contributed to his success and led to the establishment of several new industrial branches in the USSR. For example, at a time when 60 percent of the urban population and all of the peasantry consumed home-made bread, Mikoyan brought the technology for commercial baking from America, creating a domestic revolution. In the U.S., Mikoyan also saw orange- and tomato-juice factories, milking machines, and plants producing condensed and powdered milk; these technologies were also imported to the USSR. Manufacture of American hamburgers was another Mikoyan project, though with the coming of World War II a type of meat "cutlet," called "Mikoyanovsky," was produced instead.

Mikoyan also helped to develop domestic manufacture of refrigeration systems for the production of ice cream. In the mid-1930's, the Soviet Union produced only one percent of the volume of ice cream manufactured in the United States, but Mikoyan was passionate about it. Stalin once chided him, "To you, Anastas Ivanovich, the problem of producing good ice cream is more important than communism itself!" After the war, it was Mikoyan who persuaded Stalin to begin manufacturing household refrigerators—unheard of till then—at former arms plants.

In 1939, at Mikoyan's initiative, the first Soviet cookbook, titled *Kniga o Vkusnoi i Zdorovoi Pishche (The Book on Tasty and Healthy Food),* was published. It was reprinted almost yearly thereafter, in millions of copies, until almost every family owned one. A huge brown volume of more than 400 pages, its epigraph was a quotation from Stalin—"A distinctive feature of our revolution is that it gave people not only freedom but also material goods and an opportunity for a wealthy and civilized life."—and each of its sections was introduced by a quotation from Mikoyan. The sections covered cold dishes and appetizers; stocks and soups; fish; meat; poultry and game; vegetables and mushrooms; grains and pastas; peas, beans, and lentils; dairy and eggs; baked goods (types of dough, pie fillings, blinis, pancakes, sweet rolls, cookies, pastries, cakes, and icings); and desserts (kissels, compotes, jellies, and mousses, ice creams, puddings, and dessert sauces). There are also sections on baby food and food for pregnant and nursing mothers; medicinal nutrition; and jams, marinades, and pickles, including mushroom preservation.

In addition, *Tasty and Healthy Food* contained "marginal notes" and recommendations for housewives, articles on various products and dishes, menu planning, and table settings. The appetizing full-page color photographs showed not only delicacies but also such basics as frankfurters with tomato sauce and green peas. And the book was written in inspired language—a real hymn to food. It became the tabletop reference of every Soviet housewife, and, although times have changed, views on nutrition and other food-related issues have been modified, and many other cookbooks have been published since, *The Book on Tasty and Healthy Food* remains a basic work that can answer any question.

The apple of Mikoyan's eye, however, was a meatpacking plant built in 1933 and named after him, a gigantic complex producing sausages, canned meats, and "cutlets"—a term that in Russian refers to a product made with chopped meat and filler. Mikoyanovsky cutlets created a real revolution in domestic as well as institutional food in the USSR: They were cheap at six kopeks apiece, readily available, and easy to prepare, providing low-income families with access to meat, albeit not meat of the best quality. The cost and quality of meat supplies had always been problematic in the Soviet Union, but the Mikoyanovsky cutlet helped millions of people at least alleviate the problem.

The Mikoyanovsky plant is still in operation, and is today one of the ten largest meat-products companies in Russia. Even though most food products can be had in Moscow and other large cities, including a wide selection of imported sausages, the factory's products—sausages, hams, canned meats, pâtés, and partially prepared foods—remain competitive and widely preferred for their high quality.

— Irina Glushchenko

Mithaecus

C. 400 BC

M

Mithaecus was a cook and author of recipes. He lived about 400 BC, which makes him the first named culinary author anywhere in the world. Only one of his recipes is now on record.

Mithaecus was a Sicilian. At this period the coastal regions of Sicily were largely occupied by Greek colonies. It was a rich and fertile island, and these colonies, notably Syracuse, enjoyed a luxury lifestyle envied by the people of Greece itself. Among the features of Sicilian luxury were the emergence of gastronomy and the development of the arts of entertainment. Some Sicilian cooks, it appears, having learned their trade, migrated back to Greece, and earned a living there while spreading the knowledge of good food and luxury eating.

The only known contemporary reference to Mithaecus comes from the philosopher Plato, a highly respectable source, though Plato's remark is not intended favorably. In his dialogue *Gorgias*, Plato depicts Socrates poking fun at anyone who would take seriously the contribution to civilization made by three then-famous people: "Thearion the baker, Mithaecus who wrote the book on Sicilian cookery, and Sarambus the wine-dealer." Socrates goes on to say that by seducing us with fine flavors people like these encourage our physical decline. Incidentally, Mithaecus is in interesting company here. Thearion was credited with inventing an oven for the mass production of bread, and with introducing this idea to Athens. He became widely famous, and so did the aroma and flavor of the fine fresh bread that anyone could buy in the Athenian marketplace as a result of his innovation.

Plato's words are the only evidence we have concerning the date at which Mithaecus worked, and they are difficult to interpret: The dramatic setting of *Gorgias* could be as early as 427 BC, but it contains various anachronisms, so it is safer to say merely that Mithaecus must have become famous at some time before Plato wrote the dialogue, in the 390's BC.

According to an anecdote told by a much later source, Mithaecus had at first attempted to introduce his skills to the city of Sparta, in southern Greece. He spoke the language—Sparta, like much of western Sicily, used the Doric dialect of Greek—but the culture defeated him. The *ephors*, the all-powerful governors of Sparta, expelled him from the city. Luxury was not wanted there: Sparta was famous throughout the Greek world for its strict and militaristic lifestyle.

Thanks to Plato, Mithaecus finally achieved fame not as a cook but as a cookbook author. Sadly, no copy of his book survives from the ancient world. Its last known reader was that tireless compiler of gastronomic information, **Athenaeus**. In his *Deipnosophists*, Athenaeus cites Mithaecus a total of three times and quotes one recipe in full from the historic text. Mithaecus' recipe, as follows, is not the oldest recorded recipe in the world—that honor goes to the Babylonian cuneiform recipe collection—but it is the oldest authored recipe in the world:

Tainia: gut, discard the head, rinse and fillet; add cheese and olive oil.

In this brief, practical sentence, Mithaecus gives instructions for dealing with the ribbon-like fish that the Greeks called *tainia*. (It is *Cepola rubescens;* in French, *cépole*.) His laconic recipe required just 13 words of Doric Greek. The addition of cheese and oil is exactly what Mithaecus' countryman, **Archestratus**, disliked about Sicilian fish cookery. Fifty years later, having given a recipe for sea bass, Archestratus added: "Allow no Syracusan…to come near you when you are preparing this dish: They do not know how to prepare good fish, but wickedly spoil it by adding cheese to everything."

— ANDREW DALBY

Elena Ivanovna Molokhovets

❧ 1831–1918 ❧

ELENA IVANOVNA MOLOKHOVETS IS THE AUTHOR OF RUSSIA'S MOST FAMOUS cookbook, *A Gift to Young Housewives*, first published in 1861. Few facts about her life are known. Born in 1831 into a military family by the name of Burman in the far northern city of Arkhangelsk, she received a good education. From the dedication in the first edition of her book, we know that she attended a school run by the Imperial Educational Society for Noble Girls. Her husband, an architect, was apparently supportive of her writing. Together they had ten children. Molokhovets' old age coincided with the turmoil surrounding the 1917 Russian Revolution. She died in St. Petersburg in 1918.

Her cookbook, however, endures. Up to the revolution, *A Gift to Young Housewives* went through 29 editions before it was deemed too bourgeois for publication under the Soviet regime. Family copies continued to be treasured, though, and when faced with food shortages, the joke-loving Russians often quoted Molokhovets' prescription to go down to the cellar and fetch a joint of meat to serve unexpected guests. By the 1950's, Molokhovets had become almost a mythical figure—so much so that she was immortalized in a disparaging poem by the poet Arseny Tarkovsky. But it was not until the late 1980's, under *perestroika*, that Molokhovets' recipes were reprinted. A new edition of her book finally appeared in 1991.

Molokhovets originally published *A Gift to Young Housewives* anonymously. Its immediate success caused other volumes with the same title to flood the market. This appropriation of her work distressed her, and to ensure that readers were getting her recipes, rather than someone else's, beginning with the second edition she had each copy stamped with her initials. According to Joyce Toomre's introduction to the English translation of *A Gift to Young Housewives*, Molokhovets had not wanted her name to appear, as she felt some ambivalence about having written a cookbook: "Most educated Russian women of her generation were uninterested in acquiring domestic skills, preferring instead to give their energies to cultural pursuits or philanthropic activities."

Until Molokhovets published her book, the only popular cookbooks were those written by Katerina Avdeeva, who had published four of them between 1842 and 1848. Molokhovets' volume differs from Avdeeva's in that it goes beyond culinary matters to emphasize domestic life. She equates an efficient household with a good family life and makes it clear that the responsibilities of a woman are moral as well as domestic. In this regard Molokhovets' work may be compared to that of the American writer **Catharine Beecher**, who in her popular *Treatise on Domestic Economy* (1841) takes pains to connect good Christian behavior and women's familial duties. Molokhovets guides young housewives through what she perceives as the pitfalls of domestic life, and her sympathetic understanding of the daily dilemmas of kitchen management endeared her to her readers and likely accounted for the enormous popularity of her book. Writing from a position of both practical and moral authority, Molokhovets reassures the novice by allaying anxiety over food preparation and familial relations.

The first edition of *A Gift to Young Housewives* offered fifteen hundred recipes; by the twentieth edition of 1897 there were 3218, beginning with soups and ending with recipes for fast days when meat and dairy products were proscribed. The subheadings for the soup chapter alone reveal the book's extraordinary range: Hot Meat-Based Soups; Meat-Based Puréed Soups; Fish Soups; Butter-Based Soups (Without Meat); Milk Soups; Sweet, Hot Soups from Milk, Beer, Wine, and Berries; and Cold Soups. The soups are followed by an entire chapter devoted to their accompaniments. There is also an informative chapter on vegetarian cookery. Of greatest interest to the social historian, however, are the detailed sections on maintaining a household, including the treatment of servants, food storage, table settings, kitchen floor plans, and so on. *A Gift to Young Housewives* offers great insight into the lives of middle- and upper-class Russians in the nineteenth century, as well as into the evolution of Russian cuisine.

— DARRA GOLDSTEIN

Frontispiece of the 1909 edition of Molokhovets' Podarok Molodym Khozyaikam (A Gift to Young Housewives)

Podarok molodym khozjajkam (A Gift to Young Housewives), 1861

Francisco Martínez Montiño   ❋ C. EARLY 17TH CENT. ❋

WOEFULLY LITTLE IS KNOWN ABOUT THE BIOGRAPHY OF FRANCISCO MARTÍNEZ Montiño (or Motiño or Moriño). It is supposed, from etymology, that his family was from northern Spain, but beyond that, nothing is known. His legacy derives from being chef to King Philip III of Spain (1598–1621), and from the publication of his 1611 cookbook, *Arte de Cocina, Pastelería, Vizcochería, y Conservería (Art of Cooking, Pastrymaking, Biscuit-Making and Conserving)*. The book, published in Madrid, was immensely popular, due in part to its straightforwardness and simplicity, and 22 editions were printed by 1760.

Montiño cooked and wrote during *el siglo de oro*, a time in Spain when the country and the crown were reaping the outward prestige of the *reconquista* and rule over the New World. Madrid became the final location for the capital and, under Philip III, the opulent Plaza Mayor was constructed, where one could shop and watch the *corridas* (bull-fights) and *autos-da-fe* (public execution of heretics). Spain's economy, however, was in decline, increasing the gulf between social classes. A plague in the closing decades of the sixteenth and first of the seventeenth century wiped out a tenth of the population of Castile, and in 1610, the king also ordered the expulsion of any remaining *Moriscos* (Moorish converts to Christianity) from the country.

Montiño reflected the age's quixotic paradox of power, status, steadfastness, frugality, austerity, and orthodoxy in his cookbook. He included more than five hundred recipes, consciously leaving out several because they were ordinary, some because he did not want to overwhelm the reader, and a few that he found disagreeable. And although he had a pantry of unsurpassed scope, he was concerned with waste and his dishes remain relatively simple and humble.

His book also advises on the running of a kitchen, its cleanliness, the tools needed to successfully prepare feasts, and the proper presentation of banquets. Perhaps expressing a bit of culinary rivalry (his rival is usually thought to have been Diego Granado Maldonado, author of *Libro del Arte de cozina,* published in Madrid in 1599), Montiño writes, "The intent that I have in writing this little book is that there are no books which can assist those who serve the Office of the Kitchen, and that they cannot commit all of it to memory. Only one have I seen, and so mistaken, that it is enough to ruin whoever uses it, and composed by an Official who is almost unknown in this Court; and in this way the things of the Book are not practiced in a way that any Apprentice can benefit from, least of all the Spanish."

Montiño's writing lies between Spain's past and its future, for the cookery book is rich with recipes using foodstuffs introduced by the Arabs, including rice, artichokes, spinach, garbanzo beans, lemons, oranges, pomegranates, and almonds, but has not yet incorporated many ingredients that Spain gained in the Columbian Exchange. It immortalizes recipes that have come to represent Spanish cooking, including *tortilla, empanadas, chorizo,* and *olla podrida*, uses flavorings of red pepper, garlic, and saffron, and includes menus for banquets at Christmas and in May and September. In addition, the *Arte de Cocina* reflects a growing sense of nationality in cuisine, with some recipes identified as foreign, such as Portuguese and English stews, stuffed leg of lamb in the French style, and Moorish chicken.

— BETH FORREST

Arte de Cocina, Pastelería, Vizcochería, y Conservería (Art of Cooking, Pastrymaking, Biscuit-Making and Conserving), 1611

Bipradas Mukhopadhyay ❦ 1842–1914 ❦

M

IF ANYONE CAN BE CALLED THE UNSUNG HERO OF BENGALI GASTRONOMY, IT IS Bipradas Mukhopadhyay. Born in Jessore, in modern Bangladesh, he traveled to various parts of India and spent many years as a teacher. A truly Renaissance figure, his writings encompassed an enormous variety of topics. He was also part of what historians now call the Bengal Renaissance, a period of enlightenment and burgeoning nationalism in British-ruled India.

Today he is remembered as the man who first wrote about Bengali cuisine in a comprehensive, yet precise and analytical, fashion. There is an irony to this achievement. Although Bengalis have an extraordinary culinary tradition, going back many centuries, there were no books on Bengali cooking until Bipradas took it upon himself to write them. (In Bengal, well-known figures are often referred to by their first name.) Traditionally, recipes were part of treasured family lore, handed down through generations from mother to daughter or daughter-in-law. This oral transmission provided a framework but omitted precise details—the classic "a bit of this and a pinch of that" method of cooking that relies on the cook's inherent creativity for success. Outside the home, the absence of a restaurant culture meant that professional chefs mostly worked in royal kitchens and the homes of the wealthy. These chefs were not literate enough to be motivated as writers, nor keen to give away their secrets.

In such a context, Bipradas' magisterial work *Pak Pranali* (*Methods of Cooking*) was nothing less than revolutionary. The book, which he edited himself, is an anthology of pieces he wrote between 1885 and 1902. To describe it as merely a cookbook or a collection of recipes for Bengali cooking would be to do it an injustice. Bipradas started with a historic perspective, analyzing the role of food in Indian civilization and expounding the various beliefs about food and the qualities of different foods as set out in the ancient Indian Ayurvedic tradition. A discussion of food and health naturally followed, including specific foods for patients or convalescents. In providing instructions for the cook, Bipradas began with the fundamentals—organization of the kitchen, proper equipment, hygienic handling of food, and the preservation of food.

Writing at a time when the dietary habits of Hindus and non-Hindus, vegetarians and non-vegetarians, rich and poor were well distinguished, Bipradas took great pains to be inclusive. This descendant of an orthodox Hindu Brahmin family, who was educated at Calcutta's Sanskrit College and himself taught there for several years, found nothing wrong in describing elaborate methods of cooking meat and chicken. Many of his recipes are distinctly part of India's Muslim cuisine and he refers to some as being the favorites of Muslim rulers. As a subject of colonial British India, Bipradas also taught his readers how to make stews and puddings and jellies. This indicated an astute assessment of his readership, for the Bengali elite of the nineteenth and early twentieth century was becoming rapidly more westernized. Moving up the socio-economic ladder entailed familiarity with the manners, foods, and habits of the British rulers.

In a second volume, *Mishtanno Pak* (*Making Sweets*), Bipradas presented recipes for more than five hundred sweets. This book too is remarkable for its range and attention to detail. At a time when refrigerators were largely unknown and even ice was not available to many households, Bipradas explained how to preserve something as perishable as milk. In accordance with Ayurvedic principles, he recommended avoiding the consumption of milk simultaneously with items that were hard to digest—fish, meat, date-palm sugar, radish greens, and plums. And like any great artist, he took pleasure in creative adaptations of traditional dishes. One delightful example is his recipe for making *luchi*s (a fried bread Bengalis adore), by adding the thick extract of jackfruit to the dough. And as in his earlier book, he also included many recipes from the Western world—cakes, biscuits, and breads.

Bipradas' cookery books reflect the lively curiosity and polymath's talent evident in the subjects of his other books. These include a compilation of humorous anecdotes, mystery stories, and numerous treatises—on avoiding accidental death, grafting plants, kitchen gardening, female hygiene and health, sex education for young women, and wedding rituals. He was also noted for his witty conversation. Making a sly dig at the inhumane custom that rigidly forbade the remarriage of widows in Bengal and condemned them to lifelong vegetarianism, he quipped that a man could only have a truly delicious vegetarian meal when his wife became a widow. Given his exquisite culinary knowledge, we can hope that he himself did not have to wait for such a sad event.

— CHITRITA BANERJI

Pak Pranali (Methods of Cooking), 1885–1902 (as essays), 1904 (collected)
Mishtanno Pak (Making Sweets), 1906. Reprinted, 1981

Angel Muro

ANGEL MURO GOIRI WAS BORN IN MADRID ON JUNE 1, 1839. HE WAS BAPTIZED in the Church of San Sebastian, the legitimate son of Tomas Victor Muro, of the region of La Rioja, and Maria de Loreto Goiri of Madrid. His place of birth is indicative of his family's heritage and its entrance into comfortable prosperity.

His mother died when he was very young and his father later married Valentina Carratala. May 6, 1849 marked the birth of his half-brother, Jose Muro Carratala, whose work is sometimes confused with his own. Angel pursued an education in Latin studies and humanities and in 1855 obtained a bachelor's degree in philosophy. Following the death of his father he received an inheritance as well as a share of his mother's legacy, but soon thereafter he began to experience serious financial difficulties.

Despite a very small income, he went to Belgium and studied engineering at the University of Liège. To make ends meet, he found it necessary to alternate between studying and authoring numerous technical publications. He married in Liège, but his marital life was beset with difficulties of all kinds from the outset. His wife, a distinguished literary figure in her own right and the author of a controversial book titled *L'origine végétale des animaux (The Vegetable Origin of Animals)*, must have been too unconventional for his peers. It was rumored that her book might have contributed to the intimate drama of his marital separation.

Orphaned early on, financially beleaguered, and in a conflicted marital relationship, Muro also had to endure the death of three of his four children. In spite of his travails, nothing seemed to dampen his excellent health and indomitable spirit. A man of integrity, he knew how to follow an argument with energy and intelligence, and was blessed with joy and a sense of humor. His inspiration was a source of motivation and his desire to be productive egged him on.

He pursued writing as a source of income and became a journalist, a translator, and a writer. He lived in Paris for 21 years, where he was a correspondent and writer for major Spanish newspapers, as well as a contributor to the leading French papers. In 1882 he published a novel, *Los dos galanes rusos (The Two Russian Suitors)*. While he wrote about many topics, he never ceased to perceive the world through an epicurean lens.

Muro began his journalistic forays in the world of gastronomy in 1890. His writings are collected under the title *Conferencias Culinarias (Culinary Conversations)*, and this allowed him to develop the original idea of an *1892 Culinary Conversations Almanac*. He was the first to illustrate each day of a calendar for that year with recipes and other current topics. He gathered recipes from such luminaries as Lord Byron, Alexandre Dumas, Molière, **Francisco Martínez Montiño**, Count Tolstoy, Talleyrand, and Napoleon III.

Muro spent the last years of his life living in Madrid, where he produced the greater part of his work. In the illustrated publication, *La cocina por gas. Agenda de cocina para 1897 (Cooking With Gas. A Culinary Daybook for 1897)*, he offers 730 accounts of meals and food in addition to 365 recipes. Not only does this work provide a systematic classification of the new cuisine's advantages, it also aims to improve standards of hygiene and modify cooking times, and opens the door to new cooking formulas and combinations.

Others of Muro's important works, which played a key role in the tastes and habits of his contemporaries, are *Diccionario General de Cocina (General Dictionary of Cookery)* and *El Practicon (Practical Manual)* (1897). There were 33 subsequent editions of the *Manual*, with amendments, new recipes and formulas. It is an authoritative guide that sets forth the principles and rules that are required to recognize, purchase, cook and recycle food, as well as serve at table. The *General Dictionary of Cookery* encompasses the complete nomenclature of Castilian elements in the culinary arts. It contains thousands of formulas for selecting and creating dishes made with products of the air, land, and water. It also includes notes regarding human nutrition and rules for the installation and operation of kitchens and dining rooms.

Death came to Angel Muro in Bouzas, a serene hamlet on the Galician coast near the city of Vigo. The industrial engineer, journalist, prolific intellectual and culinary chronicler died on August 13, 1897, leaving a legacy of formulas, recipes and commentaries which to this day are part of the Spanish body of knowledge.

— ALICIA RIOS

Los dos galanes rusos (The Two Russian Suitors), 1882

Conferencias Culinarias (Culinary Conversations), 1892

Diccionario General de Cocina: Obra igualmente util para las mujeres de gobierno de su casa, para los mas expertos jefes de cocina, para los aficionados y hasta para las cocineras de poco saber (General Dictionary of Cookery: A Work Equally Useful for Women Maintaining a Household, for the Most Expert Chefs, for Devotees, and Even for Beginning Cooks), 1892

La cocina por gas. Agenda de cocina para 1897 (Cooking With Gas. A Culinary Daybook for 1897), 1897

El Practicon: Tratado completo de cocina al alcance de todos y aprovechamiento de las sobras (Practical Manual: A Complete Cooking Treatise Accessible to All and the Best Use of Leftovers), 1897

N

N

Ruperto de Nola   ❧ SECOND HALF, FIFTEENTH CENTURY ❧

ALSO CALLED: Mestre Robert

RUPERTO DE NOLA HAS BEEN DESCRIBED AS A MAN WHO SEEMS TO HAVE appeared from nowhere. According to Juan Cruz, in *La Cocina Mediterranea en el Inicio del Renacimiento (Mediterranean Cooking at the Beginning of the Renaissance),* the only thing we know with certainty is what appears at the front of his work: "Mestre Robert, al servicio del rey de Nápoles llamado Ferrando (Master Robert, in the service of Ferrando, King of Naples)."

It is believed that Nola's book, *Libre del Coch (Book of the Cook)*, was originally written in Catalan or Limousin and, judging by references to it by other authors, it may have first appeared as early as 1477. This would be extremely early, as the first book of any kind printed in Spain probably dates to 1473. There are, however, no extant copies of this first version; the earliest known edition was printed in 1525 in the Castilian language. Several other editions followed, including in 1529, 1538, 1544, 1549, 1566, and 1577. The popularity of this work shows that Spain was a country whose ambition was to cook well and to eat well, and to create a good table at all times and in all places.

The *Libre del Coch* mixed recipes from Aragon, Catalonia, Valencia, Provence, and Italy. Ruperto de Nola wrote for his peers and communicated his knowledge and experience, specifying cooking times and amounts for ingredients, and giving the reasoning behind certain procedures. He writes meticulously, with a respect for the quality of life that overrides any other circumstance. Nola appears to be modest, simple, dutiful, eager, and not without elegance and style. There is no doubt that his life was shaped by his involvement with royalty. His advice and descriptions demonstrate his conviction that the time set aside for sharing lunch or dinner is a great human moment.

The era of Ruperto de Nola represents the integration of culinary and gastronomic methods and thoughts reigning at the end of the Middle Ages with those of the new spirit of the Renaissance. In Spain, Arabic, Christian, and Jewish cultures coexisted and, between the first publication of his book and the edition of 1525, a radical new element was added: access to the New World. The aroma of renovation was pervasive in all Mediterranean kitchens. However little we know about him, Nola is to be given his due. The mental or spiritual basis for a man's desire to make manifest his ideas and actions on paper makes that man a historical figure, permanently. This impulse, added to his search for new mixtures and methods, makes a great cook who influenced what we know as our modern-day Mediterranean diet.

— ALICIA RIOS

Libre del Coch (Book of the Cook), 1477?

Nurallah

❧ 16TH/17TH CENTURY ❧

Detail of "Barbad, the concealed musician" from Shah Tahmasp's Shahnameh, *attributed to Mirza 'Ali. Tabriz, c.* 1535

NURALLAH WAS CHEF TO SHAH ABBAS SAFAVI, who reigned from 1588 to 1629. He is the author of the cooking manual entitled *Maddat al-hayat: resaka dar 'ilm tabbakhi (The Substance of Life: a Treatise on the Art of Cooking).*

Little is known about the life of Nurallah. In his introduction to his cookbook, Nurallah says that from the time of Shah Isma'il (reigned 1501–1524) his ancestors had been chefs in the Safavid court. It is possible that he is a descendent of the author of the first manual of Persian cooking, a chef named **Bavarchi**. This is likely as generally occupations were hereditary in families.

Nurallah's treatise was written in 1594 after his return from *Hajj,* the holy pilgrimage to Mecca. As part of *Ashpazi-yi dawra-yi safaviya: matn-i du risala az ān dawra (The Cuisine of the Safavid Period: The Text of Two Treatises From That Time),* edited by Iraj Afshar and published in Tehran in 1981, the available copy of *Maddat al-hayat* is compiled from two original copies of the manuscript: one in a private collection and the other in the Kitabkhaneh-yi Majlis Shurā-yi Milli, the library of the Iranian parliament. There are distinguishing marks by each recipe indicating from which manuscript they have been derived.

Maddat al-hayat shows Nurallah as a Renaissance man. Not only was he passionate about his profession and his religion, but he also possessed knowledge of history and literature. His introduction starts by extensive praise of God, the prophets, the imams and the shah, interspersed by lines of poetry from famous

Persian poets such Sa'di (1184–1292) and others. He continues with a list of qualities essential for being a master chef. Primary among essential qualities are that from the beginning to the end he should not neglect his work or delegate it to others. He should have faith and be honest. He should observe the *shari'a* (Islamic law) and abstain from committing any sins. He should be pure and clean both internally and externally. At all times he must keep all kitchen utensils clean and wash the ingredients, particularly meat. It is essential for this profession that the chef be honorable, zealous, patient, and charitable with his subordinates. Agility and generosity are God-given gifts. He must refrain from being immodest. Nurallah continues with some lines of poetry and concludes that whoever possesses the above qualities can be called a master chef.

The recipes are interesting as they contain information about other chefs, living or dead, who may have invented a dish, or from whom Nurallah learned a dish, or who knew best how to prepare a particular dish. In addition there are dishes which are specified as having been modified by the shahs or invented by Nurallah. He also provides information as to which dishes were prevalent and popular under which Safavid shahs At the same time, in the midst of the recipes, there are tidbits of personal information. For instance he says that he cooked such a wonderful *ghaymeh* (a ragout of finely chopped meat) for Sultan Hamza Mirza (a Safavid prince) that the prince gave Nurallah an elegant blue-black horse.

— SHIREEN MAHDAVI

Maddat al-Hayat: resaka dar 'ilm tabbakhi (The Substance of Life: a Treatise on the Art of Cooking), 1594

Richard Olney

※ 1927–1999 ※

From his book Reflexions*, 1998*

RICHARD OLNEY WAS A GIANT IN THE WORLD OF FOOD and wine. He was known for the depth of his knowledge and the clarity and passion of his writing. He had a tremendous impact on a number of people who would themselves become important and influential in the world of food and wine, Alice Waters and Kermit Lynch among them. Waters used Richard's recipes at Chez Panisse and has said of him "He has lived to please himself, and in doing so, he has created an irreplaceable body of work. His generosity to like-minded gastronomes is legendary." Indeed, in reading his books, one has the sense that he is writing for himself. His work is very personal.

Throughout his career he taught cooking at Lubéron College in Avignon and at **James Beard**'s in New York, among other venues, wrote regularly for *Cuisine et Vins de France*, *La Revue du Vin de France*, *The London Sunday Times* and was an active member in a number of prestigious gastronomic societies such as La Confrérie des Chevaliers du Tastevin, La Commanderies du Bon Temps de Médoc et des Graves, Les Amitiés Gastronomiques Internationales and l'Académie Internationale du Vin. He received a number of awards including Le Prix Littéraire des Relais Gourmands in 1986 for *Yquem* and Le Prix de l'Académie Internationale du Vin de France in 1992 "*pour l'ensemble de son oeuvre et de son action internationale de faveur du vin.*" While all of his books were equally informative and well written, perhaps the most influential were his first, *The French Menu Cookbook* and *Simple French Food*, which won the 1974 Best Cookbook of the Year Tastemaker Award and the James Beard Cookbook Hall of Fame Award in 1992.

Richard edited the 27-volume Time-Life Good Cook series. Time-Life had a policy that all of the recipes had to come from a published source and that no more than four recipes in each volume were to be from the same source. Richard wanted to include a recipe for a traditional French eggplant gratin in the *Vegetables* volume but could find no published source. He discussed this with food historian

Alan Davidson, who suggested bringing out a little food history journal, publishing one issue with the recipe, written by Richard, using a pseudonym. It could then be cited. Thus was born *Petits Propos Culinaires* (*PPC*) which is still being published. Richard used *PPC* for other recipes to be included in the Time-Life series, writing under a variety of pseudonyms such as Nathan d'Aulnay and Tante Ursule.

He was born in 1927 in Marathon, Iowa, one of eight children, with whom he remained close throughout his life. Richard moved to Paris in 1951 to paint and in 1961, using the money from an Ingram-Merrill fellowship for his painting, bought a house in the south of France, in Solliès-Toucas, where he was to live for the rest of his life cooking, writing, and teaching. He was an excellent cook who shared his table with his numerous siblings, who often stayed in Solliès-Toucas, and with friends. He died in his sleep in on August 3, 1999.

— PATRICIA M. KELLY

The French Menu Cookbook, 1970. Revised edition, 1985
The Good Cook Series, 1977–1983
Simple French Food, 1974
Yquem, 1986
Ten Vineyard Lunches, 1988
Romanée Conti, 1991
Provence the Beautiful Cookbook. Recipes and text by Richard Olney, regional text by
    Jacques Gantié, 1993
Lulu's Provençal Table: The Exuberant Food and Wine from the Domaine Tempier Vineyard, 1994
Richard Olney's French Wine and Food: A Wine Lover's Cook Book, 1998
Reflexions, 1999

Maria Parloa

1843–1909

In this group portrait taken in 1909, Parloa is seated at right. The central figure is **Ellen Richards**.

MARIA PARLOA WAS PART OF A REMARKABLE group of women in and around Boston in the latter part of the nineteenth century whose reforming efforts changed both the way Americans cooked and the way they thought about the kitchen and its role in family and community life. These women included **Mary Lincoln** and **Fannie Farmer** of the Boston Cooking School and Mary Hinman Abel and **Ellen Richards**, founders of the New England Kitchen.

Miss Parloa's views are less well known than those of Ellen Richards, the first woman admitted to MIT, who is credited with the invention, more or less, of home economics, but Parloa was a colleague who was fully committed to the movement and an enthusiastic supporter of the mission of the New England Kitchen. Indeed, Richards herself said that she developed her material on the chemistry of cooking and cleaning precisely at Parloa's request for her classes at the Boston Cooking School. Along with her associates, Parloa believed early on that technology would transform women's lives by simplifying housekeeping activities, especially in the kitchen, although she later apparently changed her mind as she came to see that labor-saving technology had in fact done little to reduce kitchen work.

If Richards was the dominant intellectual figure in the reform movement, Parloa seems to have been content with a more Martha-like role, quietly but with great authority lecturing on diet and health and on the importance of cleanliness and order in the kitchen and the home, giving cooking classes and demonstrations that were very popular, and writing cookbooks and books of household management, which were usually one and the same thing. The one photograph known of Parloa is a group portrait taken at the 1909 Lake Placid Convention, which set the seal on home economics as a science worthy of study. In the photograph, Richards is front and center, dominating the group (as well she might), while Parloa, by then 66 years old, hovers in the background, sitting in a rocker, smiling slightly, hands clasped, an elusive, almost a humble figure.

Parloa's biography remains obscure. Her dates are almost exactly contemporary with those of Richards (1842–1911), but it is not clear where she was born or what her ethnic background was. In 1871, she apparently attended the Maine Central Institute, a boarding school in Pittsfield, so she may have been a Maine native. At that point she already had some years of experience as a cook and it is tempting to think she may have gone back to school to prepare herself to write her first cookbook, which was published the following year.

That book was *The Appledore Cook Book*, published in Boston in 1872. In it, she reveals that she had worked as a cook in private families and as a pastry chef in several New Hampshire hotels. Since the cookbook deals with a good deal more than pastry, it's my guess that she had been the cook (today we might say "chef") at Appledore House, a summer resort on the Isles of Shoals off the coast of Maine and New Hampshire that was popular with the Boston literati. The resort was a summer destination for dignitaries like Emerson, Longfellow, and James Russell Lowell, who came in part because of Celia Laighton Thaxter, an admired late-nineteenth-century poet whose family owned the inn. Following a pattern that persists to this day, Miss Parloa seems to have established herself as a cooking teacher in Boston at least in part to publicize *The Appledore Cook Book* and in part because of the publicity her book created.

By 1879, when the Boston Women's Education Association was seeking to establish a cooking school to train professional cooks, domestics, and housewives, Maria Parloa was already well-known. She had been lecturing to the public since 1876 and gave her first courses in "domestic science" at Lasell Seminary, now Lasell College, in that year. The following year, she had established a cooking school on Tremont Street in Boston and quickly gained renown as a cooking teacher, so much so that she could charge $20 for two lessons, at a time when city school teachers (if women) earned $10 a week.

She was obviously the right person for the new cooking school the Women's Education Association was struggling to set up, but much too expensive for the regular classes. Instead, Miss Parloa was hired to train a group of teachers for three months, in order to develop a faculty for the school when it opened in the autumn. Later, she gave weekend public lecture-demonstrations at the school, but the daily classes were taught by others. Although Parloa is often cited as the founding director, or one of the founding directors, of the Boston Cooking School, author Laura Shapiro's meticulous research has shown that she was nothing of the sort, although she later called herself "Principal of the School of Cooking in Boston" on the title page of *Miss Parloa's New Cook Book*.

Nor was she the first cookbook writer to include a recipe for tomatoes in an American cookbook, although this too has often been claimed. According to tomato historian Andrew Smith, there had been thousands of tomato recipes published in American cookbooks by 1872, the presumed date of Parloa's first cookbook with its recipe for tomato chowder.

Over the course of her long career, Parloa wrote many influential cookbooks, among them especially *Miss Parloa's New Cook Book: A Guide to Marketing and Cook-*

ing, first published in 1881 and reprinted for nearly three decades thereafter. She wrote a column called "Everything About the House" for *Ladies' Home Journal* (of which she may have been a part owner), and also published or contributed to any number of promotional cookbooks and pamphlets, presumably paid for by such manufacturers as Gold Medal flour (then known as the Washburn Crosby Company, but already sporting a gold medal in its logo), **Liebig**'s beef extract and the Walter F. Baker chocolate company, under whose aegis *Choice Recipes* was published in 1893. She also wrote "Canned Fruits, Preserves And Jellies," a U.S. Department of Agriculture bulletin that is described as "surprisingly up-to-date."

— NANCY HARMON JENKINS

The Appledore Cook Book: Containing Practical Receipts for Plain and Rich Cookery, c. 1872
Camp Cookery, c. 1878
First Principles of Household Management and Cookery, 1879
Miss Parloa's New Cook Book: A Guide to Marketing and Cooking, 1881
Practical Cookery, 1884?
An Ideal Kitchen: Miss Parloa's Kitchen Companion: A Guide for All Who Would Be Good Housekeepers, 20th ed., c. 1887
Miss Parloa's Young Housekeeper, c. 1893
Choice Recipes, 1893
The New England Cook Book, co-authored with Mary Lincoln, 1894
Home Economics, 1898

Louis Pasteur

1822–1895

LOUIS PASTEUR'S INFLUENCE ON THE WAY WE EAT HAS BEEN profound. His name has become part of the vocabulary of food preservation and sanitation; pasteurization has prevented countless cases of illness. He worked directly with the French wine, vinegar and beer industries, as well as improving the production of alcohol from sugar beets.

In the mid-nineteenth century, when Pasteur began his scientific work, scientists recognized that living creatures, visible under a microscope, were present in spoiled foods, but there was fundamental disagreement about how they came to be there: Did they come from outside or were they generated spontaneously within the foods? Pasteur, with his genius for devising experiments, demonstrated conclusively that these microorganisms came from the surrounding air, finally laying to rest the age-old theory of spontaneous generation.

Pasteur worked out strict hygienic procedures for manufacturers that reduced bacterial infection of foodstuffs, and he further developed scientific guidelines for careful, controlled heating of wine, milk, and beer, which killed off the dangerous microbes without significantly altering the taste of the food. This practice is widespread and accepted today; in fact, it is often legally required.

Pasteur was born on December 27, 1822 in Dole, a tiny village in the Jura region of France, near Switzerland; the family later moved to the nearby, larger town of Arbois. His father had served in Napoleon's army and remained passionately devoted to his emperor and to France. Both Pasteur's parents encouraged his education. At first he was a mediocre student, more inclined to art than science, although he must have absorbed some basic principles of chemistry by observing his father's work as a tanner. With starts and stops at various schools, he gradually grew more interested and more serious about his studies. Taking a year to prepare himself, he managed to achieve admission to the Ecole normale supérieure in Paris, with a high rank on the entrance exam. There he performed so well that one of his professors chose him to work as an assistant in his chemistry lab.

Pasteur was first recognized for his investigation of tartaric acid crystals, work which revealed his genius for devising scientific experiments. He firmly believed that all theories must stand up to extensive testing in the laboratory.

At the end of 1848, Pasteur was given a position as acting professor of chemistry at the University of Strasbourg. There he met Marie Laurent, daughter of the rector, and in May, 1849, he married her. She was a devoted wife, enthusiastically supporting Pasteur's work throughout the rest of his life. She discussed his work with him, he dictated his scientific papers to her; she managed the household and kept daily distractions from him. The couple had five children, only two of whom survived to adulthood.

Believing that "there are no such things as applied sciences, only applications of science," Pasteur was always ready to consider practical problems. He began a long investigation of fermentation when he was consulted by an industrialist in Lille about the production of alcohol from sugar beets. In 1863, the Emperor Napoleon III asked Pasteur to investigate the diseases of wine, which were troubling French winemakers. Pasteur demonstrated that the diseased wines were infected by various yeasts and other microorganisms; he became so familiar with these microbes that he could relate the presence of certain organisms to the taste of the wine. Later, he turned his study of fermentation to the making of vinegar and beer.

Pasteur received the **Rumford** Medal of the Royal Society of London, and was elected to the Académie des sciences and the Académie française. A steady stream of prizes and awards continued throughout his career, but they did not come automatically: Pasteur often had to defend his theories, which he did not hesitate to do, forcefully and aggressively. He made his base in Paris from 1857, with appointments at the Ecole normale supérieure, Ecole des beaux arts, and the Sorbonne.

At about age 45, Pasteur suffered a stoke which paralyzed his left side. He gradually recovered, but was left with a limp. He did not allow this to slow down his work. He is quoted as saying, "Let us all work; it is the only fun there is," and he lived accordingly.

During the Franco–Prussian War, Pasteur took his family to Arbois, and returned his honorary doctorate to Bonn University. Years later, shortly before his death, he refused the Order of Merit offered by Prussia.

Pasteur's work extended to medicine. In 1881, he conducted a dramatic experiment in which half a flock of sheep was vaccinated with the weakened anthrax germ and the other half was not. Then—with the farmers, the press, and the public carefully monitoring the results—a usually lethal dose of anthrax was administered to the whole flock. The trial was a complete success: All the vaccinated sheep survived and all the unvaccinated sheep succumbed to the disease.

Pasteur theorized that the same technique would work in cases of rabies. Although his microscope revealed no rabies microbes, he nonetheless assumed that they existed but were simply too small to see. He was testing his rabies vaccine on dogs in 1885 when he was approached by the desperate parents of Joseph Meister, age nine, who had been bitten by a rabid dog. Pasteur hesitated to test his theories on a human subject prematurely, but the situation was dire, rabies being a particularly painful, horrifying, and fatal disease. He agreed to vaccinate Joseph Meister, and the boy survived. With this success, Pasteur received the gratitude of the whole world. Victims of rabid-animal bites came to him for treatment from all over France and from as far away as Russia and the United States.

The Pasteur Institute, a non-profit independent research institution, was opened in 1888, funded by an international public campaign. Pasteur served as its director until his death in 1895. His tomb is located in Paris inside the Institute. Today there are 29 Pasteur Institutes on five continents.

— ALICE ARNDT

Elizabeth Robins Pennell

❈ 1855–1936 ❈

"IT WAS WITH SOMETHING OF A SHOCK THAT I WOKE ONE MORNING AND found myself a collector of cookery books," Elizabeth Robins Pennell wrote in a story published in *The Atlantic Monthly* in 1901. "Outstanding collector" would have been more accurate. Before water damaged her collection in a London warehouse during World War I, Pennell had more than 1000 rare cookbooks. In *My Cookery Books*, illustrated with decorative title pages and a few portraits, she described important books in the collection. The 433 books that escaped damage are now in the rare books collection at the Library of Congress.

Pennell was born February 21, 1855 in Philadelphia, and died February 7, 1936. She is buried in the Quaker cemetery in Germantown, Pennsylvania. The death of her mother, Margaret Holmes Robins, in 1863, caused Pennell's father to send her and an older sister, Anna Matilda, to Eden Hall, a Catholic convent outside Philadelphia. The sisters remained at the convent until their graduation on June 23, 1872.

After graduation, Elizabeth moved in with her father and struggled to fit into Philadelphia's secure but somber society. She did not seek employment, since a

Sketch by James McNeill Whistler

proper Philadelphia father would have felt the social structure totter had he allowed his daughter to work.

Pennell credits one event—the 1876 centennial celebration with its art galleries and Hall of Machinery—and one person—her uncle, Charles Godfrey Leland—for stimulating her imagination and introducing her to a world beyond Philadelphia. Because writers worked in the privacy of their homes, she choose writing as a "ladylike" career that would receive her father's approval. She made a good choice: Pennell became a successful journalist and the author or co-author of more than twenty-five books. Her first major book, *The Life of Mary Wollstonecraft,* was published in 1884.

A commission from *The Atlantic* to write a story about Philadelphia led to a meeting with the illustrator and graphic artist Joseph Pennell, a meeting which led to collaborative writing assignments and eventually marriage.

During most of their marriage the Pennells lived in London. Their travels, frequently on a bicycle, took them to the continent. Pennell credits work, with its "fresh commissions," as providing the funds for their trips. *Our House and the People In It* is an account of their life in London. *Nights* describes their social adventures in Rome, Venice, Paris, and London. Other important books include *A Canterbury Pilgrimage; Charles Godfrey Leland, A Biography; The Life and Letters of Joseph Pennell; Our Philadelphia;* and *The Life of James McNeill Whistler.* "My days went to the making of books which, whether I wrote them alone or in collaboration with J., required my undivided attention," she wrote in the preface to *Nights*.

Pennell, who admitted she could not boil an egg, entered the culinary world when the editor of *The Pall Mall Gazette,* a London newspaper, asked her to write a series of articles on cookery. The columns ran for five years. A selection of some of the best essays was published in 1896 as *The Feasts of Autolycus* (later changed to *Delights of Delicate Eating*). Reviewers considered it "one of the wisest and wittiest of the literary products of the famous [18]90's." It set the stage for cookery books filled with wit, wisdom and humor.

Pennell stumbled into her career as a serious cookbook collector when William Henley, who knew of her helplessness in the kitchen, presented her with a copy of Alexandre Dumas' *Dictionnaire de cuisine.* So that she would not bore her readers by borrowing too often from Dumas, Pennell purchased more old cookbooks. She admitted to being hooked when, instead of purchasing a new gown, she "carried off at Sotheby's, from the clutches of the dealer," one of the few first editions of eighteenth-century cookery writer **Hannah Glasse**.

Elizabeth Pennell's strong-willed spirit could easily be that of the twenty-first century rather than the prudish and proper Victorian era. Whether writing about art, travel, gypsies, or food, she conveys an authoritative style, an intense interest in her subject, and a determination to be considered a professional woman.

— JACQUELINE B. WILLIAMS

Many of the books below were illustrated by Joseph Pennell
To Gipsyland, 1893
The Life of Mary Wollstonecraft, 1884
A Canterbury Pilgrimage, 1885
The Feasts of Autolycus: The Diary of a Greedy Woman (later retitled Delights of Delicate Eating), 1896

Over the Alps on a Bicycle, 1898
My Cookery Books, 1903
Charles Godfrey Leland: A Biography, 1906
The Life of James McNeill Whistler, 1908
French Cathedrals, Monasteries and Abbeys, and Sacred Sites of France, 1909
Our House and the People In It, 1910
Our House and London Out of Our Windows, 1912
Our Philadelphia, 1914
Lithography and Lithographers: Some Chapters in the History of the Art, 1915
Nights: Rome, Venice, in the aesthetic eighties; London, Paris, in the fighting nineties, 1916
Lovers, 1917
Italy's Garden of Eden, 1927
The Art of Whistler, 1928
The Life and Letters of Joseph Pennell 1929
Whistler the Friend, 1930

Platina

1421—1481

ALSO CALLED: Bartolomeo Sacchi

BARTOLOMEO SACCHI OF PIADENA WAS KNOWN FROM HIS OWN TIME TO OURS by his nickname, Platina, the Latin word for his home town. Born to a poor and obscure family, he was able to rise by intelligence and sheer facility in speaking and writing Latin, by great opportunism and sycophancy, and by a volatile and eccentric personality which inspired bitter hatreds and devoted friendships alike, to a significant place among the humanists of his time. After the age of forty-five, when in Rome, he was twice sentenced to imprisonment in Castel Sant' Angelo under orders of Pope Paul II, the second time under threat of death, but under Pope Sixtus IV he became so important a favorite that he was employed in the Vatican Library, ultimately becoming the prefect responsible for its modern organization. He died in office of plague in 1481 and was interred in Santa Maria Maggiore. He wrote about forty remaining Latin works, some slight essays of praise for patrons and some so ambitious as the entire history of the papacy, but his most famous work turned out to be his first attempt at a serious and extended book, written in his earliest years in Rome, *De Honesta Voluptate et Valetudine (On Right Pleasure and Good Health)*, a guide to foodstuffs, cooking, dining, and health, all subjects of which he knew virtually nothing—though he must have loved good food. He never attempted such a subject again.

Little is known of Platina's early life except for snippets in his works. He must have had a good Latin education in Piadena and nearby Cremona, but his first employment was as a mercenary soldier in the constant petty wars among rival Italian dukes. Eventually he decided to go to Mantua, to the famous school that the Gonzaga had established there, but its current master left, and he soon found himself tutor to the family's older sons, the future Duke Federigo and Cardinal Francesco

Gonzaga. When Cosimo de' Medici hired one of the Greek refugees from the Ottoman conquest of Constantinople in 1453 to teach Greek and philosophy at Florence, the Gonzaga sent Platina to join the sons of the great Florentine families in his classes. Those five years in Florence, bringing Platina into the new world of Greek letters and the well-established literary and artistic circles of the city, was the foundation of his later career, for here he began to write, perhaps even the beginning of his epitome of Pliny the Elder's vast *Natural History,* which exists in fragment, with the dedication, at London. And here he met many of the most important humanists and leaders of their time, including his young classmate, Lorenzo de' Medici.

Late in 1461, the seventeen-year-old Francesco Gonzaga was made a cardinal at Rome, where Platina also arrived about the same time. For the next ten years, Platina lived with Gonzaga much of the time, becoming as familiar with the curial and papal circles in which his patron moved as with the humanists who belonged to an informal group they called the "Roman Academy," and who soon welcomed him into their midst.

Their leader, Giulio Pomponio Leto, a brilliant professor at the university and bastard son of a ruling Naples family, became his closest friend for life. Platina himself was given an appointment to the College of Abbreviators, an international papal sinecure. This was perhaps the most calm and secure period of his life, and in it Platina turned to more complex scholarship on food, health and right living.

On Right Pleasure and Good Health falls into two not very well connected parts. Its ten books suggest acquaintance with the ten books of Apicius, which Leto probably edited, but Books 1–5 and 7 are drawn chiefly from Pliny's *Natural History,* and probably from Platina's own *Epitome,* because the quotations may be as short as a sentence from a long original entry. In this section he described the foods, plant and animal, eaten in his time along with their places of origin and related anecdotes. Then—since from the time of Galen in late Greek antiquity, diet and health had been a part of medicine—each plant was related to its humor, that is, to its content of one of the four elements, blood, yellow bile, black bile and phlegm, which dominate health and personality in each of us. Illustrative anecdotes were then drawn from about fifty of Platina's wide circle of acquaintances, and medical generalizations were added. This may be the material which a vituperative poem in Milan accused him of pirating from a fellow Abbreviator who was a Knight of Malta, that is, both a doctor and a probable reader of Arabic.

The second part of Platina's volume, Books 6, part of 7 and 8–10, are a Latin translation of the Italian cookbook of Martino de' Rossi of Como, with three bits of praise of Martino and an invented story of Platina's finding a stained and scarcely legible manuscript of a cookbook. Actually, Martino was a famous chef who had served the Sforza duchy in Milan and was then employed by the wealthy Cardinal Trevisan of Aquileia, who kept the best table in Rome, where Cardinal Gonzaga (and Platina) often dined. In fact, by 1465, when Platina's work was finished, the pair had spent summer holidays with Trevisan and Martino at Marino. Martino's work exists in four known manuscripts, which reveal that Platina's Latin translation sometimes missed the sense or omitted important instructions. He, after all, was using a great deal of material which he himself did not fully understand.

Platina had been appointed to the Abbreviators and flourished in Rome under Pope Pius II, but in 1464 that pontiff died and was succeeded by Paul II, who must also have been known to Platina from the dinners of the cardinals. Paul II soon abolished the Abbreviators, who chose the glib but hot-headed Platina to represent them in a protest, but Platina could not hold his tongue and so insulted the pope that he was thrown into Castel Sant' Angelo on pain of death. Gonzaga finally got him released, but in 1468 he was again imprisoned, probably falsely, as a conspirator against Paul II in a supposed plot involving other members of the Roman Academy. Again Platina was released, in 1469. All papal records of the "Conspiracy of 1468" have disappeared from the Vatican archives, possibly because of Platina's later librarianship, but we know that in this period, *De Honesta Voluptate et Valetudine* was being copied and circulated in manuscript. It may have circulated among the Academy, for we have a Milan manuscript in which the names of the friends who may have been guilty of conspiracy (because they fled Rome) have been erased and substitutions inserted. (Ultraviolet light performs miracles.)

About 1470, an undated edition of the revised version, without identification of the typographer, was printed at Rome, which was a serendipitous event: Print was very new in Italy and the subject matter of this work was neither religious nor a major survival from antiquity. The first dated edition was printed in 1475, and from that point on there were about forty editions and translations into French and German over many years. No attempt was made to translate *On Right Pleasure* into English until 1967.

Martino personally fared less well in the new medium of print, for his name was lost until very recent scholarship rescued it. Bruno Lauioux, a leading French scholar, has found 27 reprints of his work under the names of Giovanni de Roselli and Maestro Giovane, while another, in English, by A. I., was printed in 1958 at London under the title *Epulario,* the same title it bears in its Vatican manuscript. This was reprinted in 1990 at Albany, New York. Martino of course belongs near the end of a tradition of western cookery that had been growing in manuscripts at least from the early thirteenth century. He acknowledges some of his recipes to be Catalan, as seen also in Platina, but scholars are still mining more than fifty extant collections, in a number of languages, for a complex history of relationships in the developments of Western European cuisines.

But Platina may have had a far deeper effect upon the subsequent history of food in the West than his piracy from his contemporaries can taint. In his mid-forties Platina was in easy contact with most of the persons and themes of Italian Renaissance humanism of his century. He knew the debates on Epicureanism, which had attempted to restore the philosophy of Epicurus from the stigma of the sin and wantonness of pleasure under which it had labored in the Middle Ages and which lingered in the conservative viewpoints of many of the clergy around him in Rome. He knew well the storm of controversy Lorenzo Valla's *De Voluptate (On Pleasure)* had met, and found refuge in the suggestion Filelfo had made, that there were two types of pleasure, one of which was *honesta* (right, based upon honorable conduct and self-control), hence *De Honesta Voluptate.* The entire history of Italian dietary advice had followed the Greco-Arabic medical tradition of controlling the humors; hence *et Valetudine* (good health) strove for the same ideal.

Another theme in Platina's introduction may be original but may also relate to earlier royal guidelines: He places great emphasis upon the aesthetics of dining, the decoration and appointments. He seems also to have been less conventionally religious than some of his peers, for, while he had entered minor orders on advice to strengthen his employment as an Abbreviator, *De Honesta Voluptate* never mentions God and only mentions Christ once, to suggest that He would not approve the rich outbidding the poor at the fishmarket! But by marrying the etiquette and aesthetic appeals of dining to an essentially Epicurean definition of pleasure, by which it was not necessarily sinful, Platina had, in his title and introduction, suggested a theme far beyond any of the collections of recipes in many languages that preceded him—that is, the entire concept of gastronomy as one of the legitimate pleasures of life—which had not been seriously entertained with philosophic support in the West since the ancient world.

— MARY ELLA MILHAM

De Honesta Voluptate et Valetudine (On Right Pleasure and Good Health), 1465

V. V. Pokhlebkin

❦ 1923–2000 ❦

A METICULOUS AND DISTINGUISHED HISTORIAN SPECIALIZING IN RUSSIAN AND Scandinavian foreign policy, V. V. Pokhlebkin is renowned in the former Soviet Union for his cookbooks and culinary writings. In the course of his career he published more than fifty books with a combined estimated worldwide circulation of 100 million copies. For over thirty years, this reclusive author wrote books, essays, and articles for home cooks, professional chefs, and history buffs. In effect, Pokhlebkin single-handedly created, and then dominated, the little-known field of Russian-language culinary literature. Among his most celebrated works are histories of tea and vodka, a handbook of seasoning and spices, and a cookbook outlining the culinary cultures of the Soviet republics. Culinary writing was the ideal outlet for his exceptional talents as historian, gastronome, writer, and teacher. His pattern was to painstakingly research a historic recipe, prepare and present the dish, write about it compellingly, and thus share and preserve another bit of culinary heritage for future generations.

Pokhlebkin served in the Red Army on the Western front during World War II and graduated from Moscow State University of International Relations (MGIMO) in 1949. During his research assignment at the Academy of Sciences' Institute of History, which lasted more than a dozen years until 1962, Pokhlebkin founded the journal *Scandinavian Collection* and served on the editorial board of *Scandinavica*. Described as a one-man encyclopedia, Pokhlebkin could as easily write about steak tartare as he could about Genghis Khan. *The Chronology of the Golden Horde;*

Foreign Policy of Rus', Russia, and the USSR*;* and *Tatars in Rus'* are his most acclaimed historical works. From 1963 to 1968, he lectured at MGIMO, Moscow State University, and the Foreign Ministry's Diplomatic School. From 1969 on, he was able to support himself independently as an author.

With no family or children, he threw himself into the secrets and obscurities of history inaccessible to most Soviet citizens. Culinary research was his hobby. He traced many events in history back to food, most notably connecting Russian military defeats and victories to the absence or presence of yeast starter for black bread: When the troops ate black bread, they were victorious.

Pokhlebkin was an unwavering patriot. Contrary to worldwide belief, he maintained that the French cultural influence of the eighteenth and nineteenth century had a deleterious effect on Russian cuisine. It is no surprise that his finest culinary histories are about the drinks most dear to Russians—tea, *kvass,* and vodka. His first foray into culinary literature was in 1968, when the book *Tea: Types, Characteristics, and Uses* was released. For four months while writing *Tea,* Pokhlebkin drank only tea and ate only three pounds of black bread daily to prove the stimulating and fortifying effects of tea. *All About Spices* followed in 1974, a colorful description of herbs, spices, and their culinary uses. For a country that used mainly dill, bay, and black pepper, this work opened a fresh world of flavors.

His most famous work, *National Cuisines of the Peoples of the* USSR, appeared in 1978. It was his attempt to preserve and to restore the recipes of national cuisines as they were at the end of the nineteenth century. Many cite its contribution to the reawakening of national self-identity in the republics. Food, one of the few non-threatening elements of culture in the Soviet regime, marked cultural boundaries more realistically than Stalin's geographic borders of the republics, and thus reinforced the differences among ethnic groups in the Soviet Union. While developing a menu for cosmonauts, Pokhlebkin recommended a varied and invigorating diet composed of regional dishes from the republics. Remarkably, his book outlived the USSR, snappily renamed *National Cuisines of Our Peoples.*

Following the success of *Tea,* the USSR Ministry of Foreign Trade commissioned *The History of Vodka* as an internal document in 1979. Pokhlebkin was not particularly interested in the moral or medical aspects of this spirit, nor its social effects. He was more concerned with the events that led to its discovery, and whether vodka was a historical inevitability. He was struck by the destructive power of vodka on intellect, concluding that he respected the strength of alcohol and despised the weakness of the mind. During the Gorbachev anti-alcohol campaign in the late 1980's, all references to drink in Pokhlebkin's *Culinary Dictionary* were removed. After the fall of the USSR, his *Dictionary* was restored, *The History of Vodka* was issued publicly, and the author received the Langhe Ceretto Prize, an international award that honors outstanding culinary writing, in 1993.

Though he ate modestly himself, Pokhlebkin ardently believed that fine cuisine was achievable to the home cook. He attempted to teach the importance of food beyond recipes. To that end, he wrote a series of often-quoted domestic cookery books. He contributed to the landmark *Book on Tasty and Healthy Dishes,* the Russian analogue of *The Joy of Cooking,* from its fifth edition onwards. In 1979 he published *Secrets of Good Cooking*, a unique book explaining the logic and theory of cooking methods. Soviet cookbooks usually listed the ingredients for each recipe with no explanations, and Pokhlebkin asserted that generations of poor directions and recipes had led to a decline in Russian cuisine and in the cooking profession. *Good Cooking* was later adapted for use in cooking schools. A follow-on publication called *Interesting Facts about Food* covered the history of cooking, including kitchen equipment, tools, recipes, dishes, and advice. *Good Cooking* and *Interesting Facts* have become the biggest sellers among his works.

Pokhlebkin, though past retirement age, published most of his culinary books after the demise of the USSR, when culinary writing came into vogue in Russia after decades of gastronomic neglect and deprivation. By the late 1990's, many of his earlier works had been republished in a multi-volume set. In 1999, he became a member of the New York Academy of Sciences. His final culinary book, *Cuisine of the Century*, was published in 2000. It is a critical and detailed study of Russian culinary history in the twentieth century, tracing the changes in food products, preparation, and menus. As with all his culinary writings, his goal was to help the reader gain a better understanding of Russia and its people through their cuisine.

Many readers believed that "Pokhlebkin" was a pseudonym, since it translates roughly as "Mr. Pottage." He was an outspoken traditionalist when it came to food. He claimed that all wholesome, good, and natural food products are ancient. Everything new was artificial, created by man and not nature, and therefore should be eschewed.

As much as the fall of the Soviet Union contributed to his success as a culinary writer, it may have also played a role in his death. The social and economic turmoil in post-Soviet Russia led to a staggering increase in crime. Tragically, Vilyam Pokhlebkin was found murdered in his apartment in Poldolsk, on the outskirts of Moscow, in 2000, apparently the victim of a robbery. His only possessions of value were his books and his thoughts. Investigators discovered nothing missing from his residence. Though his works have been translated into at least 14 languages, a tribute to Pokhlebkin and culinary history would be to increase that number dramatically.

— GLENN R. MACK

Finliandiia (Finland), 1974

SSSR–*Finliandiia: 260 let otnoshenii 1713–1973 (USSR–Finland: 260 Years of Relations, 1713–1973*, 1975

The Chronology of the Golden Horde 1236–1481, 1999

Tainii khoroshei kukhi (Secrets of Good Cooking), 1979

Zanimatel'naia kulinariia (Interesting Facts about Cooking), 1983

A History of Vodka (Renfrey Clarke, translator), 1992

Vneshnaia Politika Rusi, Rossii, i SSSR (Foreign Policy of Rus', Russia, and the USSR, 1992

"*Kushat' podano!: repertuar kushanii i napitkov v russkoi klassicheskoi dramaturgii s kontsa XVIII do nachala XX stoletiia.*" ("*Dinner is Served! Repertory of Food and Drink in Russian Classical Plays from the Late 18th to the Beginning of the 20th Centuries.*"), 1993

Chai i vodka v istorii Rossii (Tea and Vodka in Russian History), 1995

Sobranie Izbrannykh Proizvedenii: Povarennoe Iskusstvo i Povarskie Priklady (Selected Works: Culinary Arts and Cooking Methods), 1996

Sobranie Izbrannykh Proizvedenii: Istoriia Vazhneishikh Pishchevykh Produktov (Selected Works: History of the Most Important Food Products), 1996

Sobranie Izbrannykh Proizvedenii: Natsional'nye Kukhni Nashikh Narodov: Povarennaia Kniga

(Selected Works: National Cuisines of Our People: Recipes), 1996
Sobranie Izbrannykh Proizvedenii: Kulinarnyi Slovar' (Selected Works: Culinary Dictionary), 1996.
Velikii psevdonim: kak sluchilos', chto I. V. Dzhugashvili izbral sebe psevdonim "Stalin" (The Great Pseudonym: How I. V. Dzhugashvili Became "Stalin"), 1996
Chai—ego tipy, svoistva, upotreblenie (Tea: Types, Characteristics, and Uses), 1968, 1969, 1981, 1997
Kukhni pribaltiiskikh i moldavskogo narodov (Cuisine of Baltic and Moldovan Peoples), 1997.
Kukhni slavianskikh narodov (Cuisine of Slavic Peoples), 1997
Kukhni zakavkazskikh i sredneaziatskikh narodov (Cuisine of the Caucasus and Central Asia), 1997
O kulinarnii ot A do IA: slovar'-spravochnik. (Culinary Dictionary from A to Z), 1988
Spetsii i pripravy (Spices and Seasonings), 1997
Vse o prianostiakh (All About Spices), 1974, 1997
"New principles of a national law approach in Russia's nationality policy in the Northern Caucasus," Moscow Journal of International Law, 1997
Moia kukhnia i moe meniu (My Food and My Menu), 1999
Tatary i Rus: 360 let otnoshenii Rusi s tatarskimi gosudarstvami v XIII—XVI vv., 1238-1598 gg. (Tatars and Rus': 360 Years of Relations Between Rus' and Tatar States in the 13th to 16th Centuries), 2000.
Kukhnia veka (Cuisine of the Century), 2000

Edouard de Pomiane

❦ 1875–1964 ❧

ALSO CALLED: Edouard Pomian Pozerski | Edouard Pozerski de Pomiane

EDOUARD DE POMIANE WAS A POLISH–PARISIAN DOCTOR AND biologist, a pioneer food scientist and amateur food anthropologist, an inspired cook, and a prolific writer. A charter member of Curnonsky's acclaimed Academy of Gastronomes, he was the first food writer to broadcast a popular radio program. Ahead of his time in thinking about food, his liberating and stimulating ideas anticipated much that is common wisdom today.

Pomiane, whose birth name was Edouard Pomian Pozerski, was born in Montmartre, Paris on April 20, 1875, the son of Polish nationalists who had fled to France after participating in the 1863 Polish revolution against Russia. Although the daughter of a Russian general, his mother had been condemned to death and his father to exile in Siberia. Pomiane grew up within the Polish exile community in Paris, and attended the Ecole polonaise and the Lycée Condorcet. He studied biology and medicine at the Faculties of Science and Medicine of the Sorbonne, specializing in food chemistry and dietetics and earning doctorates in medicine (1902) and natural science (1908).

Except for his military service during World War 1, Pomiane spent the next fifty years on the faculty of the Institut Pasteur in Paris, lecturing and writing extensively on bacteriology, food hygiene, and the physiology of digestion. He developed a new field of study he called gastrotechnology, which he defined as the scientific explanation of accepted principles of cookery.

Complementing his scientific career, Pomiane made cooking and food writing his hobby and his second profession. He was enthusiastically prolific, writing at least a dozen cookbooks as well as vast numbers of articles, lectures, and broadcasts. From 1923 through 1929, he starred in weekly programs on Radio-Paris, in which he told his listeners stories about his kitchen experiences and provided recipes that illustrated his precepts. Despite the fact that he was neither French nor a trained chef, these broadcasts contributed to his reputation as one of the most popular and widely respected cooks in France at the time, and made him, arguably, the food world's first media personality.

During the occupation of France in World War II, he organized public lectures and cooking demonstrations at the Institut Pasteur on how to cook and eat under the severe rationing then in force: how to make rationed food items go furthest, in nutritional terms, and how to make the best use of unrationed foods. In view of the shortage of cooking gas, the lectures included advice on energy-efficient cooking techniques and such energy-saving utensils as the "Norwegian stewpot," a well-insulated box in which casseroles could continue to cook till done without further heat input. The titles of the books he published in this period reflect his concerns: *Cuisine et restrictions (Cooking and Restrictions)* and *Manger quand-même (Eating Anyway)*.

Pomiane's widespread popular appeal is not difficult to comprehend. Drawing on his two passions, he had a genius for explaining sound scientific principles in engaging, straightforward language and applying those principles to dishes and menus that were creative and easily accomplished. "Art demands an impeccable technique; science a little understanding."

Pomiane married Charlotte Raymonde Watier, a fellow scientist with whom he collaborated on a couple of scientific papers. They had one daughter, Wanda. Mme. Pozerska—by Polish tradition, she used the feminine form of her husband's real name—seems to have joined him in his culinary endeavors; in *Cooking with Pomiane* he humorously portrays her on the day they are to give a dinner party, raging at hitches in her arrangements in the morning, then smiling serenely and welcoming the guests in the evening.

In addition to advocating a simple and healthful cuisine, Pomiane wholeheartedly believed in cooking and eating for the sheer joy of it, and he extolled the emotional benefits of cooking for loved ones. "To prepare a dinner for a friend is to put into the cooking pot all one's affection and good will, all one's gaiety and zest, so that after three hours' cooking a waft of happiness escapes from beneath the lid."

Pomiane was a staunch debunker of the then-ironclad rules of classical French cuisine; he disapproved of the unhealthy excesses of French menus and delighted in providing scientifically sound modifications of the canon without sacrificing interest or flavor. He was not, however, an advocate of unadulterated folk cooking and described ways to improve and expand upon its limitations.

Although admired by English and American interpreters of French food such as **Elizabeth David** and **Richard Olney**, only three of Pomiane's books have been translated into English. *Cooking with Pomiane*, translated by Peggie Benton in 1962, is a compendium of recipes and essays taken from the radio shows. In the foreword, Elizabeth David writes that Pomiane "takes the mystique out of cooking and still contrives to leave us with the magic."

French Cooking in Ten Minutes, or Adapting to the Rhythm of Modern Life (1930) was translated by Philip and Mary Hyman in 1977. This is the English version of one of Pomiane's most popular volumes, in which he presents simple recipes and menu ideas designed to help busy modern French housewives prepare pleasing meals.

In 1985, Josephine Bacon translated *The Jews of Poland: Recollections and Recipes* from the 1929 original. Throughout his life, Pomiane remained close to his Polish roots, and he was fascinated by the anthropological development of cuisines. "I sought to find in various national dishes the colors of the skies under which they had been born, the reflections of the psychology of the races which had created them." He spent time in urban ghettos and rural settlements in Poland, eating, observing, and collecting recipes. Although his politics are somewhat naïve and his observations too often prejudiced, this collection presents a unique view of Polish–Jewish food in context. Josephine Bacon described it as "…the only memoir of Polish Jewry between the wars written by a non-Jew, the only authentic collection of Polish-Jewish recipes, the only kosher cookbook ever written by a non-Jew."

After his retirement from the Institut Pasteur, Pomiane devoted himself entirely to the study of cooking, continuing to practice and write until his death in Paris at 89 on January 1, 1964. His papers are housed in the archives of the Institut Pasteur, where they are available to the public.

— M M P ACK

Bien manger pour bien vivre, 1922, 1932

Le code de la bonne chère: 700 recettes simples publiées sous les auspices de la Société Scientifique d'Hygiène Alimentaire, 1924, 1957

La cuisine en 6 leçons ou l'initiation à la cuisine familiale, 1926

Cuisine Juive: Ghettos modernes, 1929, 1949

La cuisine en dix minutes ou l'adaptation au rythme moderne, 1930; translated by Philip and Mary Hyman as *French Cooking in Ten Minutes, or Adapting to the Rhythm of Modern Life*, 1977, 1994

La cuisine pour la femme du monde en 10 conférences, 1932

La cuisine et le raisonnement, vol. dix: Conférences faites à l'hotel des Sociétés Savantes sous les auspices de la Société du Gaz de Paris, 1934

Vingt plats qui donnent la goutte, 1935

Pour mieux manger, 1935

La cuisine en plein air, 1935

Curnonsky, Lettres de noblesse, Préface du Dr. de Pomiane, 1935

Radio cuisine, 1ère et 2ème séries, 1936

365 Menus, 365 Recettes, 1938

Réflexes et réflexions devant la nappe, 1940

Cuisine et restrictions, 1940

Manger quand-même, 1941

La goutte au compte-gouttes ou 47 adaptations gastronomiques, 1943

Conserves familiales et microbiologie alimentaire, 1943

Bien manger pour vivre, 1948

Radio cuisine: Conférences gastronomiques diffusées par T.S.F., 1949

Le monde à table, 1952

La cuisine polonaise vue des bords de la Seine, 1952

Le carnet d'Anna: histoire naturelle d'Anna, 1967

Cooking with Pomiane, translated by Peggie Benton, foreword by Elizabeth David, 1962; 1994
The Jews of Poland: Recollections and Recipes, translated by Josephine Bacon, 1985

Procope

⚜ 1650—SOMETIME AFTER 1717 ⚜

Francesco Procopio dei Coltelli | François Procope Couteau

NATIVE TO EAST AFRICA, THE COFFEE PLANT *COFFEA ARABICA* CROSSED THE REA SEA to Yemen perhaps in the sixth century. The custom of drinking coffee had reached Mecca and Medina by the end of the fifteenth century, and from there spread rapidly throughout the vast Ottoman empire from the sixteenth century on. In the mid-seventeenth century, a French merchant named de la Roque described drinking it in Constantinople from "little cups of fine porcelain of great beauty with muslin napkins embroidered in gold, silver and silk."

Coffee was introduced to Marseille in 1644 by travelers from the Orient, and arrived in Paris by 1657. In those early days coffee was drunk in the households of a privileged few connoisseurs and was not widely known: One might be served coffee at the court and at the homes of the Marechal de Gramont and of the Cardinal de Mazarin. Then in 1669, the Ottoman sultan sent an envoy, Süleyman Ağa, to the court of Louis XIV. The French were fascinated by the luxurious and exotic lifestyle he displayed as he made his way from his debarkation in Toulon to his arrival in Paris. During his six-month stay in Paris, he received members of the court at his salons where, in a silk tent, a magnificently costumed coffee-maker prepared the brew from the beans the envoy had imported. When Süleyman returned to Constantinople, he left behind in Paris a rage for *à la turque* clothing and décor—satirized by Molière in *Le Bourgeois Gentilhomme*—and the fashion of drinking coffee.

Strolling vendors with coffee pots and spirit lamps sold coffee on the streets to Parisians well beyond the ladies and gentlemen of the court who were first taken with the appeal of the hearty beverage. At the Foire St. Germain in 1672, an Armenian named Pascal created a very successful temporary café with carpets, cushions and an Ottoman ambiance. When the Foire was over, Pascal opened an establishment serving coffee on the quai de l'Horloge. At the time, most coffee houses were dark and grim places where the patrons' lives and pockets were far from safe; Pascal's new venture, with its tavern ambiance, did not succeed, and Pascal moved on to England. But his original idea translated perfectly into the café created by a young Italian, Francesco Procopio dei Coltelli.

Procopio was born in Palermo in 1650. His parents were Onofrio Coltelli and Domenica Semarqua Procopio. At the age of 22, he arrived in Paris without money or possessions but with a great deal of foresight and courage and a taste for literature. He married Marguerite Crouin at the Eglise Saint Sulpice in 1675. In 1676 he joined the guild of the "distillateurs-limonadiers" and became a "maitre-distillateur". He began his culinary career as a waiter at the café of the aforementioned Pascal at the Foire Saint Germain. When Pascal left Paris for London, Francesco was out of work. He rented a space in the Foire Saint Germain and later a shop on the rue Tournon, where he sold coffee in bean, powder and liquid form.

When his grandfather came to Paris to serve at the French court, Procopio had the funds to create a new café on the rue des Fossés Saint Germain (now rue de l'Ancienne-Comédie). Luxurious and elegant, decorated with mirrors, marble tables and tapestries, and lit by crystal chandeliers, the café, named Le Procope, attracted honest people with an interest in fine food. The Italians connected to the court were early and loyal patrons. In addition to coffee, Procopio served wines from Spain and the Rhône Valley as well as coffee and lemonade. He also served two liqueurs, Rossoly and Populo, both made by macerating anise and various other herbs in an *eau-de-vie* base; these were perhaps the ancestors of today's *pastis*. In addition, Procopio made exotic sorbets and ice creams, using saffron and flower petals for flavoring.

In 1689 Procopio had the great luck to have the Comédie Française set up shop across the street. It inaugurated its new theater with triumphant performances of *Phèdre* and *Le Médecin malgre lui*. Le Procope became the "foyer" for the actors and artists of the theater as well as for generations of theatergoers. The café became a meeting place for people of intellect and sensibility, and the first literary coffee house was born. Not only did men of letters become habitués, but artists, musicians, politicians, and statesmen ate and drank at its tables. This was a comfortable and agreeable place to see and be seen, to read the *Mercure Gallant*, and to discuss the ideas of the day. Le Procope attracted Racine and La Fontaine and later would serve Diderot, Voltaire, Robespierre, Benjamin Franklin, Bonaparte and Rousseau.

Procopio changed his name to François Procope Couteau. His life was happy and full. He had eight children with his first wife. He was widowed in 1696, but remarried in 1697 and had four children with his second wife, Anne Françoise Garnier. In 1717, an old and tired man, he retired, and his son Alexandre took over the family business. Around the time of the French Revolution the café was sold. The date of Procope's death is unknown.

Le Procope is now a restaurant rather than a café. It attracts a general, touristic and less literary clientele. But kept alive in many ways is the design, the spirit, and the history of this place of great importance in the culinary history of Paris.

— SANDRA FAIRBANK

Pythagoras

PYTHAGORAS WAS BORN ON THE ISLAND OF SAMOS, CLOSE TO THE COAST OF Asia Minor, around 580 BC. His parents were educated and fairly well-off and he was a bright child, so when still a youth he was sent away to Syros to study with Pherekydes, a distinguished theologian and a firm believer in metempsychosis, a doctrine of reincarnation which was to become a central tenet in the Pythagorean diet and philosophy. Pythagoras continued to travel and next studied under Thales in Ionia and under his pupil Anaximander at Miletus, who claimed that "everything is full of gods." These three philosophers forged Pythagoras' thoughts and beliefs.

At the age of 22, he journeyed on to Egypt, where he studied mathematics, astronomy, and botany. He was not welcomed at first, and only after he had submitted to harsh tests was he accepted by the priests at Diospolis; he had to observe with scrupulous care all their taboos. Many of these demanded abstention from certain foods, but the Egyptian priests were also particular about not wearing any clothing that derived from animals. Wool was banned, even as a burial shroud; their clothes were made from linen and their sandals from papyrus. From them, Pythagoras would have learned geometry, the rites of purification, and the rites of Osiris.

Pythagoras depicted on a silver coin of Abdera, fifth century BC

In 525 BC, when the Persians invaded Egypt, they imprisoned Pythagoras and took him to Babylon, possibly in adherence to a policy of deporting all Greeks living in Egypt. However, he was not a captive for long—his father was a rich merchant and may have paid a ransom—for he began his studies under the Chaldeans, who taught him secret Magian rites that involved ritual cleansing through drugs and herbs. Cleansing involved not eating meat or beans; the use of hallucinatory drugs from plants was the preparation for mystic union with the gods. These teachings remained an integral part of his own rituals.

A few years later, Pythagoras left Babylon and returned briefly to his home on Samos. Then he continued to travel and study throughout the Greek world until he founded his own school at Croton, a city on the ball of the Italian boot, when he was around sixty years old. Croton was famous for its medical knowledge and gave Pythagoras an enthusiastic welcome. He soon gathered around him over two thousand students, both men and women—they were treated equally—and an inner circle of six hundred philosophers. There he taught a system of mathematics, music and a compelling philosophy based on nonviolence and mystic union with all living things; this last concept was the foundation of his vegetarianism (a word not invented then). He was the first to argue that the world was a sphere, and that the moon shone with reflected light. He believed the universe was governed by laws that could be expressed in mathematical formulas: "All is number." He was the first musical numerologist and laid down the foundations of acoustics, discovering the relationship between the length of a string and the note sounded when it was plucked.

Pythagoras promulgated the dogma that the soul was immortal and could endlessly transmigrate into other living creatures. All life forms, therefore, should be treated as kindred. To kill and eat any living creatures, be they bird, mammal or fish, was to murder one's cousins and eat their flesh, for all people are reborn in the time-flow of life on earth. The notion that a human being has only one life is an illusion caused by lost memories.

There are a number of possible explanations for the Pythagorean abstention from bean-eating. It might partly be traced back to the Egyptian priests, as Herodotus observes. The authors of *Food: The Gift of Osiris* remark that the priests merely wished to avoid the impurity of flatulence. Also, the Egyptian word for bean, *iwryt*, is similar to the word *iwr*, meaning "to conceive" or "to generate," and this association may have endowed the bean with a sacred aspect. Pythagoras also forbade them because, two theories suggest, beans were generated by the same putrefactive material that generates human beings or, according to Pliny, because he thought that the souls of the dead dwelt in them. A more prosaic explanation is that the bean was used as a voting token in elections; thus abstention from beans meant abstention from politics. Another is that foods which can at times be toxic tend to become taboo, and favism, a hereditary disorder involving an allergic reaction to the broad bean, is frequently found in Mediterranean peoples. But the ban on fava beans is summed up best by Marcel Detienne, who points out that this is the only plant whose stem is totally devoid of nodes, making it a means of communication between Hades and the human world, between the living and the dead.

The school at Croton was a flourishing religious school with its own buildings outside the city. It centered on Pythagoras and the cults of Apollo and the Muses, patrons of poetry and culture. The ritual was rigorous and the ethical observances strict; the rites and much of the wisdom were kept secret. Pythagoras played the lyre, sang and composed, and employed music and dancing to cure the sick. He was also very fond of reading aloud from Homer and Hesiod. He was said to be passionate about not inflicting violence on animals. Pythagoras lived to an advanced age and died at Metapontum, but the year of his death is unknown.

Throughout the Mediterranean countries and across Europe, until the middle of the nineteenth century, people who eschewed meat were called "Pythagoreans." The word was a term of abuse in Christian medieval Europe—the heretical Cathars, for example, ate no meat—but was used by the poet Shelley to describe an ideal way of life. The Pythagorean diet was formally renamed "vegetarianism" in 1847, when the Vegetarian Society was established at a meeting in Ramsgate, England.

— COLIN SPENCER

R

François Rabelais

❧ C. 1494–1553 ❧

THIS SATIRICAL WRITER OF EPIC PROPORTIONS WAS BORN AT THE BEGINNING of the Renaissance in Chinon in the vicinity of Tours. The area is still renowned for the excellent wine he so lyrically celebrated. Generally associated with laughter, wine in Rabelais' texts is a symbol of conviviality, of hidden spiritual truth, and ultimately of artistic inspiration. On occasion, however, the writer actually insists on moderation, as prescribed by some Renaissance dietetic treatises that hold that sound intellectual activity is incompatible with overindulgence. **Balzac** would make this theory his way of life about three centuries later.

As a boy, Rabelais was educated either by the Benedictines at the abbey of Saint-Pierre de Seuilly or by the Franciscans at La Baumette. At the age of 26, with a solid mastery of Greek and Latin, he became a Franciscan monk and at some time thereafter was ordained a priest. Though his training steeped him in late-medieval scholasticism, which relied on the received knowledge and authority of Aristotle and the church fathers, he found himself in trouble with church authorities over his devotion to the possibly heretical "new learning" of humanism, his correspondence with one of the leading humanists of the day, and his small classical library, which was confiscated and later—after the intervention of some powerful patron—returned to him. By papal dispensation, Rabelais was allowed to transfer to the more liberal Benedictine order.

In 1530 he entered Montpellier's medical school and two years later we find him in Lyon, then an important literary center, where he was promoted to doctor at the Grand-Hôtel-Dieu, or municipal hospital. Under the name Alcofribas Nasier—an anagram of François Rabelais—he produced *Pantagruel, King of the Dipsodes, Restored to the Life with His Deeds and Dreadful Feats of Prowess.* In this book, as in his next, the text starts with a discussion of the origins of its main characters within the convivial and leveling atmosphere of a country fair, where sitting down at table with friends defines social birth. The theme of food and its abundance is coupled with that of fertility and reproduction. In many instances, food is directly linked to sexuality, as in the war of the sausages, an unequivocal metaphor for sex. Rabelais' knowledge of medicine allows him to describe with precision many of his giant characters' bodily functions, including ingestion and excretion. Interestingly, the relationship between alimentary and reproductive questions will resurface during the first half of the nineteenth century, notably in the writings of **Brillat-Savarin** and Balzac.

While in Lyon, Rabelais also published Hippocrates' *Aphorismes* with his own notes on the Greek original in the margins. In 1534, under his same anagrammatic pseudonym, Rabelais published *The Most Horrific Life of the Great Gargantua, Father of Pantagruel*, with its famous prologue dedicated to "most illustrious drinkers and you, most precious syphilitics." In it, drinking and reading are reconciled as are the pleasures of the body and the mind. One of the most relished passages of this book detailing the fantastic adventures of Pantagruel's father, the giant Gargantua, relates the episode of the *fouaces*, a locally baked delicacy altogether responsible for an unimaginable war. Set in Chinon, at the time of the grape harvest, the tale tells how the *fouace*-makers were forced to sell some of their baked goods to Grandgousier's shepherds, inciting King Picrochole's Homeric campaign against the large-throated Grandgousier.

The theologians of the Sorbonne suppressed *Pantagruel* as being obscene and sacrilegious; Rabelais escaped to Rome under the protection of the Bishop of Paris, Jean du Bellay, a humanist scholar and perhaps a friend of his youth. While in Rome, Rabelais authored the *Sciomachie*, in which he recounts a grandiose feast given by his patron. It is thus travel—his travels in France as a monk as well as his multiple trips to Italy during his lifetime, plus various literary trips taken through his giant characters' bodies—that impels Rabelais to demonstrate the richness of his literary world.

In 1546, under his real name, Rabelais' *Book Third: Of the Heroic Deeds and Sayings of the Worthy Pantagruel* appeared. Like both *Pantagruel* and *Gargantua*, it was condemned by the Sorbonne, forcing Rabelais to seek refuge in Metz. Between 1548 and 1552, he published various chapters of *Book Fourth,* including a passage about a certain Sir Gaster, who allegedly invented all forms of art for the sole purpose of satisfying his stomach. The end of the fourth book also contains a text in which Rabelais inventories his numerous linguistic inventions. The multiple lists found in his writings not only explore the limits of language, they also chronicle the rich gastronomic tradition of the sixteenth century, as when he paints for us in great detail the dishes served at banquets, or various sauces and preparations such as *saulpicquet*, *paimperdu*, *grasboyau* and *carbonnade*.

Rabelais' chronicles continue to inspire gastronomes today. For a taste of the famous *fouaces*, look for the right *boulangerie* behind the cathedral in one of the sinuous medieval streets of Tours.

— Philippe C. Dubois

Les horribles et espouvantables faictz & prouesses du tresrenommé Pantagruel Roy des Dipsodes, filz du grand geant Gargantua, Composez nouvellement par maistre Alcofrybas Nasier (The Horrible and Appalling Deeds & Feats of the Very Famous Pantagruel, King of the Dipsodes, Son of the Great Giant Gargantua. Recently Written by Master Alcofrybas Nasier), 1532
La vie inestimable du grand Gargantua, pere de Pantagruel, iadis composée par l'abstracteur de quinte essence. Livre plein de Pantagruelisme (The Invaluable Life of Great Gargantua, Father of Pantagruel, Written in Times Past by the Isolator of the Quintessence. A Book Full of Pantagruelisms), 1534
Aphorismorum Hippocratis (Aphorisms of Hippocrates), 1545
Sciomachie (War Games), 1549

Le tiers livre des faicts et dicts héroïques du bon Pantagruel Composé par M. Fran. Rabelais docteur en Medicine (The Third Book of the Heroic Deeds and Dicta of Good Pantagruel, Written by M. Fran. Rabelais, Doctor of Medicine), 1546

Le quart livre des faicts et dicts heroïques du bon Pantagruel. Composé par M. François Rabelais docteur en Medicine (The Fourth Book of the Heroic Deeds and Dicta of Good Pantagruel. Written by M. François Rabelais, Doctor of Medicine), 1552

Elizabeth Raffald

R

BY ANYONE'S STANDARDS, ELIZABETH RAFFALD LED A NOTEWORTHY LIFE. She was the author of a major eighteenth-century English cookbook, *The Experienced English Housekeeper*, and was at various times a professional housekeeper, confectioner, shopkeeper, and innkeeper. She also ran an employment agency for servants and developed a business directory. She and her husband were the parents of six daughters. All of this was accomplished in a life that lasted just 48 years.

Born in Doncaster, England in 1733, Elizabeth was one of five daughters of Joshua and Elizabeth Whitaker. Her father was a schoolmaster. The girls all learned to read and write and when Elizabeth was fifteen, she went into service. In 1760, after working for several well-to-do families, she became housekeeper at the estate of Sir Peter and Lady Elizabeth Warburton in Cheshire. John Raffald was the estate's head gardener. They were married in 1763, and moved to Manchester.

There, in addition to running a confectionery shop and an employment agency for servants, she wrote *The Experienced English Housekeeper, for the Use and Ease of Ladies, Housekeepers, Cooks, &c. Written purely from Practice and Dedicated to the Hon. Lady Elizabeth Warburton, whom the Author lately served as Housekeeper.*

Mrs. Raffald says she writes in "my own plain language," so the book may be used by anyone from noble ladies to everyday cooks. In her frontispiece portrait, she looks as straightforward and matter-of-fact as her prose reads. With the barest hint of a smile, she looks directly ahead as she reaches through the oval frame of the portrait and offers her book to the reader.

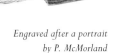

Engraved after a portrait by P. McMorland

First published in 1769, the book sold well and was soon reprinted. Seven editions were published during her lifetime, and it remained in print well into the nineteenth century. A comprehensive work, it includes recipes for soups, meats, fish, pies, puddings, custards, and cakes. She has one recipe for ice cream. Her experience as a confectioner is evident in the section on table decorations, in which she explains how to make a gold or silver web of spun sugar designed to be set atop a dish of sweetmeats on a grand table. She molds fish from flummery, a popular jellied dessert made from almonds, cream, and sugar, and sets them afloat in a sea of clear jelly. She displays flummery hens and chickens on a nest of lemon rind straw, and makes "Moonshine" with a flummery moon and stars in a lemon cream sky. She also includes instructions on such housekeeper's skills as pickling, preserving, distilling, and table setting as well as "A correct list of every thing in season in every month of the year."

In 1772, Mrs. Raffald compiled and published the first Manchester directory, a listing of area merchants, tradesmen, and residents or, in her own words, "a complete guide for the easy finding out of every Inhabitant of the least Consequence." She called it "an arduous task." Later, she compiled and published two more editions of the directory.

Mrs. Raffald died, probably of a stroke, in April of 1781.

As if her accomplishments were not enough, Elizabeth Raffald has been falsely credited with others. Many sources claim she had fifteen or sixteen children, which would have been amazing in view of her many occupations, especially since she was married only eighteen years. However, the British food historian Roy Shipperbottom, who wrote a biography of Mrs. Raffald for *The Oxford Companion to Food* as well as the introduction to the 1997 reprint of her book, noted that church records indicated she had six daughters, only three of whom survived their mother.

Her professional achievements have also been exaggerated. Some sources give Mrs. Raffald credit for publishing the first recipe for ice cream in English. She did not. Unless an earlier work comes to light, the first was in *Mrs. Mary Eales Receipts*, published in 1718. Others say Mrs. Raffald's was the first published English cookbook, a statement that is clearly incorrect.

These claims are easily dismissed, but another is more serious and destructive. Two well-regarded nineteenth-century authors, **Friedrich Christian Accum** and Dr. Arthur Hill Hassall, claimed that Mrs. Raffald's pickling recipes were poisonous. Writing about the dangers of adulterated foods, they each disparaged Mrs. Raffald, quoting her as advocating putting a copper coin in with her pickles or using un-tinned copper pans to make them turn green. They used the same quotation, although Hassall misidentified her as "Mr. E. Raffeld."

Mrs. Raffald advocates no such thing; in fact, she introduces her section on pickling by warning of the dangers of using un-tinned copper because, in her words, "it is poison to a great degree, and nothing ought to be avoided more than using brass or copper that is not well tinned." Throughout the book, she emphasizes the importance of using well-tinned pans and in her introduction, she writes: "I have made it my study to please both the eye and the palate without using pernicious things for the sake of beauty."

Mrs. Raffald's achievements should neither be maligned nor exaggerated. She deserves to be remembered as the author of one of the most important eighteenth-century English cookbooks, as well as a successful businesswoman, wife, and mother. Her life was short but most impressive.

— JERI QUINZIO

The Experienced English Housekeeper, 1769
The Experienced English Housekeeper, A New Edition: In which are inserted some celebrated receipts by other modern authors, 1834
The Experienced English Housekeeper, With an introduction by Roy Shipperbottom, 1997

Mary Randolph

THE AUTHOR OF *THE VIRGINIA HOUSE-WIFE* (1824), WHICH MANY REGARD AS the finest cookbook to ever come out of the American kitchen, was born to Thomas Mann Randolph of Tuckahoe and Anne Cary Randolph August 9, 1762, in Amptill, Virginia, the last according to her gravestone. The Randolphs were prominent in Virginia, and were related to almost everyone of note in the state.

In 1782, Mary married David Meade Randolph, a cousin. They had seven children, only four of whom survived to adulthood. The Randolphs made Moldavia, their imposing home in Richmond, celebrated for their displays of "lavish hospitality." However, political differences with President Jefferson caused David Randolph to lose his appointment as U.S. Marshal. In financial difficulty, Mary took the bold step of opening a boarding house, which her skills as hostess and cook made an immediate and enormous success.

After about a decade, Mary and David moved to Washington, D.C. to live with one of their sons. There, in 1824, Mary Randolph published her cookbook, at first without her name, but adding it to later editions. The importance of this work, which seems to have been the earliest published Southern cookbook, can hardly be exaggerated. It went through at least nineteen editions by 1860. The general acceptance of the iron range probably made it seem a bit old fashioned, but it was massively plagiarized in virtually all Southern cookbooks well into the first years of the twentieth century.

Not only did this book record the best of Virginia cookery, both of the essentially English gentry and their enslaved African cooks—containing perhaps the earliest published recipes for African okra, for example—but it introduced imposing elements of French royalist cuisine. Mary Randolph can be said to have been the amanuensis of the cuisine of Monticello. Many of her recipes contain entire tell-tale verbatim passages from recipes attributed by Thomas Jefferson's granddaughters to Étienne LeMarie and Honoré Julien, *maître d'hôtel* and *chef de cuisine*, respectively, at the President's House during his terms of office (1801–1809). While Mrs. Randolph had long been estranged from Thomas Jefferson, her cousin, his daughter Martha married Mary Randolph's brother David Mann Randolph, and they remained close. In addition, the work contains Spanish recipes that can only have come from her sister Mrs. Harriet Hackley, whose husband was stationed in Cadiz during those years.

Mary Randolph died January 23, 1828, in Washington, and was buried in Virginia across the river on the estate of George Washington Parke Custis and Mary Lee Custis, her cousin. Her grave was the first in what became the Arlington National Cemetery.

— KAREN HESS

The Virginia House-wife. Washington, 1824, 1825, 1828; 1824 edition in facsimile with additional material from the editions of 1825 and 1828, edited by Karen Hess

Ellen H. Richards

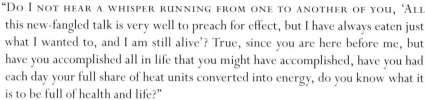

1842–1911

ALSO CALLED: Ellen Henrietta Swallow Richards

"Do I not hear a whisper running from one to another of you, 'All this new-fangled talk is very well to preach for effect, but I have always eaten just what I wanted to, and I am still alive'? True, since you are here before me, but have you accomplished all in life that you might have accomplished, have you had each day your full share of heat units converted into energy, do you know what it is to be full of health and life?"

Thus Ellen Richards challenged her audience during a lecture on food. She herself met this challenge squarely, applying all she learned from her studies of chemistry, nutrition, and sanitation to her home and to her personal life. She excelled at science, becoming the first woman graduate of the Massachusetts Institute of Technology and later the first female member of its faculty; she was instrumental in setting up the Woman's Laboratory, and the Hyannis Marine Laboratory, which became Woods Hole. But at the same time, she believed in the practical application of science, and she consulted for industry and participated in a Massachusetts state survey of the water supply for almost the entire population of the state. She headed the science section of the Society to Encourage Studies at Home; set up the New England Kitchen in Boston and the Rumford Kitchen at the 1893 World's Columbian Exposition; and assisted in the formation of the American Home Economics Association. In addition, throughout her career, she mentored and otherwise assisted countless individual women who aspired to an education in science. She died at home of heart disease March 30, 1911.

Ellen Swallow was born in Dunstable, Massachusetts, on December 3, 1842, the only child of New England schoolteachers. She was educated at home and at a traditional village academy, and also by her own efforts at study and observation. She worked with characteristic diligence on the farm and with her father in his general store and with her mother in the house until 1868, when she enrolled in Vassar College, the pioneering college for women which had opened only three years earlier. Somewhat older and certainly better prepared than most of the student body, she received her degree (in chemistry) in just two years, after which high praise from her teachers led to her becoming the first female student at the Massachusetts Institute of Technology.

In 1875, Ellen Swallow married Robert Hallowell Richards, a young professor of mining engineering at MIT. They purchased a home in Jamaica Plain, where they lived their entire married life; the couple set up housekeeping according to scientific principles, eschewing dust-collecting carpets and drapes and paying particular attention to ventilation, especially over the gas stove and the gas lighting. They embraced up-to-date conveniences such as the telephone, vacuum cleaner, and hot-water heater. Prof. and Mrs. Richards had no children of their own, but their home was filled with students, who exchanged household chores for room and board. (Ellen Richards' friend and biographer, Carolyn L. Hunt, records that Prof. Robert Richards admitted to her that they had found it expensive to hire students in this way. "But," he added, "we decided that that was *what we were here for*.")

In 1890, Mrs. Richards joined with Mary Hinman Abel and others in establishing the New England Kitchen in Boston. This well-funded enterprise, modeled after the public kitchens of Europe, was intended to provide nutritious, inexpensive meals to the working poor, serving dietary education along with the food. Sanitation as well as cooking techniques were demonstrated. In the end, the New England Kitchen was not a success; the founders paid careful attention to health and to cost, but they neglected another important aspect of the meal: the identity of the eater. The typical New England lunches served there did not appeal to the palates of workers from southern Europe and elsewhere. "You needn't try to make a Yankee of me by making me eat that," one man asserted, pointing to an Indian pudding.

Nevertheless, the lessons of the New England Kitchen were applied in establishing a school lunch program, and to the Rumford Kitchen, an educational lunch service at the 1893 World's Columbian Exposition in Chicago. Mrs. Richards was in charge of this part of the Massachusetts state exhibition, named in honor of Massachusetts native Benjamin Thompson, later **Count Rumford** of Bavaria, the esteemed scientist whose work included the study of human food and its preparation. In just two months of operation, the Rumford Kitchen served ten thousand 30-cent lunches. The daily menus gave the food value of each dish, listing "proteid, fat, carbohydrates, and calories." (Vitamins had not yet been discovered.)

As a result of her work with the Rumford Kitchen, she became associated with **Wilbur O. Atwater**, then director of the Office of Experiment Stations at the U.S. Department of Agriculture, and Mrs. Richards contributed information on nutrition and food values to several government publications. The last years of her life were extremely busy and productive: In addition to writing numerous books and articles, she was instrumental in founding the new discipline of home economics. At the culmination of a series of conferences at Lake Placid, New York, attended by prominent cooking teachers and other educators in the domestic sciences, including **Fannie Farmer**, **Mary Lincoln**, and **Maria Parloa**, the American Home Economics Association was formed with Ellen Richards as president. After serving in that office from 1908 to 1910, she insisted on stepping down.

Mrs. Richards participated in the advancement of women during her lifetime, and she envisioned even better things in the years ahead. She put her faith in women's education rather than suffrage and, looking ahead, she saw "The College Woman of 1950" as one who will blend "art and science in a way we do not dream of; the science will steady the art and the art will give charm to science.... This young woman will not run at the sight of a cow, scream at the sound of a mouse...." She will have control of her own mind and body. She will marry, "but she will take her pick of the men, who will by that time have begun to realize what sort of men it behooves them to be.... Freedom to live out her life will bring with it a new zest in life, a new wish to make it of service.... She will be so fair to look upon, so gentle and so quiet in her ways, that you will not dream that she is of the same race as the old rebels against the existing order, who, with suspicion in our eyes and tension in our hearts, if not in our fists, confront you now with the question, 'What are you going to do about it?'"

— ALICE ARNDT

The Chemistry of Cooking and Cleaning: A Manuel for Housekeepers, 1881
Food Materials and Their Adulterations, 1886
Domestic Economy as a Factor in Public Education, 1889
Food as a Factor in Student Life, 1894
Science of Nutrition, 1896
Laboratory Notes: Sanitary Chemistry and Water Analysis, 1898
The Cost of Living as Modified by Sanitary Science, 1899
*University Laboratories in Relation to the Investigation of Public Health Problems and to
    Commercial Work*, 1900
The Cost of Food; A Study in Dietaries, 1901
Dietary Computer, 1902
Air, Water, and Food From a Sanitary Standpoint, with Alpheus C. Woodman, 1904
First Lessons in Food and Diet, 1904
The Cost of Shelter, 1905
Good Luncheons for Rural Schools Without a Kitchen, 1906
Meat and Drink, 1906
Sanitation in Daily Life, 1907
The Efficient Worker, 1908
Cost of Cleanness, 1908
Laboratory Notes on Industrial Water Analysis: A Survey Course for Engineers, 1908
Tonics and Stimulants, 1909
*Euthenics, the Science of Controllable Environment; A Plea for Better Living Conditions as a First
    Step Towards Higher Human Efficiency*, 1910
*Conservation By Sanitation: Air and Water Supply, Disposal of Waste (Including a Laboratory
    Guide for Sanitation Engineers)*, 1911

César Ritz   ⁂ 1850–1918 ⁂

CÉSAR RITZ WAS BORN IN THE SWISS VILLAGE OF NIEDERWALD, WHERE AS A
young boy he herded his father's cows. When he was sixteen years old, his father
arranged for him to be apprenticed as a wine-waiter in a hotel restaurant. Several
months after his apprenticeship began, he visited the Exposition Universelle in
Paris, and he never returned to his job in Switzerland. Ritz stayed in Paris to em-
bark on a vagabond life that lasted for the next ten years.

In Paris, Ritz landed a menial job at a hotel; he held the position for only
about two months before leaving to work at a succession of restaurants, ending up
as an assistant waiter at Voisin, one of the best restaurants in Paris; he later spoke
of it as his *alma mater*. At Voisin, Ritz learned the basics of the hotelier's repertoire—most important, how to please a sophisticated clientele. Ritz remained in
Paris during the Franco-German War in 1871, but left during the seventy-two day
uprising that established the Paris Commune. He returned to Paris in 1872, becoming a waiter at the Hôtel Splendide, then one of the most luxurious in Europe.
There, Ritz catered to American nouveaux riches touring Europe.

When the International Exhibition opened in Vienna in 1873, César Ritz found work in that city as a waiter at Trois Frères Provençaux, where he met the heredity royalty of Europe. When the Exposition ended, Ritz moved to Nice, where, at the unlikely age of 23, he became the maître d'hôtel at the Grand Hôtel. From Nice, he returned to Switzerland to work at the Rigi-Kulm Hôtel, then to the Hôtel de Nice in San Remo, where he controlled the hotel's expenditures. Under his direction, the hotel vastly improved its sanitation and plumbing.

In 1877, Ritz became general manager of the Grand Hôtel National in Lucerne, and his life at last settled into a pattern: He managed this hotel during the summer and worked at the Grand Hôtel in Monte Carlo during the winter. The Grand Hôtel's competition in Monte Carlo was the less successful Hôtel de Paris. The owners of the Hôtel de Paris, knowing that the Grand Hôtel's excellent cuisine was a strong draw, hired away their competitor's chef, leaving César Ritz with a serious problem at the height of the season. The departing chef had recommended **Auguste Escoffier** as his replacement and, based on this recommendation, Ritz hired Escoffier as chef de cuisine. Thus began one of the most famous and successful partnerships in the history of the hotel/restaurant profession.

Ritz had developed his own way of running a deluxe hotel: He had innovative ideas about construction, furnishings, and staff organization and deportment, and he was convinced of the importance of food in such an establishment. Auguste Escoffier was not yet a renowned chef, but he had his own ground-breaking ideas about running a professional kitchen. Ritz provided the hotel restaurant's clientele, and Escoffier fed them elegantly, refining the flavors of the food, eliminating cumbersome and inedible garnishes, and instituting *service à la russe,* in which dishes are served sequentially rather than simultaneously. He organized his kitchen into departments run by specialist chefs and reorganized the kitchen routine.

Ritz was one of the first hotel-keepers to be greatly concerned with hygiene; Escoffier was the first chef to consider the effects of his culinary creations on his customers' digestion. Both men catered to women. Ritz created hotels and restaurants of such elegance and restraint that famous and fashionable women could comfortably be seen in them. Many of Escoffier's creations were named for prominent women, such as pêches Melba, named for Nellie Melba, the Australian-born prima donna of London's Covent Garden.

During the following years, Ritz opened several restaurants and hotels, including the Hotel Minerva and the Hotel de Provence in Baden Baden. From 1889 until 1897 he managed the Savoy Hotel in London, with Escoffier as chef. He later ran the Carlton Hotel in London, again with Escoffier as chef, and launched the Grand Hotel in Rome, the Frankfurter Hof in Frankfurt, and several others. To help manage these enterprises, he created the Ritz Hotel Development Company. Ritz had dreamed of building a perfect hotel in Paris, and this dream was fulfilled when the Hôtel Ritz was completed in 1898.

In 1903, Ritz had a mental breakdown, from which he did not recover. He had little to do with the new hotels that bore his name, such as London's Ritz

Hotel, which opened in 1905, or New York's Ritz-Carlton, which opened in 1907. He lingered until his death in 1918.

César Ritz redefined the concept of a "luxury hotel" and for this he is remembered as "king of hoteliers and hotelier to kings." His legacy lives on in the terms *ritz* and *ritzy*, which are synonymous with luxury, and his name has been immortalized in the song "Puttin' on the Ritz" and the movie of the same name released in 1930; Nabisco attempted to capitalize upon this legacy by producing Ritz Crackers in 1934.

— ANDREW F. SMITH

Robert Roberts ❦ BETWEEN 1775 AND 1780—1860 ❦

ROBERT ROBERTS WROTE *THE HOUSE SERVANT'S DIRECTORY*, ONE OF THE VERY FIRST books written by an African-American and published by a commercial press, in 1827. Quickly going into second and third editions, it established itself as the standard guide for servants and employers alike for managing a large household before the Civil War. Beyond its immediate use as an etiquette book or household directory, it had influence in the antebellum North among members of the emerging black middle class.

Between 1825 and 1827, Roberts was the butler for Christopher Gore, former senator and governor of Massachusetts, at the center of power and influence. At his beautiful Federalist mansion and country estate, Gore Place, in Waltham outside Boston, Gore entertained prominent guests, among them former President James Monroe. Roberts' experience, skill, and professionalism commanded the respect of his employer, who died two years later: He asked Roberts to witness his will. Gore supported and approved of Roberts' book, which appeared two weeks after Gore's death with a testimonial letter written only shortly before.

From the wealth of detail, readers of the *Directory* can learn much about life above and below stairs in such a household. Roberts gives directions on marketing for food, cleaning oil lamps, polishing silver candlesticks, and getting spots out of mahogany furniture. He explains at length how to burn coal, which had just come into use. He encourages servants to rise early to do their heavier work, with time left over to clean and tidy their own shoes and clothing, comb their hair, and look respectable. "In order to get through your work in proper time," he writes, "you should make it your chief study to rise early in the morning; for an hour before the family rises is worth more to you than two after they are up."

Although not a cookbook, Roberts' book includes several recipes for the lemonades, punches, sauces, and beers that the butler's pantry was expected to provide. He gives extensive directions for setting the table for every occasion and for carving fish, birds, and meat, along with instructions for hangover remedies and breath sweetener to cover the smell of liquor. "For those that are given to drink," his cure is to put three live eels into the accustomed alcoholic drink. After the eels are "quite dead," the servant can give "this liquor unawares to those you wish to reform, and they will get so disgusted against it," writes the temperate Roberts, that "they will now have quite an aversion to it afterwards."

With psychological acumen and tact that seems quite modern, Roberts considers the relationships between everyone within the household. Readers learn how servants should address and behave to their employers, who in turn should respect the skills of their loyal servants. Starting with the butler and cook, he emphasizes the importance of servants getting along with each other. He advises them how to dress—and how *not* to dress: A servant's clothing, "though neat and tidy, should never be foppish, or extravagant." His tone is moralistic, his attitude towards his work honorable. Roberts helped to maintain the decorum and gentility of the family even as he maintained the dignity of his race, particularly among black male servants.

One subject never mentioned in the book is slavery, abolished in Massachusetts in 1776. But abolition and civil rights played an important part in his life. Recent scholarship, supported by The Gore Place Society, has uncovered fascinating new information. Roberts was born in Charleston, South Carolina, around 1775 or 1780, and somehow obtained an education. Whether or not he himself was born into slavery, he observed at close hand its injustices. After making his way north to New England and at some point traveling in Europe, probably in service, he married in 1805 the daughter of a celebrated black Revolutionary War veteran. Three of her brothers were kidnapped and sold into slavery, but the family, despite many legal efforts, failed to rescue them. After her death, he married the daughter of another black veteran, an abolitionist, and by her had twelve children. Subsequently, at her death, he married a third wife, then divorced her for desertion and adultery. Once again he remarried, this fourth time a much younger woman, to his family's consternation.

Exactly what happened to Roberts after Gore's death is unclear, but apparently he never again worked in domestic service. Between 1828 and 1860 his name appears in Boston city directories as a stevedore. According to his family's oral history, he was an importer, presumably at the Boston docks, a job description that seems to fit better than "stevedore." Certainly Roberts had the literacy and sophistication in management and commerce that work as an importer would require, and such employment would also explain his growing wealth. At the time of his death in 1860, he owned two houses on Beacon Hill (on what is now Napier Street) and an estate worth about $7500, a large amount for an African-American at that time.

Roberts had long involvement with the Masons (Christopher Gore was also a Mason), the African Baptist Church, and, increasingly after Gore's death, in civic affairs and the abolitionist movement. In 1831, living then in Boston, he opposed the movement to colonize blacks, that is, to move them back to Africa and Haiti. Later the same year, he became a delegate to the First Annual Convention of People of Color in Philadelphia. In 1848, his son Benjamin filed suit against the city of Boston to force the admission of his young daughter into the public school system. Although this test case for desegregation failed, Robert Roberts must have been fully a part of their effort. It also shows the moral climate and self respect he created for his family—another dimension of his influence far beyond that of his *House Servant's Directory*.

— Elizabeth Riely

The House Servant's Directory, 1827

Irma S. Rombauer

ALSO CALLED: Irma von Starkloff Rombauer

Irma Rombauer (left) and Marion Rombauer Becker in the late 1950's

ROMBAUER'S *THE JOY OF COOKING* BECAME ONE OF THE BEST-SELLING, BEST-LOVED cookbooks of the United States during her lifetime. Its position was later consolidated by the work of her daughter and sometime collaborator, Marion Rombauer Becker (1903–1976).

Rombauer, born in St. Louis on October 30, 1877, grew up in an affluent and progressive wing of the city's large German-American community. Aside from five years in Europe while her father was American consul in the north German port of Bremen (1889–1894), her entire life was spent in St. Louis. Her formal education was limited to the unsystematic mélange of public and private instruction common among privileged girls of her generation. At 20, on a visit to relatives in Indianapolis, she had a brief romance with the young Booth Tarkington, but eventually (October 14, 1899) married a lawyer from her own St. Louis German set, Edgar R. Rombauer. Their children were Roland (who died at eight months in March, 1901), Marion (born January 2, 1903) and Edgar, Jr. (August 15, 1907).

Known as a hostess of flair and sophistication, Rombauer nonetheless had no culinary training except for reportedly having attended one or more summer cookery courses at a Michigan Chautauqua Institute. Her real passion was civic and cultural activities. But when she was unexpectedly thrown on her own resources by her husband's suicide in early 1930, the plan she devised for supporting herself was to publish a cookbook at her own expense and sell it from her apartment. Marion, together with their friend Mary Whyte (later Hartrich), helped in production arrangements for the first *Joy of Cooking,* a modest recipe compilation published late in 1931 that drew on various modern and old-fashioned strains of American and German-American cooking.

Rombauer spent several years expanding *The Joy of Cooking* into a more ambitious manual, published by the Bobbs-Merrill Company of Indianapolis and New York in 1936. Marked by an unconventionally breezy, lighthearted tone and the first use of Rombauer's own unusual recipe format (with the necessary ingredients worked into the directions, not listed first), it placed a strong emphasis on shortcuts and "convenience" foods but also covered enough culinary basics and a wide enough spectrum of general American cooking to be competitive with such reigning bibles as *The Settlement Cook Book* (compiled by Mrs. Simon Kander and Mrs. Henry Schoenfeld) and **Fannie Farmer**'s *Boston Cooking-School Cook Book.*

Rombauer's next work, *Streamlined Cooking* (1939), was a brief collection of quickie recipes with heavy use of canned and other pre-processed ingredients. It was unsuccessful in its own right, but during World War II Rombauer combined most of its contents, the bulk of the 1936 book and a smattering of recipes meant to address wartime meat and sugar rationing into a new version of *Joy* (1943) that became a national best-seller.

In 1946 Rombauer published *A Cookbook for Girls and Boys,* one of the more successful American children's cookbooks, as well as another *Joy* edition that was essentially the 1943 version minus the war-emergency recipes. She then embarked on a further-reaching revision on which she eventually asked her daughter to collaborate. Extensively revamped to include new technical developments (e.g. blenders and home freezers), emphasize nutritional priorities like conserving vitamins through careful handling of food, and encompass what was then a large international range of tastes, it was published in 1951 and reaffirmed *Joy*'s standing as the most popular kitchen bible of the day.

Rombauer died on October 4, 1962, having been incapacitated by successive strokes since the late 1950's. Unlike her best-known contemporaries among American cookbook writers, she had never really considered herself a culinary professional. She did not attempt to write as anything but one amateur Midwestern cook encouraging other people in the kitchen by virtue of vivacious personality and common sense rather than infallible expertise. This informal stance enabled her to address many competing levels of American taste at once without glaring inconsistency, cheerfully combining different elements—can-opener creations, sweet gelatin salads, old-fashioned German favorites and a certain amount of solid basic instruction—in one triumphantly miscellaneous book.

Becker, who assumed the work of revision after about 1956, shied away from publicity and never became as well known as her mother. She shared Rombauer's Midwestern German-American background and such interests as gardening and liberal political causes and would, like Rombauer, see her status as an amateur cook, able to enter into other amateur cooks' difficulties, as an asset and not a liability. Educated at the Mary Institute (St. Louis) and Vassar College (class of 1925), she had variously worked in St. Louis as a department-store gofer, *Women's Wear Daily* local stringer and art-history teacher when she married a young architect, John William Becker (June 18, 1932), and moved to Cincinnati. They had two sons, Mark (born January 16, 1937) and Ethan (August 6, 1945).

Becker was working as director of the Cincinnati Modern Art Society when in 1948 Rombauer asked her to participate in the next revision of *Joy*. From the start she brought her own convictions to bear on the work, together with a taste for painstaking instruction that her mother did not possess. She persuaded Rombauer to delete many recipes based on canned or "convenience" ingredients and to increase the coverage of from-scratch basics like fish stock or sourdough rye bread, while admitting ingredients and approaches usually associated with the health-food movement.

With the aid of her husband (her unofficial editor and collaborator), Becker produced two massive revisions. Because of a crisis in author-publisher relations, which had been strife-ridden since 1936, the first of these appeared in 1962 in an unauthorized form filled with errors; a corrected version was issued in 1963 and achieved impressive sales. Becker next wrote *Little Acorn* (1966), a short informal history of *The Joy of Cooking*. Her lifelong interest in natural history, gardening and environmental issues culminated in *Wild Wealth* (1971), a lavishly illustrated work on wild plants focusing on the upper Ohio Valley and done in collaboration with Paul Bigelow Sears, Frances Jones Poetker, and the artist Janice Rebert Forberg. Despite advancing illness and the death of her husband in 1974, she managed to complete a second highly successful *Joy* revision which was published in 1975. Becker died on December 28, 1976, after a long battle with cancer.

Her accomplishment had been to successfully graft onto *The Joy of Cooking* many purposes quite different from Rombauer's priorities of the 1930's and 40's, while retaining to a surprising degree the distinctive personal charm of the original work. The period when her editions sold most briskly coincided with the first decades of the highly publicized "gourmet revolution," when the amount of knowledgeable writing about food (as distinct from recipe-formulas) was much smaller than the hunger for it. Luckily understanding the growing demand for information, Becker turned *Joy* into something prized by American cooks of all persuasions—including many influential food professionals—as the most encyclopedic American culinary reference work of the late twentieth century, an unparalleled source of knowledge about all sorts of exotica like mangosteen or bear meat as well as about simple kitchen basics. The 1963 and 1975 editions also had a strong across-the-board appeal to cooks in quest of both American and cosmopolitan recipes rather than erudition, and spoke to countercultural types who distrusted the hold of agribusiness and industry on the nation's kitchens.

After Becker's death, her son Ethan began work on a new revision of *Joy*, much impeded by the decline of Bobbs-Merrill and, after its demise in 1985, by corporate games of musical chairs with what remained of it. In 1997, Scribner, a Simon & Schuster subsidiary, issued a revised version overseen by a New York editor, Maria Guarnaschelli, containing a drastically updated selection of recipes by several dozen professional contributors, with very little remaining from earlier editions. In 1998 the same company issued a reprint of the original 1931 *Joy of Cooking*. Becker's last edition remains in print as a paperback, and copies of older editions are eagerly sought by many who still cherish the memory of "Irma and Marion."

— ANNE MENDELSON

The Joy of Cooking, 1931 (Rombauer)
The Joy of Cooking, 1936 (Rombauer)
Streamlined Cooking, 1939 (Rombauer)
The Joy of Cooking, 1943 (Rombauer)
A Cookbook for Girls and Boys, 1946 (Rombauer)
The Joy of Cooking, 1946 (Rombauer)
The Joy of Cooking, 1962 (Rombauer and Becker, unauthorized)
The Joy of Cooking, 1963 (Rombauer and Becker)
Little Acorn, 1966 (Becker)
Wild Wealth, 1971 (Becker)

Sarah Tyson Rorer

SARAH TYSON HESTON RORER, COOKBOOK AUTHOR AND DOMESTIC SCIENTIST, was born in Richboro, Pennsylvania on October 18, 1849, and as a very young child moved with her family to the vicinity of Buffalo, New York. Educated conventionally at East Aurora Academy, where she graduated in 1869, Sarah moved back to Pennsylvania, this time to Philadelphia. There she married William Rorer, with whom she had three children. Only two, both sons, lived to adulthood. Much of Rorer's life was dogged by her own ill health or that of a family member and by financially straitened circumstances. Her father, who had served as druggist of a hospital unit in the Civil War, returned home in poor health. Her elder son was prone to illness, and she lost her only daughter when the child was two. She herself suffered digestive problems, which she recalled in an article for *Ladies' Home Journal* in 1905. The Rorers spent some of their marriage living in boarding houses or with relatives and separated in the late 1890's.

Uninterested, by her own admission, in cooking or housekeeping, she was nonetheless recruited by friends in 1879 to join the New Century Club in Philadelphia, which had founded a cooking school. This era saw the birth of domestic science as a profession and the establishment of cooking schools in many large American cities. Rorer became director of the New Century Club's school within a year and in 1883 left that post to start her own school, the Philadelphia Cooking School. Students included homemakers, cooks, younger women, and eventually teachers of domestic arts as well.

Rorer apparently educated herself in chemistry and medicine, relying on the resources of the medical school in Philadelphia's University of Pennsylvania and the Women's Medical College. This enabled her to teach hygiene and nutrition, and during the 1890's she increasingly promoted scientific cooking at a time when nutritional science was in its infancy. She and other diet reformers of the era focused, early in their careers, on digestibility, measured by how long it took the human digestive system to process a particular food. Her early menus and recommendations were much colored by the question of digestibility, and she promoted rice, for example, on the grounds that rice was quickly digested, but discouraged eating pork because it took up to five hours to digest.

Rorer was a prolific writer, beginning with a small recipe book, used at her school, which eventually became her *Philadelphia Cook Book: A Manual of Home Economies* in 1886, variations of which were in print for many years, and which gained the fame and affection in the Middle Atlantic states that **Fanny Farmer**'s *Boston Cooking School Cookbook* would achieve in New England. She was also the original publisher, with Finley Acker, a Philadelphia grocer, of *Table Talk*, which assured her reputation as a food writer. Around 1893, she sold *Table Talk* to found and edit *Household News,* which was ultimately incorporated into *Ladies' Home Journal,* where Rorer was the domestic arts editor. Rorer left *Ladies' Home Journal* in 1911 at age 62, but returned to writing in 1914 with *Good Housekeeping* magazine.

During her professional life she wrote nearly two dozen books, from the comprehensive *Philadelphia Cook Book* to smaller works covering everything from eggs to chafing dishes, vegetables to leftovers, and oysters to ice cream, as well as *Mrs. Rorer's Diet for the Sick: Dietetic Treatment of Diseases of the Body: What to Eat and What to Avoid in Each Case,* published around 1914. She has been recognized by the American Dietetic Association as a pioneer in the field, particularly for her 1893 "diet" kitchen. The Philadelphia Dietetic Association made her an honorary member and granted her a small pension in her declining years.

As dedicated as she was to diet reform and scientific cooking, Rorer's fame as a cookery writer and teacher meant she was recruited by the food industry to experiment with products and make recommendations both to industry and to the public. Consequently, her name—like the names of such others as **Marion Harland**, **Mary J. Lincoln**, Emma Paddock Telford, and Christine Terhune Herrick—came to be attached to various food products. She edited at least one edition of *Home Helps: A Pure Food Cook Book,* "published in the interests of Cottolene," a commercial lard substitute made of cottonseed oil and beef tallow by **N. K. Fairbank**. A 1912 booklet published by Jell-O included her Queen Mab Frozen Pudding recipe from *Ladies' Home Journal,* and when Corning first introduced glass ovenware, the firm sent Rorer samples of the cookware for her to test.

For Rorer and other reform-minded domestic scientists of the time, collaboration with the food industry was a great opportunity for public refinement and cookery education. Rorer traveled and lectured widely, often at public expositions set up by the food industry, which was anxious to counter widespread public fears of adulteration and leaned heavily on professionals like Rorer to shed a favorable light on their products.

Sarah Tyson Rorer lived to be 88, and despite her years of professional activity, died poor. While today some of her published work seems quaint, outdated, or even tainted by her commercial connections, Rorer and her peers in domestic science laid the foundations of much of modern cookery.

— SANDRA L. OLIVER

Philadelphia Cook Book: A Manual of Home Economies, 1886
Canning and Preserving, 1887
Home Candy Making, 1889
Hot Weather Dishes, c.1888
Colonial Recipes, 1894
How to Cook Vegetables, 1891
Fifteen New Ways for Oysters, c.1894
Dainties, 1894
Twenty Quick Soups, 1894
New Salads for Dinners, Luncheons, Suppers and Receptions, with a Group of Odd Salads and Some Ceylon Salads, 1897
Dainty Dishes for All the Year Round, 1898
Good Cooking, c.1898
Home Helps: A Practical and Useful Book of Recipes with Much Valuable Information on Cooking and Serving Breakfasts, Luncheons, Dinners, and Teas, 1898
Left Overs: How to Transform Them into Palatable and Wholesome Dishes, c.1898
Made Over Dishes: How to Transform the Materials Left over in the Preparation of the Daily Meals into Palatable and Wholesome Dishes, 1898

Some Dainty Ways for Serving Crackers, c.1898
Bread and Bread-making, c.1899
Mrs. Rorer's New Cook Book: A Manual of Housekeeping, c.1902
Mrs. Rorer's Philadelphia Cookbook, 1902
Dr. Price's Wheat Flake Cook Book, 1903
Mrs. Rorer's Vegetable Cookery and Meat Substitutes, 1909
How to Use a Chafing Dish, 1912
Many Ways of Cooking Eggs, 1912
Mrs. Rorer's Sandwiches, c.1912
Ice Creams, Water Ices, Frozen Puddings, Together with Refreshments for All Social Affairs, c.1913
Mrs. Rorer's Diet for the Sick: Dietetic Treatment of Diseases of the Body: What to Eat and What to Avoid in Each Case, c.1914
Mrs. Rorer's Key to Simple Cookery, 1917

Kitaōji Rosanjin

❦ 1883–1959 ❦

CONSIDERED ONE OF JAPAN'S GREATEST TWENTIETH-CENTURY ARTISTS, KITAŌJI Rosanjin was born on March 23, 1883 in the village of Kamigamo in northern Kyoto. He became known for his natural genius in the areas of seal carving, woodwork, lacquerware, calligraphy, metalwork, painting, pottery, and cuisine. "Total devotion to natural beauty" was a credo he lived by and incorporated into his works.

Rosanjin, which means, "foolish mountain man," was named Kitaōji Fusajirō at birth. Conceived out of wedlock, the infant was left in the care of a poor farming family and then passed on from one poverty-stricken family to the other. It wasn't until Rosanjin was 20 that he was reunited with his mother, which was apparently an acutely disappointing encounter. He never knew his real father, who committed suicide out of shame five months before his birth. No doubt, Rosanjin's loveless childhood colored his ability to form lasting relationships; he would marry and divorce five times and became so cantankerous in his later years that he alienated friends and family.

While matters of the heart may have eluded Rosanjin, creative expression did not. At the age of 13, he started carving in the woodblock-carving business of his foster father, Takezō Fukuda. Several years later, he began painting western-style signboards and studying calligraphy, for which he won several prizes, including first prize for a copy of the *Thousand Character Classic* in clerical script style (*reisho*) in the calligraphy division of the prestigious Nitten Art Exhibition.

At the age of 20, Rosanjin moved to Tokyo, where he began earning a living painting shop signs and teaching calligraphy under the name Ōtei Fukuda. His brush skills would serve him well throughout his life, particularly in his later years when painting designs on ceramics and lacquerware became his primary focus.

Rosanjin was inspired to take up pottery, due to a longstanding passion for fine food. At the age of ten, Rosanjin purchased some slices of wild boar that he later remarked, "awakened me to the joys of fine food." His culinary education continued throughout the years, particularly under the influence of Seibei Naiki, a wealthy Kyoto dry-goods magnate, art collector, and avid gourmet. Together, Rosanjin and Naiki visited inns around the Ishikawa Prefecture to enjoy dishes featuring ingredients from the nearby Hakusan mountains and Sea of Japan. It was Naiki who introduced Rosanjin to potter Seika Suda, who would eventually take Rosanjin as his pupil.

In 1916 at the age of 33, Rosanjin visited the Yama-no-o restaurant in Kanazawa, which specialized in *kaiseki*, the ceremonial multi-course meal that accompanies the formal Japanese tea ceremony. There, Rosanjin met chef-owner Takichi Ōta, who would have an enormous impact on the young artist's life. Through the various kaiseki meals that Rosanjin enjoyed at the inn, Rosanjin came to appreciate the importance of buying high quality seasonal ingredients, then serving them simply to bring out their natural essence. He also learned the aesthetics of Japanese food. As he wrote, "The appreciation of fine cuisine requires an eye for beauty. First, one must appreciate how the food is arranged in its serving dishes; the freshness and balance of colors; the dexterity with which the food has been cut; and the harmony of the various serving vessels." This last point was key. Ōta served the inn's kaiseki on beautiful wares, including ceramics and lacquerware he purchased from local artists. This would have a huge influence on Rosanjin, who decided to take up pottery to showcase his cooking. "If clothes make the person, dishes make the food," he was famous for saying.

Rosanjin began to combine his passion for food and pottery when he opened up the Taigadō antique shop in Tokyo and started serving meals to special clients. Soon thereafter, he established the Bishoku Club (Gourmets' Club) as an extension of the store. Not content with serving his food on ordinary wares, Rosanjin decided to design and decorate serving pieces for the Gourmets' Club at potter Seika Suda's kiln.

In 1925, at the age of 42, Rosanjin devoted himself to cooking when he presided over the infamous Hoshigaoka Restaurant in Tokyo—an elegant oasis for government and financial elite. Once again, frustrated with the restaurant's lack of suitable serving pieces, Rosanjin began making his own. He started with celadon wares, under the guidance of potter Tōzan Miyanaga at the potter's kiln in Kyoto, then moved onto various other styles, including blue-and-white, Kutani, and Shinsha. Rosanjin's efforts with clay enabled him to properly showcase his cuisine, which he fashioned after the kaiseki cooking he had come to revere.

For reasons that are unclear, Rosanjin was forced to leave the restaurant in 1936. To earn a living, he made ceramics at his kiln on the outskirts of Kamakura that he had erected ten years earlier. While he worked, he was said to rise at dawn and retire at sundown, calling himself Mukyo (dweller in the realm of dreams). For artistic inspiration, Rosanjin often turned to his personal art collection, which by the end of his life consisted of 10,000 works. In the same way that scholars turn to their library of books for research and guidance, Rosanjin turned to his pieces to study their glazes, form, and design.

Critics have said Rosanjin was more of a decorator than a potter, since he was said to direct his assistants to create vessels, which he would pinch and shape to suit his individual style. Arguably, this had been the common practice of potters in earlier eras, and Rosanjin still designed all his pieces, oversaw the production, then painted the designs.

As a testament to his prodigious talent, Rosanjin mastered numerous styles of pottery making, including Bizen-, Iga-, and Shigarki-style pieces, silver painted bowls, and jars decorated with brush writing in cobalt blue. He also improvised according to his taste, combining clays and glazes to create a unique style. By the end of his life, he had made approximately 200,000 pieces. He showed his works for the first time in the United States, when the Museum of Modern Art in New York held an exhibition of his work in 1954. His last ceramics exhibition was in Kochūkyo in 1958.

Those who knew Rosanjin often describe him as a man of contradictions. On the one hand, he had an extremely refined artistic sensibility. On the other, he was said to be arrogant, flamboyant, and boorish. His outspoken manner and unorthodox ways made him somewhat of a maverick in a culture that values conformity. It is said when he once visited Picasso, he presented the artist with a piece of his work encased in a beautiful wooden box. When Picasso began to admire the smoothness and craftsmanship of the container, Rosanjin was said to have barked, "Not the box, not the box, you simple child! What I made is inside the box!"

When the physical stress and financial toll of making pottery became too much, Rosanjin devoted himself to calligraphy. Living alone near the mountains and woodlands, he reveled in the beauty of nature that so inspired his work.

Although the outside world may laud Rosanjin for the art he left behind, the artist wanted recognition for his more ephemeral works—the edible masterpieces he created in the kitchen. As he wrote toward the end of his life, "I have engaged in and been interested in ceramics, painting, calligraphy, and the like, but they are mere garnishes to my epicurean endeavors."

Rosanjin died of hepatitis on December 21, 1959 at the age of 76. He left behind one daughter; both of his sons died during his lifetime.

— VICTORIA ABBOTT RICCARDI

Count Rumford

ALSO CALLED: Benjamin Thompson

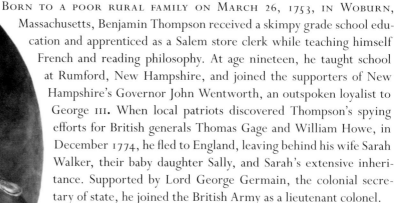

BORN TO A POOR RURAL FAMILY ON MARCH 26, 1753, IN WOBURN, Massachusetts, Benjamin Thompson received a skimpy grade school education and apprenticed as a Salem store clerk while teaching himself French and reading philosophy. At age nineteen, he taught school at Rumford, New Hampshire, and joined the supporters of New Hampshire's Governor John Wentworth, an outspoken loyalist to George III. When local patriots discovered Thompson's spying efforts for British generals Thomas Gage and William Howe, in December 1774, he fled to England, leaving behind his wife Sarah Walker, their baby daughter Sally, and Sarah's extensive inheritance. Supported by Lord George Germain, the colonial secretary of state, he joined the British Army as a lieutenant colonel.

In self-imposed exile, Thompson accepted the posts of Minister of War, Minister of the Interior, undersecretary of colonial affairs, and Royal Scientist to the British crown. For improving ordnance and inventing a mortar to gauge the explosive power of gunpowder, he was tapped by the Royal Society at age 27. After serving two years in the colonies as a military officer, his reputation suffered from charges that he sold the French secret information on the British navy, yet he weathered the uproar, received a knighthood, and settled among pro-French Bavarians to spy for the crown.

In Munich, now Sir Benjamin Thompson, he shifted allegiance to Karl Theodor, Elector of Bavaria. For his services he earned the title of Count of the Holy Roman Empire, and chose the name Rumford, from his old New Hampshire home.

Rumford was at the height of his creative genius during his sojourn in Bavaria. As minister of police and grand chamberlain, he reorganized the army and designed uniforms and insulated winter coats for the troops. He criticized the design of the masonry fireplace for excessive fuel use and heat loss up the chimney, and corrected or "Rumfordized" it, reducing the size and increasing the efficiency of its fire chamber and angling the sides to radiate more energy into the room. He created the internal ledge or smoke shelf, which kept downdrafts from chilling the room and showering the hearth and floor with cinders and live coals. Developers designed cast-iron fireplace inserts that emulated Rumford's design.

Rumford described his fireplace refinement in *Essays, Political, Economical and Philosophical* (1795). In addition, he supplied details of an experimental baking of rye bread at the military bakehouse. In an addendum dated May 1796, he reported on an experimental dinner cooked on a four-hundred-gallon iron boiler for 927 inmates of Calecannon, a Dublin workhouse. The menu consisted of boiled or mashed potatoes mixed with greens "cut fine with sharp shovels, and seasoned with butter, onions, salt, pepper, and ginger."

In 1784, when Munich's streets harbored two thousand homeless, he established a public-works program and organized workhouses to rid the area of beggars while forcing them to cut and sew uniforms. To lessen the cost of feeding them, he introduced the white potato in Europe and concocted *Rumfordsuppe*, a palatable, satisfying peasant soup made from white potatoes, pearl barley, peas, crumbs from donated *semmel* bread, vinegar, water, and salt. He invented a double boiler with tinplate steamer, a two-stage filtered coffee percolator, an insulating bottle, and a kitchen range that he installed in workhouses, orphanages, and hospitals in Europe and the British Isles.

With the intent of feeding people with less effort and waste, Rumford set out to revolutionize domestic chores. In his opinion, working at open flame cooked the cook more than the food. To improve preparation and storage of foodstuffs, he upgraded the pressure cooker, created a portable field kitchen, invented an oil lamp and a kitchen plaque for hanging pots, and devised the "Rumford roaster" for cooking meat, a forerunner of the hot-air convection oven. His kettles, set in a tight-fitting brick flue, were topped with a conical lid that completed the seal, containing heat below.

In addition to kitchen items, Rumford advanced kitchen science and architecture. After remodeling two hospital kitchens in Verona, he published a treatise, "On the Management of Fire and the Economy of Fuel" (1797), which redesigned the standard chimney into a boxy, insulated stove, which George Bodley patented in England in 1802. Rumford's main contribution to physics was a new theory of calorics, an explanation of heat flow based on his observations of a copper-bulbed thermometer and overheated cannon during combat. He devised a calorimeter to measure the release of heat.

At age 46, Rumford accepted an appointment as minister plenipotentiary to England and returned to London. During his tenure, Rumford worked at refining English fireplaces to improve coal-burning efficiency and created a hot plate heated on a firebox attached to a flue. He and the botanist Sir Joseph Banks organized a technical college, the Royal Institution, to train scientists.

His American wife having died, Rumford married Marie Anne Paulze Lavoisier, widow of the renowned French chemist Antoine Lavoisier, in 1805. While they were living in Paris, Rumford was inducted into the National Institute of France. The marriage was a disaster and lasted only a short time; when his wife divorced him, Rumford rewrote his will to support a Rumford professorship at Harvard and the Rumford Medals, given by the Royal Society and Boston's Academy of Arts and Science. (Later, Harvard professor Eben Horsford developed a formula for a chemical leavening which is still sold commercially under the name "Rumford Baking Powder.")

Rumford died suddenly of fever on August 21, 1814, in Auteuil, France. His extant writings include treatises on lamps, room heating, warm baths, experiments with gunpowder, color harmonics, fuel economy, illumination, double-glazed windows, flues and chimney fireplaces, silk, frigate building, soup kitchens, and reform measures to relieve society of the burden of the poor. A bronze statue on Maximilianstrasse in Munich represents him in field marshal's uniform and bears the inscription "Erected 1867 by Maximilian II, King of Bavaria"; a copy of the statue can be found in Woburn, Massachusetts.

— MARY ELLEN SNODGRASS

Essays, Political, Economical and Philosophical, 1795
Essays on Chimney Fire-Places: With Proposals for Improving them to Save Fuel, to Render Dwelling-Houses More Comfortable and Salubrious, and Effectually to Prevent Chimnies From Smoking, 1796
Proposals for Forming by Subscription in the Metropolis of the British Empire, a Public Institution for Diffusing the Knowledge and Facilitating the General Introduction of Useful Mechanical Inventions and Improvements, and for Teaching, by Courses of Philosophical Lectures and Experiments, the Application of Science to the Common Purposes of Life, 1799
Philosophical Papers: Being a Collection of Memoirs, Dissertations, and Experimental Investigations Relating to Various Branches of Natural Philosophy and Subjects Connected with Science and Useful Improvements, 1802
Mémoires sur la chaleur, 1804
Recherches sur la lumière qui se manifeste dans la combustion des substances inflammables, 1811
Of the Excellent Qualities of Coffee, and the Art of Making it in the Highest Perfection, 1812
Recherches sur la chaleur développée dans la combustion et dans la condensation des vapeurs, 1813
An Enquiry Concerning the Nature of Heat, and the Mode of its Communication, 1814

Rumi

✦ 1207–1273 ✦

ALSO CALLED: Mevlana | Maulana Jalaluddin Rumi | Muhammad Jalaluddin

THE GREAT SUFI TEACHER, POET AND PHILOSOPHER, THE FOUNDER of the Mevlevi brotherhood ("the whirling dervishes"), was born in the region of Balkh in today's Afghanistan, the son of the eminent religious scholar and jurist Baha'uddin Walad and, on his mother's side, the grandson of the amir of Balkh. When Jalaluddin was five or six years old, his father moved the family and a small community of followers to Samarkand; this was the first step in a series of emigrations that ended when the group settled in Karaman, in today's Turkey, where Baha'uddin continued to teach. At eighteen, Jalaluddin married Gevher Hatun, a fellow emigrant from Balkh; they had two sons, Sultan Walad (later his father's biographer) and Ala'uddin.

In 1228, the Seljuk sultan Ala'uddin Kaykobad invited Baha'uddin Walad to settle in Konya with his circle, where he taught and enjoyed great respect for his remaining years. On his death, one of his former students moved to Konya to continue Jalaluddin's spiritual training, which included studies in Aleppo and Damascus. When his studies were finally complete, his teacher told Jalaluddin, "Go and, while you live upon the earth, use your vision and your love to bring back to life those who walk about lifeless."

Rumi's doctrine advocates unlimited tolerance, positive reasoning, goodness, and charity. Like all mystics, Rumi's followers seek the personal experience of God; their doctrine teaches love as the path to this experience, and their *sema,* the whirling "dance," represents humans' mystical ascent toward the "Perfect."

Rumi wrote that "Sufis remain hungry in the kitchen [called] 'intellect,'" meaning that their food is emotional and spiritual. In his poetry and his teaching, Rumi made extensive use of food imagery and symbolism, describing his own spiritual development with the words, "I was raw, I cooked, I became done." One of his most famous writings is the story of the chickpeas, an extended metaphor for the necessity of enduring being "cooked" by God's wrath in order to move up the ladder of His creation. He also uses the fermentation of wine and the cutting and grinding of grain, the kneading of dough and the baking of bread as other examples of the suffering necessary for spiritual growth. Familiar dishes from Konya appear in his verse—he apparently disliked both eggplant and sheep's trotters—and the cooking pot is a frequent metaphor, as when he wrote that a pot might be blackened by the kitchen's heat and smoke, but if it were made of gold its value would be unaffected. He was personally fond of sweets, for which Konya was famous, and often used sweet dishes too in metaphors. His funeral was celebrated—as is each anniversary of his death—by preparation of *halva,* a traditional sweet. He often compared his intoxication with God with intoxication from wine, and wrote (in Annemarie Schimmel's translation),

> If wheat grows from my dust, and if it's baked
> As bread—intoxication will increase.
> The dough: intoxicated! and the baker!
> The oven too will sing ecstatic hymns!

In the organization of the Mevlevi dervish lodges, members' roles are defined in culinary terms, with the head of the lodge referred to as "Chef," his lieutenant as "Cauldron Keeper," and other officers as "Baker," "Fruit-Drink Maker," "Coffee Roaster," and so on. The kitchen is a sacred site, and is the first stop for those who want to join the order: The aspirant must sit there for three days, observing, before he decides to apply. If he is accepted by the Chef, his 1,001 days of training begin in the kitchen. The brotherhood's communal meal, silent and sacramental, is eaten from a single pot; it begins and ends with prayer and a taste of salt.

From Rumi's works, and from the detailed rules of the Mevlevi order that were codified after his death, much information can be drawn about the cuisine, the foodways, and the utensils of thirteenth-century Anatolia—including three recipes. When he describes the druggist who, though he holds much greater volumes of it in store, sells precious sugar in very small quantities, wrapped in paper, according to his customers' needs, Rumi is drawing a parallel with God's great stores of sweet treasure—but food historians catch a glimpse of life as it was lived more than 800 years ago.

— NEVIN HALICI

Carl Friedrich von Rumohr

ALSO CALLED: Baron von Rumohr

THE POLYMATH BARON CARL FRIEDRICH LUDWIG FELIX VON RUMOHR IS BEST known as a generous patron of the arts and as the art historian whose innovative *Italienische Forschungen* (*Italian Studies*, 1827–1831) attempted to bring objectivity and consistency to the analysis of painting. Like his French contemporary **Brillat-Savarin**, author of *La Physiologie du goût* (*The Physiology of Taste*, 1825), Rumohr published a single, influential treatise on cooking and eating, entitled *Geist der Kochkunst* (*Spirit of the Art of Cooking*, 1822). In the effort to promote a healthful, specifically German cuisine, Rumohr recommended moderation, simplicity, and traditional though not rule-bound preparation of fresh, local ingredients.

Born in Reinhardsgrimma, near Dresden, Saxony, Rumohr in fact spent most of his childhood close to the Baltic coast, on land held for generations by his wealthy, aristocratic family. Rumohr's father Henning von Rumohr served as a local government official in the duchy of Holstein. Both he and his second wife, Wilhelmine Caroline von Fersen, Rumohr's mother, were thought attractive, pleasantly outgoing, and sociable. Their son, on the contrary, would later be described by his contemporaries as mercurial, overbearing, stubborn, and difficult. Rumohr admitted that his girth and appetites were positively Falstaffian.

When his father died in 1803, Rumohr inherited an estate at Rothenhausen, near Lübeck, and began receiving the large income that made him financially independent. These happy circumstances left him entirely free to travel and pursue his varied interests. At the University of Göttingen he studied languages and history and took drawing lessons from Domenico Fiorillo, who also taught art history and oversaw the German translation of Vasari's *Lives of the Painters*. Several voyages through Bavaria culminated in lengthy stays in important Italian cities (1805–1806, 1816–1821, 1828–1829, 1837, and 1840–1841). These travels shaped Rumohr's thought in art history, literature, and agronomy as well as gastronomy. In the course of his travels Rumohr cultivated an intimate though platonic friendship with Bettina von Arnim, and in Munich he met Ludwig of Bavaria. The von Humboldt brothers received Rumohr at their house in Rome while Wilhelm was posted there as the Prussian ambassador. Rumohr traveled extensively with the writer Ludwig Tieck and the artists Johannes and Franz Riepenhausen, who influenced him to begin collecting drawings and engravings.

Born Protestant, Rumohr converted to Catholicism, possibly in order to facilitate his studies of Italian art. In Rome he frequented both neoclassical and Nazarene artists, although he did not approve of the sentimentality to which the latter were prone. Among his contemporaries he admired the painting of Joseph Anton Koch and Johannes Christian Reinhart, who developed a new, heroic style for landscape. Rumohr held that "one cannot enjoy a work of art without having clarified the circumstances accompanying and conditioning its creation." He also paid close attention to the technical and formal aspects of a work of art. For these precepts, with their regard for historical context as well as technique, he is considered the initiator of a "scientific" mode of art appreciation. Commissioned by Friedrich Wilhelm IV of Prussia, Rumohr bought the paintings and conceived the installation for the great Berlin Museum.

Rumohr extended to food the same practical brand of connoisseurship that characterized his art studies. *Geist der Kochkunst* is as much a cookbook as it is a learned treatise on food. Chapters on "Meat stock in general" and "Vegetables which [...] affect flavor" give methods of preparing ingredients or components of dishes, as well as tips for improving the final presentation and mix of flavors. Rumohr connects his dishes to places and local traditions, and his book as a whole to an "ethical, philanthropic, and patriotic" impulse. *Geist* touts a uniquely German cuisine that Rumohr describes as nourishing and healthful, conducive to the development of happy, prosperous families. The recommended German foods thus differ from the relatively simplistic cooking he describes as prevalent in the recently united American states. Nor do they resemble the "overly sophisticated" preparations he states are typical of French cuisine, which he implies are a prodigal, decadent extension of older Italian principles. As some of his contemporaries continued to search for a particularly German mode of expression in art and literature, Rumohr sought common principles and distinctive features in local German cuisines so he could unite them in a newly defined art of the table. Reflecting aspects of contemporary aesthetic theories, Rumohr's cuisine combines a classical respect for simplicity and fundamental forms with a romantic heterogeneity.

Rumohr had published *Geist* under the name of his personal cook Joseph König, only admitting authorship ten years later in the second edition of 1832. In the preface to that edition, Rumohr explains that he wanted to assist his cook, who was raising a family, by giving him the book's proceeds. It is telling that he republished *Geist* under his own name shortly after finishing another work which reflected his awareness of his responsibilities as a landowner. In *Die Besitzlosigkeit der Kolonen in Toscana* (*The Lack of Property of the People in Tuscany*, 1830), Rumohr argues that industrialization followed directly upon the neglect of traditional agricultural practices. In *Geist*, Rumohr describes optimal ways of using the best local ingredients. It is clear that Rumohr views the artisanal practice of cooking and the aesthetics of eating as part of a complex system including agriculture and economics, which in turn contribute to or reflect political ideology.

After *Geist* he did not return to the topic of food. His writings are remarkable for their scope, though all manifest the attention to history that characterizes his studies of art. Under the title *Italienische Novellen* (*Italian Tales*, 1823) he published translations of *trecento* novellas before writing his own historical tales set in Italy (1833–1835). The novel *Deutsche Denkwürdigkeiten* (*Reminiscences of Germany*, 1832) takes place in the mid-eighteenth century and depicts the travels of a diplomat throughout Germany and France. The milieu reflects Rumohr's urbane background, although his manners were sometimes far from diplomatic and, indeed, he never visited France. In the same year he published the travel book *Drey Reisen nach Italien* (*Three Journeys to Italy*), whose title recalls Goethe's *Italienische Reise (Italian Journey,* 1816–1817). In the etiquette manual *Die Schule der Höflichkeit (The School for Manners,* 1834) Rumohr advised beggars, burghers, and barons alike how to behave in accordance with their station in life. He even tried his hand at epic poetry with *Der Hunde Fuchsenstreit (The Quarrel of Dog and Fox,* 1835).

Rumohr did not marry, but lived with his sister Friederike von Rumohr at the Rothenhausen estate. Aggravated by declining health, he grew ever more temperamental as he aged. Following a falling out with Friederike in 1842, he broke up their household and moved by himself into a house in Lübeck proper. The following year, overcome with the swelling symptomatic of dropsy, he was obliged to cut short a visit to Friedrich Wilhelm IV in Berlin. He traveled toward Bavaria and Bohemia with the aim of taking a cure at the mineral spas, but only got as far as Dresden before his doctor called a halt to the journey. Upon Rumohr's death on July 25, 1843, his friend King Christian VIII of Denmark had a marble stone erected at his grave in Dresden.

— JULIA ABRAMSON

Geist der Kochkunst (Spirit of the Art of Cooking), 1822
Italienische Novellen (Italian TalesO, 1823
Italienische Forschungen (Italian Studies), 1827–1831
Deutsche Denkwürdigkeiten (Reminiscences of Germany), 1832
Drey Reisen nach Italien (Three Journeys to Italy), 1832
Die Schule der Höflichkeit (The School for Manners), 1834
Der Hunde Fuchsenstreit (The Quarrel of Dog and Fox), 1835

Marx Rumpolt

SIXTEENTH CENTURY

MARX RUMPOLT CAN BE REGARDED AS THE FOUNDER OF GERMAN ELITE gastronomy, and his *Ein New Kochbuch (A New Cookery Book),* published in 1581 by Sigmundt Feyerabendt, as the precursor of works by modern-day star chefs. The many vignettes and woodcuts that illustrate the book are by Jost Amman and other artists highly regarded in their time—the sixteenth-century equivalent of full-color, glossy printing. In spite of the high selling price that such production values presumably entailed, Rumpolt's book was reprinted at least four times, in 1582, 1586, 1587, and 1604. If he were alive today he would probably relish making television appearances: He wrote, *"Bin auch dessen erbötig, wenn sich einer nicht genugsam, seinem verstandt nach, darauß richten kann, der verfüge sich zu mir, will ich es alsdenn ihm nach der läng erklären, unnd mit eygener Handt solche Speiß zu machen, zeigen unnd lehren."* ("Should someone be unable, according to his understanding, to follow these instructions adequately, let him come to me, and I will explain it to him in detail, and show and teach him with my own hand how to make a certain dish.")

Rumpolt's nearly 500-page work is not the oldest German cookery book, but it is the first which is more than a mere collection of recipes. Instead, it is a guide for professional cooks written by a professional cook. Instructions on staging banquets for members of different social classes, on the correct seating order and behavior of servants, on shopping for provisions, and similar tasks precede approximately 2,000 systematically organized recipes, while the appendix includes detailed instructions on winemaking. *"Ohne allen zweiffel aber ist unter den gedachten Künsten nit die geringste Kochen oder Küchenmeisterey,"* he writes. *"Denn dieses können weder hohes noch nidriges Standts, weder Reiche noch Arme, one nachtheil irer Gesundtheit entrahten."* ("But without any doubt, cooking or kitchen mastery is not the least of the arts. For neither highborn nor low, rich nor poor can dispense with it without disadvantage to their health.")

With its emphasis on the relationship between cookery and medicine, Rumpolt's work is still very much in the spirit of the Middle Ages. However, the inclusion of a recipe for a potato dish, almost certainly the first in German culinary literature, marks him as a member of the avant-garde. That he wrote down and printed professional recipes makes him a daring reformer, as well. *"Weil aber, wie gesagt, sonst niemandt diese mühe und sorge, andere in kochen Schrifftlichen zu unterrichten, auff sich nemmen hat wöllen, unnd man es doch nicht, one grossen nachtheil, der Jugendt entrahten kann, hab ich endtlich wolgedachter Herrn bitt und begeren raum und statt geben."* ("But because, as stated, no one else was willing to take on the effort and trouble of teaching others cooking in written form, and [yet] one cannot deprive young people of it without great disadvantage, I finally acceded and surrendered to the request and desire of thoughtful gentlemen.") He was almost certainly the first to break the rules of the guild of chefs, which protected its knowledge by passing it on only by word of mouth and practical training in professional kitchens.

Rumpolt's exceptional position in his profession makes it very frustrating to realize just how little is known about his life. The sole certain date is that of the first appearance of *Ein New Kochbuch*. In its introduction, the personal chef of the elector of Mainz names Aschaffenburg, in the diocese of Mainz, as Rumpolt's place of residence at the time of writing. Rumpolt's employer must have been Daniel Brendel von Homburg, archbishop of Mainz and archchancellor of the empire. Rumpolt himself writes that he is Hungarian by birth and that his forefathers were driven out of "Little Wallachia" (today part of western Romania) *"vom grausam Wütrich unnd Erbfeindt Christliches Namens, der Türck"* ("by the cruel brute and he-

This detailed kitchen scene, from the title page of Rumpolt's Ein New Kochbuch, *was popular with cookbook publishers. A modified version, featuring two female cooks, illustrated the title page of* Ein köstlich new Kochbuch von allerhand Speisen *(1597) by* **Anna Weckerin**.

reditary enemy of Christianity, namely the Turk"). The lives of his relatives were threatened, forcing him to travel extensively: *"von Jugend auff unter frembden müssen erhalten, darauff geflissen und bedacht seyn, wie ich heut oder morgen meinen unterhalt und außkommen haben möchte"* ("from my youth forced to live among strangers, to be intent and aware, how I might earn my maintenance and livelihood"). He had devoted himself to cookery *"mit grosser mühe und arbeit...nun viel Jar lang"* ("with great effort and work...for many years now)", which suggests that, by the time his book appeared in 1581, he was no longer a young man. There are references in his recipes which clearly suggest that he had been, at some time, personal chef to the elector of Saxony and possibly also to the German emperor, and he states that he had been *"an vieler Herrn Höfen...und etwas in Italien, Niderlanden, Reussen, Preussen, Polen, Ungern, Böhem, Osterreich und Teutschlandt gesehen und erfahren"* ("at many lords' courts, and seen and experienced a bit in Italy, the Netherlands, Russia, Prussia, Poland, Hungary, Bohemia, Austria, and Germany").

This makes him a cosmopolitan and a self-made man in a period when both these things were exceptional. Furthermore, he insists that he has tested everything that he has written down, thereby distancing himself from contemporary cookery books in which recipes were merely copied from earlier works: *"Denn mich betreffendt, kann ich mit gutem Gewissen bezeugen, daß ich zum aller trewlichsten diß, so ich gefasset und gelerhnet, andern darzuthun, und auffs förderlichste mitzutheilen, mich unterstanden. Und hab diß, so ich allhie beschrieben, nicht auß andern Büchern entlehnet und entfrembdet, sondern mit eygener Handt, an der Herrn Höfen, so ich gedienet, zugerichtet und gemachet."* ("As for me, I can testify in good conscience that I have most faithfully presented to others and communicated in the most useful way that which I have understood and learned. And have not borrowed and taken from other books what I have described here, but have made and prepared it all with my own hand at those lords' courts where I served.")

Martin Luther's revolutionary Protestantism and the Catholic counter-reformation deeply divided Europe in the second half of the sixteenth century. On which side of this conflict did Rumpolt stand? Mainz was staunchly Catholic, and Rumpolt's employer was a vigorous supporter of the counter-reformation. On the other hand, Rumpolt's work was published in Frankfurt, one of the centers of the Protestant reformation. Four years after publishing his first edition of Luther's German Bible in 1560, Sigmundt Feyerabendt published an edition with woodcuts by Jost Amman that espoused a strongly anti-Catholic position. Does Rumpolt's choice of this publisher suggest that he was a secret Protestant? Are his frequently repeated instructions about an employer's duties, and his admonitions always to treat the servants of visitors politely and with respect, part of a tacit campaign to propagate Protestant values? It is certainly striking that, in the typically Baroque long-winded title of his book, he dedicates it to *"allen Menschen hohes und nidriges Standts"* (all people of high and low rank"). And he emphasizes in the introduction how well aware he is that there are *"der Armen allezeit mehr als der grossen Herrn"* ("always more of the poor than of great lords") and that he wishes that *"beydes den Armen und Reichen mit dieser meiner Arbeit möge nützlich unnd dienlich seyn"* ("with this my work to be useful and helpful to both poor and rich"). Is there some parallel between Rumpolt's break with the exclusionary traditions of the guild of cooks and Luther's break with the primacy of the Pope?

Against these tempting speculations must be set the fact that Feyerabendt was a very successful publisher of "bestsellers" and that his partnership with Rumpolt may have been based purely on business considerations. It is certainly interesting that Rumpolt tried to protect his work against unauthorized republication for ten years by obtaining a Holy Roman Privilege, and that, in spite of this, Feyerabendt himself published a virtual copy of Rumpolt's work, called *Koch- und Kellermeystery (Cooking and Cellarmastery)* and attributed to a certain Master N. Sebastian, in the same year as Rumpolt's original. It is hard to avoid the conclusion that this abridged version of Rumpolt's work (whose chapter on winemaking is nonetheless reprinted almost word for word) was published with Rumpolt's knowledge and approval. It too contains woodcuts by Amman and displays the same title woodcut; perhaps this was a cheaper edition for the lower classes after the expensive "coffee-table" edition skimmed the cream from the market.

Until today, posterity has barely acknowledged Rumpolt's achievement. In contrast to Sigmundt Feyerabendt, there is no entry under Rumpolt's name in the relevant reference works, nor is his *Ein New Kochbuch* listed amongst Feyerabendt's publications.

— URSULA HEINZELMANN

Ein New Kochbuch (A New Cookery Book), 1581. Reprinted 1582, 1586, 1587, 1604

Linda D. Russo

1949–1999

LINDA RUSSO WAS A POPULAR NEW YORK PUBLIC RELATIONS PERSONALITY WHO represented the International Olive Oil Council. She is remembered for her spirit and wit, and for organizing extraordinary expeditions for food professionals.

Linda D. Russo was born in Spanish Harlem, New York City, in April, 1949. Orphaned at a very early age, she was raised first by her Hungarian grandmother, who taught her to cook, and then, upon the grandmother's death, by an older sister. As a young adult, Russo worked for several years as administrative assistant at the New York City campus of Rockefeller University before serving as office manager for a New York printing company. Meanwhile, exercising savvy foresight for the 1970's, she took night courses in computer science at Hunter College. She married John Russo in the early 1980's.

Russo embarked upon her culinary career in 1980 when her neighbor and friend, food writer Grace Young, introduced her to Arlene Wanderman, president of Foodcom, Inc., a New York public relations agency that represented food-related businesses. Wanderman hired Russo as assistant and became a friend and mentor. Wanderman and her business partner, Howard Helmer, were well connected in the food business, and they launched Russo into that world. According to Helmer, "Linda did whatever needed to get done; she could accomplish anything and was so eager to learn it all." As a result of her hard work, inquisitiveness, and abiding interest in food, Russo eventually became a partner in Foodcom and, after Wanderman's death in 1996, she took over as president of the company.

For Foodcom, Russo worked primarily with the International Olive Oil Council (IOOC), a United Nations-chartered body that regulates the standards for and production of olive oil throughout most of the world. She energetically promoted the organization in the United States through presentations and writing, and she organized and led tours for culinary professionals in the countries and regions that produced olive oil.

These tours became the stuff of legend; Russo was well-known in the food community for the unusual and comprehensive experiences she organized under the auspices of IOOC, where, following her informed and enthusiastic lead, the participants were completely immersed in the culture and cuisines of the areas they visited. She populated the tour groups with food people—writers, scholars, chefs, and teachers—who would most capitalize on the opportunities, exchanging ideas and experiencing education upon exposure to food in the context of olive-producing cultures, and taking the knowledge back to their readers and students.

Andrea Clurfeld, a New Jersey food writer who participated in these culinary excursions, said, "Linda Russo had more moxie mixed with kindness than anyone. She had spirit, she had spit, and she had polish. On these trips, everyone lived as she did—running on adrenaline, getting little sleep, and eating 47 meals a day."

Linda Russo died very suddenly in New York in March 1999.

In the late 1990's, Russo had formed a committee in conjunction with Barbara Haber, Diane Harris Brown, and Andrea Clurfeld to promote the establishment of a grant for food writers to do culinary research, to be sponsored by the **James Beard** Foundation. After her death, the committee named the grant in her honor; it is jointly funded by the Beard Foundation and the International Association of Food Professionals (IACP).

— MM PACK

Sarah Rutledge

1782–1855

A TRUE CHARLESTON ARISTOCRAT, MISS RUTLEDGE WAS THE DAUGHTER OF the wealthy and prominent Edward Rutledge and Henrietta Middleton Rutledge. Her father and her maternal uncle, Arthur Middleton, were both signers of the Declaration of Independence, and Miss Rutledge could claim close kinship to Charleston's most prominent families, including the Pinckneys, Middletons, and Horrys. Known as "Sally" to her family and friends, she was very well educated and widely traveled, taking a tour of Europe with relatives in the early nineteenth century. She never married.

The Carolina Housewife, her only endeavor in food writing, was published anonymously in 1847, the title page giving its author only as "a Lady of Charleston." Though the book was written as a fund-raising project for charity, Miss Rutledge's anonymity was probably more a matter of social form than of modesty, since a lady's name in old Charleston did not properly appear in print more than three times: to announce her birth, her marriage, and her death. At any rate, it was widely known among her friends and relations that Miss Rutledge was the author of the work, but her name was not officially associated with it until shortly after her death in 1855.

The book enjoyed numerous editions, the last as late as 1960, and was widely influential throughout South Carolina and Georgia. Miss Rutledge's recipes even turn up as far away as New Orleans. She was very likely of some influence on **Annabella Hill** (*Mrs. Hill's New Cook Book*, 1867). Since 1979, the first edition has been reprinted in facsimile by the University of South Carolina Press.

Miss Rutledge's cousin, Anna Wells Rutledge, who wrote the foreword to this facsimile edition, liked to repeat the family lore that "Cousin Sally" was "a terrible cook," but women of her station were seldom taxed with cooking beyond the making of breads, cakes, and pastries, if that, and the importance of her work lies less in her knowledge of actual cooking practice than in her exceptional editorial eye for characteristically regional cookery. Miss Rutledge's collection of recipes, gleaned from her friends, family, and, significantly, from the manuscript household notebooks and receipt books of their ancestors, remained peculiarly regional. Many of them are quite old, too—probably pre-Revolutionary, but this has never been extensively documented.

In her own foreword, Miss Rutledge emphasizes that her intention was not to provide a general purpose cooking manual, but to record for posterity those dishes that were peculiar to Charleston and the surrounding Lowcountry (the flat, tidewater regions of lower South Carolina and Georgia). There are, for example, dozens of recipes for rice, in breads, savory pies, sweets, and pilaus (the Lowcountry version of pilaf), including one of the earliest printed records of such unique local dishes as "hoppin' John"—a pilau of peas and rice—and rice and wheat bread, once the staple daily bread of Charleston. From the end of the seventeenth century until the beginning of the twentieth, a major source of wealth for the region was the legendary Carolina Gold rice, once held to be the finest rice in the world.

For historians, an interesting and telling aspect of Miss Rutledge's work is contained in the many dishes that point directly back to their West African origins. Most contemporary historians and archeologists agree that the complex rice culture of the region was developed by slaves from the rice-growing nations of West Africa, and indeed the cultures and cuisines of those nations permeate the culture of the region. A study of the cuisines of these cultures and of Miss Rutledge's work shows many parallels, and demonstrates how deeply African slave cooks influenced the tables of the Lowcountry, particularly those of the wealthy planter class. "Hoppin' John," for example, clearly originates in West Africa, and many historians believe its name is an Anglicized corruption of an older West African name.

However, it is not merely rice that points the way, but numerous ingredients that are indigenous to West Africa, such as sesame seeds (locally known as "benne" seeds), okra, and eggplant. That last is not strictly native to Africa but was common in West Africa long before the slave trade. Miss Rutledge even called eggplant "Guinea Squash," a suggestive reference to a possible West African origin.

Lowcountry Carolina and Georgia cookery was unique among the myriad cuisines of America's regional melting pot, and Miss Rutledge's work, in chronicling it, provides a unique and vital link in the melting pot's history.

— DAMON LEE FOWLER

The Carolina Housewife, or House and Home, 1847

Bartolomeo Scappi

❦ ?−c. 1570 ❦

BARTOLOMEO SCAPPI WAS THE AUTHOR OF THE LONGEST AND MOST comprehensive cookbook of the sixteenth century, which may be regarded as the apogee of late Renaissance culinary culture. His origins and date of birth are unknown, though it is often assumed that he came from Lombardy or Emilia-Romagna because of the proliferation of recipes he includes from these regions. It is sometimes claimed that he was a native of Bologna, where a Scappi family is known to have existed at the time, although this may merely be guilt by association, this city having long been regarded as the culinary capital of Italy. Recently a stone was discovered in the church of San Giorgio in Runo di Dumuenza (near Lake Maggiore) referring to a perpetual mass to be said for the soul of one Bartolomeo Scappi. This may be concrete evidence of his Lombard origins.

From Opera dell' arte del cucinare, *1570*

It is known that he entered the service of various cardinals in the 1530's, and cooked a banquet in honor of Emperor Charles v in 1536. He remained in the papal court under several popes and eventually became near the end of his life the personal chef or "cuoco secreto" for Pope Pius v (Antonio Ghislieri). The appointment seems totally incongruous because this particular Pope (and saint), associated with the Catholic Reformation, was noted for his austerity and ascetic eating habits and would hardly have needed an expert chef. Either Scappi cooked primarily for other members of the Papal Curia or this position was merely honorific, recognizing his years of outstanding service by providing a sinecure.

Scappi's collected works, the *Opera Omnia*, were first published in Venice in 1570, around which time the author died. It is a massive encyclopedic volume, divided into six books, with over a thousand recipes systematically organized, delineating meat and non-meat recipes and even a section on cooking for the infirm. It is the first cookbook ever to offer extensive illustrations of cooking implements and the physical space where various duties were undertaken—bread and pasta making, cheese making, roasting, etc. The text also offers ample evidence that Scappi presided over an enormous staff divided into various departments of specialty. He even lists the equipment necessary to run such an operation.

Scappi's unique connoisseurship is also apparent in his detailed knowledge of where to find the best ingredients, how to choose them in their prime and he shows an unprecedented appreciation for the importance of using foods in season and at the peak of freshness. Beyond this, the technical precision of his instructions reveal that cookery had indeed been raised to a high art. Such procedures as how to roll hollow macaroni on a pointed iron, how to cook a zabaglione in a bain marie, and how to make exotic foods such as couscous from scratch are merely a few of the techniques meant to impress his readers and no doubt the fortunate prelates who enjoyed the fruits of his toil. There are even careful measurements in many recipes and illustrations showing how the mechanical devices and cooking tools were used. Scappi's approach to his topic can even be considered scientific, which invites comparison with the other monumental publications of this epoch by Vesalius and Copernicus.

The culinary style of the *Opera* betrays roots in medieval cookery, particularly in the heavy use of spices and sweet and sour sauces. But the sophistication of many recipes goes far beyond that of earlier eras. There is, for example, a proliferation of exotic foods like turkey, foreign dishes, and even recipes for porcupine, dormice, and bear. In fact Scappi does not neglect a single ingredient that would have been available, including every edible part of the animals he discusses, from the head and eyeballs to the testicles and tail. Obviously diners had not yet acquired a revulsion for such items. The recipes are also distinctively Italian and many dishes we commonly associate with that country today are already present: various forms of pasta such as tagliatelle, gnocchi, ravioli, numerous soups redolent with fresh greens, frittatas and pies, and fish cooked in every conceivable manner.

An entire book of the work is also devoted to planning meals in each month based on the food in season, which specifies the number of servers and carvers required and plates to be used. In general the structure of meals included a number of foods laid out on a credenza as diners arrived which might include biscuits, cold antipasti like sausages, proscuitto, olives, and cheese as well as salads. The first course from the kitchen would include about 10 different dishes each prepared in a different manner— both fish and meat when the church allowed, boiled, fried, roasted, in pies, soups, etc. The second course would be about the same size and with the same variety. Lastly came a second course on the credenza, items that need not be heated, which were mostly vegetables, fruits, dairy products, and confections. For grander occasions there might be four courses each from the kitchen and credenza. The larger meal of the day was generally dinner (pranzo), but supper (cena) in the late afternoon could be equally lavish, as could an evening's collation though it included only cold prepared dishes.

In sum, Scappi provides the model upon which subsequent celebrity chefs in a long line down to the present would be based. He was a mastermind whose experience, technique,and organizational skills not only graced the table of the wealthy and powerful, but whose knowledge could be passed on in the form of a popular cookbook.

— KEN ALBALA

Opera Omnia, 1570

Margarete Schütte-Lihotzky ❧ 1897–2000 ❧

One of twentieth-century Europe's socialist visionaries, Margarete Schütte-Lihotzky incorporated the rational-housekeeping revolution into boldly minimalist architectural design.

Born January 23, 1897 in Vienna, daughter of a municipal civil servant, Lihotzky avoided womanly stereotypes from early childhood. After leaving school she studied painting, then, in 1916, became the only female enrolled at the Vienna School of Arts and Crafts. "In 1916," she said, "no one—including me—could imagine commissioning a woman to build a house." Yet with the acquiescence of her teachers, architects Oskar Strnad and Heinrich Tessenow, she studied working-class tenements before competing in a contest for public housing. Her design earned the Max Mauthner Award, followed in 1920 by a prize for the design of allotment gardens.

With her elder sister Adele, Lihotzky furthered an altruistic project to feed the children of Holland's urban poor. In 1922, she returned to Vienna to collaborate with Adolf Loos, head of the Vienna Housing Authority, and worked in the settlement movement, which had grown out of returning Austrian soldiers' near-revolutionary response to Vienna's catastrophic post-war housing shortage. She designed expandable basic residence units, working in the construction office of the Friedensstadt Settlement, and helped build the Winarsky-Hof housing project, which replicated some of the spare functionality of Walter Gropius' L-shaped kitchen, an element of the Bauhaus style.

Lihotzky styled apartment interiors for author Hans Margulies and drew plans for Hermann Neubacher's apartments and single-family houses in the Werkbundsiedlung. She successfully out-planned competition by producing the smallest and least expensive experimental units for the working class. Her experience benefited architect Anton Brenner when he accepted a municipal commission in 1924 to erect minimalist apartments in the Sechshauserstrasse suitable for a family of four. He fitted them with prefabricated cabinetry, folding beds, and shower.

In 1926, at the height of German feminist influence on home economics, Lihotzky was called to Frankfurt am Main by architect Ernst May to contribute her expertise to a domestic movement known as *Neues Leben,* or New Life. The previous year, for his journal *Schlesisches Heim (Silesian Home)*, she had proposed a factory-assembled modular concrete kitchen, to be lowered by crane onto a homesite. May was so impressed by her bold, fresh minimalism that he offered her a post on the design team working on Germany's largest public-housing initiative. Her kitchen design thus had to be easily replicated, compact, and cheap.

Lihotzky's "Frankfurt kitchen" was a milestone in domestic design, and is now considered the forerunner of modern built-in kitchens. It was conceived as a separate room—not then the norm—connected to the living area by pocket doors, in keeping with her view that life "consists, on the one hand, of work and, on the other, of rest, company, and pleasure." She made formal time-and-motion studies of household operation, took into account the latest information on hygiene and scientific domestic management, sought input from housewives' organizations and from Georg Grumbach, manufacturer of unitized kitchen fittings and cabinetry, and calculated that 66 square feet of space, in a narrow room measuring six by eleven feet, would suffice. She equipped the rectangle with clean metal surfaces and fittings that were functional, easily maintained, and visually engaging.

Like railway dining cars and ship's galleys, her labor-saving, one-operator niche kitchen ran on gas and electricity and required no additional furniture for rapid meal preparation. She used oak for fitted flour canisters to keep away vermin and beech for continuous countertops to resist burns and cuts. Tile, glass, and metal created the sanitized ambience of a laboratory. A fireless cooker heated food; a refuse chute received kitchen waste and guided it into the garbage pail. In natural light from a window, the homemaker sat at the cutting board on a revolving stool on casters to perform a maximum of different tasks without standing up or walking. Below glass-fronted overhead cupboards, wet dishes dripped through a wooden plate holder onto a drainboard and sink, ending the need for hand drying. Tools hung on cup hooks; staple foodstuffs fit into eighteen labeled drawers or bins.

"The problem of rationalizing the housewife's work," she wrote, "is equally important for almost all classes of the population. Middle-class women, who often have to run the house entirely without help, as well as working-class women, who frequently also have outside jobs, are so overloaded that their stress cannot, in the long run, fail to have consequences for public health in general."

Lihotzky's design was the culmination of a current of thought that began with **Catharine Beecher** in the mid-nineteenth century and which viewed household work as a profession. As such, it could be rationalized and optimized just as industrial work could be. Christine McGaffey Frederick's articles in *The Ladies' Home Journal* and her resulting book, *The New Housekeeping* (1913), espoused standardization and scientific management of household tasks; the book was translated into German as *Die Rationelle Hausfrau (The Rational Housewife)* in 1923.

In 1927, after demonstration at Frankfurt's annual trade fair in an exhibition called "The New Home and Its Interior Design," May's Römerstadt project opened 10,000 well-proportioned apartments to Frankfurt residents. Lihotzky married architect Wilhelm Schütte in that year and the couple settled in one of the apartments, Schütte-Lihotzky demonstrating her project to visiting international teams of experts. Ernst May constructed 4,000 more of the apartments, which were setting a new standard throughout Europe. In 1928, the French labor minister Louis Loucheur, who modernized France, bought 200,000 prefabricated units for a housing project; Swedish designers drafted their own version of the Frankfurt kitchen; Belgian firms added standardized interchangeable cupboard units in their Cubex kitchens; and Dutch architect Pieter Zwart of the Bruynzeel company put Lihotzky's kitchens into mass production by 1936.

The Frankfurt kitchen was not entirely without critics. Lihotzky was accused of mechanizing housewives like cogs in a machine. The kitchen was not flexible enough. Designed for one person, it could not be used by two people simultaneously, and it was not childproof. Instead of helping to emancipate the housewife, it tended to isolate her. Partly in response to such criticism, Schütte-Lihotzky designed larger—and more expensive—kitchens that were nonetheless based on the same principles.

Despite the overwhelming success of the Frankfurt kitchen, Schütte-Lihotzky's coterie began to crumble in 1929. Accompanying Ernst May on his self-exile to the Soviet Union to build new Soviet industrial cities, she designed workers' homes, schools, and kindergartens there. In 1938, like some 150 other German-speaking anti-Nazi academics, she accepted Atatürk's offer of refuge in Turkey and, at Istanbul's Academy of Fine Arts, designed schools for rural Anatolia and pediatric clinics for France. In 1939, she joined the Austrian Communist Party and, feeling impelled to oppose the Nazis actively, traveled back to Vienna in December, 1940 and joined a communist resistance group. She was immediately arrested and sentenced to 15 years imprisonment.

Freed in 1945, Schütte-Lihotzky spent some months in treatment for the tuberculosis she contracted in prison, then spent 1946 in Bulgaria, where she established a department for children's facilities at the municipal construction office in Sofia. In 1947, her husband was able to leave Turkey to join her, and the couple returned to Vienna. There, her career stalled. She received few architectural commissions in the following years: two residential buildings, two kindergartens, and collaboration on the Globus publishing house building on Vienna's Höchstädtplatz. Public acceptance of the sleek, Germanic, functional kitchen had been replaced by a desire for the homey clutter of the family kitchen-dining room complex, a symbol of tradition. Schütte-Lihotzky lectured and consulted on projects in Bulgaria, China, Cuba, and East Germany, where her socialist politics were no disadvantage.

It was only in the 1980's that her role in architectural history began to receive official recognition. At age 83, she received the Architecture Award of the City of Vienna. In 1985, she won the Prechtl Medal from the Technical University of Vienna and published her memoirs, *Erinnerungen aus dem Widerstand, 1938–1945 (Memories From the Resistance, 1938–1945)*; in 1986, her resistance work was the subject of a television film, *Eine Minute Dunkel Macht uns Nicht Blind (One Minute of Darkness Does Not Make Us Blind)*; in 1989 she received an honorary doctorate from the Technical University of Graz and the IKEA Prize for her life's work; and 1992 brought her another honorary doctorate, this one from the Technical University of Munich, and the Gold Medal of Honor of Vienna. In 1988 she had been offered the Austrian Medal for Science and Art, but refused to accept it from the hands of Austrian President Kurt Waldheim, a former Nazi officer accused of complicity in war crimes; she accepted it in 1993 from Waldheim's succesor. Before her hundredth birthday, she was named to membership in the Austrian Fine Arts Society.

When Margarete Schütte-Lihotzky died, aged nearly 103, she had earned a place among the idealists of the century. Today, a small park in Vienna's Fifth District is named after her.

— MARY ELLEN SNODGRASS.

Sen no Rikyū

UNIVERSALLY HERALDED AS THE GREATEST JAPANESE TEA MASTER WHO EVER lived, Sen no Rikyū was born in 1522 in the commercial port city of Sakai. His father was a warehouse owner and fish wholesaler who catered primarily to the military class.

Rikyū's birth name was Tanaka Yoshirō, which he used throughout his youth. He began studying tea at an early age, perhaps influenced by his grandfather, Tanaka Sen'ami, who reportedly made tea for the shōgun Ashikaga Yoshimasa (1435–1490) when serving as the leader's *dōbūshū,* or social retainer. Rikyū first studied *chanoyu* (the way of tea, literally meaning, "tea's hot water") under Kitamuki Dōchin (1504–1562) in the formal *shoin* style suited to a large reception room. Later, Rikyū studied under Takeno Jōō (1502–1555) in the more modest thatched-teahouse style that Murata Shukō (or Jukō, 1422–1502) founded. Jōō and Shukō's practice of imbuing the tea ceremony with Zen Buddhism would have a tremendous influence on Rikyū, who would ultimately see the tea ceremony as a vehicle for reaching enlightenment.

Rikyū began studying Zen in his early twenties under Dairin Sotō, the ninetieth chief abbot at Daitokuji, a major temple and monastery in Kyoto. Soon thereafter, Rikyū took the name Sōeki for its Buddhist associations, along with the name Sen from his grandfather. Rikyū later studied Zen under Kokei Sōchin, also an abbot at Daitokuji.

In 1570, Rikyū met the country's provincial warlord Oda Nobunaga, who would influence the course of Rikyū's life. Nobunaga was an avid collector of tea utensils and partook in the ceremony both to polish his boorish public image and to gain access to the wealthy merchant class, who could supply the warlord with tea wares and help fund his military campaigns. Nobunaga must have been impressed with Rikyū, for soon after meeting the tea master, Nobunaga appointed Rikyū as one of his *sado,* or tea practitioners. Following Nobunaga's death in 1582, warrior Toyotomi Hideyoshi swiftly assumed power and added Rikyū to his own entourage.

For the next several years, Rikyū performed numerous tea ceremonies for Hideyoshi primarily in the formal shoin style. For Hideyoshi, the tea ritual was a useful form of social entertainment, as well as political medium in which to exert his influence and celebrate military victories. Like his predecessor Nobunaga, Hideyoshi often flaunted his power through his extensive collection of tea utensils, many of which he had seized from his captives or received as gifts.

Hideyoshi further manipulated the tea ceremony to serve his political aims when in 1585 he engaged Rikyū to help him prepare tea for the Emperor Ogimachi (1517–1593). To avoid having a commoner in the presence of the imperial leader, Ogimachi bestowed upon Rikyū the enlightened layman's title of *kojigo* for the occasion. Soon after, Rikyū was considered the premier sado of Japan.

Although Rikyū indulged Hideyoshi's preference for lavish tea ceremonies, the Zen monk favored the small-hut style called *wabicha,* which he ultimately refined. Based on the aesthetic ideal of *wabi,* which sees beauty in things that are natural, rustic, and spiritually rich, Rikyū's wabicha was a humble expression of the heart, instead of a showy display of wealth and power. In Rikyū's own words, "Chanoyu of the small room is above all a matter of practicing and realizing the way in accord with the Buddha's teaching. To delight in the splendor of a dwelling or the taste of a sumptuous meal belongs to a worldly life. There is enough shelter when the roof does not leak, and enough food when it keeps one from starving. This is the Buddha's teaching and the fundamental intent of chanoyu."

For Rikyū, the tea ceremony was ultimately a spiritual experience. Through the making and serving of whipped green tea he sought to promote a profound communion with nature that embodied harmony, respect, purity, and tranquility, the essence of Zen Buddhism. To achieve his ideal, Rikyū altered numerous aspects of the tea ceremony. He reduced the size of the teahouse to create a small space, often two tatami mats in size, to foster intimacy. He made the entrance to the tearoom so tiny, all guests, including the emperor, had to crawl inside, thus putting everyone on equal footing, mentally and physically. The garden leading to the teahouse he rendered smaller and more spare, thus reflecting the subtle beauty of nature. Along the path to the teahouse he placed a stone water basin for purification and lowered it so guests would have to crouch down and shift their perspective.

Rikyū also made many of his own tea utensils, preferring them free of ornamentation and often with slight imperfections. He also commissioned local artists to make tea bowls, serving dishes, and implements in basic shapes and natural subdued colors.

For the kaiseki, a ritualized multi-course meal served before a formal tea ceremony, Rikyū chose simple temple-style fare over the extravagant multi-tray feasts the aristocracy favored. Using local, fresh, seasonal ingredients, Rikyū's ideal kaiseki consisted of one soup and three side dishes. The food was prepared in a simple manner to allow the essence of the ingredients to shine forth, along with the spirit of the person who prepared it.

In 1587, Rikyū officiated at one of the most significant events in tea history, when Hideyoshi hosted a tea gathering at the Kitano Shrine in Kyoto for all sincere tea practitioners, almost 800 guests. Numerous tearooms were employed for the event, including a fancy gold one for Hideyoshi to show off his famous utensils and a simple grass hut for Rikyū, who used his rustic wares. This event was the first time both extreme forms of tea had come together to be appreciated.

For reasons that are unclear, Rikyū's relationship with Hideyoshi began to waver in 1590. Several theories have arisen, including that the tea master engaged in various political intrigues. At the height of Rikyū's tea career, he was reportedly transmitting secret messages for the leader, serving as one of his personal advisors, and even engaging in confidential negotiations.

Another potential cause of Rikyū's downfall involves a statue at Daitokuji temple. In honor of his father's death, Rikyū contributed funds to help rebuilt the temple's gatehouse. In a gesture of thanks, the temple built a life-size wooden statue of the tea master to stand in the room above the temple entrance. Hideyoshi was said to have been so angry about having to walk under the wooden image of Rikyū that he ordered the statue removed and decapitated. Additional theories suggest that Rikyū had demanded exorbitant prices for some of his tea utensils, or refused to allow his daughter to become Hideyoshi's mistress. Whatever the reason(s) for Rikyū's falling out with Hideyoshi, in 1591, the leader ordered Rikyū into house arrest in Sakai and then demanded he return to Kyoto to commit ritual suicide by his own sword.

Rikyū was survived by his second wife and their daughter. His three grandsons established three major tea schools in Kyoto: Omote Senke, Ura Senke, and Mushanokoji Senke. To this day, they promote and carry on the wabicha that Rikyū refined and hoped to leave as his legacy.

— Victoria Abbott Riccardi

Mary Li Sia ❈ 1899–1971 ❈

Born in 1899 in Honolulu, Hawaii, of Cantonese immigrant parents, Mary Li attended school in that territory and graduated from its university in 1922, majoring in home economics. The eldest of nine children, both of whose parents were obstetricians, she furthered her education at Yale University, taking postgraduate classes in music, and at Cornell University, continuing her studies in home economics. In 1923, at a Chinese student conference at Brown University, Mary met Richard H. P. Sia, a medical researcher from Peking. She accompanied his singing on the piano, and they became engaged a week later. They were married the following year, after he completed his work at the Rockefeller Institute in Manhattan. The Sias honeymooned in Hawaii, and then left for Peking, where they lived for the next fifteen years. Two years after getting there, they had their first child, Sylvia, the following year a son named Calvin, and two years later still, their third and last child, named Julia.

In Peking, Mary Li Sia was fascinated by the differences of local northern food from that of her Cantonese background. She began to familiarize herself with northern cuisine and also studied other Chinese cuisines. She invited international faculty members and their wives, most members of the International Women's Club, to local Chinese restaurants. She then went home and tried to make many of the dishes they had eaten there. Preparing the successful ones, she invited the same guests and others to come and try those dishes in her home.

These experiences were the basis of her first cookbook, *Chinese Chopsticks*. Published in 1935, it was probably the very first English-language Chinese cookbook published in China. A second, considerably expanded, edition was put out in 1938 by the Peking International Women's Club. Both of these books not only included many recipes, they also had local menu items priced per table.

While in Peking, Mrs. Sia was a member of Peking's Eastern Star and became a Worthy Matron of that order; she also played the piano and organ for her husband, who formed and directed a medical-school chorus. Together, the couple won a mixed-doubles championship at the summer resort Peitaho.

In 1939, Mary Li Sia returned to Honolulu when her husband accepted a visiting professorship at the university there. She began teaching Chinese cooking at the local YWCA and at a local high school's adult-education classes. She also demonstrated cooking at community festivals, took students on tours of Chinatown and its markets, and appeared on local television programs. She gave many talks about Chinese cuisine, and continued with her interests in music as the organist at her church as well. In later years, she was honored by the Chamber of Commerce as American of the Week, another time as Mother of the Year by the Honolulu United Chinese Societies, and yet another as a Woman of Achievement, an award of the Honolulu chapter of Theta Sigma Phi.

In 1956, the University of Hawaii published *Mary Sia's Chinese Cookbook*. Demand exceeded expectations and the university put out a second hardbound edition in 1957. That volume was reprinted in 1959 and in 1961. A third edition followed in 1964 which was reprinted in 1967 and in 1972. After Mrs. Sia died in 1971, the University Press of Hawaii reprinted the book in spiral-bound and paperback editions in 1975, 1977, and 1980.

Mary's son Calvin, a pediatrician, said that his mother once wrote that she "derived great satisfaction from transmitting to thousands of women and men, the background for practicing the delicate art of palate-pleasing in the Chinese way."

— JACQUELINE M. NEWMAN

Chinese Chopsticks, 1935
Mary Sia's Chinese Cookbook, 1956

Amelia Simmons

❧ ACTIVE 1796 ❧

AMELIA SIMMONS WAS THE AUTHOR OF *AMERICAN COOKERY* (1796), THOUGHT TO BE the earliest published cookbook actually written by an American. Previously, cookbooks published in the colonies had been straightforward re-editions of English works, with no deference to American readers. But Amelia Simmons changed all that. The bibliographer Eleanor Lowenstein dates the second edition to the same year as the first, citing an advertisement in the *Albany Gazette* of October 31, 1796. Lowenstein lists thirteen editions of *American Cookery*, in addition to pirated editions.

Considering her importance, we know very little about Amelia Simmons. The title page of the first edition introduces her as "An American Orphan," and she emphasizes this fact in the preface. In the second edition, Miss Simmons discusses the fate of "those females in this country, who by loss of their parents, or other unfortunate circumstances, are reduced to the necessity of going into families in the line of domestics." She explains that she wrote this second edition because "the call has been so great," and "hopes that this second edition, will appear, in a great measure, free from those egregious blunders, and inaccuracies, which attended the first: which were occasioned either by the ignorance, or evil intention of the transcriber for the press." Clearly, she was barely literate. I suggest that she was almost surely an indentured servant, which would go far to explain why no vital statistics for her have been found.

The fact that the first edition was published in Hartford, Connecticut, gave rise to speculation that she lived there. The second edition, however, was published in Albany, New York, and I suggest that a far more persuasive case can be made for her having been a resident of the Hudson River Valley rather than New England. The most notable elements supporting this hypothesis are what are regarded as the first appearances in published English of a number of words of Dutch origin, beginning with "slaw," specifically referring to cabbage salad—that is "coleslaw" or "cole slaw" (from Middle Dutch *cole,* meaning cabbage, and *sla,* meaning salad)—and "cookey" and "cookies" (from *koekje,* meaning cookie) rather than either of the corresponding English terms, "small cake" and "biscuit," which are still in use in England today. In time, those terms came to be quintessentially American, although much later perhaps in Southern cookery, and never to the same extent.

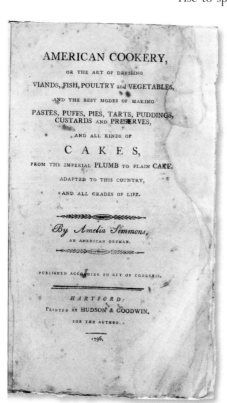

Title page of the first edition of American Cookery, *published in Hartford in 1796*

Most of the recipes in Miss Simmons' work are actually English; indeed, seven recipes, beginning with "to make a fine Sullabub from the Cow" are taken verbatim from *The Frugal Housewife* by Susannah Carter, which had been appearing in American editions since 1772. Even her famous "Election Cake"—the recipe for which did not appear until the Albany edition and so cannot be directly associated with Hartford, as it so often is—was, simply a "Great Cake" from historical English baking, recipes for which abound in sixteenth- and seventeenth-century English cookbooks and family manuscripts. Elsewhere, however, there was a distinctive use of American elements, such as serving "crambery-sauce" with roast turkey and particularly that of using "Indian meal" (cornmeal) in place of other meals, most typically oatmeal. This is nicely demonstrated by three recipes for "A Tasty Indian Pudding" following strictly traditional English method in making puddings of other meals. Likewise, while various hearth cakes using Indian meal had been made by the colonists from the beginning and are often referred to in literature, her three recipes for "Johnny Cake, or Hoe Cake" may be the earliest to actually see print. (The very word *johnny* comes from *jonniken,* a term from northern England meaning oaten bread.) She also gave recipes for gingerbread made light with pearlash (potassium carbonate), a precursor of baking soda in baking, a type which came to be the American style for gingerbread. Her work further demonstrates that the use of alkali as leavening in baking must already have been in long-standing use, and this is perhaps the most American element of all.

— KAREN HESS

American Cookery: or, the Art of Dressing Viands, Fish, Poultry and Vegetables, and the best modes of making Puff-Pastes, Pies, Tarts, Puddings, Custards and Preserves, and all kinds of Cakes, From the Imperial Plumb to plain Cake. Adapted to this Country and all grades of Life. By

Amelia Simmons, an American Orphan. Hartford, 1796. Also in facsimile, as The First America Cookbook, with an admirable essay by Mary Todd Wilson. New York: Oxford University Press, 1958. Reissued by Dover Publications, 1984

American Cookery... The Second Edition, Published according to Act of Congress. Albany: Printed by Charles R. & George Webster, At their Printing-Office and Bookstore, in the White-House, Corner of State and Pearl-Streets: For the Authoress, n.d.

André L. Simon

‡ 1877–1970 ‡

ANDRÉ LOUIS SIMON WAS BORN IN PARIS. HIS FIRST JOB WAS AS A trainee in a publishing office. As he was to write almost 50 years later, "printer's ink" was his first love. Hoping to improve his English-language skills, he traveled briefly to England, where he met his future wife, Edith Symons. Simon returned to France, where he served three years in the army: He spent three months training and the remainder of his time editing and writing a military journal. When he left the army, he moved to Reims to work for Pommery et Greno, the eminent Champagne producers. He stayed for two years, learning everything he could about the Champagne trade. He married Edith Symons in 1900 and moved to London, where he became the company's representative.

Simon's first book, *The History of the Champagne Trade in England*, was a collection of his articles on the history of Champagne that had been published in *Wine Trade Review*. It was sold to the trade and was not a commercial success. Simon went on to self-publish a three-volume work, *The History of the Wine Trade in England*. Although these books did not sell well either, they remained Simon's favorites of the dozens he wrote in his long career.

1933

When World War I erupted in August 1914, Simon joined the French army and served as a translator throughout most of the war. After the war, he returned to London, where he continued working with Pommery and resumed his writing. In 1919 the Wine Trade Club published two of his small pamphlets, *Food and Drink* and *Alcohol*. He expanded the former into a volume called *Wine and Spirits: The Connoisseur's Textbook;* it was his first book to be sold by a commercial publisher and it reached a wide audience. The following year he published *The Blood of the Grape: The Wine Trade Text Book*, a compilation of a series of lectures that he had given at the Wine Trade Club. In 1926 Simon completed *Bottlescrew Days*, which was, in effect, the fourth volume of his *History of the Wine Trade in England*.

Simon's first book to deal extensively with food was *The Art of Good Living*. In it, he defined gastronomy as "the intelligent choice and appreciation of whatever is best in food and drink...." The quality of the food and wine, in his view, was of the first importance. Expense, on the other hand, was not a consideration, although he did point out that the best food or wine was not necessarily the most expensive.

Throughout the 1920's and 1930's, Simon had been sponsoring lunches and dinners for those interested in wine and food. Many of these were held in his office and were paid for by Pommery. Beginning in the 1930's, he began keeping a record of what he ate and drank, taking pen in hand immediately after the meal to write an evaluation. His most memorable meals of the time were collected and published in *Tables of Content: Leaves from My Diary*, which included more than one hundred menus of splendid dinners and luncheons. In 1932, Simon was let go by Pommery, mainly due to the firm's financial problems related to the Depression. For a few months he served as the chairman of the Madeira Wine Association. He also edited Constable's Wine Series, to which he contributed three volume: *Madeira Wine, Cakes and Sauce*, *Champagne*, and *Port*.

The Madeira Wine Association folded nine months after its birth, but Simon had already begun setting up the organization to which he would devote the next 30 years of his life—The Wine and Food Society. It was launched in October 1933 as a two-man operation: Simon, as president, was responsible for arranging luncheons, dinners, and tastings, and edited the Society's magazine. His friend A. J. A. Symons (no relation to Simon's wife, Edith) served as the first secretary and was responsible for routine business; he also provided the premises and staff. To help establish the Society, Simon recruited a body of connoisseurs to form an advisory council and placed their names on the Society's letterhead. By January 1934, the Society had about 500 members. That spring the first issue of *Wine and Food* was published. The Society also began tours of continental wine districts, offered lectures on gastronomic topics, and conducted an annual conference. The first was held in October 1934, on the first anniversary of the organization's founding. The lavishness of the event gave the Society great visibility, and by the end of the year membership exceeded 1000. During the following years, the Wine and Food Society expanded into other countries. Its quarterly magazine, edited by Simon for almost 30 years, was an important publication, particularly in England, where it helped launch a gastronomic revolution.

During the late 1930's, Simon continued to write books, including *A Catechism Concerning Cheeses*. He set to work on his magnum opus, *A Concise Encyclopedia of Gastronomy*, which was published in sections. The first to appear was *Sauces* (1939); the *Fish* section was completed, but its publication was postponed due to the outbreak of World War II. The Society continued to sponsor lunches—the blackout made dinners unfeasible—for the first six months of the war. It then became dormant, but Simon continued to publish *Wine and Food*. The journal's size was reduced due to paper shortages, but it retained its quality, mainly because many of the articles were written by Simon, under his own name and pseudonyms.

The Society held its first dinner after the Normandy invasion in October 1944, and its membership revived after the war. Simon had continued writing sections of the *Concise Encyclopedia* during the war, and in 1952 the entire work was published by Collins. During the 1950's, Simon continued to publish books, including *Mushrooms Galore, A Wine Primer, The Gourmet's Week-end Book, How to Enjoy Wine in the Home, Wines and Liqueurs from A to Z*, and *English Fare and French Wine*.

To conduct the extensive research necessary for his writing, Simon became a bibliophile, amassing one of the world's largest private collections of books on wine and food. In 1953, he compiled a bibliography of works on food and wine, which was published as *Biblioteca Gastronomica: A Catalogue of Books and Documents on Gastronomy*. It remains one of the most important bibliographical sources on food and drink in Western Europe.

Simon continued editing *Wine and Food* until he retired in 1960. The Wine and Food Society changed its name to the International Wine & Food Society in 1968, and its quarterly magazine was folded into the British publication *House & Garden* in 1970.

— ANDREW F. SMITH

The History of the Champagne Trade in England, 1905
The History of the Wine Trade in England, 1906–1909. Three volumes
Wine and Spirits: The Connoisseur's Textbook, 1919
The Blood of the Grape: The Wine Trade Text Book, 1920
Bottlescrew Days, 1926
The Art of Good Living: A Contribution to the Better Understanding of Food and Drink Together with a Gastronomic Vocabulary and a Wine Dictionary, 1929
Tables of Content: Leaves from My Diary, 1933
Madeira Wine, Cakes and Sauce, 1933
Champagne, 1934
Port, 1934
A Catechism Concerning Cheeses, 1936
André Simon's French Cook Book, 1938
A Wine Primer, 1946
Mushrooms Galore, 1951
A Wine Primer, 1951
The Gourmet's Week-end Book, 1952
How to Enjoy Wine in the Home, 1952
Wines and Liqueurs from A to Z, 1952
A Concise Encyclopædia of Gastronomy, 1952 (editor)
Biblioteca Gastronomica: A Catalogue of Books and Documents on Gastronomy, 1953
English Fare and French Wine, 1955
The Commonsense of Wine, 1966

Upton Sinclair

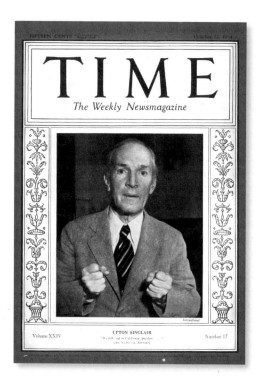

TIME *issue of October 22, 1934*

IN ORDER TO UNDERSTAND WHY UPTON SINCLAIR BELONGS in a collection of culinary biographies, we must also look at the life of Phillip Danforth Armour (1832–1901). Together, they represent two extreme examples of primary forces that determine American eating habits: the ethical and the economic.

P. D. Armour used his unique insights about developments in food production, transportation systems, control of markets, and technology to create something we now recognize as modern agribusiness. He was one of the first to recognize the value of refrigerated railcars, invented by Gustavus Swift (1839–1903), which led to fundamental changes in the way meat was delivered to cities and, indeed, to the disappearance of slaughterhouses from most eastern cities. Armour's ideas about capitalism, however, were so unencumbered by ethics, morality, or even the later Sherman Antitrust Act (1890) that he believed that anything he could get away with was just an ordinary business practice. For example, in 1888, his company was accused—though never convicted—of selling "embalmed beef" to the U.S. Army.

Armour used money he had made in California's gold fields to start his first meat-packing operations in Milwaukee. He moved his plant to Chicago in 1870, just five years after the infamous Union Stockyards opened. The combination of the stockyards, a first-rate rail hub, easy access to all the grain from the Great Plains, and an unlimited supply of cheap immigrant labor virtually guaranteed his success.

He was also a ruthless exploiter of those workers, a fact that enhanced the profitability of his empire of meat. His Chicago stockyards were often the scene of strikes. However—like other "robber barons" such as Swift and Henry Clay Frick (1849–1919)—he was a master at keeping ethnic, linguistic, and racial groups separate and channeling their anti-company energies into suspicion and distrust of each other. After his death, Armour & Co. continued to collude with Swift and three other companies to fix prices and undermine the organizing effectiveness of the labor movement.

Upton Sinclair was born in Baltimore, Maryland, but grew up in Bound Brook, New Jersey and New York City. His mother came from a well-to-do family, but his father was an alcoholic, a circumstance that forced them to live in a series of run-down boarding houses. Even as a child, he was struck by the differences between his life and that of better-off children: In his autobiography, he wrote, "Readers of my novels know that I have one favorite theme, the contrast between the social classes…and the plots are contrived to carry you from one to the other."

Sinclair graduated from the City College of New York, then went on to Columbia University, where he became interested in muckraking journalism, especially that of Jacob Riis (1849–1914). When he was 26, he wrote an account of the

1904 strike at the Chicago meat-packing plants for the socialist magazine *Appeal to Reason*. As a result, the magazine's editor, Fred D. Warren, commissioned him to do a series of articles examining the labor conditions in the plants.

Sinclair spent most of November and December of that year interviewing workers. While there, he met a man who had worked in Armour's "killing beds." The man had written an exposé of what he had seen there, but "old P. D. Armour had paid him five thousand dollars not to publish it."

Sinclair's research for the *Appeal to Reason* articles became his 1906 novel, *The Jungle*. The packing plants in Chicago were called "Durham's" in the novel, but readers all knew they were reading about Armour's. The book is ugly, dark, and squalid—much like Riis' 1890 book, *How the Other Half Lives*, which had made a big impression on Sinclair when he was a student in New York—and the slaughterhouse scenes were horrific. The magazine articles and the novel outraged the American public—not as much about the worker's situation as about the sanitary conditions in the plants, and what those conditions implied about the plants' products.

For the preceding three years, the U.S. Senate had considered a pure food and drug bill, but there had been little public support for it until Sinclair's book appeared. Suddenly the bill was pushed forward—in part by Theodore Roosevelt, who sent the Neill-Reynolds Commission to investigate *The Jungle*'s allegations. Roosevelt told Sinclair that the commission had been able to confirm everything in the book except one particularly graphic scene in which a worker falls into a vat used for rendering lard. Sinclair confirmed the story, explaining that "the men who had fallen into lard vats had gone out to the world as Armour's Pure Leaf Lard, …the families were paid off and shipped back to Lithuania, or whatever European land they had come from…."

Roosevelt's concern, combined with the fact that meat sales in the U.S. dropped by fifty percent in the weeks following release of *The Jungle*, was more than enough to lead to the successful passage of the Pure Food and Drug Act of 1906, and its corollary, the Beef Inspection Act. While industry lobbyists managed to make these acts relatively toothless, with fines as low as $500 for some violations, the acts did lead to the restructuring of existing agencies, like the Bureau of Chemistry, into what has been known since 1930 as the Food and Drug Administration.

Sinclair, always a supporter of a compassionate approach to life, was a vegetarian and a crusader, writing on moral and ethical issues such as slavery and the Sacco and Vanzetti trial, and about corruption such as the Teapot Dome scandal. In 1905, together with Jack London (who had already published *The Call of the Wild*), Sinclair founded the Intercollegiate Socialist Society. He was also ready "to put his money where his mouth was": In 1906, with the royalties from *The Jungle*, Sinclair founded Helicon Hall in Englewood, New Jersey. Unfortunately the utopian community failed the next year when its building was destroyed by a fire.

Sinclair wrote an article about fasting for health for *Cosmopolitan Magazine* in 1910, and published *The Fasting Cure* the next year. In fact, he met his future wife, Mary Craig Kimbrough, at the **Kellogg** Sanitarium in Battle Creek, Michigan. They married in New York City in 1913, the year her first novel, *Sylvia*, was published. He addressed his vegetarianism in 1918 in *The Profits of Religion*. When asked, Sinclair said he did not become a vegetarian as a result of his research for *The Jungle*—although Roosevelt claimed that *he* had upon reading the book.

In 1934, five years before John Steinbeck wrote *The Grapes of Wrath*, Sinclair ran for governor of California on the platform "End Poverty in California." He was defeated by a coalition of groups that used negative campaign ads in a coordinated manner that foreshadowed modern political campaigns, but he was among the first to succeed in drawing attention to the plight of California's migrant farm workers.

Sinclair published more than 80 books—so many under pseudonyms that the exact number is uncertain—in all genres, but most memorably in the fictionalized journalistic genre he created. He received the Pulitzer Prize in 1943 for *Dragon's Teeth*, about the early years of Nazism.

To the end of his life, Sinclair found it ironic that he had researched and written about the stockyards in an attempt to improve the laborers' working conditions there, but had instead improved the quality of the food served on tables across the country. He had, in effect, "aimed at the public's heart, and by accident hit it in the stomach."

— GARY ALLEN

On Guard, 1903
Strange Cruise, 1905
The Jungle, 1906
The Fasting Cure, 1911
The Profits of Religion: An Essay in Economic Interpretation, 1918
Letters to Judd, an American Working Man, 1920
100%: The Story of a Patriot, 1920
The Book of Life, Mind and Body, 1921
The Book of Love, 1923
Goose-Step: A Story of American Education, 1923
I, Governor of California, and How I Ended Poverty: A True Story of the Future, 1933
Way Out: A Solution of Our Present Economic and Social Ills, 1933
What Can be Done About America's Economic Troubles? 1939
Is the American Form of Capitalism Essential to the American Form of Democracy? 1940
Peace or War in America? 1941
Dragon's Teeth, 1943
The World of 1949 and What to Do About it, 1949
My Lifetime in Letters, 1960
Affectionately, Eve: A Novel, 1961

Alexis Benoît Soyer

❧ 1809–1858 ❧

ALEXIS BENOÎT SOYER WAS THE FIRST OF THE GREAT SHOWMAN CHEFS, AN eccentric combination of **Julia Child**, Thomas Alva Edison, and Baron Münchausen. He was born to French shopkeepers in Meaux-en-Brie on October 14, 1809. His mother hoped he would enter the priesthood, but a practical joke with a church bell put an end to that plan. Instead Alexis joined his brother, Philippe, a cook in Paris. By the age of 17 he was *chef de cuisine* with twelve cooks working under him.

Around 1830 Philippe moved to England, where he easily found employment. Alexis soon followed him, leaving behind his mistress, Adele Lamain. After working for various noblemen, Soyer was chosen to be the first chef of the Reform Club in London. He helped the architect, Sir Charles Barry, design the club's vast kitchens, ingeniously introducing all manner of labor-saving and food-conserving arrangements. To keep seafood fresh, Soyer and Barry devised a sloping chilled marble slab with fine jets of iced water playing upon it. Large fireproof cupboard doors concealed a massive rotisserie, set before a wall of burning charcoal, where barons of beef and game of all sorts slowly roasted to perfection on individual spits turned by clockwork. Hot water for the entire kitchen was obtained by running the pipes alongside this roasting cupboard.

In 1837 Soyer married Emma Jones, a portrait painter. She died in childbirth in 1842 while Soyer was in Belgium. His monument to her still stands in Kendal Green Cemetery.

Soyer became known for his flamboyant bias-cut clothes, "à la zoug-zoug," as he called them. His outlandish style was caricatured by Thackery in the figure of Mirobolant, the French chef, in *Pendennis.* With the help of two secretaries, F. Volant and J. R. Warren, and the staff of the Reform Club, Soyer began writing a series of cookbooks.

In 1847 the out-of-work Spitalfields weavers and the Irish potato famine called forth Soyer's genius for charitable organization. He created model soup kitchens in London, charming matrons into contributing their time and resources, and the British government commissioned him to open a huge soup kitchen in Dublin, which served 6000 portions a day. Soyer published a little cookbook selling for sixpence subtitled *The Poor Man's Regenerator*, donating a penny from each copy to the feeding of the poor.

Throughout his life Soyer concocted, invented, and marketed an array of sauces, nectars, and gadgets, all bearing his name. Whatever he did attracted comment, and Soyer thrived on praise and celebrity, which he increased with regular letters to the press. Soyer left the Reform Club in 1851 at the time of the Great Exhibition at the Crystal Palace in London. He leased Gore House, a large estate adjacent to the Exhibition, and created "The Gastronomic Symposium of All Nations." Although thousands of meals were served to visitors, Soyer's decoration scheme consumed all the profits of the undertaking and left him £7000 in debt. Soyer paid his creditors from his savings and the royalties on his books.

The fame of the Gastronomic Symposium extended to France, and one day Soyer received a letter from an Alexis Lamain in Paris, who claimed to be Soyer's son by his long-abandoned mistress. Soyer invited him to the symposium, and two years later gave Lamain his name. In 1911 Lamain's son, Nicolas Soyer, started a craze for "paper bag cookery," promoting it with familial hyperbole.

In 1854 the Crimean War began, the first conflict to be covered by photographic and telegraphic reporting. News of the death of soldiers from "Crimean

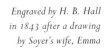

Engraved by H. B. Hall in 1843 after a drawing by Soyer's wife, Emma

fever" and their starvation in filthy hospitals appeared in the British press long before individual letters could reach home. The public outcry was deafening. In response, the government sent Florence Nightingale to reform the care of the wounded. Soyer used his Reform Club connections to arrange to follow her at his own expense. Before his departure, Soyer designed and tested a prototype camp-cooker, leaving plans behind for its manufacture in great quantity. It used one-quarter the fuel of previous arrangements and, with slight fuel modifications, is still in use today.

On arriving in Scutari (today's Üsküdar, Turkey), Soyer posted recipes and trained overseers to supervise the soldiers who served, in rotation, as cooks . He made sure that even the weakest men had food they could digest. Instead of using unsavory dried vegetables, Soyer taught the soldiers to cook soup from a vegetable mixture that was added to boiling water. Eschewing the practice of using the same pots to boil meat and make tea, he invented the "Scutari teapot," which had a removable perforated cylinder for holding the leaves. Within a month, Soyer had greatly improved the quality of the meals and become the most popular man in the camp. Like Florence Nightingale, however, he fell ill with Crimean fever and barely survived. But by the time his camp stoves arrived, he was well enough to teach the men to use them.

When the war ended in 1856, Soyer returned to London and helped Nightingale reform barracks cookery. He designed a traveling camp cook-wagon and a new method of canning cured meat. But Crimean fever had undermined his health. The combination of demands from Florence Nightingale's projects—plus frequent dinner parties and late nights at the ballet—took their toll. He died, surrounded by friends, on August 5, 1858.

Florence Nightingale wrote of him, "His death is a great disaster. Others have studied cooking for the purpose of gourmandizing, some for show, but none but he for the purpose of cooking large quantities of food in the most nutritious manner for great numbers of men. He has no successor."

— ANN ARNOLD

The Gastronomic Regenerator: a Simplified and Entirely New System of Cookery… Suited to the Incomes of All Classes, 1846

Soyer's Charitable Cookery, or the Poor Man's Regenerator, 1848

The Modern Housewife or Méngagère, 1849

The Pantropheon, or History of Food and Its Preparation, 1853

A Shilling Cookery for the People, 1854. Reprinted as *Soyer's Cookery Book*, with an introduction by **James A. Beard**, 1959

Soyer's Standard Cookery for the People, 1859. (A revised and enlarged American edition of A Shilling Cookery for the People)

Soyer's Culinary Campaign, Being Historical Reminiscences of the Late War…, 1857

Instructions to Military Hospital Cooks in the Preparation of Diets for Sick Soldiers…the Receipts by G. Warriner and A. Soyer, 1860

Violetta Symphort

ALSO CALLED: Violetta Pamphille

BORN ON THE ISLAND OF GUADELOUPE TO A CULINARY FAMILY IN THE FIRST quarter of the last century, Violetta Symphort, also known as Violetta Pamphille, was destined to cook. She learned at an early age and in the traditional manner from her mother and relatives to prepare the classic dishes of the French Caribbean culinary lexicon. She developed her own style and was soon cooking in various kitchens of the island, where her masterful hand with the traditional wooden whisk—the *baton lele*—and her gift with seasoning singled her out. Eventually, she began her own restaurant in the resort area of Gosier; it became known as one of the *chief lieux*, or capitals, of Creole gastronomy. The gossamer-light fritters known as *accras de morue* and her spicy, but not mouth-numbingly hot, *boudin*, her savory *blaff* of traditional Caribbean fish, and her stuffed crabs of unrivaled delicacy are enough to rate her a mention in any dictionary of masters of the culinary world. Violetta Symphort, though, was more than a chef and a restaurateur; she was also a visionary.

Having attained fame for her own endeavors, she went on to serve as culinary ambassadress of the cuisine of the French Caribbean. She traveled to France and beyond, spreading the tastes of her world. In her later years, she founded the Cordon Madras, a culinary order given to those whose mastery of the food of the French Caribbean rivaled her own. The order celebrated the genius of the oft-unheralded Creole cooks from Guadeloupe, Martinique, St. Martin, and Guyane and gave many the first validation that they had ever publicly received. Founding the Cordon Madras and spreading the gospel of *la bonne cuisine créole* was simply another feather in her already well-decorated headtie.

The summum of her achievements, though, was her multi-year presidency of the Cuistot Mutuel, a Guadeloupean culinary organization that began as a self-help group. Such groups were common in the post-emancipation African-Atlantic world and were designed to take care of ill or disabled members of a profession or an area, as well as provide burial insurance for its members in uncertain times. The Cuistot Mutuel, founded in 1916 in Pointe-à-Pitre, was and remains a self-help organization for the culinary community. The private face of the organization is virtually unknown today to outsiders, but many summer visitors to Guadeloupe have witnessed its public face: the Fête des Cuisinières or feast of the [women] cooks, held annually on the Saturday closest to the feast day of Saint Lawrence, the organization's patron—chosen for his martyrdom on a grill over hot coals.

The feast, little known in the English-speaking world, is a high point in the culinary calendar of the French-speaking Caribbean and brings together members of the organization and traditional Creole cooks from neighboring islands and as far away as Guyane in South America. It's also a major feature on French television news, adding its warmth and color to the detailing of the happenings in the various departments of France.

On the day of the feast, the members of the organization assemble for a high mass at Pointe-à-Pitre's Cathedral of St. Peter and St. Paul. Dressed in traditional Creole splendor—brilliant-hued fabric worn over starched blinding-white petticoats of intricate eyelet and adorned with a ransom of flashing jewelry: ropes of necklaces, dangling earrings, and brooches pinned to satin scarves on ample bosoms—the members are identifiable by their aprons, symbols of their profession, which are embroidered with the grill, the symbol of their patron, and by their baskets, filled to overflowing with a profusion of Creole treats and hung with miniature pots, pans, whisks, and other symbols of their trade.

Following the high mass, the members of the Cuistot Mutuel parade through the streets of Pointe-à-Pitre amid a growing serpentine of admirers and gastronomes to a venue where they host a public luncheon featuring an ever-changing menu, which might include fricasséed conch or stewed crab or a well-stewed chicken or a perfectly seasoned leg of lamb. Champagne and rum flow, and soon the small orchestra tunes up and the beguines begin. The ladies dance with their husbands or each other as whimsy and circumstances dictate, and they laugh, tease, eat, and drink well into the afternoon. They know only too well that the following day they will be standing facing the stoves in their various establishments, acquainting visitors with the mysteries of Creole cooking. But for that one day in August, they, as did Violetta Symphort before them, celebrate the vast and little-known culinary legacy of those of African descent in the New World.

— JESSICA B. HARRIS

T

Taillevent

❦ C. 1312–C. 1395 ❦

ALSO CALLED: Guillaume Tirel

MUNDANE ACTIVITIES OF DAILY LIFE HAD LITTLE PLACE ON the vellum or parchment of Europe's scriptoria before the middle of the fourteenth century. The practical crafts of the time relied upon both closed shops and a system of oral apprenticeship for their preservation and enhancement. Yet celebrity depends as much upon a broadly recognized reputation as upon the substance of that reputation.

In the late Middle Ages no single cook enjoyed a broader and more lasting influence on civilized dining than Guillaume Tirel, alias Taillevent ("Wind-Slicer," in recognition of his skill at carving). In large measure this influence can be explained by two interrelated circumstances: the man worked for the royal house of France; he wrote his *Viandier (Book of Foods)* at a time when few recipes were ever written down.

As chief cook in the king's kitchens, Taillevent enjoyed exceptional privileges in the matter of facilities, labor, ingredients, creativity and standards. His exalted position in a profession which was firmly hierarchical conferred immortality on his name and the set of some 150 recipes called the *Viandier of Taillevent*.

Guillaume Tirel was born about 1312, perhaps a year or two later. A few documented dates mark the progress of his career in various royal households: in 1326 and 1327, he was a scullion in the kitchen of Jeanne d'Évreux (Queen of Charles IV); in 1330, a kitchen hand for Jeanne de Bourgogne (Queen of Phillip VI of Valois); in 1346, a household cook for Phillip VI; in 1349, personal cook for Phillip VI; in 1355, 1361, 1364, and 1371, cook for Charles V, at first prince, later king; in 1378, chief personal cook for the same; in 1387, kitchen clerk—responsible for, among other things, menus, provisions, and supervision of all kitchen operations and personnel—for Charles VI; and finally, in 1388 and 1392, first kitchen clerk for the same. He died before 1398, in which year a document submitted by his

Tombstone of Taillevent and his two wives, Jeanne Bonard and Isabeau le Chandelier

widow described him as both first kitchen clerk and a sergeant at arms to the King. In all likelihood, Tirel came from a Norman family of modest nobility. Granted a coat of arms for his culinary services, he is portrayed on his tombstone armed as a knight, at his breast a shield emblazoned with three cauldrons, a hound at his feet, a wife to each side.

The manuscript containing the earliest version of the recipes that form the basis of the *Viandier* antedates Taillevent's life; the latest manuscript versions of the work postdate his life. He neither "originated" the collection's material and layout nor gave it the extensive fifteenth-century revisions and additions which ensured the celebrity of the book in printed form. At some moment in his career Taillevent came across an anonymous recipe collection that still exists in a small manuscript roll from about 1300; he modified a number of the recipes in it and added a few new ones.

The layout of the collection is clear and generic: boiled meats, meat pottages and broths, roasts of meat, roasts of fowl, *entremets* (special preparations), lean pottages and broths, freshwater fish, saltwater fish. His dishes depend upon beef, pork, and mutton, a variety of game meats and fowl, and (especially for lean meals) a surprising range of fish from both sources. Few recipes for fruits or vegetables appear, their preparation being simple: leafy vegetables are occasionally stewed, a few roots are boiled. Herbs and spices appear as admixtures or as deliberate moderating elements in a sauce.

Taillevent's style remains terse. These are practical memoranda for the cook or kitchen clerk: boil the foodstuff, cut it up, fry it, make a sauce of various condiments, boil the foodstuff in it. No quantities are specified: No professional cook would need such precise directives. Cooking temperatures (always with a wood fire) and times, both impossible to define in any case, are likewise not Taillevent's concern. The stewpot, the spit, and the grill are fundamental; the oven (a breadbaker's preserve) is only very rarely resorted to, for a whole fish or a flan.

Fifteenth-century manuscript copies (of which two subsist) and printed versions vastly enlarged the *Viandier*'s bulk with pastries, somewhat more complex dishes, wondrous centerpieces, and cures for sick wines. Printers in particular, inventing a variety of titles for Taillevent's augmented collection, appealed to a broader readership by inserting new dishes—as well as a multiplicity of errors that made blatant nonsense of many of the recipes.

— TERENCE SCULLY

Viandier (Viandier of Taillevent), fourteenth century

Alice B. Toklas

ALSO CALLED: Alice Babette Toklas

BORN IN SAN FRANCISCO, THE GRAND DAUGHTER OF A pioneering '49er, Alice Toklas always considered California "God's country," and believed that her home state had given her an independent spirit. Perhaps this independence was also fostered by her experience of running the household for the men of her family after her mother died in 1897. She had studied music seriously but abandoned it on her mother's death. For several years thereafter she enjoyed her friends and amused herself; she was interested in food but not in cooking, and in general—in the words Gertrude Stein later put in her mouth in the sham *Autobiography of Alice B. Toklas*—"was not very ardent...." Then came the 1906 San Francisco earthquake and fire; it spared the family home, but changed her life.

Toklas (right) and Gertrude Stein in 1944, with their standard poodle, Basket.

Michael Stein, Gertrude's older brother, came to San Francisco after the fire to check on property he owned there. He met Alice Toklas, and his stories of life in Paris intrigued her so much that in 1907 she and a girlfriend set out to live there. They met Gertrude Stein, and soon Toklas moved into Stein's home as her secretary, occasional cook, companion and partner, creating an environment in which Gertrude Stein wrote prolifically. Toklas even set up a company, called Plain Edition, to publish Stein's work in inexpensive volumes, since "Gertrude Stein's readers are writers, university students, librarians, and young people who have very little money."

When Toklas and Stein met, Gertrude and her brother Leo were already known as early appreciators and collectors of modern art. Many artists, among them Picasso, Matisse, Braque, and Gris, were among the notable guests the two ladies entertained. Later, writers such as Sherwood Anderson, Ford Madox Ford, and Hemmingway also came to call.

The outbreak of World War I found Toklas and Stein in England at the home of Alfred North Whitehead. After several weeks they made their way back to Paris, where they assisted the American Fund for French Wounded by distributing supplies, driving fearlessly around the countryside in a Ford Model T truck that Stein had had shipped from America. They were ultimately recognized for their war work by the French government.

In 1934, Stein was invited to give a series of lectures in the United States. The two women spent seven months traveling around their home country, visiting old and new friends, and learning how American cuisine had expanded in their absence. On this trip, they ate wild rice in Connecticut, mint jelly in Minnesota, oysters Rockefeller in New Orleans, corn sticks in Texas, and abalone, avocado, and passion fruit in California—all for the first time. Typically, they impulsively took a day's detour from their itinerary in California just to see the desert flowers in bloom.

During the German occupation of France in the Second World War, Toklas and Stein lived in their summer house in the Bugey, their identity as Jewish Americans kept secret by their neighbors and friends. Toklas tended an extensive garden of vegetables and fruit trees, which supplemented a diet of fish—until fishing was no longer allowed—and the ration of one quarter pound of meat per week. (The French authorities also gave a ration card to their standard poodle, as to all pedigreed dogs.) In the midst of this privation, Toklas passionately read cookbooks. She kept the ingredients for a Liberation Fruitcake hidden in the pantry, confident they would one day be called for. After the liberation, the women returned to their apartment in Paris to find that their art treasures remained, but that Toklas' prized iron pan for baking corn sticks was gone. "What did the Germans...expect to do with it?" she complained.

Gertrude Stein died soon after the war, in 1946. Toklas continued to live in France for the rest of her life. Years later, when Toklas was asked to write a book about her life, she refused, saying that Gertrude Stein had already written her autobiography; she did, however, offer to write "a cookbook with memories." Toklas was by no means a trained cook. Her work in the kitchen had begun with simple American suppers made for herself and Stein on Sunday evenings when their Vietnamese cook was out, but later circumstances had often made it necessary for her to do much more of the cooking. She had a deep appreciation of food and a good memory for flavors, and over the years had assembled a huge collection of recipes. Included were several for gazpacho, which she had first encountered in Spain. (She looked for gazpacho recipes in Spain, but was told only peasants and Americans ate it.)

The Alice B. Toklas Cook Book, published in 1954, was very successful, only in part because of a recipe contributed by a friend for "Haschich Fudge." (The first American edition of the *Cook Book* omitted this recipe, but it was retained by the British publisher and word of it crossed the Atlantic.) Written primarily for American cooks, it was not really a French cookbook; Toklas believed that the French were too tightly bound by tradition in their cooking, although she admired their respect for the quality and flavor of ingredients. Nevertheless, most of the recipes are for the French dishes she had been eating, and it is interesting to note how at that time, seven years before Julia Child helped Americans master French cooking, so many items were thought to need identifying: celeriac, Dutch oven, marinade, morels, sesame oil, and zucchini, for example, all appear in explanatory footnotes. Her recipes do not use standard culinary terminology, but they make the processes clear enough.

Encouraged by the reception of her cook book, Toklas wrote a few culinary pieces for *House Beautiful* magazine. Then her publisher asked her to write a second cookbook, and the food editor of *House Beautiful*, **Poppy Cannon**, was sent to work with Toklas on it. Cannon described Toklas as tiny, beautifully dressed, with large, bright eyes and short dark hair which also appeared on her upper lip—a magnetic person who quickly became the center of attention in any gathering.

Poppy Cannon was well known in America as a prominent advocate of speed and efficiency in the kitchen, and Toklas told her that "she disagreed with me about almost everything and particularly with my basic belief that it is possible to be an epicure, even an epicure-cook, in a hurry." In the final form of the book, which appeared as *Aromas and Flavors of Past and Present* in 1958, Toklas' recipes were each printed with an introductory note by Cannon explaining how one might make the dish easier, faster or with more American ingredients. Alice Toklas was not pleased.

Meanwhile, *The Alice B. Toklas Cook Book* continued to do well. In 1960 it was re-issued in America in paperback, this time with the marijuana fudge recipe included, and 24 years later, long after Toklas' death, a new edition appeared with an introduction by **M. F. K. Fisher**. Fisher, who had never met Alice Toklas, gave a physical description of her very much along the lines of Poppy Cannon's, but added that Toklas had a large, fleshy, hooked nose, and "was probably one of the ugliest people anyone had ever seen."

Alice Toklas lived out her life in Paris, surrounded by modern art and memories, receiving many visitors and occasionally lecturing. She died in 1967 after a long illness, and was buried in Paris beside Gertrude Stein.

— ALICE ARNDT

The Alice B. Toklas Cook Book, 1954
Aromas and Flavors of Past and Present, 1958

Catharine Parr Traill

❧ 1802–1899 ❧

CATHARINE PARR TRAILL, NÉE STRICKLAND, WAS AN ENGLISH IMMIGRANT into Canada who became a pioneer icon. A novelist, poet, and writer for periodicals, as well as an amateur naturalist and cookbook author, she was born at Rotherhithe, Kent, on January 9, 1802, and died at Lakefield, Ontario, on August 29, 1899. Much of Traill's Canadian writing was about adjusting to the privations of the harsh wilderness. Her *Female Emigrant's Guide, or Hints on Canadian Housekeeping* (Toronto, 1854 and 1855) was the only cookbook and household manual written for Canadian pioneer conditions. It was the first English-Canadian culinary voice, and is a Canadian classic.

Growing up in idyllic rural Suffolk, Catharine and her younger sister Susanna learned in between school lessons how to milk cows, grow vegetables, and bake cakes, which only partially prepared them for their unexpected lives as impoverished genteel settlers in the rough backwoods of Upper Canada, now Ontario. Catharine and Susanna both married half-pay officers, with whom they emigrated to Upper Canada in 1832; they settled in log houses in Douro Township, near present-day Peterborough, near their younger brother Samuel Strickland.

Unlike their brother-in-law Sam, neither Thomas Traill nor John Moodie were competent farmers, causing frequent destitution for their large families. Already published authors before emigration, both sisters thus returned to writing to support their families. Catharine Parr Traill's first Canadian book was *The Backwoods of Canada:*

*Catharine in her early
twenties in Suffolk*

being letters from the wife of an emigrant officer, illustrative of the domestic economy of British America (London: 1836). Although in hindsight she considered it naïve, she established in it the main elements of her adult Canadian writing: narrative descriptions of local life, study of native flora and fauna, and practical household instruction.

Not realizing it personified rural English Canada's culinary character for much of the century, literary academics without a background in culinary history have usually dismissed *The Female Emigrant's Guide* as a mere housewifery book and a minor document of backwoods life that was unequal to Traill's other fine output. However, as a blend of applicable English, Scottish, American, and Canadian information, *The Female Emigrant's Guide* was a regional book of housewifery totally suitable to the backwoods context. "As this work was not intended for a regular cookery-book, I have limited myself to such [recipes] as are in common use in the farm-houses."

Drawing upon 22 years of hard-won personal experience and advice from many established settlers, Traill captured on paper the advice she would have liked to have as a novice colonist. She explained what to do with the meager and humble ingredients available, and how to supplement them with native plants and animals, like wild strawberries and wild duck. Her audience was middle-class English gentlewomen like herself, their servants, and the wives of mechanics, farmers and laborers, all of whom were totally unprepared for the subsistence bush housekeeping they would undertake in Canada. Traill's *Guide* was an unequalled view into the empirical details of women's daily "customs and occupations." They already knew how to make decent gravy and good pound cake, but were clueless about tapping maple trees for sap, substituting local cornmeal for the familiar white flour or oatmeal, cooking indigenous wild rice, curing fish for winter use, preserving wild purple plums with maple sugar, and making medicinal teas from forest herbs—and about how to feminize a log cabin and turn a flour barrel into a comfortable armchair. Many immigrants did not understand how to make basic bread, let alone bake-kettle breads. She included appropriate receipts from published books, such as Lydia Maria Child's *American Frugal Housewife*, and recycled her own material from periodicals like *Canadian Agriculturist*. Her most famous quote epitomizes her spirit: "In cases of emergency, it is folly to fold one's hands and sit down to bewail in abject terror: it is better to be up and doing."

Desperately seeking income, Traill produced her book rapidly in less than a year; however, she realized little revenue from its success, because a dishonest publisher repeatedly swindled her. Through the 1850's and 1860's ten editions appeared, of which the fifth (1855) was retitled *The Canadian Settler's Guide*, the title by which it is commonly known today, although not Catharine's choice. She started an updated version in the early 1880's, but it was not published; her handwritten notes, however, survive in the National Archives of Canada.

Catharine Parr Traill and her sister Susanna Moodie are Canadian literary icons because their many fine works form the core of nineteenth-century Canadian pioneer writing. Traill's *The Female Emigrant's Guide* was the first genuine culinary voice of English Canada.

— FIONA LUCAS

The Female Emigrant's Guide, or Hints on Canadian Housekeeping, 1854

Barbara Tropp

Tropp in her garden in Napa

THOSE WHO KNEW THIS ARTICULATE SCHOLAR, ASPIRING chef, cookbook author, writer, student, or colleague, all referred to her as a woman passionate about Chinese food. She was also passionate about educating other women culinary professionals. This latter passion focused her on founding the Women Chefs and Restaurateurs organization and on being a mentor to many of its members and other aspiring chefs.

Barbara was born in the late nineteen forties and grew up with sister Nhumey in Springfield, New Jersey, daughters of podiatrists, in a town with one Chinese restaurant. As a studious child eager to learn, she showed an early interest in things Chinese, particularly after taking a high-school course on Asian culture. She went on to Barnard College, where she was granted a bachelor's degree with honors in oriental studies. Thereafter, she continued graduate work on a Woodrow Wilson Fellowship, earned a master of science degree at Princeton University in the Department of East Asian Studies, concentrating on Chinese literature and art history, and worked on a doctorate.

Improving her language skills and studying poetic structure for the doctorate, she went to Taipei, Taiwan and said she was both bitten by and smitten with Chinese food. She gave credit in part to the two families she lived with. Describing these two hosts, she commented that one was a great cook, the other a discriminating gourmet. After their tutelage, she often reiterated that "the Chinese taught me how to eat and how to live."

When she returned to Princeton in 1973, circumstance saw her fellowship end, so to augment her income she became, as she called herself, the Pearl Mesta of the department. Enjoying it so, she spent more time on culinary matters and less on her thesis until she abandoned her studies in 1978. But she never gave up her love of Tang poetry.

Soon thereafter, she moved to San Francisco to immerse herself in both Chinese food and the Mandarin language of those selling and preparing food there. Shortly after arriving, she signed a book contract for what became *The Modern Art of Chinese Cooking*. This massive and authoritative volume, published by William Morrow in 1982, was loaded with things cultural. It was complete with a chapter on East-West desserts and a contributed one on wines by Gerald Asher.

During this time and thereafter, Tropp wrote articles for *Gourmet* and other food magazines and for newspapers. She taught cooking classes and led tours of San Francisco's Chinatown; somewhat later, she took people on a culinary tour of China. The *San Francisco Chronicle* bestowed on her the title of "the Julia Child of the Chinese kitchen." Some years later she married Bart Rhoades, helping him to raise his two sons and a daughter.

In 1986, Barbara Tropp opened a Chinese bistro in San Francisco called China Moon. With Tropp serving as its number-one chef for a decade, it earned critical acclaim. This art-deco coffee shop on Post Street, complete with counter stools and booths, served foods that married French with Chinese culinary concepts. She authored the *China Moon Cookbook*, published by Workman in 1992, further bringing Chinese and European cooking together. This book won an award from the International Association of Culinary Professionals. Heartsick and physically ill with ovarian cancer, she closed the bistro in 1996.

Believing in both Western and Chinese medicine, Barbara sought out chemotherapy and a Chinese doctor who specialized in cancer treatment. When the cancer was in remission, she stayed on her recommended herbal regimen. Then her illness flared again on a trip to China and she said the herbal way was no protection, so she pitched those items and went back to chemotherapy, and survived. Frustrated that her life-long good diet had not protected her from illness, and that later restricted diets did not make her well, she continued cooking, writing, and teaching until she succumbed in 2001, at the age of 53.

Diminutive in stature, she called herself a peanut, but felt a good five feet tall when teaching anyone who wanted to learn, and she wielded gargantuan influence in both Chinese and Western culinary worlds. Barbara Tropp would be proud to know that a scholarship in her name now exists. It is thanks to many colleagues, even acquaintances, and to an organization she founded, that her name and legacy continues to educate aspiring chefs.

— JACQUELINE M. NEWMAN

The Modern Art of Chinese Cooking, 1982
China Moon Cookbook, 1992

Friedrich Unger

🎇 ACTIVE 1830'S 🎇

FRIEDRICH UNGER WAS *HOFCONDITOR,* OR ROYAL CONFECTIONER, TO OTTO I, a young Bavarian prince of just eighteen who was elected the first king of Greece by the European powers in 1832, three years after Greece gained its independence from the Ottoman Empire. Unger accompanied Otto's German household to Athens, and spent the next five years researching eastern confectionery for his book *Conditorei des Orients,* written in 1837 and published in 1838. In his introduction, he explains that his aim was "to give the public insight into a subject of which little is known and about which so many mistaken opinions exist." This book is the only source of information about Friedrich Unger's life and work.

During this period Unger also compiled material for a book about western confectionery that he proposed to write if his first book was well received. This second book, to be entitled *Conditorei des Occidents,* was apparently never published.

Unger departed for Greece eager to investigate Eastern confectionery: "When opportunity arose for an extended residence in Hellas, a country that is so close to the Orient, I was overjoyed to have the opportunity to enrich my knowledge of Eastern confectionery through learning about the preparation of many of its articles, and from the very start I missed no opportunity wherever it arose that would advance me in this object." Indeed he began his investigations even before arriving in Greece, at Trieste, where he "had the opportunity to taste a few preserves which were supposedly prepared from Oriental recipes."

Greece proved disappointing, confectionery-wise, however, and Unger resolved to go to Istanbul: "Although I was very disappointed in my expectations of gaining new illuminating experiences in the craft of confectionery in Greece, I still did not dare to judge Oriental confectionery, and from then on, not mistakenly, considered the city of Constantinople to be the place where I was most likely to be able to finally satisfy my hunger for learning."

Title page of Unger's Conditorei des Orients, *1838*

In the summer of 1835, on grounds of ill health, Unger obtained leave of absence and on 27 July, sailed from Greece to Izmir aboard the English schooner *Elizabeth*. The ship ran aground entering the harbor, and Unger completed the voyage to Istanbul on an English steamer, the *Levante*. After spending a few days seeing the sights in Istanbul, he devoted the rest of his time to "the achievement of my principal objective, that of acquainting myself with the Oriental craft of confectionery."

In Istanbul, as well as observing and questioning confectioners of all kinds, he obtained information from "a Greek confectioner who had worked for a long time in the Imperial Sugar Bakery," and was a guest at several grand dinners, as we know from the bills of fare at the end of his book.

Although Unger tends to be scornful, sometimes acidly sarcastic, and displays the arrogant assurance of European superiority typical of the era, he was also an acute and knowledgeable observer with an avid interest in the smallest details. As a professional confectioner, he largely understood the techniques and materials that he observed, and painted a vivid picture whose accuracy is abundantly corroborated. He does make errors on occasion, some arising from his misjudged reliance on Joseph von Hammer's *Constantinopolis und der Bosphoros*, but these are exceptions proving the rule, none being of a kind to cast doubt on his good faith or the thoroughness of his investigations.

He provides detailed descriptions of confectioners at work, sweet shops, street vendors, culinary utensils, and ingredients, as well as recording recipes for a total of 97 confections—34 fruit preserves, 29 sherbets, eleven *helva*s, two toffee-like sweets with sesame and chickpeas, four Turkish delights, eight miscellaneous candies, and nine sweet pastries—plus nine non-confectionery items. Some of the confections he describes have disappeared without a trace, others have changed, and some can be found in almost identical form today.

His account of *lohuk şerbet* is of particular interest, since this is none other than fondant by another name. Since fondant was unknown in Europe until the mid-nineteenth century, the possibility that Unger was instrumental in introducing *lohuk şerbet* into Europe from Turkey cannot be dismissed. As chief confectioner at a royal court which fascinated Europeans of the time, any agreeable new confections served by Unger to his royal employer, courtiers and aristocratic guests would have been likely to spread rapidly through European high society and its confectioners, even without the help of his book. Indeed, one of Unger's stated aims in investigating oriental confectionery was to seek out new items worth introducing. Fondant was, moreover, simple to prepare, as Unger notes: "I will only quote the favorites that I tasted in Constantinople and whose precise recipes I collected, and the reader will find that when he understands some of the preparations, he will be able to make all kinds of *lohuk scherbet* with the greatest of ease."

Another notable aspect of Unger's book is that he visited and described an otherwise unknown and no longer extant confectionery kitchen at Topkapı Palace. His unique description throws light on a famous engraving by Antoine-Ignace Melling depicting a line of figures carrying trays on their heads emerging from a gateway. On Unger's evidence they must have been carrying confectionery, probably for one of the numerous palace ceremonies involving the distribution of sweet dishes of diverse kinds.

Friedrich Unger's book is not only an exceptional source for the history of Ottoman confectionery, but also opens new lines of inquiry into reciprocal influence of the confectionery traditions of the Near East and Europe during the nineteenth century. In view of the professional knowledge, keen observation and dedication poured into this book, we can only regret that Unger never wrote his promised *Conditorei des Occidents*, which was to be "a thorough instruction containing all the branches of our European craft of confectionery."

— PRISCILLA MARY IŞIN

Conditorei des Orients, 1838

U

Gregory Usher

🌸 1950–1994 🌸

GREGORY USHER IS KNOWN AS AN AMERICAN EXPERT IN THE FIELD OF FRENCH gastronomy. As an educator and director at La Varenne, Le Cordon Bleu, and the Ritz-Escoffier schools in Paris, he not only improved the image of Americans in France, he changed the way the French taught the world to cook. He was well respected by the French culinary community and was an energetic emissary of French food and culture. Patricia Wells said, "He made Paris more Parisian and France more French, without ever losing the best qualities an American can have—honesty, enthusiasm, a sense of humor."

Gregory Clydesdale Usher was born on August 15, 1950 in Montclaire, New Jersey, the third of four brothers. In 1962, the family moved to Portland, Oregon, where he established his own catering business while still in high school. He studied art history at the University of Oregon.

Usher arrived in Paris in 1970 to study at the Sorbonne and began his lifelong immersion in and dedication to French gastronomy and culture. He apprenticed at three notable Parisian restaurants: La Barrière Poquelin, L'Orangerie, and Régine's, where he worked under Chef Michel Guérard. In 1976, he joined the staff of Anne Willan's cooking school, La Varenne, as teacher and translator; he was named director in 1980.

In 1983, he founded a consulting business, Gregory Usher Cooks and Co., which promoted French cuisine and assisted American restaurants in hiring French chefs. During this period, he organized demonstration tours for chefs in Europe and North America, translated menus for restaurants, was a guest speaker at culinary trade shows and on French radio and television, and hosted a weekly radio show in Paris.

In 1985, Usher was appointed administrative director at Le Cordon Bleu—the first non-French director in the Paris school's history. He was engaged in

1987 by the Hotel Ritz to be founding director of the Ritz-Escoffier Ecole de Gastronomie Française. He created and nurtured all aspects of the school, from its design and construction in the hotel's basement, to writing the curriculum and hiring the chefs.

In addition to writing articles for American and French periodicals, Usher contributed, in collaboration with Isabelle Bachelard, to *France: A Culinary Journey* (Collins), which won both the James Beard and Julia Child cookbook awards in 1993.

In recognition of his service to "la vraie cuisine française," the French government named Usher a Chevalier du Mérite Agricole in 1989. He was also named Chevalier du Tastevin in 1993, the same year he was inducted into James Beard's Who's Who in Food and Beverage, as well as into Who's Who in American Cooking.

Gregory Usher died in Paris in 1994 after a long illness. In 1995, the Franco-American culinary community held a commemorative celebration at the Paris home of the American ambassador, Pamela Harriman. The French chapter of the American Institute of Wine & Food (of which he had been chairman) established the Gregory Usher Gastronomic Research Grant. The IACP Foundation created a scholarship in his name.

His library became the Gregory Usher Collection at the American Library in Paris, and remains one of the largest English-language culinary collections in Europe. The non-English volumes of the collection went to the Schlesinger Library of the Radcliffe Institute for Advanced Study, Harvard University, in Cambridge, Massachusetts.

— MM PACK

France: A Culinary Journey, 1992

Varro

116BC—27BC

MARCUS TERENTIUS VARRO WAS A ROMAN POLITICIAN AND SCHOLAR. HIS BOOK about farming is full of information about Roman food sources.

Varro was born in 116 BC in the Italian country town of Reate (modern Rieti), fifty miles north of Rome. Exactly one hundred years earlier, in 216, his ancestor Gaius Terentius Varro had been elected Consul and, in the same year, was killed by the Carthaginians at the head of a Roman army at the disastrous battle of Cannae. It's not surprising, perhaps, that Varro was passionately interested in Roman culture and history. He studied at Rome and then, like many young Romans, pursued advanced studies at Athens, where his teacher was the philosopher Antiochus of Ascalon.

Varro's political career coincided with the most interesting period of Roman political life: He was lucky to come through it alive. He was a faithful supporter of Pompey in peace and war. In Rome's sea battles against the Mediterranean pirates in 67 BC, Varro personally earned a decoration for bravery, the "naval crown". He also fought twice for Pompey in Spain, first against the charismatic rebel Sertorius, then against the even more charismatic Julius Caesar. He was captured twice by Caesar, who generously set him free on both occasions. In 48, Varro wisely retired from active politics. Caesar, now in control of Rome, chose him to supervise the creation of Rome's first public libraries of Greek and Latin literature. This appointment is evidence that Varro's scholarly eminence was already well known, outweighing political rivalries. Even so, he was on the list of those "proscribed"—destined for death—by Mark Antony after Caesar's assassination in 44. He was spared thanks to the personal intervention of Caesar's adopted son Octavian, the future emperor Augustus. He died in 27 BC, aged 89.

Varro wrote a total of 74 works, on many subjects, in prose and verse. Only two survive: *De Lingua Latina (On the Latin Language)*, dealing mainly with the origins and meanings of words, and *Res Rusticae (Country Work)*. The remainder of his works are lost, though some are known indirectly because they were read and cited by later Roman scholars: For example, Varro's *Histories, Human and Divine* are often quoted by Saint Augustine.

Res Rusticae, written when Varro was 80, is divided into three books and is in dialogue form: It reports a series of imaginary discussions between Varro himself and various friends. In spite of this format, Varro's work is much more systematic than **Cato**'s earlier *De Agri Cultura*. It was a major source for **Columella**'s even more comprehensive work *Res Rustica*. Book 1 is dedicated to Varro's wife Fundania, who had just inherited a farm.

Among the many aspects of farming dealt with in *Res Rusticae*, Varro focuses on some that are especially relevant to food. The section on conserving, at the end of Book 1, is much more informative than Cato's earlier notes on the subject. Not only does Varro give instructions for conserving grapes, olives, apples, quinces, pomegranates, pears, sorbs (*Sorbus domestica*) and walnuts; he also advises on the selection of suitable fruit, the length of time it can be stored, and, once the jars are opened, the way the fruit should be prepared and served to best possible effect. In Book 2, on the keeping of cows, sheep, goats, swine and donkeys, Varro includes information on milk and on the making of cheese. Book 3 is in some ways the most interesting: It is the first extensive study in Latin (and perhaps in any language) of the keeping of other animals, both domesticated and semi-wild. Some of these specialized practices, such as beekeeping and the keeping of geese and hens, were already hundreds of years old, but most of them were quite new in Varro's time. In many cases Roman farmers were the first to attempt them. The "aviary" section of the book deals with peafowl, ducks, pigeons, turtle-doves (*Streptopelia turtur*) and many smaller waterbirds and wild birds that Romans liked to eat. There is detailed advice on the force-feeding of geese and pigeons. The "warren" section begins with the keeping of hares, which was evidently a traditional practice, and continues with newer ideas, including rabbits, wild boars and that famous Roman delicacy, the edible dormouse (*Glis glis*). The keeping of snails and the production of honey are also discussed at this stage. Finally, there is a brief "fishpond" section. Although Varro includes very few recipes, the reader learns a great deal about the Romans' favorite foods and flavors.

— ANDREW DALBY

Res Rusticae, 36 BC

Vatel

⚜ MID-SEVENTEENTH CENTURY ⚜

ALSO CALLED: François Watel

"THE NEWS IS THAT VATEL——THE GREAT VATEL, THE MAÎTRE D'HÔTEL OF MONSIEUR FOUQUET AND MORE recently of Monsieur the Prince, that man of such outstanding ability, head and shoulders above all the rest, that man whose good head was capable of handling affairs of state——Vatel, the man whom I knew——Vatel, when he discovered, at eight o'clock this morning, that the seafood shipments which he had ordered had not come, could not face the disgrace he knew

would be sure to follow and, to sum it up, he ran himself through with his poignard. You can imagine the horrible dismay that so terrible an accident caused at that royal fête. And to think— the seafood shipments arrived just as he was expiring."

[translation by Frances Mossiker, *Madame de Sévigné: A Life and Letters*]

Thanks to Madame de Sévigné's letter, dated April 26, 1671, Vatel gained immortality. Without it, we might never have learned of the man reputed to have killed himself because the seafood didn't arrive. As it is, we don't know much more about him than that. The lack of facts, however, has encouraged speculation. He has been called, variously, Jean, Jean-François, or Fritz Karl; Vatel or Watel; Swiss or Flemish. He's been labeled a cook or pastry chef rather than a *maitre d'hotel*. According to the French film "Vatel" (2000), he died for love, not seafood. Some thought his suicide irresponsible; others considered it courageous. His name has been given to restaurants, organizations, awards, dishes. In culinary circles today, being called "a Vatel" is a high compliment.

According to Dominique Michel, author of *Vatel et la naissance de la gastronomie*, we now know that Vatel was born François Watel and was the son of Pierre Watel, a laborer, and Michèle Caudel. The couple were married on March 13, 1624 and lived in Alaigne, near Péronne in the north of France. The date of their son's birth is not known, nor do we know how he rose to such eminence. When he died, he was not an impoverished cook: He was financially well-off, and a confidant of nobles.

Vatel first came to public attention as the *maitre d'hotel* for Nicolas Fouquet, superintendent of finance for Louis XIV. He managed Fouquet's estates and financial affairs, supervised security and oversaw every detail of the lavish entertaining Fouquet favored. On August 17, 1661, when king and court arrived at Fouquet's recently completed estate at Vaux-le-Vicomte for a spectacular banquet, Vatel was in charge of the event. He overlooked no detail, spared no expense. The guests, who numbered several thousand, were entertained by a Molière première introduced by the playwright himself. Jean Baptiste Lully wrote a concerto for the occasion. Beautifully decorated tables offered hundred of dishes, hot and cold, sweet and savory.

It was an event fit for a king, but outshining the Sun King was not wise. Louis was so impressed with the magnificence of Vaux that he created Versailles in its image and employed many of the same artisans to do so. But since Vaux was built at least in part with revenues Fouquet had skimmed from royal taxes, the king had Fouquet and many of his associates arrested. Fouquet died in prison. Vatel left the country.

In 1669, Vatel returned to France as *contrôleur général* of the household of Louis II de Bourbon, prince de Condé, and two years later, he was again put in

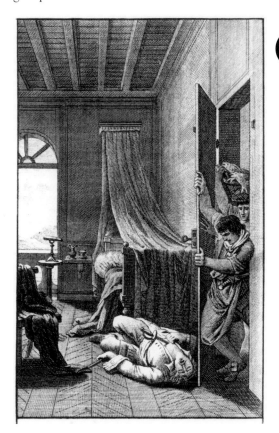

Engraving from Berchoux's La Gastronomie, *1805*

charge of entertaining the king, this time for a three-day-long festival at Chantilly. He planned lavish settings, brilliant entertainment and elegant feasts with meticulous attention to detail. It was said that he did not sleep for eleven nights prior to the royal arrival. On the first night, according to Sévigné, "the hunt, the lanterns, the moonlight, the promenade, the collation served in a spot carpeted with jonquils—all went off perfectly." However, she added, due to a number of unexpected guests, a few tables lacked roasts. Vatel was distraught, even though the king was unaware of the gaffe and Condé was unconcerned.

Later that evening, the fireworks failed. In one letter, Sévigné said the moon was too bright; in another, the sky was veiled in clouds. (Sévigné got her information from her confidant the Abbé d'Hacqueville. She was not actually at the feast.)

Since the next day was a fast day, Vatel had ordered fresh seafood. He was up all night with anxiety, and toward morning went out to check on its arrival. One purveyor was bringing in two containers. "Is that all there is?" Vatel asked. "Yes, Monsieur." By then, Vatel was beside himself. "I will not survive this disgrace," he said. "I have my honor and my reputation to lose." He waited for more seafood to arrive. When it did not, he went to his room, put his sword against the door and ran himself through. It took three attempts, according to Sévigné, before he succeeded. Shortly afterward, when the rest of the fish arrived, people looked for Vatel. They couldn't find him. They went to his room and discovered his bloody body.

Since the king would not stay in a house where there was a corpse, Vatel's body was quickly removed and buried in a nearby cemetery without ceremony. The priest recorded that he acted on orders of the prince, because a suicide is not supposed to be buried in church ground. Vatel's death was not reported in newspapers.

The festival went on just as Vatel had arranged it. Sévigné wrote, "They dined very well; they partook of a collation; they supped, they promenaded, they gambled, they hunted. Jonquils perfumed the air; there was enchantment everywhere."

Why did Vatel commit suicide? Some said he could have improvised something else if the fish hadn't arrived. However, serving thousands of guests on a day when meat was forbidden would have been nearly impossible without fish. He couldn't have had the seafood delivered a day earlier because there was no refrigeration and ice was needed for sorbets, then the fashionable dessert. Having seafood delivered fresh on the day of the banquet was the only way.

At any rate, Vatel's suicide wasn't simply about seafood. No doubt Vatel was haunted by the ghosts of Vaux. A portrait of Fouquet was found in Vatel's residence after his death and this was his first big event since that one. An enormous amount of money had been spent; the fireworks alone had cost 16,000 francs. Newspapers were quick to report flaws at these events, and nobles loved to gossip. Vatel knew the festival was important to Condé's relationship with the king. A scandal would have been ruinous.

Michel writes that when Vatel chose the sword, symbol of his office, he signaled that he was acting to preserve his honor and reputation. Molière had said honor was more important than life. Vatel agreed.

— JERI QUINZIO

Joseph Dommers Vehling

BEST KNOWN AS THE FIRST ENGLISH-LANGUAGE TRANSLATOR of **Apicius**' ancient Latin cookery book, Joseph Dommers Vehling was also artist, poet, armchair scholar, linguist, reformer, and culinary bibliophile. Most of all, he was a passionate cook.

Born in 1879 in Dülken, Germany, a hamlet near the Dutch border, Vehling's education and training are murky. He left public school at fourteen with a knowledge of Latin and some acquaintance with Greek. It appears that he spent the next fifteen years in a jumble of vocational training and liberal-arts study. Some (including Vehling himself) cast him as a German **Antonin Carême**, toiling in cookery and pastry apprenticeships for five years but stealing free moments in libraries. He cooked professionally for another five years in various cities and mastered English, Italian, and French, in addition to his native German. At some point he studied art in Düsseldorf, Vienna, and Italy, and published a volume of poems in Munich, *Aus Hohlwegen und von stillen Höhen: Dichtungen.*

From the translation of Apicius

Around the age of 23, Vehling abandoned the kitchen due to, in his own words, "bad rheumatism contracted there" and a desire to study. He embarked on a management career at prestigious European hotels, including the Bristol in Vienna and the Dremels Hotels in Aix-la-Chapelle and Brussels, and this period may overlap with his art studies. Brought to New York because of his secretarial skills (in the old-fashioned sense), he worked at the Plaza and Hotel Astor. Anthropologist Frederick Starr, who wrote the introduction to Vehling's translation of Apicius, claims that, "were we writing Mr. Vehling's biography, we would have ample material for a startling and racy narrative." Unfortunately the discreet professor remained mute on the details.

Vehling's past as a kitchen laborer guided his subsequent work. In certain ways a German-American **Auguste Escoffier**, Vehling sought to professionalize cooking beyond "mere stupid drudgery" and spent much of his energy advancing the hospitality and food-service industries. In 1911, Vehling, along with his brother, Paul, organized the International Hotel Workers' Union in New York and began publishing a monthly newsletter. Opposed to strikes, tipping, and open class warfare, their philosophy was reform through litigation, suing abusive employers to improve working conditions. Modest successes piqued the more radical American Federation of Labor; members of the AFL infiltrated the IHWU and criticized Vehling's moderate tactics. The AFL elements staged a coup, driving the brothers Vehling from the increasingly syndicalist IHWU on charges of self-dealing and arrogance.

Vehling retreated to the world of management and relocated to the Midwest. For the rest of his life, he would supervise major hotel kitchens in Chicago and Milwaukee, lecture, write, and act as a consultant to various chain restaurants and institutional kitchens. In 1923, he published the immodestly titled *Food Cost Finding and Controls for Hotels, Restaurants, Cafeterias, Clubs, Institutions, Department Stores, Industrial Eating Places, Transportation Companies and All Other Modern Eating Establishments.* In 1931, the monthly trade journal *Hotel Bulletin* added a food section, "The Nation's Chefs," and soon named Vehling its food editor. Vehling quickly dominated its pages, addressing issues ranging from food and drug laws, catering management, and practical food-service advice to esoterica such as the "dasheen fruit." He lobbied for educating cooks, boasting of the intellectual foundation of cookery, and fueled debates that still rage today, such as whether America has a "cuisine." He promoted food shows and culinary competitions to portray cooking as a high art and a profession.

Vehling's real love, however, was the then under-appreciated realm of culinary history. He collected cookery books and manuscripts dating from the fifteenth century onward, and in 1927 published *A Catalogue of Abridged Titles and Descriptions of a Collection of Gastrosophical and Magiric Documents Dating from the 15th to the Middle of the 19th Century.* This tracked much of his private collection, judged one of the world's finest. He ultimately donated nearly 500 rare and historical volumes to Cornell University's budding School of Hotel Administration, where he was a guest lecturer from 1933 through 1938.

The year 1936 saw the publication of Vehling's *Apicius: Cooking and Dining in Imperial Rome*, the first English translation of *De re coquinaria*. Vehling's art background was put to practical use: He illustrated the volume with 49 workman-like pen-and-ink drawings of ancient culinary paraphernalia, each signed with his stylized monogram.

Platina and the Rebirth of Man is Vehling's monograph-length homage to the author-editor of the world's first printed cookery book, *De honesta voluptate et valetudine*. One cannot help but think that Vehling identified with his subject, lauding "the many-sided **Platina** [who], by his selection of cookery as a subject of study and investigation displayed a singular genius." Vehling's real genius was not his flowery prose, but his practitioner's sense that a scholar such as Platina could hardly write so confidently about kitchen labor. Aided by a bit of serendipity, Vehling discerned that fully half of Platina's work was, essentially, a translation into Latin of an Italian recipe manuscript written two decades earlier by Maestro Martino of Como, the cook of the Patriarch of Aquileia.

Vehling's last book, *America's Table*, is a culinary dictionary astonishing in its scope. The inaptly-named volume reflects Vehling's belief that the golden age of "America's social and gastronomical history and practices [is] based on the best European traditions." The work does more to educate Americans about European culinary traditions than to explore American cookery. Nor can the frustrated scholar resist peppering the 882-page tome with *bons mots* dating as far back as Athenaeus and some rather peculiar digressions into European history, in addition to the descriptions of French, Italian, Spanish, and German preparations. Consistent with his broad knowledge, Vehling offers information on nutrition, dining customs, and Asian and exotic ethnic ingredients well before *nouvelle cuisine* and fusion cookery made such influences ubiquitous. *America's Table* tantalizingly promotes Vehling's two-volume companion culinary history entitled *Survey of Dining*.

It seems likely, however, that his death on September 20, 1950, in Milwaukee interrupted the publication of the *Survey*, as no trace of it is found in current library collections. Vehling was seventy-one and was survived by his widow, Johanna.

Latinists have roundly condemned Vehling as a dilettante for his non-literal translation of Apicius. (He willingly pleaded guilty to the charge of infusing practical kitchen knowledge into the sketchy recipes.) Students of Renaissance cookery, when they even acknowledge his "popular" but "significant" work on Platina and Martino, carp about its lack of footnotes. His terse obituaries describe him as a "cooking authority and cook-book collector" and the very undistinguished-sounding "catering manager of a Milwaukee hotel." All this would probably have wounded Vehling, who so clearly longed for recognition from academics and acceptance from his vocational peers. Depending on his audience, Vehling could be self-effacing or pompous, calling himself "an ex-student who drifted into the waiting business," a "foremost food specialist," or "an editor-translator and technical expert" who, most unconvincingly, wished "to stay *hors de combat*" in "the competition for scholastic laurels." Ultimately, Vehling, like his favorite subject, was a Renaissance man who vigorously lived by the creed that fine cookery was a noble and intellectually all-encompassing endeavor.

— Cathy K. Kaufman

Food Cost Finding and Controls for Hotels, Restaurants, Cafeterias, Clubs, Institutions, Department Stores, Industrial Eating Places, Transportation Companies and All Other Modern Eating Establishments, 1923
A Catalogue of Abridged Titles and Descriptions of a Collection of Gastrosophical and Magiric Documents Dating from the 15th to the Middle of the 19th Century, 1927
Apicius: Cooking and Dining in Imperial Rome, 1936
Platina and the Rebirth of Man, 1941
America's Table, 1950

Josefina Velázquez de León   ❧ 1899–1968 ❧

THE FOREMOST AUTHOR OF MEXICAN COOKBOOKS, JOSEFINA VELÁZQUEZ DE León helped to create modern Mexican cuisine by integrating recipes from diverse provinces and ethnic groups into a single national repertoire. Her career spanned more than thirty years, from the 1930's until her death in 1968, a period in which economic development, mass media, and internal migration unified Mexico. In more than 150 cookbooks, she provided a culinary voice for the nation, combining traditional Spanish dishes such as flan and *arroz con pollo* (chicken with rice) with previously scorned Native American favorites, including tamales and enchiladas, into a uniquely Mexican cuisine.

Doña Josefina, heiress of one of Mexico's most illustrious families, traced her ancestry back to the conquistador Diego Velázquez and the colonial mining official Joaquín de Velazquez Cárdenas de León. The oldest of four sisters, she was born in 1899 on an Aguascalientes hacienda and grew up in a fashionable Mexico City home. Her family lost its land during the revolution of 1910 and, in the 1920's, her marriage to an aging and unhealthy businessman, Joaquín González, ended tragically with his death in less than a year. In the mid-1930's, Josefina began to teach cooking classes in order to support her family.

Her classes featured both everyday Mexican dishes and elaborate European concoctions to satisfy the aspirations of the growing middle classes. Thus, she explained *sopa de fideos* (noodle soup) alongside veal croquettes and cakes decorated with the latest Hollywood icons like Snow White and the Seven Dwarves. This eclectic mix also characterized her first book, published in the late 1930's, *Manual práctico de cocina y repostería (Practical Manual of Cooking and Pastry)*, an instant classic that went through five editions. Her other early works included *Los 30 menus* and *La cocina económica*. By the mid-1940's, she had established her own press, Ediciones J. Velázquez de León, which ultimately offered more than 140 separate titles.

Josefina's early works, like the vast majority of Mexican cookbooks published before 1946, had concentrated on international cuisine and largely ignored national dishes made of corn because of the stigma of their lower-class, Native American origins. The rich regional variations of Mexican cooking had likewise been condensed to a few archetypal dishes, the seafood of Veracruz and Campeche, the *moles* of Puebla and Oaxaca, the roasted meats of Monterrey and Guadalajara, and little more.

Frontispiece from Platillos Regionales de la Republica Mexicana

Following the revolution of 1910, forging a unified national culture became a government priority, and Velázquez de León dedicated much of her career to overcoming the regional and ethnic chauvinism that had impeded the formation of a Mexican national cuisine. Her classic 1946 work, *Platillos regionales de la República mexicana (Regional Dishes of the Mexican Republic)*, collected for the first time the country's diverse cuisines in a single volume, placing enchiladas and tamales on an equal footing with dishes of Spanish origin.

The goal of social and culinary unification was greatly aided by mass media and highway construction. Josefina first took to the radio in 1946, and the following year she collected the recipes as *La cocina en el aire (Cooking on the Air)*. The popularity of her radio broadcasts inspired a television show in the early 1950's called "El Menu de la Semana" ("The Menu of the Week"). Josefina also used Mexico's expanding highway system to explore regional cuisines. In the 1940's, she purchased an automobile, hired a chauffeur, and set off with her loyal servant and traveling companion Luisa. Together they gave cooking classes to women throughout Mexico, usually to benefit local Catholic charities. At the same time they collected local recipes, which provided the material for a series of regional cookbooks ultimately covering more than half the states of the Republic.

Tremendous rural-urban migration in the 1940's and 1950's encouraged women to build a sense of community by sharing with new neighbors their hometown dishes, such as distinctive *moles* associated with family rituals and village festivals.

In a volume on *Cocina oaxaqueña (Oaxacan Cooking),* for example, Josefina empha-sized the authenticity of her recipe for Oaxaca's black *mole,* which she labeled the "*legítimo mole negro antiguo.*" Her 1950 work *Cómo cocinar en los aparatos modernos (How to Cook with Modern Appliances)* likewise sought to create links with the past by juxtaposing modern housewives with stereotyped historical figures. The book's illustrations showed fashionable women effortlessly using blenders and pressure cookers to make tamales with peasant girls and sweets with colonial nuns.

Josefina's Christian benevolence extended beyond the middle classes to Mexi-co's impoverished masses. She published inexpensive cookbooks such as *Cómo coci-nar en tiempos de carestía (How to Cook in Hard Times)* and *Cómo aprovechar los sobrantes de la comida (How to Use Leftover Food).* Her final work, *Cocina para enfermos (Cooking for the Ill),* appeared shortly before her death in Mexico City, on September 19, 1968, at the age of 69.

— JEFFREY M. PILCHER

Manual práctico de cocina y repostería (Practical Manual of Cooking and Pastry), late 1930's
Los 30 menus
La cocina económica
Platillos regionales de la República mexicana (Regional Dishes of the Mexican Republic), 1946
La cocina en el aire (Cooking on the Air), 1947
Manual práctico de cocina y repostería (Practical Manual of Cooking and Pastry), 1947
Mexican Cookbook Devoted to the American Homes, 1947
La cocina española en México: selección de 75 recetas de platillos (Spanish Cooking in Mexico: 75 Selected Recipes), 1947
Cocina oaxaqueña (Oaxacan Cooking),
Antojitos mexicanos: selección de 100 recetas de los principales platillos de la cocina mexicana (Mexican Savories: 100 Selected Recipes for the Principal Dishes of Mexican Cuisine), 194?
Cómo cocinar en los aparatos modernos (How to Cook with Modern Appliances), 1950
Concina de Chihuahua Chihuahuan Cooking), 195?
Repostería alemana y vienesa (German and Viennese Pastry), 1951
Cómo cocinar en tiempo de carestía (How to Cook in Hard Times), 1951
Academia de cocina y reposteria Velázquez de León (The Velázquez de León School of Cooking and Pastrymaking), 1952
Smörgåsbord, 1952
Cocina mexicana de abolengo (Mexican Heritage Cooking), 1952
Cocina criolla de Nueva Orleans (Creole Cooking of New Orleans), 1952
Cocina veracruzana (Cooking of Vercruz), 1952
Cocina regional de Michoacan (Region Cooking of Michoacan), 1952
Cocina yucateca (Cooking of the Yucatán), 1952
Cocina de Campeche (Cooking of Campeche), 1953
Cómo cocinar en tiempos de carestía (How to Cook in Hard Times)
Cómo aprovechar los sobrantes de la comida (How to Use Leftover Food)
Tamales y atoles, 1956
Concina de San Luis Potosí (Cooking of San Luis Potosí), 1957
Concina de Sonora (Cooking of Sonora), 1958
Arte y decoración de pasteles (The Art and Decoration of Cakes), 195?
Cocina para enfermos (Cooking for the Ill), 1968
Cocina oaxaqueña (Cooking of Oaxaca), 1984
Platillos de vigilia: Josefina Velázquez de León (Dishes for Fasting Days), 1988

Thomas Walker

1784–1836

THOMAS WALKER AUTHORED A SERIES OF GASTRONOMIC MUSINGS THAT MELDED **Brillat-Savarin**'s quasi-medical tone and poeticism with a curmudgeonly, Benjamin Franklin-esque pragmatism. These articles, which first appeared in London in 1835 as part of a periodical called *The Original*, do not directly paraphrase *La Physiologie du goût,* published nearly a decade earlier, but betray its influence in their spirit. Indeed, the two authors had much in common.

Walker was one of six children born at Barlow Hall in Charlton-cum-Hardy, outside Manchester, England on October 10, 1784. Like Brillat-Savarin, he trained in the law and worked professionally as a magistrate. His father, Thomas Walker the Elder (1749–1817), was a successful cotton merchant who outspokenly led the local Whig Party and founded the Manchester Constitutional Society. Thomas Walker the Younger continued his father's quest for liberal social reform, and studied the Poor Laws with special interest. After receiving his B.A. in 1808, and an M.A. in 1811 from Trinity College, Cambridge, he was called to the bar at the Inner Temple in 1812. He moved to Longford Hall, Stretford upon his father's death and there occupied himself with town politics. He later became a magistrate of Middlesex County, then of the Worship Street Police Court, and lastly of the Lambeth Police Court. In 1826 he published "Observations on the Nature, Extent, and Effects of Pauperism, and on the Means of Reducing It," and eight years later, "Suggestions for a Constitutional Reform in Parochial Government."

With a view to expanding the scope of his literary endeavors, on May 20, 1835, Walker released his first issue of *The Original*, which he single-handedly authored and published nearly every Wednesday at noon until December 2 of that year. In it, he declared his intention "to treat, as forcibly, perspicuously, and concisely as each subject and my own ability will allow, of whatever is most interesting and important in Religion and Politics, in Morals and Manners, and in our Habits and Customs." Articles devoted to the "Regulation of Charity" and the "Domestic Economy of the Labouring Classes," and serialized extracts of his treatise on the Poor Laws, were interspersed with descriptions from his travels to the continent in 1822, popular sayings, and short, often hastily written diatribes on matters as diverse as "Marriage in Low Life," latter-day Judas Iscariots, and the advantages of the two-penny post. Such unapologetic statements as "Liberty is a super-excellent thing, very much talked about, and very little understood, generally least of all by those who make the most noise about it; indeed, I should say, it is an unerring rule, that a noisy advocate for liberty is never a sincere one" typified the intolerance for hypocrisy and the unwillingness to submit to the status quo that Walker evinced throughout his pages.

More than any other topic, *The Original* devoted special attention to the "art of dining," for the study of which he invented the word "aristology," because "according to the lexicons, the Greek for dinner is Ariston." The subject was inextricably bound to the "art of attaining high health," in its author's mind. Sick and weakly as a child, Walker as a young man transformed his health through a methodical reform of diet and lifestyle, which inspired his articles. "My care," he explained, "was neither to anticipate my appetite, nor to overload it, nor to disappoint it—in fact, to keep it at the best possible humour." The success of this experiment led him to conclude that careful attention to diet could improve the smoothness of both skin and temper, reduce blistering and swelling of the feet, and even protect the weary traveler from the stress of unknown adventures.

Walker provided his readers with only a handful of recipes—a baked, fruit-filled rice pudding; stewed vegetables; a salad of cooked onions, celery, and beetroot; and another of simply dressed lettuce. Instead, Walker prescribed guidelines to "ensure the greatest quantity of health and enjoyment."

The expression "Enough is as good as a feast" embodied Walker's approach to the table. In contrast to the numerous dishes that typically comprised any course in his era, Walker preferred to dine on one food at a time, successively. In his no-nonsense opinion, "A chief maxim in dining with comfort is, to have what you want when you want it." Toward this end, Walker decried the grand formality of fashionable London dinners for sixteen and advised a maximum of eight guests (preferring Brillat-Savarin's ideal of six) and limiting the selection of foods and wines consumed on any given day to a good quantity of the best local, affordable, and seasonal foods. An ideal Christmas dinner he organized for three consisted only of crimped cod, woodcock, and plum pudding, all accompanied by champagne. He contrasted this to contemporary menus that offered delicate woodcock after a substantial roast, when the appetite was already sated.

Walker bowed neither to tradition nor to fashion in his aristological recommendations. He enjoyed a good glass of table-beer as much as a fine glass of claret and endorsed sparkling champagne at a time when snobbish oenologists of his generation lauded the still variety. He deplored the fact that good vegetables only appeared in a secondary way at formal dinners; admitted he held little affection for dessert at all, deeming fruit more enjoyable at any other moment of the day; and denigrated lunch, then just coming into vogue, as "a joyless dinner." He painstakingly explained the importance of having every accompaniment on the table before the main dish arrived steaming hot from a kitchen situated close to the dining room, and the hospitality afforded by a cheerfully blazing fire in winter. He thought wine should be placed within easy reach on the table, rather than poured out by the butler at the sideboard. Among his most innovative recommendations, Walker insisted that guests be given an invitation that included the names of other attendees, the menu, wines, and in what quantity they would be served, in order to allay any disappointment or niggling misapprehension in advance.

Other suggestions—the importance of clarity of décor, a well-proportioned dining room and table, proper lighting, and punctuality—reprise those in *La Physiologie du goût*. Although he never mentioned Brillat-Savarin, Walker had traveled in France; noted the advantages of the *cabinets particuliers* of Parisian restaurants; quoted Madame de Staël; and considered French vegetables and undecorated white porcelain worthy of English emulation. Although he admired the attractiveness and lightness of French cuisine, he nevertheless concluded, "I do not think, from my own experience and observation, that the French mode of cookery is so favourable to physical power as the English."

Walker thought the art of dining especially important for women to study, but warned, "There is one female failing in respect to dinners, which I cannot help here noticing, and that is, a very inconvenient love of garnish and flowers, either natural or cut in turnips and carrots, and stuck on dishes, so as to greatly impede carving and helping." No woman could ever have lived up to the idealized image Walker presented of his mother, who, he nostalgically recalled, tirelessly and uncomplainingly waited up for him until any hour to greet him cheerfully by the fire, with a supper tray waiting ready in the kitchen.

It is hardly surprising that Walker remained a lifelong bachelor who retreated to the masculine confines of his club, the Athenaeum, to dine and to write. The gentleman's club, an innovation he deemed "one of the greatest and most important modern changes in society," made a cheerful alternative to lonely evenings perched on a cane chair in the bedroom of his hotel, where he wrote late into the night. But the burden of completing an entire periodical, week after week, wore on him increasingly. By September 16, Walker confessed to his readers that he did not always take his own advice regarding the importance of regulating diet, sleep, and exercise and felt great panic at needing four more pages by the next morning. On November 18 he revealed that "the dangers of good cheer" had increasingly tempted him, resulting in a flurry of all-nighters to release his publication on time. At half past four in the morning, he still needed six additional pages by the next day. On December 2 he proclaimed, "London living and authorship do not go well together," and announced he was taking an extended holiday.

He intended to resume work in March of the following year, after a restorative trip to the continent. However, he died of pulmonary apoplexy on January 20, 1836 in Brussels, where he is buried. Despite ill health, Walker's innate curiosity, interest in social reform, and love of a good meal continued until the very end. He took time out from sightseeing to visit local prisons. On the eve of his death he attended church, dined at his inn, and retired to rest.

Popular from the time of its publication, *The Original* was reprinted through the nineteenth century in numerous editions, many of which reorganized and edited the somewhat jumbled order of Walker's articles. Long after his opinions on the Poor Laws were forgotten, Walker's gastronomic writing continued to be read. As early as 1837, a selected edition of these was published in Philadelphia with the title *The Art of Dining and of Attaining High Health*. An 1881 edition, edited and annotated by Felix Summerly (i.e., Sir Henry Cole), which appeared as *Aristology; or the Art of Dining*, included an appendix with Brillat-Savarin's aphorisms. Further editions were published in 1921, 1928 (including illustrations by J. M. Dixon) and 1965 (with drawings by Lynton Lamb). Walker's influence extended into such works as the anonymously published *Art of Dining; or Gastronomy and Gastronomers* (1852) and has been excerpted in anthologies such as *The Epicure's Companion* edited by Ann Seranne and John Trebbel (1962).

— CAROLIN C. YOUNG

The Original, weekly from May 20 until December 2, 1835

Artemas Ward

❦ 1848–1925 ❦

ARTEMAS WARD WAS BORN ON MAY 20, 1848, IN NEW YORK CITY, WHERE HE lived his early life, with the exception of a year in Europe. He was named for his great-grandfather, a Revolutionary War general. In 1863, at the age of fifteen, Ward began working at the New York Soldiers' Depot, caring for soldiers returning from the Civil War. He later moved to Philadelphia and became an employee of the shipping house of Isaac Hough & Morris, which imported and exported goods from and to Cuba. In Philadelphia he married Rebecca Dunwoody Robinson; they had one son, also named Artemas Ward.

In 1874, Ward founded *The Philadelphia Grocer*, a periodical which he edited for several years. At the time, the grocery trade in America was in flux. As American cities grew larger, grocery stores proliferated. Staple foods, such as flour, grains, and sugar, were sold from barrels or sacks. Grocery stores also carried specialty items, such as tea, wine, spices, and sugar, as well as such domestic products as syrups, jellies, and nuts. The stores themselves, as well as the range of goods they stocked, expanded after the Civil War. It was difficult for grocery-store owners to understand all the changes that were under way in the trade—hence the success of publications like *The Philadelphia Grocer*. Ward concluded that grocers needed general information about food, and he compiled data about specific products and published them in a book titled *The Grocer's Hand-Book* (1882); a second edition was published four years later.

Ward's work in publishing *The Philadelphia Grocer* and *The Grocer's Hand-Book* gained him wide recognition, which resulted in his appointment in 1885 as general manager of the firm Enoch Morgan's Sons' Company. *The Philadelphia Grocer* continued and was subsequently renamed *The National Grocer*. In 1894 it merged with

From The William Ward Genealogy; The History of the Descendants of William Ward of Sudbury, Mass., 1638–1925, *published in 1925. In it,* Artemas Ward *is described as "Publisher of this Genealogy."*

The American Grocer, which was the most important source of information about food products through the mid-twentieth century.

Enoch Morgan's Sons' manufactured Sapolio soap, and Ward engaged in a number of unusual promotional stunts to advertise the product. In 1892, Ward sent Captain William Andrews across the Atlantic on a 14-foot sailboat named *Sapolio*; Andrews left with great fanfare from Atlantic City and sailed to Palos, Spain, the port from which Christopher Columbus had sailed 400 years earlier on his first voyage of discovery to the New World. Newspapers covered the voyage, and Ward and Andrews wrote a book about it. Thanks to promotional stunts like this, Sapolio became one of the most popular soaps in America.

In 1899, Ward established an advertising agency, Ward & Gow, later renamed Artemas Ward, Inc. He obtained the right to advertise in Brooklyn's elevated trains and later acquired the rights to advertising and merchandising on New York City's subways. To supply the vending machines and news-stands in the subway, he began manufacturing chocolate and chewing gum. The profits from these activities made him wealthy, and he bought a dairy in Orange County, New York and an apple orchard in Virginia.

Throughout his life, Ward retained an interest in food. When he retired from Enoch Morgan's Sons' in 1910, he immediately began work on *The Grocer's Encyclopedia*, a 748-page work that was the first food encyclopedia published in America. True to his interest in advertising, the front cover was a promotion for the Puritan Chocolate Company, which he owned. Ward added many color illustrations to this work and twelve years later published the revised work as *The Encyclopedia of Food*, which, according to Charles Martyn, was "the most lavishly illustrated volume on the subject that has ever been produced, a standard reference work in libraries and the higher education institutions."

Ward was also interested in American history and biography, particularly in the Revolutionary War period. In 1921 he published Charles Martyn's *The Life of Artemas Ward* (a biography of his great grandfather), and in 1925, Martyn's *The William Ward Genealogy*. Ward died in New York in 1925, but his *Encyclopedia of Food* outlived him: It was reprinted in 1929 and again in 1941. His four food books remain some of the best historical material on American grocery stores and the products they sold.

— ANDREW F. SMITH

The Grocers' Hand-Book and Directory for 1883, 1882
The Grocer's Hand-Book and Directory for 1886, 1886
The Grocer's Encyclopedia, 1911
The Encyclopedia of Food, 1923

Cajsa Warg

ALSO CALLED: Anna Christina Warg

ANNA CHRISTINA WARG, AFFECTIONATELY KNOWN BY HER NICKNAME, CAJSA, has been called "the mother of the art of Swedish cooking," thanks to her book *Hjelpreda i Hushållningen för Unga Fruentimber (Housekeeping Advice for Young Wives)*. Although not the very first, Warg's tome was one of the earliest Swedish cookbooks and is arguably the most famous. Published in 1755, it was immediately successful and went on to be reprinted fourteen times, the last time in 1822. It included some 800 recipes, as well as practical advice on such matters as how to make ink and remove wine stains. A modern reprint, minus the household tips, was released in 1993 by Rabén & Sjögren under the title *Cajsa Wargs Kokbok: Man Tager Vad Man Haver (Cajsa Warg's Cookbook: One Takes What One Has)*.

The subtitle refers to a famous saying popularly attributed to Warg, though scholars have not found it in her writings. Still, the sentiment would probably sit well with the resourceful author, whose life's work—in addition to writing her book—was running the household of her maternal cousin Catharina and her cousin's husband, Baron Leonard Klinckowström. Warg managed the kitchens both in the town house on Hercules Street in Stockholm and at the family's country estate, Löfsta, in Uppland, north of the capital. Together with several kitchen-maids and manservants, she would have been responsible not only for preparing banquet dinners but also for the daunting task of preserving enough of the food grown on the family's lands to get the household through the long Swedish winters.

Born in Örebro, Cajsa was one of two daughters. Her father, Anders Warg, died when she was only five years old; several years later Cajsa's mother, Catharina, remarried and moved to the country estate of her new husband, Erik Rosenstråle. Cajsa may have moved with her mother or she may have then gone to live with other relatives to begin her training in household management. Lacking a dowry to attract a gentleman, yet too well bred to be married to a farmer or a smith—not to mention that the country's wars had left a gender imbalance of three men to every five women—Warg never married. Instead, at age sixteen, she went to live with her newlywed cousin, with whom she spent the rest of her days. She was 52 years old when her cookbook was published.

Its success has been attributed to the eighteenth-century public's interest in food and drink, to the comprehensiveness of the volume, and to Warg's detailed measurements and instructions. For the 21-century reader, some of Warg's recipes are more curious than useful: how to salt mutton, stuff a pig, make blood soup, stew milk thistles, or brew beer. But many others represent dishes that are still part of Sweden's traditional cooking repertoire known as *husmanskost*—home cooking. These include recipes for rose-hip soup, rye crisps, ginger snaps, rice pudding, caper sauces for fish dishes, and instructions for cooking an artichoke. Interestingly, while Warg included several recipes for ice cream, then a new fad, she did not even mention what would become the foremost Swedish staple: the humble potato.

On her death at age 66, Cajsa Warg was buried in the Klinckowström family plot in Stockholm's Klara Kyrka.

— JUDITH PIERCE ROSENBERG

Hjelpreda i Hushållningen för Unga Fruentimber (Housekeeping Advice for Young Wives), 1755. Reprinted under the title *Cajsa Wargs Kokbok: Man Tager Vad Man Haver (Cajsa Warg's Cookbook: One Takes What One Has)*, 1993

Anna Weckerin

❧ C. 1535–1596 ❧

ALSO CALLED: Anna Wecker

*Down to the cat, the kitchen scene on the title page of Anna Weckerin's cookbook is almost identical to the title illustration of **Marx Rumpolt**'s* Ein New Kochbuch *(1581), except that here the image was altered to make both cooks women.*

ANNA WECKERIN IS THE AUTHOR OF THE FIRST known printed cookbook written by a woman. She was born in Basel, Switzerland, the daughter of one Isaac Keller; she became the wife of a very well known physician of the time, Johann Jacob Wecker of Colmar, in Alsace, and later his widow.

Wecker's wealth, prominence, and wide acquaintance gave his wife the responsibility of running a large household, and also the opportunity to learn about dishes and recipes that were beyond the means of working- or middle-class households. Far more important, she learned through him about the physical and spiritual needs of the sick, and probably assisted him in their dietetic treatment.

Weckerin's cookbook thus presents no humble dishes, but rather a healthful cuisine intended for the urban upper-middle class and aristocracy, with particular attention to the sick and those needing special care. It is clearly written by a woman well acquainted with the medical practices of the time.

After Wecker's death in 1586, Weckerin (she used the feminine form of his family name) was probably left in comfortable circumstances and apparently continued to run her household and to collect recipes. It may have been the economic and social straits in which her daughter and son-in-law found themselves that made her decide to publish her collection. Certainly she moved from Colmar to their home in Altdorf, near Nürnberg, near the end of her life, and the dedication of her cookbook is dated "Altdorf, Anno 1596."

She gave the collection the title *Ein köstlich new Kochbuch von allerhand Speisen... (A Delightful New Cookbook of All Kinds of Dishes...)* and asserted her authorship with the phrase "Mit Fleiss beschrieben durch F. Anna Weckerin" (Industriously described by Mrs. Anna Weckerin). A local noblewoman under whose patronage the book was to appear was the addressee of a most humble dedication, in which

Weckerin recalled her husband's "industry and effort" in the practice of medicine and his extensive writings, and pointed out that he had known that "good order in eating and drinking" was of the greatest importance, especially for the sick, and that he had always preferred "to cure and help [his patients] from the kitchen rather than from the apothecary." She continued, "Because he noticed not only that I had always had great enjoyment from cooking, but also that God had given me the rare grace and gift of serving and waiting upon sick people through my preparation of various useful and acceptable dishes, and that I had by such means and by God's grace brought many weak people, including some of high degree, back to their strength, he was always glad to have me at his side at the sickbed, and he also frequently urged me to describe and write down what I had observed and used for the sick and had found effective."

The cookbook is in four chapters, the first on almonds, grains, and vegetables, and the second on dried and fresh fruit. The third chapter deals with meat dishes, and the last with fish and sauces. Recipes for almond milk and blancmange establish a firm connection to medieval cuisine, as do some of the multiple cooking methods used for meat: boiling followed by mincing, steaming, sieving, and finally roasting. Less typical is the fact that meat recipes make up only twenty percent of the book, and that, in many recipes, there are changes of ingredients or cooking methods specified for the sick. Some recipes are specifically curative: "Eggs good for the feverish," "For purging," "Food for those losing weight," and so on. And Weckerin was no armchair cook: she specifies the size of dishes, describes what utensils should be made of and how they should be used, and explains how to distribute the fire coals.

Published the year after Weckerin's death, the cookbook was apparently a success, for the second edition is dated the next year, 1598. It contains a second, much more concise, dedication to the same noble lady, signed by Weckerin's daughter, Katharina Taurellus, but probably composed by her son-in-law, Nicolaus Taurellus. He was a quarrelsome and usually impecunious nonconformist professor of medicine at the University of Altdorf who spent much of his income producing pamphlets to argue the causes he espoused and publicize the injustices he suffered; the income from Weckerin's cookbook was no doubt welcome to him and his large family, as was the public association with his well-remembered father-in-law.

Though Weckerin's is the earliest printed cookbook by a woman, it is certain that there were other women in that time who were also writing down their recipes and observations in the kitchen. For example, Sabina Welserin, a member of the prominent Welser family of Augsburg, began her cookbook in 1553 with a prayer for wisdom, reason and common sense. She wrote a fine cookbook, clear and concise, with an emphasis on showy presentation, but it languished in manuscript form for centuries, and was first published only in 1980 as part of a study of the development of the German language.

— JULIUS ARNDT

Ein köstlich new Kochbuch von allerhand Speisen an Gemüsen, Obs, Fleisch, Geflügel, Wildpret,
Fischen und Gebackens. Nit allein vor Gesunde: sondern auch und fürnemlich vor Kranke,
in allerlei Krankheiten und Gebrästen: auch Schwangere Weiber, Kindbetterinnen, unnd

alte schwache Leute, künstlich und nützlich zuzurichten unnd zugebrauchen (A Delightful New Cookbook of All Kinds of Dishes, of Vegetables, Fruit, Meat, Fowl, Game, Fish and Baked Goods. How to Prepare and Use These Artfully and Practically Not Only for Healthy Persons, but Also and Especially for the Sick, Suffering From All Kinds of Illness or Injury, Also Pregnant Women and Those in Childbed, and Old Weak People), 1597. Second edition with additional dedication, 1598. Subsequent editions 1600, 1606, 1609, 1667, 1679, 1697

Frances Virginia Whitaker

❦ 1895–1962 ❦

Whitaker's silhouette on the Frances Virginia Tea Room's pink and green sign signified elegance and good food for more than thirty years.

BORN IN CARTERVILLE, GEORGIA AS THE DAUGHTER OF A PHARMACIST, FRANCES Virginia Wikle combined propriety with unconventionality in her life and brought healthy and tasty food to an underserved portion of the Southern public.

She studied at Wesleyan College but received a diploma in collegiate industrial home economics from Georgia Normal and Industrial College in Milledgeville (later Georgia State College for Women), and in 1918 received a degree in dietetics from the Pratt Institute in Brooklyn, New York. At a time when vitamin-deficiency diseases were common in the South and research in nutrition was as full of exciting promise as DNA research today, she was called to head the first nutrition and dietetics department in Atlanta at the Piedmont Hospital, working with the hospital's famous Dr. James Paullin, planning menus, devising preparation methods, and training and supervising dietetic interns, nurses, and kitchen staff.

In the early 1920's Wikle moved briefly to Bartow, Florida, where she opened her first "tea room." She returned to Atlanta late in the decade as the wife of Toxey Whitaker and, in 1929, in the depths of the Depression but with the help of her sisters, hired dependable home cooks and opened the Frances Virginia Tea Room and Tray Shop on Poplar Street. The tea room served light fare, fresh vegetable salads, low-fat appetizers and soups; the availability of electric toasters and refrigerators enabled the staff to make toasted sandwiches quickly and to offer gelatin salads and aspics. Frances Virginia herself greeted diners; her mother presided at the cashier's desk.

In the 1920's—and indeed even into the 1960's in the South—department-store grills, public hotel dining rooms, bars, and drugstore counters were off limits to ladies, especially if unescorted. The "tea room," with its air of gentility and decorum and its female ownership and operating staff, provided a socially sanctioned place where women could eat in public with propriety and safety. Ladies—escorted or unescorted—and gentlemen—often including gay men—and families could eat lunch and dinner there, as well as afternoon tea, in an understated and elegant decor and a comfortable atmosphere. At a time when businessmen in Atlanta, and even their secretaries, went home for "dinner" at noon, and when the city's upper crust entertained at home or in their clubs, the tea room offered to others relatively fast food that was also nutritious and healthy, as well as tasteful presentation of excellent and familiar dishes. Besides lunching ladies, customers of the Frances Virginia soon included workers on their lunch break from downtown offices.

Whitaker soon moved "The Frances Virginia," as it came to be called, to Peachtree Street, occupying the entire third floor of the Collier Building and taking space in the basement for butchering and vegetable preparation. Every plate that left the kitchen was inspected by Whitaker or her assistant for adherence to the standards of quality, cleanliness, and esthetics she had learned in college. There was no lukewarm soup, no limp lettuce, and the fancy green olive was centered in every pre-measured mound of chicken salad. There were children's menus and long-legged "junior chairs" for young ladies and gentlemen. The menu, changed daily, was relatively light and included a plenitude of fresh Southern dishes such as turnip greens, pole beans, and fried chicken; "exotic" items such as deviled crab, eggplant casserole, harvard beets, and asparagus aspic; and petite hot muffins. There was no alcohol except in some post-Prohibition desserts, of which sherry chiffon pie, rum cream pie and fluffy wine sauce were favorites. The Frances Virginia seated 350 and by 1943 was serving more than 2,000 people a day.

Whitaker brought in friends and other family members to help run the tea room, including Louise Nabell and Ruth Pannell from secretarial jobs and Agnes New, who held degrees in home economics and dietetics, from the food service department at Emory University Hospital. In the late 1930's, as her health began to fail, Whitaker sold her own shares in the tea room to her sister, who in turn, in the early 1940's, sold the thriving operation to Nabell, Pannell, and New. Nabell became the tea room's manager, Pannell ran the front of the house, and New was in charge of the kitchen, and the Frances Virginia continued as an Atlanta landmark for another sixteen years, maintaining its reputation for elegance and excellent food. Many customers assumed that Nabell and Pannell were "Frances" and "Virginia," and asked which of them had posed for the famous silhouette on the tea room's sign.

Frances Virginia Whitaker retired to New Smyrna Beach, Florida, in the 1950's and died on July 4, 1962, a year after the construction of Georgia's first shopping mall on Peachtree Road. The tea room's three operating partners retired in the same year and closed the operation, taking recipes, records, and memories home.

The Frances Virginia's corner of Peachtree and Ellis had been the Times Square of the South, a center for movies, hotels, and shopping, and history marched past three decades of diners at their window tables: the glamorous stars of *Gone With the Wind*, World War II brides in gloves and girdles, teenaged girls in crinolines. In its heyday, the tea room was *the* place to hold the annual "Girls' High" Senior Tea, to propose marriage, interview a candidate, or celebrate a birthday or graduation. Its pink and green sign, with Whitaker's own bobbed-hair silhouette, was a feature of Peachtree Street and a symbol of accessible elegance and excellent food.

— MILDRED HUFF COLEMAN

Harvey Washington Wiley

c. 1910

HARVEY WASHINGTON WILEY WAS BORN IN INDIANA ON October 18, 1844. He earned his A.B. degree from Hanover College, an M.D. degree from Indiana Medical College, and a B.S. degree from Harvard University. After Harvard, he returned to Indiana to become professor of chemistry at Purdue University. He remained at Purdue from 1874 to 1883, focusing on tests to detect the adulteration of sugars and syrups.

In large part because of his interest in sugar chemistry, Wiley was offered the position as the seventh Chief Chemist for the United States Department of Agriculture. He held this position for 29 years, from 1883 to 1912. The USDA Division of Chemistry was the predecessor organization to the current Food and Drug Administration, and the Chief Chemist was the predecessor for the current Commissioner of Food and Drugs.

Laws to regulate food and drugs had been enacted from the very beginning of the United States at the state and local level. At that time the prevailing interpretation of the Commerce Clause in the United States Constitution was that the production of food and drugs was an entirely local matter, over which Congress had no jurisdiction. It wasn't until 1879 that the first national legislation to regulate the food and drug supply was even introduced in Congress.

Wiley came into his position four years later. He became an unflagging proponent for national legislation and a towering figure of his era, traveling throughout the country to champion his cause, commanding the attention of the entire nation with the force of his personality. It would still take 27 years before the law would be enacted. The 1906 Act is properly regarded as a landmark in American history; it transformed the American food and drug supply by prohibiting all adulteration and misbranding throughout the country.

Soon after he came to Washington, Wiley focused the work of the Division of Chemistry on a systematic study of food adulteration. He and his staff published numerous studies demonstrating food adulteration throughout the country, thereby gathering public support for national legislation.

Wiley transformed a small scientific staff focusing on agricultural chemistry into a powerful advocacy organization encompassing the safety and labeling of all food and drug products marketed in the United States. Because he was such a zealot, with a deep and unfailing certitude in the righteousness of his cause, even pursuing his own interests to the exclusion of others, his presence quickly polarized groups into opposing camps. People were either for him or against him. His arrogance and contentious nature permitted no middle ground.

Wiley's genius for publicity led to undoubtedly the most widely publicized safety test in American history: the 1902–1904 human feeding study on twelve young USDA employees—popularly referred to as the Poison Squad—of the five most often used food preservatives. Although the results of these feeding studies were undoubtedly uninterruptible from a purely scientific standpoint, the testing itself clearly captured the imagination of the American public and helped prepare the way for the national law.

Although Wiley is credited with being the "father" of the Food and Drugs Act of 1906, this is only partly true. However extraordinary Wiley's work may have been, the 1906 Act would almost certainly have become law anyway, enacted as a direct result of the national publicity about unsanitary meat-packing following publication of **Upton Sinclair**'s novel *The Jungle* in 1906.

Following enactment of the 1906 Act, Wiley sought to enforce it vigorously. He strongly felt that his work was thwarted by others in the USDA who advocated a more moderate approach. His constant confrontations with his colleagues culminated in charges brought in 1911 that he had illegally paid too much for a consultant. After his vindication, he left the USDA in 1912 to become an associate editor of *Good Housekeeping Magazine* where he became director of the Bureau of Foods, Sanitation and Health, the predecessor to the Good Housekeeping Institute, and helped make Good Housekeeping an American institution. He authored *The History of a Crime Against the Food Law* in 1929 and *An Autobiography* in 1930, just before his death on June 30, 1930, the 24th anniversary of the 1906 Act.

— PETER BARTON HUTT

The History of a Crime Against the Food Law, 1929
An Autobiography, 1930

Hannah Wolley

❦ 1622 OR 1623–1674 OR LATER ❦

ALSO CALLED: Hannah Woolley

IN HER BOOK, *THE QUEENE-LIKE CLOSET*, HANNAH WOLLEY ADDRESSES WOMEN WHO have been "impoverished by the late Calamities, *viz.* the Late Wars, Plague, and Fire." It is likely that she herself lived in precarious financial circumstances at several periods during her life, particularly before she went into service at age seventeen and after the deaths of her two husbands. At the same time, the social turmoil of the mid-seventeenth century permitted a more public role for women, and she was able to earn an income by writing cookbooks and household manuals and to attain a certain renown from her books. She is, in fact, the first female author of a printed cookbook in the English language. (She was preceded, however, by **Anna Weckerin**, writing in German more than half a century earlier.)

Hannah was born about 1622 and learned cooking and housekeeping from her mother and elder sisters, women who were skilled in making medicines and

Title page of The Queene-Like Closet, *1670*

treating the sick. We do not hear of her father. Later, in the service of Anne, Lady Maynard, of Essex, her abilities were encouraged and she was allowed expensive ingredients for her potions; she also met physicians and was given access to books by her employer. It was while in service to this royalist family that Hannah participated in serving the king, Charles I.

When she was 24, Hannah married a schoolmaster named Wolley from a nearby village. The marriage was a happy one, producing several children, including four sons. The couple moved to Hackney, where they ran a boarding school for 60 pupils, thereby giving Hannah further opportunity to perfect her domestic skills.

When Hannah Wolley's husband died in 1661, she self-published *The Ladies Directory,* presumably to help support herself and her children. In this work, she offered recipes for cakes, comfits, and preserved and candied fruits and flowers, as well as medicines and perfumes. The book went into a second edition, encouraging her to write *The Cooks Guide* (1664), which contained many more recipes for all kinds of dishes, including some for "Kickshaws" and "Ho-good [*Haut-Goût*] Sawces," in the French taste.

In 1666, Hannah married Francis Challiner (or Chaloner), but within four years she was widowed for the second time and again took up her pen, publishing *The Queene-Like Closet* in 1670 and *The Ladies Delight* in 1672. Having established some reputation under the name Hannah Wolley, she continued to write under this name. Evidence of the value of her name as author is seen in the publication of *The Gentlewomans Companion* in 1673, attributed to "Hannah Woolley." Though based on her earlier books and possibly begun with her consent, this book was clearly written by someone else. The frontispiece portrait that appears in the second edition of the work is also not of Hannah.

At the end of her life, Hannah Wolley lived with one of her sons, supplementing her income from writing by selling medicines and giving lessons in preserving and embroidery. In 1674, she published her final book, *A Supplement to the Queene-Like Closet,* in which she included a brief autobiographical sketch.

— ALICE ARNDT

The Ladies Directory, 1661
The Cooks Guide: or, Rare Receipts for Cookery, 1664
The Queene-Like Closet; or, Rich Cabinet, 1670
The Ladies Delight; or, Rich Closet of Choice Experiments and Curiosities, 1672
The Gentlewomans Companion; or, A Guide to the Female Sex, attributed to Hannah Woolley, 1673
A Supplement to the Queene-Like Closet; or, A Little of Every Thing, 1674

Y

Yuan Mei

❊ 1716–1798 ❊

The poet Yuan Mei lived in China in the eighteenth century, during the Qing dynasty. As he neared the end of his life, he was expressively vocal about old age. (Translations are by Arthur Waley, from *Madly Singing in the Mountains*, edited by Ivan Morris, 1970.)

On people's insistence that he still write poems for them and his continued willingness to do that:

Can it be that though my body sinks to decay,
My writing brush alone is still young?

On frailty:

If I step into the garden, a servant rushes to hold me;
If I climb the stairs, the whole household panics.

On being unable to sleep:

Now that I am old, I am frightened of the night, for it seems longer than a year.

On diminished abilities:

This winter cricket's wings must both be there,
Or it would not be able to fashion its songs.

When he was 78 (or so: In East Asia, a newborn is considered to be "one year old"), his sight improved for no accountable reason and he was able to give up his spectacles. Perhaps encouraged by this miracle, he was finishing his cookery book at the end of 1796, though parts of it had been circulating in manuscript for years. It is called *Shih Tan (The Menu).*

Yuan Mei had always cadged recipes from his friends' cooks by sending his own cook to learn how to make especially delicious dishes that he had tasted in their houses. He was no easily satisfied gourmand: He tells tales of being offended by lavish display of endless but tasteless dishes, but also of a host who was begged by a (rude!) guest never to be invited again because the food was so bad. He delivers quite obvious cautions for the cook: His hands must be clean, the ingredients "fresh and in good condition"; he must not let ashes from his pipe get into the food. He cautions that it is impossible to make more than four dishes in a day without allowing quality to suffer, and that assistants are no good, for they will have their own ideas. He praises chicken, pork, fish, and duck as "the original geniuses of the board" and dismisses sea-slug and swallow's nest as having no character, served only to impress by their expense. There are two paragraphs about black-groats wine, called *wu-fan* in Chinese. This is made with "dark-cooked millet," and he could not stop drinking it, though drunkenness was not his habit.

Yuan Mei had always been known for his joviality and his love of company:

> *If you want to call, you need only pause outside the hedge and listen;*
> *The place from which the most laughter comes is certain to be my house!*

All that was important to him—truth; absolute honesty; the inclusion of all things, no matter how improper; loyalty to those he loved—went into his verse, as well as humor, for which he was criticized. He did not bother with politics but his views, which Arthur Waley says were typical of his time, included "the right of women to be educated," and he and his friends sometimes had "lady-pupils."

Yuan Mei left detailed instructions about the disposition of his property and especially the manner of marking his death: no priests, scriptures, or chanting; notices for certain people on colored paper, for other on small slips; and so on.

Curiously, because a few excerpts from *Shih Tan* appeared in English in Herbert A. Giles' *History of Chinese Literature* (1901) and because the whole volume appeared in French in 1924, thanks to an unknown translator who called himself Panking, Yuan Mei has been known in the West more for the cookery book than as a poet. He would have laughed: There were at least 6300 poems.

— ANN F. WOODWARD

Shih Tan (The Menu), c. 1796

Zhang Qien

⚜ DIED C. 115 BC ⚜

ALSO CALLED: Chang Ch'ien

ZHANG QIEN, CHINA'S MARCO POLO, WAS THE FIRST EXPLORER TO REPORT TO the Chinese court on Central Asia, Persia and the fringes of the Roman Empire.

In 138 BC, Wu Ti, the "Martial Emperor" of the Han Dynasty, sent Zhang Qien, commander of the guard at the imperial palace gates, some two thousand miles west on a diplomatic mission. With one hundred retainers and his "barbarian" slave Kan-fu, he was to find the Yuechi people, who had been driven out of northwestern China by the Xiongnu, or Huns, a confederation of nomadic steppe tribes with whom the Han, like the Chin before them, were intermittently and unsuccessfully at war. Zhang was to form an alliance with the Yuechi against the Xiongnu, but the Xiongnu soon captured the envoy and his entourage and kept Zhang in diplomatic captivity for ten years. When they moved him to the western edge of their territories, Zhang was able to escape, with some of his retainers and the wife and family he had meanwhile acquired, and he carried on his mission.

Traveling through several Central Asian states whose rulers expressed interest in trade with China, Zhang finally found the Yuechi in Bactria (in today's Afghanistan), but though he spent a year trying to persuade them, they remained uninterested in an alliance with China against the Xiongnu. Returning to China, Zhang was again captured by the Xiongnu, from whom he escaped after only a year, returning to Wu Ti's court with his wife and Kan-fu after a twelve-year absence.

But Zhang's travels were not in vain. He returned with a wealth of firsthand political and economic information about Central Asia and indirect knowledge of Persia, Arabia, India and the Roman Empire, as well as word of the magnificent horses bred in the Ferghana Valley—horses that Wu Ti could use against the barbarians of the steppe.

Zhang Qien later accepted a second mission, this time among the Indo-European–speaking Wu-sun of the Tarim Basin, in today's Xinjiang Province of China. Accompanied by three hundred horse soldiers, he set out with silk, precious metals, and other enticements. He delegated visits to various parts of Central Asia to an aide. On his own, he assembled a dossier on Parthia, Bactria, and India and returned to Wu Ti with news of a diplomatic link with Greece. Because of his persistence, China gained ambassadorial status with Central Asia.

Though Wu Ti did not obtain his Ferghana horses until the year 102, after Zhang's death, the envoy brought the Chinese people a host of new foods from his forays into the West. To a diet based on rice, beans, and millet, Zhang added grapes and pomegranates, walnuts, sesame and caraway, cucumber and coriander, peas, and onions, as well as alfalfa. New foods expanded the variety of plants grown in China's kitchen gardens and made possible a new era of refined food flavors, aromas, and textures in Chinese cuisine.

— MARY ELLEN SNODGRASS

Shih Tan (The Menu), c. 1796

Ziryab

✦ C. 789–C. 857 ✦

ALSO CALLED: Abu al-Hasan 'Ali ibn Nafi' | "Blackbird"

THE CUISINE OF MEDIEVAL ARAB SPAIN—AND EVENTUALLY OF EUROPE AS A whole—was profoundly influenced by one of the great musicians of the time, a man known as Ziryab or "Blackbird."

So named because of his dark complexion and beautiful singing voice, Ziryab performed and taught music in Cordoba under the patronage of the Umayyad emir of al-Andalus, Abdul Rahman II. The musician became widely known as an arbiter of style; historians have compared him to Beau Brummel and Petronius. He introduced revolutionary changes in music, dining, fashion, grooming, hairstyles, cosmetics and other aspects of courtly life. Many of his innovations spread to other social classes and communities, and eventually throughout Western Europe. In the ninth century, Cordoba was the capital of the civilized West, just as Baghdad was the cultural center of the Arab East. Cordoba's fads, fashions and creations were widely emulated. Ziryab's innovations were more than fads, and a number of them survive in the West to this day, as enduring parts of our everyday life.

Ziryab's real name was Abu al-Hasan 'Ali ibn Nafi'. He was born in Mesopotamia, probably near Baghdad, in about 789 AD. Details of his early years are sketchy. He was most likely a freed slave, in the service of the Abbasid caliph Harun al-Rashid. Some Arab historians say he was of African ancestry; others claim he was Persian or Kurdish. As a member of the caliph's court, Ziryab was well schooled in poetry, astronomy, geography, physics and other fields. Music was his first love. He studied under a living legend, court musician Ishaq al-Mawsili. Eventually forced to flee Baghdad because of the hostile jealousy of his teacher, Ziryab traveled to Kairouan in North Africa and then to Arab Spain, where he was invited to the Umayyad emir's court at Cordoba in 822. He opened the country's first musical conservatory, as well as an academy of beauty and cosmetology.

Ziryab's impact on Spanish society was swift and powerful. As music historian Julian Ribera (1929) observed, Ziryab "knew all branches of literature, his social contacts were most delicate and courteous, his conversation very agreeable, and his urbanity exquisite, thus combining all the qualities needed for a gentleman of the court." Many were his musical contributions, including new song styles and a fifth course of strings for the Arabian lute or 'ud. Thanks to Ziryab, Spaniards became acquainted with such social innovations as toothpaste, the shaving of beards, short hair styles with bangs and the concept of seasonal clothing.

Ziryab was also celebrated as a gourmet, possessing detailed knowledge of the sophisticated cuisine of Baghdad. With the emir's blessing, he took charge of the kitchens of the Cordoba court and revolutionized the arts of the table in ways that survive to this day. Before Ziryab's influence, Spanish dining was a somewhat crude affair, inherited from the Visigoths, Romans and local custom. Platters of assorted foods were piled together on wooden tables sometimes covered with rough cloth, sometimes not.

Modern artist's vision of Ziryab in the Court of Harun al-Rashid in Baghdad.

Ziryab taught the palace cooks how to prepare Spain's delectable ingredients—meats, fish and fowl, vegetables, cheeses, soups, nuts and fruits—in imaginative recipes inspired by Baghdad's haute cuisine. He delighted courtly diners by elevating a humble spring weed called asparagus into a succulent dinner vegetable. One of his popular dishes, meatballs and small triangular pieces of dough fried in coriander oil, came to be called *taqliyat Ziryab*, or "Ziryab's Fried Dish." Another, an *asado* or roast of seasoned broad beans, survived into modern times as a Cordoba classic called *ziriabí*. A thirteenth-century Andalusian cookbook preserves a dish named *baqliyyat Ziryab* ("Vegetables Ziryab"), a "casserole" of lamb chunks, cabbage, onion and spices, topped with a crispy crust of ground meat, eggs, almonds and breadcrumbs.

Ziryab arranged for palace dinners to be served in courses—one after another, beginning with soup, continuing with meat entrees alternating with fowl dishes, and ending with sweet desserts which, in the words of one historian, included "cakes of walnuts, almonds and honey, or fruit patés," with pistachios and hazelnuts.

This orderly presentation style—unheard of even in Baghdad—steadily gained popularity, spreading through the upper and merchant classes, then among Christians and Jews, and even the peasantry. In time, the custom became the rule throughout Europe. Our expression "from soup to nuts," indicating a lavish meal of successive courses, can be traced back to Ziryab's innovations at the Andalusian table.

Dressing up the plain dinner table, Ziryab instructed local craftsmen how to produce tooled and fitted leather table coverings. He replaced the bulky gold and silver drinking goblets of the aristocracy—a holdover from the Goths and Romans—with delicate, hand-cut crystal ware. He redesigned the wooden soup spoon, substituting a trimmer, lighter-weight model. Ziryab's dining innovations made his social evenings the talk of al-Andalus.

Ziryab died in about 857 at the age of 68. He had several wives and concubines; most of their names are unknown. Ziryab was survived by eight sons and two daughters, all of whom pursued musical careers. His son Abdul Rahman took over management of the music school. His daughter Hamduna, a famous singer, married a vizier and helped publish a collection of her father's music, *Kitab Ma'ruf fi Aghani Ziryab* (*The Book of Ziryab's Known Songs*).

As the centuries passed, popular memory of Ziryab faded, but his innovations remained deeply entrenched in Western custom.

— ROBERT W. LEBLING

Contributors

JULIA ABRAMSON, PhD from Princeton University. Teaches food studies and French literature at the University of Oklahoma; has published innovative articles on French gastronomic writing; her book *Learning from Lying: Paradoxes of the Literary Mystification* was published in 2005; currently at work on the book *Food Culture of France*.

KEN ALBALA, PhD. Associate professor and chair of the History Department, University of the Pacific; author, *Eating Right in the Renaissance* and *Food in Early Modern Europe*; currently working on a culinary history of the sixteenth century.

GARY ALLEN. Author, *The Resource Guide for Food Writers*; editor, *Remarkable Service* for the Culinary Institute of America; associate editor, *The Oxford Encyclopedia of Food and Drink in America*; *The Herbalist in the Kitchen* and *Just Like Mom Used to Make* are forthcoming. Currently food history editor at *Leitesculinaria.com* and webmaster for the Association for the Study of Food and Society, he teaches at New York's Empire State College.

MARIO ANDERS. Free-lance and ghost writer, specializing in science; contributor to several books and national and international magazines.

ALICE ARNDT. Food historian; author, *Seasoning Savvy: How to Cook with Herbs, Spices, and Other Flavorings*; contributor, Scribner's *Encyclopedia of Food and Culture* and the 1997 *Joy of Cooking*; editor and mind behind, *Culinary Biographies*.

JULIUS ARNDT, PhD. Newspaper publisher and bibliophile, the late Julius Arndt, with his wife, **Erna Horn**, assembled the most significant private collection of culinary books in Germany, publishing facsimiles of selected volumes from the collection.

ANN ARNOLD. Author and illustrator, *The Adventurous Chef: Alexis Soyer*; illustrator, *Fanny at Chez Panisse* by Alice Waters. She lives in Berkeley, California, and her oil paintings of still-life subjects are shown at the North Point Gallery in San Francisco.

CHITRITA BANERJI. Writer and food historian specializing in Bengali food and culture; author, *Life and Food in Bengal*, *Bengali Cooking: Seasons and Festivals*, and *The Hour of the Goddess: Memories of Women, Food and Ritual in Bengal*; contributor to *Gastronomica*, *Gourmet*, *Granta*, and *Boston Globe*; recipient, Sophie Coe Prize at 1998 and 1999 Oxford Symposium on Food and Cookery.

KARI W. ÇAĞATAY. Native Norwegian and educator in early childhood development; author of five children's books and some translations; currently employed at Swedish Research Institute in Istanbul.

MILDRED COLEMAN. Culinary historian; as "Miss Millie," she appears on radio and television and at conventions and historical meetings to talk about food, cooking, and eating in the twentieth-century South; past president of the Georgia Nutrition Council; niece of the last dietitian partner of the Frances Virginia Tea Room, and author, *The South's Legendary Frances Virginia Tea Room Cookbook*.

NICOLE CROSSLEY-HOLLAND. Dr. Crossley-Holland has lectured in the Universities of the Sorbonne, Cambridge, and London. She is an honorary fellow of the University of Wales, where she teaches medieval history, and is the author of *Living and Dining in Medieval Paris: The Household of a Fourteenth-Century Knight*.

NANCY CARTER CRUMP. Culinary historian specializing in Virginia and North Carolina foodways. Her first book, *Hearthside Cooking*, is in its second printing, and another book is in progress. Her articles have appeared in the *Journal of Early Southern Decorative Arts*, *Virginia Cavalcade*, and other publications.

KATHLEEN CURTIN. The food historian at Plimoth Plantation, where she has worked since 1987, toiling over iron pots and badly photocopied sixteenth- and seventeenth-century cookbook manuscripts; author (with Sandra Oliver) of *Giving Thanks: Thanksgiving Recipes and History, From Pilgrims to Pumpkin Pie*.

KATARZYNA CWIERTKA, PhD. Expert in food culture and food history of Japan and Korea at Leiden University; editor, *Asian Food: The Global and the Local*.

ANDREW DALBY. Historian and linguist; author, *Siren Feasts: A History of Food and Gastronomy in Greece*, *Dangerous Tastes: The Story of Spices*, *Empire of Pleasures*, *Cato: On Farming*, *Dictionary of Languages*, *Language in Danger*, and *Food in the Ancient World from A to Z*; co-author of *The Classical Cookbook*.

HELEN DAY, PhD. Specializes in Mrs. Beeton and Victorian bourgeois consumption. She teaches English literature at Lancaster University (U.K.) and bakes exceedingly good cakes.

ELIZABETH DRIVER. Toronto-based author of *A Bibliography of Cookery Books Published in Britain 1875–1914*, the forthcoming *Culinary Landmarks: A Bibliography of Canadian Cookbooks, 1825–1949*, and introductions in the Classic Canadian Cookbooks Series (Whitecap Books); director, foodways program in the 1838 kitchen at Montgomery's Inn; President, Culinary Historians of Ontario.

PHILIPPE C. DUBOIS, PhD. Associate professor of French, Bucknell University; author, articles on Balzac and Brillat-Savarin in *Nineteenth-Century French Studies*, and on tables of the Mediterranean in the special issue on gastronomy of the journal *Critique*.

SANDRA FAIRBANK. Designer of restaurants and kitchens, based in Cambridge, Massachusetts; she has an abiding interest in the history of the restaurant in terms of food, design, and clientele.

PRISCILLA PARKHURST FERGUSON. Professor of sociology, Columbia University; author, article on Carême in *Gastronomica* and "La gastronomie en revues" (review of four food journals), *Critique* special issue on gastronomy; author, *Accounting for Taste: The Triumph of French Cuisine*.

ELIZABETH FIELD. Food writer and researcher; contributor to *The New York Times*, *The Boston Globe*, *Irish Times*, *Gourmet*, *Gastronomica*, etc.; contributing editor, *The 100 Best Restaurants/Places to Stay in Ireland*; lecturer and contributor to the Oxford Symposia on Food and Cookery; at work on a study of immigrant food in Ireland; secretary of Irish Food Writers Guild.

BEATRICE FINK. Professor of French emerita, University of Maryland/College Park; Secretary-General, International Society for Eighteenth-Century Studies, 1979–1987; two scholarly areas: political thought of Benjamin Constant and French eighteenth-century culinary history; numerous publications in both areas.

CHERYL J. FOOTE, PhD from the University of New Mexico. Teaches at Albuquerque Technical Vocational Institute Community College; author, *Women of the New Mexico Frontier, 1846–1912*; she is very interested in the culinary history of the American Southwest.

BETH MARIE FORREST. Boston University, Boston, Massachusetts.

DAMON LEE FOWLER. Cookbook author, food writer, and culinary historian; founding member of the Southern Foodways Alliance; historical commentator to reprint of Mrs. Hill's *Southern Practical Cookery and Receipt Book*.

BETTY FUSSELL. Food historian specializing in American history; author, *Masters of American Cookery*, *I Hear America Cooking*, *The Story of Corn*, and *My Kitchen Wars*.

IRINA GLUSHENKO. Journalist, translator, member of Writers Union of Russia.

DARRA GOLDSTEIN. Professor of Russian at Williams College; founding editor of *Gastronomica: The Journal of Food and Culture*; author of three cookbooks, *A Taste of Russia* (nominated for a Tastemaker Award), *The Georgian Feast* (winner of the 1994 IACP Julia Child Award for Cookbook of the Year), and *The Winter Vegetarian*; currently food editor of *Russian Life* magazine and general editor of California Studies in Food and Culture (University of California Press).

BARBARA HABER. Former Curator of Printed Books, Schlesinger Library, Harvard University; author, *From Hardtack to Homefries*; board member, IACP Foundation.

NEVIN HALICI. Food writer and researcher; author, *Traditional Dishes of Konya*, *Dishes of the Aegean Region*, *Dishes of the Mediterranean Region*, *Dishes of the Southeast Anatolia Region*, *Turkish Cookery*, *Nevin Halıcı's Turkish Cookbook*, and *Sufi Cuisine*.

JESSICA B. HARRIS, PhD. Professor, food historian, lecturer, and cookbook author with a specialty in the food of Africa and its diaspora; her most recent works are *Beyond Gumbo: Creole Fusion Food From the Atlantic Rim* and *On the Side, A Celebration of Side Dishes and Condiments;* her website is africooks.com.

URSULA HEINZELMANN. Independent scholar and culinary historian; trained chef, sommelier and ex-restaurateur, now a wine and food writer and journalist based in Berlin, with special interest in helping her contemporaries get in touch with their culinary roots. Winner of the Sophie Coe Prize 2004.

KAREN HESS. Food historian; author of *The Carolina Rice Kitchen: The African Connection; Martha Washington's Booke of Cookery and Booke of Sweetmeats;* "Okra in the African Diaspora of Our South" in *Cornbread Nation 1: The Best of Southern Food Writing;* "The First American Cookbook, Second Edition, Albany [1796]: Historical Notes on the Work and Its Author, Amelia Simmons," paper for Culinary Historians of New York; "A Century of Change in the American Loaf: Or, Where Are the Breads of Yesteryear?" keynote address at Smithsonian symposium; and of historical notes for facsimile editions of Hannah Glasse's *The Art of Cookery Made Plain and Easy,* Mary Randolph's *The Virginia House-wife,* and Abby Fisher's *What Mrs. Fisher Knows About Old Southern Cooking.*

SHARON HUDGINS. Author, food writer, culinary historian. Author, *The Other Side of Russia: A Slice of Life in Siberia and the Russian Far East* and *Spanien: Küche, Land und Menschen (Spain: Cuisine, Land and People).* Former editor, *Chile Pepper* magazine and food columnist, *The Stars and Stripes* newspaper; currently food columnist for *German Life* magazine. Contributor to *The Oxford Encyclopedia of Food and Drink in America, The Oxford International Encyclopedia of Cheese,* and *Gastronomica.* Recipient of a Sophie Coe Subsidiary Prize in Food History, 1996.

VINOD K. HURIA. Senior scientist at the Central Food Technological Research Institute, Mysore (India), with interests in food development and history of foods; a student of Dr. K. T. Achaya and a friend for a quarter of century; held a senior position at the National Dairy Development Board at Anand. Gained immensely from Dr. Achaya's professional approach and his wide knowledge of food science and technology and the history of foods.

PETER BARTON HUTT. Partner in the Washington, D. C. law firm of Covington & Burling, specializing in food and drug law; teaches food and drug law each winter term at Harvard Law School; author (with Richard A. Merrill), *Food and Drug Law: Cases and Materials;* from 1971 to 1975 he was chief counsel for the Food and Drug Administration; serves on a wide variety of academic and scientific advisory boards, including the Institute of Medicine of the National Academy of Sciences.

PRISCILLA MARY IŞIN. Native of England and resident of Istanbul, she has translated over 150 books, mostly on art, architecture, and history, from Turkish to English; she has researched the history of Turkish cuisine for more than two decades, and published a Turkish cookery book, as well as an annotated transcription of an Ottoman cookery book into modern Turkish (*Mahmud Nedim bin Tosu: Aşçıbaşı*); and an annotated edition of an early nineteenth-century German book on Turkish confectionery (*Friedrich Unger: A King's Confectioner in the Orient*).

TOM JAINE. Publisher, Prospect Books and *Petits Propos Culinaires*; food writer and author.

NANCY HARMON JENKINS. Writer and food historian with a special interest in the foods of the Mediterranean, particularly Italy; her most recent publication is *The Essential Mediterranean*.

LISA JONES. Collections cataloger for 25 years at the Harry Ransom Center, University of Texas at Austin; free-lance writer and researcher with particular interest in foodways and culinary history; owner, Perfect Ganesh, a vegetarian catering company.

CATHY K. KAUFMAN. Former lawyer turned chef and culinary historian; instructor, Institute of Culinary Education; senior editor, *The Oxford Encyclopedia of Food and Drink in America*; currently working on a culinary history of the ancient world from Babylon to Byzantium.

PATRICIA M. KELLY. Professor of culinary arts (retired), North Shore Community College, Massachusetts; long-time editor, Culinary Historians of Boston Newsletter; co-editor, *Current Research in Culinary History: Sources, Topics, and Methods*; co-author (with Barbara Wheaton), *Bibliography of Culinary History: Food Resources in Eastern Massachusetts*; editor, *Luncheonette: Ice-Cream, Beverage and Sandwich Recipes from the Golden Age of the Soda Fountain*.

BRUCE KRAIG, PhD. Emeritus Professor of History, Roosevelt University, Chicago.

RACHEL LAUDAN. Before turning to culinary history, she taught science history at Carnegie-Mellon, Virginia Tech, and the University of Hawaii. Her book *The Food of Paradise: Exploring Hawaii's Cultural Heritage* won a Julia Child Prize in 1997.

ROBERT W. LEBLING. Graduate of Princeton University; graduate work in Middle East studies at University of Chicago; lived and worked as a journalist in Egypt, Lebanon, Saudi Arabia, the United States and the United Kingdom; writer and editor based in Dhahran, Saudi Arabia; co-author of *Natural Remedies of Arabia*.

MARGARET (MARGE) LEIBENSTEIN. Culinary historian and author of three cookbooks; chairman of the Culinary Historians of Boston; at the time of her death in 2001 she was engaged in writing her memoirs.

JANICE BLUESTEIN LONGONE. Curator of American culinary history, Clements Library, University of Michigan, Ann Arbor, where she is developing the Longone Center for American Culinary Research, a large and diverse collection and a major resource for scholars; founder, Wine and Food Library, the oldest antiquarian bookshop in the U.S. devoted solely to gastronomy; founder and honorary chair of the Culinary Historians of Ann Arbor; on boards and advisory committees, including AIWF, *Gastronomica*, Dover Press, IACP, James Beard Foundation, Tabasco Community Cookbook Awards, and *The Oxford Encyclopedia of Food and Drink in America*; international consultant, collection developer, exhibition curator, lecturer, and writer.

FIONA LUCAS. Culinary historian working for the Museums of the City of Toronto, Ontario; co-founder of the Culinary Historians of Ontario; holds a master's degree in Canadian history.

BOB LUCKY. Former editor of *The Asian Foodbookery*, he counts himself fortunate to have known the late K. T. Achaya. He is currently teaching in Bahrain at the Ibn Khuldoon National School and writing about food and culture.

MÁIRTÍN MAC CON IOMAIRE. Lecturer and chairman of the BA (Hons) in Culinary Arts program at the Dublin Institute of Technology; over 15 years experience working as a chef in Ireland and abroad; writer on food and consultant on food training. Areas of interest include mentoring, Irish food history and customs, oenology, education, ethnic cookery, and ballad/traditional "seannós" singing. He is currently researching an oral history of Dublin restaurants between 1922 and 2002 for his PhD at the Dublin Institute of Technology.

GLENN R. MACK. Chef instructor, researcher, and writer with a special interest in the Silk Road and the history of professional cookery; Director of Education at Le Cordon Bleu-Miami, and chair of the Food History Committee of IACP; former photojournalist with *TIME* magazine in Moscow and Central Asia; trained in the culinary arts in Uzbekistan, Russia, Italy, and the United States; author, *Uzbek Cuisine* and *Food Culture Around the World: Russia and Central Asia*.

SHIREEN MAHDAVI, PhD. Department of History, University of Utah; author, "Women, Shi'ism and Cuisine in Iran" in *Women, Religion and Society in Iran*.

MARTY MARTINDALE. Social anthropologist, currently a free-lance food writer, travel writer, and operator of www.FoodSiteoftheDay.com, now in its fifth year; she specializes in chef profiles and individual foods and their origins.

ANNE MENDELSON. Food historian; author, *Stand Facing the Stove* and a forthcoming history of the foods of New York.

WALTER METHLER. A native of Wengern, the birthplace of Henrietta Davidis; pastor of the Evangelical Church congregation in Volmarstein/Oberwengern until his retirement in 2001; founder of the Henriette Davidis Museum, Wetter; author (with Eckehard Methler) of the award-winning bibliography *Von Henriette Davidis bis Erna Horn*.

ECKEHARD METHLER. Son of Walter and Erika Methler; antiquarian bookseller; student of economics and special education for children with learning disabilities; co-author, *Von Henriette Davidis bis Erna Horn*.

MARY ELLA MILHAM. Professor of classics and linguistics; taught at University of Wisconsin–Madison and University of New Brunswick; her many books and articles include editions of Apicius and Platina.

JACQUELINE NEWMAN, PhD. Professor emeritus and past chairperson of the Family, Nutrition and Exercise Sciences Department, Queens College, CUNY; author, numerous books, articles, and restaurant reviews; editor-in-chief, *Flavor and Fortune*, the only English-language magazine in the United States dedicated to Chinese cuisine; board member, James Beard Foundation, Queens Botanical Garden, Association for the Study of Food and Society, American Institute of Wine and Food; advisor to the board of directors, Food Exhibition Museum, Suzhou, China; author, *Food Culture in China*.

JILL NORMAN. Founder of the influential Penguin cookery list in the U.K.; she was Elizabeth David's publisher and editor for many years, and is literary trustee of the David estate; she is also a writer with a special interest in spices and herbs.

SANDRA L. OLIVER. Working in food history since 1971, specializing in New England regional foods, and in maritime foodways; founding editor of *Food History News*; author, *Saltwater Foodways: New Englanders and their Food in the 19th Century at Sea and Ashore* (winner of the Jane Grigson Award for distinguished scholarship), *Giving Thanks: Thanksgiving Recipes and History, From Pilgrims to Pumpkin Pie* (with Kathleen Curtin), and the volume on *Food in Colonial and Federal America* in the series "Food in American History."

MM PACK. Attended the California Culinary Academy following a career as librarian, technical writer, and information architect; private chef; has contributed food articles to *The San Francisco Chronicle, Austin Chronicle, Scribner's Encyclopedia of Food and Culture*, and the anthology *Cornbread Nation*. Her culinary interests include foodways of the Pacific Islands, American regional foods, and food writing in the early twentieth century.

CHARLES PERRY. Widely published food historian specializing in the Islamic world; contributed translation of an unstudied thirteenth-century cookbook to *Medieval Arab Cookery*; a major contributor to *The Oxford Companion to Food*; in an earlier life, he was editor and staff writer at *Rolling Stone*, and today is a staff writer for the food section of *The Los Angeles Times*.

KYLE PHILIPS. Went to Italy in 1982 for what was to be a year of post-grad study; is still there, working as a food, travel, and wine writer; translator, *The Art of Eating Well* by Pellegrino Artusi.

JEFFREY M. PILCHER. Professor of history at The Citadel in Charleston, South Carolina; author, *¡Que Vivan Los Tamales! Food and the Making of Mexican Identity.*

JERI QUINZIO. Free-lance writer whose articles on various aspects of food history have appeared in publications including *The Radcliffe Culinary Times* and *Gastronomica*; contributor, *Scribner's Encyclopedia of Food and Culture* and *The Oxford Encyclopedia of Food and Drink in America.* Her book on the history of ice cream is forthcoming from the University of California Press.

JOAN REARDON, PhD. Professor emeritus, Barat College, Lake Forest, Illinois; culinary historian and cookbook author; biographer of M. F. K. Fisher; recently wrote the introduction for the 50th-anniversary edition of Fisher's *Art of Eating.*

VICTORIA ABBOTT RICCARDI. Graduate of Harvard, studied classical French cooking at Le Cordon Bleu in Paris, tea *kaiseki* (a ritualized form of cooking that accompanies the formal tea ceremony) at Mushanokoji tea school in Kyoto, and food styling at The New School University, New York; author, *Untangling My Chopsticks: A Culinary Sojourn in Kyoto*; former restaurant critic; free-lance food, travel, and health writer for numerous magazines and newspapers.

ELIZABETH RIELY. Editor, *Radcliffe Culinary Times*; author, *The Chef's Companion: A Culinary Dictionary* (now in its third edition) and *A Feast of Fruits*; journalist; past president of the Culinary Historians of Boston.

ALICIA RIOS. Food historian, food artist, and international food performer; former lecturer in history of psychology, Universidad Complutense de Madrid; former owner and chef, Los Siete Jardines; author (with Lourdes March), *The Heritage of Spanish Cooking*; gastronomic consultant; designer of ceremonies of logophagy.

JUDITH PIERCE ROSENBERG. Teacher; author, *A Question of Balance: Artists and Writers on Motherhood* and *A Swedish Kitchen: Reminiscences and Recipes*; her website is www.swedishkitchen.com.

ALICE ROSS, PhD. Director and teacher, Alice Ross Hearth Studios for the pursuit of historic, hands-on hearth cooking; adjunct professor, New York University and other universities; museum consultant and curator; editor for *The Oxford Encyclopedia of Food and Drink in America.*

ARTHUR SCHWARTZ. Longtime host of the United States' only daily radio food program, WOR, New York; leader of culinary tours of Campania; teaches cooking at many New York venues, including the Culinary Institute of America; author of four cookbooks, the latest titled *Naples at Table: Cooking in Campania,* and of *Arthur Schwartz's New York City Food.*

TERENCE SCULLY. Author of a number of works on late-medieval and renaissance European cookery; his *Early French Cookery*, in collaboration with his wife Eleanor, presents recipes from Taillevent, Ménagier de Paris, and Chiquart.

COLLEEN TAYLOR SEN, PhD. Free-lance writer specializing in Indian cuisine; author of *Food Culture in India* and many articles; currently writing a handbook on Indian restaurants.

MARGARET SHAIDA. Food writer and culinary historian; author, *The Legendary Cuisine of Persia*, winner of the Glenfiddich Award for best cookery book in Britain, 1993; lecturer and contributor to the Oxford Symposia on Food and Cookery, etc.

LAURA SHAPIRO. Journalist and historian; author, *Perfection Salad: Women and Cooking at the Turn of the Century* and *Something from the Oven: Reinventing Dinner in 1950s America.*

SANDRA SHERMAN. Professor of British literature, University of Arkansas; culinary historian; author, *Fresh From the Past: Recipes and Revelations From Moll Flanders' Kitchen.*

ANDREW F. SMITH. Author or editor of eight books on food history and two biographies; teaches culinary history at the New School University; general editor of the University of Illinois Press's Food Series and editor-in-chief of *The Oxford Encyclopedia of Food and Drink in America.*

MARY ELLEN SNODGRASS. English and classics teacher; former columnist for *The Charlotte Observer*; reference book author specializing in literature and women's history; has published *Encyclopedia of Kitchen History, Historical Encyclopedia of Nursing*, and literary companions to the works of Barbara Kingsolver and Amy Tan. Works in progress include *Encyclopedia of Feminist Literature* and *Encyclopedia of the Underground Railroad.*

COLIN SPENCER. Novelist, painter, playwright, and food historian; his last book is *British Food: An Extraordinary Thousand Years of History.*

NANCY C. STUTZMAN. Nutritionist; president, Culinary Historians of Boston; member, Society for Nutrition Education and American Association of Family and Consumer Sciences; student of art history.

BARBARA KETCHAM WHEATON. A pioneer of culinary history; co-founder (with Joyce Toomre) of the Culinary Historians of Boston; author, *Savoring the Past* and (with Patricia Kelly) *Bibliography of Culinary History: Food Resources in Eastern Massachusetts;* honorary curator of the culinary collection, Schlesinger Library, Harvard University.

ELIZABETH BORST WHITE. Resident of Houston, Texas with nearly thirty years' professional experience in developing collections of medical history, particularly Texas history, for the Houston Academy of Medicine–Texas Medical Center Library. Of personal interest is the history of Texas foodways and a burgeoning collection of cookbooks documenting Texas' culinary history; member, Texas Medical Association's History of Medicine Committee and the Endangered Treasures Committee of the IACP Culinary Trust.

JOHN WILKINS. Head, Department of Classics and Ancient History, Exeter University; specialist in the history of food in Greco-Roman culture, with current interests in literature and medicine (especially nutrition); publications include *Euripides: Heraclidae, Archestratus: The Life of Luxury* (with Shaun Hill), *Food in Antiquity* (editor), *Food in European Literature* (editor), *Athenaeus and His World* (editor), *The Rivals of Aristophanes* (editor), *The Boastful Chef: The Discourse of Food in Ancient Greek Comedy.*

JACQUELINE B. WILLIAMS. Award-winning author of *Wagon Wheel Kitchens: Food on the Oregon Trail* and *The Way We Ate: Pacific Northwest Cooking, 1843–1900;* contributor to historical journals and newspapers; lectures widely about pioneer life in the Pacific Northwest; author, introduction to University of Illinois paperback edition of *The Delights of Delicate Eating* by Elizabeth Robins Pennell.

SUSAN MACDUFF WOOD. Co-author, *Business and Social Etiquette With Disabled People* (1989 Barbara Jordan Award for excellence in the communication of the reality of disabled people) and a number of scientific publications; first president of the Houston Culinary Historians; host of "Thoughts on Food" radio program for KHOU, Houston; currently resides in Walnut Creek, California.

ANN F. WOODWARD. Longtime member of the Culinary Historians of Ann Arbor; fiction writer specializing in mysteries set in medieval Japan.

CAROLIN C. YOUNG. Writer and cultural historian specializing in European table arts; author, *Apples of Gold in Settings of Silver: Stories of Dinner as a Work of Art*; lecturer at numerous venues including Sotheby's Institute of Art, New York, for whom she produces elaborate recreations of historic banquets; recipient, Royal Society of Arts Diploma, Christie's Education, London.

ILLUSTRATION CREDITS

Accum—National Portrait Gallery, London

Achaya—Courtesy of Vinod K. Huria

Acton—National Portrait Gallery, London

Adanson—Courtesy of Barbara Ketcham Wheaton

Aitken—Courtesy of Robert G. Hortop

Akabori—Courtesy of Katarzyna Cwiertka

Alexander—Museo Archeologico Nazionale, Naples; Scala / Art Resource

Allen—Culver Pictures

Altamiras—Courtesy of Alicia Rios

Apicius—Division of Rare and Manuscript Collections, Carl A. Kroch Library, Cornell University

Appert—France International; with permission of La Poste; Scott 759, Yvert 1014

Arbuckle—Courtesy of Historical Society of Western Pennsylvania, Heinz Pittsburgh Regional History Center

Arcimboldo—Copyright © 2003 National Gallery in Prague

Artusi—Courtesy of Kyle M. Phillips III

Atwater—Culver Pictures

Aunt Sammy—National Archives and Records Administration, 16-G-93-2-34155C

Balzac—Culver Pictures

Barlow—Connecticut Historical Society, New Haven

Beard—Courtesy of The James Beard Foundation

Beauvilliers—Courtesy of Emilie Arndt-Meislinger and Theresia Dengler-Arndt

Beck—Photo by Arnold Newman; Getty Images

Beeton—National Portrait Gallery, London

Bekir—Courtesy of Priscilla Mary Işin

Benoît—*The Gazette* (Montreal)

Betty Crocker—Courtesy of General Mills Archives

Bircher-Benner—Bircher-Benner-Archiv, Medizinhistorisches Institut und Museum der Universität Zürich

Borden—Culver Pictures

Brady—Hulton Archive / Getty Images

Brillat-Savarin—Courtesy of Emilie Arndt-Meislinger and Theresia Dengler-Arndt

Chen—Courtesy of Helen Chen

Child, J.—Courtesy of Joan Reardon

Child, L. M.—Culver Pictures

Chiquart—Médiathèque Valais, Sion, Switzerland, ms S103, fol 2r

Chu—*The New York Times*

Claiborne—Photo by Arthur Schatz / Time Life Pictures; Getty Images

Cobbett—National Portrait Gallery, London

Coe—Courtesy of Sarah Coe

Columbus—Library of Congress, USZ62-39304

Colwin—Photo by Nancy Crampton

Dalén—Courtesy of and copyright © by the Nobel Foundation

Das—Courtesy of the Das family.

David—Courtesy of Jill Norman

Davidis—Courtesy of Walter Methler and Eckehard Methler

Davidson—Photo by Michel Porro; Getty Images

Davis—Photo by Henry Clarke; Condé Nast Archive / Corbis

Delmonico—Engraving after a photo by Mora; Culver Pictures

Drummond—National Portrait Gallery, London

Eisai—Courtesy of Kennin-ji Tacchu Ryōsoku-in Temple, Kyoto, and Kyoto National Museum

Emy—Library of Congress, TX795.R54

Epicurus—Photo by Brogi; Culver Pictures

Erken—Courtesy of Aschehoug Forlag, Oslo

Escoffier—Library of Congress, USZ62-87367

Fairbank—Special Collections Research Center, Morris Library, Southern Illinois University Carbondale

Farmer—Culver Pictures

Fisher, M. F. K.—Photo by George Hurrell; Culver Pictures

Fitzgibbon—*The Irish Times*

Francatelli—National Portrait Gallery, London

Gandulfo—Courtesy of Rebekah E. Pite and Marcela Elisa Massut

Gilbert—Archives and Special Collections Department, New Mexico State University Library, Las Cruces

Gilbreth—Library of Congress, USZ62-101773

Glasse—Courtesy of Emilie Arndt-Meislinger and Theresia Dengler-Arndt

Gogol—Culver Pictures

Goodnight—Panhandle-Plains Historical Museum, Canyon, Texas

Graham—The Granger Collection

Grigson—Courtesy of Sophie Grigson

Haber—Courtesy of and copyright © by the Nobel Foundation

Harland—Valentine Richmond History Center, Richmond, Virginia

Harvey—Heard Museum, Phoenix, Arizona

Hazelton—Photo by Ralph Crane; Time Life Pictures / Getty Images

Horn—Courtesy of Emilie Arndt-Meislinger and Theresia Dengler-Arndt

Jefferson—Library of Congress, USZ62-200

Kellogg—Courtesy of the Michigan Women's Historical Center & Hall of Fame

Knopf—Culver Pictures

Kroc—Photo by New York Times Co.; Hulton Archive / Getty Images

Kump—Courtesy of Jerry Ruotolo and the Institute of Culinary Education

La Chapelle—Bibliothèque nationale de France; courtesy of Dr. Beatrice Fink

La Varenne—Courtesy of Emilie Arndt-Meislinger and Theresia Dengler-Arndt

Legrand d'Aussy—Bibliothèque nationale de France, ms. 3415; courtesy of Dr. Beatrice Fink

Liebig—Hulton Archive / Getty Images

Lincoln—Courtesy of Mary Mark, Celebration of Women Writers

Lo—Stanley Devon, *The Times*

Lucas—Photo by George Karger; Condé Nast Archive / Corbis

MacAusland—Culinary Archives & Museum at Johnson & Wales University

Markham—National Portrait Gallery, London

Marshall—Courtesy of Robin Weir

Maurizio—Courtesy of Katarzyna Cwiertka

Ménagier de Paris—Bibliothèque nationale de France, fr. 12477, fol. 1r

Merigot—Courtesy of Dr. Beatrice Fink

Messisbugo—New York Academy of Medicine

Mikoyan—Photo by Ed Clark; Time Life Pictures / Getty Images

Molokhovets—Courtesy of Sharon Hudgins

Nurallah—Courtesy of the Nasser D. Khalili Collection of Islamic Art; mss. 1030.9, fl. 731a

Olney—Courtesy of John Colby; copyright © Brick Tower Press

Parloa—Division of Rare and Manuscript Collections, Carl A. Kroch Library, Cornell University

Pasteur—Library of Congress, USZ62-29316

Pennell—Library of Congress, USZ62-61046

Pomiane—Copyright © Institut Pasteur

Rabelais—Culver Pictures

Raffald—National Portrait Gallery, London
Randolph—The Library of Virginia
Richards—Photo by G. Walden Smith; Special Collections, Vassar College Libraries
Ritz—Photo by Studio René; National Portrait Gallery, London
Rombauer—Courtesy of Ethan Becker
Rorer—Culinary Archives & Museum at Johnson & Wales University
Rumford—National Portrait Gallery, London
Rumi—The Granger Collection
Rumpolt—Courtesy of Emilie Arndt-Meislinger and Theresia Dengler-Arndt

Scappi—Courtesy of Emilie Arndt-Meislinger and Theresia Dengler-Arndt
Simmons—Clements Library, University of Michigan
Simon—Photo by Howard Coster; National Portrait Gallery, London
Sinclair—Time Life Pictures / Getty Images
Soyer—National Portrait Gallery, London

Toklas—Photo by Carl Mydans; Time Life Pictures / Getty Images
Traill—National Archives of Canada, C67337
Tropp—Photo by Elena Dorfman

Vatel—Courtesy of Emilie Arndt-Meislinger and Theresia Dengler-Arndt
Vehling—Division of Rare and Manuscript Collections, Carl A. Kroch Library, Cornell University

Ward—Courtesy of Robert Klein
Weckerin—Courtesy of Emilie Arndt-Meislinger and Theresia Dengler-Arndt
Whitaker—Courtesy of Mildred Huff Coleman
Wiley—Library of Congress, USZ61-730
Wolley—British Library; 1037.d.42

Ziryab—Illustration by Norman MacDonald; *Saudi Aramco World* / PADIA

Endpapers—Marbled paper made in 1973 by Mustafa Düzgünman, Istanbul

CATEGORICAL LISTING

Agriculturalist/Farmer
Cato
Cobbett
Columella
Jefferson
Markham
Varro

Butler/Maitre d'Hôtel/Scalco
Latini
Messisbugo
Roberts
Vatel

Chef/Cook/Confectioner
Altamiras
Baldwin
Bavarchi
Bekir
Bockenheim
Carême
Chiquart
Das
Emy
Escoffier
Favre
Fisher, Abby
Kellogg
La Chapelle
La Varenne
Lucas
Marshall
Massialot

Mithaecus
Montiño
Nurallah
Parloa
Pomiane
Rosanjin
Rumpolt
Scappi
Sia
Soyer
Symphort
Taillevent
Tropp
Unger
Usher
Vehling

Cookbook Author
Acton
Adanson
Aitken
Akabori
Al-Baghdadi
Allen
Altamiras
Anthimus
Apicius
Artusi
Bavarchi
Beard
Beauvilliers
Beck
Beecher

Beeton
Benoît
Blot
Bockenheim
Brown
Carême
Chao
Chen
Child, Julia
Child, Lydia Maria
Chiquart
Chu
Claiborne
Corson
DasGupta
David
Davidis
Davis
Duckitt
Emy
Erken
Escoffier
Farmer
Fisher, Abby
FitzGibbon
Gandulfo
Gilbert
Glasse
Grigson
Hale
Harland
Hazelton
Hill

Howland
Horn
Kellogg
Kump
Kushi
La Chapelle
Latini
La Varenne
Leslie
Lincoln
Lo
Lucas
Makhmudov
Markham
Marshall
Massialot
Ménagier
Mérigot
Messisbugo
Mithaecus
Molokhovets
Montiño
Mukhopadhyay
Muro
Nola
Nurallah
Olney
Parloa
Pokhlebkin
Raffald
Randolph
Rombauer
Rorer
Rumpolt
Rutledge
Scappi
Sia
Simmons
Soyer
Toklas
Traill
Tropp
Unger
Velázquez de León

Warg
Weckerin
Wolley
Yuan Mei

Cookbook Collector

Bitting
Brown
Coe
Horn
Pennell
Simon
Usher
Vehling

Diplomat, Politician,
Government Official or Leader

Barlow
Cato
Davidson
Jefferson
Mikoyan
Varro
Zhang

Encyclopedist

Achaya
Benoît
Davidson
Favre
FitzGibbon
Simon
Ward

Entrepreneur

Accum
Aitken
Appert
Arbuckle
Borden
Butt
Chen
Cochrane
Dalén

Das
Fairbank
Fisher, Abby
Glasse
Goodnight
Harvey
Kroc
Kump
Kushi
Liebig
Lo
MacAusland
Marshall
Raffald
Roberts
Usher
Ward

Exchanger/Introducer/
Culinary Ambassador

Alexander
Columbus
Eisai
Jefferson
Sia
Symphort
Unger
Velázquez de León
Zhang
Ziryab

Food Historian

Achaya
Coe
Davidson
Drummond
Hartley
Horn
Legrand d'Aussy
Makhmudov
Maurizio
Mukhopadhyay
Pokhlebkin
Vehling

Gourmet/Gastronome/Epicure

Apicius
Archestratus
Brady
Brillat-Savarin
Grimod de la Reynière
Jefferson
Lucullus
Pokhlebkin
Pomiane
Simon
Walker
Ziryab

Home Economist/ Domestic Scientist

Beecher
Corson
Erken
Gandulfo
Gilbert
Parloa
Richards
Rorer

Imaginary Character

Amphitryon
Aunt Sammy
Betty Crocker

Nutritionist/Dietitian

Achaya
Atwater
Davis
Drummond
Graham
Kellogg
Richards
Rorer
Whitaker

Philosopher

Athenaeus,
Avicenna
Brillat-Savarin
Epicurus
Galen
Makhmudov
Platina
Pythagoras
Rumi

Physician

Anthimus
Avicenna
BircherBenner
Chao
Galen
Pomiane

Publisher

Knopf
Toklas
Velázquez de León
Ward

Radio/Television Presenter

Akabori
Aitken
Allen
Aunt Sammy
Beard
Benoît
Betty Crocker
Child, Julia
Gandulfo
Lucas
Pomiane
Usher
Velázquez de León

Reformer

Accum
BircherBenner
Child, Lydia Maria
Cobbett
Corson
Davis
Escoffier
Favre
Graham
Kellogg
Kushi
Maurizio
Schütte-Lihotzky
Sinclair
Soyer
Vehling
Wiley

Restaurateur

Beauvilliers
Butt
Delmonico
Gujral
Harvey
Jammet
Lo
Procope
Symphort
Tropp
Whitaker

Scientist

Accum
Achaya
Appert
Atwater
Avicenna
Bitting
Dalén
Drummond
Gilbreth
Haber
Liebig

Maurizio
Pasteur
Pomiane
Richards
Rumford
Wiley

Teacher
Akabori
Allen
Beard
Beck
Beecher
Benoît
Blot
Child, Julia
Chu
Corson
Erken
Farmer
Gandulfo
Gilbert
Hartley
Kump
Kushi
Lincoln
Lucas
Marshall
Mukhopadhyay
Parloa
Pokhlebkin
Richards
Rorer
Rumi
Tropp
Usher
Velázquez de León

Writer/Poet
Archestratus
Balzac
Barlow
Benoît
Brillat-Savarin

Brown
Bushaq
Chao
Claiborne
Cobbett
Columella
Colwin
Corson
David
Davidson
Escoffier
Fisher, M. F. K.
Galen
Gilbert
Gogol
Graham
Grigson
Grimod de la Reynière
Hale
Harland
Hartley
Hazelton
Kump
Leslie
Lincoln
Markham
Mukhopadhyay
Muro
Platina
Pennell
Pokhlebkin
Pomiane
Rabelais
Roberts
Rumi
Rumohr
Simon
Sinclair
Traill
Vehling
Walker
Wolley
Yuan

Other
Arcimboldo (*Artist*)
Brillat-Savarin (*Jurist, Musician*)
Cochrane (*Inventor*)
Eisai (*Monk*)
Grimod de la Reynière (*Food Critic*)
Hale (*Editor*)
Lo (*Tennis Champion*)
Lucullus (*Roman General*)
Marshall (*Inventor*)
Ménagier (*Householder, Knight*)
Platina (*Vatican Librarian*)
Ritz (*Hotelier*)
Rosanjin (*Artist*)
Rumi (*Sufi*)
Rumohr (*Art Historian*)
Russo (*Food Publicist*)
Schütte-Lihotzky (*Architect*)
Sen no Rikyū (*Tea Master*)
Varro (*Scholar*)
Vehling (*Artist*)
Ziryab (*Musician*)

GEOGRAPHICAL LISTING

NOTE:
Those who moved
from one country
to another will be
listed under both.

Hungary
Rumpolt

India
Achaya
Das
DasGupta
Gujral
Mukhopadhyay

Ireland
Butt
FitzGibbon
Jammet

Italy
Arcimboldo
Artusi
Columbus
Hazelton
Latini
Messisbugo
Platina
Procope
Rumpolt
Scappi

Japan
Akabori
Eisai
Kushi
Rosanjin
Sen no Rikyū

Kenya
Butt

Mexico
Velázquez de León

Netherlands
La Chapelle
Rumpolt

Norway
Erken

Persia
Avicenna
Bavarchi
Bushaq
Nurallah

Poland
Maurizio
Pomiane
Rumpolt

Roman Republic/Empire
Anthimus
Apicius
Athenaeus
Cato
Columella
Galen
Lucullus
Varro

Russia
Gogol
Mikoyan
Molokhovets
Pokhlebkin
Rumpolt

Savoy
Chiquart

South Africa
Duckitt

Spain
Altamiras
Columbus
Montiño
Muro
Ziryab

Sweden
Dalén
Warg

Switzerland
Bircher-Benner
Delmonico
Favre
Maurizio
Ritz
Weckerin

Turkey
Bekir
Rumi
Unger

United States
Allen
Arbuckle
Atwater
Aunt Sammy
Barlow
Beard
Beecher
Bitting
Chao
Chen
Child, Julia
Child, Lydia Maria
Chu
Claiborne
Cobbett
Cochrane
Coe
Colwin
Corson
Davis
Delmonico
Fairbank
Farmer
Fisher, Abby
Fisher, M. F. K.
Gilbert
Gilbreth

Goodnight
Graham
Hale
Harland
Harvey
Hazelton
Hill
Howland
Jefferson
Kellogg
Knopf
Kroc
Kump
Kushi
Leslie
Lincoln
Lucas
MacAusland
Parloa
Pennell
Randolph
Richards
Roberts
Rombauer
Rumford
Russo
Rutledge
Sia
Simmons
Sinclair
Toklas
Tropp
Usher
Vehling
Ward
Whitaker
Wiley

USSR
Makhmudov
Mikoyan
Pokhlebkin

Uzbekistan
Makhmudov

Significant Culinary Texts
AND THEIR AUTHORS, ARRANGED CHRONOLOGICALLY

NOTE:
See the authors'
biographies for
more information
on these works.

PUBLICATION DATE	TEXT	AUTHOR
C. 1700 BC	*Babylonian cuneiform recipe collection*	Anonymous author(s)
C. 400 BC	*Sicilian cookery book*	**Mithaecus**
C. 330 BC	*The Life of Luxury*	**Archestratus**
C. 200	*Deipnosophists (Professors at Dinner)*	**Athenaeus**
FIRST HALF OF 2ND CENTURY BC	*De Agri Cultura (On Farming)*	**Cato**
1ST CENTURY	*Res Rustica (Country Work)*	**Columella**
4TH CENTURY	*De Re Coquinaria (On Cookery)*	**Apicius**
6TH CENTURY	*De Observatione Ciborum (Observations About Foods)*	**Anthimus**
LATE 8TH CENTURY	*Ch'a Ching (The Classic of Tea)*	Lu Yu
13TH CENTURY	*Kitâb al-Tabîkh (The Book of Dishes)*	**Al-Baghdadi**
END OF 13TH/ BEGINNING OF 14TH CENTURY	*Liber de Coquina (Cookery Book)*	Anonymous author in Naples
14TH CENTURY	*Viandier (Book of Foods)*	**Taillevent**
1350	*Daz buoch von guoter spîse (The Book of Good Food)*	Anonymous
C. 1390	*The Forme of Cury (The Art of Cookery)*	Master Cooks of King Richard II
EARLY 15TH CENTURY	"A Treasury of Appetite"	**Bushaq**
C. 1470	Printed edition of *De Honesta Voluptate et Valetudine (On Right Pleasure And Good Health)*	**Platina**
SECOND HALF OF 15TH CENTURY	*Libre del coch (Book of the Cook)*	**Ruperto de Nola**
EARLY 16TH CENTURY	*Karnameh dar bab-i tabbakhi va san'at an (Manual on Cooking and Its Craft)*	**Bavarchi**

PUBLICATION DATE	TEXT	AUTHOR
1532	*Les horribles et espouvantables faictz & prouesses du tresrenommé Pantagruel Roy des Dipsodes, filz du grand geant Gargantua, Composez nouvellement par maistre Alcofrybas Nasier (The Horrible and Appalling Deeds & Feats of the Very Famous Pantagruel, King of theDipsodes, Son of the Great Giant Gargantua. Recently Written by Master Alcofrybas Nasier)*	**François Rabelais**
1570	*Opera Omnia (Collected Works)*	**Bartolomeo Scappi**
1581	*Ein new Kochbuch (A New Cookery Book)*	**Marx Rompolt**
1597	*Ein köstlich new Kochbuch von allerhand Speisen (A Delightful New Cookbook of All Kinds of Dishes)*	**Anna Weckerin**
1611	*Arte de Cocina, Pastelería, Vizcochería y Conservería (Art of Cooking, Pastrymaking, Biscuit-Making and Conserving)*	**Francisco Martinez Montiño**
1651	*La Cuisinier françois (The French Cook)*	**La Varenne**
1661	*The Ladies Directory*	**Hannah Woolley**
1745	*Nuevo Arte de Cocina (The New Art of Cooking)*	**Juan Altamiras**
1747	*The Art of Cookery Made Plain and Easy*	**Hannah Glasse**
1755	*Hjelpreda i Hushållningen för Unga Fruentimber (Housekeeping Advice for Young Wives)*	**Cajsa Warg**
1769	*The Experienced English Housekeeper*	**Elizabeth Raffald**
1793	*The Hasty Pudding*	**Joel Barlow**
1796	*American Cookery*	**Amelia Simmons**
1803–1812	*Almanach des Gourmands (The Gourmands' Almanac)*	**Grimod de la Reynière**
1814	*L'Art du Cuisinier (The Art of the Cook)*	**Antoine Beauvilliers**
1824	*The Virginia Housewife*	**Mary Randolph**
1825	*La Physiologie du goût (The Physiology of Taste)*	**Jean-Anthelme Brillat-Savarin**
1827	*The House Servant's Directory*	**Robert Roberts**
1829	*The American Frugal Housewife*	**Lydia Maria Child**
1833	*L'art de la cuisine française au dix-neuvième siècle (The Art of French Cuisine in the Nineteenth Century)*	**Antonin Carême**
1837	*Treatise on Bread and Bread-Making*	**Sylvester Graham**
1837	*Directions for Cookery*	**Eliza Leslie**
1845	*Modern Cookery in all its Branches*	**Eliza Acton**

PUBLICATION DATE	TEXT	AUTHOR
1845	*Praktisches Kochbuch (Practical Cookbook)*	**Henriette Davidis**
1854	*The Female Emigrant's Guide*	**Catharine Parr Traill**
1861	*Book of Household Management*	**Isabella Beeton**
1861	*Podarok molodym khozjajkam (A Gift to Young Housewives)*	**Elena Ivanovna Molokhovets**
1867	*Mrs. Hill's New Cook Book*	**Annabella Powell Hill**
1869	*The American Woman's Home*	**Catharine Beecher** *and* **Harriet Beecher Stowe**
1871	*Common Sense in the Household*	**Marion Harland**
1881	*What Mrs. Fisher Knows About Old Southern Cooking*	**Abby Fisher**
1884	*Mrs. Lincoln's Boston Cook Book*	**Mary J. Lincoln**
1885	*Miss Corson's Practical American Cookery and Household Management*	**Juliet Corson**
1891	*Hilda's "Where is It?" of Recipes*	**Hildagonda Duckitt**
1891	*La Scienza in Cucina e l'Arte di Mangiar Bene (The Science of Cookery and the Art of Eating Well)*	**Pellegrino Artusi**
1896	*The Boston Cooking-School Cookbook*	**Fannie Farmer**
1903	*Le Guide Culinaire (The Culinary Guide)*	**Auguste Escoffier**
1904	*Katei jûnikagetsu ryōrihō (Home Recipes for Twelve Months)*	**Akabori**
1906	*The Jungle*	**Upton Sinclair**
1912	*Stor Kokebok (The Big Cookbook)*	**Henriette Schønberg Erken**
1930	*Der neuzeitliche Haushalt (The Modern Household)*	**Erna Horn**
1931	*The Joy of Cooking*	**Irma Rombauer**
1934	*El libro de Doña Petrona (The Book of Doña Petrona)*	**Petrona Carrizo de Gandulfo**
1935	*L'Art culinaire moderne (Modern Culinary Art)*	Henri-Paul Pellaprat
1939	*The Englishman's Food*	**Jack Drummond**
1939	*Gastronomic Bibliography*	**Katherine Golden Bitting**
1939	*Kniga o Vkusnoi i Zdorovoi Pishche (Book on Tasty and Healthy Dishes)*	*Collective authorship (see* **Mikoyan** *and* **Pokhlebkin**)
1945	*How to Cook and Eat in Chinese*	**Buwei Yang Chao**
1946	*Platillos regionales de la República mexicana (Regional Dishes of the Mexican Republic)*	**Josefina Velázquez de León**
1950	*The Betty Crocker Picture Cook Book*	**Betty Crocker**

PUBLICATION DATE	TEXT	AUTHOR
1950	*A Book of Mediterranean Food*	Elizabeth David
1952	*The Can-Opener Cookbook*	Poppy Cannon
1954	*The Art of Eating*	M. F. K. Fisher
1954	*Food in England*	Dorothy Hartley
1959	*The James Beard Cookbook*	James Beard
1961	*Mastering the Art of French Cooking*	Simone Beck, Louisette Bertholle, *and* Julia Child
1961	*The New York Times Cookbook*	Craig Claiborne
1963	*L'encylopédie de la cuisine canadienne* *(The Encyclopedia of Canadian Cuisine)*	Jehane Benoît
1982	*Bangla Ranna (Bengali Cooking)*	Minakshie DasGupta
1994	*Indian Food: A Historical Companion*	K. T. Achaya
1999	*The Oxford Companion to Food*	Alan Davidson

General Index

NOTE:
Names in bold type are of principal biographees. Here you will also find variant names and spellings, as well as persons mentioned in someone else's biography.

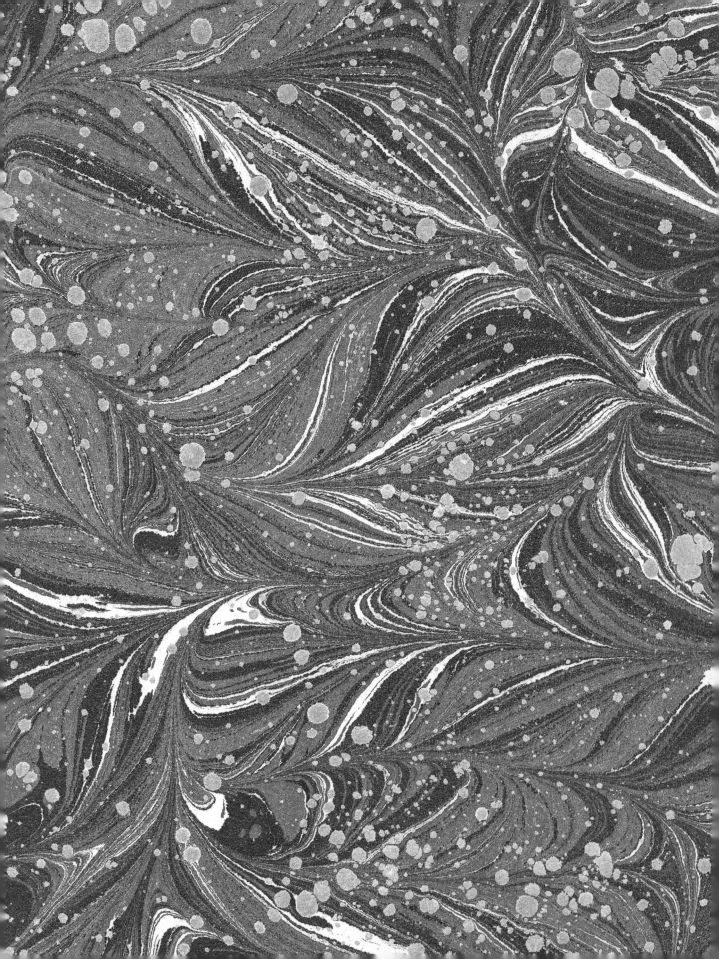